W9-DAS-059

THE
NEW
AMERICAN
NATION
1775–1820

A Twelve-Volume Collection of Articles on the Development of the Early American Republic

Edited by

PETER S. ONUF
UNIVERSITY OF VIRGINIA

A GARLAND SERIES

THE NEW AMERICAN NATION
1775–1820

Volume

7

★

ESTABLISHING THE NEW REGIME:
The Washington Administration

Edited with an
Introduction by

PETER S. ONUF

GARLAND PUBLISHING, INC.
NEW YORK & LONDON
1991

Library of Congress Cataloging-in-Publication Data

Establishing the new regime : the Washington administration / edited
with an introduction by Peter S. Onuf.
     p.   cm. — (New American nation, 1776–1815 ; v. 7)
     Includes bibliographical references.
     ISBN 0-8153-0442-0 (alk. paper) : $49.99
     1. United States—Politics and government—1789–1797.   2. United
States—Politics and government—1783–1789. I. Onuf, Peter S. II. Series.
     E164.N45   1991 vol. 7
     [E311]
     973 s—dc20
     [973.4]   91-3515
                    CIP

Printed on acid-free, 250-year-life paper.
Manufactured in the United States of America

THE NEW AMERICAN NATION, 1775–1820

EDITOR'S INTRODUCTION

This series includes a representative selection of the most interesting and influential journal articles on revolutionary and early national America. My goal is to introduce readers to the wide range of topics that now engage scholarly attention. The essays in these volumes show that the revolutionary era was an extraordinarily complex "moment" when the broad outlines of national history first emerged. Yet if the "common cause" brought Americans together, it also drove them apart: the Revolution, historians agree, was as much a civil war as a war of national liberation. And, given the distinctive colonial histories of the original members of the American Union, it is not surprising that the war had profoundly different effects in different parts of the country. This series has been designed to reveal the multiplicity of these experiences in a period of radical political and social change.

Most of the essays collected here were first published within the last twenty years. This series therefore does *not* recapitulate the development of the historiography of the Revolution. Many of the questions asked by earlier generations of scholars now seem misconceived and simplistic. Constitutional historians wanted to know if the Patriots had legitimate grounds to revolt: was the Revolution "legal"? Economic historians sought to assess the costs of the navigation system for American farmers and merchants and to identify the interest groups that promoted resistance. Comparative historians wondered how "revolutionary" the Revolution really was. By and large, the best recent work has ignored these classic questions. Contemporary scholarship instead draws its inspiration from other sources, most notable of which is the far-ranging reconception and reconstruction of prerevolutionary America by a brilliant generation of colonial historians.

Bernard Bailyn's *Ideological Origins of the American Revolution* (1967) was a landmark in the new historical writing on colonial politics. As his title suggests, Bailyn was less interested in constitutional and legal arguments as such than in the "ideology" or political language that shaped colonists' perception of and responses to British imperial policy. Bailyn's great contribution was to focus attention on colonial political culture; disciples and critics alike followed his lead as they explored the impact—and limits—of "republicanism" in specific colonial settings. Meanwhile, the social historians who had played a leading role in the transformation of colonial historiography were extending their work into the late colonial period and were increasingly interested in the questions of value, meaning, and behavior that were raised by the new political history. The resulting convergence points to some of the unifying themes in recent work on the revolutionary period presented in this series.

A thorough grounding in the new scholarship on colonial British America is the best introduction to the history and historiography of the Revolution. These volumes therefore can be seen as a complement and extension of Peter Charles Hoffer's eighteen-volume set, *Early American History*, published by Garland in 1987. Hoffer's collection includes numerous important essays essential for understanding developments in independent America. Indeed, only a generation ago—when the Revolution generally was defined in terms of its colonial origins—it would have been hard to justify a separate series on the "new American nation." But exciting recent work—for instance, on wartime mobilization and social change, or on the Americanization of republican ideology during the great era of state making and constitution writing—has opened up new vistas. Historians now generally agree that the revolutionary period saw far-reaching and profound changes, that is, a "great transformation," toward a more recognizably modern America. If the connections between this transformation and the actual unfolding of events often remain elusive, the historiographical quest for the larger meaning of the war and its aftermath has yielded impressive results.

To an important extent, the revitalization of scholarship on revolutionary and early national America is a tribute to the efforts and expertise of scholars working in other professional disciplines. Students of early American literature have made key contributions to the history of rhetoric, ideology, and culture; political scientists and legal scholars have brought new clarity and sophistication to the study of political and constitutional thought and practice in the founding period. Kermit L. Hall's superb Garland series, *United States Constitutional and Legal History* (20 volumes, 1985), is another fine resource for students and scholars interested in the founding. The sampling of recent work in various disciplines offered in these volumes gives a sense of the interpretative possibilities of a crucial period in American history that is now getting the kind of attention it has long deserved.

Peter S. Onuf

INTRODUCTION

The First Federal Congress continued the work of the Constitutional Convention by drafting the amendments that would become the Bill of Rights and by enacting the Judiciary Act and other legislation required to put the federal Constitution into operation. The stability and survival of the "first new nation" depended on a variety of circumstances, some fortuitous. An economic recovery that began well before George Washington's presidential inauguration in April 1789 gave the new regime an aura of legitimacy, which was further enhanced by the vast expansion of neutral trade made possible by the onset of the French Revolutionary wars. The very existence of an effective central government strengthened American credit in European markets and promised to protect and promote the new nation's vital economic interests at home and abroad.

Perhaps the most important factor in securing the new regime was the unanimous and enormously popular choice of George Washington as chief executive. Washington presided at the Philadelphia Convention, and his imprimatur gave the new charter a badly needed boost. The framers' certainty that the hero of the Revolution would become the first President enabled them to overcome classical republican anxieties about the dangers of concentrated, despotic power and create an "energetic," unitary executive with wide-ranging authority. As Ralph Ketcham argues in his excellent study of the early presidency, *Presidents above Party* (1984), Washington firmly intended to stand above the struggle for political or economic advantage. Parties were anathema to patriotic republicans because they supposedly sought to promote a "partial" or selfish interest at the expense of the whole. Washington therefore hoped to moderate, if not eliminate, sectional or personal rivalries in his government by a judicious choice of Cabinet officers, including Secretary of State Thomas Jefferson of Virginia and Secretary of the Treasury Alexander Hamilton of New York.

Washington's sensitivity to the need for sectional balance reflected an accurate assessment of the union's continuing vulnerability. In retrospect, historians have been able to trace the formation of political parties to congressional debates over such issues as national commercial policy and the funding of state debts that reflected personal and political splits in Washington's Cabinet. But opposition to Hamilton's economic policies—and to his alleged influence over the President—was at first neither consistent nor coherent. Congressmen were more attuned to the particular interests of their states and regions. The decision to locate the new national capital on the Potomac reflected this awareness of the need to accommodate powerful sectional interests. The Washington administration also had good reason to doubt the loyalty of settlers in western regions, particularly in the wake of the Whiskey Rebellion.

When the embryonic party system began to take shape with Jefferson's resignation from the Cabinet late in Washington's first term, it was the disproportionate sectional strength of the opposing parties that seemed most threatening to the union. Federalist supporters of the administration were strongest in the commercial Northeast, while the Republicans dominated the staple-producing states of the upper South. Yet the impetus of party formation was to transcend these sectional identifications by building truly national coalitions. A forthright espousal of sectional interests was tantamount to the kind of self-interested factiousness that revolutionary republicans disdained and despised. In any event, an opposition party could never hope to gain control of the national government on a sectionalist platform. Jefferson and his friend James Madison thus focused their partisan and polemical energies on questions of principle—for instance, on the proper interpretation of the Constitution—that transcended immediate interests. More significantly, in light of Hamilton's aggressive management of the Treasury, the Jeffersonians elaborated a radically distinct and broadly appealing vision of the new nation's political economic development.

The most important recent work on early national history has been devoted to assessing the implications of Hamiltonian and Jeffersonian political economy and identifying their constituencies. Much of the literature has been centered on the putative "republican" or "liberal" character of Jeffersonianism, a historiographical debate that is fully discussed in earlier volumes of this series. The case for a liberal Jefferson is most vigorously presented in the writings of Joyce Appleby, while Drew R. McCoy explores the dilemmas faced by Jefferson and Madison in their efforts to sustain a republican political economy through the promotion of commercial agriculture. Divergent portraits of Hamilton, as modernizer or Anglophile avatar of a neo-mercantilist fiscal and commercial policy, emerge from these studies and from the works of Forrest McDonald and John R. Nelson, Jr.

As the historiographical dust settles, the richness and complexity of opposing ideological persuasions becomes increasingly apparent. Most striking is the deadly seriousness with which Federalists and Hamiltonians advanced their positions. Political economic visions, as we will see in the next volume, pointed toward radically different foreign policies in a period of world war. Both parties agreed that the survival of the republic was at stake, even while they challenged each other's loyalty and partriotism. The great irony of party formation in the first party system was that integrative programs and appeals that transcended sectional interest simultaneously promoted deep divisions in the national political community that in turn jeopardized the survival of the American union.

Peter S. Onuf

ADDITIONAL READING

Joyce Appleby. *Capitalism and a New Social Order.* New York: New York University Press, 1984.

Joseph Charles. *The Origins of the American Party System: Three Essays.* Williamsburg, VA: Institute of Early American History and Culture, 1956.

Ralph Ketcham. *Presidents above Party: The First American Presidency, 1789–1829.* Chapel Hill: University of North Carolina Press, 1984.

Seymour Martin Lipset. *The First New Nation: The United States in Historical and Comparative Perspective.* New York: Basic Books, 1963.

Drew R. McCoy. *The Elusive Republic: Political Economy in Jeffersonian America.* Chapel Hill: University of North Carolina Press, 1980.

Forrest McDonald. *Alexander Hamilton: A Biography.* New York: W.W. Norton, 1979.

———. *The Presidency of George Washington.* Lawrence: University Press of Kansas, 1974.

John R. Nelson, Jr. *Liberty and Property: Political Economy and Policymaking in the New Nation, 1789–1812.* Baltimore: Johns Hopkins University Press, 1987.

Thomas P. Slaughter. *The Whiskey Rebellion: Frontier Epilogue to the American Revolution.* New York: Oxford University Press, 1986.

CONTENTS

Volume 7—Establishing the New Regime: The Washington Administation

John Garry Clifford, "A Muddy Middle of the Road: The Politics of Edmund Randolph, 1790–1795," *Virginia Magazine of History and Biography*, 1972, 80(3):286–311.

Mary K. Bonsteel Tachau, "George Washington and the Reputation of Edmund Randolph," *Journal of American History*, 1986, 73(1): 15–34.

Jacob E. Cooke, "The Compromise of 1790," *William and Mary Quarterly*, 1970, 27(4):523–545.

Howard A. Ohline, "Slavery, Economics, and Congressional Politics, 1790," *Journal of Southern History*, 1980, 46(3): 335–360.

Gerard Clarfield, "Protecting the Frontiers: Defense Policy and the Tariff Question in the First Washington Administration," *William and Mary Quarterly*, 1975, 32(3) (Third Series): 443–464.

Paul David Nelson, "General Charles Scott, the Kentucky Mounted Volunteers, and the Northwest Indian Wars, 1784–1794," *Journal of the Early Republic*, 1986, 6:219–251.

William D. Barber, "'Among the Most Techy Articles of Civil Police': Federal Taxation and the Adoption of the Whiskey Excise," *William and Mary Quarterly*, 1968, 25(1):58–84.

Richard H. Kohn, "The Washington Administration's Decision to Crush the Whiskey Rebellion," *Journal of American History*, 1972, 59(3):567–584.

Mary K. Tachau, "The Whiskey Rebellion in Kentucky: A Forgotten Episode of Civil Disobedience," *Journal of the Early Republic*, 1982, 2:239–259.

ACKNOWLEDGMENTS

Volume 7—Establishing the New Regime: The Washington Administation

Gordon C. Bjork, "The Weaning of the American Economy: Independence, Market Changes, and Economic Development," *Journal of Economic History*, 1964, 24(4):541–560. Reprinted with the permission of the Cambridge University Press. Courtesy of Yale University Sterling Memorial Library.

James F. Shepherd and Gary M. Walton, "Economic Change after the American Revolution: Pre- and Post-War Comparisons of Maritime Shipping and Trade," *Explorations in Economic History*, 1976, 13(4):397–422. Copyright by Academic Press, Inc. Courtesy of Yale University Sterling Memorial Library.

Michael Lienesch, "The Constitutional Tradition: History, Political Action, and Progress in American Political Thought 1787–1793," *Journal of Politics*, 1980, 42(1):2–30. Reprinted with the permission of the author and the University of Texas Press. Courtesy of Yale University Sterling Memorial Library.

John F. Hoadley, "The Emergence of Political Parties in Congress, 1789–1803," *American Political Science Review*, 1980, 74(3):757–779. Reprinted with the permission of the Academy of Political Science. Courtesy of Yale University Law Library.

James C. Riley, "Foreign Credit and Fiscal Stability: Dutch Investment in the United States, 1781–1794," *Journal of American History*, 1978, 65(3):654–678. Reprinted with the permission of the *Journal of American History*. Courtesy of Yale University Sterling Memorial Library.

Jacob E. Cooke, "Tench Coxe, Alexander Hamilton, and the Encouragement of American Manufactures," *William and Mary Quarterly*, 1975, 32(3) (Third Series):369–392. Originally appeared in the *William and Mary Quarterly*. Courtesy of Yale University Sterling Memorial Library.

John R. Nelson, Jr., "Alexander Hamilton and American Manufacturing: A Reexamination," *Journal of American History*, 1978–79, 65(4):971–995. Reprinted with the permission of the *Journal of American History*. Courtesy of Yale University Sterling Memorial Library.

Merrill D. Peterson, "Thomas Jefferson and Commercial Policy, 1783–1793," *William and Mary Quarterly*, 1965, 22(4) (Third Series):584–610. Originally appeared in the *William and Mary Quarterly*. Courtesy of Yale University Sterling Memorial Library.

Drew R. McCoy, "Republicanism and American Foreign Policy: James Madison and the Political Economy of Commercial Discrimination, 1789 to 1794," *William and Mary Quarterly*, 1974, 31(4):633–646.

Originally appeared in the *William and Mary Quarterly*. Courtesy of Yale University Sterling Memorial Library.

Lance Banning, "THE HAMILTONIAN MADISON: A Reconsideration," *Virginia Magazine of History and Biography*, 1984, 92(1):3–28. Reprinted with the permission of the Virginia Historical Society. Courtesy of Yale University Sterling Memorial Library.

John Gerry Clifford, "A Muddy Middle of the Road: The Politics of Edmund Randolph, 1790–1795," *Virginia Magazine of History and Biography*, 1972, 80(3):286–311. Reprinted with the permission of the Virginia Historical Society. Courtesy of Yale University Sterling Memorial Library.

Mary K. Bonsteel Tachau, "George Washington and the Reputation of Edmund Randolph," *Journal of American History*, 1986, 73(1):15–34. Reprinted with the permission of the *Journal of American History*. Courtesy of Yale University Sterling Memorial Library.

Jacob E. Cooke, "The Compromise of 1790," *William and Mary Quarterly*, 1970, 27(4):523–545. Originally appeared in the *William and Mary Quarterly*. Courtesy of Yale University Sterling Memorial Library.

Howard A. Ohline, "Slavery, Economics, and Congressional Politics, 1790," *Journal of Southern History*, 1980, 46(3):335–360. Reprinted with the permission of the Southern Historical Association. Courtesy of Yale University Sterling Memorial Library.

Gerard Clarfield, "Protecting the Frontiers: Defense Policy and the Tariff Question in the First Washington Administration," *William and Mary Quarterly*, 1975, 32(3) (Third Series):443–464. Originally appeared in the *William and Mary Quarterly*. Courtesy of Yale University Sterling Memorial Library.

Paul David Nelson, "General Charles Scott, the Kentucky Mounted Volunteers, and the Northwest Indian Wars, 1784–1794," *Journal of the Early Republic*, 1986, 6:219–251. Reprinted with the permission of Indiana University, Department of History. Courtesy of Yale University Sterling Memorial Library.

William D. Barber, "'*Among the Most Techy Articles of Civil Police*': Federal Taxation and the Adoption of the Whiskey Excise," *William and Mary Quarterly*, 1968, 25(1):58–84. Originally appeared in the *William and Mary Quarterly*. Courtesy of Yale University Sterling Memorial Library.

Richard H. Kohn, "The Washington Administration's Decision to Crush the Whiskey Rebellion," *Journal of American History*, 1972, 59(3):567–584. Reprinted with the permission of the *Journal of American History*. Courtesy of Yale University Sterling Memorial Library.

Mary K. Tachau, "The Whiskey Rebellion in Kentucky: A Forgotten Episode of Civil Disobedience," *Journal of the Early Republic*, 1982, 2:239–259. Reprinted with the permission of Indiana University, Department of History. Courtesy of Yale University Sterling Memorial Library.

The Weaning of the American Economy: Independence, Market Changes, and Economic Development*

Notwithstanding the actual prosperity of the United States of America at this time, it is a fact which ought not to be concealed that their affairs had fallen into a very disagreeable condition by the year 1786.

TENCH COXE, 1794.[1]

I see in the public newspapers of different States frequent complaints of hard times, deadness of trade, scarcity of money, etc. It is not my intention to assert or maintain that these complaints are entirely without foundation. . . . But let us take a cool view of the general state of our affairs and perhaps the prospect will appear less gloomy than has been imagined.

BENJAMIN FRANKLIN, 1784.[2]

DISAGREEMENT on the state of the economic health of the new nation has persisted since contemporary observers disputed over the changes wrought by the end of the War for Independence. In recent years, diagnosis has ranged from the gloomy picture of commercial depression painted by Curtis Nettels[3] to the rather different evaluation of Merrill Jensen, who found the period "one of extraordinary economic growth."[4]

There was, obviously, much room for differing opinions about the health of the economy by contemporary observers during the rapidly changing conditions of the period. Economic prospects differed greatly from region to region, and even in the same town some prospered while others did not. One cannot move with certainty from an appraisal of the fortunes of one sector of the economy to conclusions about the economy as a whole. The inevitable necessity

---

* Financial assistance for the research underlying this paper was provided by the Lincoln Educational Foundation while the author was a graduate student at the University of Washington.
   [1] Tench Coxe, *A View of the United States, in a series of papers* . . . (Philadelphia, 1794), p. 3. Hereafter cited as *A View of the United States*.
   [2] A pamphlet entitled, *The Internal State of America; Being a true Description of the Interest and Policy of that Vast Continent.* Reprinted in John Bigelow, ed., *The Works of Benjamin Franklin* (New York: G. P. Putnam's Sons, 1904), X, 394-400.
   [3] Curtis P. Nettels, *The Emergence of a National Economy, 1775-1815* (New York: Holt, Rinehart, and Winston, 1962).
   [4] Merrill Jensen, *The New Nation* (New York: Alfred A. Knopf, Inc., 1950), pp. 423-24.

for selectivity and judgment by the historian makes generalizations about the American economic scene during these years of flux hazardous and tentative. And the economist who would interpret the changes taking place finds difficulty in assessing the quantitative magnitudes of many conflicting trends.

There are three separate considerations which might lead one to expect economic difficulties during the period: (1) The war wrought widespread disorganization and damage to the productive capacity of the economy. (2) The loose Confederation which preceded federal union allowed states to regulate interstate commerce. Because Hamilton argued in the Federalist Papers that a federal union was necessary to promote internal commerce, it has been said that the absence of federal union during the period constricted internal commerce. (3) The exclusion of the former colonies from the mercantilist system of the British Navigation Acts meant that certain markets for American exports were closed. The loss of these commercial privileges caused Lord Sheffield to prophesy commercial doom for the former colonies, and Thomas Jefferson lamented the exclusions and prohibitions at great length.[5]

In considering the changes taking place in the economies of the thirteen states during the Confederation period, this paper will be concentrated on foreign commerce. The structure of the economy during the period was such as to give overriding importance to the fortunes of American exports in world markets. Although more than 90 per cent of the population was in agricultural production, the population which participated in the market economy to any significant extent found that foreign markets were of paramount importance in determining how far above the level of frontier subsistence would be their standard of living. There was much discussion during the period by contemporaries as to whether exclusion from the British mercantile system had been harmful or beneficial to the foreign trade of the American states. While no final answer can be given to this question, because of the impossibility of knowing what the volume and terms of trade would have been if the thirteen colonies had remained within the British Empire, it is possible to compare the level and composition of trade before and after the Revolution and to note the changes which were taking place.

[5] Paul L. Ford, ed., *The Writings of Thomas Jefferson* (New York: G. P. Putnam's Sons, 1892-1899), V, 413. Hereafter cited as *Jefferson*.

In order to identify the differential impact of the changed commercial situation following the war, it is useful to distinguish four economic regions.

The lower South was centered on the port of Charleston and included parts of the present states of Georgia and the Carolinas. The areas along the coast were concentrated in the production of rice and indigo. Both crops were produced on large plantations. A sizable amount of capital was sunk in physical improvements to the land used for rice paddies. The labor supply for rice production was made up entirely of slaves. Thus, the rice planter found himself with a large percentage of his costs of production in the form of fixed expenses—interest on the capital tied up in land and slaves and provision of food and supplies to the slaves whether they were employed or not. Add to this the fact that rice lands were not adaptable to the production of alternative commodities and it is easy to see that the rice economy of the lower South was not readily adaptable to short-run changes in economic conditions.

Indigo, like rice, required very intensive cultivation. Prior to the war there had been a bounty on indigo shipped to England, and the discontinuance of the subsidy coupled with the encouragement of the industry in the West Indies combined to reduce the profitability of indigo production after the Revolution.

The back country of the lower South was different in character from the coast plantations. Deerskins, lumber and staves, tar, pitch and turpentine, corn, and increasingly tobacco comprised the commodities upon which the frontier farmers depended for cash income. The back country may have been a fairly important source of food for the plantation slaves. The value of their exports is quantitatively unimportant in comparison to that of rice and indigo. There was a rapid increase in the production of tobacco after 1783, and tobacco culture in the lower South was sufficiently great to lower prices in the older tobacco regions of Maryland and Virginia after 1787.

The upper South—Virginia, Maryland, and the part of North Carolina contiguous to the Virginia border—had been the great tobacco-producing region in Britain's North American colonial empire. Prior to the war, the trade had been dominated by British factors who acted as agents for the planters. Tobacco was required by law to be shipped to Britain, where it was heavily dutied; but a large part of the duty was remitted when tobacco was reexported.

The major change wrought in the export markets of the upper South in the postrevolutionary period was release from the necessity of shipping all tobacco through Britain. The British merchants' monopoly of markets for tobacco in Europe was effectively broken after the Revolution.[6]

Just prior to the war, the average annual export of tobacco from Virginia was estimated by Winterbotham at 55,000 hogsheads.[7] The average export from 1784-1790 was slightly greater. The amount of tobacco released for export from the several state warehouses in the postwar era is given below in hogsheads, each year beginning and ending October 1:[8]

1783-84	49,497	1786-87	60,041
1784-85	55,624	1787-88	58,544
1785-86	60,380	1788-89	58,673

It can thus be seen that the postwar Virginian tobacco exports were substantially equal to prewar.

From 1790 to 1792, total U. S. exports of tobacco averaged 110,000 hogsheads per year. This was a slight increase over the prewar average of 102,000 hogsheads per year. Until 1840, American exports of tobacco never again reached the high average level of 1790-1792.[9]

Although there is much qualitative and quantitative evidence to indicate that the upper South was shifting out of tobacco into production of wheat, corn, flaxseed, and foodstuffs, it is difficult to quantify the extent of the shift.

The middle Atlantic states of Pennsylvania, Delaware, New Jersey, New York, and Connecticut had not been tied to the production of an export staple in the colonial period. With the exception of New York, where there were large proprietary estates up the Hudson, the area was characterized by a farming yeomanry carrying on diversified agriculture. The two largest cities in North America prior to the Revolution, Philadelphia and New York, were the important

[6] For the extent of the decline, see Elizabeth B. Schumpeter, *English Overseas Trade Statistics* (Oxford: Clarendon Press, 1960) Table 18, p. 62.

[7] William Winterbotham, *An Historical, Geographical, Commercial and Philosophical View of the United States of America, and of the European Settlements in America and the West Indies* (New York, 1795), III, 111. Hereafter cited as *An Historical View.*

[8] Lewis C. Gray, *History of Agriculture in the Southern United States to 1860* (Washington: The Carnegie Institution, 1933), II, 573. Hereafter cited as *Southern Agriculture.*

[9] *Ibid.,* II, 605.

commercial centers of the region. New York grew from 22,000 in 1775 to 33,000 in 1790, while Philadelphia grew from 21,000 to 42,000 during the same period.

Independence led to major reorientation of markets. The European demand for American wheat was highly unstable, since the American supply was needed only during years of bad harvests in Europe. The West Indian markets were reestablished, and there was some additional business from the French islands; but southern markets were altered by increased production of foodstuffs in the upper South and by a shift into self-subsistence in the lower South. The market for salt meat was considerably diminished by the prohibition against its import in the British islands, although smuggling and the connivance of local governors kept the vent partly open.

The effect of market reorientation was to shift resources into import-competing industries. Grist mills were built, and wheat was increasingly exported in processed form as bread or flour. Distillation of cereals into beer, porter, and whiskey made possible a lessened import of rum, wines, and gin. In addition to supplying their own population with manufactured goods, the middle Atlantic states began exploiting the southern markets formerly dominated by British merchants. There even began to be talk of supplying the West Indies with manufactures, and the diversification of Philadelphia and New York exports is evident in their customs house returns.[10]

The economy of the New England states depended on the sea. Lacking staple agricultural exports, the New Englanders in the colonial period had relied on exports of codfish and whale oil, coupled with the sale of ships and shipping services to pay their import bill. The changed commercial situation following the war hit hard at the bases of the New England economy.

Jefferson's report on the cod fisheries[11] reveals the changed character of the postwar markets. In 1786, the industry was operating at approximately 80 per cent of the prewar level, with the French West Indies, Spain, and Portugal the most important markets in that order. By 1790, it had surpassed the prewar size.

[10] For customs-house records cited, see Gordon C. Bjork, "Stagnation and Growth in the American Economy, 1784-1792" (unpublished Ph.D. dissertation, University of Washington, 1963), appendices III-2-2 and III-3-1.

[11] Timothy Pitkin, *A Statistical View of the Commerce of the United States of America* (New Haven, 1835) pp. 84-85.

Turning our attention once again to the economic situation of the nation as a whole, it would seem fair to say that the people recovered rapidly from the economic effects of the war and of the changed market situations which obtained from 1784 to 1792. Speaking of the change which had taken place since the Revolution, the British consul in Philadelphia wrote to his Foreign Office in 1789:

> During the troubles, my Lord, a number of useful labourers were taken from the pursuits of agriculture and employed as soldiers; the diminution of useful labour occasioned a diminution of the crops and the farmer sustained a heavy loss thereby . . . but a very considerable discouragement to agriculture existed during the war, the intercourse with Europe and the West Indies was so frequently obstructed by the cruizers that the farmer found no certain vent for his produce and fearful that the little he raised might perish on his hands he looked scarcely further than to the nurture of his family and became careless of cultivating more than their wants required . . . farm houses fell into decay, so that upon the accession of peace those means which were formerly exerted for the purpose of tillage and improvement were appropriated to the discharge of old debts . . . . These inconveniences are gradually wearing away . . . the eyes of the people seem now to be opened to their true interests . . . .[12]

An American, writing in the same year, told the story in more glowing terms:

> There is a spirit of emulation, of industry, of improvement, of patriotism, raised throughout the states . . . . In no period have they made a more rapid progress than within this year or two . . . . Every nerve and sinew seems to be at its utmost stretch, and this is not by the interposition of the legislature but by the patriotic or interested and enterprising spirit of the individuals: perhaps, even by the want of an effective government, I might almost have added; for it might have meddled and, as in most similar cases, might have marred.[13]

This, then, is a thumbnail sketch of the United States economy during the period following the War for Independence. Before it is possible to make any conclusions, we must develop some quantitative estimates of the changes which were taking place.

The period has for many years been the "dark ages" of American economic history as far as quantitative work has been concerned.

---

[12] Letter to Lord Carmarthen, Philadelphia, May 17, 1787. Found in J. Franklin Jameson, ed., "Letters of Phineas Bond, British Consul at Philadelphia to the Foreign Office of Great Britain, 1787, 1788, 1789," *American Historical Association, Annual Report . . . 1896.*

[13] A letter in *The American Museum*, a periodical published by Matthew Carey in Philadelphia from 1787 to 1792, VI, 238.

This can easily be understood by reference to the gaps which exist in any of the standard statistical sources between 1775 and 1790. What is presented in this paper is an attempt to bridge that gap with some fragmentary returns.

The first approach to estimating the foreign trade of the thirteen states during the period is directly from the customs-house returns of individual states. These estimates are presented in Table 1. Briefly, these estimates were prepared by valuing customs-house estimates of export quantities by average annual prices of the important staple commodities in the ports concerned.[14] The ratio estimates appearing in the bottom line of the table are estimates of what the trade of the thirteen colonies would have been from 1784 to 1788 if the partial returns were in proportion to their average of 1790 to 1792. No great faith is placed in this procedure, but it is interesting to note that the ratio estimate presented for 1789 to 1790 tallies quite closely with customs-house returns for the whole United States for the year when they have been altered to allow for the fourteen-month year.

The only figures for domestic imports available for the pre-1790 period are those constructed from customs-house returns from New York and Philadelphia. My estimates for the value of imports into the port of New York for 1784-1787 indicate that the annual average value of imports for those years was about $4 million.[15]

Estimates of imports for three separate years are available for Philadelphia. In 1784, the value of imports into Philadelphia is estimated at $8.8 million. The figure dips to $3.2 million per year in 1786-1787 and then climbs back up to $4.6 million in 1789.[16] One remarkable thing about these figures is the stability of the value of enumerated West Indian and tropical commodities during these three very disparate years. The fluctuation in the value of imports is due entirely to huge changes in the volume of imported manufactured goods. The behavior of the Philadelphia import series agrees very closely with the series of British exports to the U. S.— showing the same boom in 1784, depression in 1786-1787, and recovery in 1789.[17]

[14] For a more complete account, see Bjork, *Stagnation and Growth*, appendices to ch. iii.
[15] *Ibid.*, appendix III-6.
[16] *Ibid.*, appendix III-7.
[17] *Ibid.*, Table 4-B.

TABLE I
EXPORTS BY STATE 1784-1792
(IN $000)

State	1784	1785	1786	1787	1788	1789-90	1790-91	1791-92	Average Proportion of Trade by States (percentage) 1790-92
Georgia	$2,148						$ 491	$ 459	2.4
South Carolina		$1,892	$2,303	$2,717	$2,551		2,693	2,428	12.9
North Carolina			506				525	528	2.6
Virginia							3,132	3,553	16.8
Maryland						$2,028	2,240	2,624	12.2
Delaware							120	134	0.6
Pennsylvania	3,725	2,509	2,059	2,142	2,427	3,511	3,436	3,821	18.2
New Jersey							27	23	0.1
New York					1,925	2,000	2,505	2,536	12.7
Connecticut							710	880	4.0
Rhode Island							470	698	2.9
Massachusetts							2,520	2,888	13.6
New Hampshire				1,588	1,969		143	181	0.8
Official total value of exports, in $000						17,450	19,012	20,753	
Ratio estimate of total value of exports in $000,000's	18.9	14.2	14.4	14.4	15.5	17.5			

When we add to the evidence on the volume of imports (1) the behavior of the foreign exchanges[18] and (2) the estimates of the volume of exports already presented, the picture of Philadelphia trade during the Confederation period fits together very nicely. The premium of sterling over Pennsylvania currency advances slowly from 1783 until March 1786, when it reaches its high. Pennsylvania currency remains at approximately a 6 per cent discount until the spring of 1788, when it starts to move back toward par. The tremendous rise in exports during 1789 caused sterling to sink to a sizable discount during the spring of 1790, reflecting the favorable balance of trade which Pennsylvania had established during the previous autumn.

The fall in the exchange rate between 1783 and 1786 resulted from the adverse balance of trade. The high postwar prices of American exports and the shipment of specie kept the exchange discount from becoming greater than it was. The heavy discount on Philadelphia currency in 1786 coincided with the low level of exports for that year and the low level of imports in the following year. The decline of the discount in Pennsylvania currency and the occurrence of a premium in 1790 were the monetary indicators of the recovery which had taken place after 1787.

Another way of attacking the problem of estimating the level of trade is from a survey of the records of the countries with which the new nation carried on commerce.[19] Foremost among the customers of the United States during the Confederation period was Britain. British trade policy was very favorable as regards trade between the United States and Great Britain as opposed to the restrictions imposed on the West Indian trade. The same bounties on exports to the United States were given as on exports to the British colonies. Imports from the United States could be carried in either British or American bottoms and were subject to the same duties and drawbacks as goods imported from the British colonies. The trade policies were aimed at securing as large a proportion as possible of the trade of the former colonies.[20] The value of U. S. exports to Britain and the British West Indies following the war is of partic-

---

[18] See Anne Bezanson, *Prices and Inflation During the American Revolution, 1770-1790* (Philadelphia: University of Pennsylvania Press, 1951), p. 346.

[19] See Bjork, *Stagnation and Growth*, Table 4-D.

[20] Richard Champion, *Considerations on the present situation of Great Britain and the United States of North America, with a view to their future commercial connections* (London, 1784).

ular importance because it has been claimed that exclusion from the privileges of the mercantile system was a serious blow.

Economic historians have been led astray on British export statistics during the period because of the British practice of reporting "official" rather than market values.[21] The estimated market value of British imports from the United States is shown in Table 2.[22]

TABLE 2
BRITISH TRADE WITH THE U. S.
(ESTIMATED MARKET VALUE OF BRITISH IMPORTS FROM THE UNITED STATES, 1770-75, 1784-92)

Year	Estimated Market Value (in thousands)	Value Relative (1790 = 100)
1770	$3,248	55
1771	5,978	86
1772	5,078	86
1773	4,960	84
1774	4,842	82
1775	6,555	111
1784	4,429	75
1785	4,901	83
1786	4,134	70
1787	4,488	76
1788	4,901	83
1789	4,901	83
1790	4,905	100
1791	4,724	80
1792	4,311	73

Source: Estimated market value of British imports from the United States was obtained by converting British "Official" values into a volume series (1790 = 100) and valuing this with a Laspeyres price index (1790 = 100) weighted by the composition of U. S. exports to Britain. For complete discussion see Bjork, *Stagnation and Growth*, appendix IV-1.

From a survey of the changed postwar commercial situation, one would expect the U. S. exports to Great Britain would decline. Tobacco, indigo, and naval stores no longer were required by law to be shipped to England for reexport. The decline of the reexport trade in tobacco has already been alluded to. Rice shipments to European ports north of Cape Finisterre no longer had to be sent first to England. What is interesting, therefore, is—not that American exports to Britain were marginally lower in the postwar period—

[21] See Albert H. Imlah, *Economic Elements in the Pax Britannica: Studies in British Foreign Trade in the Nineteenth Century* (Cambridge: Harvard University Press, 1958).

[22] For a description of the sources and methods used in the construction of these values, see Bjork, *Stagnation and Growth*, appendix IV-1.

but that they were as high as they were when Britain lost mercantilist control of American trade. The estimated annual average market value of exports from the thirteen colonies to Britain in the six years preceding the revolution is $4.96 million, while the estimated annual average value in the period from 1784 to 1792 is $4.74 million.

Of crucial importance to any discussion of the changed situation of the foreign trade of the U. S. after the war is the trade of the British West Indian islands. Before the war, the thirteen colonies had been practically the sole supplier of the sugar islands in foodstuffs and lumber. Trade deficits with Britain had been offset by surplus in the West Indian trade. After the war, U. S. ships were excluded from the carrying trade to the British islands, and the import of salt meat and fish was prohibited in order to favor Irish and Canadian producers. Several writers have called attention to the circumvention of the Navigation Acts following the Revolution by temporary relaxation of restrictions, connivance of colonial officials, and smuggling. It is fair to infer that the extent of illicit trade was fairly considerable. In 1785, Horatio Nelson wrote to the Admiralty:

. . . nearly the whole trade between the British colonies and the United States of America was carried on in American bottoms. To see the American ships and vessels with their colours flying in defiance of the Laws, and by permission of the officer of the customs, landing and unloading in our ports was too much for a British Officer to submit too [sic].[23]

My calculations (see Table 3) indicate quite conclusively that the extent of legal trade was considerably lower after the Revolution than before. What is very interesting, however, is that the value of trade from 1785 to 1787 was greater than it was in 1793 after restrictions were lifted. The series and contemporary qualitative evidence point to a cyclical low in U. S. exports in 1786.

A careful consideration of the economic situation of the British West Indies soon leads one to the conclusion that their reported trade with the U. S. considerably understates the actual extent of commercial intercourse. The plantation economy had certain requirements for cereals, proteins, and lumber. A good measure of those requirements can be seen in the imports from the thirteen colonies in 1771-1773.

[23] Letter from Horatio Nelson to Lord Sydney, November 17, 1785, Nevs, B.W.I. Colonial Office 152/64.

TABLE 3

EXPORTS TO THE BRITISH WEST INDIES

VALUE OF EXPORTS FROM THE UNITED STATES, 1771-73, 1785-87, AND 1793

Commodity	Average of 1771-73			Average of 1785-87			1793		
	Volume	Price	Value	Volume	Price	Value	Volume	Price	Value
Lumber (000 board feet)	25,500	$14.00	$357,000	9,320	$15.75	$146,790	14,747	$12.75	$187,000
Shingles (000)	19,800	1.33	26,334	13,500	1.33	17,955	23,472	1.33	31,000
Staves (000)	19,300	17.90	345,470	13,500	20.80	280,800	8,864	21.00	144,000
Corn (bu.)	401,000	.50	200,500	221,000	.59	130,390	242,000	.48	116,000
Bread & Flour (bbl.)	112,000	4.75	627,000	139,000	5.60	778,400	131,000	5.00	655,000
Rice (bbl.)	35,000	5.00	175,000	7,850	6.00	67,000	13,000	3.90	51,000
Dried fish (bbl.)	7,100	2.20	15,620				5,000	2.50	12,000
Pkld. fish (bbl.)	84,000	2.50	210,000				426	3.00	1,200
Naval stores (bbl.)	5,700	3.60	20,520	3,500	3.00	10,500			
Beef and Pork (bbl.)	15,000	12.00	180,000	120	5.80	1,536	140	11.00	1,500
Whale oil (bbl.)	1,060	20.00	20,120	24	15.00	360			
Total value			$2.2 million			$1.4 million			$1.2 million

Sources: The main source of volume figures for 1771-73 and 1793 is Bryan Edwards, *The History of the British West Indies* (London, 1818-1819), Vols. II and V. For 1785-87, volume figures are taken from a document in the British Public Record Office, C.O. 318/1, "A Comparative State of the Trade between the West Indies, and North America. . . ." Prices are taken from A. H. Cole, *Wholesale Commodity Prices in the United States, 1700-1861, Statistical Supplement* (Cambridge: Harvard University Press, 1938).

For a more complete discussion see Bjork, *Stagnation and Growth*, Appendix IV-2

At the same time that the British were discouraging trade between the United States and their West Indian colonies, the French were encouraging trade with theirs. Jefferson estimated that value of trade to the French West Indies in 1790 at $3.3 million as against $2.3 million with the British West Indies.[24] In 1790, goods worth about $1.9 millions were exported to Holland and her possessions. The largest part of these were bound for St. Eustatia—the entrepôt port of the West Indies from which the British islands were supplied in contravention of the Navigation Acts. It would appear that the U. S. was shifting toward increased trade with the non-British West Indies during the period.

Any conclusions about the value of American trade with the West Indies after the Revolution must inevitably be tentative. There can be little doubt that the legal trade with the British islands was diminished from its prewar level—the largest part of the diminution being in the export of fish. There was probably some loss of the lumber trade to the Canadian colonies. Balanced against the loss of this legal trade was the rapid expansion of trade with the French West Indies and indirect trade through St. Eustatia.

Writing at the close of the Confederation period, Tench Coxe observed that the United States was obtaining many of its imports at cheaper prices than before the Revolution. He particularly called attention to East Indian goods, wines, and manufactures from England. He then went on to observe that the tobacco trade was bringing more profit to the planter than it had before the Revolution.[25]

Evidence on trends in relative prices seems to indicate that the states enjoyed a definite improvement in the net barter terms of trade in the postwar period (see Table 4). Import price index A, comprising eight commodities at their annual average wholesale prices in various U. S. cities, shows definite cyclical behavior both before and after the war but is appreciably lower in the postwar period. There was a general downward trend in most prices after the war, with lows coming in 1788-1789; the import price index turns up again after 1790, agreeing with D. C. North's figures on the prices of imports, which show them rising during the period of the Napoleonic Wars to levels considerably above the Confederation

[24] Ford, *Jefferson*, V, 413.
[25] Coxe, *A View of the United States*, p. 340.

TABLE 4
IMPORT AND EXPORT PRICES AND THE TERMS OF TRADE

Year	Import Price Index A	Import Price Index B	Composite Import Price Index	Export Price Index	Terms of Trade
1770	123	98	110	69	63
1771	108	100	104	75	72
1772	103	102	102	83	81
1773	114	104	109	78	72
1774	115	100	108	73	68
1775	123	96	109	70	64
1784	109	98	103	115	112
1785	101	101	101	106	105
1786	98	104	101	97	96
1787	97	105	101	92	91
1788	94	103	99	87	88
1789	94	105	99	87	88
1790	100	100	100	100	100
1791	107	99	103	92	89
1792	120	99	110	86	78

Sources and methods: Import price index A is a Laspeyres index (1790 = 100) composed of U. S. prices for tea, coffee, sugar, salt, molasses, Madeira wine, rum, and Russian duck. Import price index B is also a Laspeyres index (1790 = 100) based on British prices for blue cloth, common shoes, stockings, and hats modified to take into account changes in the rate of exchange between sterling and the dollar. Indices A and B are given equal weight in the composite index.

The export price index is a Laspeyres index composed of fourteen commodities accounting for 86.8 per cent of the value of total exports in 1790. For a complete discussion of weights, sources, and procedures for export price indices, see Bjork, *Stagnation and Growth*, appendices V-1 and V-2.

years.[26] Import price index B is constructed from English price series on shoes, stockings, woolen cloth, and hats and then is corrected for American use by taking into account changes in the rate of exchange between sterling and American currency.

It is in the prices of export commodities that the important changes are to be noted. The first thing which springs to the reader's attention from looking at the export price index is that the postwar price relatives are higher than the prewar level in every single year. Turning to individual commodities, one of the largest increases in relative prices is in the price of tobacco—just as noted by Coxe. The increase in tobacco prices would be even more noticeable if the prices were to be pushed back before 1770, for prices in the prewar years quoted were an all-time high. One of the reasons for the higher prices of tobacco in the postwar era was the end of the British

[26] D. C. North, *The Economic Growth of the United States, 1790-1860* (Englewood Cliffs, N. J.: Prentice-Hall, 1961), p. 229.

monopoly in the tobacco trade and the release of the commodity from numerous charges connected with its reexportation.

The extremely high prices which tobacco commanded in 1784-1785 doubtlessly reflected a diminished production in the older tobacco areas of Virginia and Maryland, but demand was also very buoyant after the reopening of the English market by the proclamation of the King in Council in September 1783.[27] The high prices during 1784-1785 frustrated the attempts of Robert Morris to buy tobacco, and he was unable to ship any tobacco to the French Farmers General in 1784.[28] Tobacco prices continued at a high level until 1790. Research on prices at Amsterdam by N. Posthumus indicates that the postwar behavior of tobacco prices in European markets was similar to that in American. Tobacco prices were 50 per cent above their prewar level in 1784 in Amsterdam and at their low in 1786 were still above their 1770-1775 level, which was reached again only after 1791.[29]

There are two inferences to be drawn from the behavior of tobacco prices at Amsterdam. First, the European price of tobacco was a primary determinant of American prices. But secondly, the end of the British control of the trade meant that even when price dropped to its prewar level in the United States, American producers benefited from the reorganization of the distribution of the commodity.

The relatively higher level of prices for wheat and flour was also an important contributor to the postwar improvement in the terms of trade.

Taken together, the high prices of the farm crops of the middle states reflected a very favorable turn in the terms of trade for the farming yeomanry, from the back country of Virginia to southern Connecticut. It must have created hardships, however, for New England and for the plantation economy of the lower South, in that both regions were now importers of cereals from the middle states.

In New England, export prices were higher than would be expected from the changed commercial situation facing the New Englanders, because of restrictions on the West Indian trade.

[27] Bezanson, *Prices and Inflation*, p. 259.
[28] Frederick L. Nussbaum, "American Tobacco and French Politics 1781-1789," *Political Science Quarterly*, XL, No. 4 (Dec. 1925), 501.
[29] N. W. Posthumus, *Inquiry into the History of Prices in Holland* (Leiden: E. J. Brill, 1946), p. 86.

An overview of the general trend of prices of export commodities in the postwar period suggests a general downward trend from the high levels which prevailed in 1783-1784. The trend was interrupted by a precipitate rise in the price of food in 1789-1791 due to the effect of a temporary shift in European demand resulting from widespread crop failures. The beginnings of the Napoleonic Wars initiated another period for the American economy which is beyond the scope of this study.

The general conclusion to be made from a study of prices during this period is that slightly lower import prices coupled with significantly higher export prices resulted in a marked improvement in the net barter terms of trade for the new nation during its formative years. Let us draw some conclusions from the evidence which has been presented.

As shown in Table 5, the value of exports from the lower South showed no market tendency to expand during the period under consideration. The official values of British imports from the Carolinas and Georgia were far below their prewar level in 1788. The figure for the Carolinas is 50 per cent below prewar, and the exports from Georgia to Great Britain were only one third of what they had been from 1770 to 1775. The figures understate market values, and undoubtedly there was some expansion of trade with the other European countries in rice, indigo, naval stores, and tobacco; but the amount was certainly far from large enough to make up for the decline in exports to Britain. The difficulties faced by the plantation economy of the lower South were nowhere better seen than in the population statistics of South Carolina, where there was an absolute decline in the slave population between 1775 and 1790.

The effects of the Revolution and the end of the imperial connection were not favorable to the export economy of the lower South. The physical destruction and disorganization during the period of hostilities and the loss of subsidies for the export of indigo and naval stores were a definite setback. The low volume of rice exports in the immediately postwar period was compensated by high prices, so that total revenue from rice exports did not suffer.[30] Expansion of tobacco production took up some of the slack created by the relative decline of indigo and naval stores. But the lower South faced definite problems in the Confederation period, arising

---

[30] Bjork, *Stagnation and Growth*, appendix III-1.

TABLE 5

OFFICIAL VALUE OF BRITISH IMPORTS FROM THE UNITED STATES BY REGIONS
(£ STERLING)

Year	New England	New York	Pennsylvania	Maryland and Virginia	Carolinas	Georgia	Total
1770	148,011	69,882	28,109	435,094	288,907	55,532	1,015,535
1771	150,381	95,875	31,615	577,848	420,311	63,810	1,339,840
1772	126,265	82,707	29,133	528,404	425,923	66,083	1,258,515
1773	124,624	76,246	36,652	589,803	456,513	85,391	1,369,229
1774	112,248	20,008	69,611	612,030	432,302	67,647	1,373,846
1775	116,588	187,018	175,962	758,356	579,349	103,477	1,920,750
						Scottish, for 1783	37,932
1783	26,350	83,412	30,053	93,888	74,589	5,784	351,988
1788	267,146	111,848	32,807	504,671	282,248	25,057	1,023,789

Sources: For 1770-1775, *Senate Report No. 259* (Washington, 1894), Table 1. For 1783, MacPherson, *Annals of Commerce* (London, 1805), IV, 40. For 1788, Great Britain, Board of Trade, 6/20, p. 176.

from the fact that there were no expanding markets for the primary staple exports of the region. This, coupled with the relative increase in the price of foodstuffs they imported from the other regions, was responsible for an increasing shift into production of domestically consumed foodstuffs, and the increase in exports was well below the increase in population.

The years up to 1790 were a time of real prosperity for the tobacco planters of the upper South. A slight diminution in volume of exports for the region, coupled with exceptionally high prices, resulted in greatly increased returns from the sale of tobacco. The temporary nature of prosperity is stressed because, by 1791, the increase in production in the lower South had driven prices almost back to their prewar level and the usual pattern of agricultural price behavior was being accomplished as high prices stimulated expansion of production for the industry.

The level and pattern of economic activity for the middle Atlantic region may be inferred from several of the series for the port of Philadelphia. The export series in Table 1 shows the value of exports falling from a high in 1784 to a low in 1786 and then rising again to another peak in 1789-1790. Most of the fluctuation in the value of exports is traceable to changes in the price and volume of flour and wheat exports.[31]

Interacting with the cyclical forces introduced by the erratic shifts in the European demand for wheat were the monetary effects of the Revolution. The accumulation of specie during the war and the inability to buy imported goods had resulted in a rise in the domestic price level relative to the European, and at the end of the war there was a tremendous influx of imported goods—especially manufactured soft-goods from Great Britain. If we use our figures on the estimated value of Philadelphia exports and imports for 1784, 1787, and 1789, an estimate of the balance of trade for Philadelphia may be obtained (in millions):

	1784	1787	1789
Estimated value of exports	$3.7	$2.1	$3.5
Estimated value of imports	8.8	3.2	4.6
Estimated deficit in the balance of trade for Philadelphia	−5.1	−1.1	−1.1

The balance of trade does not allow us to make any estimates

31 *Ibid.*, appendix III-2 and pp. 160-62.

directly of the balance of payments. However, given the above estimates of the balance of trade, the consistent discount of Pennsylvania currency of sterling during the Confederation period is understandable. So is the shipment of specie to Europe, so widely depreciated by the debtor sections of the community.

The postwar adjustment of the American economy required an equilibration of the American price level with the world level of prices. This was accomplished by the classical mechanism of a trade deficit and an outflow of specie until the domestic price level had been reduced. The adjustment was complicated and modified by the abnormal supply-demand relationships for the most important of the staple commodities produced by the United States—wheat, tobacco, and rice.

One of the most interesting things about the foreign trade of the New England states in the postwar period is the tremendous increase in exports to England. Table 5 shows the official value of exports from New England to Britain in 1788 at double their prewar level. In fact, New England was the only section of the United States which exported more to Britain after the Revolution than before.

An overall view of the economic fortunes of the various states during the period makes clear much of the background against which the formulation of the Constitution and the formation of the Federal Union can be considered. Prices were falling both because of the outflow of specie and because of the behavior of European prices of important export staples. The differential effects of a falling general price level on the community are well known. The burden of governmental debt becomes heavier. The dissatisfaction of the debtor class with the resultant redistribution of income is expressed in civil unrest. The effect on profits is protested by the merchants, and trade is slow in expectation of further price decreases. All these complaints are rife in the writings of the period.

A time of disorganization of traditional markets (even when coupled with the rise of new economic opportunities) is protested as having disastrous effects, because those who are hurt by the changes are more vocal in their complaints than those who are benefiting. When this is coupled with a cyclical recession resulting from world market forces acting on the economy, it is altogether understandable that there should have been widespread dissatisfaction from 1783 to 1787 and that the weakness of the national government under the Articles of Confederation in controlling the money supply, paying interest on the public debt, and regulating and encouraging the foreign and domestic commerce should be blamed for the hardships, real and imagined, of the nation during the "critical period of American history."

After an analysis of the evidence on the period, one is inclined to agree with Benjamin Franklin that "taking a cool view of the general state of our affairs" the fortunes of the United States were "less gloomy than has been imagined." There was a modest increase in the value of American exports in the postwar period, and the terms of trade were certainly much more favorable than they had been prior to the Revolution.

The peculiar characteristics of the period from 1784 to 1792 should not be allowed to divert consideration from the longer-run problems facing the United States during the years after the War for Independence. True, commerce recovered remarkably quickly after the war, and the Federal Union was borne in on a wave of prosperity. True, the terms of trade were significantly altered, at least temporarily, by changed market conditions and by fluctuations in world prices. Nevertheless, the southern states did not have a bright future, and the growth of the middle Atlantic and northeast states would not have proceeded significantly faster than the rate of expansion of domestic markets. And if there was no necessity for a strong federal government for commercial reasons, there were still the matters of national defense, western lands, Spanish control of the Mississippi, and the Indians to be dealt with.

Taking a long view, it becomes evident that while there was a modest increase in exports between the pre- and postrevolutionary periods, the increase in exports was far below the rapid increase in population.[32] The value of per capita exports was considerably less in 1790 than it had been prior to the war.

If we were to postulate some model for the analysis of economic growth in which an expanding export sector was given causal importance in stimulating the growth of the economy, the United States during the period under consideration would not have appeared to be a very likely candidate for economic growth based on rapidly expanding demand for her products in world markets.

GORDON C. BJORK, *Columbia University*

[32] Population estimates are presented in Bjork, *Stagnation and Growth*, appendix II-3.

Explorations in Economic History 13, 397–422(1976)

Economic Change after the American Revolution: Pre- and Post-War Comparisons of Maritime Shipping and Trade*

JAMES F. SHEPHERD

Whitman College

AND

GARY M. WALTON

Indiana University and University of California, Berkeley

I. INTRODUCTION

In 1775, restrictions implemented by both the British and the American governments eliminated all direct and legal trade between the revolting 13 colonies and Great Britain and her loyal possessions. One cost of the American Revolution from the viewpoint of historians was the lapse in quantitative information on commodity trade and shipping. Not until August, 1789 did the American government take up where British officials had left off in the collection of data on shipping and trade at North American ports. Customs data for South Carolina and Pennsylvania for several years in the 1780's provide some clues to changes in the external economic relations of these states before the adoption of the Constitution, but for the most part there is a lack of sufficient statistical evidence with which to obtain a reasonably sound overall view of overseas trade and shipping for the period from 1775 to 1790. The lack of quantitative information for these years is most unfortunate, for few periods are more deserving of scholarly interest.

Of course, the levels of wartime commerce moved with the changing fortunes of war. By mid-1775 acute shortages were already felt, not only for war-related goods such as powder, flints, muskets, and knives, but also for other items like salt, shoes, woolens, and linens. To procure arms and ammunition, Congress authorized limited trade late in 1775 with the foreign West Indies, and unrestricted trade to any foreign area was allowed the following spring. Consequently, France, Spain, The Netherlands, and their American possessions became important trading partners of the revolting

*Earlier drafts of this paper have been presented to the Johns Hopkins University History Seminar on the Atlantic Economy, to the Berkeley–Stanford Economic History Workshop, to the University of Pennsylvania Economic History Seminar, to the Indiana University Economic History Seminar, and to the 49th Annual Meetings of the Western Economic Association. We are grateful to the participants at these events, who offered advice and encouragement. We also wish to thank Lawrence A. Harper, Robert L. Sexton, Gloria L. Main, Jackson Turner Main, and Gordon Philpot for comments and suggestions on an earlier version of this paper. Lastly, we are grateful to Albert Fishlow and Roger L. Ransom, who judiciously and nonanonymously acted as referees of this paper. Responsibility for any remaining errors rests solely with the authors.

397

colonies. Despite these new ties, the lowest levels of trade were reached in 1776 and 1777. These were years in which the British maintained an effective though incomplete naval blockade of American ports.[1] The main central ports from southern New England to Philadelphia were blockaded for most of the War, especially before 1778. Boston remained open after mid-1776, and it was a stronghold of American trade and privateering for the remaining years of the War. In addition the southern ports were open off and on until Savannah was taken in December, 1778, and Charleston in May, 1780; but these centers of trade generated little activity until commercial bonds with Europe were strengthened. Moreover, although some trade continued at British-occupied ports, such as New York, the levels of trade were low, especially for exports.

From a casual policy of open ports to foreigners, the American colonies came to sign formal treaties of commerce. The first such alliance was with France in 1778, and from this date until early 1782 American *wartime* commerce was at its zenith. Paralleling and reinforcing the rise of French–American commerce was the growth of trade with Spain and The Netherlands, especially after they entered the war against England in 1779 and 1780, respectively.

The Dutch were particularly active as carriers of tobacco from the Chesapeake, and the Dutch island of St. Eustatius took on the characteristics of an entrepôt in the Caribbean. In fact, the lively trade there contributed to Britain's decision to declare war against The Netherlands late in 1780. Pre-War commercial contacts between New England and Spain were maintained throughout the War, although normal trade between Spain and the colonies was on a reduced level, especially in fish, salt, and wine. Nevertheless, Spain was a center for the sale of captured prizes by American privateers, and similar to the Dutch island of St. Eustatius, Spanish Cuba became an important trade center in the Caribbean, particularly for Philadelphia and Baltimore merchants.

The revolting colonies suffered heavy losses at sea in 1782 as a result of the new southern deployment of the Royal Navy, which seized American vessels trading in the Caribbean. This reinforced the earlier effect of the British conquest of St. Eustatius, which severed trade with that important entrepôt in 1781. In general, British naval action was much more intensive in the last year of war, which brought insurance costs and risks at sea to an all-time high. Accordingly, the wartime flow of goods in and out of the colonies probably peaked before 1782.

Although direct firsthand evidence is lacking, there can be little doubt that wartime trade was considerably below pre-War levels. First, available quantitative evidence on earlier periods of conflict in North America shows

[1]For an interesting account of British blockades and their similar dislocating effects on the economies of Continental Europe during the Napoleonic Wars, see Crouzet (1964).

that wartime brought about sharp reductions in commerce, especially exports. For instance, the official values of colonial exports from 1751 to 1755 were over 40% higher than during the following 5 years of war (*Historical Statistics*, 1960, p. 757). It should be emphasized that this decline was precipitated *without* legal restrictions and blockades, effects that tended further to reduce exports during the American Revolution. Second, it could be expected that trade would be directly affected by the great reduction in shipping activity and the higher risks and costs of shipping that resulted from British blockades and naval action. It must be remembered that the export trades, especially in southern staples, were largely carried by British vessels before the war. The absence of British shipping plus the diversion of American ships from freight carriers to privateers greatly reduced the supply of ships for commerce. French, Dutch, and Spanish shipping activity only partly compensated for these reductions. In addition, the loss of ship sales to England, and the loss of bounties on particular colonial products, such as indigo and naval stores, depressed production for export. Even the coastal trade fell off because of the lack of ships, the blockades, and the embargoes imposed by the individual colonies. It should not be overlooked that the sharp rise in ocean freight rates affected the delivered cost of colonial exports, which were goods typically of low value relative to their bulk, proportionately more than imports. Third, transaction costs and uncertainty were increased, and exchanges were made more difficult to negotiate because of the hyperinflation brought about by wartime finance. The general level of prices in the colonies rose at an unprecedented rate, increasing several hundred times from the beginning of the War to the withdrawal of Continental currency and the return to hard money in 1781. Lastly, the flood of imports entering North America, especially from Britain, when peacetime trade resumed, demonstrates the deprivation that the War imposed on American consumers.[2] Clearly wartime trade was substantially below normal peacetime levels; but because the degree of decline will never be known precisely, disagreement on the magnitudes of wartime trade undoubtedly will persist.

[2] In addition to this indirect evidence we know that because of the reduced level of imports into the colonies, American resources were channeled into import-competing industries and economic self-sufficiency increased in the 13 colonies. Examples of such adjustments abound. For instance, Bezanson notes the increase of artisan workshops in and around Philadelphia. She also states that the putting-out system became general early in the War, especially in spinning for the textile plants. By the middle of 1776, 4,000 women were reputed to be employed in their homes under this system in the Philadelphia vicinity alone (see Bezanson, 1951, p. 17). The use of cereals in making beer, whiskey, and other alcoholic beverages lessened dependence upon imported wines and West Indian rum, as well as upon domestically produced rum made from imported molasses. Further evidence on external trade reduction during the 1770's and 1780's is reflected in the evidence on slave imports (see Fogel and Engerman, 1974, p. 25). Also, see Jensen, 1958, pp. 219–220.

23

Similarly, disagreement on the health of the new United States economy after the War has abounded, both among contemporary observers and among historians. For instance, Tench Coxe contended that affairs reached "... a very disagreeable condition by the year 1786."[3] Benjamin Franklin, on the other hand, upon returning from Europe, said that perhaps the state of the economy was "... less gloomy than has been imagined."[4] Historians, too, have voiced sharp differences of opinion. Curtis Nettels has painted a picture of a commercial depression,[5] whereas Merrill Jensen has called the period "... one of extraordinary economic growth."[6] The reasons for such differences of opinion again have stemmed from the lack of any overall statistical picture of output and trade for the United States during the 1780's.

Clearly, the Confederation period was one of change and readjustment. The new nation was forced to adjust both to peacetime conditions and to being outside the British Empire. The latter fact meant that the United States was subject, as any other foreign country, to British mercantilist restrictions. The impact of these adjustments had differing effects upon the several regions and the various trades. Gordon Bjork, who has recently examined the American economy of the 1780's, has stated:

> There are three separate considerations which might lead one to expect economic difficulties during the period: (1) The war wrought widespread disorganization and damage to the productive capacity of the economy. (2) The loose Confederation which preceded federal union allowed states to regulate interstate commerce. Because Hamilton argued in the Federalist Papers that a federal union was necessary to promote internal commerce, it has been said that the absence of federal union during the period constricted internal commerce. (3) The exclusion of the former colonies from the mercantilist system of the British Navigation Acts meant that certain markets for American exports were closed. The loss of these commercial privileges caused Lord Sheffield to prophesy commercial doom for the former colonies, and Thomas Jefferson lamented the exclusions and prohibitions at great length.[7]

Bjork's study was an attempt by a "new" economic historian to construct a quantitative view of the economy during the formative years of the New Nation. The purpose of the present paper is to give an alternative statistical perspective to developments which took place between the colonial years and the time of the adoption of the Constitution. The procedure followed is to use the statistical information on trade and shipping from the American Inspector-General's Ledgers[8] for the years 1768 through 1772 as a benchmark to compare with customs data for the years 1790–1792.[9]

[3]Quoted from Bjork, 1964, p. 541.
[4]Quoted from Bjork, 1964, p. 541.
[5]Nettels, 1962; see especially Chaps. 3, 4.
[6]Jensen, 1958, p. 423.
[7]Bjork, 1964, p. 542.
[8]Great Britain, Public Record Office, Customs 16/1.
[9]*U.S.A.S.P.*, 1832.

Before presenting this new statistical view of the comparative patterns and composition of trade, and of the magnitudes of trade, a critical evaluation of Bjork's evidence and analysis is presented in Section II. The statistical portrayal then follows in Sections III, IV, and V. Finally, a summary and conclusions are briefly set forth in Section VI.

II. THE PERIOD OF CONFEDERATION: FRAGMENTARY EVIDENCE

It has now been more than a decade since Bjork first presented his quantitative picture of the external economic relations of the United States for the 1780's. His attempt to give a quantitative assessment of economic change during this critical decade was an important break with previous studies of the period; earlier inquiries had been limited primarily to qualitative evidence. In contrast to these earlier investigations, Bjork boldly offered "hard numbers" to buttress his analysis. Two pillars of evidence form the basic structure of Bjork's study. The first pillar comprises estimates of exports derived from the customs-house returns of individual states. To obtain current values of trade Bjork valued the customs-house export quantities with average annual prices of the major staple commodities of the relevant ports. His account of the foreign trade of the 13 states is reproduced here in Table 1. As is evident from the table, only information from South Carolina and Pennsylvania exist for many years in the 1780's.

Of particular interest are the aggregate estimates at the bottom of Table 1. These should be viewed with extreme caution, if not total skepticism. They have been constructed by assuming that the total trade of the 13 states paralleled the trades of South Carolina and Pennsylvania, and that the partial returns for these 2 states from 1784 to 1788 remained in constant proportion to total trade, 1790–1792. By this procedure these aggregates suggest a rather severe business cycle that bottomed out in 1786 and 1787; generally, they support the pessimistic views of Coxe and Nettels quoted above in Section I.

As Fishlow (1964) has noted, several flaws mar Table 1's aggregates. First, the trade of only two states was observed. These two states were important ones, to be sure, but a mere 31% of total trade in 1790–1792 is too small a proportion of the total, even appropriately adjusted, to give a convincing view of total trade. Second, the adjustment procedure using constant shares of 1790–1792 is directly at odds with the observations for 1786 and 1788, which indicate that South Carolina's exports exceeded rather than were lower than Pennsylvania's exports for each year.. Bjork's selection of 1790–1792 weights therefore bestows greater importance to Pennsylvania's trade than would result if he had used weights from other years. Third, other evidence used by Bjork on British trade with the United States shows an increase in trade from 1784 to 1785 rather than a decline of 25% shown in his

TABLE 1
Bjork's Estimates of Exports by State 1784–1792
(in $000)

State	1784	1785	1786	1787	1788	1789–90	1790–91	1791–92	Average proportion of trade by states (percentage) 1790–92
Georgia							491	459	2.4
South Carolina	2,148	1,892	2,303	2,717	2,551		2,693	2,428	12.9
North Carolina			506				525	528	2.6
Virginia							3,132	3,553	16.8
Maryland						2,028	2,240	2,624	12.2
Delaware							120	134	0.6
Pennsylvania	3,725	2,509	2,059	2,142	2,427	3,511	3,436	3,821	18.2
New Jersey							27	23	0.1
New York					1,925	2,000	2,505	2,536	12.7
Connecticut							710	880	4.0
Rhode Island							470	698	2.9
Massachusetts				1,588	1,969		2,520	2,888	13.6
New Hampshire							143	181	0.8
Official total value of exports, in $000						17,450	19,012	20,753	
Ratio estimate of total value of exports in $000,000	18.9	14.2	14.4	14.4	15.5	17.5			

Source: Bjork, 1964, p. 548.

aggregates (Bjork, 1964, p. 550). Similarly, the estimates of United States trade to France and to Holland do not support the view of an extended depression in trade. Instead, the mid-1780's appear as years of modest advance (see Buron, 1932; and Kohlmeier, 1925).

Since Great Britain, France, and The Netherlands were major overseas trading partners of the United States, and exports to these countries formed more than one-half of total United States trade, Bjork's portrayal of a nationwide depression in 1786 is questionable. Similarly, as Table 1 shows, South Carolina apparently did not suffer the sharp drop in trade experienced by Pennsylvania. Perhaps the more pessimistic portrayals of a nationwide depression in 1786 reflected in Bjork's estimates of total trade have resulted from too much concentration on Pennsylvania.

Aside from these shortcomings, Bjork's Table 1 does not permit direct comparisons with trade of the later colonial period. For instance, no adjustment was made to show exports in real terms, nor was any evidence on total real exports from the late colonial period presented. Moreover, no adjustment was made for population growth. Were real per capita exports higher in the 1780's than in the early 1770's? Because Bjork's estimates are given in isolation, their usefulness has been severely limited.

By comparison, Bjork's second pillar stands more sturdily. It shows estimates of the terms of trade for the years 1770–1775 and 1784–1792. This evidence, reproduced here in Table 2, nicely complements and increases the usefulness of his estimates of the current value of exports in Table 1. If exports in the late colonial period were not significantly different from those in the 1780's, then the improved terms of trade between these periods signified an increase in total U.S. import capacity. Whether or not the increase occurred in per capita terms was left unanswered, however.

Also, the finding of relatively constant import prices, 1770–1775 to 1784–1792, with higher export prices between these periods is not free of bias. Similar to the export aggregates of Table 1, Bjork weighted his export price series by the share of commodities in total exports for the years 1790–1792. It is quite possible that the 1770–1775 weights would substantially alter this favorable terms of trade picture. For instance, favorable markets abroad for wheat and flour and breadstuffs in 1791 and 1792 give these items unusually large weights. In contrast, tobacco was no longer the leading export in 1790–1792 (in current prices), and its price was weighted less than it would have been with an earlier selection of weights. As suggested by Fishlow, these and other alterations would leave the terms of trade higher in the 1780's than in the early 1770's, "but with considerable difference in magnitude."[10]

In any case, without making the proper link between the evidence given in

[10]Fishlow, 1964, p. 563. For a more complete account of these and other criticisms of Bjork's study, see Fishlow (1964, pp. 561–566).

TABLE 2
Bjork's Import and Export Prices and the Terms of Trade

Year	Import price index A	Import price index B	Composite import price index	Export price index	Terms of trade
1770	123	98	110	69	63
1771	108	100	104	75	72
1772	103	102	102	83	81
1773	114	104	109	78	72
1774	115	100	108	73	68
1775	123	96	109	70	64
1784	109	98	103	115	112
1785	101	101	101	106	105
1786	98	104	101	97	96
1787	97	105	101	92	91
1788	94	103	99	87	88
1789	94	105	99	87	88
1790	100	100	100	100	100
1791	107	99	103	92	89
1792	120	99	110	86	78

Source: Bjork, 1964, p. 554.

Notes: Import price index A is a Laspeyres index (1790 = 100) composed of U.S. prices for tea, coffee, sugar, salt, molasses, Madeira wine, rum, and Russian duck. Import price index B is also a Laspeyres index (1790 = 100) based on British prices for blue cloth, common shoes, stockings, and hats modified to take into account changes in the rate of exchange between sterling and the dollar. Indices A and B are given equal weight in the composite index.

The export price index is a Laspeyres index composed of 14 commodities accounting for 86.8% of the value of total exports in 1790.

Tables 1 and 2, and without the necessary adjustments of the estimates, one is left uncertain about the comparable conditions of trade between the periods, especially in real per capita terms. It would appear from the evidence that quite possibly conditions were worsening, particularly from a longer-run perspective when the early 1770's are compared to the early 1790's. Table 1 suggests little improvement in the absolute levels of total trade, 1784–1792, and Table 2 suggests that by 1790–1792 the more favorable terms of trade enjoyed in the early and mid-1780's had been dissipated. To investigate more thoroughly this possible worsening of conditions, we now turn to newly assembled evidence on aggregate U.S. maritime trade and shipping.

III. PRE- AND POST-WAR COMPARISONS: PATTERNS AND COMPOSITION OF AMERICAN EXPORT TRADE

In contrast with the 1780's, the early 1790's offer the possibility of a much more systematic comparison with pre-War trade. This results from the availability of customs data which the new American government began to collect in August 1789. With this evidence, the patterns, magnitudes, and composition of foreign trade for the years 1790–1792 can be compared with the statistical picture of trade in 1768–1772.

An interval of 17 years between these records of trade is appropriate for giving perspective to the longer-run effects of independence. Of course, changes in trade were a persistent feature of pre-Revolutionary America, and some of the changes to be noted were a consequence of pre-War trends. The West Indian trade, for example, increased in relative importance over the entire 18th century. Consequently, though independence was an important factor in altering trade patterns and magnitudes, it is impossible to isolate the impact of independence from earlier trends and changes which would have occurred had the 13 colonies remained within the British Empire. The effects of the adoption of the Constitution and the emergence of a stronger central government had important consequences for the United States economy, especially over the longer run.[11] Still, one would expect that the basic economic structure of the country, and the patterns of its foreign trade in the early 1790's, was shaped more importantly, first, by a resource base and the existence of an Atlantic economy which were the heritage of earlier years; and second, by modifications brought about by recovery and independence, and the consequent readjustments which took place in the 1780's. Beginning in 1793, however, the situation pertaining to the country's external economic relations changed as the major European powers entered into the Napoleonic Wars. Because the effects of this conflict were so great, any changes which had been brought about by the War and independence would be obscured by the effects of the Napoleonic Wars on American trade.

Thus, to begin this comparison of American overseas trade, the annual average values of exports from the 13 colonies to major overseas areas in 1768–1772 are compared with those values from the United States in 1790–1792,[12] in Table 3. In order to make the values comparable, the dollar values from 1790–1792 have been converted to pounds sterling, and to 1768–1772 prices.[13]

[11] Important shorter-run consequences followed from such actions by the federal government as the funding of the national debt and the assumption of the state debts.

[12] The fiscal years in the customs records were August 1789, through September 30, 1790; October 1, 1790, through September 30, 1791; and October 1, 1791, through September 30, 1792. The first customs year thus contained from 13 to 14 months, but this should have only a slight upward bias on the 3-year averages.

[13] There are certain factors that make the values in Table 3 less than perfectly comparable. For example, export values to the Canadian colonies are not available for 1768–1772; Florida and Louisiana are included in the trade with the foreign West Indies in 1790–1792 (they were not included for 1768–1772); and legal trade with other areas, such as the East Indies, did not exist in 1768–1772. Nevertheless, these qualifications are minor and the broad patterns of trade with overseas areas can be contrasted. (See footnote 17 for a discussion of the computation of real values.) Note that a "national" or overall export price index is used to compute real values

TABLE 3

Average Annual Exports to Overseas Areas: The 13 Colonies, 1768–1772, and the United States, 1790–1792[a] (Thousands of Pounds Sterling; 1768–1772 prices)[b]

Destination[c]	1768–1772	Percentage of total	1790–1792	Percentage of total
Great Britain and Ireland	1616	58	1234	31
Northern Europe	—		643	16
Southern Europe	406	14	557	14
British West Indies	759	27	402	10
Foreign West Indies			956	24
Africa	21	1	42	1
Canadian colonies	—[d]		60	2
Other	—		59	1
Total	2802	100	3953	100

Source: Average annual exports for 1768–1772 are taken from Shepherd and Walton (1972, pp. 94–95); and exports for 1790–1792 are taken from *U.S.A.S.P.* (1832).

[a] The annual average exports for 1790–1792 are taken from export values given in the source for the following periods: (1) various days in August, 1789, to September 30, 1790; (2) October 1, 1790 through September 30, 1791; and (3) October 1, 1791 through September 30, 1792.

[b] Values for 1790–1792 were converted to pounds sterling and 1768–1772 prices on the basis of a Paasche price index implicit in the calculations of real values of the more important commodity exports in Table 4. This implicit Paasche index is 4.924, which includes the exchange rate between sterling and dollars, and the change in the average level of prices of those exports (listed in Table 4) between 1768–1772 and 1790–1792 (see footnote 17 for a discussion of the exchange rate and changes in the general level of export prices). This index stems from revaluing the quantities of those annual average commodity exports in 1790–1792 with average prices of the same commodities exported in 1768–1772 (Table 4).

[c] Northern Europe includes continental European countries north of Cape Finisterre. Southern Europe includes Spain, the Canary Islands, Portugal, Madeira, the Azores, the Cape Verde Islands, Gibraltar and other Mediterranean ports in Europe (except French ports). The Foreign West Indies includes the Swedish, Danish, Dutch, French and Spanish Caribbean possessions, and Florida and Louisiana. Africa includes North Africa, the west coast of Africa, and the Cape of Good Hope. The Canadian colonies include the British American colonies, including Newfoundland and the British fisheries; and St. Pierre, Miquelon, and the French fisheries. Other destinations include the East Indies, the northwest coast of America, and unknown destinations.

[d] Not available.

of 1790–1792 exports destined for each overseas area. An error is committed using this estimation procedure because of the different mix of commodities going to each overseas area. The share of tobacco was larger in exports to Europe than in total exports to all overseas areas. The price of tobacco decreased relative to flour. As a result, the use of an overall export price index tends to understate the real value of exports to Europe and to overstate the real value of exports going to the West Indies (to which flour was a relatively more important import than tobacco). Such errors could only be avoided if separate indexes were prepared for the trade with each overseas area. The same problem occurs below on the American side when we estimate exports by colony/state and region.

From Table 3, it is clear that by 1790 the United States had taken advantage of its new freedom to trade directly with other northern European countries. The major part of this trade was with France and the Netherlands, and the major commodity exported to these countries was tobacco, though exports of rice, flour, wheat, and Indian corn (maize) were important.[14] The establishment of this trade with northern Europe, however, did not preclude the major share of American exports from reverting to Great Britain, though pre-War levels of exports to Britain were not reached by 1790–1792. The reversion of much of American foreign trade to Britain probably occurred soon after the War ended.[15] The reasons for this have long been discussed by historians.[16] Many of the imports desired by Americans were found in greatest variety and at the best price and quality there. British woolens, Irish linens, and the vast array of hardwares of British manufacture are examples. British merchants, too, through a common language, established contacts, and a knowledge of American markets, regained a competitive edge over French and Dutch merchants after the War. Still, the emergence of a large direct trade with other northern European countries must stand as a major consequence of independence.

By 1790 trade with the West Indies had surpassed its relative pre-War role, and trade with southern Europe, which had been severely disrupted by the War, had just regained its relative position. The major difference after the War is one not shown in Table 3 because a precise breakdown between exports to the British and foreign West Indies is not available for 1768–1772. Before the Revolution, trade with the British West Indies had been greater than with the foreign islands. By 1790 the situation was reversed. The exclusion of American shipping from the British West Indies after the War was a major factor. Undoubtedly, this shift is overstated by the statistics. Many American ships clearing for foreign islands went illegally to British Caribbean areas. Also, in the 1780's Saint Eustatius remained an entrepôt from which British islands were supplied, as it had during the War. Consequently, any conclusions about changes in the important West Indian trade brought by independence must be tentative. It would appear, however, that the United States was shifting towards increased trade with non-British areas of the Caribbean during the 1780's. The War and independence must have played a part in such a shift; but this trend had been going on before the Revolution, and was likely only accelerated by independence and restrictions upon American shipping.

The changes in the composition of trade that accompanied these changing

---

[14]The late 1780's and early 1790's appear to have been times of poor crops in Europe. Demand for American foodstuffs may have been abnormally high as a result.

[15]See Bjork, 1964, p. 550, for evidence on British–American trade during the 1780's.

[16]Johnson, 1915, pp. 125–127; Gray, 1933, pp. 599–602.

31

TABLE 4

Annual Average Exports of Selected Commodities from the 13 Colonies, 1768-1772, and the United States, 1790-1792

Commodity	Thirteen Colonies, 1768-1772			United States, 1790-1792		
	Quantity (1)	Value (thousands of current pounds sterling) (2)	Value (thousands of dollars; 1790-1792 prices) (3)	Quantity^a (4)	Value (thousands of current dollars) (5)	Value (thousands of pounds sterling; 1768-1772 prices)^e (6)
Beef^b	26,036 bbl	51	209	60,457 bbl	367 }	159
Pork^b				29,741 bbl	285 }	
Bread	38,634 tons	410	2,534	3,823 tons	221 }	712
Flour				63,256 tons^c	4,178^c }	
Cotton	29,425 lb	1	7	163,822 lb^c	41^c	8
Fish, dried^d	308,993 quintals	154	740	375,619 quintals	900	187
Flaxseed	233,065 bu	42	189	352,079 bu	286	64
Grain:						
Indian corn	839,314 bu	83	424	1,926,784 bu	974	191
Rice^e	140,254 bbl	311	1,971	129,367 bbl	1,818	287
Wheat	599,127 bu	115	654	998,862 bu	1,090	192
Indigo^f	547,649 lb	113	567	493,760 lb	511	101
Iron:						
Bar	2,416 tons	36	195	300 tons	24	4
Pig	4,468 tons	22	116	3,667 tons	95	18
Livestock:^g						
Cattle	3,433	21	63	4,861	89	29
Horses	6,048	60	240	7,086	282	71
Naval Stores:						
Pitch	11,384 bbl	5	21	7,279 bbl	13	3
Tar	90,472 bbl	34	135	68,463 bbl	102	25
Turpentine	19,870 bbl	9	42	51,194 bbl	108	24
Oil, whale	3,841 tons	46	212	1,826 tons^h	101	22
Potash	1,381 tons	35	134	4,872 tons	472	123

Rum, American	342,366 gal	22	132	441,782 gal	170^i	28
Tobacco	87,986 hhd	766	3,093	110,687 hhd	3,891	964
Wood Products:						
Pine boards^k	38,991 M ft	70	228	45,118 M ft	264	81
Staves and headings^l	21,585 M	65	275	31,554 M	401	95
Total, above commodities		2,471	12,181		16,683	3,388
All exports		2,802			19,465	

Source: See Table 3.

[a] Five commodities (bread, flour, flaxseed, rice, and whale oil) were given in different units in the two sources; see Table 3). The following amounts were recorded in the *U.S.A.S.P.* (1832), and the following ratios have been used to convert to equivalent units for purposes of comparison.

Amounts recorded in *U.S.A.S.P.*		Conversion equivalencies
Commodity		
Bread	85,644 bbl	1 bbl = 100 lb
Flour	722,923 bbl	1 bbl = 196 lb
Flaxseed	50,297 casks	1 cask = 7 bu
Rice	113,196 tierces	1 tierce = 600 lb = 1.1429 barrels (of 1770)
Whale oil	460,114 gallons	1 ton = 252 gal = 8 barrels

Tons of bread and flour were interpreted as long tons of 2240 lb. Sources for these conversions have been several. The reader may wish to see *Historical Statistics* (1960, Chap. Z); Cole (1938, p. x); Gray (1933, p. 610); and Shepherd and Walton (1972, p. 206).

[b] Quantities of beef and pork were given in barrels in both sources for the two periods. However, Cole (1938, p. x) states that barrels of beef averaged 225 pounds and pork 217 pounds until 1789, and 200 pounds thereafter. No adjustments were made in the quantities of barrels for beef and pork in this table, but the appropriate adjustment, based upon these weights (as stated by Cole) were made in computing the value of 1768–1772 exports in 1790–1792 prices, and the value of 1790–1792 exports in 1768–1772 prices.

[c] The source listed the 1790 quantity of cotton exports as 2027 bales, and the 1790 value as $58,408. No attempt was made to convert the 1790 quantity to pounds. Consequently, the average quantity and value of cotton exports shown in this Table are for 1791 and 1792 only. The average value of cotton exports for 1790–1792 was $46,733.

[d] Dried fish was recorded in quintals in both the American customs records, 1768–1772, and the *U.S.A.S.P.* (1832) for 1790–1792. The latter source, however explicitly states for 1791 that these quintals were hundred weights of 112 pounds. Cole (1938, p. x) states that quintals of dried codfish were 100 pounds during both these periods. This raises the possibility that in the 1768–1772 records, quintals were 100 pounds, and 112 pounds in the 1790–1792 source. In view of the lack of any other evidence bearing upon this question, however, no adjustment was made of the quantity data for dried fish exports for either period.

continued

TABLE 4—Continued

e Rice exports for 1790 and 1791 may be understated because one quarterly return for 1790, and two consecutive quarterly returns for 1791 (April 1–September 30), for Charleston, South Carolina had not been submitted, according to the source (U.S.A.S.P., 1832). The source gave the following annual data on rice exports.

	Quantity (tierces)	Value ($)
1790	100,845	1,753,796
1791	96,980	1,503,190
1792	141,762	2,197,311
Average 1790–1792	113,196	1,818,099

If rice exports in 1790 and 1791 were as large as in 1792 (162,014 barrels of 1770 valued at 359,000 pounds sterling in 1768–1772 prices), then annual rice exports in the early 1790's would have averaged more than in 1768–1772.

f With regard to indigo exports for 1792, the source stated: "There is reason to believe that an error of clerkship has arisen in some of the returns of indigo, as the quantity shipped in the several years last past has been much greater, on a medium, than 371,442 pounds." The source gave the following data on indigo exports.

	Quantity (lb)	Value ($)
1790	612,119	537,379
1791	497,720	570,234
1792	371,442	425,558
Average 1790–1792	493,760	511,057

Consequently, annual indigo exports in the early 1790s may have averaged more than in the years, 1768–1772. Indigo exports averaged 554,920 pounds and $553,807 in 1790–1791 (115,000 pounds sterling in 1768–1772 prices).

g Livestock, especially cattle, probably was overvalued in the 1768–1772 source. In view of the small amounts involved, no attempt was made to correct the values in this Table.

h The 1790 quantity of whale oil exported was given as 15,765 barrels. It was assumed these were barrels of 31.5 gallons.

i The average quantity of American-produced rum exports is for 1790 and 1791 only. Exports in 1792 were not given in the source.

j Tobacco exports were given in both hogsheads and pounds in the source for 1769–1772. The average weight of a hogshead in these years was 1,015 pounds per hogshead.

k The quantities of pine boards are given in thousands of feet. The average quantity of exports for 1790–1792 included both pine boards and plank. The 1790 quantity did not distinguish pine from oak and other boards and plank. Pine boards and plank were 94% of all boards and plank exported in 1791 and 1792. In view of the probable small amounts involved, no adjustment was made to the 1790 quantity and value of boards and plank exported.

l The quantities of staves and headings are given in thousands.

patterns of trade can be seen in Table 4.[17] Though not all commodity exports are listed, those that comprised the major proportion of the value of exports are given (over 88% in 1768–1772, and over 85% in 1790–1792). Contrary to popular belief, the great pre-War staple, tobacco, was no longer the single most valuable export by the early 1790's in terms of current values, though tobacco exports came to exceed pre-War levels and reached an all-time high in 1790–1792.[18] Tobacco production may have equaled or perhaps exceeded pre-War levels by the mid-1780's.[19] Higher prices of tobacco in the later 1780's together with higher levels of output resulted in modest recovery in the tobacco-producing areas of Virginia and Maryland, as well as stimulating the Piedmont region of North Carolina into which tobacco production was spreading.[20]

This appears not to have been the case for the other important southern staples of rice and indigo, however, and the export trade of South Carolina may have actually fallen from 1768–1772 to 1790–1792 (also, see Table 5). This conclusion must be qualified because of incomplete customs returns from that state for 1790 and 1791 (see Table 4, footnotes *e, f;* Table 5, footnote *d*). Nevertheless, even when noting this qualification, exports of the lower south surely did not increase to the extent they did from other regions,

[17] In order to compare the magnitudes of trade as well as the composition, the real values of those commodities listed in Table 4 were computed in two ways. First, 1768–1772 exports were valued using the average dollar prices implicit in the quantities and values of the same commodities exported in 1790–1792 (column 3). Second, 1790–1792 exports were revalued in the same way, using implicit average sterling prices from 1768–1772 (column 6). Thus, there are two comparisons of real values that may be made. These two comparisons are equivalent to revaluing 1790–1792 exports by a Paasche price index, which provides a lower limit to the change in prices between the two periods, and a Laspeyres price index, which provides an upper limit to the change in prices. The Paasche index is 4.924 and the Laspeyres 4.930 (1768–1772 = 100), hence the ambiguity in the price level change is very small. It should be noted that these two index numbers include the exchange rate between sterling and the dollar, as well as the change in the level of export prices. The usual exchange rate between the U.S. dollar and sterling was $4.44 = £1 (Nussbaum, 1957, p. 32) after the U.S. dollar was established in the Coinage Act of 1792. The same exchange rate had earlier prevailed for Spanish dollars in circulation. Consequently, if this rate can be used to convert dollars to sterling, the Paasche index becomes 1.109 and the Laspeyres 1.110 (1768–1772 = 100). Hence, export prices rose on the average about 11% from 1768–1772 to 1790–1792. This price level change can be compared to the Warren-Pearson price index (*Historical Statistics*, 1960, p. 116). Taking a simple average of the Warren-Pearson index numbers for 1768–1772 and 1790–1791 (1792 is not given), the price index for 1790–1791 is 1.105 (1768–1772 = 100) very nearly the same as our Paasche and Laspeyres indexes from Table 4. For 1789–1791 (remembering that the 1790 fiscal year covered part of 1789), the Warren-Pearson price index yields a price index for 1789–1791 of 1.098 (1768–1772 = 100). Had we used the Warren-Pearson price index to compute real values, by chance, our results would have been nearly the same. The results indicate that the real value of exports increased by about 37% from 1768–1772 to 1790–1792.

[18] Robertson, 1973, p. 115; Bjork, 1964, p. 544. The 1790–1792 exports of tobacco valued in 1768–1772 prices exceeded the value of flour exports, however. Current values of flour were higher due to the increase in its price relative to tobacco between the two periods (see Bezanson, 1951, pp. 332–342).

[19] Gray, 1933, p. 605.

[20] Tobacco prices fell, however, in 1791 (Gray, 1933, p. 605).

or keep pace with the rise in population (see Table 5, footnote *d*). Higher rice prices offset to some extent the lower quantity of rice exports in 1790–1792, but indigo fell in both quantity and value. The decline in indigo production, however, was not to the very low levels that some have attributed to the loss of the British bounty and the encouragement of its production by the British in the West Indies after the War.[21]

Naval stores were other exports largely produced in the southern colonies. Average annual exports of these commodities in 1790–1792 were mixed compared with 1768–1772; but their total value was about the same in both periods, and small relative to tobacco, rice, and indigo. Though average annual exports of cotton increased by over five times from 1768–1772 to 1790–1792, the overall value of cotton exports was still relatively small before Whitney's invention of the cotton gin in 1793.

The most outstanding feature of Table 4 is the dramatic increase in the export of foodstuffs like barreled meats (beef and pork), bread and flour, Indian corn, and wheat. Because these were the more important commodities in the West Indian trade, the increase in their share of total exports should come as no surprise. These trends were under way before the Revolution occurred, however, and the shift into grain production in the upper south in the later colonial period is well known.[22] To repeat, then, not all of this increased export of foodstuffs can be attributed to independence.[23]

One sharp reversal in exports clearly due to independence was the impact of the prohibitive duty on whale oil imports imposed by the British in 1783. New England's whaling industry suffered as a result.

Overall, there was an increase in the real value of exports of about 37% from 1768–1772 to 1790–1792, assuming that the customs data upon which these comparisons have been based are reasonably accurate.[24] Did this increase in real exports keep pace with population? What were the regional effects of these changes? It is to these questions that we now turn.

IV. COMMODITY TRADE: REGIONAL AND PER CAPITA TRENDS

Comparisons of per capita values of exports from the individual colonies and states, and major regions, disclose further interesting changes in the American economy. These comparisons are shown in Table 5 in real terms

[21]See, for example, Thomas, 1965, p. 628. Indigo production did decrease greatly after 1792, however, due to competition with the West Indies for British markets (Gray, 1933, pp. 610–611). It is possible that indigo exports began to decline in 1792, and that this was the reason for the lower figure in the customs returns of this year (see Table 4, footnote *f*).

[22]Klingaman, 1969, pp. 268–278.

[23]Increased demand for foodstuffs from Europe due to poor crops in the late 1780's and early 1790's has been noted above in footnote 14. To the extent such demand came from northern continental countries, independence allowing direct trade with these countries would have been a factor.

[24]The implicit Paasche quantity index from Table 4 is 1.3696, and the implicit Laspeyres quantity index is 1.3711 (1768–1772 = 100).

TABLE 5
Average Annual Exports from Colonies and Regions of the 13 Colonies, 1768-1772;
and States and Regions of the United States, 1791-1792[a]
(Thousands of Pounds Sterling; 1768-1772 Prices)[b]

	1768-1772			1791-1792		
Origin	Total exports	Percentage of total	Per capita exports[c]	Total exports	Percentage of total	Per capita exports[c]
New England						
New Hampshire	46	2	0.74	33	1	0.23
Massachusetts	258	9	0.97	542	14	1.14
Rhode Island	81	3	1.39	119	3	1.72
Connecticut	92	3	0.50	148	4	0.62
Total, New England	477	17	0.82	842	22	0.83
Middle Atlantic						
New York	187	7	1.15	512	14	1.51
New Jersey	2	—	0.02	5	—	0.03
Pennsylvania	353	13	1.47	584	16	1.34
Delaware	18	1	0.51	26	1	0.44
Total, Middle Atlantic	559	20	1.01	1127	30	1.11
Upper South						
Maryland	392	14	1.93	482	13	1.51
Virginia	770	27	1.72	678	18	0.91
Total, Upper South	1162	41	1.79	1160	31	1.09
Lower South						
North Carolina	75	3	0.38	104	3	0.27
South Carolina	455	16	3.66	436	12	1.75
Georgia	74	3	3.17	97	3	1.17
Total, Lower South	603	22	1.75	637	17	0.88
Total, all regions	2802	100	1.31	3766	100	0.99

Sources: See Table 3 for sources of export data. Population data used to compute per capita exports were taken from *Historical Statistics* (1960, pp. 13, 756).

[a] The annual average exports for 1791-1792 are taken from export values given in the source for the following periods: (1) October 1, 1790, through September 30, 1791; and (2) October 1, 1791, through September 30, 1792. Note that Table 5 differs from Tables 3 and 4 in that average exports are computed for only 2 fiscal years, 1791 and 1792, rather than 3 years, 1790 through 1792. This is because exports were not given by state or region of origin in the source for fiscal year 1790.

[b] See Table 3, footnote *b*.

[c] The population of Maine was included with that of Massachusetts for computing per capita exports in 1768-1772 and 1791-1792. The population of Vermont was included in that of New England for computing the regional per capita exports of that region, but Vermont's population was not allocated among the other New England colonies and states for computing per capita exports of the individual colonies and states for 1768-1772 and 1791-1792. Per capita exports are given in pounds sterling.

[d] Because of incomplete returns from Charleston, South Carolina, for 1790 and 1791, and errors which may have affected the returns for indigo (see Table 4, footnotes *e* and *f*), exports from South Carolina and the lower south may be understated in this table. If rice exports had been as great in 1790 and 1791 as in 1792 (for which a full year's returns presumably exist), then total exports from South Carolina and the lower south would have been greater by 77,000 pounds sterling. If indigo exports had been as high in 1792 as they averaged in 1790-1791 (see Table 4, footnote *f*), then total exports from South Carolina would have been greater by about 9000 pounds sterling. Additional exports of 86,000 pounds sterling from South Carolina would have resulted in per capita exports for the state of 2.10 pounds sterling in 1791-1792, and per capita exports for the lower south of 0.99 pounds sterling.

in order to adjust for inflationary effects and sterling–dollar exchange. It is clear that the increase in real exports from 1768–1772 to the early 1790's was due almost entirely to increased exports from New England and the Middle Atlantic regions. Compared to pre-War proportions among the regions, therefore, overseas trade gained slightly in relative importance to the northern regions, and especially to the Middle Atlantic states. It might be noted that this occurred despite the depressed economies of Pennsylvania and New Hampshire, which suffered because of the falling off in shipbuilding and the lumber trade.

As indicated by the fall in per capita exports, the export trade of the southern regions did not keep pace with a growing population. Though the export trades of these regions just about regained their pre-War absolute levels of exports by the early 1790's, per capita exports were significantly below pre-War levels. In contrast, and with the exceptions of New Hampshire, Pennsylvania, and Delaware, the export trades of the northern states increased relatively more than their populations. In particular, exports from New York boomed, reflecting the increased agricultural output of that state. This contrast among the states makes generalization difficult, if not impossible. Clearly, the decline of more than 25% in real per capita exports between 1768–1772 and 1790–1792 hides as much as it reveals. Moreover, the fall in per capita export values for the south was likely the result of a slowing in the growth of demand for southern staples rather than the direct consequence of market alterations stemming from independence and new economic and political alliances. It should be emphasized that it was the export trade in southern staples which was stagnating—not the aggregate size of the southern economies. Population growth and settlement were rapidly taking place; but this vigorous growth was in the western parts of the original southern states, and in the future states of Kentucky and Tennessee, rather than in the older staple-producing areas. Soon there would be a great new southern staple; but, at this moment in the early 1790's, the older staples were beginning to fall into eclipse.

This discussion also illustrates the fact that the new United States, like the 13 colonies, did not comprise a single, integrated national economy. Political and social, rather than economic, ties primarily bound the new nation together.

V. SHIPPING FLOWS AND INVISIBLE EARNINGS

Paralleling the growth of commodity trade was the growth of mercantile and shipping activities which had been so important to New England and the middle colonies before the War. Although tonnage statistics of vessels clearing American ports are not available, there is information on tonnages of entering vessels after 1789. Alexander Hamilton described this entering shipping as "vessels employed . . . in the import trade of the United States . . ." (*U.S.A.S.P.*, 1832, p. 50). Table 6 compares these tonnage flows with ones from before the War. According to the *American State Papers*, the total tonnage of shipping entering U.S. ports in the years 1790–1792 averaged about 587,000 tons per year. Due to a change in the definition of tonnage measurement between 1768–1772 and 1790–1792, however, the tonnage data from the *American State Papers* are not comparable with those from the pre-War years.[25] This relationship has been investigated by McCusker (1967), Walton (1967), and French (1973), who found that pre-1786 registered tonnage was substantially less for any vessel, on the average, than post-1786 measured tonnage (based upon the 1773 formula). To account for this change of definition, all tonnages taken from the *American State Papers* have been multiplied by correction factors of 0.75, 0.65, and 0.55 to obtain tonnage ranges comparable with the registered tonnage of 1768–1772. This range of correction terms is used because the relationship between registered and measured tonnage varied systematically by size category of ships (Table 6, footnote *a*).

Because American vessels typically were smaller—certainly smaller than British vessels—an appropriate comparison of pre-War American-owned tonnage is most likely with the range set forth by columns (4) and (5). For comparisons of foreign-owned tonnages, however, column (6) should most likely be compared to the range specified by columns (8) or (9) because foreign vessels were normally larger.

What does this comparison of tonnage flows suggest about shipping earnings before and after the Revolution? Existing estimates are based upon evidence pertaining to the volume of American-owned tonnage and average earnings per ton.[26] Unfortunately, evidence on average earnings per ton for 1790–1792 is scanty and incomplete. There are no data on utilization of shipping capacity for this period, nor do freight rate series for U.S. shipping routes exist. Rates in the Baltic timber trade declined about 30% from 1770–1790 (North, 1965). Consequently, one is led to conclude that any increase in shipping earnings must have come from an increase in the volume of American-owned shipping engaged in overseas trade.

Table 6 does support the view that there was a considerable growth of shipping volume between these periods. Not only did the absolute amount of tonnage increase with all areas, but as shown in Table 6 the proportion of American-owned shipping increased in all overseas trades except for the important West Indies trade. Here the British restrictions on American shipping precluded direct legal trade with the British islands. Of course, American ships may have gone illegally to the British islands, or American

---

[25]See Walton, 1967; French, 1973.

[26]The estimated average annual shipping earnings for 1768–1772 (Shepherd and Walton, 1972, p. 128) are less than half the estimated shipping earnings for the United States in 1790–1792 of 6.5 million dollars (North, 1960, p. 600). The 1768–1772 estimate employs data on tonnage flows into and outward from the American colonies. The 1790–1792 estimate is based upon the stock of American-owned tonnage.

TABLE 6

Annual Average Shipping Tonnage^a (by American and Foreign Ownership)^b Entering Major Regions^c of the 13 Colonies, 1768–1772, and the United States, 1790–1792, from Foreign Areas (in Hundreds of Tons)^e

	American-owned					Foreign-owned				
	1768–1772	1790–1792				1768–1772	1790–1972			
	(1)	(2) (Unadjusted)	(3) (0.75 of (2))	(4) (0.65 of (2))	(5) (0.55 of (2))	(6)	(7) (Unadjusted)	(8) (0.75 of (7))	(9) (0.65 of (7))	(10) (0.55 of (7))
Overseas area of origin: American region of destination										
Great Britain & Ireland										
New England	95	165	124	107	91	45	36	27	24	20
Middle Atlantic	104	207	155	135	114	61	213	160	138	117
Upper South	34	180	135	117	99	349	346	260	225	190
Lower South	22	59	44	38	32	200	155	116	101	85
Total	256	611	458	397	336	655	750	563	488	413
Northern Europe										
New England	—	108	81	70	59	—	9	6	6	5
Middle Atlantic	—	106	80	69	58	—	38	29	25	21
Upper South	—	109	82	71	60	—	102	77	66	56
Lower South	—	34	26	22	19	—	51	38	33	28
Total	—	358	268	232	197	—	200	150	130	110
Southern Europe										
New England	58	143	107	93	79	11	8	6	5	4
Middle Atlantic	90	207	155	134	114	29	85	64	55	47
Upper South	21	92	69	60	51	43	47	35	30	26
Lower South	6	21	16	14	12	25	19	15	13	11
Total	176	462	347	301	254	108	160	120	104	88

West Indies										
New England	437	938	703	610	516	18	134	100	87	74
Middle Atlantic	183	374	281	243	206	35	370	278	241	204
Upper South	97	230	172	149	126	62	294	220	191	162
Lower South	56	337	253	219	186	130	341	256	222	188
Total	774	1879	1409	1221	1033	246	1139	854	740	626
Africa, Total	—	8	6	5	4	20[b]	5	4	3	3
Canadian Colonies, Total	—	21	16	14	12	—[d]	207	155	134	114
Other, Total	—	48	36	31	26	—	27	20	17	15
Total from foreign areas										
New England	590	1389	1042	903	764	74	280	210	182	154
Middle Atlantic	378	923	692	600	508	125	815	611	530	448
Upper South	153	622	467	404	342	459	808	606	525	444
Lower South	84	453	340	294	249	370	585	439	380	322
Total	1205	3387	2540	2202	1863	1028	2488	1866	1617	1368

Sources: For 1768–1772, Shepherd and Walton (1972, pp. 118–119); and for 1790–1792, U.S.A.S.P. (1832, pp. 51–63, 206–216, 254–263).

[a] The tonnage data for 1768–1772 are based upon the pre-1786 measure of registered tonnage used to record the size of British vessels. After 1786 British vessels were required to register on the basis of the 1773 formula for measured tonnage. The relationship between pre-1786 registered tonnage, and the measured tonnage calculated from the 1773 formula, has been investigated by McCusker (1967), Walton (1967), and French (1973). In the samples observed by French, pre-1786 registered tonnage for the same ships averaged approximately 25.45% less than their post-1786 measured tonnage. However, as noted by French, the relationship between registered and measured tonnage differed from ship to ship, and varied systematically by size classification of ship. The difference tended to be larger for smaller ships; registered tonnage was approximately 43 to 45% less than measured tonnage for ships ranging from 51 to 150 registered tons, and 30 to 32% less for ships in the range of 151 to 250 registered tons (French, 1973, p. 440). Therefore, in order to present a probable range within which 1790–1792 tonnage estimates comparable to the 1768–1772 data fell, we have presented three different sets of estimates, the tonnage data from the U.S.A.S.P. (1832) were multiplied by correction factors of 0.75, 0.65, and 0.55 to obtain the 1790–1792 tonnage estimates in columns (3)–(5) and (8)–(10).

Actual reporting years for the 1790–1792 data were October 1 of the preceding year through September 30 of the stated year. Tonnage returns for three states, Rhode Island, New Jersey, and North Carolina, were incomplete for 1790 due to the fact that these states did not ratify the Constitution before October 1, 1789. Average annual estimates of tonnage entering each of these three states were based upon 1791 and 1792 data only.

continued

TABLE 6—Continued

In some instances the totals for a state differed from the detailed data due to errors of addition. In all cases, the detailed data were accepted. It should be noted that the aggregation of tonnage in the above table differs substantially from the aggregation given in the source (*U.S.A.S.P.*, 1832, p. 250), where the average annual American-owned tonnage entering the states during 1790–1792 was 375,601 tons (unadjusted) compared with the figure for American-owned tonnage of 338,700 tons in this table. The average annual foreign-owned tonnage estimated was nearly the same (247,994 from *U.S.A.S.P.*, p. 250, compared with 248,800 in this table). The difference may be due (or partly due) to the fact that the aggregation in the source (*U.S.A.S.P.*, p. 250) pertains to the *calendar* years, 1790 through 1792, and not to the fiscal years beginning with October 1, 1789, through September 30, 1792.

*b*Tonnage was recorded in the *U.S.A.S.P.* (1832), the source of the 1790–1792 data, by place of ownership. In a very few instances, tonnage was indicated to be jointly owned by foreign and U.S. residents. These observations were classified as foreign-owned tonnage in this table. The breakdown between colonial and foreign-owned tonnage for 1768–1772 was not given in the American customs records. Estimates therefore were made on the basis of ownership data taken from samples of recorded entries of ships from naval office lists of various colonial ports; see Shepherd and Walton (1972, pp. 122–123). Evidence to estimate the ownership of the annual average of 1,974 tons entering the colonies from Africa was incomplete. Consequently, this tonnage was listed in the table as being all foreign-owned, though some unknown proportion unquestionably was owned in the colonies. The largest part of this tonnage (an annual average of 1440 tons) entered the lower south, and probably the greatest part of this was British-owned.

*c*The major foreign areas are defined in Table 1, footnote *c*, except that Florida and Louisiana were included in the "other" category in this table. The "other" places of origin included China, the East Indies, the South Seas, Bourbon and Mauritius, and Florida and Louisiana. The data were available to present regional breakdowns for Africa, the Canadian colonies, and "other" places of origin, but it was not deemed worthwhile because of the small amounts of tonnage involved. Definitions of regions are given in note *c* to Table 2.

*d*Not available.

*e*Tonnage for regions may not add to totals because of rounding.

goods may have been reexported from the foreign islands, but the consequence of the restrictions seems to have been an increased relative importance of foreign-owned shipping (nearly all British).

A comparison of American-owned tonnage inflows in 1768–1772 (column
(1)) with the probable range of American-owned tonnage inflows in
1790–1792 (columns (4) and (5)) in Table 6 suggests that American-owned
tonnages did increase perhaps by 50–80%. It may well be that the growth of
foreign and American-owned tonnage inflows approximated the 80%
increase of United States population between these two periods, and that
per capita shipping earnings varied little. Of course, such comparisons and
conclusions depend upon the tonnage correction factor selected in Table 6;
but even the most conservative estimates suggest substantial growth in shipping volume. The regional patterns, too, conform to those discussed earlier.
The northern colonial regions clearly experienced greatly increased shipping
activity. Tonnage entering the southern regions in the early 1790's was
greater (even by the most conservative estimates in Table 6), but the
increases were relatively smaller than for the northern regions.

In summary, it seems probable that in the early 1790's shipping earnings
and mercantile profits had recovered from the doldrums of the 1780's. This
recovery, though not dramatic, was important to the maintenance of the
strong commercial base of the New England and Middle Atlantic regions,
and to the recovery from the troublesome years of the 1780's.

VI. SUMMARY AND CONCLUSIONS

In conclusion, what were the important consequences of the American
Revolution and independence on American maritime trade and shipping? It
led to the beginnings of direct trade with northern European countries other
than Britain. During the 1780's these countries became markets of moderate
importance for American products which no longer had to be routed through
Great Britain. Trade with southern Europe recovered and regained its relative importance, while the West Indian trade became relatively more important. Had not British restrictions been placed upon American shipping to
the West Indies, this trade would have been even greater. Together with the
relative decline of trade with northern Europe went a relative decrease in the
importance of the traditional southern staples. Because these trends had
existed before the Revolution, however, such changes cannot be attributed
solely to the War and independence.

Certainly, the War itself led to lower levels of trade and increased self-
sufficiency for the country. This increase in American self-sufficiency
persisted into the 1780's as the United States adjusted to independence. Not
only does the direct evidence upon trade support this conclusion, but the evidence of declining agricultural productivity in Pennsylvania (Ball and
Walton, 1976, p. 100) over this period indicates that economic improvement

was interrupted by War and readjustment which necessitated greater self-sufficiency. Many examples of increased domestic manufacturing activity exist, as well.[27]

Whether one views the years between 1768–1772 and 1790–1792 as a period of economic stagnation, or decline and then recovery, it is apparent that these were years of economic difficulty and perhaps depressed living standards for the New Republic. The new evidence presented here is not consistent with the perspectives given by Jensen (1958), who asserts that "by 1790 the U.S. had far outstripped the colonies of a few short years before" (p. 218); or "by 1790 the export of agricultural produce was double what it had been before the war. American cities grew rapidly . . ." (p. 224).[28]

Total exports were 37% above their pre-War level by the early 1790's, but this was far short of the 80% increase in population increase for the period. Overall, the United States economy of the early 1790's does not appear to have been a prime example of export-led growth. The relative overall importance of foreign trade was declining, both in export values per capita, and most likely as a share of per capita income. For the American colonies, and the United States before the Civil War, such a large fall in per capita export values was an unusual peacetime experience. These changes were noticeably different by region, however, and great caution must be taken when dealing with trade in the aggregate. The southern decline of exports relative to population was sharp; the New England states (except for New Hampshire) and New York more than fully recovered from trade disruptions, but overall there was a significant decline in the relative importance of foreign trade. All this was to be drastically changed, however, by two events that occurred in 1793: the beginning of the Napoleonic Wars, and Eli Whitney's invention of the cotton gin; but the dramatic consequences of these events could not have been foreseen in 1792—or in 1775.

In closing, it is important to note that the commercial base that had developed in the United States before 1790 played a crucial role in the ability of the new nation to take advantage of economic possibilities which arose in following years. The development of this commercial base, especially in New England and the Middle Atlantic regions, stood in sharp contrast to the lack

[27]Jensen, 1958, pp. 219–227. One might also wonder if the failure of the population of the three largest cities (Philadelphia, New York, and Boston) to keep pace with general population growth is also indicative of a greater reliance on domestic production. Philadelphia increased from about 40,000 to 42,500 from 1775 to 1790, New York from 25,000 to 33,000, and Boston from 16,000 to 18,000 (Bridenbaugh, 1955, p. 216; Jensen, 1958, p. 116). Baltimore, on the other hand, more than doubled in population between these dates. This slower growth of these northern cities does not seem consistent with the greater growth of overseas trade of the northern regions. Obviously, however, many other factors would influence their growth.

[28]Jensen's comments seem more appropriate for the Middle Atlantic region than representative of the overall state of the economy. Nevertheless, they are too optimistic even for this region.

of similar developments in other colonies in Latin America and elsewhere. Surely this was an important aspect of the differential economic success of North America. United States prosperity in trade and shipping during the period of the Napoleonic Wars was to come and go, but the nation would soon embark upon an irrevocable course of industrialization and a path of development that would result in material standards of living undreamed of in 1790.

REFERENCES

Ball, D. E., and Walton, G. M. (1976), "Agricultural Productivity Change in Eighteenth-Century Pennsylvania." *Journal of Economic History* 36, 102–117.

Bezanson, A., *et al.* (1951), *Prices and Inflation during the American Revolution: Pennsylvania, 1770–1790.* Philadelphia: University of Pennsylvania Press.

Bjork, G. C. (1964), "The Weaning of the American Economy: Independence, Market Changes, and Economic Development." *Journal of Economic History* 24, 541–560.

Bridenbaugh, C. (1955), *Cities in Revolt: Urban Life in America, 1743–1776.* New York: Knopf.

Buron, E. (1932), "Statistics on Franco-American Trade, 1778–1806." *Journal of Economic and Business History* 4, 571–80.

Cole, A. H. (1938), *Wholesale Commodity Prices in the United States, 1700–1861: Statistical Supplement.* Cambridge, Mass.: Harvard University Press.

Crouzet, F. (1964), "Wars, Blackade, and Economic Change in Europe, 1792–1815." *Journal of Economic History* 24, 567–588.

Fishlow, A. (1964), "Discussion." *Journal of Economic History* 24, 561–566.

Fogel, R. W., and Engerman, S. L. (1974), *Time on the Cross: The Economics of American Negro Slavery.* Boston: Little, Brown.

French, C. J. (1973), "Eighteenth-Century Shipping Tonnage Measurements." *Journal of Economic History* 33, 434–43.

Gray, L. C. (1933), *History of Agriculture in the Southern United States to 1860.* 2 Vols. Washington, D.C.: Carnegie Institute of Washington.

Jensen, M. (1958), *The New Nation: A History of the United States during the Confederation, 1781–1789.* New York: Knopf.

Johnson, E. R., *et al.* (1915), *History of Domestic and Foreign Commerce of the United States.* Washington, D.C.: Carnegie Institute of Washington.

Klingaman, D. (1969), "The Significance of Grain in the Development of the Tobacco Colonies." *Journal of Economic History* 29, 268–78.

Kohlmeier, A. L. (1925), "The Commerce of the United States and the Netherlands, 1783–1789." *Indiana University Studies* 12, 3–47.

McCusker, J. (1967), "Colonial Tonnage Measurement: Five Philadelphia Merchant Ships as a Sample." *Journal of Economic History, 27,* 82–91.

Nettels, C. P. (1962), *The Emergence of a National Economy 1775–1815.* New York: Holt, Rinehart and Winston.

North, D. C. (1965), "The Role of Transportation in the Economic Development of North America," in *Les grandes voies dan le monde,* XVe–XLXe *siecles.* Paris: SEVPEN.

North, D. C. (1974), *Growth and Welfare in the American Past,* 2nd ed. Englewood Cliffs, N.J.: Prentice-Hall.

Nussbaum, A. (1957), *A History of the Dollar.* New York: Columbia University Press.

Robertson, R. M. (1973), *History of the American Economy,* 3rd ed. New York: Harcourt Brace Jovanovich.

Shepherd, J. F., and Walton, G. M. (1972), *Shipping, Maritime Trade, and the Economic Development of Colonial North America.* London: Cambridge University Press.

Thomas, R. P. (1965), "A Quantitative Approach to the Study of the Effects of British Imperial
    Policy Upon Colonial Welfare: Some Preliminary Findings." *Journal of Economic His-
    tory,* 25, 613–638.
United States, *American State Papers* (1832), Class IV, *Commerce and Navigation,* Vol. VII.
    Washington, D.C.: Gales and Seaton. [Cited as *U.S.A.S.P.* (1832).]
United States, Bureau of the Census (1960), *Historical Statistics of the United States, Colonial
    Times to 1957.* Washington, D.C.: U.S. Government Printing Office, Chap. Z. [Cited as
    Historical Statistics (1960).]
Walton, G. M. (1967), "Colonial Tonnage Measurement: A Comment." *Journal of Economic
    History* 27, 392–397.

The Constitutional Tradition:
History, Political Action,
and Progress
in
American Political Thought
1787-1793

MICHAEL LIENESCH

F EW CONCEPTS are talked about more these days than tradition. Few are so seldom defined. Among political theorists there is an interest again in the history of theory, with scholars doing historical research, teachers dusting off the classics, students, including the ones who used to speak so often of "relevance," talking now about "the tradition." Yet for those concerned with the concept of tradition, recent theorists have had little to offer. Few have written about the idea. Most who have leave us with several misconceptions. First, that tradition is an organic force, mystical spirit, or scientific inevitability. Second, that it is a product of the ancient past or long-forgotten history. Third, that it is inexorable, an ancient curse or genetic code that we today can only accept, presumably without protest. But tradition need be none of these. Instead tradition can sometimes be a political strategy designed to legitimate a decision by demonstrating its continuity with past, present, and future policies. Such a tradition creates the impression of con-

* For their ideas and encouragement, I want to thank Norman Jacobson, Michael Rogin, Joel David Schwartz, Robert Holsworth, Eric Herzik and my colleagues in the Comparative Politics Study Group at the University of North Carolina at Chapel Hill.

tinuity by recalling the influence of the decision on past events, emphasizing its significance for present behavior, and predicting its effect on future actions. Hence its creation requires an idea of history, a concept of political action, and a theory of progress. This study investigates the example of the American Constitutional tradition. It describes the source of the tradition in the Constitutional concept of founding. Then it analyzes the development of the idea by those who used it to defend the new Constitution in the years immediately following the framing. The arguments of these Constitutionalists are examined in a review of their public writings. Finally the study evaluates the effect of the Constitutional tradition on later Americans, in particular those of the next generation, but also, at least by extension, of every later age.[1]

INTRODUCTION: THE CONSTITUTIONAL CONCEPT OF FOUNDING

From the moment of founding the creators of the Constitution showed an acute awareness of the importance of the future. Founding took place in an instant, while implementation required years. decades or centuries. The Constitution was written to last for ages, its precepts designed to endure, John Adams confidently predicted, for "many thousands of years." It was clear to the framers that they would not live to see the final outcome of their creation. "We, who are now actors on the theater of life," said Dan Foster in 1789, "shall soon be called off;—a new set of comedians will rise and take our places." By 1787 most of the founding generation, having entered public life fifteen or more years earlier, were already old for their day. "The evening tide of life is fast approaching," Samuel Whitwell suggested, "a few more days will remove us from the theatre of action.—Annually do our numbers diminish." Death came to the signers as to anyone. "Though you are called Gods," Josiah Bridge advised them, "yet you must die like men." As to the results of their founding, they would never know. The completion of the American experiment, said Thomas Jefferson, would ". . . require time, temper, wisdom, & occasional sacrifice of interest; & how far these will be ours, our children may see, but we shall not."[2]

[1] One recent political theorist who has described the misuse of tradition is John G. Gunnell, *Political Theory: Tradition and Interpretation* (Cambridge, Massachusetts: Winthrop Publishers, Inc., 1979), esp. 66-93.

[2] John Adams, "A Defence of the Constitutions of Government of the United States of America [1787]," *The Works of John Adams*, ed. Charles Francis

As early as the Revolution the idea of posterity was a preoccupation of American republicans. Most Revolutionary republicans talked of posterity as a theory of obligation according to which citizens of the present acted in the interest of citizens of the future by providing examples for them to emulate. The theory, which was similar to the classical Greek conception, held that succeeding generations were to act as protégés, carrying on the work of their predecessors by following their examples. In 1787, however, this interpretation was challenged by another, the Greek theory of obligation giving way to a Roman concept of authority in which those of the present acted for the benefit of those of the future by providing rules to obey rather than examples to follow. The writers who developed this concept spoke of future Americans less as protégés than rivals, referring to what they called "the rising generation" as an independent power which could either implement or subvert the work of constitutional government. Posterity was to hold a decisive role in American constitutional politics. For the ultimate course of events, Jefferson wrote solemnly, "Our children or grand children will answer."[3]

In 1787 Americans faced the irony of founding, the irrefutable fact that ultimate responsibility for founding lies not with the founders who frame the constitution but with the citizens who live under the new government. Americans of the time were conscious of the problem, most assuming that no future generation would equal that of the founders; that no future age could expect to boast a Washington, Franklin, Hancock or Adams: "Posterity may have reason to rue the day," wrote Benjamin Austin, "when their political welfare depends on the decision of men who may fill the place of these worthies." Even as the Constitution was being signed many realized

Adams (Boston: Charles E. Little and James Brown, 1851-65), IV, 297; Dan Foster, A.M., *An Election Sermon; Delivered Before the Honorable Legislature of the State of Vermont* . . . *October 8, 1789* (Windsor [Vermont]: Alden Spooner, 1790), 22; Samuel Whitwell, *An Oration Delivered to the Society of the Cincinnati* . . . *July 4, 1789* (Boston: Benjamin Russell, 1789), 18; Josiah Bridge, A.M., *A Sermon Preached Before his Excellency John Hancock, Esq. Governor* . . . *of the Commonwealth of Massachusetts, May 27, 1789* . . . (Boston: Adams & Nourse, 1789), 47; Thomas Jefferson to Edward Rutledge, June 24, 1797, *The Writings of Thomas Jefferson*, ed. Paul Leicester Ford (New York: G. P. Putnam's Sons, The Knickerbocker Press, 1892-99), VII, 154.

[3] David Ramsay, M.D., *The History of the American Revolution* [1789] (Philadelphia: R. Aitken & Son, 1789), II, 353; Jefferson to [Francois] d'Ivernois, Feruary 6, 1795, *Writings*, VII, 5.

that through ignorance or incompetence future citizens might weaken its character, undermine its institutions, even destroy its fragile form altogether. When they looked to posterity they saw little that was comforting. "In short my dear Friend you and I have been indefatigable Labourers through our whole Lives," wrote Adams to Jefferson, "for a Cause which will be thrown away in the next generation, upon the Vanity and Foppery of Persons of whom we do not know the Names perhaps."[4]

Yet the persistence of the Revolutionary concept of posterity made the dilemma of founding even more extreme. Revolutionary theory had been premised on the assumption that future citizens would be activists; that they would oppose tyrants, guard against corruption, fight to limit the power of government. Revolutionary republicans believed that the inspiration to action would be political ambition, the desire of citizens to win personal fame by performing in the public realm. Revolutionaries held that such ambition was imperative if free government was to survive. As late as 1787 many Americans of the Revolutionary generation assumed that history would follow a continuous cyclical course of founding, corruption, and revolt. Thus they expected a future marked by periodic insurrection. In fact some positively insisted on future revolutions, arguing even twenty years too long to wait without another. According to the theory future republicans had a right to revolution. Indeed Americans of the future had a positive responsibility to carry out revolutions of their own. "The tree of liberty must be refreshed from time to time," Jefferson declared in the most eloquent statement of the theory, "with the blood of patriots and tyrants."[5]

---

[4] "Candidus [Benjamin Austin]," letter to the *Boston Independent Chronicle,* December 6, 1787, *The Antifederalist Papers,* ed. Morton Borden (East Lansing: Michigan State University Press, 1965), 55; Adams to Jefferson, October 8, 1787, Jefferson, *The Papers of Thomas Jefferson,* ed. Julian P. Boyd (Princeton, New Jersey: Princeton University Press, 1950-), XII, 221. See James Madison, Federalist 10, James Madison, Alexander Hamilton and John Jay, *The Federalist Papers,* ed. Clinton Rossiter (New York: The New American Library, Mentor Books, 1961), 80, Madison, Federalist 49, *Federalist Papers,* 315, and Hamilton, Federalist 73, *Federalist Papers,* 441.

[5] Jefferson to William Stephens Smith, November 13, 1787, *Papers,* XII, 356. The description of revolutionary republicanism is derived from Bernard Bailyn, *The Ideological Origins of the American Revolution* (Cambridge, Massachusetts: Harvard University Press, The Belknap Press, 1967), esp. 93-143. It relies also on Gordon S. Wood, *The Creation of the American Republic, 1776-1787* (Chapel Hill: The University of North Carolina Press, 1969), 18-45, 53-70, 118-124. See too Hannah Arendt, *On Revolution* (New York: The Viking Press, 1963), 26.

Nonetheless in 1787 the Revolutionary concept was challenged by the Constitutional version of posterity. The founders argued that the Constitution had put an end to the need for republican activism, having overthrown tyranny, halted corruption, and limited permanently the power of government. Hence they saw political ambition as less a necessity than a threat. The champions of the Constitution who took up the argument in 1787 feared that future Americans would seek to play the roles of revolutionaries and constitutionalists, emulating the example of the framers by destroying their government and preempting their places as founders. They assumed that future citizens would fall prey easily to the power of political ambition. In his *Discourses on Davila,* published in 1791, John Adams argued that the passion for distinction, the "desire to be observed, considered, esteemed, praised, beloved, and admired by his fellows," remained one of the most potent forces in public life, "one of the earliest as well as the keenest dispositions discovered in the heart of man." Constitutionalists knew well the power of the desire for distinction, feeling it deeply, speaking almost reverently of the love of fame as "the ruling passion of the noblest minds," yet seeing in it danger from the popular demagogue, Hamilton's "man of irregular ambition." Thus they argued that government must limit the influence of the ambitious, not only preventing them from using their talents to destroy the established order, but indeed capturing and expropriating their abilities, setting one against another in a continuing struggle to wih personal fame that within the Constitutional system became a struggle to serve the public good. It was, wrote Adams of the desire for distinction, "a principal end of government to regulate this passion, which in its turn becomes a principal means of government."[6]

The American founders, relying on Enlightenment assumptions, had insisted that ambition could be controlled by the introduction of rational institutions. Even in 1791 John Adams could make the case. But as early as 1787 some supporters of the Constitution had begun to recognize a fundamental weakness in the assumption. The

---

[6] Adams, "Discourses on Davila [1791]," *Works,* VI, 232; Hamilton, Federalist 72, *Federalist Papers,* 437, 440; Adams, "Davila," *Works,* VI, 234. See Martin Diamond, "Democracy and *The Federalist*: A Reconstruction of the Framers' Intent," *The American Political Science Review,* 53 (March 1959), 67-68 and Douglass Adair, "Fame and the Founding Fathers," *Fame and the Founding Fathers: Essays by Douglass Adair,* ed. Trevor Colbourn (New York: W. W. Norton & Company, Inc., 1974), 3-26.

debate over ratification made it clear that rational rules would not be enough to assure wide acceptance for the Constitution. Especially following ratification, however, as American politics began to degenerate into partisanship and violence, supporters were forced to reconsider Constitutional theory, admitting that good laws alone would not create good government. All the checks ever created, all the balances ever devised could not restrain the ambition that lay in the hearts of talented citizens. Laws, as Peres Fobes would remark, "cannot reach the heart." The effective government relies not on written rules only, but on an unwritten ethic, the shared expectations that make government necessary, the conventions that make it acceptable, the agreements that make it work. This unwritten ethic is the basis of political legitimacy, residing, according to Samuel Miller, "not in the words and letters of the *Constitution;* but in the temper, the habits, and the practices of the people." In the years after 1787 supporters of the Constitution realized their responsibility to define not just what Americans thought about their government, but what they felt about it as well. Having constructed laws, they set about to build loyalty, a personal commitment to government that would ensure the Constitutional order "with far more efficacy, and incomparably more ease," as Timothy Dwight would put it, "than the post and the prison, the gibbet and the cross."[7]

The creation of constitutional legitimacy required a change from the existing concept of founding. Most modern theorists prior to the American founders relied on the definition set down by Aristotle in the *Politics,* according to which foundings were exercises in legislation in which lawgivers handed down constitutions to grateful

[7] Peres Fobes, L.L.D., *A Sermon, Preached Before his Excellency Samuel Adams, . . . May 27th, 1795 . . .* (Boston: The Mercury Press, Young & Minns, 1795), 13; Samuel Miller, A.M., *A Sermon, Preached in the New Presbyterian Church, New-York, July Fourth, 1795 . . .* (New-York: Thomas Greenleaf, 1795), 23; [Timothy Dwight], *A Sermon, Delivered on the 7th of July, 1795, before the Connecticut Society of Cincinnati* (New-Haven: T. & S. Green, [1795]), 16. On the dissolution of Constitutional politics in the 1790s, see John R. Howe, Jr., "Republican Thought and the Political Violence of the 1790s," *American Quarterly,* 19 (Summer, 1967), 147-165, Marshall Smelser, "The Federalist Period as an Age of Passion," *American Quarterly,* 10 (Winter, 1958), 391-419, and Smelser, "The Jacobin Phrenzy: Federalism and the Menace of Liberty, Equality, and Fraternity," *The Review of Politics,* 13 (October, 1951), 457-482.

publics. The legitimacy of these constitutions, their authority or
sanction, was achieved through the extraordinary status of the
legislators themselves, from the fact that they stood outside the
states for which they legislated, acting at their own behest, or under
the aegis of some superhuman power like an oracle, or sometimes
even on the direct command of the gods. Indeed in a few cases
the lawgivers, presumably because of their intimacy with the deities,
were seen as gods themselves. But even where this did not happen
the legislators remained figures from outside the normal realm, the
Greek states relying on foreigners to give laws or in those cases
where founders were not foreigners requiring banishment or allowing exile. The American Constitutional founding, however, because
it was based on impersonal scientific authority, required no such
superhuman founders. The framers, John Adams announced, had
never pretended to have held "interviews with the gods, or were
in any degree under the inspiration of Heaven." They acted instead according to the principles of Enlightment science, relying
on "principles of human nature," as Hamilton described them, "as
infallible as any mathematical calculations." The founders, acting
less as lawgivers than scientists, could remain therefore safely in
their state, assured, according to Hamilton, that their government
was "as perfect as human forms can be."[8]

Yet the American Constitution demanded more of its founders.
Because the Constitution was scientific and infallible the framers
were allowed to retain a place in the new republic. But to the
extent that the Constitution was human and imperfect they were
positively required to maintain an active role in the new government. Hence in 1787 constitutional theorists began to develop a
definition of founding similar to one used by Roman republicans
like Cicero, in which the act of founding was seen to include not
only the establishment of a form of government but also the creation of a process of governing. Madison and Hamilton, writing as
"Publius" for the Roman lawgiver Valerius Publicola, developed
the point in the last numbers of The Federalist. Constitutions need

---

[8] Adams, "Defence," Works, IV, 292; Alexander Hamilton, Address to the
New York Ratifying Convention, The Debates in the Several State Conven-
tions on the Adoption of the Federal Constitution . . ., ed. Jonathan Elliot (2d
ed.; Philadelphia: J. B. Lippincott & Company, 1861-63), II, 366; II, 348.
See also for the Greek concept, Aristotle, The Politics of Aristotle, trans. Ernest
Barker (New York: Oxford University Press, Galaxy Books, 1962), 87-90.

a period of operation during which new governments can win the loyalty of their citizens. The founders had no illusion that their Constitution would meet with unanimous or even wide acceptance. The debate in many of the states was long and rancorous. The commitment to state sovereignty remained strong. Time alone would tell whether the idea of federal government would win popular support. The American Constitution required a period of testing during which its principles could be adopted, its institutions embraced, its operations accepted. "TIME," as Hamilton put it, "must bring it to perfection."[9]

In the years following the founding, however, supporters of the Constitution saw that they had not the luxury of a period of acceptance. The debate over ratification followed by the conflict of the 1790s suggested that time alone would not suffice; that dissolution threatened. Hence they faced the task of creating legitimacy by inventing their own tradition, creating instant but enduring commitment by building in a moment the loyalty of ages. This task required a new theory of the Constitution. Before 1787 constitutional theory had been the work of philosophers who formed specific principles, institutions, and processes. Afterward it became the responsibility of supporters who explained the principles, described the institutions, and clarified the processes, a role taken not only by the few important theorists, but also by the many local ministers, elected officials, and community leaders who introduced the Constitution to the public audience. These Constitutionalists, mostly Federalists but including many Republicans, formed no political party, held no common ideology, used no secret handshake. Most knew one another probably only by reputation. But the works of more than fifty of them show striking similarities. The Constitutionalists argued that the Constitution provided the truest source of continuity in American political life; that it had defined the past, was shaping the present, and would continue to influence the future. To make the case they created constitutional concepts of history, political action, and progress. They brought their arguments to the public in their letters, orations, and sermons. The result of their efforts was the constitutional tradition.

[9] Hamilton, Federalist 85, *Federalist Papers*, 526. See for the Roman idea of founding, Cicero, *De Re Publica*, trans. Clinton Walker Keyes (Cambridge, Massachusetts: Harvard University Press, Loeb Classical Library, 1928), 11-13, 129-131, 145.

HISTORY: REINTERPRETING THE PAST

The first consideration in the making of constitutional tradition
was the creation of a sense of continuity between past and present.
This continuity was provided by a constitutional theory of history,
designed to show how American life had been marked since Independence by the continuous development of constitutional principles. During the period preceeding the convention the proposed
Constitution had been seen by most Americans as a rejection of the
Revolution. Opponents saw it as anti-Revolutionary, a symbol of
betrayal, repudiation, or counter-revolution. But as late as 1787
many supporters as well could describe it as non-Revolutionary,
few arguing that Revolution and Constitution were compatible. On
the contrary the very genius of the constitutional position was that
Revolution and Constitution were different; that the new government announced a break with the mistaken assumptions of the past.
Most supporters saw it as a correction for Revolutionary excess, "the
proper antidote for the diseases of faction," as Madison called it.
Many suggested that it was an entirely new creation, "a new and
more noble course." Almost all agreed, Constitutionalist and anti-
Constitutionalist alike, that it signalled a break with the past and a
new beginning, "not a mere revision and amendment . . . but a com-
pleat System for the future government of the United States."[10]

In the debate over ratification, however, the argument began to
change. Before 1787 Revolution and Constitution had been discontinuous. Afterward they became inseparable, Constitutionalists
showing how Revolution had led inexorably to Constitution. American history had been based previously on a periodicity in which
events before, during, and after the war formed distinct historical
eras. In constitutional history all were subsumed into a single age.
Thus David Ramsay would deliberately delay publication of his
study of Revolutionary America until after ratification so that his
History of the American Revolution, rather than conclude at the
attainment of Independence in 1783, could continue with a description of the Confederation period, include a survey of the events

[10] Madison, Federalist 14, *Federalist Papers*, 99; 104; "John de Witt," letter
to the *Boston American Herald*, October 27, 1787, *The Antifederalists*, ed.
Cecelia M. Kenyon (Indianapolis: The Bobbs-Merrill Company, Inc., 1966),
96. See Richard Henry Lee to General John Lamb, June 26, 1788, *The
Letters of Richard Henry Lee*, ed. James Curtis Ballagh (New York: The
Macmillan Company, 1911-14), II, 475. Refer also to Wood, *Creation*, 273-
282, 532-536, 606-615.

leading up to the Philadelphia Convention, and end with the text of the Constitution itself. According to Ramsay the decisions of these years showed remarkable continuity, the transition from Revolution to Constitution having been carried out "without a sigh or groan." The Constitution did not reject Revolutionary precepts but rather adopted and developed them. "The people of the United States gave no new powers to their rulers," he maintained, "but made a more judicious arrangement of what they had formerly ceded." In the new history the Constitution, far from signalling a reversal of the Revolution, announced its culmination. "Till this period," confided Aaron Hall, "the revolution in America, has never appeared to me to be completed; but this is laying on the cap-stone of the great American Empire."[11]

Constitutional historians made the Revolution look distinctly less revolutionary than before, their arguments going to place the Revolutionary War within a sequence of events culminating in the Constitutional Convention, making revolution constitutional by picturing a passionate violent revolt as a rational deliberate reform. "This single circumstance . . . will stamp a peculiar glory on the American revolution, and make it as a distinguished era in the history of mankind," wrote Joel Barlow; "that sober reason and reflection have done the work of enthusiasm, and performed the miracles of gods." This was a radical reinterpretation, through which a theory of politics inspired by revolutionary passion became in retrospect an idea of government informed by enlightened reason. Constitutionalists described the American Revolution as another Glorious Revolution, a "revolution by reasoning" in which Americans had "*reasoned* before they have *felt*"; had followed "the *still small voice*, the voice 'of rational reflection." They explained how the War of Independence had proceeded from "the permanent principles of sober policy," "a well digested knowledge of civil rights," "philosophical reflection, and speculative enquiry." The new historians drained the blood from the Revolutionary War, reclaiming its ardor, stressing instead its "philosophic composure." Constitutional history transformed Revolutionary passion into Constitutional rationality. "No circumstance of whim or passion moved us," declared

[11]Ramsay, *History*, II, 344; 341-342; Aaron Hall, M.A., *An Oration, Delivered at the Request of the Inhabitants of Keene*, June 30, 1788 . . . (Keene, [New Hampshire]: James D. Griffith, 1788), 6-7. See also Merrill Jensen, *The New Nation: A History of the United States During the Confederation, 1781-1789* (New York: Alfred A. Knopf, Inc., Vintage Books, 1950), 96.

William Pierce, "no frantic zeal enraged us,—no cause of a popular demagogue inflamed us, . . . —no, —all was the result of reason."[12]

Constitutional historians created a Revolution different from the one that had actually taken place. The Constitutional Revolution was waged not by separate divided colonies but one united nation. It was fought not for independence but strong central government. In 1787 the New York pamphleteer "Caesar" began to argue that the desire for national government had been the primary purpose of the War. Revolutionaries, he wrote, "sought to obtain liberty for no particular State, but for the whole Union, indissolubly connected under one controlling and supreme head." According to the historians Americans had felt little sense of national identity before the war: "Country religion, local policy, as well as private views," wrote Ramsay, "operated in disposing the inhabitants to take different sides." The common experience of British oppression had drawn them together, however, setting people "thinking, speaking and acting, in a line far beyond that to which they had been accustomed." With the creation of national institutions like the Army and Congress and the appearance of national leaders like Hamilton and Madison a national purpose began to be defined. Local prejudices gave way to continental loyalties. Out of the common experience of war emerged an American nation: "The great body of the people," Ramsay allowed, "as soon as reason got the better of prejudice, found that their best interests would be most effectually promoted by such practices and sentiments as were favourable to union."[13]

Constitutional historians found the spirit of Constitutionalism long before the Constitution. It then became their task to explain how that spirit had been waylaid along the road to strong government during the Confederation period. The historians described

---

[12] Joel Barlow, *An Oration, Delivered at the North Church in Hartford, . . . July 4th, 1787* . . . (Hartford: Hudson and Goodwin, [1787]), 6; Enos Hitchcock, A.M., *An Oration: Delivered July 4, 1788* . . . (Providence: Bennett Wheeler, [1788]), 11; Barlow, *An Oration*, 6; 7; Alexander C. Macwhorter, *An Oration Delivered on the Fourth of July, 1794.* . . . (Newark, [New Jersey]: John Woods, 1794), 16; Major William Pierce, *An Oration, Delivered at Christ Church, Savannah, on the Fourth July, 1788.* . . . (Savannah: James Johnston, 1788), 5; 7-8.

[13] "Caesar," letter to the *New York Daily Advertiser*, October 17, 1787, *Essays on the Constitution of the United States*, ed. Paul Leicester Ford (Brooklyn, New York: Historical Printing Club, 1892), 290; Ramsay, *History*, II, 310; 315; 317.

how the Confederation had been a misguided detour into excess
and error. It must have come as a surprise to Americans of the time
to learn how bad the Confederation had been. In the years from
1783 to 1787 numerous writers had shown dissatisfaction with the
course of American affairs. But in the public pronouncements of
the day there had been no suggestion of desperation, contemporary
writers speaking of the Confederation period not with despair but
uncertainty. Before 1787 events had seemed neither encouraging
nor ominous, but ambiguous and indefinite. In the new history,
however, the period took on a definite personality indeed. Constitutionalists were candid about their plan to depict the Confederation as a period of calamity, the Constitution as the document that
redeemed the age of discontent. Fisher Ames wrote a friend that
he for one intended to convince Americans that before the federal
government, "The corn would not grow, nor the pot boil." The
historians told how credit had expired, gold vanished, and property
depreciated, how commerce had fallen off and produce dropped in
value, how government had become totally inadequate. Only afterward did people begin to realize how critical this critical period had
been. "I believe it is not generally known on what a perilous
tenure we held our freedom and independence during that period,"
wrote James Wilson. "The flames of internal insurrection were
ready to burst out in every quarter; . . . and from one end to the
other of the continent, we walked on ashes, concealing fire beneath
our feet."[14]

The Constitutional historians left no doubt that Confederation
government had subverted the true tradition of American politics,
but they made it clear as well, that in spite of this reversal the spirit
of constitutional government had survived. Throughout the war
Americans had maintained their commitment to national union, the
tie that held the states together during troubled times. "Not that
Confederation, but common danger, and the spirit of America, were
the bonds of our union," wrote Edmund Pendleton. "Union and
unanimity, and not that insignificant paper [the Articles of Con-

[14] Fisher Ames to George Richards Minot, July 23, 1789, *Works of Fisher
Ames*, ed. Seth Ames (Boston: Little, Brown, and Company, 1854), I, 66;
James Wilson, Address to the Pennsylvania Ratifying Convention, *Debates*, II,
521. See Ramsay, *History*, II, 339, Edmund Randolph, Address to the Virginia
Ratifying Convention, *Debates*, III, 27, and Frank I. Schechter, "The Early
History of the Tradition of the Constitution," *The American Political Science
Review*, 9 (November, 1915), 707-734.

federation], carried us through that dangerous war." Errors in government had been only temporary aberrations, the product of what Benjamin Rush called "very unfavorable circumstances." The American states had just emerged from a corrupt monarchy and their people were inexperienced in republican government. "Although we understood perfectly the principles of liberty," said Rush, "yet most of us were ignorant of the forms and combinations of power in republics." The nation was in the midst of war, the British army "in the heart of our country, spreading desolation wherever it went." In these circumstances mistakes in government became inevitable. It was not to be wondered, declared John Jay, ". . . that a government instituted in times so inauspicious should on experiment be found greatly deficient and inadequate to the purpose it was intended to answer."[15]

The Constitutional Convention, however, had reasserted the rationality that had been the true character of American republicanism. Constitutionalists did yeoman labor in interpreting political passion as philosophical rationality, rewriting politics to make it look like philosophy. The Convention itself, an intense and partisan congress, was pictured as a dispassioned philosophical gathering, "an assemblage of wisdom and philanthropy." Party politicians were made out to be unbiased philosophers, men "distinguished by their patriotism, virtue, and wisdom," "commanding all the sources of information," "unawed by fear, unbiassed by self-interest." Partisan debate became intellectual discussion. "In the mild season of peace," wrote Jay, "with minds unoccupied by other subjects, they passed many months in cool, uninterrupted, and daily consultation; and finally, without having been awed by power, or influenced by any passions except love for their country, they presented and recommended to the people the plan produced by their joint and very unanimous councils." Constitutional historians re-wrote the history of the Convention, depicting the Constitution as the product not of expediency and compromise but theory and philosophy. It was as if the founding had been the result of revelation by some Enlightenment deity. In fact, in Constitutional history calculating politicians became themselves almost rationalistic gods. The act of founding, William Hunter would conclude, ". . . required minds,

[15] Edmund Pendleton, Address to the Virginia Ratifying Convention, *Debates*, III, 38; Rush, "On the Defects of the Confederation [1787]," *The Selected Writings of Benjamin Rush*, ed. Dagobert D. Runes (New York: Philosophical Library, 1947), 26; Jay, Federalist 2, *Federalist Papers*, 39.

rarely gifted, and richly endowed, but a prudence, a forbearance, a discretion, too seldom bestowed on Mortals. —It almost required," he wrote, "men to be like the God of the Stoics, all Intellect, and no Passion."[16]

POLITICAL ACTION: SHAPING THE PRESENT

The second element in the creation of the Constitutional tradition was a new definition of political action. Having re-written the past, Constitutionalists turned to the present, re-defining political action in contemporary affairs. This required a new philosophy of political education. For a hundred years colonials had been schooled in classical political theory, a training that had been one of the greatest inspirations to the American Revolution. Classical republican theory held that citizens were required constantly to guard their freedom, be vigilant against the corruption of their leaders, come forward to fight when liberty was threatened and return to their homes only when it was secured. Revolutionary writers adopted these classical ideas as basic precepts. The classical republicans maintained that free government required civic virtue, the commitment of citizens to defend freedom at any cost against the power of government. Revolutionaries looked especially to the Roman republic for examples of this civic virtue—to Cato, Cicero, and Cincinnatus —modelling themselves on these classical characters, imitating their oratorical styles, even adopting their names as pseudonyms. In the years before 1787 it was still common to find veterans of the Revolution exhorting their children to look to Livy, Plutarch, or Tacitus for the same precepts that they themselves had followed in Revolutionary days. Indeed, even after 1787 there were those who championed the classics, entreating others to "recur to the page of history" to find those "universal principles" that had "stood the shock of ages."[17]

[16] Hitchcock, *An Oration*, 14; Jay, Federalist 2, *Federalist Papers*, 39; Harrison Gray Otis, *An Oration, Delivered July 4, 1788* . . . (Boston: Benjamin Russell, 1788), 15; Jay, Federalist 2, *Federalist Papers*, 39; William Hunter, *An Oration, Delivered in the Baptist Meeting-House in Newport, July 4, A.D. 1795* . . . (Newport [Rhode Island]: Henry Barber, 1795), 14.

[17] George Mason, Address to the Virginia Ratifying Convention, *Debates*, III, 380; Patrick Henry, Address to the Virginia Ratifying Convention, *Debates*, III, 385; Henry, Address to the Virginia Ratifying Convention, *Debates*, III, 137. On the idea of classical virtue see Wood, *Creation*, 18-28 and for the

Following the founding, however, Constitutionalists began to question the need for classical education. Throughout the ratification debate they argued that the examples of classical politics were at best inappropriate and at worst harmful to the realities of constitutional government. Ancient theory did not apply to modern practice. Besides, civic virtue, with its emphasis on popular participation, had led Greek and Roman republics alike down the road to anarchy. Thus in 1787 some Constitutionalists set out to eliminate altogether such assumptions from republican theory by purging their classical sources from republican education. "Let us try the effect of banishing the Latin and Greek languages from our country," wrote Benjamin Rush, who spoke for many in 1789. "They consume the flower of human life, and by enabling us to read agreeable histories of ancient crimes often lead us to imitate or to tolerate them." The ancient languages were detriments to society, to be classed, Rush went on, "with Negro slavery and spirituous liquors." By 1791 he was arguing for the complete abolition of the classics from American education. "It is high time to cease from idolizing the idolatry of Greece and Rome," Rush advised. "Truth alone is knowledge, and spending time in studying Greek and Roman fictions, is only labouring to be more ignorant."[18]

Constitutionalists argued that classical education had little to offer a modern developing nation. Ancient terms seemed inadequate to describe contemporary concepts. "Where shall we find Latin words to convey just ideas of the many terms which electricity—chemistry—navigation—and many other sciences have intro-

---

classical background Richard M. Gummere, "The Heritage of the Classics in Colonial North America: An Essay on the Greco-Roman Tradition," *Proceedings of the American Philosophical Society*, 99 (April, 1955), 68-78, Charles F. Mullett, "Classical Influences on the American Revolution," *The Classical Journal*, 35 (November, 1939), 92-104, and H. Trevor Colbourn, *The Lamp of Experience: Whig History and the Intellectual Origins of the American Revolution* (Chapel Hill: The University of North Carolina Press, 1965), 21-25.

[18] Benjamin Rush to John Adams, June 15, 1789, *Letters of Benjamin Rush*, ed. L. H. Butterfield (Princeton, New Jersey: Princeton University Press, 1951), I, 516; Rush to Adams, July 2, 1789, *Letters*, I, 518; Benjamin Rush, M.D., "Observations Upon the Study of the Latin and Greek Languages . . . [1789]," *Essays, Literary, Moral & Philosophical* (Philadelphia: Thomas & Samuel F. Bradford, 1798), 34. On the inapplicability of classical politics see also Madison, Federalist 37, *Federalist Papers*, 226, James Wilson, Address to the Federal Convention (Madison's Notes), *Debates*, V, 219, and Benjamin Randall, Address to the Massachusetts Ratifying Convention, *Debates*, II, 69.

duced into our modern languages?" asked Rush. Old irrelevant classics contributed little compared to new practical scholarship. No American youth had need of "lectures upon the ruins of Palmyra and the antiquities of Herculaneum, or in disputes about Hebrew points, Greek particles, or the accent and quantity of the Roman language," Rush wrote. Instead, "The youth of America will be employed in acquiring those branches of knowledge which increase the conveniences of life, lessen human misery, improve our country, promote population, exalt the human understanding, and establish domestic, social, and political happiness." Constitutionalists referred often to the potential for national development. "Here the opportunities of acquiring knowledge and of advancing private and public interest are so numerous," Rush said, "and the rewards of genius are so certain, that not a particle of time should be mis-spent or lost. We occupy a new country. Our principal business should be to explore and apply its resources, all of which press us to enterprise and haste." The study of history, language, and classical literature consumed time better spent gaining command of agriculture, manufacturing, or international trade. "Under these circumstances," Rush concluded, "to spend four or five years in learning two dead languages, is to turn our backs upon a gold mine, in order to amuse ourselves in catching butterflies."[19]

The Constitutional concept of education was designed for nation-building. Whereas classical education had emphasized political activism, a role appropriate to republican revolution, Constitutional theory called for private enterprise, a condition essential to national development. The Constitutional citizen, Rush explained, was to be taught that "study and business should be his principal pursuits in life." Where Revolutionary republicans had relied for inspiration on civic virtue, Constitutional republicans looked to self-interest. The good citizen was required, Rush continued, to "love life, and endeavour to acquire as many of its conveniences as possible by industry and economy." Revolutionaries had assumed that private

[19] Rush, "Observations on the Study of Latin and Greek," *Essays*, 35; Rush, "To the Friends of Federal Government: A Plan for a Federal University," October 29, 1788, *Letters*, I, 494-495; Rush, "Observations," *Essays*, 39. It should be noted that not all Constitutionalists made the case for the banishment of classical education. See for example John Adams replying to Rush, October 13 and 15, 1810, *The Spur of Fame: Dialogues of John Adams and Benjamin Rush, 1805-1813*, ed. John A. Schutz and Douglass Adair (San Marino, California: The Huntington Library, 1966), 170-171.

interest was inimical to public interest; Constitutionalists held to a primitive utilitarian calculus in which the interests of each accumulated arithmetically to create the interest of all. Thus the Constitutional American was required "to amass wealth," declared Rush, "but it must be only to encrease his power of contributing to the wants and demands of the state." Private enterprise was a political obligation, Constitutional educators calling on Americans to seek personal profit in the service of public prosperity. "A particular attention to the virtues of economy, temperance, and industry, are peculiarly necessary in a country like ours," concluded William Atkinson. "The farmer who will make three ears of corn grow where nature gave only one, is more deserving of a statue than the conqueror of a world."[20]

Constitutionalists faced the task of creating private citizens. John Adams set the example for their efforts. The pre-Revolutionary letters of Adams to his wife had shown his determination to educate their children in the tenets of classical republicanism. As late as 1783 Adams was demanding that they take up the public life. But beginning about 1780 there began to enter his correspondence a nagging intimation that these earlier principles had become somehow inappropriate. In the early letters Adams had demanded republican frugality from his children, and even in the 1780s he was insisting that they despise the pursuit of personal fortune. But as Adams made clear after 1780, the creation of wealth in the interest of national development was another matter altogether, for when the future of the country was at stake, Adams announced to his wife, "I would have my children attend to duits and farthings as devoutly as the merest Dutchman upon earth, if such attention was necessary to support their independence." Of public life there was little said in the later letters, Adams writing increasingly of private affairs, how the ideal citizen was the "honest, sensible, humane man." After 1783 Adams could be found encouraging a notion of private enterprise far removed from his earlier advocacy of public virtue. In the last analysis, he advised, the man who lived ". . . in a moderate simplicity clearly within his means, and free from debts

[20] Rush, "Of the Mode of Education Proper in a Republic [1786]," Essays, 12; 11-12; 12; William King Atkinson, An Oration, Delivered at Dover, New-Hampshire, on the Fourth of July, 1791 . . . (Dover, New-Hampshire: E. Ladd, 1791), 19.

or obligations, is really the most respectable man in society, [and] makes himself and all about him the most happy."[21]

Constitutional education was created to provide for stable government. To build stability, Constitutionalists turned to a theory of obligation unlike that of most earlier republicans. Revolutionary Americans, believing that the greatest threat to freedom came from the power of government, looked skeptically at their rulers. Constitutionalists maintained that such skepticism was unnecessary; that because Constitutional rulers relied on the ultimate authority of the people, their power could never pose a threat to freedom. Indeed it followed that freedom was secure only when citizens were obedient, the liberty of Americans under the Constitution consisting of "nothing more than obedience to the authority and majesty of the laws," as Chandler Robbins described it, "—and laws too, made by themselves." Under the Constitution leaders were representative and responsible. Hence citizens had the obligation to respect them, "a *respectful* behavior," Robbins went on, being "unquestionably due to those in authority." Subordination ensured liberty, for, "When the people are submissive to their laws and rulers," Israel Evans explained, "their liberties will be permanent." Constitutional citizens, far from revolutionary, were champions of order, dedicating themselves, according to Bridge, to "the support of order, peace and good government." They stayed away from protest, concentrated on the home, their primary responsibilities, as Hitchcock summed them up, to establish the "best cultivated farm" and "best regulated family." Constitutional republicans, William Linn concluded, had one overriding duty: "to be obedient subjects."[22]

[21] John Adams to Abigail Adams, December 18, 1780, *Letters of John Adams, Addressed to his Wife,* ed. Charles Francis Adams (Boston: Charles E. Little and James Brown, 1841), II, 76; Adams to Abigail Adams, April 8, 1783, *Letters,* II, 96.
[22] Chandler Robbins, A.M., *A Sermon, Preached Before his Excellency John Hancock, Esq. Governour . . . of the Commonwealth of Massachusetts, May 25, 1791* . . . (Boston: Thomas Adams, 1791), 27; 25; Israel Evans, A.M., *A Sermon, Delivered at Concord, Before the Hon. General Court of the State of New-Hampshire . . .* (Concord, [New Hampshire]: Geo. Hough, 1791), 21; Bridge, *A Sermon,* 53; Enos Hitchcock, D.D., *The Farmer's Friend . . .* (Boston: I. Thomas and E. T. Andrews, 1793), 270; William Linn, D.D., *The Blessings of America. A Sermon, Preached in the Middle Dutch Church, On the Fourth of July, 1791* . . . (New-York: Thomas Greenleaf, 1791), 30. See

Constitutional education seemed to promise stability. The Constitutionalists demanded that it provide permanence. Self-sustaining government required self-regulating citizens. Following the framing Constitutionalists realized that politics was influenced by psychology, that the strongest political commitment was psychological, the best social control self-control. Thus they set out to create a psychological theory to match their political thought, molding a private constitution to complement the public one. Their goal was to turn skeptical republicans into loyal Constitutionalists, to create a "happy temper of mind" in which citizens would be "cheerfully obedient to their laws." After 1787 political education became psychological management, Constitutional educators creating a new kind of American, the Constitutional republican, "the true friend of society," as Hitchcock said, who would "cheerfully submit to lawful authority," "encourage and support public officers," and "cultivate . . . those benevolent dispositions so necessary to . . . the preservation of peace and harmony."[23]

The builders of the tradition created a Constitutional psychology to perpetuate Constitutional government. Their theory of personality internalized their model of politics. Constitutional government had created a balance between political extremes, "the happy medium between oppression and licentiousness." Constitutional self-government introduced in turn a balance between psychological states, a medium of personal moderation. As early as

---

also Joseph Lyman, A Sermon, Preached Before his Excellency James Bowdoin, Esq. . . . , May 30, 1787 . . . (Boston: Adams and Nourse [1787]), 18-19, Elizur Goodrich, D.D., The Principles of Civil Union and Happiness considered and recommended. A Sermon, Preached . . . May 10th, 1787 (Hartford: Hudson and Goodwin, 1787), 11, and Nathan Strong, A.M., A Sermon Delivered in the Presence of His Excellency Samuel Huntington. . . . May 13th, 1790 (Hartford: Hudson and Goodwin, 1790), 25.

[23] Evans, A Sermon, 15; Hitchcock, An Oration, 18-19; 19. The development of constitutional psychology is seen best in the numerous election sermons of the period, for example Samuel Miller, A.M., Christianity the Grand Source, and the Surest Basis, of Political Liberty: A Sermon, Preached in New-York, July 4th, 1793 . . . (New-York: Thomas Greenleaf [1793], 14, Nathan Williams, A.M., Carefully to observe the signatures of Divine Providence, a mark of wisdom. Illustrated in a Sermon . . . (Hartford: Hudson and Goodwin, 1793), 22, Caleb Blood, A Sermon Preached Before the Honorable Legislature of the State of Vermont; . . . October 11th, 1792 . . . (Rutland, [Vermont]: Anthony Haswell, [1792]), 32-33, and Timothy Dwight, D.D., Virtuous Rulers a National Blessing. A Sermon, Preached at the General Election, May 12th, 1791 (Hartford: Hudson and Goodwin, 1791), 36.

1725 in his *Dissertation on Liberty and Necessity, Pleasure and Pain*
the young Benjamin Franklin had applied the idea of balance to
the psychological realm, devising a Newtonian psychology based
on the principle of the pendulum, according to which every human
emotion would move between poles of pleasure and pain, each sentiment seeking out its opposite as required by the laws of physics.
When people embraced pleasure they condemned themselves thereby to equal pain, for the pendulum promised to swing back to its
opposite state. Thus those who insisted on ecstasy consigned themselves to despair, while those willing to accept moderate happiness
suffered only limited sorrow. The ideal condition was the balanced
pendulum, the psychological state in which pleasure was controlled,
pain limited, and perpetual moderation assured. "Men should endeavor at a *balance* of affections and appetites," wrote Adams,
"under the monarchy of reason and conscience, within, as well as at
a balance of power without." The model Constitutional character
was defined by this prudent balance, a "happy mediocrity," according to the tradition-makers, "an *animated moderation*."[24]

Yet a few Constitutionalists sought an even stronger Constitutional psychology, arguing that balance was not enough, that if
Newtonian physics had defined the shape of Constitutional government, post-Newtonian technology offered a better metaphor for
Constitutional psychology. Benjamin Rush in particular began at
this time to bring to political thought ideas from applied science.
Revolutionary republicanism, written for a simple agrarian world,
had been individualistic and libertarian. Constitutional republicanism, the product of an increasingly technological society, seemed to
stress homogeneity and social order. Education should be designed,
Rush advised, to "render the mass of the people more homogeneous,
and thereby fit them more easily for uniform and peaceable government." Where Revolutionary theorists had emphasized personal
freedom, Constitutionalists talked of social uniformity; how the wills
of the people had to be "fitted to each other" to "produce regularity
and unison in government." The creators of the Constitutional

[24] Linn, *The Blessings of America*, 17; Adams, "Defence," *Works*, IV, 407;
David Osgood, A.M., *A Sermon, Preached at the Request of the Ancient and
Honorable Artillery Company in Boston, June 2, 1788* . . . (Boston: Benjamin
Russell, 1788), 6; John Dickinson, "The Letters of Fabius. . . , IX [1788],"
The Political Writings of John Dickinson, Esquire . . . (Wilmington, [Dela-
ware]: Bosnal and Niles, 1801), II, 165. On Franklin, see *A Dissertation on
Liberty and Necessity, Pleasure and Pain* (London: n.p., 1725), 15.

tradition, like Americans of every previous period, believed that
times of achievement would be followed by those of backsliding,
strong generations leading to weak ones, extraordinary parents to
unexceptional offspring. They looked cynically at the next generation: "Wise men beget fools," warned a gloomy John Adams, "and
honest men knaves." Hence they set out to banish the threat of
generational decline by creating a Constitutional ethic that would
eliminate the possibility of generational declension. The Constitution required no ages of achievement, allowed none of backsliding.
Constitutionalists saw to it that strong and weak generations, wise
men and fools alike would disappear, replaced by a succession of
mediocre generations, an unending line of obedient citizens. With
these prudent people, balanced government would never falter,
holding instead to controlled, self-sustaining, perpetual moderation.
The Constitution had created a Newtonian machine. To run it the
Constitutionalists provided Newtonian parts: "I consider it is possible," concluded Rush, "to convert men into republican machines.
This must be done, if we expect them to perform their parts properly, in the great machine of the government of the state."[25]

PROGRESS: DEFINING THE FUTURE

The final ingredient in the creation of the Constitutional tradition was a theory of progress, the idea used by Constitutionalists to
gain control of the future. Progress was an idea new to most Americans in 1787, for while, before that time, many had made statements
about the possibility of development, few had talked of the likelihood of continuous or cumulative advance. Revolutionary thinkers
in particular assumed the certainty of declension, holding that all
political institutions grew corrupt; that personal liberty gave way
inevitably to governmental power; that freedom declined everywhere into tyranny. Most described the Revolution as a last desperate attempt to end the declension brought on by colonial rule,
turning back corruption by re-claiming original liberties. But even
after Independence, while a few hoped for progress, many more
were certain of decline. Thus the theorists of the Constitution

[25] Rush, "Of the Mode of Education Proper in a Republic," *Essays*, 8; 15;
Adams, "Defence," *Works*, IV, 396; Rush, "Of the Mode," *Essays*, 14-15. See
also John F. Kasson, *Civilizing the Machine: Technology and Republican
Values in America, 1776-1900* (Harmondsworth, Middlesex, England: Penguin
Books Ltd., 1977), 28-36.

devised a form of government to do away with declension by establishing a perpetual balance between counterpoised powers. The American Constitution, designed to negate corruption, required no theory of progress. Its intention instead was a timeless order, a system, as Joel Barlow described it, "which will stand the test of ages."[26]

After 1787, however, the idea of perpetual Constitutional equilibrium began to change. The tradition-makers did not doubt that the Constitution had brought permanence to American politics. Yet this was not to say that Constitutional government made no allowance for improvement. Rather it was precisely the permanence of the system that made adaptation possible, in that while the structure of the republic promised to vary almost not at all, the character of the nation was certain to alter dramatically. The Constitutionalists knew that they themselves would not be present to determine the nature of the change. Thus unable to provide continuing personal direction for their system, they did the next best thing, creating a theory of progress to define the future in advance. By extending the Constitutional tradition, adding to it a theory of socio-economic development, the tradition-makers offered not only the end to corruption and the assurance of stability but also the promise of progress, "the progress of science, agriculture, manufactures, and all the pleasing and useful arts of refined society," as Hitchcock suggested, "which naturally flow from independence."[27]

The ratification of the Constitution allowed a place for the idea of progress in American political theory. Before this time economic expansion, meaning urbanization and industrialization, had been seen as a corrupting influence, a process certain eventually to destroy the hardy yeoman virtues of agrarian America. With the Constitution, however, the concern with corruption seemed to yield to a fascination with development. The Constitutional Convention, having reconciled longstanding disputes over control of the western territories, had cleared the way for further settlement of the trans-Allegheny West. Constitutionalists spoke of the West as an open invitation to economic growth, arguing that the American states could experience now the wealth of an advanced Eastern economy while still maintaining the simplicity of an agrarian Western society

[26] Barlow, *An Oration*, 19. On the idea of corruption see Bailyn, *Ideological Origins*, 45-54. On the Constitutional theory of equilibrium, see Wood, *Creation*, 606-615.

[27] Hitchcock, *An Oration*, 19.

through repeated expansion. In popular language the word "progress," which before had meant almost exclusively spatial movement, became a temporal term meaning development. Economic improvement went hand-in-hand with territorial expansion, first agriculture, then commerce, then manufacturing proceeding, as James Wilson described it, "in rapid succession from east to west." In 1787 Constitutionalists began to define a notion of temporal progress, substituting space for time, looking away from the inevitable corruption of the civilized East toward the limitless opportunity of the agrarian West, predicting the progress of America, "that America which but a few years past was a lonely wilderness—rising to the zenith of her lustre."[28]

The Constitutionalists introduced an American idea of progress. Throughout the eighteenth century many Americans had talked of progress, by which they meant development. Only in 1787, however, did Constitutionalists begin to define an idea of progress, meaning a theory of continuous development. The idea was but a small first step in the direction of later deterministic theories. It was not a concept of historical inevitability. Instead it was a notion of progress based on human action, the Constitutionalists arguing that continuous development would follow from self-conscious direction, that cumulative innovation could be attained only through constant application of human initiative. "Whatever attainments are already reached," declared Wilson, "attainments still higher should be pursued." Earlier Americans had relied on the hand of God for the advance of civilization. Constitutionalists took that role upon themselves. "The gradual progress of improvement fills the mind with delectable ideas," Arthur St. Clair told a Western audience. "Vast forests converted into arrable fields, and cities rising in places which were lately the habitations of wild beasts; gives us a pleasure something like that attendant on creation, if we can form an idea of it."[29]

[28] James Wilson, "Oration," Francis Hopkinson, "An Account of the Grand Federal Procession. Performed at Philadelphia on Friday the 4th of July 1778 (sic) [1788]," *The Miscellaneous Essays and Occasional Writings of Francis Hopkinson, Esq.* (Philadelphia: T. Dobson, 1792), II, 417; Whitwell, *An Oration,* 12. See also Alex. Macwhorter, D.D., *A Festival Discourse, . . . In the Town of Newark* (Newark, [New Jersey]: John Woods, 1793), 12-14, and Elias Boudinot, L.L.D., *An Oration, Delivered at Elizabeth-town, New Jersey . . .* (Elizabeth-town, [New Jersey]: Shepard Kollock, 1793), 26.

[29] Wilson, "Oration," Hopkinson, "An Account," *Miscellaneous Essays,* II, 415-16; Arthur St. Clair, "The Speech of his Excellency Arthur St. Clair,

The Constitutional idea of progress required continuous human action. Attainment of future progress demanded commitment from future citizens. As early as 1780 John Adams had outlined the role of future Americans in securing national development. Adams predicted that political founding would be followed by socio-economic improvement, which would be followed in turn by cultural and artistic advances. Each stage would require appropriate efforts. He described them in a letter to his wife concerning the education of their children. "I must study politics and war," he wrote, "that my sons may have liberty to study mathematics and philosophy. My sons ought to study mathematics and philosophy, geography, natural history and naval architecture, navigation, commerce and agriculture, in order to give their children a right to study painting, poetry, music, architecture, statuary, tapestry and porcelain." Political founding had been secured. Cultural advances seemed at least a generation in the future. Thus there remained the responsibility of economic development, the role of the next generation, who would act diligently in building the nation, developing its social life, establishing economic prosperity. Even conservative assessments showed extraordinary potential. It was, as Adams claimed, "like contemplating the heavens through the telescopes of Herschell. Objects stupendous in their magnitude and motions strike us from all quarters, and fill us with amazement!" Constitutional government, having provided exceptional resources, insisted in return on exceptional efforts. The creators of the Constitutional tradition thought it little to ask of the next generation. "A profligate American youth," Adams wrote, "must be profligate indeed, and richly merits the scorn of all mankind."[30]

There lay a paradox, however, in the Constitutional theory of progress, in that socio-economic development was possible only with political stability, future Americans having the responsibility to build the private realm while remaining outside the public, their role economic, not political. Even where they were allowed the chance for political action, it was limited. Constitutionalists believed that citizens could advance their politics incrementally,

Esquire. . . ," James M. Varnum, *An Oration Delivered at Marietta, July 4, 1788* . . .(Newport, [Rhode Island]: Peter Edes, 1788), 10. See Joseph Blake, jun., *An Oration, Pronounced July 4th, 1792, at . . . Boston* . . . (Boston: Benjamin Russell, 1792), 16.

[30] John Adams to Abigail Adams, n.d. [fixed by content in 1780], *Letters*, II, 68; Adams, "Defence," *Works*, VI, 218.

though any change they made would be presupposed by the principles of the Constitution. Indeed even within the private realm
innovation was incremental, progress being possible only when
citizens suppressed any desire to reject the efforts of the previous
generation, giving up the demand for sudden or discontinuous
change and consigning themselves to a cautious course of step-by-
step development. Constitutionalists made allowance for economic
innovation by doing away with political instability, provided for
reform by outlawing rebellion. Progress demanded prudence. The
role of future Americans, as Josiah Whitney put it, was to make "a
wise, and discreet improvement of our constitutional privileges."[31]

Most Americans accepted the role assigned them by the makers
of the Constitutional tradition, many taking up eagerly their new
political status. With ratification a period of protest, conflict, and
uncertainty had come apparently to a close. Revolutionary republicans, veterans of political action, turned willingly, like Cincinnatus
returning to his plow, to private enterprise. Especially among the
young the desire to look from public to private concerns was strong,
Americans of the post-founding generation recognizing that the end
of an age of self-sacrifice would mark the beginning of a period of
self-interest. The Constitutional tradition found a receptive audience among the young. John Quincy Adams, age twenty-five,
speaking for many of his generation, addressing an audience of his
father's peers in a 1793 oration at Boston, announced their acceptance: "From the present prosperous appearance of our public
affairs," he confessed, "we may admit a rational hope that our
country will have no occasion to require of us those extraordinary
and heroic exertions which it was your fortune to exhibit."[32]

The makers of the Constitutional tradition announced that from
that time heroic politics existed only in the past, the duty of Americans being to revere the Founders, remembering their illustrious
deeds, applauding their magnificent government, cherishing their
hallowed Constitution. The Constitutional tradition secured immortality for the government the Founders had handed down, "per-
petuated in our posterity," as Foster said, "to the latest age." In
the same way the tradition won immortality for the Founders them-

[31] Josiah Whitney, A.M., *The essential requisites to form the good Ruler's
Character, illustrated and urged. A Sermon, Preached . . . at Hartford, . . .
May 8th, 1788* (Hartford: Elisha Babcock, 1788), 35.

[32] John Quincy Adams, *An Oration, Pronounced July 4th, 1793, at . . . Boston
. . .* (Boston: Benjamin Edes & Son, 1793), 14.

selves, "whose prudence, integrity, and virtue," Whitwell declared, "will ever make them renowned to posterity." The Constitutional tradition granted immortality to the founding, Americans remembering it, revering it, remaining grateful always, according to Whitney, for "the great, and good things which have been done for us." To succeeding generations it would be as if their fathers were always present, while they remained forever children: "Secure in their prosperity," wrote James Sullivan, "they weep for joy, that Heaven hath given them—Fathers!"[33]

The creators of the Constitutional tradition made it clear that the Founding Fathers, a term they introduced at this time, deserved alone the godlike immortality attributed to founders. Future Americans would be mortal figures, the Constitutionalists seeing to it that their children would live from that time in the shadow of the Founding. As early as 1783 John Adams had written to his sons concerning their responsibility to be private citizens, promising that if they ever shirked their duty or offered even one word of complaint he would disinherit them. "Work, you rogues, and be free," he wrote. "You will never have so hard work to do as papa has had." As late as 1798 Adams was still repeating the theme, though by this time it had become a political argument directed not to his own children but to all young Americans. Addressing a group of young men who had created a club to inspire youthful participation in politics, Adams was paternal and benign. Taking note of their enthusiasm and having, he said, no wish "to deny the ardor of curiosity," he lauded their intentions. But he went on to imply politely that their efforts were futile, even somewhat pathetic. "I will hazard a prediction," he concluded, "that, after the most industrious and impartial researches, the longest liver of you all will find no principles, institutions, or systems of education more fit, in general, to be transmitted to your posterity, than those you have received from your ancestors."[34]

The children of the Founding Fathers accepted the status of mortals descended from demigods. But while most endorsed their new position, some admitted reservations. There was a definite cost in accepting the Constitutional tradition. For future Americans

[33] Foster, *An Election Sermon*, 24; Whitwell, *An Oration*, 13; Whitney, *The essential requisites*, 35; "Cassius [James Sullivan]," letter to the *Massachusetts Gazette*, December 25, 1787, *Essays*, 48.

[34] Adams to Abigail Adams, April 8, 1783, *Letters*, II, 95; John Adams to the Young Men of the City of Philadelphia. . . , May 7, 1798, *Works*, IX, 188.

the price was that they themselves would never be allowed to define
a political role of their own. The Founders had laid the basis for
permanent government. "The seeds of Liberty are plentifully
sown," as John Quincy Adams said, and promised "eventually to
flourish with luxuriant profusion." But in this promise of success
came a dilemma for future citizens, in that the republic would
prosper with or without their efforts. The framers of the Constitution, having done their work too well, had left future Americans
no significant political role, an oversight, John Quincy Adams implied, that had consigned the citizens of succeeding generations to
perpetual inferiority. Under the Constitutional system Americans
were never again to undertake extraordinary political actions. From
that time there were, at least in theory, no more revolutions to be
fought, no more constitutions to be founded. Hence from that time
there was no more fame to be won. "The field is extensive; it is
fruitful," explained the young Adams, "but the copious treasures of
its fragrance have already been gathered by the hands of genius;
and there now remains for the gleaning of mental indigence, nought
but the thinly scattered sweets which have escaped the vigilance of
their industry."[35]

Yet the decision had been no oversight. The creators of the Constitutional tradition had set out to end the menace of ambition, re-
voking from succeeding generations the chance for glory by purging from them the desire for fame. They did not falter in carrying
out the task. The most painful punishment in life, John Adams
wrote, was to be denied the opportunity for fame. The citizen with
no standing in public affairs was like the consumer of no wealth in
economic life, a creature not so much despised as neglected. "Mankind takes no notice of him," Adams wrote. "He rambles and
wanders unheeded. In the midst of a crowd, at church, in the
market, at a play, at an execution, or coronation, he is in as much
obscurity as he would be in a garret or a cellar. He is not dis-

[35] John Quincy Adams, *An Oration*, 19; 20; 7. Adams' metaphor was
adopted later by Abraham Lincoln in his address to the Young Men's Lyceum
of Springfield, Illinois. But where Adams, speaking for the second generation
of American republicans, counseled acceptance and resignation, Lincoln, representative of the next generation, argued ominously that the time was ripe for
protest and a renewal of heroic action: "This field of glory is harvested, and
the crop is already appropriated. But new reapers will arise, and *they*, too, will
seek a field." Abraham Lincoln, "Address Before the Young Men's Lyceum
of Springfield, Illinois," January 27, 1838, *The Collected Works of Abraham
Lincoln*, ed. Roy P. Basler (New Brunswick, New Jersey: Rutgers University
Press, 1953), I, 113.

approved, censured, or reproached; *he is only not seen.*" The
founding generation had feared this obscurity, a fate, as Adams
described it, "mortifying, painful and cruel." But the Constitutionalists did not hesitate to leave it as a legacy to the succeeding generations of Americans who would be unacquainted with distinction
and incapable of fame. Constitutional citizens were deferential,
retiring, unobtrusive, in private life solid and respectable, in politics
anonymous. The Constitutional tradition replaced the love of fame
with the desire for anonymity. After all, advised Charles Backus,
there was always "much more to praise in the good man, who passes
all his days in the vale of obscurity, than in some who are recorded
as the boast of their nation or age."[36]

Nevertheless Constitutional education did not eliminate the desire
for fame. John Quincy Adams admitted readily that he and his
peers were unprepared to follow the example of their parents. But
that did not mean they were unable to match the deeds of the
previous generation. The Founders would make a grave mistake,
Adams told his listeners, to conclude ". . . from the greater pre-
valence of private and personal motives in these days of calm se-
renity, that your sons have degenerated from the virtues of their
fathers." Rather the opposite was true, it being, he supposed, "a
subject of pleasing reflection" to them to know their children were
their equals. The fire of ambition had not been extinguished in the
hearts of young Americans. Instead, as Adams informed his audience, the flame burned low but brightly: "The generous and disinterested energies, which you were summoned to display, are permitted by the bountiful indulgence of Heaven to remain latent in
the bosoms of your children."[37]

The creators of the Constitutional tradition had done all they
could to eradicate Revolutionary ambition. In his Boston oration
John Quincy Adams showed that they had not succeeded completely. Adams recalled for his Independence Day audience the
events of the American Revolution. He spoke at length of the
character of the Revolutionary patriots, their dedication to republican principles, their love of liberty. Then he assured his aging
listeners that his own generation stood ready to emulate the example of these heroes. The Revolution had been fought and won,

[36] John Adams, "Davila," *Works*, VI, 239; Charles Backus, A.M., *A Sermon,
Preached Before His Excellency Samuel Huntington, Esq. L.L.D. Governor . . .
of the State of Connecticut . . . May 9th, 1793* (Hartford: Hudson and Goodwin, 1793), 6.
[37] John Quincy Adams, *An Oration*, 14.

but liberty was fragile, never secure, and Americans were certain to be called on again to protect their Revolutionary freedom. Adams promised they would be ready "should the voice of our country's calamity ever call us to her relief." In times of crisis patriots would come forward to defend the old Revolutionary principles, resisting oppression, maintaining liberty. Adams swore to his audience that he and his generation would be among those patriots; that they would remain loyal to the memory of the Revolutionary generation, faithful to what he called "the precious memory of the sages." Americans would not forget their true political heritage. Rather he promised they would keep alive the legacy of the Revolution, emulating their Revolutionary ancestors, defending the old republican principles, acting, Adams declared, "as the faithful disciples of those who so magnanimously taught us the instructive lesson of republican virtue."[38]

CONCLUSION:
SUCCESS AND FAILURE OF THE CONSTITUTIONAL TRADITION

Already in 1793 there were signs that the Constitutionalists had both succeeded and failed in their attempt to create a Constitutional tradition. Americans of succeeding generations had been given a new identity, become private citizens, made Constitutional republicans. From that time the concept of Constitutional citizenship would be a dominant influence in American politics. But Revolutionary ambition did not disappear after 1787, for while the memory of the Revolution faded, its example remained to inspire Americans in times of protest, crisis, and war, animating insistent Abolitionists, determined Populists, radical reformers. These Americans of later ages would look to the Revolution for their principles, guarding against tyranny, defending liberty, pursuing the common good. In doing so, they would keep alive the spirit of rebellion, questioning and challenging the Constitutional system. The tradition-makers succeeded in their strategy to create Constitutional tradition, but they failed in their campaign to erase Revolutionary ambition, which was taken up, hidden away, cherished, nurtured, and protected. And even now there are those who keep alive within themselves the quiet faith that one day they too will win fame for themselves by joining with others in the cause of liberty.

[38] *Ibid.*, 14; 14-15; 15.

The Emergence of Political Parties in Congress, 1789-1803

JOHN F. HOADLEY
Duke University

Although the political leaders who wrote the Constitution did not hold the idea of party in high regard, these same individuals (according to many historians) became the founders of a new party system within the first decade of the new government. This article considers the question (on which no consensus exists) of whether parties did develop. The analysis focuses upon one aspect of party development, namely, the agreement among members of Congress in their roll-call voting records. Spatial analysis (multidimensional scaling) permits a visual picture of the increased clustering of congressmen into two party blocs from 1789 to 1803, especially after the Jay Treaty debate in 1796. This very clear trend supports the idea that politics was moving away from a sectional basis to one founded more clearly on partisan grounds.

Scholars have differed considerably in assessing the development of American political parties during the period immediately following ratification of the Constitution. The date marking the emergence of parties has been placed anywhere between the beginning of the new government and the time 50 years later when Whigs and Jacksonian Democrats were competing for power. Despite disagreements over the precise date when parties first appeared, most observers have agreed that important divisions did materialize in the first decade of the new nation. Varying explanations have been offered for these divisions, ranging across economic factors, regionalism, personalities, issues, and even the boardinghouse residences of members of Congress.[1]

This article explores the question of when and why political parties first appeared in the United States. I examine the development of parties for the period between 1789, the first year of the new government under the Constitution, and 1803, a year which directly followed the first transition of government from one party to another. This span of 14 years is of particular interest because it was dominated by individuals who themselves did not believe parties could be a positive force in a governmental system. It was also a critical era of national development when the United States was trying to establish itself as a newly independent nation under a democratic government, a form generally untested at that time.

To reach conclusions concerning party development which may resolve some of the confusion in the literature, I have undertaken two tasks. First, I examine carefully the concept of "party" and distinguish it from the idea of "faction." Second, I apply a new methodological approach to consider empirical evidence on the question of party development. I use spatial analysis (multidimensional scaling) of roll-call voting because it avoids some of the limitations in other methods of roll-call analysis. I then examine spatial maps of congressional voting to answer questions concerning the state of party development in the early years of the nation.

An earlier version was presented at the 1976 meetings of the Southern Political Science Association, Atlanta. I have benefited greatly from the comments of many friends from Chapel Hill, especially Beth Fuchs, George Rabinowitz, Bill Keech, Duncan MacRae, Forrest Young, Don Searing, Whit Ayres, Ed Crowe, Nelson Dometrius, as well as several referees. Acknowledgement is also due to the Historical Archive of the Inter-University Consortium for Political and Social Research for the compilation of roll-call votes and to the Institute for Research in Social Science at the University of North Carolina at Chapel Hill for computing support. Nevertheless, tradition requires me to take responsibility for all remaining errors.

[1] According to one traditional interpretation of American party development, political parties existed from the beginning of the national government (Beard, 1915; Ryan, 1971). Other scholars have cited the Jay Treaty as the issue which marked appearance of parties, thus placing the date at about 1795 (Bell, 1973; Chambers, 1963; Charles, 1961; Cunningham, 1957). Still others have pointed to events and issues during the Adams administration as crucial in the emergence of parties (Dauer, 1953; Libby, 1912). Finally, a group of party historians has argued that true parties did not exist in this early period and has placed the date of party emergence after 1830 (Formisano, 1974; Hofstadter, 1969; Nichols, 1967). In many cases, these different conclusions can be attributed to varying definitions of party and an assortment of methodological approaches.

757

Toward a Definition of Party

As of 1789, a clear distinction between party and faction had not been established. According to eighteenth-century usage, "faction" (for which the word "party" was often substituted) usually referred to a group involved in the political arena but working toward private ends. Party, on the other hand, was "a new name for a new thing" (Sartori, 1976, p. 64). As the idea of party developed in the seventeenth and eighteenth centuries, the word gradually acquired a more distinct and positive meaning than "faction." That this distinction was not commonly recognized in 1789 is illustrated by the writings of James Madison in *The Federalist*, where he cautioned against both the "violence of faction," and the "rage of party." Although he used the terms interchangeably, he clearly had in mind the old idea of faction and not the new idea of party (Hofstadter, 1969; Sartori, 1976).[2]

Today the distinction between "party" and "faction" is much clearer. "Faction" tends to be used in two different contexts. In one, it retains the negative connotations of the old concept, referring to a self-seeking and contentious group. In a nonpartisan setting or within a single party, it may denote a group which forms around a single issue or personality, but with limited durability and minimal organization. A political party, on the other hand, is a more permanent group which generally has a positive role in the political system. Parties "are instrumental to collective benefits.... [They] are functional agencies—they serve purposes and fulfill roles—while factions are not" (Sartori, 1976, p. 25). There are in fact two important and strongly related roles which can be fulfilled by parties. One is an involvement in elections. Parties may help to recruit and screen candidates, supply symbols and names to help identify candidates to voters, and provide victorious candidates a mechanism for working toward policy goals once in office. The other role is serving as what Sartori calls "channels of expression" (p. 27). The party is one institution which helps people communicate their demands to the government. Furthermore, because a party can simultaneously channel the demands of a number of people, it adds a degree of

pressure which aids popular control of public policy.

While these roles are normally associated with the concept of party, the term itself is generally defined from a more structural perspective. Although numerous definitions of "party," emphasizing a variety of themes, can be found in the literature, several components are common to most of them. The following elements of the concept should be considered in any investigation of party development.[3] All parties have:

1. a common symbol or label,
2. a group of leaders in office,
3. a group of supporters in elections,
4. an organization, however minimal.

Several theories have been put forth to explain how parties come into being (Chambers, 1966; Duverger, 1959; Huntington, 1968; LaPalombara and Weiner, 1966). Integrating these considerations leads to the view that party development is a process taking place in four stages.[4] In the first stage, *factionalism*, groups form in the legislature over a variety of issues and personalities.[5] These factions are rarely organized and last for only a short time. In the second stage, *polarization*, these factions are stabilized into more permanent legislative groups which oppose each other over a broad range of issues. This coalescence into polar groups is frequently set off by a single issue of overriding importance or by the cumulation of several cleavages. In the third stage, *expansion*, the public is drawn into the process of party development, usually after the extension of suffrage. Electoral committees may arise at the local level to influence decision makers or may be created by office holders to strengthen their own positions. In either case, at this stage party affiliations become significant factors in the electoral process. In the fourth and final stage, *institutionalization*, a permanent linkage is cre-

---

[2]References are taken from *The Federalist*, No. 10 (Madison et al., 1961, p. 77) and No. 50 (p. 320). Elsewhere Madison clearly shows that he equates the two words, referring to "the most numerous party, or in other words, the most powerful faction..." (No. 10, p. 80).

[3]This discussion on definitions of party was strongly influenced by comments of Formisano (1974, p. 475), who in turn drew heavily from Chambers (1967) and Sorauf (1967), whose ideas were also important in the present effort. An alternative definition is provided by Sartori (1976, p. 63).

[4]Huntington's terminology (1968, pp. 412–20) is used here, but the meaning of the stages has been modified to incorporate other views, particularly Duverger's (1959) idea of the parliamentary origin of parties.

[5]This use of "factionalism" is not intended to carry the negative connotations often attached to the term.

ated between the parliamentary group and its electoral committees. At this point some type of national organization should begin to direct and coordinate the party activities.

This article examines the transition of American political parties from factionalism to polarization and therefore focuses on parties emerging within the Congress. The expansion of partisanship into the electorate and the institutionalization of parties are considered only where they amplify the party development taking place in Congress.

Methodology

The principal data for this investigation are the records of how members of Congress voted on roll calls taken between 1789 and 1803. While there are inherent limitations in using roll calls, the official nature of these votes makes them a valuable source of information.[6] The chief analytic method is multidimensional scaling of measures of agreement between legislators. Since this method has been fully discussed elsewhere,[7] I will give only a brief summary of the approach. Multidimensional scaling employs a matrix of agreement scores, defined simply as the proportion of times two legislators agree in their votes, out of the total number of bills on which both vote. These agreement scores are transformed into distances in a geometric space of some given dimensionality. The legislators are then represented as points in this multidimensional space in such a way that those who *agree* most often in voting are *closest* to each other in the resulting configuration of points, while those who *disagree* most are *farthest* away in the space.

Interpretation of a multidimensional scaling configuration is perhaps the most important and most difficult part of the analysis. First, the quality of a solution, or the fit between the data (agreement scores) and the configuration, is indicated by a statistic called "stress," which measures the degree to which the configuration fails to reproduce accurately the relationships present in the data. Stress can range theoretically from 0.0, for a perfect fit, to 1.0, for a total lack of fit. Second, the appropriate dimensionality of a solution must be determined with respect to its stress. A solution can be derived in any number of dimensions, and the stress will always be lower when a higher dimensionality is allowed. Thus the analyst must determine the most appropriate dimensionality, according to the conflicting standards of good fit (low stress) and parsimony (a small number of dimensions). Finally, the interpretation of a configuration involves a search for meaningful dimensions, clusters, or other structural patterns. It must be emphasized that a two-dimensional solution should *not* automatically be discussed in terms of two linear dimensions, such as a factor analysis would be. The analyst must be attentive in searching for that structural interpretation which best represents the information contained in the scaling solution.

An alternative method, cluster analysis, is used to aid the interpretation and explication of the configurations derived by multidimensional scaling. In clustering, legislators are placed into blocs or clusters, based on their level of agreement with each other. Those grouped in a particular cluster are more likely to agree with others in that cluster than with those outside it. Once clusters have been obtained, it is possible to compute the average level of agreement within them. Because cluster analysis is based on the same agreement scores, the results should help to support conclusions reached from multidimensional scaling.

While cluster analysis can be used to discover blocs that exist on the basis of voting patterns, the cohesion of parties and sectional blocs, defined externally to the voting records, is of equal interest. For each group, I calculate several standard indices of partisanship, including the average level of agreement, Rice's index of cohesion, Rice's index of difference, and Lowell's party vote.[8]

---

[6]Some limitations of roll-call analysis are immediately obvious. Roll-call votes may not always be accurate records of either the scope of activity in Congress or the true positions of members. Also, for a variety of reasons, roll calls are not taken on every issue before the legislature. Furthermore, when votes are recorded, members may sometimes misrepresent their positions, for reasons such as friendship or future reelection. Roll calls nevertheless do provide an official record of positions taken on a variety of issues and thus may be more important than a legislator's own preferences in cases where they differ.

[7]A more detailed presentation and justification of the methodology used here is found in Hoadley (1979). A good general discussion of multidimensional scaling is provided by Rabinowitz (1975). The use of cluster analysis for studying legislative blocs has been evaluated by MacRae (1970).

[8]Rice's index of cohesion is the absolute difference between the percentage "yes" and percentage "no" for a particular group. His index of difference is the absolute difference between the percentage "yes" for any two groups. A party vote, according to Lowell, is one where more than 90 percent of one party opposed more than 90 percent of the other. MacRae (1970, pp. 177—84) provides a fuller discussion of these indices.

Another means of studying party development is to consider the party identification of congressmen. This process is, however, far more difficult in studying the eighteenth century than the twentieth, since party labels were not commonly used in those early years of our nation. There were no formal party caucuses in Congress, nor were party labels used in most congressional elections. Nevertheless, information on the party affiliations of members of Congress has been compiled in the historical archives of the Inter-University Consortium for Political and Social Research (ICPSR), the *Biographical Directory of the American Congress, 1774–1961* (U.S. Congress, 1961), and several monographs on the early party system (Bell, 1973; Dauer, 1953). This information remains incomplete and occasionally inconsistent, particularly for the earliest years.[9] Nevertheless, party labels can aid in the assessment of partisan development. The extent to which congressional voting blocs correspond to those labels is one indication of the emergence of a party system.

Spatial Analysis of Roll-Call Voting

Once the scaling and clustering solutions are obtained, it is necessary to assess whether the resulting configurations show the existence of parties. As I have indicated, this article concentrates on the stages of factionalism and polarization. In the factional stage, congressional voting is expected to be fairly unstructured. Stress should be relatively high, as votes are cast for idiosyncratic reasons. Furthermore, the legislators should not be divided into two or three very distinct blocs. Since different issues presumably produce different divisions, the individual points should be distributed fairly uniformly across the space.

As party development evolves from factionalism to polarization, the configurations should change correspondingly. In the second stage,

groups of legislators are expected to be voting together across a set of issues, rather than shifting alignments from one issue to the next. Thus the configurations should reveal much tighter clusters of legislators corresponding to these party groups. Of course, the lines of division may still shift somewhat from one issue to another, but there should be a clear consistency of groupings, which was not true in the earlier stage of development. It is impossible to denote specific thresholds of agreement or distinctive patterns which would mark the existence of a party, for many factors affect these results. But careful examination of patterns over time should allow reasonable conclusions to be drawn regarding trends in partisanship.

With the establishment of these criteria for party development, I can examine the multidimensional scaling analysis of congressional voting. Configurations have been generated in one, two, and three dimensions for both the Senate and House of Representatives of the First through the Seventh Congresses (1789–1803). In each case, all roll calls were included and weighted equally,[10] and all members were included except those who were absent on a large proportion of roll calls. The stress for each configuration, with the number of legislators and number of roll calls involved, is presented in Table 1. Configurations for the House are presented in Figures 1 through 5, and Senate configurations for illustrative years[11] are presented in Figures 6 through 9.

The two-dimensional configuration has been selected as the best representation of voting patterns in each congress, with the sole exception of the First Senate. For several congresses, three-dimensional solutions yield a distinct improvement in stress, yet in every case but one the added accuracy is counteracted by increased difficulty in visualizing the resulting configuration. In the case of the First Senate, however, a two-dimensional configuration would not accurately represent the patterns of

[9]It is clear, from comparisons with primary research reported in several monographs on state party development, that there are frequent errors in the ICPSR file and in the *Biographical Directory*. I have estimated an error rate of greater than 10 percent for some years, and that complete and accurate information is generally available for only about 60 percent of the congressmen. A compilation of party labels from primary sources is needed, indicating the party with which a member of Congress identified at the time of each election. In the absence of such a compilation, the party codes used in this article represent the best information available in published sources.

[10]The inclusion of all roll calls with equal weight may introduce a bias into the analysis, although its degree and nature are unknown. Because any scheme of exclusion or weighting would be difficult to justify, all votes have been included. Given the nonmetric assumptions of MDS and the strength of the results, it seems unlikely that any resulting bias has seriously affected the conclusions.

[11]Configurations for the Third, Fifth, and Sixth Senates are not included here, to conserve space. Patterns for these years differ little from those of surrounding years, and the configurations fit clearly within the overall pattern of party development.

voting agreement, and a three-dimensional configuration is presented instead. One-dimensional configurations would be adequate in some cases on the basis of stress, but there is no advantage in restricting the figures to a single dimension.

It is important to reemphasize that these configurations are *not* to be interpreted in terms of two orthogonal linear dimensions. Thus I have not labeled the vertical or horizontal dimensions of the figures. Although such labeling can be appropriate in certain instances, it does not provide the best description of patterns in the period under consideration. Rather, the configurations should be seen as clusterings of legislators in a two-dimensional (or three-dimensional) space. A closely grouped cluster of congressmen indicates a cohesive voting bloc, and the relationships among voting blocs and unattached legislators are displayed in the configurations.

The series of configurations across the seven congresses, both in the House and the Senate, provides convincing evidence for the development of political parties during this period. The pattern which emerges is a clear progression from factionalism to polarization. In the following sections, the configurations are examined in greater detail.

Factionalism, 1789–1791

After the new Constitution was proposed at the Philadelphia Convention in 1787, it had to be ratified by at least nine states to become effective. The ensuing process involved considerable disagreement and very close votes in several states. This conflict between supporters and opponents of the Constitution became the major issue affecting the elections for the First Congress in 1788 and 1789. While personalities and local issues were often decisive, nearly every state experienced contests between Federalists and Antifederalists. The Federalists, who generally had more incentive to become involved in the new government, were victorious in most contests. In fact, only 10 (of 65) seats in the House and only 2 (of 26) seats in the Senate were won by Antifederalists (Paullin, 1904).

Despite the importance of divisions over the Constitution, this issue did not dominate voting in the First Congress. While Antifederalist members of the House are separated roughly at the top of the voting configuration (Figure 1), this division clearly was not the major one. This is illustrated by noting that the average agreement between Federalists and Antifederalists (49.3 percent) was not much below the average agreement within either group (Federalists, 55.1 percent; Antifederalists, 57.9 percent).

To the extent that there was any consistency in voting patterns, it was along sectional lines. In the First Senate, there is minimal evidence of consistent voting (Figure 6). Those alignments that do exist, which require three dimensions to represent spatially, are geographical and cannot

Table 1. Quality of Fit between Agreement Scores and Spatial Configurations
(in 1, 2, and 3 Dimensions)

Congress	Level of Stress			Number of Members	Number of Roll Calls
	1 Dim.	2 Dim.	3 Dim.		
House of Representatives					
First (1789–1791)	.468	.337	.263	62	109
Second (1791–1793)	.438	.304	.249	65	102
Third (1793–1795)	.278	.237	.201	100	69
Fourth (1795–1797)	.282	.233	.213	100	83
Fifth (1797–1799)	.084	.070	.066	100	155
Sixth (1799–1801)	.059	.055	.053	100	96
Seventh (1801–1803)	.041	.040	.040	100	141
Senate					
First (1789–1791)	.711	.489	.275	26	100
Second (1791–1793)	.420	.275	.185	27	52
Third (1793–1795)	.278	.191	.159	29	79
Fourth (1795–1797)	.179	.161	.142	30	86
Fifth (1797–1799)	.202	.162	.150	31	202
Sixth (1799–1801)	.207	.173	.151	36	120
Seventh (1801–1803)	.107	.097	.091	33	88

Source: Derived from multidimensional scaling of recorded roll-call votes in the United States Congress (collected by the Inter-University Consortium for Political and Social Research).

be considered evidence of party voting. With certain exceptions, senators from New England, the Middle States, and the South are each isolated in a distinct region of the space. The exceptions, however, foreshadow the coming party alignment. William Maclay, from Pennsylvania's more developed party system, is aligned rather closely with Virginia's senators, an alignment consistent with the future Jeffersonian Republican party.

While it is difficult to find even factional patterns for voting in the First Senate, voting in the House of Representatives is far more structured (Figure 1). Although the stress in two dimensions is not perfect, it is far better than the stress for a two-dimensional representation of the Senate. Evident from either multidimensional scaling or cluster analysis are three principal voting blocs, which are best described as sectional groupings. One bloc

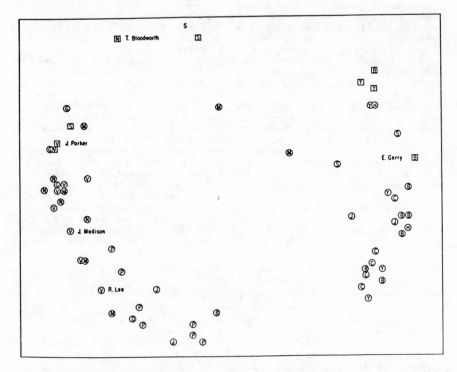

Source: Spatial configuration, derived from multidimensional scaling of recorded roll-call votes in the United States Congress (collected by the Inter-University Consortium for Political and Social Research).

Key: Each symbol indicates the state represented by a particular congressman. The circle or square drawn around the letter indicates party affiliation.

B = Massachusetts	J = New Jersey	R = Rhode Island
C = Connecticut	K = Kentucky	S = South Carolina
E = Vermont	M = Maryland	T = Tennessee
G = Georgia	N = North Carolina	V = Virginia
H = New Hampshire	P = Pennsylvania	Y = New York

Ⓧ = Federalist
Ⓧ = Antifederalist
X = None/Unknown

Figure 1. Voting Patterns in the First Congress,
United States House of Representatives, 1789–1791

includes mostly members from New England and New York. The second consists almost exclusively of southern congressmen, and the third is dominated by members from Pennsylvania and several neighboring states. The principal exceptions to this alignment come from New Jersey, Maryland, and South Carolina. The four New Jersey congressmen are divided between the New England and Pennsylvania blocs, according to their proximity to the cities of New York and Philadelphia. Maryland congressmen are placed with or near each of the three voting blocs, perhaps in accordance with the state's location between North and South. Finally, the South Carolina delegation contained two members (both representing coastal towns, Charleston and Georgetown) who voted in agreement with the New England bloc. Throughout the early years, South Carolina had the strongest Federalist party of any southern

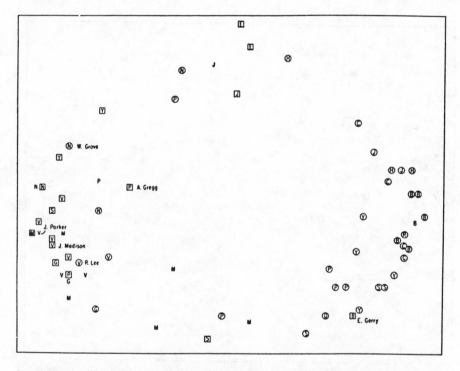

Source: Spatial configuration, derived from multidimensional scaling of recorded roll-call votes in the United States Congress (collected by the Inter-University Consortium for Political and Social Research).

Key: Each symbol indicates the state represented by a particular congressman. The circle or square drawn around the letter indicates party affiliation.

B = Massachusetts	J = New Jersey	R = Rhode Island
C = Connecticut	K = Kentucky	S = South Carolina
E = Vermont	M = Maryland	T = Tennessee
G = Georgia	N = North Carolina	V = Virginia
H = New Hampshire	P = Pennsylvania	Y = New York

Ⓧ = Federalist
☒ = Republican
X = None/Unknown

**Figure 2. Voting Patterns in the Second Congress,
United States House of Representatives, 1791–1793**

state, a fact best explained by the existence of trading interests centered in the port of Charleston.

These patterns of congressional voting in the House provide evidence that factionalism was present. At least two major sets of issues in the First Congress contributed to the appearance of this stage. One was the location of the new capital. The choice between New York, Philadelphia, the Susquehanna valley, and the Potomac valley contributed to the sectional divi-

sions, particularly the separation of the various Middle States delegations. Another large set of votes in the First Congress concerned domestic economics, specifically relating to Hamilton's fiscal proposals. These votes have been cited as the first on which new partisan alignments arose, and they also demonstrate the lack of continuity between the old divisions over the Constitution and the newly emerging divisions. While majorities of both the North Carolina and Virginia delegations had been supporters of the

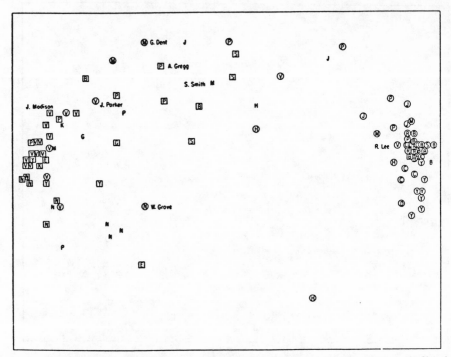

Source: Spatial configuration, derived from multidimensional scaling of recorded roll-call votes in the United States Congress (collected by the Inter-University Consortium for Political and Social Research).

Key: Each symbol indicates the state represented by a particular congressman. The circle or square drawn around the letter indicates party affiliation.

B = Massachusetts	J = New Jersey	R = Rhode Island
C = Connecticut	K = Kentucky	S = South Carolina
E = Vermont	M = Maryland	T = Tennessee
G = Georgia	N = North Carolina	V = Virginia
H = New Hampshire	P = Pennsylvania	Y = New York

Ⓧ = Federalist
☒ = Republican
X = None/Unknown

Figure 3. Voting Patterns in the Third Congress,
United States House of Representatives, 1793–1795

Constitution, they were "federalists only in support of the Constitution and not federalists in upholding all of the centralizing measures of the new government" (Gilpatrick, 1931, p. 45).

A Period of Transition, 1791–1793

By the Second Congress, voting patterns were still best described as factional, but sectionalism was beginning to give way to partisanship. There was not yet, however, a clear movement toward polarization of legislators into two cohesive groups. Nor was there much evidence of partisanship in elections for this congress.

The circular pattern evident in the configuration for the Second Senate represents a transitional stage in the development of party voting (Figure 7). The circle actually consists of four distinct blocs of senators plus one isolated individual (Aaron Burr). These blocs are clearly dominated by senators from particular regions: a South bloc, a South-plus-Middle bloc, a

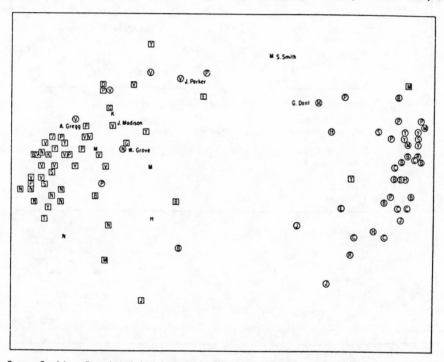

Source: Spatial configuration, derived from multidimensional scaling of recorded roll-call votes in the United States Congress (collected by the Inter-University Consortium for Political and Social Research).

Key: Each symbol indicates the state represented by a particular congressman. The circle or square drawn around the letter indicates party affiliation.

B = Massachusetts	J = New Jersey	R = Rhode Island
C = Connecticut	K = Kentucky	S = South Carolina
E = Vermont	M = Maryland	T = Tennessee
G = Georgia	N = North Carolina	V = Virginia
H = New Hampshire	P = Pennsylvania	Y = New York

Ⓧ = Federalist
☒ = Republican
X = None/Unknown

Figure 4. Voting Patterns in the Fourth Congress, United States House of Representatives, 1795–1797

A. Fifth Congress, 1797–1799

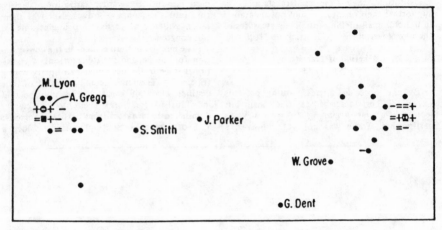

Key: Each symbol represents the number of congressmen at a particular point in the space.

Symbol	Number of Members	Symbol	Number of Members
●	1	+	4
–	2	⊜	5
≈	3	⊗	7
		■	9

B. Sixth Congress, 1799–1801

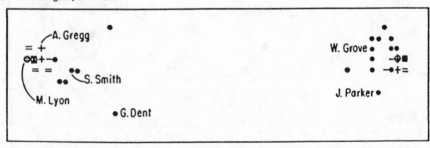

Key: Each symbol represents the number of congressmen at a particular point in the space.

Symbol	Number of Members	Symbol	Number of Members
●	1	⊜	7
–	2	⊕	9
≈	3	⊗	16
+	4	■	19

Source: Spatial configuration, derived from multidimensional scaling of recorded roll-call votes in the United States Congress (collected by the Inter-University Consortium for Political and Social Research).

Figure 5. Voting Patterns in the United States House of Representatives, 1797–1803

Figure 5. Voting Patterns in the United States House of Representatives, 1797–1803, *continued*

C. Seventh Congress, 1801–1803

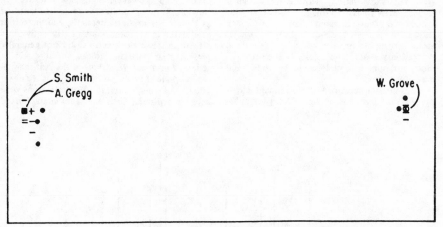

Key: Each symbol represents the number of congressmen at a particular point in the space.

Symbol	Number of Members	Symbol	Number of Members
●	1	+	6
–	2	⊗	34
▪	4	▪	43

Middle-plus-New England bloc, and a New England bloc. Furthermore, the third of these blocs consists exclusively of senators who were being identified as Federalists or were friendly toward Hamilton's fiscal programs. While no bloc is exclusively Republican, there is a tendency for Republicans to be at the opposite side of the figure from the Federalist core group. Clearly, voting in the Second Congress was still more determined by sectional groupings than by party, but the origins of the two parties are already evident in the configuration for this Senate.

Aaron Burr's isolated position is particularly intriguing given his special role in early American politics. His position in the spatial configuration is even more isolated than it appears in Figure 7. In a three-dimensional configuration, Burr alone defines the third dimension, showing his individualized voting in this congress. Chosen as a senator from New York because of a "reputation for independence which fascinated substantial men of both par-

ties" (Young, 1967, p. 189), Burr's record in the Second Congress was truly one of independence from partisanship. Only in later years did he become a confirmed Republican, both in his congressional voting and in his political ambitions.

The configuration for the Second House (Figure 2) is not very different from that of the First House. The principal features are still the regional blocs, particularly the New England and southern blocs. Once again, the South Carolina delegation provided the main exceptions, with the continuing alliance of those from coastal districts with northern congressmen. A second notable exception was the two-member delegation from the newly admitted state of Vermont, the first state without direct access to the coast.

Delegations which changed the most from the First to the Second Congress were those from the Middle States. No longer was each state delegation a cohesive voting bloc. The New York and Pennsylvania delegations had become internally divided, with three Pennsylvanians in both the southern and northern blocs, and two others between the two blocs. In New York's delegation, two members aligned themselves with the South, and the other four voted with New England. The New Jersey delegation remained divided, but no longer along geographic lines. Finally, the Maryland delegation was still much closer to the southern bloc, but only half of it could be considered part of that bloc.

Sectionalism remained the dominant cleavage in the Second Congress. Yet geographic lines were becoming less important in certain states, especially New York and Pennsylvania. Whether this new diversity was truly a sign of partisanship, however, remains a question. In New York, most candidates could be identified as Federalists or Antifederalists, and victorious candidates later voted consistently with these affiliations. But the elections did not generally present clear partisan choices, and it would be at least two more years before the Antifederalists became known as Republicans (Young, 1967). In Pennsylvania, the 1791 elections were held on a district basis and were characterized

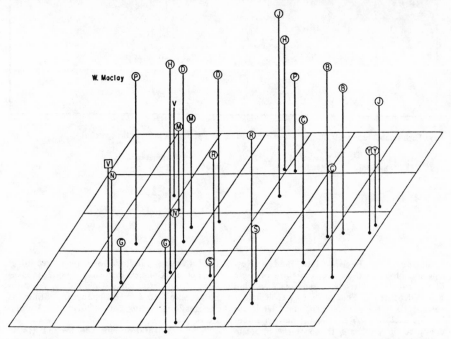

Source: Spatial configuration, derived from multidimensional scaling of recorded roll-call votes in the United States Congress (collected by the Inter-University Consortium for Political and Social Research).

Key: Each symbol indicates the state represented by a particular congressman. The circle or square drawn around the letter indicates party affiliation.

B = Massachusetts	J = New Jersey	R = Rhode Island
C = Connecticut	K = Kentucky	S = South Carolina
E = Vermont	M = Maryland	T = Tennessee
G = Georgia	N = North Carolina	V = Virginia
H = New Hampshire	P = Pennsylvania	Y = New York

Ⓧ = Federalist
☒ = Antifederalist
X = None/Unknown

Figure 6. Voting Patterns in the First Congress,
United States Senate, 1789–1791

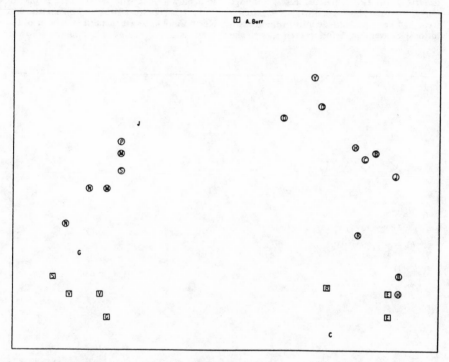

Source: Spatial configuration, derived from multidimensional scaling of recorded roll-call votes in the United States Congress (collected by the Inter-University Consortium for Political and Social Research).

Key: Each symbol indicates the state represented by a particular congressman. The circle or square drawn around the letter indicates party affiliation.

B = Massachusetts	J = New Jersey	R = Rhode Island
C = Connecticut	K = Kentucky	S = South Carolina
E = Vermont	M = Maryland	T = Tennessee
G = Georgia	N = North Carolina	V = Virginia
H = New Hampshire	P = Pennsylvania	Y = New York

Ⓧ = Federalist
☒ = Republican
X = None/Unknown

**Figure 7. Voting Patterns in the Second Congress,
United States Senate, 1791–1793**

by little political activity of any sort. Again, the candidates' political leanings were probably known to the more well-informed voters, but there was no open partisanship.

This lack of partisanship can be further illustrated by two individual cases. Elbridge Gerry, from the Middlesex district in Massachusetts, had been an Antifederalist in the Constitutional Convention, refusing even to sign the

final document. He later became a leader in the Republican party, eventually serving as vice-president under James Madison. But in the Second Congress, Gerry voted more often with the Federalist bloc than with his nominal Republican allies. The second case is that of William Barry Grove, who had been elected in North Carolina as a Federalist supporter of the Constitution, defeating an incumbent who was

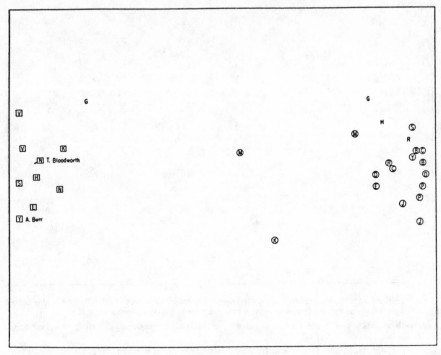

Source: Spatial configuration, derived from multidimensional scaling of recorded roll-call votes in the United States Congress (collected by the Inter-University Consortium for Political and Social Research).

Key: Each symbol indicates the state represented by a particular congressman. The circle or square drawn around the letter indicates party affiliation.

B = Massachusetts	J = New Jersey	R = Rhode Island
C = Connecticut	K = Kentucky	S = South Carolina
E = Vermont	M = Maryland	T = Tennessee
G = Georgia	N = North Carolina	V = Virginia
H = New Hampshire	P = Pennsylvania	Y = New York

Ⓧ = Federalist
☒ = Republican
X = None/Unknown

Figure 8. Voting Patterns in the Fourth Congress,
United States Senate, 1795–1797

one of North Carolina's leading Antifederalists.[12] In spite of his Federalist label, his voting record placed him at the edge of the cluster of

[12]Grove and his opponent, Bloodworth, were in sharp opposition over the wisdom of the Constitution, and the campaign was accented by a series of newspaper advertisements. In spite of an apparently heated contest where Grove won 65 percent of the 3166 votes cast, the election was very one-sided at the county level. In only two of the 12 counties in the district did the leading candidate get fewer than 90

southerners, who mostly became known as Republicans. These two cases help to indicate that the patterns of voting in the Second Congress were not yet clearly determined by partisan affiliations.

percent of the votes, with each candidate winning those counties nearest to his home county. This "friends and neighbors" voting pattern is another clear sign of the lack of partisanship at this time (Gilpatrick, 1931; *North Carolina Chronicle*, 1791).

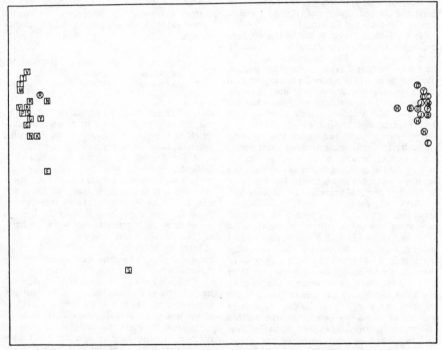

Source: Spatial configuration, derived from multidimensional scaling of recorded roll-call votes in the United States Congress (collected by the Inter-University Consortium for Political and Social Research).

Key: Each symbol indicates the state represented by a particular congressman. The circle or square drawn around the letter indicates party affiliation.

B = Massachusetts	J = New Jersey	R = Rhode Island
C = Connecticut	K = Kentucky	S = South Carolina
E = Vermont	M = Maryland	T = Tennessee
G = Georgia	N = North Carolina	V = Virginia
H = New Hampshire	P = Pennsylvania	Y = New York

(X) = Federalist
[X] = Republican
X = None/Unknown

Figure 9. Voting Patterns in the Seventh Congress,
United States Senate, 1801–1803

Polarization and Party Politics, 1793–1797

The polarization of congressmen into two political parties occurred during Washington's second administration, from 1793 to 1797. This process is clearly indicated by the lower levels of stress for the Third and Fourth Congresses, both in the House and the Senate (Table 1). But it is even more obvious from a comparison of configurations. There is a distinctly tighter clustering in configurations of the Third and Fourth Congresses (Figures 3 and 4, House; Figure 8, Senate), as compared to the First and Second Congresses (Figures 1 and 2, House; Figures 6 and 7, Senate).

In the Fourth Congress, the Senate configuration has a clearly bipolar structure (Figure 8), with two voting blocs corresponding to the emerging Federalist and Republican parties. The parties generally retained a highly sectional character, for the Republican bloc consisted almost entirely of southern senators, while the Federalist bloc included mostly senators from New England and the Middle States. Because of this overlap of party and region, there is some difficulty in determining whether these voting blocs formed because of partisan or regional affiliation. Nevertheless, for most cases where a senator's party ties and sectional loyalties were in conflict, he voted according to his party ties.

The configurations for the House of Representatives, like that for the Senate, show a clear movement toward a pattern of polarization (Figures 3 and 4). In each congress, two distinct polar groups form the cores of the two emerging parties. In addition, there are a number of individuals who do not clearly belong to either group. While this basic pattern appears for both the Third and Fourth Congresses, voting in the latter is more polarized. Instead of a large number of individuals who vote with neither cluster, nearly everyone in the Fourth Congress can be placed in one group or the other, although the groups are still not highly cohesive.

Something can be learned about the polarization process by a careful look at those congressmen who were not clustered with either polar group. In the Third Congress, over 20 of the 100 congressmen were in this intermediate position. Among these individuals, two particular categories are represented. The first type is the northern Republican (such as Gregg of Pennsylvania), who was moving toward his partisan allies from a position of regional loyalty. The second type is the southern Federalist (Parker of Virginia, Grove of North Carolina), moving in the opposite direc-

tion but again toward a position of partisan consistency. By the Fourth Congress, most northern Republicans had reached at least the fringe of the Republican bloc. The small group of southern Federalists was also loosely aligned with the Republicans, showing that partisanship was developing more slowly in the South.

Several general observations can be made about the progress of party development by the end of the Fourth Congress. First, the Federalists had developed quickly into a unified voting bloc, while cohesive voting emerged more slowly for the Republicans. This conclusion, supported by the spatial configurations, can be further confirmed by comparing the average agreement within the Federalist and Republican groups.

	Federalist	Republican
Third Congress	83.3%	73.5%
Fourth Congress	77.0%	72.7%

This difference might be partially attributed to the advantages of being in power. Because much of the agenda was set by the Federalist administration (with the active role of Hamilton), the Republicans in opposition had more difficulty reaching any kind of unity.

Second, both new parties retained a distinctive sectional character. In both the Third and Fourth Congresses, a majority of those in the Federalist bloc came from New England, and a majority of the Republican bloc were southerners. Given the great cultural and economic differences between regions, it should not be surprising that the parties were so distinctively regional.

Yet, in spite of the dominance of regionalism, partisan diversity had clearly emerged within several states. This was particularly true in the larger Middle States: New York, Pennsylvania, and Maryland. In each, elections were revolving around partisan concerns, and they were sending to Congress delegations which included partisans from both emerging groups. For the other regions at this time, partisan diversity was far more limited. New Hampshire, Vermont, and even Massachusetts (a center of Federalist strength) had elected a few men who voted together with the Republicans. South Carolina continued to provide virtually the only exceptions to Republican solidarity in the South. The sole remaining southerner to vote with the Federalist bloc was Richard Bland Lee, of Virginia, who was rewarded for his Federalist leanings with defeat in the election of 1795 (Cunningham, 1957). Most who identified themselves as Federalists in Virginia or North

Carolina still voted more frequently with their Republican neighbors.

By the end of the Fourth Congress, the American party system had reached the level of development labeled "polarization." Nearly every member of Congress could be classified with one party or the other, either by the political leaders of the time or on the basis of this analysis of voting agreement. Party organization and party discipline were growing, although still with limited effectiveness. Furthermore, political leaders such as Jefferson, Madison, and Giles were regularly discussing party activities in their correspondence (Cunningham, 1957). The issue which dominated the Fourth Congress and which several historians have regarded as crucial in party development was the contest over ratification and appropriation of funds for the Jay Treaty (Bell, 1973; Chambers, 1963; Charles, 1961). This treaty with Great Britain marked one of the first organized attempts by the opposition to defeat an important administration policy proposal. With Madison as party leader, Republican strategists tried to coordinate their opposition and defeat the treaty. In the end, they lost by a single vote, but their effort marked a critical point in partisan development (Cunningham, 1957).

The Emergence of Parties, 1797–1803

The Jay Treaty conflict (with its final vote on April 30, 1796) had a significant impact on subsequent congressional elections. These elections, held in late 1796 and early 1797, were dominated by the Jay Treaty issue and were characterized by a level of partisanship not previously seen. George Washington's retirement from politics, and the resulting choice between Adams and Jefferson for president, also tended to raise the level of partisanship. Thus these elections were important for the expansion of party politics into the electoral arena.

Spatial analysis of congressional voting in the Fifth, Sixth, and Seventh Congresses reveals a set of patterns which lend support to the idea that the 1796–97 elections began a new period of partisan politics. Voting in the House had become highly polarized and extremely well defined. The stress for these three configurations is very low and supports an excellent fit even in a single dimension (Table 1). The actual configurations (Figure 5) reveal two very tight clusters with only a few individuals outside of both blocs. In fact, the clustering is so dense

that individual points in these figures cannot be labeled. For this reason, the partisan and regional distributions of the major voting blocs are provided in Table 2. In the Senate (Figure 9), the voting was also polarized into two groups, although the clusters are less well defined than in the House.

Cluster analysis of House members in these three congresses helps to demonstrate further the cohesiveness of the emerging parties. Average levels of agreement within the two voting blocs are shown below.

	Federalist	Republican
Fifth Congress	82.7%	86.9%
Sixth Congress	86.4%	86.0%
Seventh Congress	89.9%	79.6%

These levels of intra-group agreement are extremely high and far above comparable levels in previous years (or in fact, in modern times). The only real exceptions to the polarization into partisan voting blocs were in the Fifth Congress, where three individuals were noticeably unaligned: Dent (Md.), Parker (Va.), and S. Smith (Md.). All three served in Congress for several terms and had a history of inconsistent partisan ties. Yet, by the Sixth Congress, even these three men were clearly aligned with one of the party blocs.

There remains, of course, the question of whether these voting alignments can appropriately be called party blocs. This question can be examined by looking at the relationship between party labels and voting blocs, and by considering the sectional composition of these blocs. If voting blocs result from party alignments, they should be very consistent with party labels and relatively diverse in their geographical composition. The relationships in Table 2 are clearly consistent with the designation of the voting blocs as partisan.

At an individual level, this conclusion is illustrated by looking again at the voting record of Grove (N.C.). He was first elected to Congress in 1791 and was always regarded in his home state as a Federalist, the only North Carolina Federalist chosen before 1798. Yet in the Second, Third, and Fourth Congresses, his voting record was more in line with the Republican bloc and the rest of his state delegation. By the Fifth Congress his votes placed him on the edge of the Federalist bloc; and in the Sixth and Seventh Congresses, he was clearly a partisan Federalist. Furthermore, in the latter two congresses, Grove was joined in the Federalist camp by several other North Carolina Federalists. A second southern Federalist, Parker (Va.), followed a similar path, moving from his sectional group to his party affiliation.

The issue which seems to symbolize the emergent partisanship was the passage of the Alien and Sedition Acts in 1798. These acts were at least partially an attempt by the Federalists to destroy the opposition party. Votes on these laws coincided almost perfectly with the blocs shown in the configurations, providing further evidence that these blocs were partisan groupings.

Indices of Partisanship

A more traditional type of roll-call analysis may help to amplify further the multidimensional scaling results. Three indices of party voting are employed here—Rice's index of cohesion, Rice's index of difference, and Lowell's concept of the party vote. The utility of these indices for studying partisanship across time has been demonstrated by MacRae (1970, pp. 200–07), who showed that the degree of partisanship in Congress (as measured by party votes) rose to its highest levels immediately following party realignments. Because the emergence of new parties might be regarded as a special case of partisan realignment, a similar pattern might be expected between 1789 and 1803.

The values of the index of cohesion, the index of difference, and the percentage of party votes are presented for the House and Senate from 1789 to 1803 in Figure 10. These data

readily show that cohesion in both legislative parties increased dramatically during this period, while party differences grew simultaneously. The indices of party cohesion and difference rose constantly during the first five congresses, leveling off after 1797. The timing of these changes corresponds rather closely with the polarization observed in the MDS configurations. Parties developed steadily from 1789 until 1796, the year of the Jay Treaty controversy. By the Fifth Congress, they had reached a high level of development on any measure of congressional voting, a level sustained through 1803.

For purposes of comparison, I have also calculated indices of cohesion and difference for the three regional groups: New England, Middle States, and the South. Regional cohesion remained reasonably constant across this period, although some changes did occur in the Sixth and Seventh Congresses, reflecting large partisan swings within several states in the elections of 1798 and 1800. The average regional cohesion for the entire period was 49.3, a level higher than party cohesion in the first two congresses but exceeded by party cohesion in all the remaining years. This result confirms the earlier conclusion that partisanship had become more important than sectionalism after about 1793.

In order to make a better assessment of party development in these early years, comparisons can be made between the cohesion of the early parties and twentieth-century parties. During the entire period from 1921 to 1969, the average index of cohesion of the two

Table 2. Partisan and Regional Distributions of Members of the United States House of Representatives, by Multidimensional Scaling Blocs

Multidimensional Scaling Bloc	Total	Party			Region			
		Federalist	Republican	None	New England	Middle States	South	West
Fifth Congress								
Federalist	52	51	1	0	25	21	6	0
Republican	45	0	44	1	3	12	27	3
None	3	2	1	0	0	2	1	0
Sixth Congress								
Federalist	51	51	0	0	22	15	14	0
Republican	49	6	43	0	3	21	22	3
Seventh Congress								
Federalist	38	37	1	0	20	10	8	0
Republican	62	3	59	0	8	26	25	3

Source: Derived from multidimensional scaling of recorded roll-call votes in the United States Congress (collected by the Inter-University Consortium for Political and Social Research).

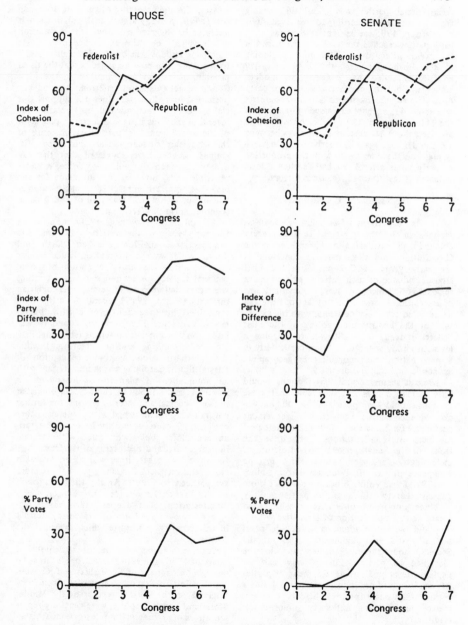

Source: Computed from recorded roll-call votes in the United States Congress (collected by the Inter-University Consortium for Political and Social Research).

Figure 10. Trends in Partisanship, United States Congress,
House of Representatives and Senate, 1789–1803

congressional parties was about 66, ranging from 55 to 77.[13] According to this standard of comparison, 1795 seems to mark the year when early parties reached the level of unity found in the twentieth century. Furthermore, beginning in the Fifth Congress, the level of party cohesion exceeded that in nearly any modern congress. Similarly, the average index of party difference for the twentieth-century congresses was about 41, a figure surpassed by the time of the Third Congress. The number of party votes averaged about 10 percent of all votes between 1921 and 1969; again, the early parties generally matched these levels. In fact, the proportion of party votes after 1797 had reached a level obtained at few times in American history.

Discussion and Conclusions

The loose patterns of association known as factionalism had been present in nearly every colonial and national assembly predating the Constitution, and these patterns continued in the early years of Congress. For the First House, evidence of such patterns existed in the regional voting blocs. At least minimal patterns of association characteristic of factionalism can be detected for every congress, with the exception of the unstructured voting of the First Senate. Indeed, it is difficult to imagine a legislative body without factions, particularly in a new nation with considerable geographic, economic, and cultural diversity.

While it seems natural that factions should have arisen, it was not inevitable that these factions should have polarized. Yet the empirical evidence shows that such a movement occurred. Examination of the chronological sequence of configurations, for either the House or the Senate, reveals a vivid picture of increasing polarization, culminating in the emergence of two highly cohesive voting blocs by 1797. These voting blocs were in fact more cohesive than twentieth-century parties.

Three important questions can be raised regarding this polarization of legislative voting: Why did particular alignments develop, or in fact why did any alignments appear at all? Second, should these polarized voting blocs be identified as parties? Finally, how can we explain the anomalous development of parties (if that is indeed an appropriate term) during a period when most political leaders were immersed in a strong anti-party philosophical tradition?

[13]The averages for the congresses of the twentieth century were computed from tables in Cooper, Brady, and Hurley (1977, pp. 138–39).

Reasons for the Emerging Alignments. Huntington (1968, p. 415) argues that polarization is likely to be triggered by either "the cumulation of cleavages" or "the emergence of a single dominant issue which overshadows all others." In the American case he suggests that the fiscal program presented by Hamilton to the First Congress met this latter criterion. The evidence presented here, however, does not support this claim, for the factions did not polarize for several years. This issue was merely a precursor of the new alignments, particularly in terms of the leadership of Madison and his fellow Virginians. Others have suggested that the Jay Treaty provided the polarizing force. A more plausible case, however, can be made for the idea that polarization resulted from the cumulative effect of several issues, all of which came together in the Jay Treaty conflict.

Several cleavages were generally important in the early years of the new republic. One was the sectional division between North and South, which was manifested on issues such as the location of the capital for reasons of simple regional loyalty. A second significant conflict was that between commercial and agrarian interests (Beard, 1915), economic differences intensified by their convergence with the regional divisions. The northern economy was built upon commercial interests (shipping, fishing, trade, banking, and manufacturing), while the southern economy (with exception of coastal South Carolina) was more agrarian, with an abundance of plantations dependent on slavery (Dauer, 1953). A third cleavage existed between coastal and interior regions, the former naturally more concerned with trade and other commercial interests, and the latter, with agrarian economies, being concerned with internal improvements and protection of the frontier. A fourth cleavage set those wishing to maintain close relations with England against those more sympathetic to France. Against the background of the French Revolution, this division was a manifestation of a deeper philosophical disagreement over the form of democracy desired in this country, a dispute which provided the fifth major cleavage.

All five divisions were present in the political arena of 1795, and each tended to reinforce the emerging alignment of Federalists and Republicans. Federalists, coming most often from New England or the coastal regions of the Middle States and South Carolina, were generally representatives of commercial interests, sympathizers with the English, and supporters of a more aristocratic political system. Republicans, on the other hand, came generally from the interior or the South, and they were mostly allies of agrarian interests and believers in the direct democracy symbolized by the French Revolution.

At a time when these blocs of interests were coalescing, controversy arose over ratification and implementation of the Jay Treaty. The treaty itself was the outcome of negotiations with Great Britain over a number of concerns, including British activity on the western frontier, British seizure of slaves during the war, American trade debts dating to before the war, the neutrality of American shipping in the war between Britain and France, and the general status of British-American trade. As the product of the Federalist administration, the treaty was opposed by the Republicans, who were particularly concerned about the favorable trade status granted to Britain at the expense of France and the failure to provide compensation for slaves seized by Britain (Chambers, 1963; Charles, 1961; Varg, 1963). The Jay Treaty, therefore, represented in a single issue the cumulation of dominant cleavages in early American politics. The subsequent polarization of congressional voting and increased partisanship in electoral contests made this issue a crucial factor in the development of American political parties.[14]

The Existence of Party. While there should be little question about the polarization of alignments in the early American congresses, reasonable objections can be raised to the designation of polar voting blocs as parties. Formisano (1974), for example, has suggested that voting blocs may have formed not along party lines, but rather along lines related to such factors as regionalism and boardinghouse residences. Obviously, region and party were highly related during this period, a fact which itself does not run counter to the existence of parties. But the multiplicity of cleavages and the persistence of voting alliances would seem to deny a simply regional explanation. In fact, by the end of this era, the voting blocs had become less dominated by a single region (see Table 2). And, as long as the capital remained in New York or Philadelphia, boardinghouses were not a salient factor in congressional voting. Furthermore, when Congress did move to Washington in 1800, there is no evidence of distinct voting blocs corresponding to boardinghouse membership. Indeed, it is more likely that congressmen

chose as messmates their established partisan allies.[15]

Nevertheless, there is more to the idea of party than simply the existence of congressional voting blocs. The several aspects of party identified early in this article include common symbols or labels and groups of supporters in the electorate. Formisano (1974, p. 478) has pointed out that

> multivariate analysis of roll calls needs to be accompanied by evidence that men ran for Congress as openly identified members of a party. To show convincingly that the core factions of Federalist and Republican interests came to think of themselves in party terms, consideration must be given to legislators' self-images. . . .

Although there was not a consistent use of party labels in election campaigns across the entire nation, it is clear that party labels were becoming more meaningful as legislators polarized into voting blocs. Gradually people were beginning to think about politics in explicitly partisan terms (Cunningham, 1957; Young, 1967).

The determination of whether parties existed in the 1790s has become in effect a game of definitions. Evidently, this was a decade of party development, and whether the word "party" is appropriate at any particular time is not crucial. What is important is to document the continually increasing prominence of parties in the politics of this era. In 1790, members of Congress were voting together in regional groups whose composition shifted considerably from one issue to the next. By 1792, patterns of voting were shifting from a regional basis to a more partisan basis built on a set of issue positions. By 1796, these voting patterns had polarized so that two blocs of congressmen opposed each other on nearly every issue. As the cohesiveness of party groups in Congress increased, party affiliation became a more significant factor in congressional elections. These trends continued until at least 1803. Only thereafter, with the decline of the Federalists, did the country experience a temporary hiatus in the process of party development.

[14]For further discussion, see Hoadley (1979).

[15]The boardinghouse explanation of voting cohesion was advanced by Young (1966), but his conclusions have been recently challenged (Bogue and Marlaire, 1975; Cunningham, 1978). A comparison of boardinghouse residence (found in Goldman and Young, 1973) with the location of members in the configurations for the Philadelphia and Washington years (to 1803) fails to reveal any pattern supporting Young's thesis for this period.

Parties in an Anti-Party Era. When the new government was created by the Constitution, most political leaders shared a strong anti-party tradition. Parties were perceived as agencies which would hinder the progress of good government, a view expressed forcefully by Madison in *The Federalist*, No. 10 (1961, p. 77): "Among the numerous advantages promised by a well constructed Union, none deserves to be more accurately developed than its tendency to break and control the violence of faction." Yet in spite of such sentiments, parties very quickly became a prominent feature of the political system. This anti-party stigma does, however, help to account for the fact that parties had not reached the highest stages of development during this period. The reluctance of candidates to run openly for office as members of a party and the failure of leaders to develop any substantial national organization were two factors that might be explained in part by this distrust of the idea of a party system.

One explanation for the anomaly of party development within the context of an anti-party tradition lies in the lack of any positive historical precedent. Nowhere in the eighteenth-century world did parties exist by any modern definition. There was considerable factionalism, both in Great Britain and in colonial America, but no clear development of parties beyond this stage. Therefore, in their anti-party statements, American political thinkers were dealing with a concept of "party" which today would be characterized as "faction." They simply did not recognize the possibility of a more constructive political party until some time after they had actually created such parties.

A second explanation for this anomaly lies in the emerging idea of legitimate opposition. Some of the philosophical objections to the idea of party were based on the belief that parties might hinder development of the unanimity considered essential for the stability of a state. Gradually people realized that unanimity was impossible in a diverse society and that the right of opposition had to be recognized. Sartori (1976, p. 11) has suggested that "parties presuppose—for their acceptance and proper functioning—peace under a constitutional rule." The first set of elections for Congress (between 1788 and 1790) showed that the Constitution was quickly being accepted. In spite of the large numbers opposing ratification in some states, most of the new congressmen were supporters of the Constitution. Furthermore, even an Antifederalist such as Elbridge Gerry could be found arguing in debate that, "If this constitu-

tion, which is now ratified, be not supported, I despair of ever having a government for these United States" (Austin, 1829, p. 103).

When it became clear that the opposition was concerned only with specific policy alternatives within the existing constitutional system, it was far easier for such opposition to be tolerated. Once the legitimacy of opposition was established, the acceptance of parties followed. This was, of course, a slow process. The Sedition Act, passed by Federalist majorities in 1798, represented the old tradition; at least one Republican congressman (Lyon of Vermont) won reelection after being convicted and jailed under this act. Nevertheless, the progress of party development was not deterred seriously by this act of a declining Federalist majority. Only two years later, the Republicans were victorious in both presidential and congressional elections. That a transfer of power occurred peacefully in 1801 reflects growing acceptance of the legitimacy of opposition and the idea of party.

In 1804, Thomas Jefferson wrote in a letter, "The party division in this country is certainly not among it's pleasant features. To a certain degree it will always exist. . ." (quoted in Cunningham, 1965, p. 19). By this time, nearly everyone in Congress was clearly associated with one of the new parties. Acceptance of these parties, however, came reluctantly as their inevitability became more apparent. Whether recognized by those involved or still regarded as an undesirable development, the changing voting patterns exhibited by members of Congress between 1789 and 1803 present strong evidence that a true party system had emerged.

References

Austin, James T. (1829). *The Life of Elbridge Gerry*, Vol. 2. Boston: Wells and Lilly.

Beard, Charles A. (1915). *Economic Origins of Jeffersonian Democracy*. New York: Macmillan.

Bell, Rudolph M. (1973). *Party and Faction in American Politics: The House of Representatives, 1789–1801*. Westport, Conn.: Greenwood Press.

Bogue, Allan G., and Mark Paul Marlaire (1975). "Of Mess and Men: The Boardinghouse and Congressional Voting, 1821–1842." *American Journal of Political Science* 19: 207–30.

Chambers, William Nisbet (1963). *Political Parties in a New Nation: The American Experience, 1776–1809*. New York: Oxford University Press.

——— (1966). "Parties and Nation-Building in America." In Joseph LaPalombara and Myron Weiner (eds.), *Political Parties and Political Development*. Princeton, N.J.: Princeton University Press, pp. 79–106.

——— (1967). "Party Development and the American Mainstream." In William Nisbet Chambers and

Walter Dean Burnham (eds.), *The American Party Systems: Stages of Political Development.* New York: Oxford University Press, pp. 3–32.

Charles, Joseph (1961). *The Origins of the American Party System: Three Essays.* New York: Harper.

Cooper, Joseph, David W. Brady, and Patricia A. Hurley (1977). "The Election Basis of Party Voting: Patterns and Trends in the U.S. House of Representatives, 1887–1969." In Louis Maisel and Joseph Cooper (eds.), *The Impact of the Electoral Process.* Beverly Hills: Sage Publications, pp. 133–65.

Cunningham, Noble E., Jr. (1957). *The Jeffersonian Republicans: The Formation of Party Organization, 1789–1801.* Chapel Hill: University of North Carolina Press.

——, ed. (1965). *The Making of the American Party System: 1789 to 1809.* Englewood Cliffs: Prentice-Hall.

—— (1978). *The Process of Government under Jefferson.* Princeton, N.J.: Princeton University Press.

Dauer, Manning J. (1953). *The Adams Federalists.* Baltimore: Johns Hopkins University Press.

Duverger, Maurice (1959). *Political Parties,* rev. ed. Translated by Barbara North and Robert North. New York: Wiley.

Formisano, Ronald P. (1974). "Deferential-Participant Politics: The Early Republic's Political Culture, 1789–1840." *American Political Science Review* 68: 473–87.

Gilpatrick, Delbert H. (1931). *Jeffersonian Democracy in North Carolina.* New York: Columbia University Press.

Goldman, Perry M., and James S. Young, eds. (1973). *The United States Congressional Directories, 1789–1840.* New York: Columbia University Press.

Hoadley, John F. (1979). *The Development of American Political Parties: A Spatial Analysis of Congressional Voting, 1789–1803.* Ph.D. dissertation, University of North Carolina, Chapel Hill.

Hofstadter, Richard (1969). *The Idea of a Party System: The Rise of Legitimate Opposition in the United States, 1780–1840.* Berkeley: University of California Press.

Huntington, Samuel P. (1968). *Political Order in Changing Societies.* New Haven: Yale University Press.

LaPalombara, Joseph, and Myron Weiner (1966). "The Origin and Development of Political Parties." In Joseph LaPalombara and Myron Weiner (eds.), *Political Parties and Political Development.* Princeton, N.J.: Princeton University Press, pp. 3–42.

Libby, Orin G. (1912). "A Sketch of the Early Political Parties in the United States." *Quarterly Journal of the University of North Dakota* 2: 205–42.

MacRae, Duncan, Jr. (1970). *Issues and Parties in Legislative Voting.* New York: Harper and Row.

Madison, James, Alexander Hamilton, and John Jay (1961). *The Federalist Papers.* New York: New American Library.

Nichols, Roy F. (1967). *The Invention of the American Political Parties.* New York: Macmillan.

North Carolina Chronicle or Fayetteville Gazette (1791). February 7, 1791.

Paullin, Charles O. (1904). "The First Elections Under the Constitution." *Iowa Journal of History and Politics* 2: 3–33.

Rabinowitz, George B. (1975). "An Introduction to Nonmetric Multidimensional Scaling." *American Journal of Political Science* 19: 343–90.

Ryan, Mary P. (1971). "Party Formation in the United States Congress, 1789 to 1796: A Quantitative Analysis." *William and Mary Quarterly,* 3rd ser. 28: 523–42.

Sartori, Giovanni (1976). *Parties and Party Systems: A Framework for Analysis,* Vol. I. Cambridge: Cambridge University Press.

Sorauf, Frank J. (1967). "Political Parties and Political Analysis." In William Nisbet Chambers and Walter Dean Burnham (eds.), *The American Party Systems: Stages of Political Development.* New York: Oxford University Press, pp. 33–55.

United States Congress (1961). *Biographical Directory of the American Congress, 1774–1961.* Washington, D.C.: Government Printing Office.

Varg, Paul A. (1963). *Foreign Policies of the Founding Fathers.* Baltimore: Penguin Books.

Young, Alfred F. (1967). *The Democratic Republicans of New York: The Origins, 1763–1797.* Chapel Hill: University of North Carolina Press.

Young, James Sterling (1966). *The Washington Community, 1800–1828.* New York: Harcourt, Brace and World.

Foreign Credit and Fiscal Stability: Dutch Investment in the United States, 1781–1794

James C. Riley

T HE importance of foreign credits and subsidies to war and peacetime finance during the Confederation is well established. Compared to the nominal value of paper currency and interest-bearing note issues, those credits and subsidies produced rather little. But a more accurate comparison would be based on the specie value of fiat money and domestic loan certificates, and would acknowledge the difficulty of finding domestic resources for such essential foreign purchases as military supplies.

Little attention has been given foreign borrowing in the early years of the federal government, another critical period in which domestic resources were inadequate. In attempting to achieve financial stability for the new regime, Alexander Hamilton had to cope with a bequest from the Confederation combining a debt-revenue ratio unparalleled in Europe with tenuous or wholly exhausted domestic credit resources. Nor until the mid-1790s could sufficient tax revenues be collected, for the authority given Congress by the Constitution could not be transformed quickly into enough income to meet military, naval, administrative, debt service, and other expenditures. Save default, the only option left was to turn to the reputation for financial dependability which, ironically, had been built for the Confederation on the Amsterdam capital market since 1781. Hamilton's program of national public finance, an adept compromise among conflicting interests, succeeded not merely because it satisfied many potential antagonists, but because Hamilton, recognizing the necessity of foreign credit, took advantage of Dutch loans and the readiness of Dutch rentiers to invest heavily in the American domestic debt. Revenue and expenditure reconstructions show that Hamilton's establishment of a reliable system of public finance was funded substantially by foreign capital, for which there was no substitute, and from which important monetary and economic benefits were also drawn.

James C. Riley is assistant professor of history in Indiana University.

654

Congress' first loan in Amsterdam was raised long after other states, beginning at least as early as 1616, had drawn on Dutch savings. Only after about 1740, however, was there substantial growth in Dutch involvement in foreign government finance. Attracted by high yields, rentiers converted part of their savings from trade, commercial credit, and other areas into the essential prop of an international government credit structure in which loans raised in the Dutch Republic were combined with intensified credit exploitation within debtor states.[1] Using Dutch investment capital, European governments leveraged income from taxation, bank note issues, and loans on domestic capital markets. Until capital supply contracted in the early stages of the wars of the French Revolution, the international government credit structure replaced the traditional instability of monarchical and public finance in much of Europe with deficit spending programs that inspired confidence.

Similar techniques were employed by the United States during the War of Independence, but with a different short-term outcome. Congress supplemented credits and subsidies from its allies and the inadequate proceeds of assessments on the states by currency inflation, long-term borrowing, and confiscation.[2] Unable to attract foreign resources in sufficient volume to duplicate European leveraging, the United States was forced into unrestrained seigniorage. In hyperinflation, American paper currency lost most of its nominal value, and in 1780 was established against specie at a ratio of 40:1. During 1781 recognition of that paper was for the most part withdrawn.[3]

[1] On Dutch capital supply see P. W. Klein, "Stagnation économique et emploi du capital dans la Hollande des XIIIe [sic] et XIXe siècles," *Revue du Nord*, LII (1970), 33–41. The operation in the Dutch Republic of a strong social imperative toward savings is well established in an impressionistic fashion. See, for example, Violet Barbour, *Capitalism in Amsterdam in the Seventeenth Century* (Baltimore, 1950), 28–29. Some specific cases of its operation may be found in B. E. de Muinck, *Een regentenhuishouding omstreeks 1700* (The Hague, 1965), 50–52, 79; and Marten G. Buist, *At Spes non Fracta: Hope & Co., 1770–1815* (The Hague, 1974), 520–25.

[2] Davis Rich Dewey offers a breakdown for 1775–1783 in specie values:

Paper money issues	$37,800,000
Domestic loans	11,585,506
Foreign loans	7,830,517
Tax revenues	5,795,000
Miscellaneous	2,852,802
	$65,863,825

Davis Rich Dewey, *Financial History of the United States* (New York, 1939), 35.

[3] On the currency issue see Joseph Albert Ernst, "Currency in the Era of the American Revolution: A History of Colonial Paper Money Practices and British Monetary Policies, 1764–1781" (doctoral dissertation, University of Wisconsin, 1962), 398–404; Curtis P. Nettels, *The Emergence of a National Economy, 1775–1815* (New York, 1962), 24–33; and Charles J. Bullock, "The Finances of the United States from 1775 to 1789," *Bulletin of the University of Wisconsin*, I (1897), 132–37.

Interest-bearing notes issued first in 1776 by the loan office failed to attract lenders on the desired scale despite an increase of the yield from 4 to 6 percent. Service on that paper was suspended in 1782, and in 1784 Congress began to pay interest with indents. In 1780 depreciated loan office notes had been related to a table intended to reflect specie values at the time of purchase. That operation conveyed to those notes the label "liquidated debt," although in fact what was involved was a prolongation of the debt under revised terms rather than a liquidation.[4] Not until 1790 did Congress fund the liquidated debt, and not until 1791 did it begin repayments. Through 1788, loan office notes and various paper issued during and after the War of Independence to pay military contractors and personnel and others circulated far below face value while they tended to flow away from initial recipients into the hands of investors willing to take the risk of speculative gains or repayment above current market value.[5]

Thus, while European states managed to create public finance programs that permitted them to expand liabilities without losing the confidence of lenders, the United States exhausted the credit available to it on domestic markets and potential revenues from seigniorage before finding access to Dutch capital. American representatives in Europe during the late 1770s understood the advantage that Dutch credit gave European governments, but they failed to persuade investors to subscribe to loans for Congress.

The new nation's precarious fiscal position in the late 1770s prevailed for the remainder of the war and after because the financial devices used to pay for the war had been so thoroughly discredited and because revenues from the states remained inadequate. Furthermore, France and Spain, which had supplied credit and matériel, curtailed their financial support because of the costs of their conflict with England. But in November 1781 France opened a loan in the Dutch Republic for ƒ5 million, with the proceeds earmarked for the United States.[6] That was the first occasion on which any significant sum was gotten from Dutch investors, but the 1781 loan succeeded because it was issued by France and, moreover, because the States General of the Dutch Republic added a collateral guarantee. There was little prospect that future advances

---

[4] E. James Ferguson, *The Power of the Purse* (Chapel Hill, 1961), 68–69. The indents were acceptable in tax payments to the states, and for that reason they retained value in the market.

[5] On speculation in the debt, see *ibid.*, 251–86.

[6] Rafael A. Bayley, *The National Loans of the United States from July 4, 1776 to June 30, 1880* (Washington, 1881), 13; and Ferguson, *Power of the Purse*, 127, and note 5. Repayment of the 1781 loan by France was to be completed in 1792, and by the United States to France over the period 1787–1796.

could be raised in the same fashion, however much good will toward the United States might prevail in France or the Dutch Republic. Still, the United States had been introduced to Dutch investors even if there was no assurance that those investors would take up loans secured only by the resources available to Congress.

In the spring of 1782 John Adams, American representative in the United Provinces, negotiated the issue of a loan for *f*3 million (later increased to *f*5 million) through the houses of W. & J. Willink, N. & J. van Staphorst, and De la Lande & Fynje.[7] Although at 5 percent the United States offered a premium return, the interest was only 1 percent greater than what France had paid in 1781. However, commission charges, the compensation the borrower allowed bankers and other agents for sounding the market and placing shares, were actually less than what France had paid. In both cases those charges amounted nominally to 4.5 percent, but France had agreed to an additional "gratification" that increased its total to 7.5 percent.[8] Because commissions were taken off the top of receipts, the nominal return differed from the effective return. In this comparison the United States paid an effective yield of 5.24 percent and France one of 4.32 percent. Even so, it is clear in retrospect that the entire overhead, and especially the low commission charges, were particularly favorable terms for an untested and impecunious debtor. Neither Dutch bankers nor investors fully appreciated the precariousness of America's financial position, but the bankers soon found that they had been too sanguine about the rate of placements that might be expected. To negotiate a loan was not necessarily to attract actual subscriptions. The 1782 issue moved very slowly, the full *f*4,775,000 remaining to Congress after costs becoming available only gradually over the period from 1782 until 1786.

Nonetheless, the American loan was an attractive proposition for the bankers. Business had developed political alignments in the Dutch Republic in the early 1780s, during the Fourth Anglo-Dutch War, and Adams had found it necessary to contend with the problem of partisanship in approaching houses about organizing a loan. The most substantial firms of the city in 1782 were still Orangists, supporters of the stadholder and thus identified with England. Although one of the

[7] For details on this and subsequent loans see P. J. van Winter, *Het aandeel van den Amsterdamschen handel aan den opbouw van het Amerikaansche Gemeenebest* (2 vols., The Hague, 1927–1933), I, 59–87, 133–92, II, 147–89, 476–77. That monograph is also available in a revised and translated edition, Pieter J. van Winter, *American Finance and Dutch Investment, 1780–1805, With an Epilogue to 1840,* ed. James C. Riley (2 vols., New York, 1977).

[8] Herbert Lüthy, *La banque protestante en France de la révocation de l'édit de Nantes à la Révolution* (2 vols., Paris, 1959–1961), II. 616.

most prestigious Orangist houses might have guaranteed the success of a loan to the United States merely by attaching its name to it, Adams had to turn to firms that were more congenial politically, if less imposing as bankers. He applied to a circle of houses that identified themselves as Patriots, members of an as yet loosely formed political faction wishing to attach Dutch interests to France, and therefore pro-American. The van Staphorst brothers, Nicolaas and Jacob, Hendrik Fynje, and Jacobus de la Lande were Patriots, and thus disposed to consider managing a loan for the United States. But they and the apolitical Willinks as well were attracted to Adams' proposals principally because of the business advantages available in them.[9] As long as Congress' loan did not have to be guaranteed, so that no part of it would ever have to come from their pockets, there was far less risk in managing that issue than there was potential gain. If subscriptions were filled, even very slowly, those bankers would gain the reputation of being capable of managing large-scale loans to foreign governments and thus enter a lucrative sector of enterprise. Moreover, in the pattern that had become customary in Amsterdam, one loan issue could be expected to lead to another for the same borrower and perhaps to an unofficial monopoly over a lengthy series.

None of the firms involved in Congress' early loans has left any sizable body of business papers but, from the available sources, neither Dutch bankers nor investors appears to have made any systematic attempt to investigate Congress' financial position before 1786. A willingness to open government loans without an extensive exploration of the credit worthiness of the debtor was entirely consistent with customary banking practice on the Amsterdam market. Few houses had access to reliable information about key issues of government finance, revenues, expenditures, and accumulated indebtedness, and the bankers that managed foreign loans were content to secure those advances on vague statements about revenues assigned to pay service and redemptions. Dutch investors were inclined to assume that bankers had evaluated risk and established appropriate terms. For those reasons and because the Amsterdam market was characterized by an abundance of capital and lower long-term interest rates than prevailed elsewhere, market practice in establishing loan terms revolved around a narrow margin of yields. The offer of 5 percent placed the United States in a position of rough equivalency with such borrowers as the King of

[9] This theme has been developed with care and in detail by van Winter, *Amsterdamschen handel,* I, 1–28, 59–87.

TABLE 1
Gross and Net Proceeds of Dutch Loans to the United States, 1782–1794

	Gross Proceeds	Commission (in percent)	Net Proceeds after Commission Charges
1782	ƒ 5,000,000	4½	ƒ 4,775,000
1784	2,000,000	7	1,860,000
1787	1,000,000	8–9	915,000*
1788	1,000,000	8	920,000
1790	3,000,000	4½	2,865,000
1791	8,500,000	4	8,160,000
1792	5,950,000	5–5½	5,637,500
1793	1,000,000	3½	965,000
1794	3,000,000	4½	2,865,000
	ƒ 30,450,000		ƒ 28,962,500
1791 (Antwerp)	2,050,000		1,975,375,13
Total	ƒ 32,500,000		ƒ 30,937,875,13

* Commission on the 1787 loan was increased from 8 percent to 9 percent to speed subscriptions after the loan was issued. Net proceeds are estimated because of the change in commission.

Poland, some minor German states, and the Kingdom of Spain, financially the weakest clients of the Amsterdam market.

The three original firms opened a second loan in 1784, for ƒ2 million, and Willink and van Staphorst a third in 1787 for ƒ1 million (see Table 1 and Chart 1).[10] To that point, then, loan issues had totaled ƒ8 million. After the deduction of commissions, those yielded the United States some ƒ7,550,000, or slightly more than $3 million (assuming exchange rates at par, or $.40 to the current guilder).[11] As funds became available they were used to meet obligations abroad, expenses for which domestic resources were inadequate in part because of the scarcity of specie in the United States but also because the states forwarded to Congress only about 25 percent of quotas assessed them in that period. Transfers to Europe were costly because of an unadvantageous exchange rate. On the

[10] For a presentation in tabular form of the pertinent data on the loans, see *ibid.*, II, 476–77. De la Lande & Fynje suspended payments in 1785, leaving Willink and van Staphorst to pursue the American agency on their own. See the notarial accord drawn by P. C. Nahuys, 16728/355, Municipal Archives (Amsterdam). A 4.5 percent return was paid on the loan opened in Antwerp on December 1, 1791, and commission charges were 4 percent. The net receipts, however, totaled slightly more than 96 percent. See van Winter, *American Finance and Dutch Investment*, I, 503. A 1793 loan opened for the Bank of the United States is not included here.

[11] Hamilton calculated par (via bullion content) at 35 89/100 ninetieths of a dollar to one current guilder, or $.3988 (ƒ2.51 to the dollar). Jonathan Elliot, *The Funding System of the United States & of Great Britain* (New York, 1968), 192. That has been rounded off to $.40. The dollar rate at the time of those loans was probably closer to ƒ 2.35, at which the yield would be calculated at more than $3.2 million. (See note 44.) Because loan proceeds were not transferred in their entirety to the United States, such calculations have only an hypothetical applicability.

Chart 1: Interest Rates and Commission Charges in Dutch Loans
to the United States, 1782–1794

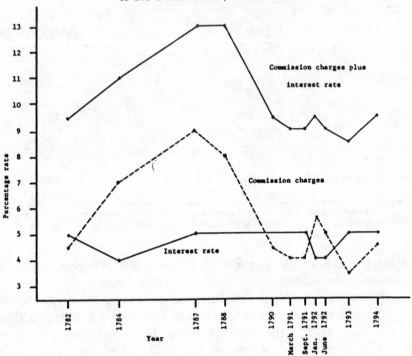

other hand, when loan proceeds could be forwarded to the United States, guilder drafts brought correspondingly larger dollar sums.

The credit evaluation implied in the 1782 loan, one that placed the United States among the least dependable borrowers floating loans in the Dutch Republic, prevailed again in 1784. Even though that loan was issued at 4 percent, Congress agreed to the addition of premiums which, together with commission charges, increased the effective cost to 6.65 percent.[12] On the Amsterdam market the adjustment of commissions tended to be more important than a variation in interest rates as a means of responding to shifts in the receptivity of investors to given issues. Although with premiums the 1784 loan returned more than 6 percent to investors, a 5 percent yield was reinstated in 1787. In contrast, commission charges, which were sometimes shared with investors but

[12] Elliot, *Funding System*, 188.

which more generally determined the enthusiasm of brokers, were increased to 7 percent in 1784, and 8 percent in 1787.[13]

What those variations indicate is that Congress' bankers were assisted in what would otherwise have been a perilous operation of establishing and maintaining investor confidence not only by the premium return that Congress agreed to pay but also by a bias characteristic of the Amsterdam market toward cheap credit, a situation favoring borrowers. That interpretation is fortified by the success Congress' bankers enjoyed in withholding from investors certain signals that would have made them substantially more apprehensive about American credit. Dutch rentiers believed punctuality in payment of service on a loan to be the key standard of credit worthiness.[14] The United States met its annuity payments in the Dutch Republic punctually, and for that reason established and preserved its ability to borrow at a time when Congress' tax authority was ludicrously weak and the public debt, even discounted as the domestic debt was in trading, wholly beyond Congress' power to redeem or even to service with specie. But the United States met service payments in Amsterdam by issuing new loans, a practice that amounted implicitly to insolvency. It was Congress' good fortune that the bankers were able to withhold knowledge of that from the public.[15]

Maintaining the appearance of solvency and credit worthiness at a time when Congress could lend little assistance was a laborious procedure, one through which the intermediaries had to tread warily.[16] Houses managing loans to other foreign governments preferred to complete subscriptions as rapidly as possible, generally over a period of several months. Congress' notes would not move that quickly, and thus van Staphorst and Willink had to dole them out in small blocs in order to avoid spoiling the market.[17] At the same time, they had always to keep up the appearance of success on the terms customary in other loans. They were adequately compensated for their care after the first loan by high commissions, and even in the issue of 1788, again for ƒ1

[13] A further 1 percent was added to the 1787 issue in 1788 as a spur toward placement.

[14] *De Koopman, of bijdragen ten opbouw van Neerlands koophandel en zeevaard* (6 vols., Amsterdam, 1768–1776), III, 172–75; Samuel Ricard, *Traité general du commerce*, M. de M[orien], ed. (2 vols., Amsterdam, 1781), I, 210; and Handschriften IV, f, 18a, University Library (Amsterdam).

[15] According to the Prussian ambassador in The Hague, Russia's failure to reimburse loans in the Dutch Republic out of its own resources, rather than out of fresh credit, had damaged the Empire's credit position in January 1782. Robert Fruin and H. T. Colenbrander, eds., *Dépêches van Thulemeyer*, 1763–1788 (Amsterdam, 1912), 294–97.

[16] Van Winter, *Amsterdamschen handel*, I, 169–77.

[17] *Ibid.*, I, 177–78, 186.

million, charges totaled 8 percent. Nonetheless, Congress could take satisfaction in the fact that the loans succeeded and that the annuity rate was held to no more than 5 percent in 1787 and 1788. It was, after all, preferable to pay higher commissions than a higher interest.

Most borrowing states conducted loan negotiations through special agents or domestic government departments, relying on individuals who were seldom well informed about the Amsterdam capital market or about capital supply in the Dutch Republic. In contrast, the United States entrusted such negotiations, even if rather vaguely, to its diplomatic agents, and beginning with Adams those agents made it a practice to inform themselves about trends on the Amsterdam market and terms accorded other borrowers.[18] Investor credulousness, banking custom, abundant capital supply, and Adams' maneuvering all contributed to American success in raising loans during the 1780s.

From the American perspective the replacement of the Articles of Confederation by the Constitution and the allocation to Congress of taxation authority far in excess of what had been permitted under the Articles could be expected to improve Congress' credit in Amsterdam. That case was argued persuasively in 1790 and 1791, and those arguments, together with a threat that the United States might transfer its banking agency elsewhere, and growing familiarity among investors with the United States as a borrower, helped gain appreciably better terms for subsequent loans opened by the federal government. More than anything else, however, it was the anxiety of the Dutch bankers about competition that established the terms under which federal government loans would be opened and set the precedent for lower costs.[19] The threat to their agency arose from a complex assortment of schemes, forwarded sometimes in concert and sometimes in opposition by Dutch, French, and American speculators, to take over the American debt to France on terms that would yield gigantic profits.[20] Provoked by

[18] John Adams' understanding of the Amsterdam market during the early years of his stay in Europe was, of course, weak, but he devoted some effort to informing himself, and by 1787 had as good a grasp as an outsider could expect to gain. On the early years of stumbling, see *ibid.*, I, 46–47; and, for an example of Adams' later knowledgeability, see Julian P. Boyd, ed., *The Papers of Thomas Jefferson* (19 vols., Princeton, 1950–1974), XII, 581–82. For a sample of the thoroughness of American representatives in exploring conditions in Amsterdam see Harold C. Syrett, ed., *The Papers of Alexander Hamilton* (25 vols., New York, 1961–1977), VII, 175–87. William Short occasionally forwarded incorrect data, but for the most part he displayed a firm grasp of market practices and current trends.

[19] Van Winter, *Amsterdamschen handel*, I, 201–03.

[20] There is no comprehensive account of the various projects aimed at cornering all or part of the American debt to France. The most useful sources that might be consulted are: *ibid.*, I, 160–67 and 193–203, and II, 150–56; Howard C. Rice, ''James Swan: Agent of the French Republic

their anxiety over that threat, and by their confidence in the degree to which America's position would indeed be improved by the Constitution, the bankers opened a loan in February 1790 wholly on their own initiative. Without having authorized such a step, Hamilton and Thomas Jefferson, then ambassador to France, nonetheless approved it after the fact. An advance was decidedly necessary in any case, and the return and commission charges established by the bankers were attractive enough to still opposition.[21]

In spite of the Constitution's psychological contribution to American credit, an evaluation of the financial standing of the United States in 1790 shows that Dutch bankers acted in hasty and premature fashion. When Congress adopted a revenue program designed to meet central government demands and to service domestic and foreign debts, the liabilities assumed from the Confederation and the states were estimated at $77.8 million.[22] The magnitude of that assumption, even scaled down by nearly $7 million as it was by more extensive data about liabilities, can be grasped both by projecting that sum and the actual total of the debt in succeeding years (1791: $75.4 million; 1792: $77.2 million; 1793: $80.3 million; and 1794: $78.4 million) against tax revenues (see Table 2),[23] and by comparing the fiscal position of the United States with that of contemporary European states.

1794–1796," *New England Quarterly*, X (Sept. 1937), 477–86; Ferguson, *Power of the Purse*, 264–67; Boyd, *Papers of Thomas Jefferson*, XV, 563–68; and Syrett, *Papers of Alexander Hamilton*, VII, 361–63. None of the projects succeeded.

[21] Van Winter, *Amsterdamschen handel*, I, 193–204; and Boyd, *Papers of Thomas Jefferson*, XVI, 134.

[22] Bayley, *National Loans of the United States*, 31, gives the following figures:

French loans	$6,324,688.89
Spanish loan	174,017.13
Dutch loans (through 1788)	3,600,000.00
Balance owed on military supplies from France	24,332.86
Interest arrears on the above	1,760,277.08
Debt to foreign military officers	186,988.78
Interest arrears thereon	11,219.32
Estimated principal of the domestic debt	28,858,180.65
Interest arrears thereon estimated	11,398,621.80
Claims against the Confederation government	450,395.52
State debts estimated	25,000,000.00
	$77,788,722.03

[23] *Report of the Secretary of the Treasury on the State of the Finances for the Year 1867* (Washington, 1868), 356–59; van Winter, *Amsterdamschen handel*, II, 476–77; and, for debt totals, Dewey, *Financial History of the United States*, 113. Proceeds of the loans raised in Amsterdam and Antwerp have been calculated after the deduction of commissions. Budgetary data

TABLE 2

Foreign Loans and Central Government Revenues and Expenditures, 1789–1794
(in thousands of dollars)

	4 March 1789– 31 Dec. 1791	1792	1793	1794	Totals
Revenues					
Ordinary revenues	4,419	3,670	4,653	5,432	18,174
Domestic and foreign loan revenues	5,791	5,071	1,068	4,609	16,539
Foreign loan revenues (by estimated date of availa- bility for disbursement)	4,410	3,042	386	1,146	8,984
Total revenues	10,210	8,741	5,721	10,041	34,713
Expenditures					
Civil list, war and miscellaneous	1,921	1,878	1,710	3,501	9,010
Interest on the public debt	2,349	3,202	2,772	3,490	11,813
Redemptions of the public debt	2,939	4,062	3,047	2,311	12,359
Total expenditures	7,209	9,142	7,529	9,302	33,182

In 1792, the first year for which figures are available on an annual basis for both revenues and expenditures, interest payments on the American debt amounted to $3.2 million, a figure equivalent to 87 percent of tax revenues totaling $3.67 million. Debt charges including redemptions equaled no less than $7.26 million, or 198 percent of tax revenues. Neither European investors nor European bankers used a consistent measure to gauge solvency or to compare the credit positions of debtor states other than that of the punctuality of service, but such ratios between tax revenues on the one hand and interest payments and total debt charges on the other exceeded current levels for even the most straitened European governments. In 1787, when Louis XVI sum-

in reports of the secretary of the treasury are more comprehensive than those offered in Walter Lowrie and Matthew St. Clair Clark, comps., *American State Papers, Finance* (Washington, 1832), I, 661–63. This account offers a variation on format and omits service on the foreign debt and expenditures toward redemption of the public debt. That latter source is to be preferred, however, for a more detailed itemization of ordinary revenues (of which, from 1789 through 1794, 93 percent was accounted for by customs revenues) and expenditures. Neither report distinguishes foreign loan from all loan proceeds. The sums entered in this table as foreign loan proceeds represent accurately the value of those to the United States at par rates of exchange, but the chronology of actual availability for disbursement from Amsterdam is sufficiently uncertain to warrant qualification of those entries as estimates. Moreover, the largest part was transferred to Paris, which means that there were two rhythms of receipt and disbursement, one operating very slowly via Philadelphia and the other with more speed directly from Amsterdam to Paris. Of the ƒ19.55 million raised in the loans of 1790–1792, nearly ƒ5,650,000 was remitted to the United States through bills drawn by the treasury. The exchange rates on those bills, including discount, averaged nearly $.41 to the guilder. Elliot, *Funding System of the United States*, 160–63.

moned an extraordinary Assembly of Notables to deal with a financial crisis in which France stood on the verge of a suspension of payments, debt service (combining interest and partial amortization) consumed about 67 percent of revenues.[24] Great Britain had appropriated a high of 66 percent of net revenues for debt service in 1784, but thereafter reduced that share to a 1792 level of 50 percent.[25] And in the Dutch Republic, the province of Holland, keystone of the Republic's finances, allotted about 70 percent of revenues to debt service in the early 1790s. In 1792, although not for the longer period from 1789 through 1794, American interest payments alone exceeded the share of tax revenues assigned to debt service by any European state in years for which data are available, while American debt service as a whole was far in excess of tax revenues for the entire six-year period.

This comparison demonstrates that the relative burden of debt service in the United States was significantly greater than in European states involved at the same time in large-scale programs of secular credit exploitation. In two important respects, however, strictly equal situations have not been measured. The appropriations necessary in the United States for non-debt-related items, principally administrative and military functions, were both absolutely and relatively lower than those faced by European states, and thus the United States enjoyed a margin within which part of its burden of debt charges could be sustained. But at the same time the credit that the United States was obliged to raise in order to cover its deficits was reliable only to the extent to which foreign credit access was reliable. Recognizing the fragile character of public confidence within the United States in federal government credit, Hamilton devised a financial program that combined interest payments on the foreign and domestic debt with small-scale but nonetheless significant redemptions of domestic indebtedness (while prolonging the foreign debt already due or falling due through renegotiation in the Dutch Republic). For the United States debt service required both interest and redemption payments, whereas among European states the share of debt-related spending devoted to amortization had been reduced during the eighteenth century and debt service was composed principally

[24] J. F. Bosher, *French Finances, 1770–1795: From Business to Bureaucracy* (Cambridge, 1970), 24, 89–90. If the amortization portion of French spending for debt service is estimated at 15 percent of the total, then French interest payments alone would have amounted to 57 percent of tax revenues in 1787.

[25] B. R. Mitchell and Phyllis Deane, *Abstract of British Historical Statistics* (Cambridge, 1971), 388, 391. Other states generally appropriated much lower shares of revenues for debt service but, like the United States, had more restricted opportunities to borrow than did Great Britain, France, or the Dutch Republic.

of interest payments. That is to say, the United States could not adopt the most efficient technique of credit exploitation available to government because, in the face of the need to establish its credit, there was no choice but to provide for those redemptions that would bolster public confidence.

In order to appreciate Hamilton's task it is also appropriate to consider the number of years' revenues necessary ultimately to redeem the debt, no other expenses intervening. The French debt in 1787, estimated at nearly 5 billion livres tournois, totaled about ten and one-half times that year's revenues. In Great Britain increased tax income after the War of the American Revolution had reduced the ratio of the nominal sum of the public debt to current revenues from 18.4:1 in 1784 to 13:1 in 1792. In 1792, in contrast, the funded debt of the United States equaled more than twenty-one times the sum of that year's revenues, a figure that most clearly evokes an understanding of the gravity of Congress' financial position. Such a situation prevailed because of the limited tax revenues that the new government deemed it could confidently raise.

While appropriations available for debt service in the United States were enlarged by smaller administrative and military spending, gains in that area were not great enough to pay debt charges or bring the federal government into approximate equality with European states in its overall public credit position. From 1789 through 1795 American spending for current operations and interest payments alone regularly equaled or exceeded tax revenues. Through 1794 those two areas surpassed the cumulative total of tax revenues by $20.8 to $18.2 million, and all spending exceeded tax revenues by $33.2 to $18.2 million. Although the United States borrowed slightly more than was necessary to cover expenditures in that period, there was nevertheless, on an annual basis and in cumulative terms, a significant deficit in ordinary revenues through 1795 (see Tables 3 and 4).

TABLE 3

Cumulative Expenditures as a Percentage of Taxation
and All Revenues, 1789–1794

	Taxation Revenues	All Revenues	Expenditures
Civil list, war, and miscellaneous	50	26	27
Interest on the public debt	65	34	36
Redemptions on the public debt	68	36	37
Totals	183	96	100

TABLE 4 '
Expenditures as a Percentage of Taxation Revenues, 1789–1796

	4 March 1789–31 Dec. 1791	1792	1793	1794	1789–1794	1795	1796
Civil list, war, and miscellaneous	43	51	37	64	50	71	30
Interest on the public debt	53	87	60	64	65	52	38
Sub total	96	138	97	128	115	123	68
Redemptions on the public debt	67	111	65	43	68	47	32
Total expenditures	163	249	162	171	183	170	100

This image of financial precariousness must also be tested against assets that do not appear in the balance of revenues, expenditures, and debts. The tax program adopted under the Constitution was based principally on duties levied against imports and an excise on commodities. There was therefore a substantial margin between the range of taxes as yet in use in the United States and the more extensive programs of assessment employed in Europe. But Hamilton properly discounted Congress' ability to increase taxes and devised a revenue structure which, through 1795, was based chiefly on foreign and domestic loans. Tax revenues increased steadily during that period and beyond, but that was due to an expanding volume of goods subject to duties rather than to an increase in the rate or an expansion in the incidence of taxation. Such a development, and in particular the marked increase of revenues resulting from enhanced shipping opportunities during the European wars of 1792 and thereafter, could not have been reliably forecast in 1790.

In a realm of more immediately measurable assets, the United States possessed vast tracts of unsettled land that might theoretically have been disposed of to the benefit of the treasury. But sales depended on such long-term developments as population increase and significant westward migration. The value of that asset in 1790 was problematic because the American land market was already glutted and a European market not yet developed. Land could not be transformed into liquid wealth that might supplement tax revenues, and land sales played an insignificant role in revenues until after 1800.

A material improvement in the American position could be projected in 1790, when Congress adopted an initial program of taxation and approved with no more than minor alterations Hamilton's skillfully designed proposals for organizing the funding and assumption of state and Confederation debts and providing fresh credit.[26] But not until 1796 were ordinary revenues sufficient to cover debt and non-debt spending. In the intervening years import duties and excise revenues increased simultaneously with foreign and domestic borrowing. As long as debt service, while fluctuating from year to year, represented virtually a fixed level of expenditures,[27] any increase in tax revenues exceeding administrative and military spending would improve the financial condition of the United States. The excess of ordinary revenues over non-debt related expenditures averaged $2.1 million from 1792 through 1795, but increased sharply in 1796 (from $1.8 million in 1795 to $5.8 million in 1796) and, although that figure fell in 1799 to a level reminiscent of the early years of the decade, it expanded again thereafter. In 1796 the American position was superior to that of the major states of Europe and improving, while in Europe the revolutionary wars were worsening an already serious situation. The share of tax revenues necessary for debt service in the United States in 1796 was only 38 percent, and the debt-revenue ratio had fallen to less than 10:1.

A balance has been struck on the liquid and potential assets and liabilities of the federal government in the years to 1796, and it is necessary to acknowledge that the calculation points to insolvency. But the important fact is that such a balance was not struck then in Amsterdam, either in regard to the United States or other debtor states. As a result, all states raised capital on the Amsterdam market on terms which, in retrospect, appear ludicrously modest, although no state was better served in that regard than the United States. It acquired and retained an image of credit worthiness that was stronger than that held by France in the 1780s and, by the early 1790s, equivalent to that held by European states accepted by Dutch investors as the most secure risks. The effective return paid on the combined foreign and domestic debt of the United States amounted in 1792 to an average of 4.1 percent, significantly less than the annual service of approximately 6.4 percent that France paid in 1787 even after deduction of French amortizations. Moreover, the rate offered by the United States in new loans fell in 1790

[26] The Funding and Assumption Act of August 4, 1790, divided the domestic debt of the United States into three categories of paper—6 percents (two-thirds of the so-called liquidated debt), deferred 6 percents bearing interest after 1800 (one-third of the liquidated debt), and 3 percents (the arrears in interest on the debt capitalized). The debts assumed from the states were also funded in those same three categories, although on a slightly different footing.

[27] Interest payments averaged $3.2 million per annum from 1792 through 1800, while tax revenues increased from $3.7 to $10.8 million.

to a level equal to the minimum acceptable to Dutch investors for long-term foreign loans of any type. To the degree that Hamilton's funding and assumption program reduced or deferred the 6 percent yield that had been established on all federal securities, the average service on the domestic debt in 1792 reflected a partial default. But that was not the view that American or European investors took. In the United States Hamilton's program was regarded favorably because it provided that paper long depreciated in trading was to be redeemed at par.[28] At the same time, Dutch investors could take pleasure in what appeared to be a confirmation of the sagacity of prior purchases of American domestic debt.

There is more than a little irony in the observation that the favorable terms of the foreign loans of 1790 and thereafter were established before it was clear that the United States would emerge from the transition to a federal government with the pretentious revenue authority granted under the Constitution intact. And there is even more irony in the observation that the favorable credit image reflected by the 1790 loan in Amsterdam was in large measure the product of developments that were unconnected with the appropriateness and potential effectiveness of the fiscal program being unfolded at the same time by Alexander Hamilton. The success of the American loans in the Dutch Republic and their success on decidedly favorable terms were central ingredients in the triumph of Hamilton's program of national public finance, and in what E. James Ferguson has termed "the Nationalist effort to achieve political centralization by fiscal reform."[29]

From 1790 through 1794 Congress raised loans in Amsterdam and Antwerp totaling ƒ23.5 million, of which some ƒ22,460,000 (or $8,984,200 at par rates) remained after costs,[30] and in addition the United States borrowed $7.56 million on the domestic market (see Table 2). The net additional credit acquired in those years was $4.18 million, or 23 percent of tax revenues. Foreign loan proceeds were counterbalanced to a degree by the cost of servicing outstanding credits, by 1793 more than ƒ1.3 million per annum. But through 1792 and

[28] For a discussion of Hamilton's program and responses to it, see Ferguson, *Power of the Purse*, 292–305.

[29] *Ibid.*, 292.

[30] The series of loans in the Dutch Republic was suspended in 1794 because, in the judgment of the Amsterdam bankers, a second issue proposed for that year could not be launched with any prospect of success. The problem lay in the impact of the War of the First Coalition on capital supply on the Amsterdam market. In successfully raising ƒ3 million in the January 1794 loan, the United States had already benefited from its aloofness from the conflict, but neither American credit nor neutrality could overcome anxiety among investors about the military position of the United Provinces.

again in 1794 there remained a significant surplus, and one that was available at the crucial point of transition to the expanded tax authority of the Constitution. The Dutch loans were used not only to pay off most of the debt and debt arrears owed France, in effect transferring those obligations to the Dutch Republic, but also to settle smaller debts owed Spain and foreign military officers who had served in the American Revolution, to pay some diplomatic expenses, and to provide funds for the purchase of American domestic debt certificates prior to the redemption program initiated in 1796.[31]

The magnitude of the credits gotten in the Dutch Republic and the Austrian Netherlands comes more sharply into focus when net proceeds are projected at par exchange rates against domestic revenues and expenditures. There was no annual balance of revenues and expenditures, although Hamilton struck a quarterly balance designed to discover what assets were on hand (see Table 2).[32] Those statements reveal that he preferred to conduct financial affairs around a contingency surplus. But more importantly Hamilton grasped the weight that should be attached to treating the domestic debt in a fashion that would enhance the stability of the new regime, and he designed a funding and assumption program that satisfied most creditors without alienating individuals and sectional areas that could not expect to benefit from it. Hamilton also grasped the importance of providing for the settlement of the foreign debt as another measure that would contribute to the regime's stability. Moreover, he understood the extent to which the market price of domestic debt certificates reflected the public image of the financial and political integrity of government. At the same time that he prepared a program of funding and assumption, Hamilton began the settlement of arrears on the debt to France and established a sinking fund that could be used to manipulate the price of domestic debt certificates.

[31] At the rates employed by Rafael A. Bayley to transfer livre tournois values into dollars, the debt to France and arrears on it, and the debt to military officers who served in the American Revolution and arrears on it, totaled 45.77 million *l. t.* or $8.3 million in 1790. Bayley, *National Loans of the United States*, 31. Of that sum and subsequent service, $5.39 million (29.72 million *l. t.*) was paid out of the Amsterdam and Antwerp loans between December 1790 and September 1792, and on terms highly beneficial to the United States. At exchange and agio rates prevailing when the French loans were raised, the sum involved in those payments, ƒ10.08 million in current money, would have brought about 21.8 million *l. t.* N. W. Posthumus, *Inquiry into the History of Prices in Holland* (2 vols., Leiden, 1946–1964), I, 607–08, 654. Although the United States did not take full advantage of the depreciation of the French assignat and evaluated the total of remittances at 24.19 million *l. t.*, it nonetheless profited from the fall of the écu of three livres against the guilder. For details on those transfers to Paris and on settlement of the remainder of the debt to France, see Elliot, *Funding System of the United States*, 211–12, 427–28; Bayley, *National Loans of the United States*, 40–41; van Winter, *Amsterdamschen handel*, II, 164–67.

[32] Elliot, *Funding System of the United States*, 194–95, 216.

Beginning with the 1790 loan, proceeds were dispatched to Paris (ƒ1.5 million) and bills were drawn by the treasury on Amsterdam (ƒ800,000) to bring the sinking fund into operation buying domestic debt.[33] That dual program was continued thereafter and, as Hamilton portrayed its results in 1793, to the benefit of the United States. Domestic debt purchases in particular were advantageous because they produced multiple gains. When paper could be bought in the United States or Europe below par, such purchases both reduced ultimate redemption costs and, since Dutch loans were raised at effective returns of 4.5 to 5.5 percent but could be used to buy notes costing the treasury 6 percent per annum, saved interest.[34] But those economies were not as important in the success of Hamilton's program as the pressure that domestic debt purchases applied toward appreciation of prices.

Between 1790 and July 1792, as Hamilton reported in 1793, all or nearly all debt purchases were funded by foreign loans.[35] Through 1794 some $3 million was spent for that purpose.[36] While that was a significant aid to driving prices toward par, coincidental developments out of the sphere of Hamilton's influence were of even more assistance. That part of the paper in question made up of loan office and settlement certificates traded in the period from 1782 to 1788 at 20 to 25 and 10 to 15 percent respectively. Both groups of paper appreciated sharply during 1789, as a result of the adoption and implementation of the Constitution, and by December the settlement certificates, generally the weaker of the two types, were trading at 45 to 50 percent of par. Prices dipped in response to Hamilton's January 1790 report on public credit but rose again after mid-year.[37] The 6 percent stocks of the funding program of 1790 reached par at the end of July 1791, and for the remainder of that year and through 1792 traded at or slightly above par.[38]

The appreciation of 1789, the decline of 1790, and the renewed appreciation of the second half of 1790 and thereafter were all influenced by foreign investment in the domestic debt, and the two upward trends appear to have been determined by foreign investment. Moreover, investment from the Dutch Republic was organized predominantly in such a fashion that it sought long-term profits, the capital gains that

[33] *Ibid.*, 184–85.
[34] *Ibid.*, 190.
[35] *Ibid.*, 195.
[36] Bayley, *National Loans of the United States*, 26–27.
[37] Ferguson, *Power of the Purse*, 252–53, 327–29.
[38] Elliot, *Funding System of the United States*, 231–32.

would be achieved as a result of reimbursements scheduled to begin in 1796. Thus most Dutch acquisitions were retained in portfolios and the market that developed in American domestic debt in Amsterdam remained small.

Dutch interest in the domestic debt may be traced to the War of Independence, but there was no significant increase in purchases until 1785–1786.[39] Then American jobbers found their way to Amsterdam and embarked on a program of selling certificates to European investors at prices far above those current in the United States.[40] Even on the terms those jobbers managed to command, the apparent return on the domestic debt was sufficiently attractive to induce Dutch bankers to explore for themselves the details of domestic finances and to acquire blocs of the debt. The leading figure in that effort was the commission agent and merchant Pieter Stadnitski who had in 1785 and 1786 arranged to purchase an allotment of $320,000 from Daniel Parker. Recognizing his ignorance of American financial affairs, Stadnitski undertook a program of self-education and prepared a publicity campaign designed to draw Dutch investors into the American domestic debt.

Stadnitski's task in preparing the investing public was eased by the care van Staphorst and Willink had taken with Congress' loans. But it was still necessary to examine the paper in which he proposed to deal and to convey a favorable impression of it. The information Stadnitski gathered was presented in two brochures that extolled both the merits of the political experiment underway in the young American republic and the benefits of investment in its domestic debt.[41] In the first pamphlet,

[39] The first large bloc of American domestic debt to pass into Dutch hands resulted from the liquidation of a trading society (the Noord Americaansche Handel Societeit) formed under the nominal direction of De la Lande & Fynje. Claims on American merchants totaling ƒ535,750 were sold to the Massachusetts jobber Daniel Parker for $500,000 in domestic debt certificates, and Pieter Stadnitski was entrusted with forming an investment management venture on behalf of the creditors of the trading society and investors who supplied additional funds necessary to settle with Parker. Those matters are discussed by van Winter, *Amsterdamschen handel*, I, 88–141. See also Archief van Eeghen, Ad4 and Bd1, Municipal Archives; Archief Stadnitski en van Heukelom, "Stukken betreffende de diverse negotiaties, 1793–1858," *ibid.*; Archief van de familie de la Lande Cremer, te Bolsward, Economic History Library (Amsterdam); and Kleine aanwinsten 1, *ibid.*

[40] In the NAHS liquidation, American securities were transferred at 65 percent (so that Parker was owed an additional sum of nearly ƒ200,000 above the amount of the claims he acquired). Archief van Eeghen, Ad4, Municipal Archives; Archief Daniel Crommelin & Soonen, "Negotiatiën van 1 October en 1 November 1789," especially H. Fynje to D. Parker, 14 Jan. and 9 March 1789, *ibid.*; Archief Stadnitski en van Heukelom, "Diverse documenten, descharges, particuliere beschieden, enz., I en II," *ibid.*; 565B14, plans d'emprunts, part 1, University Library (Amsterdam); and Boyd, *Papers of Thomas Jefferson*, VIII, 531–32.

[41] Copies of the two tracts, Pieter Stadnitski, *Ophelderend bericht wegens het fonds, genaamd Liquidated Debt, of vereffende schulden, ten lasten de Vereenigde Staaten van America, rentende 6 p. ct. in het jaar,* and Pieter Stadnitski, *Omtrent de natuur en soliditeit van welk fonds de directeur Pieter Stadnitski een omstandig bericht gegeeven heeft,* may be found in, respectively, the

which appeared early in 1787, Stadnitski offers an idyllic picture of the American colonials, motivated by love of country, striving to wrest freedom from ogreish England. As a propagandist Stadnitski lacked subtlety, but he understood how to make a blatant appeal to factional attitudes in the Dutch Republic by ascribing to America the religious and political liberty he wished to see instilled in the United Provinces, and by the use of lurid coloring in his portrayal of England, the common enemy of Americans and Dutch Patriots. Such images as Stadnitski offered about the American republic had a particular appeal in the Dutch Netherlands in the late 1780s, both before and after the abortive Patriot Revolution of 1787. Stadnitski and the van Staphorst brothers were leaders of the Patriot faction that sometimes identified the American republic as the model for refashioning the unsatisfactory regent oligarchy of Amsterdam, the province of Holland, and the pro-English stadholderate of the United Provinces.

Their own political sentiments, and the response such ideals would evoke among the investing public, were enough to draw attention to investment opportunities in the United States. But there was no sacrifice to the nobility of the American experiment in investing on the terms described by Stadnitski. As in the case of loans to the Confederation Congress, it must be assumed that the potential profits described in those two tracts and in the prospectus that announced the investment venture of 1787 had a larger role in attracting subscribers than did Stadnitski's propaganda. Much of the first brochure and most of the second were devoted to an examination of the financial position of Congress. Stadnitski admitted that the United States was more heavily in debt in proportion to its resources than European governments, but he claimed that the American form of government made the young republic more likely to fulfill its obligations because it was more responsive to the nation than a monarch would be. Stadnitski also admitted that Congress had difficulty in persuading the states to honor their commitments, and that interest on the domestic debt was paid in indents rather than in specie. But on balance he could claim that the 1787 venture "promises more advantages than any other investment known at present."[42]

According to an explanation of objectives given in 1788, the goal in such enterprises was "to make the quickest and highest possible

Economic History Library and the Archief Stadnitski en van Heukelom, "Stukken betreffende de diverse negotiaties, 1793–1858," Municipal Archives. Van Winter, *Amsterdamschen handel*, I, 229–36, reproduces the prospectus.

[42] Stadnitski, *Ophelderend bericht*, 18.

profit,'' yet to leave the investors in it ''a good gain.''[43] In terms of the yields to which Dutch rentiers were attuned in 1787, and the profits that Dutch bankers could expect from organizing foreign loans or other investment operations, the American domestic debt was a lucrative proposition. In the 1787 venture, Stadnitski offered to sell shares in a collective ownership of $840,000 in the so-called liquidated debt for a total of f1.2 million (or $504,000).[44] That was an irresistible bargain because, as Stadnitski described the benefits, participants could anticipate an appreciation in the market value of domestic debt, an improvement in the exchange rate to the advantage of the United States and thus also of holders of dollar assets, and a generous 10 percent return distributed in dividends and premiums.[45] Moreover, Stadnitski and his associate in that first investment operation, Hendrik Vollenhoven, added a guarantee of interest and reimbursement. That was a substantial risk for them, since the failure of the United States to service or repay its debts would have resulted in an assignment against the assets of their firms. But they calculated the risk and the profit with some care, and realized that although they were staking much of what they owned on the guarantee, they would get an immediate windfall. Evidently they judged, also, that they could reasonably expect Congress to abide by its obligations, at least under the terms of the investment venture that devalued the domestic debt involved. But the windfall in particular appealed to them and their successors in such operations.

Stadnitski and Vollenhoven made no less than f400,000, and perhaps more than that, on the 1787 venture. They bought the American securities at rates as low as 37.5 percent, and the total of $840,000 (face value) at a cost of no more than f800,000. Those notes were then transferred to subscribers for f1,200,000, and under the impression that the securities involved had been bought at 60 percent and were being

[43] 565B14, plans d'emprunts, part 1, University Library (Amsterdam). The memorandum in which these observations appear (''Consideratiën over het te formeerene plan der negotiatie van 200000 dollars . . . '') was composed, according to internal evidence relating to purchase prices of American paper, in 1788, and was probably written by Pieter Stadnitski. The sum alluded to in the heading, $200,000, was transferred by Stadnitski to the trustees of a venture organized by van Staphorst under the informal cooperation that developed among Stadnitski, Vollenhoven, van Staphorst, Willink, and other houses. That transfer was part of the reorientation of Stadnitski's interests toward the state debts and unsettled land in the United States.

[44] According to Stadnitski's calculations in the prospectus, the $840,000 had been acquired at 60 percent and at an exchange of 47 stuivers to the dollar, that is at $.425 or f2.35 (as opposed to par, $.40 or f2.5).

[45] Adams and Thomas Jefferson both viewed the enterprises on the domestic debt as competition for Congress' loans, one of which was opened in June 1787. But they could not seek to discredit such operations since Congress' credit was at stake in them as in the loans. See Boyd, *Papers of Thomas Jefferson*, XII, 566; and Ferguson, *Power of the Purse*, 260–61, 267.

resold at that rate.[46] In so far as they guaranteed the American paper at that rate, their subterfuge might be regarded as acceptable; since those securities were funded at par and eventually paid off under terms that also provided participants with handsome gains, there was no retrospective criticism.

Stadnitski and Vollenhoven introduced an enormously profitable field, and other firms, some associates of Stadnitski and some independent competitors, joined them as soon as sufficiently large blocs of domestic debt could be accumulated. No operations of that type were organized in 1788, but in 1789 five were opened, and competition developed among American and European buyers for domestic debt certificates.[47] As prices moved toward par, the yields that had been arranged for both organizers and investors in 1787 were reduced, but as long as federal, or later, state securities were available below implied par values there was enough incentive to form such ventures. Stadnitski's terms could be and were modified so that lower yields were offered subsequently, and so that the ratio of domestic debt to capital was lowered.

Altogether twenty-eight undertakings were organized from 1787 through 1793, either under the format Stadnitski had devised, involving the sale of American securities to the Dutch investing public, or under a format that mortgaged blocs of those securities over the long term to the same body of investors.[48] Those cannot simply be added one to another to reach the cumulative amount involved, for firms often bought shares in one venture and then withdrew the assets behind those shares for subsequent operations. That kind of duplication taken into account, it appears that a total of more than *f*18 million was drawn from the investing public, and that something between $7 and $10 million in certificates (at face value) was involved. That would account for the bulk of all Dutch holdings in the American debt as of 1803, when a balance was struck. At that point Dutch assets in 6 percent, 6 percent deferred,

[46] Notary P. C. Nahuys, 16729/520, 16732/79, 16734/27 and 87, and notary J. H. Zilver, 17297/25, Municipal Archives; Archief Stadnitski en van Heukelom, an unlabelled dossier containing documents on various American ventures, the dossiers cited in notes 40 and 41, and the journal and ledger of this undertaking, *ibid.*; 565B14, plans d'emprunts, part 1, University Library (Amsterdam); and van Winter, *Amsterdamschen handel*, I, 143–46, and appendix 2. Liquidation of the 1787 venture was completed in 1837, and the return on an investment of *f*1,000 ultimately ranged from a minimum of *f*2,340 to a maximum of *f*5,072.30, with the difference depending principally on the date on which the share was reimbursed, between 1788 and 1810. Most of the profit, which may have been shared with other houses involved in debt purchases, appears to have been reinvested in the purchase of shares in that venture, subsequently withdrawn for later ventures.

[47] Van Winter, *Amsterdamschen handel*, I, 207, II, appendix 4.

[48] Three were floated after 1793, but the boom in this sector faded with the arrival of prices that left returns roughly equal to those available in other areas.

and 3 percent stock totaled $13.1 million, all foreign holdings $29.5 million, and the total outstanding $60.9 million.[49]

The volume of purchases involved in the series of ventures initiated by Stadnitski, plus an undetermined amount acquired by individual English, French, and Dutch investors between 1787 and 1793, indicates that foreign demand led stock prices to appreciate. There was no want of speculative frenzy in the United States either in the year preceding Hamilton's first report on public credit or in 1790 and thereafter, but, on the scale of sums involved, American speculative markets did not have access to domestic capital in sufficient volume to support such price increases. To illustrate the point, examine the shift implied by that movement. In 1791 Congress' domestic liabilities amounted to about $60 million. At 1786 prices, the paper involved—loan office and settlement certificates, indents, and state debt notes—could have been bought, on the average, for less than 20 percent. Under Hamilton's program those liabilities were all to be redeemed at their full nominal value, but because of the variable returns there was not an across-the-board movement to the par levels implied by those returns. At the apex of prices, on January 25, 1792, the 6 percents were trading at 127 (or at an effective return of 4.7 percent), the 3 percents at 76 (or 3.9 percent), and the 6 percent deferreds at 77. It is conceivable of course that speculation without foreign resources might have driven prices toward par, but not conceivable that such trading levels should have been maintained on the 6 percents, as they were, after the upward advance ceased. In forcing market prices toward implied par rates, European purchases met an important requirement of Hamilton's program of simultaneous interest payments and redemptions, that being the establishment of public confidence in the credit worthiness of the federal government. Moreover, European purchases expanded the domestic market for future loans by the mere transfer of capital to the United States and by absorbing part of the outstanding debt.

Massive capital imports also had other effects. During the 1780s the United States had suffered from an exchange rate under which foreign currencies were more costly than what came to be regarded as the par rate. Under the pressure of transfers arising out of loans negotiated in the Dutch Republic and a sharp increase in grain sales to Europe in 1790, but more particularly from the demand for domestic debt, the

[49] Bayley, *National Loans of the United States*, 34. The combined foreign and domestic debt, including other categories of internal obligations, amounted in 1803 to $77 million. The part in foreign hands exceeded 50 percent.

exchange moved temporarily to the benefit of the United States.[50] From 1790 into 1792 European currencies were cheaper, with the result that smaller dollar sums were realized on the Dutch loans than would have been the case under earlier exchange rates, and that European purchases of American domestic debt were relatively more expensive.

More importantly, European domestic debt purchases transferred large quantities of investment capital to an economy impoverished for capital. Not only did the bill and specie transfers behind those purchases augment the quantity of media of payment in circulation, but the movement of domestic debt prices to par added the full volume of notes issued under the Funding Act as stable media to what had been a deficient quantity of specie or reliable paper, at once strengthening the monetary position of the United States.[51] It is also plausible to suggest that the gains to the American economy from those purchases were greater than their sum or than the profits made by American investors and speculators to the degree that the domestic debt had passed into the hands of individuals likelier than the average original creditor to reinvest profits in commerce and industry. Nor were the gains of Dutch bankers and investors a loss to the American economy, for the Dutch reinvested in unsettled land, canal building enterprises, and nascent American industry.[52] There was, therefore, through 1794 or 1795 a continual addition to Dutch assets in the United States. Directly and indirectly those reinvestments produced revenues for the federal treasury and invigorated certain sectors of the economy.

[50] On grain sales, see Ferguson, *Power of the Purse*, 268–69. At the rate of exchange employed by Stadnitski in calculations on his 1787 venture on the domestic debt, ƒ1 million would have fetched some $425,000. At the exchange rates that prevailed in 1792 the yield on ƒ1 million would have totaled only about $404,000. There was a loss on receipts insofar as the Dutch loans of 1790 and thereafter were transferred to the United States, but there was a gain with respect to all drafts on European currencies for the government and the private sector and also, ultimately, on redemption of the Dutch debt. Available data on the 1790 loans always reflect the par rate of $.40 rather than the market rate.

[51] Alexander Hamilton acknowledged the benefits of the federal securities issued in the funding program as "an engine of business, an instrument of industry and commerce." Quoted by John C. Miller, *The Federalist Era, 1789–1801* (New York, 1960), 50.

[52] P. J. van Winter surveys other investment areas that included large-scale commitments by the Dutch in unsettled lands, various canal companies, American land speculation ventures such as the Pennsylvania Population Company, the Bank of the United States, the Society for Useful Manufactures, and a host of other enterprises. Van Winter, *Amsterdamschen handel*, II, 190–435. The archival resources in the Netherlands on those investments are extensive. They center on the papers of the Holland Land Company, at the Municipal Archives (see the inventory published in 1976 and compiled by Wilhelmina C. Pieterse), but include also the Archieven Stadnitski en van Heukelom, van Eeghen, and Crommelin at the Municipal Archives, and, at the University Library (Amsterdam), 565B14, plans d'emprunts, and 566A2. The Stadnitski en van Heukelom and Crommelin collections also contain extensive information on nineteenth-century Dutch investment in the United States, specifically in bank stock, municipal loans, railroads and railroad construction bonds, canals and canal construction bonds, and federal government loans.

As Ferguson has pointed out, there was reason in 1790 to doubt "whether federal revenues would support both [the Congress' and the states'] debts, or, if taxes were raised to an adequate level, whether they would be resisted."[53] Doubts about the adequacy of revenues faded with the simultaneous elaboration of two revenue sources, domestic taxes and foreign loans. From 1789 through 1792 foreign loan proceeds nearly matched domestic tax revenues. In the two years following the adoption of the Funding Act, those advances, totaling ƒ16.5 million (some $6.6 million) in 1791 and 1792, probably exceeded domestic tax revenues.[54] They made it possible to transfer to the Dutch Republic most of the foreign debt dating from the Revolutionary era, and to transfer it under favorable costs and a redemption term that stretched to 1809. Because of that transfer and the subsequent increase of American tax revenues, there was not, after 1790, any further question about the integrity of the foreign debt, and thus no external threat to the program of national public finance pursued by Hamilton. The foreign loans also permitted profit taking on and manipulation of the domestic debt and, together with coincidental and massive purchases by Europeans, drove market prices up and held them there. Establishment of public confidence in the domestic debt, measured by market prices, lent an appearance of solvency and even reliability to American finances before that was justified by such indices as the ratio of debt service charges to revenues or of accumulated indebtedness to current revenues, and permitted a shift in the period from 1793 through 1795 to a credit system that increasingly emphasized domestic borrowing. With foreign assistance, Hamilton's fiscal program succeeded, and in 1794 and 1795 domestic resources and British capital were used together to settle the remainder of the debt due France. Hamilton's was a sound program that dealt cleverly and fairly with conflicting views in the United States about the federal and state debts and about use of the revenue authority theoretically available to Congress under the Constitution. But it could not have succeeded on the strength of the resources available within the United States alone.

[53] Ferguson, *Power of the Purse*, 326.
[54] In a 1793 report to Congress, Hamilton put 1791 revenues at $3,553,195.18, which would indicate that Dutch loan proceeds exceeded domestic tax revenues by nearly $230,000. Elliot, *Funding System of the United States*, 196.

Tench Coxe, Alexander Hamilton, and the Encouragement of American Manufactures

Jacob E. Cooke*

TENCH Coxe's contributions to the famous Report on Manufactures submitted to Congress by Alexander Hamilton on December 5, 1791, and to the conception and launching of the Society for Establishing Useful Manufactures, the new nation's pioneering experiment in industrialization, have long been subjects of inconclusive historical conjecture. Certainty has been precluded largely by the unavailability of Coxe's papers, which only recently have been opened to scholars. An examination of this voluminous manuscript collection and of Coxe's published writings suggests that in both instances his role was instrumental. Just as he was the one individual who most decisively influenced Hamilton's Report on Manufactures,[1] so he provided the inspiration for the SEUM and played an important part in arrangements for its organization, incorporation, location, and operations.

On January 15, 1790, some five months before Coxe's appointment as assistant secretary of the Treasury, the House of Representatives had requested the secretary of that department to prepare "a proper plan or plans" for the encouragement of manufactures. Knowledgeable though

---

*Mr. Cooke is a member of the Department of History, Lafayette College.

[1] This thesis is at odds with the two ablest explorations of the subject. In his authoritative biography of Hamilton, Broadus Mitchell downplays Coxe's contribution when he states that "the parts of three drafts of the Report on Manufactures, in Hamilton's papers, refute any notion that Tench Coxe or another was the real author. . . . Not only is the body of the report in Hamilton's autograph, but also recommendations concerning particular manufactures." *Alexander Hamilton: The National Adventure, 1788-1804*, II (New York, 1962), 151. In the *Hamilton Papers* the conclusion is reached that while Coxe's contribution was important, "Hamilton's final version of this Report differs markedly in both emphasis and substance from Coxe's draft and from Coxe's other writings on manufactures." Harold C. Syrett and Jacob E. Cooke, eds., *The Papers of Alexander Hamilton* (New York, 1961-   ), X, 12, hereafter cited as *Hamilton Papers*. My restudy of the subject, based on Coxe's hitherto unavailable manuscript collection, particularly an additional portion of his draft of Hamilton's report as described in n. 9 below, has persuaded me that those earlier assessments, excepting Hamilton's debate with European economists, are mistaken.

Hamilton was on economic subjects generally, he had not over the years since his boyhood mercantile apprenticeship in the West Indies acquired the kind of detailed information he believed necessary for the preparation of such a report. He promptly took steps to obtain the needed data by sending on January 25 a circular letter to promotional societies throughout the country requesting information on the state of local manufactures. Among them was the Manufacturing Society in Philadelphia whose secretary, Tench Coxe, was one of the nation's best known and most active advocates of manufactures.[2]

In response to Hamilton's queries, Coxe provided a bright picture of the condition and prospects of manufactures both in Pennsylvania and in the country at large.[3] But he also described the difficulties under which domestic manufactures labored, pointing to those the Treasury secretary would lengthily discuss in his report, among them the shortage of labor, the need for "machines and secrets in the Useful Arts," and the want of adequate capital. Although Hamilton generally endorsed Coxe's economic diagnosis, he emphatically did not share the latter's belief that dependence on British "goods and habits in trade" was a defect in the new nation's economy that must be corrected by the cultivation of France, whose own interests dictated the growth of American manufactures. Nevertheless, what Hamilton must have viewed as heretical views on foreign policy mattered less to him than the rightness of Coxe's domestic prescriptions. Certainly no American of that day was a more indefatigable advocate of Hamilton's brand of economic nationalism than was Coxe.

It was his recognition of this that prompted Hamilton to appoint Coxe assistant secretary of the Treasury in May 1790, and to assign to him, soon after the Philadelphian took office, the task of collecting additional data on American manufactures and preparing a report on their current state and the means whereby they might be encouraged. Coxe

² [Alexander] Hamilton to The President Directors and Co. of the Society for the incouragement of Manufactures etc [of] Philadelphia, Jan. 25, 1790, Tench Coxe Papers, Historical Society of Pennsylvania, Philadelphia. Aware of Coxe's repute, Hamilton had some three months earlier submitted to the Philadelphian a number of queries concerning economic conditions in Pennsylvania. (Hamilton's letter of Oct. 26, 1789, has not been found.) Coxe, always ready to discuss his favorite subject, not only answered Hamilton's specific questions but submitted a general survey of "the present state of the navigation of Pennsylvania with a comparison of the same with that of the principal Nations of Europe," as well as 8 other articles, some printed and some in manuscript form. Coxe to Hamilton, Nov. 30, 1789, *ibid.* The articles submitted are listed on the endorsement of the draft of this letter.
³ A partial draft of Coxe's letter dated Feb. 1790 is *ibid.*

swiftly began to carry out the assignment. On May 11 he addressed a circular letter to Treasury officials repeating Hamilton's request for information of the previous January, and he devised an efficient filing system for this information as well as for data on commerce, agriculture, and general economic conditions in the states and their subdivisions.[4] Although he counted on Treasury officials to supply reliable statistics, Coxe was by no means dependent on them. As secretary of the Pennsylvania Manufacturing Society, he had corresponded with similar organizations in other states, and his acquaintance both with Philadelphia's leading merchants and with the country's best known proponents of manufacturing provided him an extra-official, country-wide network of well-informed correspondents. Some of them, like Jeremiah Wadsworth and William Paterson, were members of Congress and available for informal consultation; others, such as Andrew Van Bibber of Baltimore and Nathaniel Hazard (who wrote to Coxe frequently and at length), were eager to share their knowledge of local conditions; yet others, like Thomas Fitzsimons and William Parton, were long-time Philadelphia associates. It was fortunate that Coxe could command such assistance, for the available (although doubtless incomplete)[5] evidence suggests that the Treasury officials whose aid he solicited were either uncooperative or uninformed.[6]

Unlike Hamilton, who labored over draft after draft before he was satisfied with the report he submitted to Congress on December 5, 1791, Coxe prepared only one draft which he obviously dashed off quickly, perhaps in a day or two. This celerity was owing neither to carelessness nor to indifference but rather to a mind so stocked with information on the subject that scant preparation was needed. After all, he had written article after article describing the condition of domestic manufactures

---

[4] *Hamilton Papers*, VI, 209, n. 4; Coxe to Benjamin Rush, May 16, 1790, Rush Papers, Hist. Soc. Pa.

[5] Coxe's correspondence on manufactures may have disappeared in fires that destroyed many Treasury Department records. That he collected more information than the Treasury records indicate is suggested in a "Supplementary Note" on household manufactures that was published in *A View of the United States of America, in a Series of Papers, Written at Various Times, Between the Years 1787 and 1794 . . .* (Philadelphia, 1794) and that he said was based on inquiries made in preparation for the Report on Manufactures. There is also an undated letter in the Coxe Papers that was sent to members of the Pennsylvania Manufacturing Society inquiring in detail about the manufacture of paper.

[6] In Mar. 1791 Coxe tried again, sending out another circular that stipulated more precisely the type of information needed. Coxe to Collectors of the Customs, Mar. 10, 1791, Hamilton Papers, Library of Congress. Although the replies were more satisfactory, he was obliged nevertheless to rely primarily on his own copious collection of economic data.

and the necessity and means of encouraging them, and he was also at that time sending off to the *American Museum* a series of articles, entitled "A brief examination of lord Sheffield's observations on the commerce of the united states of America," in which he gave a detailed account of the state of the American economy.[7] The nature of his draft—the generalizations that he drew from his files of statistics, and his avoidance of theoretical considerations—was attributable to his strict interpretation of the congressional mandate that the secretary of the Treasury prepare a plan for "the promotion of such manufactures as will tend to render the United States independent of other nations for essential, particularly for military, supplies."[8] Interpreted literally, this resolution merely called for the recommendation of measures to accomplish the specified goal, not for a defense of manufactures whose desirability was assumed in the resolution, much less for an analysis of the comparative advantages of agriculture and manufactures or a foray into political economy. Coxe, in sum, tailored his report to congressional specifications.

Coxe's draft for Hamilton's report was probably written during January or early February 1791. A tangle of deletions, insertions, marginal notations, and other alterations, it comprises twenty manuscript pages and is roughly two-fifths again as long as hitherto recognized.[9] After an open-

[7] "A brief examination of lord Sheffield's observations on the commerce of the united states of America" appeared as 7 articles in the *American Museum,* IX (1791).

[8] *Journal of the House of Representatives of the United States,* I (Washington, D. C., 1826), 141-142.

[9] The Coxe Papers were not officially opened until 1973. In 1965, however, Daniel M. Coxe, representative of Coxe's heirs, authorized the Hist. Soc. Pa. to make Coxe's draft of the Report on Manufactures available to the editors of the *Hamilton Papers.* Owing to the scrambled state of Coxe's manuscripts, which were then uncatalogued and only partially sorted, the draft of which the *Hamilton Papers* editors were permitted to make a copy was incomplete. See *Hamilton Papers,* X, 15-23. Additional pages of Coxe's draft had found their way into his bulky miscellaneous notes and drafts of articles on manufactures where I discovered them.

The version of Coxe's draft printed in the *Hamilton Papers* consists of its first 11 manuscript pages, exclusive of the following materials: (1) a paragraph marked by Coxe "X" and intended for inclusion on p. 6; (2) a page labeled "p. 21 *," presumably mistakenly so since it was intended for inclusion on p. 8 of his manuscript draft; and (3) a fragment of a page designed for insertion between the 11th and 12th pages of Coxe's manuscript.

The part of Coxe's draft that has not been published consists of 7 full pages plus 2 partial pages. These composed the last section of Coxe's draft and are roughly the same as the last ¼ of Hamilton's "First Draft." *Ibid.,* 43-49. For additional information on the extent of Coxe's contribution to Hamilton's "First Draft" see n. 12.

Only the first 11 pages of Coxe's draft are numbered. These also are the pages printed *ibid.,* 15-23. I have referred to this printed version when possible. Since the

ing paragraph in which he briefly stated why the "expediency of encouraging manufactures . . . appears at this time to be generally admitted," Coxe offered a survey of practices by which European nations
traditionally had sought to achieve self-sufficiency in the supply of articles
regarded as indispensable to national economic vitality and military
strength. To his list of familiar devices, such as protective or prohibitive
duties, bounties, and premiums, he joined a discussion of their appli-
cability to American conditions and needs, thus outlining a plan compounded of European precedents and domestic exigencies. Coxe then
enumerated those manufactures necessary for defense "or which may
be deemed most essential to the Government and citizens of the United
States." His discussion of the ones he regarded as vital (gunpowder, brass,
iron, wood, sailcloth, cotton goods, and linen articles, for example) included proposals on how best to encourage them. Both the articles
enumerated and the recommendations offered were essentially those that
the secretary of the Treasury would present in his report six months
later.[10]

Hamilton probably began systematic and sustained work on that
document in February 1791, soon after Coxe submitted his draft. Four
months later, on June 22, the secretary directed a circular to the newly
created Supervisors of the Revenue requesting particulars on the past,
present, and prospective state of manufactures in each revenue district;
soon thereafter he may have begun his review of European writings on
national economic policy. Although he presumably profited from the
latter, the replies to his circular letter that trickled in during the summer
and fall of 1791 did not significantly influence his report. As its closest
students remark, this was because "the information which he appeared
most anxious to obtain," such as data on the comparative costs and
profits of agriculture and manufactures, "was not readily available."[11]

Hamilton started with Coxe's draft, which had been neatly copied
by a clerk. He wrote fifteen new paragraphs (ten of them following the
first paragraph of Coxe's draft), deleted four of his assistant's paragraphs
as well as a number of sentences and phrases (some of which were then
incorporated elsewhere), and made stylistic changes. Nevertheless, Coxe's

---

previously unprinted part of Coxe's draft is unnumbered, my citations thereto read
"Coxe's 'Draft,' Coxe Papers." For the convenience of the interested student, I
have also supplied a reference to the corresponding part of Hamilton's "First Draft"
as printed in the *Hamilton Papers*, X, 23-49.
    [10] Coxe's "Draft," Coxe Papers; Hamilton's "First Draft," *Hamilton Papers*,
X, 43-46.
    [11] *Hamilton Papers*, X, 10.

draft remained virtually intact and became the basis of Hamilton's second revision.[12] Hamilton's "Second Draft," this time all in his own hand, reorganized the "First Draft" and incorporated additional material. Then came a third draft and a fourth in which Hamilton amplified Coxe's report by presenting a theoretical justification of Coxe's utilitarian arguments in support of manufactures. Although the secretary of the Treasury's indebtedness to his assistant is thus indisputable, its detailed demonstration would be tedious. To complicate matters still further, Hamilton submitted the several drafts of his report to Coxe, who made comments and corrections on them.[13]

The Report on Manufactures has been widely regarded as the greatest of Hamilton's memorable triad of reports. The judgment is a curious one. Leaving aside the considerations that it was the only one of his major reports that Congress failed to adopt and that its subsequent influence (particularly on a protective tariff) is indeterminable, it lacks the creative boldness, the conciseness and readability, of the Report on the Public Credit and the taut organization and intellectual force of the Report on the Bank. Prolix and repetitious, the Report on Manufactures was also more derivative than inventive. As the editors of the most recent edition of Hamilton's writings observe, "it contains few, if any, specific proposals that even the most enthusiastic supporters of Hamilton

[12] The note that follows will be more intelligible if the reader conjunctionally consults Hamilton's "First Draft," *ibid.*, 23-49. As stated in the text above, Hamilton took as the basis of his "First Draft" a clerk's clear copy of Coxe's draft (both that section of it printed in the *Hamilton Papers* and the hitherto unpublished part described in n. 9 above). In the *Hamilton Papers* the clerk's copy that Hamilton used is printed in roman type; Hamilton's additions are in italics. Of the portion in roman type, all but four of the printed pages correspond to Coxe's draft. It is, accordingly, highly probable that all of the document in the hand of the clerk was a copy of Coxe's draft. This likelihood is strengthened by a close examination of Coxe's manuscript draft. On the margin of p. 2 of that draft (corresponding to Hamilton's "First Draft," *ibid.*, 35) Coxe inserted next to and slightly above his words "Among the means devised . . . " four signs indicating that insertions should be made at this point. Although those insertions have not yet been discovered in the Coxe Papers, it is surely plausible to assume that, if found, they would match the four pages in the clerk's hand (*ibid.*, 30-34) that appear in Hamilton's "First Draft" and that otherwise could be attributable to neither Coxe nor Hamilton but, illogically, to a third person.

If my conjecture is correct, Coxe's draft accounted for almost 3/4 of Hamilton's "First Draft" (or 16 of the 26 printed pages), not 1/3, as previously believed. *Ibid.*, 23, n. 59.

[13] For evidence of this see the manuscript drafts of Hamilton's Report on Manufactures in the Hamilton Papers, particularly draft number IV. The material that the editors have identified as written in an unidentified hand is in Coxe's writing. *Hamilton Papers*, X, 124, n. 107.

could maintain were original. In this sense, the report is as much a product of its times as the creation of its author . . ."[14] The subject had, after all, been explored repeatedly by political economists abroad and aired time and again by American advocates of a balanced national economy, most notably by Tench Coxe.

What Hamilton did was to add to Coxe's compendium on American manufactures and his recommendation of the measures Congress should adopt to encourage them a philosophical argument for their indispensability to an essentially agricultural and underdeveloped nation. Unlike Coxe and other American economic nationalists, Hamilton was not content to infer the need for manufactures from their observable utility at home and abroad. Rather, he sought to demolish the theoretical assumptions on the basis of which European economists and philosophers —notably the Physiocrats and Adam Smith (Hamilton's principal intellectual target)—objected to the "artificial" encouragement of manufactures. If belief, and thus practice, flowed from theory, then the way to amend error was to assail false theory. Hamilton's unique accomplishment, in brief, was to present the case for manufactures not only in practical but in theoretical terms. The written record contains no hint that Coxe, although a close student of European political economists, contributed to Hamilton's exposition of economic theory. (We cannot, of course, know what transpired in their frequent conferences at the Treasury Department.) The Philadelphian's demonstrable contribution lay elsewhere: the secretary of the Treasury's more practical discussion of the utility of manufactures, including his assistant's favorite literary technique of appealing to past accomplishment as the harbinger of yet greater success, was substantively and illustratively the same as Coxe's.

To Hamilton as to Coxe the encouragement of manufactures was a prerequisite of national security and defense.[15] Hamilton recommended in his report, as had Coxe in his draft, that raw materials suitable for manufactures be free of import duties.[16] They both also suggested that the tools, implements, and possessions of immigrant artisans be exempted.[17] Hamilton's argument that protective duties on foreign articles also manufactured in the United States amounted to a virtual bounty for domestic producers was precisely, even in phraseology, that proposed in

[14] *Hamilton Papers*, X, 1.
[15] Coxe's "Draft," *ibid.*, 16; Hamilton's "Report," *ibid.*, 291ff.
[16] Coxe's "Draft," *ibid.*, 22; Hamilton's "First Draft," *ibid.*, 41; Hamilton's "Report," *ibid.*, 305.
[17] Coxe's "Draft," Coxe Papers; Hamilton's "First Draft," *Hamilton Papers*, X, 38; Hamilton's "Report," *ibid.*, 306.

his assistant's draft.[18] So, too, did Hamilton incorporate, although in different words, Coxe's cautionary remarks on the prohibition of rival articles.[19] Both men proposed drawbacks of duties levied on raw materials needed for domestic manufactures.[20] Both recommended that those who imported machinery or contrived, as Coxe put it, to secure mechanical "secrets of great value" should be granted protection the equivalent of that afforded by patent law.[21] Both urged the encouragement of European immigrants as a valuable addition to the American work force.[22] Hamilton accepted Coxe's proposal of "judicious . . . inspection" as a means of obviating frauds and improving "the quality and character of our manufactures."[23] He also adopted his assistant's recommendation for internal improvements to facilitate the transportation of goods, while adding a long quotation from Adam Smith to embroider the point.[24] The secretary of the Treasury, like Coxe, argued that the shortage of sufficient capital might be allayed, in the latter's words, by "a steady pursuit of such measures as will give full and unfluctuating value to the public funds."[25] Both men viewed the public debt as a means of acquiring capital for the promotion of manufactures, and Hamilton paraphrased Coxe in recommending an accelerated circulation of bank notes throughout the country in order to facilitate remittances of funds for the purchase of raw materials and sale of manufactured goods.[26] Finally, the section of Hamilton's report (about one-fifth of the whole) enumerating specific articles that merited encouragement and recommending appropriate measures was substantially based on, although considerably longer than, Coxe's draft.[27] In sum, Coxe made few proposals that did not wind up, although

[18] Coxe's "Draft," *Hamilton Papers*, X, 16-17, 19; Hamilton's "First Draft," *ibid.*, 35; Hamilton's "Report," *ibid.*, 296-297.

[19] Coxe's "Draft," *ibid.*, 17; Hamilton's "First Draft," *ibid.*, 35; Hamilton's "Report," *ibid.*, 297.

[20] Coxe's "Draft," *ibid.*, 20; Hamilton's "First Draft," *ibid.*, 37-38; Hamilton's "Report," *ibid.*, 306-307.

[21] Coxe's "Draft," *ibid.*, 19, 23; Hamilton's "First Draft," *ibid.*, 36-37; Hamilton's "Report," *ibid.*, 308.

[22] Coxe's "Draft," *ibid.*, 16; Hamilton's "First Draft," *ibid.*, 35; Hamilton's "Report," *ibid.*, 296.

[23] Coxe's "Draft," Coxe Papers; Hamilton's "First Draft," *Hamilton Papers*, X, 40; Hamilton's "Report," *ibid.*, 309.

[24] Coxe's "Draft," *Hamilton Papers*, X, 20; Hamilton's "First Draft," *ibid.*, 38-39; Hamilton's "Report," *ibid.*, 310-311.

[25] Coxe's "Draft," *ibid.*, 22; Hamilton's "First Draft," *ibid.*, 41; Hamilton's "Report," *ibid.*, 277ff.

[26] Coxe's "Draft," *ibid.*, 22; Hamilton's "First Draft," *ibid.*, 40-41; Hamilton's "Report," *ibid.*, 309-310.

[27] Coxe's "Draft," Coxe Papers; Hamilton's "First Draft," *Hamilton Papers*, X, 43-49.

usually in different stylistic garb and occasionally in expanded form, in the secretary of the Treasury's report.

That at least one of Coxe's ideas was rejected and several modified is scarcely surprising. Hamilton was emphatically no man's rubber stamp, and he and his assistant disagreed on some policies and approached others differently. Thus the secretary promptly ruled out one of Coxe's pet proposals—the abolition of tonnage duties on coasting vessels.[28] Nor was Hamilton as ardent an advocate of household manufactures as was his assistant. In contrast, moreover, to Coxe's assertion that there were no compelling justifications for "a strenuous recommendation" of bounties, Hamilton, who was convinced that public funds could in no way be expended more beneficially than in promoting the introduction of needed new manufactures, listed a number of reasons why bounties might be considered the most "efficacious" and "in some views, the best" means of encouraging manufactures.[29] Save for this purpose, however, he shied away from proposing any general program of "pecuniary bounties," recommending instead a policy that Coxe also endorsed: a high duty on foreign manufactures of materials whose growth the United States wished to encourage, and the allocation of the proceeds to those who either produced or manufactured them.[30] Their agreement on another aspect of the question is indisputable. Hamilton paraphrased the remark made in Coxe's draft that bounties on the manufacture of fabrics were unnecessary since their sale on the domestic market gave them a competitive advantage with European products that had to bear the heavy expense of transatlantic transportation.[31] Their disagreement over premiums was on the means of securing the necessary funds, not on the desirability of the premiums themselves. In place of Coxe's proposal for the creation of a landed fund to encourage manufactures by subsidizing "Introducers . . . of manufactories, machinery and secrets in the useful Arts," Hamilton recommended the allocation of surplus revenues accruing from import duties to achieve the same purpose.[32]

Coxe's contribution to the Report on Manufactures was confined neither to his preliminary sketch of it nor to his editorial assistance on

---

[28] Coxe's "Draft," *Hamilton Papers*, X, 21; Hamilton's "First Draft," *ibid.*, 39.

[29] Coxe's "Draft," *ibid.*, 18; Hamilton's "First Draft," *ibid.*, 36; Hamilton's "Report," *ibid.*, 298, 301.

[30] Coxe's "Draft," *ibid.*, 19-20; Hamilton's "First Draft," *ibid.*, 37; Hamilton's "Report," *ibid.*, 300.

[31] Coxe's "Draft," *ibid.*, 18; Hamilton's "First Draft," *ibid.*, 36; Hamilton's "Report," *ibid.*, 302.

[32] Coxe's "Draft," *ibid.*, 18-19, n. 52; Hamilton's "First Draft," *ibid.*, 36; Hamilton's "Report," *ibid.*, 304-305, 338-340.

the Treasury secretary's drafts. Many of Hamilton's seemingly independent ideas and recommendations were precisely the same as those that Coxe had propounded in his writings, most notably in his essays on manufactures and commerce published in 1787 and his "brief examination" in 1791 of Lord Sheffield's *Observations*.[33] One might, of course, argue that such similarity was merely fortuitous, but if so, one should at least discount the fortuity by Hamilton's familiarity with his assistant's writings.[34] And if historians remain interested in drawing analogies between the observations and proposals made by Hamilton and those made by other American authors, Coxe's writings are clearly the most likely source. If, that is, Hamilton needed information on American manufactures or sought arguments in support of their encouragement, it is surely reasonable to assume that he would have turned to one whose "great industry," "very good talents," and "extensive theoretical and practical knowledge of Trade" he respected and with whom he was in almost daily association.[35] His assistant was, in sum, the nation's most influential advocate of the ideas and program set forth in the secretary of the Treasury's report.

Certainly Coxe and Hamilton held the same view of the relation between manufactures and national power and prestige. The advantages

[33] In the annotated version of Hamilton's report a number of references are made to parallel statements in Coxe's writings. *Ibid.*, 230-340. It would be possible to make many more. See, esp., essays written by Coxe in 1787 and 1788: *An Address to an Assembly of the Friends of American Manufactures. Convened for the Purpose of establishing a Society for the Encouragement of Manufactures and the Useful Arts* . . . (Philadelphia, 1787); *An Enquiry into the Principles on which a Commercial System for the United States of America Should be Founded, to which are added Some Political Observations connected with the subject* (Philadelphia, 1787); "Address to the friends of American manufactures—ascribed to Tench Coxe, esq.," *Am. Museum*, IV (1788), 341-346; and "Thoughts on the present situation of the united states: by Tench Coxe, esquire," *ibid.*, 401-404.

[34] Coxe had sent Hamilton at least 8 of his essays before his appointment as assistant secretary. According to an endorsement on the draft of Coxe to Hamilton, Nov. 30, 1789, Coxe Papers, the articles enclosed were

1. Enquiry—(Museum)
2. An address to the friends of Amn Mans—(Museum)
3. A paper on the future legislation of Commerce addressed to R. H. Lee, Esqr.—(Museum)
4. A Continuation of the address on the Subject of American Mans.—(Museum)
5. Thoughts on the future prospect of Ama. published in Dunlaps paper of 1788 about Septr. or Octr.
6. An accot of the Navn. etc.
7. Spanish Wool
8. Succedanea for foreign liquors.

[35] Hamilton to Timothy Pickering, May 13, 1790, Pickering Papers, Massachusetts Historical Society, Boston.

Hamilton attributed to manufactures—the heart of his Report—were exactly those that Coxe had also stressed time and again: the division of labor, the utility of machines, the expansion of economic opportunity, the creation of additional modes of investment, and the enlarging of the market for agricultural produce. Their emphasis on the last of these advantages suggests both their desire to dispel the notion that an agricultural South and an industrial North were natural antagonists and their conviction, to use Hamilton's words, that the sections could so "succour" and "befriend" each other as to come "at length to be considered as one."[36] To both men, the consequence of such national unity would be economic progress, defined as the promotion of manufacturing at home and the acquisition of wider foreign markets. To neither of them, however, was such progress automatically guided, as Adam Smith believed, by some hidden hand. The impetus for desirable changes rather required "the incitement and patronage of government."[37]

But to stress their common repudiation of Smith's laissez-faire, as well as of the Physiocratic doctrine that agriculture is "the most beneficial and *productive*" economic activity,[38] is to overlook an important difference in emphasis and tone that rendered Coxe, in Leo Marx's words, "a subtler and more farsighted—if less candid—advocate of industrialization than Hamilton."[39] More attuned than Hamilton to the susceptibilities of a predominantly agrarian nation, Coxe was more intent on demonstrating the benefits of a partnership between the farm and the factory than in proving the superiority of the machine. For his part, Hamilton did not share Coxe's implied belief "that, somehow, technology would help America reach a kind of pastoral stasis."[40] The more consistent mercantilist, Hamilton argued that self-sufficiency and wealth were the sure means for achieving the ultimate goal of national power and thus American supremacy. Coxe did not disagree, but, as Marx perceptively observes, he "saw the need to couch this aim in the language of the prevailing ideology." Unlike Hamilton, he understood that his countrymen "preferred not to acknowledge wealth and power as their goals," and he recognized "that Americans would be more likely to endorse the Hamiltonian program with enthusiasm if permitted to

---

[36] Hamilton's "Report," *Hamilton Papers*, X, 293.
[37] *Ibid.*, 267.
[38] *Ibid.*, 231.
[39] Leo Marx, *The Machine in the Garden: Technology and the Pastoral Ideal in America* (New York, 1964), 168.
[40] *Ibid.*, 167.

conceive of it as a means of fulfilling the pastoral ideal."[41] But Coxe did enthusiastically champion that program, particularly its insistence on the indispensability of manufactures to a balanced economy.

Their collaboration—and such it was—on the Report on Manufactures was a natural result of Coxe's encyclopedic knowledge of the American economy and Hamilton's intellectual creativity, as well as their shared commitment to economic nationalism. The precise extent of the contribution of each is less important. The famous report indubitably bore the imprint of Hamilton's own ideas and program. Yet Coxe's role in its preparation cannot be swept aside as merely that of a compiler of useful facts and figures. Although not the kind of state paper that Coxe alone would have produced, the report clearly reflects both his industrious research and policies he had previously proposed and would continue to champion for more than two decades. An eclectic in economics as in statecraft, Hamilton doubtless relied on whatever sources were at hand, but when the lineage of the Report on Manufactures is traced, the major threads are found to lead to Tench Coxe.

Not only did Coxe collaborate with Hamilton on the Report on Manufactures, but he played a major role in the creation of the Society for Establishing Useful Manufactures, the most ambitious industrial experiment in early American history. The SEUM was a practical demonstration of arguments that would be included in the Report on Manufactures. Although Hamilton's support and participation were crucially important, Coxe must be credited with both the initial idea and the plans for its actualization. He had outlined proposals for the creation of a government-sponsored manufacturing town some months [42] before Hamilton lent the prestige of his office and his enthusiasm to such a project; long before that Coxe had been among the most active and prominent members of the Pennsylvania Manufacturing Society, whose accomplishments Hamilton attempted to nationalize.[43] Coxe had dispatched his own agent, Andrew Mitchell, to England to clandestinely make models of textile machinery, and when this attempt at industrial espionage failed,[44] he had arranged for the local construction of laborsaving

[41] *Ibid.*, 168-169.
[42] Coxe, "Plan for a Manufacturing Society" [Apr. 1791], Coxe Papers.
[43] I am indebted for this observation to Roland Baumann, "The Democratic-Republicans of Philadelphia: The Origins, 1776-1797" (Ph.D. diss., Pennsylvania State University, 1970), 316.
[44] See "Contract between Andrew Mitchell and Tench Coxe," Aug. 9, 1787;

machines patterned on British models—machines that would, in the event, be utilized by the proposed national society.

Coxe's acquisition of this machinery was made possible by George Parkinson, subsequently an employee of the SEUM, an English émigré who had brought with him to the United States purportedly valuable industrial secrets culled during his years as a weaver in Darlington, Durham. On January 11, 1790, Coxe and Parkinson signed a partnership agreement according to which the Englishman, averring that he "possessed . . . the Knowledge of all the Secret Movements used in Sir Richard Arkwright's Patent Machine" (which his own improvements made applicable also to the manufacture of hemp, flax, worsted, and silk), agreed to construct and deliver to Coxe a working model of an experimental mill. Ownership of the model, patent rights, and all profits made by its use in manufacturing were vested equally in the partners. In return, Coxe agreed to pay Parkinson £16 a month for the period required to construct the model and £400 out of the first profits earned, to furnish all requisite supplies, to procure a patent, and to arrange for the passage of Parkinson's wife and children from Liverpool to Philadelphia.[46]

Within three months the Englishman had fulfilled his part of the bargain, and Coxe promptly forwarded Parkinson's patent petition and model of a flax mill to his friend George Clymer, congressman from Pennsylvania, who was requested to present them to the secretary of state and the attorney general. Bureaucrats then as now moved slowly, but a patent finally was granted in March 1791.[46] On March 24 Parkinson announced that the American government had officially endorsed his evasion of those English laws that were intended to prevent the emigration of skilled artisans and the purveyance of industrial secrets. His patents, Parkinson's advertisement stated, consisted of "improvements upon the mill or machinery . . . in Great Britain," which were of the

---

Mitchell to Coxe, Aug. 16, Oct. 3, 24, 1787, Feb. 1, Mar. 3, 7, May 4, June 4, 1788, and two undated letters; Coxe to Mitchell, Sept. 21, Oct. 21, 1787, Coxe Papers.

[45] "Articles of Agreement," Jan. 11, 1790, ibid. See also George Parkinson to Coxe, Apr. 15, 1794, ibid. Coxe arranged for the passage of Parkinson's family through James Maury, United States consul at Liverpool. See Coxe to Maury, May 4, 1791, and Maury to Coxe, July 29, 1791, ibid.

[46] The story can be followed in William Coxe, Jr., to Coxe, Jan. 22, 1790; Fitzsimons to Coxe, Feb. 12, 1790; George Clymer to Coxe, Apr. 22, May 1, 1790; Daniel W. Coxe to Coxe, May 15, July 23, 24, 1790, ibid.; Coxe to Jefferson, Mar. 14, 1791, Jefferson Papers, Lib. Cong. See also Parkinson to Coxe, July 12, Dec. 7, 1792, Coxe Papers. Parkinson's patent is dated Mar. 17, 1791. Joseph Stancliffe Davis, Essays in the Earlier History of American Corporations, I (Cambridge, Mass., 1917), 399.

utmost importance to the United States and were now available to "any individual or company on terms to be agreed upon."[47] No one responded, however, until Parkinson's business partner prevailed on Hamilton to recommend the Englishman to the directors of the SEUM. Whether or not Coxe benefitted personally from the arrangement (and he apparently did not), he was aware of no impropriety.

Coxe regarded his efforts in support of manufactures as a form of public service, making no distinction between his private recommendation of Parkinson and his official proposal of policies that would find fruition in the SEUM.[48] For these policies he had been a tireless propagandist. In "A brief examination," for example, he had pointed to the introduction of laborsaving machines as a means of rapidly exploiting America's rich resources and of incidentally enriching its citizens, suggesting that "the public creditors, the owners of perhaps fifteen millions of sterling money of now inactive wealth, might at this moment do much towards the introduction of the cotton mills, wool mills, flax mills, and other valuable branches of machine manufacturing." For this purpose, he said, let a subscription of $500,000 in transferable stock, payable in public paper, be floated; let this be used as collateral for a loan of specie from a cooperative foreign nation; and let the capital so raised be employed in the purchase of an extensive area of land and the erection thereon of manufacturing establishments. If "persons of character" were to proceed "with judgment and system" in such a plan, Coxe concluded, "they would be sure of success in their manufactories; they would raise a valuable town upon their land, and would help, to support the vallue of the public debt."[49]

Here was proposed precisely the type of model manufacturing city Hamilton would recommend; here, as Joseph S. Davis, the foremost authority on the SEUM, comments, were foreshadowed "the features of the matured project."[50] They were also anticipated in other articles pub-

---

[47] *Federal Gazette* (Philadelphia), Mar. 24, 1791.

[48] Indeed, before his appointment to the Treasury Department Coxe had made no secret of his personal interest in Parkinson's machinery. An article in the May 1790 issue of the *Am. Museum,* perhaps written by Coxe, described the Englishman's invention, adding in a footnote that the aforesaid "mill for roping combed wool, hemp, and flax, is possessed by Tench Coxe, esq." *Am. Museum,* VII (1790), 228. Once he was appointed to the Treasury and became involved in the plans for the SEUM, however, Coxe said nothing more publicly of his partnership with Parkinson.

[49] Coxe, "A brief examination," *ibid.,* IX (1791), 179-180.

[50] Davis, *Essays,* I, 351. Davis convincingly spells out the similarities between

lished by Coxe at this time: one of his pet proposals was the importation of skilled workers and machinery; he recommended the launching of a lottery to raise supplementary funds; he repeatedly endorsed government sponsorship or support of manufactures; he threw out as bait for prospective investors in a manufacturing town the possibility of windfall profits from rising land values; and he persuasively presented the case for the practicability of proceeding initially with the manufacture of cotton goods. The Society for Establishing Useful Manufactures, in fine, was constructed according to Coxe's blueprint.

This assertion is rendered the more certain by the similarity of the Society to Coxe's "Plan for a Manufacturing Society," prepared in April 1791. First shared with Hamilton and then submitted to Jefferson,[51] the "Plan" was an elaboration of the proposal, already described, that Coxe had made in "A brief examination." He once again recommended that half a million dollars be raised by subscriptions (to funded stock of the federal government, however, he now added stock of the Bank of the United States) and that this capital be used as security for a foreign loan (Holland was now designated) of the same sum in specie. Stockholders in the corporation, he proposed, should apply for an act of incorporation to one or more of the state legislatures, which should also be asked to authorize lotteries for raising funds to improve internal navigation and to encourage settlers to move to the model city. The customary corporate structure was recommended: stockholders should elect a number of directors who in turn should appoint a manager.

The first major task of the directors would be the purchase of suitable land situated, in order to assure easy and cheap transportation, "on some river that is navigable from the Ocean" and containing streams adequate for "water machinery and works." The area should be laid out in lots to be sold, rented, or leased to manufacturers, tradesmen, and other interested settlers. Although Coxe believed that, if feasible, a variety of manufactures should be supported, he argued that under existing circumstances only those should be encouraged that were suitable for the introduction of laborsaving machines, aptly termed by Coxe his "favorite idea," or to the institution of *"labor-saving processes."* What were the advantages of his plan? Coxe ticked off the familiar ones: enhanced confidence in government and bank stock "by creating a new object for

---

Coxe's proposal and the SEUM. It is suggestive that Hamilton's published papers contain no evidence that he was considering such a society before the preparation of Coxe's plan in Mar. or Apr. 1791.

[51] Coxe to Jefferson, Apr. 15, 1791, Jefferson Papers. A draft of the "Plan" is in the Coxe Papers.

them," an increase in the value of improved land, and, above all, handsome profits from the Society's manufacturing operations.[52]

Coxe's motive in submitting such a plan to Jefferson, the country's most prominent agrarian, is puzzling, the more so since Coxe's own explanation was disingenuous, if not a ruse. He was transmitting a copy of his proposals for establishing a manufacturing society, Coxe wrote, because as a Virginian Jefferson surely would be interested in a plan that "may apply happily in the federal district," an extensive area possessing a natural source of water power. It might indeed have been applicable, but Jefferson scarcely was the man to provide either the inspiration or the support. In asserting that agriculture is the "most natural employment," Coxe was affirming a point he had repeatedly made, one that he knew the Virginian enthusiastically shared. But the further argument he drew from this premise was more an effort to please and disarm Jefferson than a candid presentation of his own views. Since manufacturers are *"often an intemperate and disorderly class,"* he wrote, "modes of manufacture which do not require them . . . appear to be very desirable." His real, although unavowed, motive may have been to elicit the secretary of state's reaction to the still-confidential but predictably controversial plans of the Treasury Department to launch the SEUM. The Treasury secretary, Coxe remarked in his covering letter to Jefferson, "has every reason to believe" that such an experiment "will be very soon attempted in New Jersey."[53] Jefferson did not reply.

Where Jefferson was silent, Hamilton was enthusiastic. Coxe's "Plan for a Manufacturing Society" dovetailed precisely with his own ideas and may, indeed, have been prepared at his request. "The more I have considered the thing," he remarked to William Duer in a letter enclosing Coxe's proposal, "the more I feel persuaded that it will equally promote the Interest of the adventurers and of the public and will have an excellent effect on the Debt."[54] Hamilton had already discussed the plan informally with a number of prominent businessmen, Duer included, and by the summer of 1791 was ready to carry it out. Leaving Coxe in charge of other Treasury affairs, he traveled in July to New York to lend the prestige of his office and his personal influence among

---

[52] Coxe, "Plan for a Manufacturing Society," Coxe Papers.

[53] Italics mine. Coxe cautioned that his plan, known only to a very few top government officials and including "several delicate points," should be considered confidential and be confined to Jefferson's "private office." Coxe to Jefferson, Apr. 15, 1791, Jefferson Papers.

[54] Hamilton to William Duer, Apr. 20, 1791, *Hamilton Papers*, VIII, 300.

that city's leading capitalists to the successful launching of the project. Whether because of the contagion of his enthusiasm or the speculative bent of New York's business community, the Society's capital stock of $100,000 was promptly subscribed, and on August 9 a number of its larger stockholders met at New Brunswick, New Jersey, to discuss ways of raising additional capital and lay plans for the formal organization of the Society. The secretary of the Treasury was authorized to begin negotiations for a suitable charter, to secure qualified artisans for the manufacture of cotton, and to advertise the project in the country's principal newspapers.[55]

Early in September, as the depressed stock market propitiously showed signs of recovery, Hamilton made public the Society's "Prospectus," a carefully contrived promotional document, already privately circulated and designed to attract investors.[56] Its purpose, like the Report on Manufactures Hamilton was then preparing, was to demonstrate that both national and individual interests would be promoted by industrialization; unlike the report, however, its focus was on private gain rather than on the public weal. Accordingly, it emphasized the current state of domestic manufacturing, pointing to its disadvantages and advantages and presenting a plan by which the former might be obviated and the latter secured. The benefits were those to which industrial propagandists had often pointed—the abundance of raw materials and the absence of foreign competition.[57] The alleged handicaps, as Hamilton, Coxe, and many others had repeatedly insisted, could be easily overcome—the labor shortage by the introduction of machines, employment of women and children, and encouragement of immigration; the lack of capital by "a proper application of the public Debt" and by a pooling of individual and corporate resources. The "Prospectus" called for seed capital of $500,000, made up of $100 shares to be subscribed either in public stock or in specie, and proposed that whenever one-fifth of this sum had been raised, a manufacturing establishment capable of producing paper, cotton goods, and other items should be chartered by New York, Pennsylvania, or New Jersey, preferably the last. To that end the "Prospectus" included a model for the charter. Like the recommended corporate structure, this included virtually all of Coxe's favorite proposals—incorporation of the manufacturing town, the establishment of a lottery, and the investment

[55] Davis, *Essays,* I, 370, 373-374.
[56] See "Prospectus," *Hamilton Papers,* IX, 144-153.
[57] Coxe, "A brief examination," *Am. Museum,* IX (1791), 180.

of company funds in the purchase of lands and the construction of the necessary buildings.

Whether Hamilton or Coxe actually drafted the "Prospectus" is neither determinable nor particularly important. More significant is the inclusion in that document, although in amplified and occasionally modified form, of Coxe's "Plan for a Manufacturing Society"—a plan whose implementation had been made possible by Hamilton's influential advocacy.[58]

Similarly collaborative was the decision to locate the manufacturing town in New Jersey. The choice was made as early as April 1791, and the "reasons which strongly recommend" that state ("it is thickly populated—provisions are there abundant and cheap . . . its situation seems to insure a constant friendly disposition" to the advancement of manufactures) were explained in the SEUM "Prospectus." But granted New Jersey's advantages, the question remained: precisely where should the town be situated—on the Passaic, the Raritan, or the Delaware River? Each location had merits and each had the support of influential landowners eager to reap the profits accruing from enhanced land values. In an effort to forearm himself with facts to counter the importunities of land speculators, Hamilton in mid-August engaged two agents to reconnoitre the more likely sites. Some weeks later they laconically reported that the Falls of Passaic offered "one of the finest situations in the world," the Delaware "several good situations," and the Raritan none at all.[59] Since without supporting evidence this recommendation was of no practical use, the secretary of the Treasury, having himself no special interest in such a comparatively minor matter, turned the problem over to his assistant. Coxe was willing to solve it, but was by no means disinterested. The extensive landholdings of his father-in-law, Charles Coxe, included property on the proposed Delaware site near Trenton, as well as on the Raritan, and Charles Coxe made no effort to disguise his eagerness that the manufacturing city be located at one place or the other. The fulfillment of his wish depended for the moment on Thomas Marshall, the agent deputized by Coxe to resurvey the various sites proposed.

Marshall, an expatriate Englishman who had served an apprenticeship under Arkwright and whom Hamilton had hired to work for the SEUM, went first to Trenton to inspect eligible locations on the Delaware. Carrying letters of introduction to Charles Coxe, to Moore Furman,

[58] The same conclusion was reached by Davis, *Essays*, I, 356.
[59] William Hall to Hamilton, Aug. 29, Sept. 4, 1791, *Hamilton Papers*, IX, 121, 171.

Tench's former mercantile partner, and to other family and business friends of the Coxes, Marshall, accompanied by Furman, carefully examined the area. The recommendation of a location in or near Trenton "received somewhat of an additional force" from the offer of Charles Coxe, at whose home Tench's agent was staying, to pay for that part of the requisite canal that would run through his estate. But Marshall, "having weighed every Pro and Con," was "Necessitated to put my Unqualified Negation to the Delaware at Trenton." In what was doubtless intended as an indirect reproach, he also reminded the assistant secretary of his determination "to divest myself of every Prejudice or Attachment Whatsoever for any particular Place" and "to leave my mind free and Unshackled." If Coxe or Hamilton disagreed with his decisions, Marshall wrote, he would be consoled by the sure knowledge that he was at least disinterested.[60]

During the next few weeks Marshall visited many other possible locations, including Charles Coxe's lands along the Raritan and on Assawpink Creek. Should Marshall see fit to recommend either of these places, he was authorized by their owner to report to Treasury headquarters that "Coxe offers every *other* Lot, free of Purchase to Col. Hamilton." Although Charles Coxe was "well convinced" that his son-in-law's reconnaissance agent "has not seen so eligible a Situation any where with so many valuable advantages" as his own land, Marshall, while politely discreet, was not persuaded. Instead, he rhapsodically endorsed a site on Second River, some three miles from the center of Newark and a mile from the Passaic, and despite Duer's preference for the falls of the latter river, stuck firmly to his recommendation.[61]

The decision lay with the yet-to-be-appointed directors of the SEUM. The appointment of directors awaited, in turn, the granting of a satisfactory charter by the New Jersey legislature. That body soon granted all that was asked, and on November 22, 1791, Gov. William Paterson, whose name tactfully was chosen for the newly chartered town, signed the bill establishing the SEUM. Its structure was roughly the same as that recommended by Coxe in his "Plan" of the previous April and iterated in the Society's "Prospectus": overall direction by a board of directors and management by a governor and deputy governor. More important than its formal organization and status as a New Jersey corpora-

---

[60] Thomas Marshall to Coxe, Sept. 18, 1791, Hamilton Papers.
[61] Marshall to Coxe, Sept. 21, 27, Oct. 10, 1791, *ibid;* Charles Coxe to Coxe, Oct. 10, 1791, Coxe Papers; Marshall to Hamilton, Oct. 2, 1791, *Hamilton Papers,* IX, 267-269.

tion was its control by a coterie of wealthy eastern businessmen, mostly New Yorkers ("I wish very much," John Kemp wrote to Coxe, "there had not been So many Speculators among them"),[62] and its establishment under federal auspices, if the quasi-official support of the secretary of the Treasury can be so construed.

At the first meeting of the board, held on December 9, 1791, Hamilton's friend Duer, the rich and influential New Yorker whose speculations covered the whole sweep of American economic activity, was elected governor,[63] the controversial question of a suitable site was debated, and the secretary of the Treasury's nominations for the Society's top jobs (William Hall, Joseph Mort, William Pearce, Parkinson, and Marshall) were endorsed. Of these, at least two were based on Coxe's recommendations. Parkinson, Coxe's "business partner," was recommended as a foreman in the cotton mill. Pearce, whom Hamilton had employed "in preparing Machines for the use of the Society" and with whom he had "advanced pretty far in Agreement," had become Coxe's protégé soon after the English inventor arrived in America in the summer of 1791.[64] It was Coxe who (through the agency of William Seton, on whom he enjoined secrecy) submitted to President Washington descriptions and drawings of Pearce's machines and who drafted Pearce's petition to Jefferson, Knox, and Edmund Randolph for patents on a number of textile inventions, including a double loom to be operated by one person.[65] It, too, was Coxe who persuaded Pearce to sell to Coxe's own partner, Parkinson, all of Pearce's "right title interest and property" in his inventions "so far as regards hemp and flax."[66] Given his acquaintance with many of the artisan émigrés in Philadelphia, Coxe may also have

---

[62] John Kemp to Coxe, Dec. 25, 1791, Coxe Papers. The directors consisted of 7 New Yorkers and 6 Jerseymen. For information on their business careers see Davis, *Essays*, I, 392-398.

[63] Nathaniel Hazard presumably was alone in the conviction that Coxe would "be at the Head of that splendid Undertaking." Hazard to Coxe, Oct. 4, 1791, Coxe Papers.

[64] See Hamilton to Governor and Directors of the SEUM, Dec. 7, 1791, *Hamilton Papers*, X, 345. Pearce had been recommended to Coxe by Jefferson. Coxe to Jefferson, July 13, 1791, Jefferson Papers. Jefferson also backed Coxe's request to reimburse Pearce for his expenses by assuring William Seton, cashier of the Bank of New York, that "all charges," including the Englishman's passage to America, "would be thankfully repaid." Seton to Hamilton, June 11, 1792, *Hamilton Papers*, XI, 506.

[65] Coxe to Seton, July 15, 1791, Coxe Papers. Secrecy was necessary, Coxe explained, because an attempt had "been made to induce Mr. Pearce to take away or give up his Machinery, and to return to Europe." The draft of Pearce's petition in Coxe's hand, undated, is *ibid.*

[66] William Pearce to Jefferson, July 25, 1791, *ibid.*

been instrumental in selecting the other three top employees proposed by the Treasury secretary, the more likely so since Hamilton, as his leading biographer concedes, "had no experience for this special task," whose successful execution "must spell success or failure for the best plan."[67]

Although Coxe was in a position to designate some of the employees of the SEUM and although Hamilton proposed that he "should partake in the Management of the New Jersey Manufg. Society," Coxe had no control, unfortunately for his father-in-law, over the location of the proposed town.[68] Charles Coxe presumably thought otherwise. The selection of directors on whose support he confidently counted, he wrote Tench early in December 1791, kindled his hopes that "we shall have the factory fixed on the banks of the Raritan."[69] Aware that rival landowners were lobbying for other sites, Charles Coxe submitted a copy of "a draught of his Sidney Estate" to the six New Jersey directors, one of whom, Furman, described it as "a more eligible place for the Manufactory than any other that can be found."[70] Another copy was given to Tench Coxe, who was requested to put it "in away of being noticed by Col. Hamilton."[71] A favorable decision, Charles Coxe reminded his son-in-law, "may be the means of fixing the attention of Some of my children and placing them and perhaps Some of their children in a situation that may be agreeable to them."[72] The Society's directors, beset by such importunate property owners and torn by "clashing personal interests," repeatedly deferred the decision but finally selected the falls of the Passaic River, next door to Newark.[73]

Neither of the Coxes need have been disappointed, for the decision was, in the event, of no great consequence. Within months the Society was in trouble; within a few years it had collapsed. Doubtless the experiment was premature; perhaps to have succeeded at all the Society would have to have been either public or quasi-public, subsidized by state funds because the application of federal funds at that time would have

---

[67] Mitchell, *Alexander Hamilton*, II, 182.

[68] Coxe to Hamilton, May 20, 1792, Hamilton Papers. In spite of Hamilton's proposal, Coxe became neither a director nor a shareholder of the SEUM.

[69] Charles Coxe to Coxe, Dec. 5, 1791, Coxe Papers.

[70] Charles Stewart to Coxe, Dec. 3, 1791; Moore Furman to Coxe, Apr. 28, 1792, *ibid*.

[71] Stewart to Coxe, Dec. 3, 1791, *ibid*.

[72] "How do you know," Charles Coxe continued, "but yourself Some years hence may wish for a little more retirement than you can have in Philada. and make choice of a spot on the Sidney farm—This thought is more pleasing to me than the thought of your following Congress to that unhealthy country on the banks of the Potomack." Charles Coxe to Coxe [1791], *ibid*.

[73] Davis, *Essays*, I, 402-405, 408, 418; Mitchell, *Alexander Hamilton*, II, 183.

been out of the question. Whatever the larger issues, more mundane things were directly responsible for the failure of this ambitious attempt to achieve national economic planning by harnessing private capital. Adequate capital was not forthcoming. Initially, SEUM stock was snapped up with the same avidity that national bank stock had been. But when the time came to make the first quarterly payment for stock, formerly eager investors had second thoughts.[74] This was owing not only to doubts about the viability of the SEUM but to a financial panic in the spring of 1792 that brought a sharp fall in government securities and also occasioned the bankruptcy of the governor of the corporation and several of its directors.

Only a group of myopic speculators could have entrusted the management of what might have been viewed as a great experiment in economic planning to Duer, one of the great risk-takers of his day, a man unlikely to forgo personal advantage for the good of any cause. With their chief administrator in debtors prison, the Society's directors, numbed by his and their own financial reverses, faced the futile task of trying to recover a large sum of money entrusted to Duer for which he failed to account.[75] As if the "financial visionary Duer" had not caused trouble enough, Pierre L'Enfant, a "talented engineering visionary," added to the Society's woes.[76] Employed to prepare a plan for the new town, the French engineer attempted to duplicate the imaginative design he had recently completed for the new federal capital, stubbornly refusing to acknowledge that the resources of a fledgling private corporation were not those of a national government. In brief, by the time the board held its third meeting in April 1792, the funds of the Society were depleted, its leadership discredited, and its affairs in confusion.

Bewildered by the hopeless disarray of the Society, those directors who were still solvent called on the St. George of the Treasury Department to slay the dragons of malfeasance and inefficiency, but although Hamilton promptly came to their rescue, not even his managerial wizardry could long arrest the downhill course of this once promising venture. His timely first aid, combined with a rising stock market, by late summer of 1792 did superficially appear to have given the Society a new lease on life, but his intervention, ironically enough, was itself a serious impedi-

[74] Of the $625,000 subscribed by Dec. 1791, Davis calculates that the stockholders actually paid in somewhere between $240,000 and $300,000. *Essays*, I, 405, 407.

[75] For an account of the effect of Duer's bankruptcy see Hazard to Coxe, Mar. 17, 1792, Coxe Papers.

[76] The quoted phrases are from Mitchell, *Alexander Hamilton*, II, 185.

ment to recovery. His political battle with Jefferson was then raging
fiercely, and his intemperate newspaper attacks on his cabinet colleague
did more to arouse hostility against himself than to discredit Jefferson. For
the SEUM, this contributed to a steady erosion of the public confidence
necessary to buoy successful stock flotations. "The newspapers of 1792,"
in Davis's words, "interestingly reveal the scope and vehemence of the
attacks which the new enterprise sustained, and their connection with
the party warfare which was just now reaching an unprecedented
height."[77] They reveal, too, the strong counterattack mounted by its
supporters, who rushed to defend Hamilton's personal integrity as well
as his policies.

The ablest of these gladiators was Coxe, who stoutly supported the
SEUM against the criticisms of George Logan, the prominent Quaker
doctor of Philadelphia. Writing as "A Farmer," Logan trained on the
SEUM the full fury of his Jeffersonian outrage. He contended that the
New Jersey legislature, in chartering the Society, had sacrificed the
interests of the majority of the state's citizens by granting to "a few
wealthy men" exclusive jurisdiction over an extended area and an un-
conscionable number of unconstitutional privileges. In Logan's view, the
charter subverted "the principles of . . . equality, of which freemen
ought to be so jealous," fostered "inequality of fortune," and strongly
suggested a predisposition "to an aristocracy."[78] Rebutting Logan, Coxe
rehearsed the arguments for the SEUM and, since his adversary had used
the Society as a springboard for an attack on Hamiltonian economics
generally, defended the Treasury policies that he had helped to formulate.
Hamilton's program, he declared, was "entitled to all the merit of being
an efficient instrument of public justice, honour, and prosperity," one
that "all the foreign world applaud and admire, as wise and efficient."[79]

[77] Davis, Essays, I, 426.

[78] George Logan, Five Letters Addressed to the Yeomanry of the United States:
Containing some Observations on the dangerous scheme of Governor Duer and
Mr. Secretary Hamilton, to establish National Manufactories (Philadelphia, 1792).
The Letters were published in pamphlet form on Aug. 21, 1792, and were reprinted
in the National Gazette (Philadelphia), Aug. 29, Sept. 5, 19, 1792, and in the
Am. Museum, XII (1792). The quotations are from Letter No. 2, ibid., 161-163.
Later, as United States senator, Logan would become one of Coxe's closest political
allies.

[79] Using the nom de guerre of "A Freeman," Coxe entitled his articles merely
"Observations on the Preceding Letters." This was made meaningful by the con-
sent of Mathew Carey to print his friend's articles immediately following the
Letters to the Yeomanry. See Am. Museum, XII (1792), 167-170, 217-221, 272-278.
Quotations are from pp. 276, 275. Coxe identified himself as the author in a letter

Not the least praiseworthy feature of this program was the SEUM. But more than rhetoric and argument was needed to save that undertaking. Plagued by a host of problems, the Society lingered a few years, finally coming to an end in 1796.[80]

By that time Coxe and Hamilton had quarreled, thus ending an official relationship that had been among the most fruitful of the new nation's early years. Together they had launched the Society for Establishing Useful Manufactures, a pilot project for an industrial economy, and produced the Report on Manufactures, a state paper "distinguished" by "its far-reaching implications and its ennobling vision of the destiny of the United States."[81]

---

to Jacob Broom on Jan. 24, 1794: "The New Jersey law is worthy of attention. I mean the act incorporating the Town of *Patterson*. I shall send you some Numbers of the American Museum in which are three papers of mine signed *'a freeman'* answering objections that have been made to it." Coxe Papers.

[80] For an able description of the reasons for the Society's failure see Mitchell, *Alexander Hamilton*, II, 191-192.

[81] *Hamilton Papers*, X, 1.

Alexander Hamilton
and American Manufacturing:
A Reexamination

JOHN R. NELSON, JR.

"HAMILTON envisaged," Nathan Schachner writes, "a nation resting on the twin foundations of agriculture and manufactories." One "pillar of Hamilton's capitalist edifice," Charles Beard adds, was "the protective tariff designed to develop American industry." "He would bring America," Broadus Mitchell concludes, "as rapidly as possible, into the new industrial age which had become the condition of national advance."[1] Historians seldom question the image of Alexander Hamilton as the foremost advocate of American manufacturing.[2] This essay reexamines that image and reopens the question of Hamilton's relationship to American manufacturing. First the essay establishes the larger context of Hamilton's political economy. It seeks to clarify the basic elements in his economic stabilization program, assess their impact upon the interests of American manufacturers, and analyze the response of the manufacturers to his policies.[3] After exploring the relationship between his political economy and American manufacturers, the essay reconsiders his famous *Report on Manufactures* and his Society for Establishing Useful Manufactures (SEUM).

This essay won the Organization of American Historians' Pelzer Award for 1977. John R. Nelson, Jr., is a Ph.D. candidate at Northern Illinois University, where his adviser is Alfred F. Young.

[1] Nathan Schachner, *Alexander Hamilton* (New York, 1946), 278; Charles Beard, *Economic Origins of Jeffersonian Democracy* (New York, 1915), 159–60; and Broadus Mitchell, *Alexander Hamilton: The National Adventure, 1788–1804* (New York, 1962), 143.

[2] William Appleman Williams has directly challenged this consensus by arguing that Alexander Hamilton "never pushed manufacturing as an integral part of the economy and in fact opposed the efforts of others to accelerate its development." William Appleman Williams, *The Contours of American History* (Chicago, 1966), 163. See also William Appleman Williams, "The Age of Mercantilism: An Interpretation of the American Political Economy, 1763–1828," *William and Mary Quarterly*, 15 (Oct. 1958), 428–32.

[3] The term "manufacturer" includes two groups in early America: the urban artisans and mechanics, and the larger, though fewer, entrepreneurs maintaining manufactories.

971

The purpose of Hamilton's political economy was the preservation of private property and the liberty to pursue it. For him the chief functions of government were to protect property, to enforce a legal framework in which it was secured, and to provide a stable environment for economic activity and growth. In the last two decades of the eighteenth century, the central issue involving both property and economic stability was government credit. "The maxims of public credit," Hamilton wrote, were "of the essence of good government, . . . intimately connected, by analogy and sympathy of principals, with the security of property in general, and . . . forming an inseparable portion of the great system of political order."[4] Although his solution to the problem of economic stabilization underwent various mutations during the 1780s, the greatest of which was his decision to press for a new national government instead of reforming the Confederation, Hamilton's basic approach remained the same. He wanted to "make it the *immediate* interest of the monied men to cooperate with government" in the restoration of currency.[5]

When he turned toward the creation of a new government, the cause of credit and that of the federal government merged. Hamilton pressed for full funding of the Confederation debt and assumption of state war debts. "If all the public creditors," he wrote in his *Report on Public Credit*, "receive their dues from one source . . . their interest will be the same. And, having the same interests, they will unite in the support of the fiscal arrangements of the government. . . ."[6] Funding and assumption realized his hopes of making the national debt "a powerful cement of our union" and strengthening the "infant Government by increasing the number of ligaments between the Government and the interests of Individuals."[7] The capstone of his stabilization program was the national bank con-

[4] Defense of the Funding System, July 1795, *The Papers of Alexander Hamilton*, ed. Harold C. Syrett (26 vols., New York, 1961–1978), XIX, 5. The term "stabilization" is used in a broad sense to include the creation of a political and economic environment conducive to business investment, economic growth, and national security. See the brief discussion in Douglass North, *Growth and Welfare in the American Past: A New Economic History* (Englewood Cliffs, 1966), 55–57.

[5] Alexander Hamilton to [?], Dec. 1779–March 1780, *Papers of Alexander Hamilton*, II, 244; see also "Letter from Phocion," Jan. 1–27, 1784, *ibid.*, III, 494; and Hamilton to Robert Morris, April 30, 1781, *ibid.*, II, 617.

[6] Report on Public Credit, Jan. 1790, *ibid.*, VI, 80.

[7] Hamilton to Morris, April 30, 1781, *ibid.*, II, 635; Report on Public Credit, *ibid.*, VI, 86; and Defense of the Funding System, July 1795, *ibid.*, XIX, 40.

ceived in the early 1780s "to engage the monied interest immediately in it by making them contribute the whole or part of the stock and giving them the whole or part of the profits." The bank would link "the interests of the state in an intimate connexion with those of the rich individuals belonging to it . . . ."[8]

This wealthy group consisted mainly of well-established merchants who accumulated their fortunes trading within the British empire during the colonial period and after the Revolution. A significant portion of this trade, though by no means all, involved the exchange of British manufactured goods for the raw and semi-finished produce of the colonies. Hamilton was solicitous of this trade not only because of the merchants' role in his stabilization program, but because it produced the 80 percent of tariff revenues that provided funds to service the debt and operate the government. These considerations led him toward a pro-British foreign policy and instilled in him a profound wariness of any action that might jeopardize the flow of English goods into America. He consistently opposed any trade discrimination and preferred "a strict national or commercial friendship with Great Britain." His program for economic stabilization made such an Anglo-American alliance in "the best interests of this Country." He thus tied his political economy, his party, and the nation itself to the greatest manufacturing power in the world.[9]

Another important element in Hamilton's political economy was its failure to formulate any adequate means of reaching out to the small property holders—the majority of the people. For those of great property he constructed a most elaborate program to engage their interests and attract their support. His attitude toward the "mass of the people," however, rested on a fear of popular passions

[8] Hamilton to James Duane, Sept. 3, 1780, ibid., II, 414; Hamilton to [?], Dec. 1779–March 1780, ibid., 248; and Hamilton to Washington, March 1791, ibid., VIII, 223. The best treatment of the character and context of funding and assumption is E. James Ferguson, The Power of the Purse: A History of American Public Finance, 1776–1790 (Chapel Hill, 1961), 220–342.

[9] Conversations with George Beckwith, Oct. 1789, Papers of Alexander Hamilton, V, 488; and Feb. 16, 1791, ibid., VIII, 43. See also Joseph Charles, The Origins of the American Party System (Williamsburg, 1956), 8–37; Julian P. Boyd, Number Seven, Alexander Hamilton's Secret Attempts to Control American Foreign Policy (Princeton, 1964), 41–84; Bradford Perkins, The First Rapprochement: England and the United States, 1795–1805 (Los Angeles, 1967), 11–26; and John C. Miller, Alexander Hamilton: Portrait in Paradox (New York, 1959), 134, 388. See also Hamilton's explanation of the importance of British imports to government revenues in "Americus No. II," Feb. 7, 1794, Papers of Alexander Hamilton, XVI, 13.

as a source of disorder. Public allegiance depended upon habits of loyalty or, at times, the armed coercion of the state.[10] Even Charles Beard, who interprets Hamilton's support of manufacturers as unqualified, commented that "Hamilton, who was so deeply concerned in the growth of manufactures, does not appear to have given that consideration to the labor [i.e., manufacturer-mechanic] vote which its importance demanded."[11] This oversight was portentous. In all Hamilton's policies and projects related to manufacturing he never sought to comprehend the manufacturers themselves. While favoring the wealthy class of merchants, he expected patriotism, coercion or some profound sense of national interest to retain popular support for his programs. "In doing so," as Cecelia Kenyon concludes, "he was not logical, he was not realistic, and he led his party straight down the road to extinction."[12]

A comparison of the exigencies of Hamilton's political economy with the manufacturers' articulation of their own interests reveals a profound tension between the two. This tension became evident with the first manufacturers' petitions to the federal government in 1789. These petitioners displayed a common pattern in their appeals for congressional aid to their nascent enterprises. They assailed "foreign luxuries," particularly British manufactured goods, as draining American wealth and causing economic hardships. They explained that since state governments were not effective in stopping this "misfortune of a foreign intercourse," they expected the national government to give "proper encouragement" to manufactures and free the country from "the commercial shackles which have so long bound her." Finally, they requested tariffs to protect· American manufactures or navigation laws to stimulate domestic shipbuilding.[13]

Hamilton and his congressional supporters were less than accommodating to these petitions. The Philadelphia "master shipwrights" wanted discriminatory duties levied upon Britain's ships to counter its Navigation Laws and make American-built ships more competi-

[10] Speech on a Plan of Government, Robert Yates' version, June 1787, *Papers of Alexander Hamilton*, IV, 200; Speech on a Plan of Government, James Madison's Version, June 18, 1787, *ibid.*, IV, 189, 192; Hamilton to Duane, Sept. 3, 1780, *ibid.*, II, 410–11; Hamilton to Washington, Feb. 13, 1783, *ibid.*, III, 254–55; and Cecelia M. Kenyon, "Alexander Hamilton: Rousseau of the Right," *Political Science Quarterly*, 73 (June 1958), 161–78.

[11] Beard, *Economic Origins of Jeffersonian Democracy*, 246n.

[12] Kenyon, "Alexander Hamilton," 170–71.

[13] U.S. Congress, *New American State Papers: Manufactures*, intro. Alfred A. Chandler (9 vols., Wilmington, Del., 1972), I, 33–37.

tive in international trade. Madison managed to move such a measure through the House over the opposition of Hamilton's chief spokesman, William Smith of South Carolina; ultimately, the Senate blocked it. Hamilton told George Beckwith, England's chief liaison to America, that he "was decidedly opposed to those discriminatory Clauses." In their stead Congress passed a general provision for equal discrimination against all foreign ships.[14]

The "tradesmen and manufacturers" of Boston asked for a tariff "intended to *exclude* such [manufactured] importations, and, ultimately, establish these several branches of manufacture among themselves."[15] These manufacturers were requesting in an extreme form what all the manufacturers wanted: a strong protective tariff. In Congress Madison proposed protective tariffs specifically directed against England, but his proposals were defeated and what was in effect a revenue tariff imposed with Hamilton's wholehearted approval.[16] Favoring a "moderate" tariff productive of revenue, Hamilton argued that when duties "are low, a nation can trade abroad on better terms—its imports and exports will be larger—the duties will be regularly paid, and arising on a greater quantity of commodities, will yield more in the aggregate, than when they are so high as to operate . . . as a prohibition. . . ."[17] The need for revenue overrode the demand for protection of manufactures.

In response to a general inquiry pertaining to manufacturing the treasury department received letters revealing the difficulties that Hamilton's economic program caused manufacturers. Peter Colt, a Connecticut manufacturer, cited the lack of capital, expense of materials and cost of labor as the chief obstructions to local development. He hoped that "when the active Stock of the Citizens shall no longer be embarked im paper Speculations, then we may expect to see part of it turned to the promoting & extending our manufactures & then those which languish and dwindle for want of being

[14] *Ibid.*, 35–36; John C. Miller, *The Federalist Era, 1789–1801* (New York, 1960), 17–19; Edward Stanwood, *American Tariff Controversies in the Nineteenth Century* (2 vols., New York, 1903), I, 39–49; Irving Brant, *James Madison, Father of the Constitution, 1781–1800* (Indianapolis, 1950), 246–47, 252–53; and Conversation with Beckwith, Oct. 1789, *Papers of Alexander Hamilton*, V, 488.

[15] U.S. Congress, *New American State Papers: Manufactures*, I, 37.

[16] Miller, *Alexander Hamilton*, 222–25. F. W. Taussig argues that the tariff was protective in intention, but admits it had no impact on manufacturers. Only the anti-British measures of 1808 had any stimulating effect on manufacturing. *The Tariff History of the United States* (New York, 1931), 15–17.

[17] "Continentalist No. V," April 18, 1782, *Papers of Alexander Hamilton*, III, 78–79.

support[e]d with proper Capitals may be expected to prosper & this Country freed from a disgracefull dependance on Europe for their ordinary Cloathing." Elisha Colt, also of Connecticut, complained of the "smallness of our capital" and the "impossibility of hiring Money on legal Interest" as well as the "Jealousy of the British Factors and agents in this Country." He too wished that "the rage for Speculation in the funds of the United States shall have ceased, [and] part of the Money of the Country, which now only circulates in paper traf[f]ic, may be directed into this channel for the aid of our infant Manufactures."[18]

Although Hamilton disapproved of the stock speculation ignited by his funding program, it nonetheless served to deprive manufacturers of capital. In reports from Rhode Island and Massachusetts, manufacturers complained of merchants enriching themselves by selling massive imports of British goods dumped by British manufacturers on the American market to stifle domestic enterprises. Moses Brown of Providence concluded that "the Actual Combination" of "the Manufacturing Interest of Great Brittain" and "Our Importing Merchants . . . forms a very great Discouragement to Men of Abilities to lay Out their propperty in Extending Manufacturies. . . ."[19] These complaints were echoed by Charleston's leather manufacturers. "The vast importations of almost every article" and "the long and general Credit given by the Importers" to buyers "strike at the root of [our] Manufactories."[20] With ample capital from Hamilton's funding program and British firms, the importers could easily use their credit facilities to undermine domestic producers. Finally the Virginia manufacturers of cordage requested a higher duty on imported cordage, but they doubted that even such protection would induce shippers to buy from them since "most of the Ships are British & give a preference to English Cordage. . . ."[21] In the minds of these American manufacturers, Britain and its American importers assumed a central role in impeding their economic development.

Throughout 1792 Hamilton confronted an increasing need for larger government revenues. This need could have been met by raising tariffs and partially fulfilling the manufacturers' demands

[18] Enclosures to Hamilton, Oct. 11, 1791, *ibid.*, IX, 323–27.
[19] Enclosures to Hamilton, Oct. 13 and 15, 1791, *ibid.*, 372–73, 436–39.
[20] Memorandum to Daniel Stevens, Oct. 1791, *Industrial and Commercial Correspondence of Alexander Hamilton*, ed. Arthur H. Cole (Chicago, 1928), 91.
[21] Enclosure to Hamilton, Oct. 4, 1791, *Papers of Alexander Hamilton*, IX, 278.

for protection. Instead his fear of antagonizing importers with higher duties led Hamilton to enforce the tax upon the large quantity of domestically manufactured liquor and snuff; the slight increases in the tariff that he recommended were predicated upon the declining cost of imports and hence were of little protective value. Moreover Hamilton noted that the tariff increase "will not be of very long continuance."[22] This small, temporary increase in tariffs and the enforcement of a relatively heavy excise tax on liquor manufactures strongly indicate that his priorities did not lie with manufacturers.

By the end of 1793 Hamilton's pro-importer political economy was driving manufacturers from Boston to Charleston into opposition to the Federalists. This opposition crystalized in the Democratic Societies which in the cities drew their largest membership from artisans and manufacturers. In Pennsylvania's Germantown Society for Promoting Domestic Manufactures Hamilton's policies, especially the SEUM, were vehemently attacked. In 1794 New York's General Society of Mechanics and Tradesmen shifted their support from the Federalists to nascent Republican organizations.[23] It was becoming apparent to many American manufacturers that Hamilton's policies contravened their interests.

This growing dissent marked the emergence of an opposition coalition that later became the Republican party. This coalition included manufacturers disenchanted with Hamilton's economic policies, merchants opposed to his acquiescence in British assaults on their trade, and the planters and farmers repelled by his economic stabilization program. Merchant opposition, though not yet explored adequately, seems to have come from those merchants trading outside the British Empire whose ships were most often victims of English attacks. They also appear to have been reaping

[22] Report Relative to the Additional Supplies for the Ensuing Year, March 16, 1792, *ibid.*, XI, 142–48; and Report on the Difficulties in the Execution of the Act Laying Duties on Distilled Spirits, March 5, 1792, *ibid.*, XI, 84–86. Compare the latter with the Report on the Subject of Manufactures, Dec. 5, 1791, *ibid.*, X, 336–37. See also Miller, *Federalist Era*, 155–57; and Miller, *Alexander Hamilton*, 393–400.

[23] Paul Goodman, *The Democratic-Republicans of Massachusetts: Politics in a Young Republic* (Cambridge, 1964), xi, 11–12, 44–45, 70–77, 97–102; Alfred F. Young, *The Democratic Republicans of New York: The Origins, 1763–1797* (Chapel Hill, 1967), 249, 368–69, 568, 579–81; and Alfred F. Young, "The Mechanics and the Jeffersonians: New York 1789–1801," *Labor History*, 5 (Fall 1964), 252–76; Roland Baumann, "The Democratic-Republicans of Philadelphia: The Origins, 1776–1797" (doctoral dissertation, Pennsylvania State University, 1970), 370–71, 385, 449–51, 472–79, 577–78; and Eugene Perry Link, *Democratic-Republican Societies, 1790–1800* (New York, 1942), x, 5–78, 93–96.

the benefits of the widening carrying trade within the Spanish and French empires after the Royal Navy had interdicted French and Spanish shipping. Their relative newness probably meant they were neither direct beneficiaries of Hamilton's economic program nor importers of British manufactures. The interest of these merchants and the manufacturers alienated by Hamilton's policies coalesced in their common opposition to Britain, its exports, and its restrictions upon non-British commerce. It is also obvious that these merchants would have much less to lose from domestic manufactures than those importing British industrial goods. Indeed, a few Republican merchants invested in manufactures.[24]

Although the desertion of much of the urban manufacturing interest is well documented, evidence for the larger entrepreneurs' response is scattered. A significant indication of their probable response appeared in 1795 when one of the chief spokesmen of these large manufacturers, Assistant Secretary of the Treasury Tench Coxe, broke with Hamilton over the Jay Treaty and other, more personal conflicts. In July 1795, under the pseudonym "Juricola," Coxe assailed the treaty's harmful impact upon American manufacturers. This attack embarrassed Hamilton and contributed to Coxe's resignation from the administration. Coxe later joined the Republican party.[25]

In response to this overall political threat Hamilton arranged to dispatch John Jay to negotiate a new settlement with Britain. He managed to defeat Madison's renewed efforts to discriminate against British ships and goods. Indeed, to avoid a conflict with Britain Hamilton offered to exempt British ships from all foreign tonnage duties and allow "the commodities and manufactures of Great Britain and Ireland . . . [to] be imported into the Ustates upon terms equally good with the like commodities & manufactures of any other nation. . . ." Finally he proposed that "the duties upon such of them as now pay ten per Cent ad valorem & upwards shall not be increased and the duties upon such of them as now pay under 10 per Cent ad valorem shall not be increased beyond 10 per

---

[24] The Republican coalition is discussed in Baumann, "Democratic-Republicans of Philadelphia," 423, 448–49, 587; Goodman, *Democratic-Republicans of Massachusetts*, xi, 70–77, 105; Link, *Democratic-Republican Societies*, 5, 53, 73–75; and Young, *Democratic Republicans of New York*, 248–50, 566–81.

[25] Hamilton to George Washington, Feb. 2, 1795, *Papers of Alexander Hamilton*, XVIII, 252; *Philadelphia Gazette and Universal Daily Advertiser*, July 31, 1795; Hamilton to Oliver Wolcott, Jr., Aug. 5, 1795, *Papers of Alexander Hamilton*, XIX, 97; and Harold Hutchison, *Tench Coxe: A Study in American Economic Development* (Baltimore, 1938), 38–42.

Cent."[26] He was again sacrificing American manufacturers to his political economy's need for continued Anglo-American rapprochement.

This foreign crisis necessitated some program for national defense. Hamilton might have seized this opportunity to aid domestic manufacturers through the dispensation of government defense contracts; instead, he turned to British importers. "It has been determined," he wrote Thomas Pinckney, "to import from Europe as expeditiously as may be the articles . . . towards the construction of six frigates. . . . the desire of dispatch principally has recommended an experiment to procure them from G Britain. . . ."[27] Although some of these imports may be explained by the lack of domestic production and credit needs, Hamilton overlooked the one American industry that could supply all the government's requirements—sailcloth manufacturing. "What sail Cloth shall we use for the Frigates," he asked Benjamin Lincoln and the other port collectors, "that of Domestic or that of Foreign Manufacture? National pride & interest plead for the former if the quality be really good. But is it really good?" Then he added, "Objections are made; that which is principally insisted upon is that it shrinks exceedingly." Lincoln quickly responded that American sailcloth was better than foreign and that there had been no problems for two years. This exchange is all the more puzzling since, in a draft of his *Report on Manufactures,* Hamilton had observed that Boston sailcloth "is asserted to be of a quality superior to any import."[28]

After his retirement from office Hamilton continued activities of dubious benefit to domestic manufacturers. He opposed Jefferson's decision to repeal internal taxes, desiring instead a reduction in import tariffs. He continued his activities in various land speculation schemes, activity that English broadsides exalted because it

[26] Hamilton to Washington, April 23, 1794, *Papers of Alexander Hamilton*, XVI, 322. Hamilton also engineered the defeat of James Madison's resolutions against Britain, which centered upon the reduction of British manufactures and the increase of American domestic production. Brant, *James Madison, Father of the Constitution*, 389–93. For Hamilton's concerns in this matter and a clear statement of his priorities see Hamilton to John Jay, May 6, 1794, *Papers of Alexander Hamilton*, XVI, 383; and Hamilton to Washington, April 14, 1794, *ibid.*, 274–76.

[27] Hamilton to Thomas Pinckney, June 25, 1794, *Papers of Alexander Hamilton*, XVI, 527. See also Stephen Higginson to Hamilton, July 10, 1794, *ibid.*, 586; Tench Coxe to Hamilton, Oct. 15, 1794, *ibid.*, XVII, 326–27; and Coxe to Hamilton, Dec. 22, 1794, *ibid.*, 455–56.

[28] Hamilton to Benjamin Lincoln, June 28, 1794, *ibid.*, XVI, 536; Hamilton to William Seton, *ibid.*, 543–44; Lincoln to Hamilton, July 5, 1794, *ibid.*, 568; and Report on the Subject of Manufactures, Third Draft, *ibid.*, X, 104.

diverted money from American manufacturing. Indeed, the numerous efforts on Hamilton's part in and out of office to promote such schemes led his biographer, John C. Miller, to question "whether Hamilton did not actually do more during his lifetime for land speculation than for American manufactures."[29]

In order to gain a better perspective on Hamilton's approach to manufacturing it is appropriate to consider the origins and nature of the Society for Establishing Useful Manufactures. The SEUM's origins can be traced to the security market situation of the early 1790s. Circumscribed by a ring of European empires not yet opened by world war, American trade declined throughout 1791. High imperial tariffs weakened American exports and, as the year progressed, imports also slackened.[30] Within this milieu of closed markets, many American merchants turned toward speculation in government securities and bank scrip to vent their surplus funds. Such speculation created a very volatile securities market whose fluctuations threatened the assets of holders and allowed large foreign acquisitions of securities at low prices. Acutely aware of this situation, Hamilton was especially concerned with the fluctuating prices of American securities which facilitated foreign acquisitions, undermined their stability, and limited their usefulness in supporting business activity.[31] When he purchased securities for the sinking fund, Hamilton was less interested in a low price than in boosting security prices in general.[32]

In early 1791 he began planning a more comprehensive method to deal with problems that his political economy had spawned in securities speculation. It would be a method to develop manufacturing as well. Thus Hamilton envisioned the Society for Establishing Useful Manufactures with a threefold purpose: to support the price levels of the speculative market by stabilizing the demand for government bonds, to provide a productive outlet in manufacturing

[29] Charles A. Conant, *Alexander Hamilton* (Boston, 1901), 90–93; Link, *Democratic-Republican Societies*, 77n; and Miller, *Alexander Hamilton*, 546.

[30] Douglass C. North, *The Economic Growth of the United States, 1790–1860* (Englewood Cliffs, 1961), 221, 228.

[31] Hamilton to William Duer, Aug. 17, 1791, *Papers of Alexander Hamilton*, IX, 75; Hamilton to Rufus King, *ibid.*, 76; Hamilton to Seton, Aug. 18, 1791, *ibid.*, 77; Hamilton to Washington, Aug. 17, 1792, *ibid.*, XII, 244. See also Hamilton to Washington, March 27, 1791, *ibid.*, VIII, 222.

[32] Joseph Stancliffe Davis, *Essays in the Earlier History of American Corporations* (2 vols., Cambridge, 1917), I, 206–07.

for surplus merchant capital, and to curb the outflow of American securities abroad by requiring their use in subscriptions to the SEUM's stock. With these considerations in mind he wrote to William Duer in April 1791: "The more I have considered the thing [SEUM], the more I feel persuaded that it will equally promote the Interest of the Adventurers & of the public and will have an excellent effect on the Debt."[33]

The problems of the debt and speculation were also the themes that Coxe took up in his defense of the SEUM. "Moreover," the assistant secretary of the treasury wrote in September 1792, "as it was manifest, that active capital was flowing into and arising in the United States very rapidly, there was a sincere and serious apprehension, that evils would arise from it, particularly in a profuse consumption, unless objects to employ it were provided. . . ."[34] The society was the ideal object to draw capital away from "profuse consumption" and reckless speculation. Perhaps, too, the necessity of providing a large enough object for surplus merchant capital explains Hamilton's inclination toward a new factory rather than piecemeal aid to smaller, existing manufacturers, incapable of quickly absorbing sufficient capital to help the security market.

The SEUM was a determined effort on Hamilton's part to integrate manufacturing into his stabilization program. The society would, if successful, constitute a very large manufactory of cotton goods. Its size and advance machinery would allow it to compete with foreign imports, particularly in providing manufactures for export. In keeping with his overall political economy, the society would stabilize security prices and lessen speculation. As he noted in his subsequent *Report on Manufactures*, the society would be eligible for government bounties if such a program were enacted. Thus, without the protective tariffs that endangered import revenues, and without other forms of aid that conflicted with his stabilization program, Hamilton could promote manufacturing. In addition, the owners and directors of the SEUM were to be the creditors and merchants upon whom Hamilton had built his program. In this way the society included all the essential elements of his political economic system.

[33] Hamilton to Duer, *Papers of Alexander Hamilton*, VIII, 300.
[34] *Gazette of the United States*, Sept. 22, 1792. Tench Coxe wrote under the pseudonym "A Freeman."

Public subscriptions to the Bank of the United States had succeeded in bringing the market out of a spring slump and inciting a
long summer upswing in prices.[35] When Hamilton released the prospectus for the society in August 1791, the bank's impact had
diminished substantially. Employing a twofold thrust to stabilize
the market and raise prices, he used treasury funds and this promise of a new investment field to support the stock prices. The prospectus described the SEUM as "a mean of public prosperity and an
instrument of profit to adventurers in the enterprise. . . ." The
document foreshadowed the basic line of argument in the *Report
on Manufactures* regarding industrial development. Regarding the
speculative market, Hamilton added that the society "at the same
time, affords a prospect of an enhancement of the value of the
debt; by giving it a new and additional employment and utility."
Finally, the prospectus and the charter itself required that "all subscriptions . . . shall be payable, one half in funded six percent stock
of the United States, or in three percent stock."[36]

Hamilton's choice of William Duer to head SEUM only reinforced its essential character. Duer, the "Prince of the Speculators"
and the great bull in the market, was heavily involved in the speculative market. He had participated in the implementation of
Hamilton's fiscal program as assistant treasury secretary; his resignation was due in part to his desire to remain in New York, one of
the centers of the creditors and security speculation, when the government moved to Philadelphia.[37] Although he knew nothing about
manufacturing, Duer's knowledge of Hamilton's fiscal program and
contacts with large merchant-creditors made him the ideal choice
for Hamilton's purposes. He brought his fellow "adventurers" into
the directorate of the society, which became in effect the headquarters of the "Six per-cent Club." According to the SEUM's definitive scholar, "a speculative spirit was strong in the whole group,"
while "in manufactures they had little experience." Nevertheless,
launching the SEUM served its purpose, ephemerally at least. It

[35] Davis, *Essays in the History of Corporations*, I, 373–74.
[36] Prospectus of the Society for Establishing Useful Manufactures, *Papers of Alexander
Hamilton*, IX, 145, 148; and *Laws of the State of New Jersey* (Newark, 1800), 105.
[37] Davis, *Essays in the History of Corporations*, I, 176. According to Robert F. Jones,
William Duer "viewed his official positions as accessories to his commercial and speculative
activities" and "approached the SEUM as if it were yet another of his stock speculation . . . ."
Robert F. Jones, "William Duer and the Business of Government in the Era of the American
Revolution," *William and Mary Quarterly*, 32 (July 1975), 414, 411.

created a bull market and brought several key supporters of Hamilton's financial system into manufacturing.[38]

From the outset the speculative interests of the directors, in this instance the land upon which the SEUM would be built, conflicted with the judgments of the skilled managers over the best location. Thomas Marshall, one of those knowledgeable about manufactures, opposed the site chosen for it. He wrote to Hamilton in a vain effort to have it changed from the Passaic, favored by Duer, to his own choice, Second River. "When the Passaic is froze," he pointed out, "Land carriage for such a distance will fall heavy. . . ." The site that Marshall advocated had "almost every thing . . . to recommend its preeminence. . . ." Thus, he concluded, "I venture to differ in Opinion from others who have gone before me. . . ."[39] The choice of a location illustrates the problems of Hamilton's synthesis of merchants and creditors with manufacturing. The society's directors lacked the experience necessary to construct a manufactory. The result was bad decision-making.[40]

In spite of Hamilton's energetic efforts, the security market collapsed in March 1792. The SEUM's organizers had advanced the venture little beyond the construction phase. With the market at its nadir their attention turned toward their own financial and, in some cases, legal plight. Duer, for example, had been jailed by his creditors. Lacking a bull market, its capital embezzled by its directors, the society slowly choked. In a final attempt to salvage his plan Hamilton wrote to William Seton of the Bank of New York and requested a $5,000 loan to the SEUM. He guaranteed "*in confidence* that the Bank of New York shall suffer no diminution of its *pecuniary faculties* from any accommodations it may afford to the Society in Question." Hamilton felt his "reputation much concerned in its welfare," and pledged the "public Stock" as perfect security.[41]

It is important to note that this and other bank loans to the SEUM were exceptions to the general rule of short-term commercial credit usually extended by these institutions. The loans were made at Hamilton's specific request, backed by the treasury depart-

[38] Young, *Democratic Republicans of New York*, 170–74, 220–21; Jones, "William Duer and the Business of Government," 412; and Davis, *Essays in the History of Corporations*, I, 370–73, 390–97, 278.

[39] Thomas Marshall to Hamilton, Oct. 2, 1791, *Papers of Alexander Hamilton*, IX, 268. See also Davis, *Essays in the History of Corporations*, I, 402–03, 408, 423.

[40] Mitchell, *Alexander Hamilton: The National Adventure*, 197–98.

[41] Hamilton to Seton, May 25, 1792, *Papers of Alexander Hamilton*, XI, 425.

ment, and therefore did not represent a general source of capital for manufacturers. Seton's reply to Hamilton reflected the special character of this loan. "Be assured My Dear Sir," he wrote, "they [the bank directors] have so much confidence in any measure pointed out by you, & take so much pleasure in promoting your Views . . . that by complying with your wishes, they have not even an opportunity of retaliating the obligations this Institution is under to you."[42]

The society's declining fortunes brought much advice from Hamilton, but little more. He appointed the French architect, Pierre L'Enfant, to design the SEUM's plant. The latter's grandiose plans led the society's new manager, Peter Colt, to complain strongly of the disruption caused by L'Enfant's presence. "An *English Manufacturer*," he insisted, "cannot bring himself to believe that a *French Gentleman* can possibly know anything respecting manufactures."[43] Hamilton's appointments to the society were inconsistent and often poor. Manufacturing was simply not his forte.

When it peacefully passed into oblivion in 1796, there remained only $19,542 of the society's original subscriptions of $600,000. Although Hamilton's funding program endured, and his central banking system survived a decade of Republican rule, the society died prior to the conclusion of Washington's second term of office. The SEUM's failure was a result of incompetence in both conception and management. It had alienated public opinion, and no manufacturing society was chartered for two years after its demise. The SEUM provided another rallying point at which the Republicans could organize American manufacturers against Hamilton's policies, another symbol upon which frustrated manufacturers could focus their wrath.[44] It had alienated the small-scale manufacturers and given little help to larger entrepreneurs who needed capital.

If the SEUM was, as Jacob E. Cooke has argued persuasively, "a practical demonstration of the arguments that would be included in the Report on Manufactures,"[45] then a reappraisal of that famous

[42] Seton to Hamilton, June 25, 1792, *ibid.*, 566–67. Herman Krooss, "Financial Institutions," *The Growth of the Seaport Cities, 1790–1825,* ed. David T. Gilchrist (Charlottesville, 1967), 122.
[43] Peter Colt to Hamilton, May 7, 1793, *Papers of Alexander Hamilton*, XIV, 420.
[44] Davis, *Essays in the History of Corporations*, I, 450–51, 480; II, 276.
[45] Jacob E. Cooke, "Tench Coxe, Alexander Hamilton, and the Encouragement of American Manufactures," *William and Mary Quarterly,* 32 (July 1975), 380. See also Cole, ed., *Industrial and Commercial Correspondence,* 231–32.

document may be in order. The report itself reveals a lack of sympathy for the problems of manufacturers and an insensitivity toward the realities that the manufacturers faced. Hamilton directed the report toward the kind of men who would own and control the SEUM.

The report's origins are usually traced to January 15, 1790, when a message from President Washington extolling the utility of domestic manufacturing induced the House to order a manufacturing report from Hamilton. There are indications, however, that it was not so much this House directive as the security market's troubles and the SEUM that actually prompted the report. Within two weeks of the directive the treasury department dispatched a circular requesting information on manufactures to Benjamin Lincoln, to the directors of the Manufacturing Society of Philadelphia, and possibly to other societies. Lincoln never received it, nor did Hamilton attempt to ascertain why there had been no response from him, though he regularly corresponded with Lincoln on treasury business. The Philadelphia society did, however, receive the circular and in February 1790, Tench Coxe responded on its behalf with an extensive discussion of domestic manufactures. Possibly this response, together with previous communications from Coxe, induced Hamilton to hire him as assistant secretary and charge him with responsibility for collecting information on manufactures. Hamilton himself did not take up the matter of the report again until 1791—over a year after the House directive.[46]

Apparently at the time of the directive and for a year or more thereafter Hamilton gave it a low priority while he worked to establish government fiscal arrangements. This impression is strengthened by a comparison with the time that elapsed between other House directives to Hamilton for reports and their completion. He presented the funding and bank reports approximately four months after the relevant directives; this speed is not surprising since he had been planning the fiscal program and bank for a decade. In the 1780s, however, he planned no manufacturing program, and the *Report on Manufactures* arrived some twenty-four months after the directive. What is even more striking about this delay is that the House ordered the bank report eight months *after*

[46] See Hamilton to Lincoln, Jan. 25, 1790, and June 8, 1790, *Papers of Alexander Hamilton*, VI, 207–08, 460; and Cooke, "Tench Coxe," 370, 373.

it ordered a manufacturing report, but Hamilton still presented the bank report one year before the one on manufacturing.[47]

While Hamilton attended to his fiscal program, Coxe, an avid proponent of domestic industry, twice sent out requests for manufacturing information in May 1790, and March 1791. At some point, probably February 1791, he drafted a report for Hamilton's perusal. Sometime thereafter Hamilton revised Coxe's draft, made some minor additions, and put it aside until he formulated the plans for the SEUM. Many of the basic arguments of the report were first articulated in the SEUM prospectus. The treasury did not receive many letters concerning manufactures until September 1791. The release of the final report coincided with the legal birth of the SEUM in December. In the report Hamilton made an explicit plea for federal aid to the SEUM.[48]

Why after one and a half years of little or no action upon the report did Hamilton suddenly begin a concerted effort to complete it? His general unresponsiveness to domestic manufacturers, his lack of interest in existing enterprises, and his prolonged delay in obeying the House directive support the inference that the catalyst of the report had to be the development of the SEUM. If the SEUM largely prompted the report and security market problems largely prompted the SEUM, then the exigencies of the stabilization program seem, once again, to be the ultimate determinants of Hamilton's activities at the treasury.

[47] Williams also stresses this time lag. Williams, Contours of American History, 166–67. Jacob E. Cooke explains the hiatus as a product of the "extensive research that went into [the report's] preparation, including hundreds of letters soliciting information on the state of manufactures in every part of the Union." Jacob E. Cooke, "The Federalist Age: A Reappraisal," American History Retrospect and Prospect, ed. George Athan Billias and Gerald N. Grob (New York, 1971), 129–30n. There is, however, no evidence beyond his correspondence with Benjamin Lincoln and general circular immediately after the House directive that Hamilton did anything further concerning the report until February 1791. He did not fruitfully solicit information until June 1791—eighteen months after the directive. As to the "hundreds of letters," there were only four different solicitations of manufacturing information, two by Hamilton and two by Coxe, and less than fifty responses to them including enclosures in letters to Hamilton. Ninety percent of these responses were to the final solicitation in June 1791. Hamilton personally corresponded with no manufacturer concerning the report. Cooke himself observed that these letters from manufacturers "did not significantly influence" the final report. His explanation thus leaves the period from February 1790 to May 1791 a mystery.

[48] For Coxe's requests for manufacturing information, see Cooke, "Tench Coxe," 371; Papers of Alexander Hamilton, VI, 209n; and Joseph Whipple to Hamilton, June 4, 1791, ibid., VIII, 434. The treasury received three letters in response to these inquiries: Lincoln to Hamilton, May 25, 1790, ibid., VI, 430, 460; Nathaniel Hazard to Hamilton, March 9, 1791, ibid., 166–67; and Whipple to Hamilton, June 4, 1791, ibid., 434–36. Hamilton's June 1791 circular received some forty responses. Ibid., IX, 162–63, 177–80, 193–94, 275–81, 300–03, 323–63, 372–74, 436–49.

Coxe's draft differed from Hamilton's report in important ways. In general, Hamilton expanded Coxe's defense of the usefulness of manufacturing while revising Coxe's concrete proposals to conform to his stabilization program. Coxe's draft concentrated upon developing a market in which domestic manufacturing could flourish. Unlike Hamilton, who depended to a great extent upon existing financial intermediaries to provide manufacturing capital, Coxe mentioned the funding program and United States Bank only as stabilizers of an expanded circulating medium. Instead he sought to stimulate investment in manufactures through the creation of a profitable market for domestically manufactured products. To create such a market raw material costs would have to be reduced, an internal transportation system built, incentives offered to potential investors, and a tariff enacted for protection from foreign imports. Within such an environment manufacturers would accumulate larger resources and profits and possibly attract capital from commerce or land speculation.[49]

A secure, profitable market is fundamental to the process of industrial development. Without access to such a market no substantial capital could be maintained in manufacturing; no one would invest in nor long sustain ventures that promised no return. Thus Coxe presented six proposals for securing a market for domestic manufacturers: a protective tariff on manufactured imports, outright prohibitions of some such imports, abolition of all duties on coastal trade, government construction of roads and canals, direct federal loans, and land grants to manufacturing entrepreneurs from a federal reserve of one-half million acres.[50] These were substantial proposals that, if implemented, would have provided a solid ground for American manufacturing. Coxe stressed the development of an internal market system to wean the domestic economy from foreign manufactures. The land grant proposal anticipated the chief method by which the government subsidized railroad con-

[49] Report on the Subject of Manufactures, Tench Coxe Draft, 1790, ibid., X, 16–18, 20–22. Cooke argues that "when the lineage of the Report on Manufactures is traced, the major threads are found to lead to Tench Coxe." He also credits Coxe "with both the initial idea and plans for [SEUM's] actualization." Cooke, "Tench Coxe," 380. The differences between the Coxe draft and Hamilton's report may be stressed because Hamilton wrote several major drafts of the report, which indicate his own arguments for the development of manufacturing. Coxe wrote Hamilton that the SEUM's plan had been "devised by you," that is Hamilton, and offered to "take but a single share." Coxe to Hamilton, May 20, 1792, Papers of Alexander Hamilton, XI, 406.

[50] Coxe Draft, Papers of Alexander Hamilton, X, 17–18, 20–21. For Coxe's loan proposal see the first draft of the report which Cooke has discovered to be part of Coxe's draft. Ibid., 47–49; and Cooke, "Tench Coxe," 372n.

struction in the latter half of the nineteenth century. During the 1790s it was land that attracted foreign, especially Dutch, capital to the United States. Thus, if used as a premium, a land reserve promised to be a strong inducement for investment in manufactures. Yet, not only did Hamilton reject the land bounty, but he rejected or emasculated all of Coxe's proposals for stimulating manufacturing and attached himself instead to proposals that Coxe had rejected. A careful analysis of the report demonstrates Hamilton's selective revision of Coxe's draft.

Hamilton began with his justifiably renowned defense of manufacturing development and a systematic discussion of contemporary theories of political economy. Although he attempted to demonstrate the interrelationship of agriculture and manufacturing, he neglected to deal at all with the problems that enlarged manufactures would present to merchants importing British manufactures and, more importantly, to the revenues those imports provided for his fiscal programs. Unlike Coxe and other manufacturing advocates, who always strove to demonstrate the benefits manufacturing would bestow upon most merchants, Hamilton did not confront this central issue. His neglect is comprehensible if one assumes that he planned no measures that would interfere with those merchants. Indeed, the enterprise he had in mind was to be composed of those merchant-creditors to the exclusion of existing manufacturers.[51]

After the introductory remarks Hamilton analyzed domestic manufacturing. He discounted the complaints of the manufacturers, who had written of labor shortages, high wage rates and capital deficiencies on the grounds that they "are not sufficient to prevent the advantageous prosecution of many very useful and extensive manufactories."[52] Historians generally interpret Hamilton's optimism about manufactures as the device of a great advocate of industrialization rallying his forces. To American manufacturers, however, swamped by British imports, debts, and high labor costs, such optimism tended to undermine the urgency of their demands for aid. Perhaps his optimism referred less to the manufacturers than to backers of the SEUM who possessed the capital and the political power to overcome, at least temporarily, many of these difficulties.

[51] Report on Manufactures, *Papers of Alexander Hamilton*, X, 230–69.
[52] *Ibid.*, 269. See also Davis, *Essays in the History of Corporations*, I, 358n.

In many respects capital was the crucial issue. Adequate capital would allow manufacturers to purchase machines to assuage labor shortages and generally expand their enterprises. But Hamilton's proposals for capital aid to manufacturers were dubious at best. Indeed, he seemed to have assumed that those interested in manufacturing had access to or already possessed the necessary capital. Such assumptions would be consistent with the report's orientation toward the SEUM. Operating upon these assumptions, Hamilton described three major capital resources: domestic banks, the funded debt, and foreign investment. The first resource promised to be of little use to manufacturers. The banks of the last quarter of the eighteenth century were basically a "clubbing together" of merchant capital to discount short-term notes during intra-voyage periods. As Bray Hammond observes, these banks "specialized in short term self-extinguishing credit, and exercised a function that was almost purely monetary." The average loan period was thirty to forty-five days. Even the United States Bank extended credit for only sixty days. A manufacturer required long-term loans to purchase land and plant equipment, and guarantee labor. To erect a factory, install machines, purchase materials, hire laborers, make products and market them were not sixty-day operations. Manufacturers found it difficult if not impossible to obtain money from banks.[53] Banks could not serve as a source of manufacturing capital, although they, as Hamilton noted, did facilitate commercial transactions and provide credit and, in effect, capital to merchants. Hamilton's orientation again appears to be toward the merchant owners of the SEUM who did have access to bank capital, and not the manufacturers.

He designated the funded debt as the second major source of capital. Government securities, "usually held by monied men," provided a capital asset to its holder that was easily liquidated for investment purposes. He argued that this transfer through taxes had increased the "active capital" in the nation and had fueled an economic recovery in industry and commerce. Most of this capital, however, went into speculation and the importation of British

[53] Bray Hammond, "Long and Short Term Credit in Early American Banking," *Quarterly Journal of Economics*, XLIX (Nov. 1934), 79–81, 89; Fritz Redlich, *The Molding of American Banking: Men and Ideas* (2 vols., New York, 1951), I, 10–18; Krooss, "Financial Institutions," 106–07, 115, 119; and Bray Hammond, *Banks and Politics in America From the Revolution to the Civil War* (Princeton, 1957), 75. As late as 1812 the New York Manufacturing Society sought a bank charter because of the difficulty of borrowing money from existing banks. Krooss, "Financial Institutions," 124.

manufactured goods, thus causing manufacturers to complain bitterly. Although Hamilton cited these investments as the rationale for the movement of some of this capital into manufacturing, the creditor, who was "possessed of a sum . . . ready to be applied to any purpose, to be embarked in any enterprize, which appear to him eligible," invested his "active capital" in commerce, land, or securities.[54]

An investor's criteria of "eligibility" are the profitability and security of his investment. If an enterprise offered a profitable and secure return, then a portion of the active capital might well flow into it. But since creditors found that commerce and speculation in land or stock adequately met these criteria, Hamilton's proposal proffered no real capital to the manufacturer, whose profits were marginal and uncertain. As long as manufacturing's rate of return was below that of other enterprises, then it was not eligible for investment. For the capital generated by his economic program to flow into manufactures, Hamilton would have had to advocate and enact a strong protective tariff or general embargo to make the importation of foreign manufactures in particular, and commerce in general, much less profitable while securing a profitable market for domestic products. This action would have struck a debilitating blow to the businesses of those merchants whom he considered the foundation of economic stability. Moreover, it would cripple tariff revenues and undermine his financial system. Hamilton simply could not condone such a tariff.

The third source of manufacturing capital, in Hamilton's view, was foreign investment. Starting with the assumption that a capital surplus existed in parts of Europe, he argued that "deficiency of employment" or "a very material difference in profit . . . operate to produce a transfer of foreign capital to the United States." Although this transfer was "induced merely with views to speculations in the funds, it may afterwards be rendered subservient to the interests of Agriculture, Commerce, & Manufacturers."[55] Foreign capital had largely found outlets in security speculation, commerce, and land purchases because they were the most profitable outlets for investment in America. The capital from Britain served chiefly to finance imports of their manufactured goods and exports of American raw materials. In short, foreign capital actually impeded

[54] Report on Manufactures, *Papers of Alexander Hamilton*, X, 277–81.
[55] Ibid., 275–76.

domestic manufacturing. Why would British investors, the greatest potential source of foreign capital, finance the development of competitors to their own industry, especially since American manufactures were not nearly as profitable as British? Certainly their government sought to retain its monopoly in world manufacturing.[56]

Despite Hamilton's expressed desire for government "incitement and patronage" of manufacturing through intervention in the marketplace, he made no proposal to insure capital for manufacturers. Once he established the general availability of capital funds in the nation, Hamilton left it entirely to the workings of the market to redirect its flow into domestic industry. Unlike Coxe or, later, Albert Gallatin, Hamilton did not suggest direct government loans to the manufacturers.[57] His fiscal priorities proscribed any such aid. He could rely only upon the "invisible hand" to put capital into the manufacturers' purses.

In the remainder of the report Hamilton discussed the manufacturing market itself. As in analyzing labor and capital problems, Hamilton denied any pressing need for the protective tariffs and prohibitions sought by manufacturers. Explaining that transportation costs, cheaper raw materials and existing revenue tariffs tended to "wear a beneficial aspect toward the manufactures of the Country," he advocated "pecuniary bounties" as "one of the most efficacious means of encouraging manufactures, and . . . in some views, the best." Yet on the grounds of preventing fraud, he excluded "every private family, in which the manufacture was incidentally carried on" and those manufacturers for whom the making of the article was not "a regular trade."[58] This exclusion might have been used to prevent the payment of bounties to many people whose efforts had a great potential for the industrial development of America. Hamilton's method would have aided only those enterprises such as the SEUM, large enough to qualify. Even without such limitations, bounties lacked the effectiveness of a protective tariff or prohibition. In his draft report Coxe rejected bounties

[56] The clearest illustrations of this antagonism were the yearly reports of Phineas Bond, the British consul at Philadelphia, expressing the English desire to maintain their monopoly of manufactures and their concerns over possible American development. *Annual Report of the American Historical Association for the Year 1896* (2 vols., Washington, 1897), I, 553–54, 581–83, 630–54.

[57] Report on Manufactures, U.S. Congress, *New American State Papers: Manufactures*, I, 124–30.

[58] Report on Manufactures, *Papers of Alexander Hamilton*, X, 291–92, 296–98, 336–37.

because he believed that they would do little to aid manufacturers. Twenty years later Albert Gallatin in his *Report on Manufactures* also rejected bounties as "more applicable to articles exported than to those manufactured for home consumption."[59] Yet Hamilton made them the centerpiece of his *Report on Manufactures*.

In his final argument for bounties Hamilton noted that "the duty upon the importation of an imported article can no otherwise aid the domestic production of it, than by giving the latter greater advantages in the home market." However "it ca[n] have no influence upon the advantageous sale of the article produced, in foreign markets; no tendency, there[fore], to promote its exportation."[60] In other words, by acting upon the domestic market alone protective tariffs did not benefit and would probably injure many merchants. Bounties had no comparable effect. They could in fact help promote the exportation of goods and serve as the link between merchants and a manufacturing company like the SEUM. Their capital could build the manufactory and their ships would export its products—subsidized by government bounties. Hamilton's emphasis upon bounties was not without good reason.

In proposing tariff changes he was cautious because the tariff directly involved both government revenues and merchants importing manufactures. In reference to iron manufactures he followed Coxe's suggestions about raising the duties on steel, nails, and iron products. He rejected any increase in the duties on brass, lead, coal, skins, hemp, and flax. With the exceptions of firearms and starch, the duties that he would have increased still remained below or at 10 percent, in no sense a protective level. He modified Coxe's suggestion about eliminating all duties on raw materials used by American manufacturers by refusing to reduce the duties "where the material is itself, an object of general or extensive consumption, and a fit and productive source of revenue. . . ." Thus any raw material used in manufacturing, regardless of its importance, would continue to be taxed to support the government. His concern for any possible loss of tariff revenues, if a domestic manufacture replaced a foreign import, led him to state that an "indemnification can easily be found . . . out of the manufacture itself. . . ."[61] Bound

[59] U.S. Congress, *New American State Papers: Manufactures*, I, 130.
[60] Report on Manufactures, *Papers of Alexander Hamilton*, X, 300.
[61] *Ibid.*, 313–27, 306, 337.

by his fiscal program Hamilton thus would have had to tax any manufacturer who did succeed in "lessening" an imported article's consumption by increasing his own sales.

In discussing Coxe's plan for government construction of canals and roads Hamilton hedged in making a commitment. "[I]t were to be wished," he wrote, "that there was no doubt of the power of the National Government to lend its aid on a comprehensive plan." He described the "Jealousies" and "local or partial spirit" which would interfere with any comprehensive plan.[62] He then dropped the matter as a plan dashed on the rocks of partisan politics. Hamilton's reticence about transportation aid followed priorities he had set for government revenues. To expend large sums of money on internal improvements would have weakened his fiscal program. Thus Hamilton allowed the proposal to pass without further discussion or future efforts to promote it.

He made no mention of Coxe's proposals to abolish duties on coastal trade and to grant land to investors in manufacturing. The former action was doubtless a product of Hamilton's concern for government revenues derived from coastal duties. Hamilton did employ Coxe's suggestion of a board "for promoting Arts, Agriculture, Manufactures and Commerce." The commissioners of the board would encourage invention, emigration of skilled workmen, and importation of machinery. Since he planned to commit revenue from land sales to the sinking fund, Hamilton could not propose a land reserve to support the board's activities. He instead suggested financing it out of any surplus revenues from his newly proposed tariff structure. Those revenues, however, would only become available after "a competent substitute" for any loss of duties now "pledged for the public debt" had been subtracted from the surplus.[63] Thus before one dollar from any source could go toward the board for manufactures, the public debt would have to be fully serviced.

In summary, Hamilton rejected Coxe's proposals for the abolition of duties of coastal trade, government loans to manufacturers, and land grants to manufacturing entrepreneurs. He advocated bounties and declined to eliminate duties on raw materials if such duties contributed significantly to government revenues. He de-

[62] *Ibid.*, 310–11.
[63] *Ibid.*, 337–40; and Coxe draft, *ibid.*, 47.

murred from any efforts to foster federal construction of an internal transportation system. He proposed tariff changes that were primarily revenue measures. While endorsing Coxe's plan for a board to promote manufactures, he offered to finance it out of "surplus" revenues. Since the government debt commanded nearly half of the revenues, and Hamilton had to borrow $2.5 million in 1792 just to meet expenses, any board would have been without funds even if one were created.

When the House received and tabled Hamilton's report, they provoked no protest from its author. Hamilton, who spared no effort to enact his other reports, did nothing to promote the *Report on Manufactures* as a comprehensive program. What energies he invested in manufactures went to the SEUM. Several of the suggested tariff revisions were incorporated in his proposal to boost revenues in the face of government deficits. In it he pointed out that "our Merchants . . . procure the supplies, which they import from abroad, upon much more cheap, and advantageous terms than heretofore; a circumstance which must always alleviate to them the pressure of somewhat higher rates of duties. . . ."[64] In other words, because the prices of foreign manufactures had declined, an increase in duties upon them would not affect the general price level. Sales would continue at the present volume, government revenues would be unimpaired, and domestic manufacturers would reap little benefit from the higher duties. The report's only offspring, the SEUM, was stillborn.

The relationship of Hamilton to American manufacturing was multifaceted. His ties to manufacturers were first strained, then severed by conflicts between their interests and his program. The SEUM and the *Report on Manufactures* appear to have been geared as much toward the merchant-creditors and the securities market as toward manufacturing. Those measures a government commonly enacted in a private enterprise economy to stimulate manufacturing, favorable tariffs, direct loans and grants, and internal improvements, Hamilton could not attempt. As his political economy compelled him to act against the manufacturers' interests, many responded by deserting his party and opposing his program.

Recent scholarship has reassessed and revised the traditional view of the Jeffersonian Republicans as exclusively agrarians. They

[64] Report Relative to Additional Supplies for the Ensuing Year, *ibid.*, XI, 142.

appealed to merchants and manufacturers as well as farmers. As this aspect of the traditional view of early national political divisions has been revised, perhaps now the other aspect, which holds Hamilton to be the political leader of manufacturers, can also be reassessed.[65] This paper has endeavored to begin the task of distinguishing the historical Hamilton from the historians' Hamilton.

[65] For suggestive leads toward revising the traditional dichotomy between Thomas Jefferson and Hamilton over manufactures, see Merrill D. Peterson, *Thomas Jefferson and the New Nation* (New York, 1970), 459, 514–15.

Thomas Jefferson and Commercial Policy, 1783-1793

Merrill D. Peterson*

On December 16, 1793, just two weeks before he resigned the office of Secretary of State, Thomas Jefferson submitted to Congress his Report on the Privileges and Restrictions on the Commerce of the United States in Foreign Countries.[1] The Report had a curious history. It was made in compliance with a resolution of the House of Representatives in February 1791. Jefferson worked it up in the ensuing months and planned to present it when Congress convened in the fall; but his colleague in the Treasury Department, Alexander Hamilton, opposed it "violently," thinking the threat of commercial warfare on Great Britain, which the Report carried, would wreck the negotiations then in process with the British minister. Jefferson agreed to defer the Report.[2] It lapsed into the catalepsy of the British negotiations. A year passed; Jefferson revised the Report and prepared to submit it at the close of the Second Congress in February 1793. But the timing troubled him. His recommendations would almost certainly get a better hearing from the Third Congress, more heavily freighted with Republicans, and in the interim the new French minister would have an opportunity to present the attractive commercial propositions he was thought to be bringing from Paris, thus strengthening the Secretary's case for differential treatment of the commerce of Britain and France. The Republican leadership in the House, prodded by Jefferson, decided not to call for the Report.[3]

*Mr. Peterson is a member of the Department of History, University of Virginia. This article is the revision of a paper presented at the Conference on Early American History, Williamsburg, Virginia, Oct. 9, 1964.

[1] The Report will be found in Paul L. Ford, ed., *The Writings of Thomas Jefferson* (New York, 1892-99), VI, 470-484. The best study of the background and the circumstances surrounding the Report is Vernon G. Setser, *The Commercial Reciprocity Policy of the United States, 1774-1829* (Philadelphia, 1937), chap. 4 especially.

[2] The Anas, Mar. 11, 1792, in Ford, ed., *Writings of Jefferson*, I, 186-187.

[3] To the Speaker of the House, Feb. 20, 1793, in Andrew A. Lipscomb and Albert Ellery Bergh, eds., *The Writings of Thomas Jefferson* (Washington, 1903-4), IX, 31-32.

Edmond Genêt did, indeed, propose a new and liberal treaty of commerce; but the circumstances of European war and American neutrality, combined with the Minister's own monumental ineptitude, put the project out of the way of serious discussion. Urgent problems of neutrality usurped the place previously occupied by the long-range problems of peacetime commerce. A discriminatory commercial policy was one thing in 1792, when the leading maritime powers were at peace; it was another thing in 1793, when they were at war. For it must then, whether founded in treaty or in statute, have the color of an unneutral act. Moreover, the injuries complained of by the United States as a neutral were different from the injuries to American trade in a world at peace. In the waning hours of his ministry, Jefferson must have pondered what to do with his twice deferred Report on Commerce. He finally decided to submit it, without further revision, based upon the conditions of American commerce in the year 1792.

It was a gesture of summation. The Report culminated a decade of unremitting labor to develop a national system of political economy independent of Britain, tied to France, and directed ultimately to a reign of free exchange and pacific intercourse among nations. This was, Jefferson had come to insist, "my system,"[4] and it was directly at odds with the fiscal system of the Secretary of the Treasury. The Report rested on a body of assumptions Jefferson had never fully articulated, and only suggested here, but which can be pieced together from his private letters, diplomatic correspondence, and other papers written over a period of years.

The subject, broadly stated, is the relationship of the American economy to the European world. As an agricultural-commercial nation, its internal trade undeveloped, its industrial base exceedingly narrow, the United States must cherish its navigation, penetrate foreign markets, and seek its economic well-being in the transatlantic trading area. Economic policy is inseparable from foreign policy. Trade is a weapon of diplomacy—the only potent weapon in the American armory—to be employed in pursuit of the national interest, including in that term not only the security and independence of the United States but also the widening acceptance of liberal commercial principles in the international community. "Instead of embarrassing commerce under piles of regulating laws,

[4] To George Washington, Sept. 9, 1792, in Ford, ed., *Writings of Jefferson*, VI, 103.

duties, and prohibitions," Jefferson wrote, "could it be relieved from all its shackles in all parts of the world, could every country be employed in producing that which nature has best fitted it to produce, and each be free to exchange with others mutual surplusses for mutual wants, the greatest mass possible would then be produced of those things which contribute to human life and human happiness; the numbers of mankind would be increased, and their condition bettered."[5]

Ideally, trade should be free; in fact it is burdened with monopolies and restrictions injurious to the United States and to the peace and happiness of mankind. In his Report Jefferson described these burdens, nation by nation, and drew up the balance sheet of American maritime commerce. France appeared as America's best friend. With republican France, though she was deeply troubled, the "system of free commerce" might be fairly begun. Britain appeared as the monstrous enemy. She supplied three quarters of American imports, took one half of our exports, re-exported the greater part, prohibited what she pleased, monopolized the navigation, and left everything at the hazard of executive decree. British command of American commerce held the nation on its tether. To break this dangerous connection, Jefferson proposed counter prohibitions, regulations, and duties, working reciprocally on all nations but in the necessity of the case working hardest on Britain. The inconveniences attending the introduction of this plan "are nothing when weighed against the loss of wealth and loss of force, which will follow our perseverance in the plan of indiscrimination." "Free commerce and navigation are not to be given in exchange for restrictions and vexations," Jefferson declared, "nor are they likely to produce a relaxation of them."[6] But by granting favors where favors were due, by meeting prohibitions with prohibitions, the United States might, in the course of serving its own interest, bring other nations to the liberal standard.

The sequel to the Report on Commerce is well known. This piece of unfinished business might have attracted little notice but for renewed British violence on the seas. Falling in with the turn of events, the Report set off a great congressional debate. In January, James Madison, Jefferson's collaborator in this enterprise as in so many others, introduced a series of resolutions based on the Report.[7] France was stamped on their

[5] Report on Commerce, *ibid.,* 479.
[6] *Ibid.,* 479, 483, 480.
[7] For the resolutions and debate, see U. S., Congress, 3d Congress, 1st session, in

face, the Federalists charged. The movement for commercial discrimination stemmed from the old unreasoning hostility to Britain, revived now solely for political effect. Hamilton's spokesman in the House, William Loughton Smith of South Carolina, decried "the impracticability and Quixotism of an attempt by violence, on the part of this young country, to break through the fetters which the universal policy of nations imposes on their intercourse with each other."[8] Whatever the disadvantages of the British trade, Federalists said, they were more than offset by the rewards in capital and credit, federal revenue, and dependable markets and supplies. But as relations with Britain deteriorated, chances for passage of the resolutions improved. Then, unfortunately for the Republicans, the deterioration was too rapid, bringing the two countries to the verge of war, causing the resolutions to be put aside in favor of an emergency embargo, and leading finally to the mission of John Jay, whose famous treaty consummated the British-centered policy of the Federalists—an astounding defeat for the Jeffersonian system.

The Report of 1793 led nowhere: it was epilogue rather than prologue. Never fairly put to the test, the Jeffersonian policy can only be appraised in the light of antecedent experience. While the underlying principle of this policy had been widely shared by America's leaders, with only shadings of difference, from the Revolution until the inauguration of the Hamiltonian system, no one had been so long or so deeply committed to it as Thomas Jefferson. It had given coherence and direction to all his work and thought on national affairs during the previous decade. How he came to this conception of commercial policy, the difficulties he encountered, the successive phases through which it passed before the eclipse of 1794, is an important but often neglected chapter in the early history of the American nation.

When Jefferson entered Congress in 1783 the prospects of American commerce, perforce of American wealth and power, were very uncertain. From the first, the hopes of the new nation had been tied to the kite of commercial freedom. The United States stood ready to trade freely with all comers who would recognize its independence and enter into liberal

---

Joseph Gales, comp., *The Debates and Proceedings in the Congress of the United States* . . . (Washington, 1834-56), IV, 155 ff.; hereafter cited as *Annals of Congress*.

[8] Jan. 13, 1794, *ibid.*, 196.

treaties. "Our plan is commerce," *Common Sense* had declared, "and that, well attended to, will secure us the peace and friendship of all Europe; because it is the interest of all Europe to have America as a free port. Her trade will always be a protection. . . ."[9] Acting on this calculation, Congress, in 1776, adopted the *i*'plan of treaties."[10] It failed of conspicuous success except in the case of France, where, however, the treaty of commerce was coupled with a treaty of alliance involving political commitments inconsistent with the "commerce only" principle of the "plan of treaties." That plan, for all the troubles it encountered, was the natural offspring of the union 'between revolutionary necessity and revolutionary aspiration. Seen in the light of the policies of nations, rather than of their forms of government, the American Revolution announced the dissolution of mercantilism and the liberation of trade, together with a new openness, trust, and pacific temper in all dealings among nations. It was this emphasis on commercial freedom that made the revolutionary event and the simultaneous publication of *The Wealth of Nations* something more than a coincidence; that gave substance to the Earl of Shelburne's abortive project for a commercial union between Britain and the United States at the conclusion of the war; and that conveyed the message of the American Revolution to many enlightened Europeans who, while they valued commercial freedom, either had little use or little hope for republican government.[11]

The "plan of treaties" was the first lineal ancestor of Jefferson's 1793 Report on Commerce. He had no responsibility for it, of course, and had not thought much on commercial questions before he returned to Congress after an absence of seven years; but he was in complete accord with the spirit of the standing policy. With the conclusion of the war, it was thought that nations that had been reluctant to treat with a rebel government would be eager to treat with a legitimate one whose only interest was mutual trade and profit. To take advantage of these friendly dispositions, Congress had appointed a three-man European Commission.

[9] Philip S. Foner, ed., *The Complete Writings of Thomas Paine* (New York, 1945), I, 20.

[10] See the discussions in Setser, *Commercial Reciprocity Policy*, chap. 2, and Felix Gilbert, *To The Farewell Address: Ideas of Early American Foreign Policy* (Princeton, 1961), chap. 3.

[11] See, in general, Vincent T. Harlow, *The Founding of the Second British Empire, 1763-1793*, I (London, 1952); Richard Koebner, *Empire* (Cambridge, Eng., 1961); and Carl Ludwig Lokke, *France and the Colonial Question: A Study of Contemporary French Opinion, 1763-1801* (New York, 1932).

Jefferson was soon engaged in drafting a report on their work and revising their instructions.[12] The undertaking had assumed a new importance. Lacking the old privileges of trade within the empire, the Americans, in 1783, had secured few privileges of trade outside of it, and so they suffered the same colonial dependence as before the Revolution. It became increasingly evident that Britain, though she had lost the colonies, was determined to hold the Americans in commercial vassalage. The Earl of Sheffield demonstrated how easily it could be done.[13] Exploit the feebleness of the Confederacy. Exploit the British merchants' mastery of the American market. Above all, destroy the American carrying trade by imposing the navigation law that had nurtured its growth within the imperial system. The crippling blow fell in July 1783. An order in council excluded American ships from the British West Indies; and this, together with the restoration of old restrictions in the French and Spanish colonies, closed off the most profitable branch of American trade.[14]

There were several possible lines of attack on the problem, and in different contexts Jefferson advocated all of them. When moral and political considerations were foremost in his mind, he held up the ideal of a hermit nation. "Were I to indulge my own theory," he wrote characteristically, "I should wish them [the Americans] to practice neither commerce nor navigation, but to stand with respect to Europe precisely on the footing of China. We should thus avoid wars, and all our citizens would be husbandmen." He thus expressed his sense of the unique opportunities of American society, which modified the orthodox canons of European political economy. "But this is theory only," he hastened to add, "and a theory which the servants of America are not at liberty to follow."[15] Foreign commerce was a necessity, all the more so if America stuck to its agricultural calling; and he never let the dreamy ideal control his search

[12] Report on Letters from the American Ministers in Europe, [Dec. 20, 1783], and Instructions to the Commissioners for Negotiating Treaties of Amity and Commerce, May 7, 1784, in Julian P. Boyd and others, eds., *The Papers of Thomas Jefferson* (Princeton, 1950—), VI, 393-400, VII, 266-271.

[13] Earl of Sheffield [John Baker Holroyd], *Observations on the Commerce of the United States . . .* (London, 1783).

[14] See, in general, Merrill Jensen, *The New Nation: A History of the United States During the Confederation, 1781-1789* (New York, 1950), chap. 7; and Curtis P. Nettels, *The Emergence of a National Economy, 1775-1815* (New York, 1962), chap. 3.

[15] To G. K. van Hogendorp, Oct. 13, 1785, in Boyd and others, eds., *Papers of Jefferson*, VIII, 633.

for a viable system of political economy. A variation on the insular approach looked to the development of internal commerce. The Americans are peculiarly blessed and have no need of foreign commerce, no cause to incur its vices, enmities, and debaucheries, Richard Price counseled in 1784. "They are spread over a great continent, and they make a world within themselves."[16] The English radical was gifted with prophecy. In time the Americans would realize the conception of a great home market —"a world within itself"—but few had as much as a glimpse of it in 1784. Jefferson was a warm advocate of internal commerce; he was thinking a good deal about it at this time in connection with Virginia's efforts to open arteries of trade with the trans-Allegheny West. Yet, like nearly everyone else, he regarded inland commerce as an accessory of foreign commerce.[17] Still another strategy called for the creation of a counteracting system of mercantilist restrictions in the United States. Jefferson was not averse to retaliatory measures of this kind. In the condition of American affairs he did not believe trade should be left to regulate itself, though that was his theoretical preference of course. He helped to draft the congressional address of April 30, 1784, recommending that the states "vest Congress with so much power over their commerce as will enable them to retaliate on any nation who may wish to grasp it on unequal terms; and to enable them . . . to pass something like the British navigation act."[18] The Confederacy must be strengthened primarily, in his opinion, for the purpose of regulating foreign commerce. But the states held back, preventing a truly national system, and regulation by the states severally raised more problems than it solved. Madison and some other nationalists inclined to believe that so long as the vacuum of commercial power existed in the Confederacy there was really nothing to do but fill it.[19] Jefferson, always sanguine, did not—not yet anyway—take this desperate view. Although the front door to commercial regulations was closed, the back door was already opened. In its power to make treaties the United States

[16] Richard Price, *Observations on the Importance of the American Revolution, and the Means of Making It a Benefit to the World* (London, 1784), 62.

[17] See Jefferson to George Washington, Mar. 15, 1784, in Boyd and others, eds., *Papers of Jefferson*, VII, 25-27; and the observations in Joseph Dorfman, *The Economic Mind in American Civilization* (New York, 1946-49), I, 248-251.

[18] To Horatio Gates, May 7, 1784, in Boyd and others, eds., *Papers of Jefferson*, VII, 225.

[19] James Madison to Jefferson, Apr. 25, 1784, and the note on Jay's attitude, *ibid.*, 123, 470.

could act as "one Nation,"[20] and so acting not only develop its commercial system but strengthen the bonds of Union as well.

On May 7, 1784, Jefferson was appointed to the European Commission, replacing John Jay. At the same time Congress approved the revised instructions he had had a hand in drafting and would soon convey to the other commissioners, Benjamin Franklin and John Adams, in Paris. These instructions, more explicit than any to precede them, carried forward the liberal policy with some modifications. The plan was founded on the principle of the "most favored nation," which only offered a guarantee against treatment *less* favorable than was accorded another nation. The principle was European, far short of the American objective, as stated in previous instructions, of "the most perfect equality and reciprocity."[21] Although the Commission was authorized to go as far toward the ultimate goal as conditions might permit, it was recognized that the "most favored nation" formula offered the only realistic starting point for negotiations. Mercantilist prejudice and practice, deeply embedded in the European states, had to be reckoned with. Jefferson willingly accepted this concession to expediency, yet was steady in his pursuit of the goal. With respect to the American colonies of European nations, however, trade was to be put on a reciprocal basis if at all possible; at the very least United States ships and productions should be admitted into direct trade with these possessions. This was asking a good deal when scarcely a foreign port in the Western Hemisphere was open to American vessels. Other provisions covered the rights of enemy aliens and neutral carriers in time of war—matters of pacific and humanitarian import under the law of nations, in which Jefferson built on the work already begun by Franklin.

Congress authorized commercial treaties with sixteen European states, as well as the Barbary powers. The decision to pursue this general European plan was of considerable importance. Freedom from British domination was to be found in the widening of markets. A strong minority in Congress, primarily New England men, advocated a different approach, one which would give precedence to a commercial treaty with Britain.

[20] For the use of this phrase, see the Report of Dec. 20, 1783, and the Instructions of May 1784, previously cited *ibid.*, VI, 394, VII, 267, and Jefferson's Notes for Consideration of the Commissioners, VII, 478-479.

[21] Compare Instructions of Oct. 29, 1783, with those of May 7, 1784, *ibid.*, VII, 265, 267.

The restoration of the British trade to something like its old footing was so vital, in their opinion, that it should not be complicated with other matters infinitely less important; and no doubt some objected to the European plan because it would pivot on France, thereby increasing that nation's influence in American affairs.[22] Jefferson opposed the re-establishment of a partial connection with Britain, even assuming, in the face of mounting evidence to the contrary, the London government was amenable. He was well aware of the importance of a British treaty both for itself and for the over-all plan, for if Britain could be drawn into the paths of progress, other nations would likely follow.[23] But Britain must come on the terms of the European-wide plan. Nor did Jefferson favor a preferential status for France. "Our interest calls for a perfect equality in our conduct towards these two nations," he wrote to Adams in 1785, "but no preferences any where."[24] He envisioned the French treaty not as a new axis of American commerce replacing the discredited British one, but rather as the point of departure for the creation of a far-flung system.

It was an incredibly ambitious undertaking: nothing less than a diplomatic mission to convert all Europe to the commercial principles of the American Revolution. The end in view was a system of purely economic relations with foreign states, which, being based on the exchange of mutual surpluses for mutual wants, need not plunge the United States into the blood-drenched rivalries of the Old World or, alternately, force the country into isolation and penury. Clearly, however, the end could not be reached along purely commercial lines. In order to overcome mercantilism it was first necessary to play the mercantilist game and exploit trade as a political weapon. Although no threats were issued, it was well understood—Congress had so declared—that nations declining to enter into treaty relations with the United States would be liable to discriminatory regulations in the American market and would, of course, be denied other valuable privileges in peace and in war. How much these considerations could be made to count in the European balance of power depended on the progress of reform at home. In the end, however, every nation, on a rational view of its own interest, must see the advantages of entering the American consortium.

Unfortunately, most of the European courts met the American over-

[22] See the editorial commentary *ibid.*, 466-469.
[23] To Edmund Pendleton, Dec. 16, 1783, *ibid.*, VI, 386-387.
[24] To John Adams, Sept. 24, 1785, *ibid.*, VIII, 545.

tures with colossal indifference. As Jefferson later recalled the experience: "They seemed, in fact, to know little about us, but as rebels, who had been successful in throwing off the yoke of the mother country. They were ignorant of our commerce, which had always been monopolized by England, and of the exchange of articles it might offer advantageously to both parties."[25] In the two years allotted to the Commission, only one European negotiation, with Prussia, on the model treaty drafted by Jefferson, was successfully concluded.[26] (A treaty was also concluded with Morocco, but that is another story.) Frustrated and discouraged, Jefferson began to question the practical wisdom of the system of treaties.

His reappraisal focused on two points. First, since it was "indispensably necessary" to gain access to the West Indies, treaties with the several colonial powers were of first importance. "Yet how to gain it," he reflected, "when it is the established system of these nations to exclude all foreigners from their colonies. The only chance seems to be this. Our commerce to the mother countries is valuable to them. We must endeavor then to make this the price of an admission into their West Indies, and to those who refuse the admission we must refuse our commerce or load theirs by odious discriminations in our ports."[27] The privilege of free trade with the mother countries would be attractive, he thought; but it would be no privilege at all, he came to realize, if every piddling kingdom in Europe could claim it on the ordinary ground of the "most favored nation." The change of tactics met with no greater success. Of the colonial powers only France and Portugal (for a brief time) showed the slightest disposition to lower commercial barriers. Months before their commissions expired, Jefferson and Adams were actually shunning the advances, earlier invited, of nations like Austria. Jefferson expressed the dilemma to John Jay, Secretary of Foreign Affairs: "Our instructions are clearly to treat. But these made part of a system, wise and advantageous if executed in all it's parts, but which has hitherto failed in it's most material branch, that of connection with the powers having American territory."[28]

The second part of the reappraisal concerned the home front. Jefferson had said, more than once, "that my primary object in the formation

[25] *Autobiography of Thomas Jefferson* (New York, 1959), 75.
[26] On the Prussian treaty, see the editorial note and the documents collected in Boyd and others, eds., *Papers of Jefferson*, VII, 463-493, 615-628, and VIII, 26-33.
[27] To James Monroe, June 17, 1785, *ibid.*, VIII, 232.
[28] To John Jay, Jan. 27, 1786, *ibid.*, IX, 235.

of treaties is to take the commerce of the states out of the hands of the states, and to place it under the superintendance of Congress, so far as the imperfect provisions of our constitution will admit, and until the states shall by new compact make them more perfect."[29] It is difficult to believe that this was the "primary object," that the treaty making in Europe was an elaborate shadow-play screening consolidation at home. Yet consolidation was certainly one of Jefferson's calculations. He had written into the Commission's instructions the article declaring the United States to be "one Nation" toward others: an implicit denial of state authority so far as American commerce was covered by treaties. Not only was he a firm friend of national authority in this sphere, but, regarding frequent war as the inevitable price of commercial power, he pleaded for the establishment of an American navy and always underscored the value of trade and navigation as resources of national defense.[30] He began to question, however, whether the approach to national strength and dignity by way of the back door was sound. In 1785 several of the states were pushing their own commercial systems; and while Jefferson applauded any retaliatory laws against British monopoly, he also reckoned their damage to the idea of "one Nation."[31] Earlier he had seen the plan of treaties as a means, however imperfect, of arming the Union. Now he stressed the limitations of this plan and wondered if it should not be abandoned for the frontal attack of nationalists like Madison and Jay. "My letters from members of Congress render it doubtful," he wrote Adams, "whether they would not rather that full time should be given for the present disposition of America to mature itself, . . . rather than, by removing the incentive, to prevent the improvement."[32] He was soon advocating coercion of the states, if need be, to strengthen the Confederacy.[33] This greater realism in no way dimmed his vision of friendly intercourse among nations, which drew him on even as he struggled for solutions within the limits of circumstance.

With the failure of the general European plan, Jefferson turned his attention to the development of a Franco-American commercial axis. In

[29] To James Monroe, June 17, 1785, *ibid.*, VIII, 231.
[30] To John Jay, Aug. 23, 1785, *ibid.*, 426-427; Report on Commerce, in Ford, ed., *Writings of Jefferson*, VI, 480.
[31] To John Bannister, Aug. 16, 1785, and to John Adams, Nov. 19, 1785, in Boyd and others, eds., *Papers of Jefferson*, VIII, 393, IX, 42-43.
[32] To John Adams, Sept. 24, 1785, *ibid.*, VIII, 545.
[33] To John Adams, Oct. 3, 1785, *ibid.*, 579-580.

part, the change of direction was a natural result of the position he now occupied, Minister Plenipotentiary to France, succeeding Franklin in 1785. But it also stemmed from the conviction, soon firmly implanted in Jefferson's mind, that France held the key to America's commercial problem. The British monopoly could be overthrown, the main avenues of American trade shifted to France and her colonies, if Versailles would abolish antiquated regulations, open the ports to American productions, and pay for them in manufactures, oils, wines, tropical produce, and other articles. France had everything to gain. Her hopes of permanently displacing Britain in the American market as a result of the war had been cruelly disappointed; but the commercial war was still on, in Jefferson's opinion, and France might yet succeed. The Vergennes ministry hated Britain, a hatred that played into Jefferson's hand, and he did not have to look far in the French capital—to Americanists like Lafayette, to physiocrats like Dupont, to philosophes like Condorcet, even to Vergennes himself—for men of influence who sympathized with the commercial goals of the American Revolution.[34] As for the United States, the infant prodigy needed France's friendship. War was an ever-present danger, especially with Britain. Aside from the economic benefits of a strong commercial union, it would undergird the treaty of alliance. "It will be a strong link of connection," Jefferson said, "the more [so] with the only nation on earth on whom we can solidly rely for assistance till we stand on our own legs."[35] He no longer talked of "perfect equality" of commerce with the two great European powers. To be sure, every improvement in Franco-American relations was so much additional leverage for working on Britain; but neither he, in Paris, nor Adams, in London, had much hope that the British could soon be moved. "Nothing will bring them to reason but physical obstruction, applied to their bodily senses," Jefferson said; and his experience during a visit to England in the spring of 1786 only served to deepen this conviction.[36] Unable to obtain equal terms from Britain, unable as yet to apply that "physical obstruction," the

[34] Louis Gottschalk, *Lafayette Between the American and the French Revolution (1783-1789)* (Chicago, 1950) is particularly informative on this subject. See also, Dumas Malone, *Jefferson and the Rights of Man* (Boston, 1951).

[35] To Ralph Izard, Nov. 18, 1786, in Boyd and others, eds., *Papers of Jefferson*, X, 541-542.

[36] To James Madison, Mar. 18, 1785, and to R. H. Lee, Apr. 22, 1786, *ibid.*, VIII, 40, IX, 398.

prudent course for the United States was to connect its commerce unequivocally to France.

When Jefferson took up commercial diplomacy at Versailles in the later months of 1785, the French economy was depressed, the mercantile community was still reeling from the disaster of its first peacetime venture in the American market, and the government was hard put to defend the limited concession it had a year earlier made to American trade in the West Indies. The circumstances demanded caution all around.[37] In the ministry's view, the Americans seemed irrevocably attached to English merchandise and English commercial practices. Jefferson combatted these ideas, saying "that were national Prejudice alone listened to, our Trade would quit England and come to France."[38] The difficulty, he insisted, was the inability of the Americans to trade directly and make exchanges in the French market. The remedy was no less obvious: the eradication of monopoly and restriction in France. Of course, this was not the whole of the problem. As a Virginian, himself deeply in debt to British merchants, Jefferson knew all too well that the chains of bondage were the invisible chains of credit.[39] The French merchants, not as adventuresome as their British counterparts, unaccustomed to advancing credit and trading on consignment, lacking established connections in American ports, were necessarily at a disadvantage. Diplomacy alone would not slay the hydra of British credit, nor could Jefferson change the conservative habits of French merchants, though he tried. Commercial restrictions were more readily assailed, and Jefferson centered his efforts on opening the French market to direct trade in American productions.

Tobacco, America's leading export, was substance and essence of the entire proceeding. France took large quantities of this commodity but granted a monopoly in its importation to the Farmers-General, the powerful company to which His Majesty's government "farmed out" the collection of several indirect taxes and customs duties, including the

[37] For Jefferson's observations, see the letters to Elbridge Gerry, May 11, 1785, James Monroe, June 17, 1785, and John Adams, Nov. 19, 1785, *ibid.*, VIII, 142-143, 228-229, IX, 42-43. George V. Taylor, Problems of an Immature Economy: France in the 1780's, a paper read at the annual meeting of the Southern Historical Association, Nov. 13, 1964, in Asheville, N. C., focuses on the industrial crisis which struck in the later months of 1786. I am indebted to this paper and also to suggestions made by Mr. Taylor in correspondence with me.

[38] Jefferson's Report on Conversations with Vergennes, [Dec. 1785], in Boyd and others, eds., *Papers of Jefferson*, IX, 139.

[39] To Nathaniel Tracy, Aug. 17, 1785, *ibid.*, VIII, 399.

lucrative tobacco duty. The Farmers-General was interwoven with the French system of finance—ministers tampered with it at their peril and the peril of the treasury—yet any attempt to free the market for American commerce must begin with an attack on the tobacco monopoly. Jefferson made a persuasive case for its abolition. The Americans, he argued, are reluctant to enter a market where there is but one buyer, who sets the price, and that buyer one who does not engage in mercantile exchange but pays in coin, which is promptly remitted to Britain, thus supporting the industry of the common enemy. "By prohibiting all His Majesty's subjects from dealing in tobacco except with a single company," Jefferson said, "one third of the exports of the United States are rendered uncommerciable here. . . . A relief from these shackles will form a memorable epoch in the commerce of the two nations. It will establish at once a great basis of exchange, serving like a point of union to draw to it other members of our commerce. . . . Each nation has exactly to spare the articles which the other wants. . . . The governments have nothing to do but *not to hinder* their merchants from making the exchange."[40]

Actually, as Jefferson soon learned, the tobacco monopoly had not one but two heads; for the Farmers-General had awarded to Robert Morris an exclusive three-year contract for the supply of American tobacco. European monopoly had straddled the Atlantic, with predictable consequences for tobacco prices and ominous forebodings for American freedom. The combined efforts of Jefferson, Lafayette, and others led Vergennes to appoint the so-called American Committee to study and recommend measures for the promotion of Franco-American trade, starting with tobacco. As a result of the Committee's work, the Morris monopoly was broken, a highly beneficial measure even if it did not go to the root of monopoly in France; and some months later, in October 1786, the government announced a host of concessions to American commerce and navigation, freeing exports as well as imports, lowering bars in France as well as in the Antilles. It was another fourteen months before this "ultimate settlement" obtained the force of law.[41] The delay, so vexatious to Jefferson and his friends, was perhaps to be expected. For the decree,

[40] To Montmorin, July 23, 1787, *ibid.*, XI, 617.
[41] The concessions are set forth in a letter from Calonne, the Comptroller General, to Jefferson, Oct. 22, 1786, *ibid.*, X, 474-478. The final decree of Dec. 29, 1787, appears *ibid.*, XII, 468-470. The negotiations are covered in Gottschalk, *Lafayette*, chaps. 15-17.

when it finally came, presaged a virtual revolution in the French commercial system.

As Jefferson said, the tobacco trade was to be the "point of union" for a flourishing commerce in many articles of American industry. The next most important of these were train oil and rice, one so vital to the New England economy, the other to South Carolina and Georgia. The whale fishery had not recovered from the damage wrecked by the Revolution. Britain levied prohibitive duties on American whale oil and under elaborate subsidy built up her own fishery. Between the two fisheries, France held the balance; but instead of freely admitting the American supply, France labored against enormous odds and at heavy fiscal sacrifice to revive her own fishery, succeeding only in further improverishing the American and enriching the British. The intimate connection between fisheries and sea power gave the issue an importance that transcended economics. "Is it not better then," Jefferson pleaded, "by keeping her ports open to the U. S. to enable them to aid in maintaining the field against the common adversary . . . ? Otherwise her supplies must aliment that very force which is keeping her under."[42] All that was needed was an order excluding *European* oil from France. The decree of December 1787 had gone some way toward this objective, only to be followed by a reaction against which Jefferson struggled for many months. He finally triumphed. In December 1788 France gave the American, together with the French oil, a monopoly of the market.[43] How the arrangement advanced the "freedom of trade" he had started out to promote, Jefferson did not explain; but it was a great stride toward Franco-American partnership. Versailles threw itself into the scales of American power against Britain, and despite formidable political and mercantile opposition left French industry to the hazard of American competition.

The American Minister's campaign in behalf of American rice reveals still another side of his commercial diplomacy. Rice exports were less than one half the pre-war figures. Britain continued to dominate the trade—a highly profitable re-export trade on her part—through the controls of debt and credit and the excellent facilities of the entrepôt at Cowes. The French, on the other hand, merely ate rice, some of it American, but the exacting requirements of the cuisine gave a preference to the

[42] *Observations on the Whale Fishery* (1788), in Boyd and others, eds., *Papers of Jefferson,* XIV, 249.
[43] The *Arrêt* of Dec. 7, 1788, appears *ibid.,* 268-269.

Mediterranean variety. Having no desire to reform the cuisine, the American Minister tried rather to educate the Carolinians in the cultivation and preparation of rice suited to the French palate. The lengths he went, even smuggling Piedmont seed across the Appenines, proved the ardor of his commitment. In addition, and despite the disappointing returns from American voyages generally, Jefferson induced solid French houses to enter the Carolina rice trade. The venture was not entirely a happy one on either side; but the Carolinians were deeply grateful to him, and far more ships and casks of rice cleared the Charleston customshouse for France in 1789 than ever before.[44]

On the whole, however, Jefferson's labors to build a Franco-American commercial system were out of all proportion to the results obtained. After five years, the French Revolution intervened, disrupting further progress along the lines he had laid out. The available statistics on the trade between the two nations during this period point to several conclusions. First, the total volume of the trade, though there were ups and downs in key articles, fluctuated little and was about the same at the end of the period as it was at the beginning. Second, the trade with the West Indies greatly exceeded the direct trade with the mother country. And third, in both branches, the Americans had much the better of it. The balance of trade in the island commerce favored the United States on a ratio of nearly two to one, the direct trade on a ratio of perhaps five or six to one.[45] A bonanza for the Americans, the trade was a small disaster for the French.

What, then, becomes of Jefferson's constant plea for markets? Obviously, it did not go to the heart of the problem. Jefferson naturally fixed his attention on obstacles to American imports to the neglect of France's difficulties in making exchanges for them. He knew very well that an enduring commerce between the two countries must be more or less equal in its benefits; and near the end of his ministry especially, he was urging the French to look beyond the luxury trade in wines and bran-

[44] The episode may be traced in Jefferson to Ralph Izard, Aug. 1, 1787, Edward Rutledge to Jefferson, Oct. 23, 1787, Apr. 1, 1789, and Brailsford and Morris to Jefferson, Oct. 31, 1787, Mar. 10, 1789, *ibid.*, XI, 659, XII, 263-264, 298-301, XIV, 633, XV, 12-13.
[45] Edmund Buron, "Statistics on Franco-American Trade, 1778-1806," *Journal of Economic and Business History*, IV (1931-32), 571-580. An article based on these figures is John F. Stover, "French-American Trade during the Confederation, 1781-1789," *North Carolina Historical Review*, XXXV (1958), 399-414.

dies, silks and linens, and to adapt their industry more deliberately to the American market.[46] But French industry was sluggish and inefficient; the Anglo-French commercial accord of 1786 flooded the market with English goods, in the process drowning many merchants and manufacturers; and in the deepening depression of the following years capital was simply not available for the improvements Jefferson had in mind.[47] At any rate, though he did not fully appreciate it, the difficulty of his system was less one of French markets than of French supplies. By 1789 the markets were open to an astonishing degree, largely due to Jefferson's efforts and the influence of American commercial ideology at Versailles; and the Americans exploited these markets, then transferred most of the money balance in their favor to the support of British industry. This was certainly not what Jefferson, or the French government, intended. And even as liberal commercial policy gained in favor, the country's merchants, manufacturers, *fabricants,* and shopkeepers who were losing by it moved toward reaction and revolution. The American Minister had little contact with the bourgeoisie. He moved in a restricted circle, the enlightened nobility for the most part—friends of agriculture and free trade, of America and republicanism—and so it is not surprising that some of the most disturbing realities of the French economy eluded him. Some years later, when these realities were more obvious, Gouverneur Morris, who succeeded Jefferson at Versailles, passed the sophisticated skeptic's slur, *visionary,* on the Jeffersonian plan of direct commerce between France and the United States.[48]

The plan was, nevertheless, an important phase of Jefferson's, and America's, search for a sound commercial system. It was oriented to France primarily by virtue of its being against Britain. Britain was still the enemy in Jefferson's eyes, and so long as she dominated the American economy, national dignity and independence were more illusory than real. The advantages of direct trade with France and her dominions were self-evident from an economic standpoint. On moral and political grounds they appeared to be overwhelming, as a means of curbing British power and of multiplying ties of interest and affection with the only nation that deserved, or was likely to justify, American friendship. The

[46] See, for instance, *Observations on the Whale Fishery,* in Boyd and others, eds., *Papers of Jefferson,* XIV, 253.

[47] Taylor, Problems of an Immature Economy.

[48] Gouverneur Morris to Robert Morris, Mar. 7, 1791, in Beatrix Cary Davenport, ed., *A Diary of the French Revolution, by Gouverneur Morris, 1752-1816* (Boston, 1939), II, 127-128.

true American policy toward foreign nations was one of perfect freedom and equality in trade and of strict political neutrality. Unfortunately, Jefferson reasoned from his own experience, the world was not ready for this policy. Young America must make the best commercial arrangements she could, and everything pointed to France, the proven friend and ally, as the best partner in a preferential system.

The French Revolution and the establishment of the new national government in the United States set the stage for the climactic phase of Jefferson's search. He returned home late in 1789 warmly attached to France and convinced that he had just witnessed in the momentous events there "the first chapter of the history of European liberty."[49] A free France was a more attractive partner than a despotic France. To the reasons the United States already had for alliance with France was now added union in the cause of freedom and self-government. And since monopolies and prohibitions would surely fall with the progress of European liberty, Jefferson expected the Revolution would clear the way for the promised new epoch of commercial freedom. In the United States the adoption of the Constitution made possible at last practical implementation of the national policy inaugurated in 1776. It was the responsibility of the new government to legislate the system that had heretofore floundered on the contingencies of treaties and could be but partially realized in diplomacy with a single foreign state. The commercial impotency of Congress had been a major factor producing the Constitutional Convention; now that Congress was well armed nearly everyone supposed it would act, indeed was obliged to act, in accordance with long declared principles and aims. Alexander Hamilton stated the common sense of the matter in the eleventh paper of *The Federalist*. Under the new government an "active commerce" would replace a "passive commerce." "By prohibitory regulations, extending, at the same time, throughout the states, we may oblige foreign countries to bid against each other, for the privileges of our markets." Hamilton threatened the prospect of "excluding Great Britain . . . from all our ports," which could not fail to "produce a relaxation in her present system" and "would be likely to have a correspondent effect on the conduct of other nations."[50]

[49] To Diodati, Aug. 3, 1789, in Boyd and others, eds., *Papers of Jefferson*, XV, 326.
[50] *The Federalist* . . . , with an intro. by Edward Mead Earle (New York, [1941]), 63-64.

With these ideas and expectations, Jefferson entered upon his duties as Secretary of State in 1790. Next to the redemption and pacification of the West, the encouragement of foreign commerce was the leading object of his ministry. The two objects were not unrelated. In order to deal with the British in the Northwest and the Spanish in the Southwest, he needed a place to stand in European politics. The French alliance provided it.[51] The power to restrict or withhold American trade, especially in times of European war, was an instrument well-nigh indispensable to force Britain to honor American independence, commercial claims, and territorial integrity. Commerce was a minor consideration in negotiations with Spain, since it could be had only by abandonment of the American claim to free navigation of the Mississippi. After the controversy of 1786 on the abortive Jay-Gardoqui negotiation, Jefferson realized that the Western trade must flow, not eastward as he had earlier hoped and planned, but down the Mississippi, and to bargain away its navigation in exchange for privileges in Spanish ports was unthinkable.[52] Foreign commerce was a primary object only on condition that it served the interests of a growing Union.

The first attempt at commercial regulation, in the form of an American navigation act, had already been made when Jefferson took his post in New York. In the debate on the tonnage bill in the previous session, Madison had proposed a discrimination between the vessels of nations in and out of commercial treaty with the United States. But Congress had turned its back on this time honored American principle and placed the trade of all foreign nations on the same footing.[53] Madison resumed the fight in 1790. Jefferson watched it closely, and from behind the scenes in the State Department worked to promote the discriminatory policy, which the Virginians always insisted was, in fact, one of reciprocity, since it only aimed to counter foreign restrictions, chiefly British, and would be altered as these restrictions fell. (Either term will do depending on the context: the policy called for discrimination on the just grounds of reciprocity.) A mixed majority in Congress—planters dependent on Brit-

---

[51] On the role of France in Jefferson's diplomacy, see especially Alexander de Conde, *Entangling Alliance: Politics & Diplomacy under George Washington* (Durham, 1958).

[52] See Jefferson's Report on Matters of Negotiation with Spain, [Mar. 7, 1792], in Ford, ed., *Writings of Jefferson*, V, 441-449.

[53] The debate in the House is reported in 1st Cong., 1st sess., *Annals of Congress*, I, 183-199, 294-302, et passim.

ish ships and credit, importing merchants and shippers tied into the old channels of trade, Anglophiles, and Treasury men eying the abundant revenue collected on British tonnage and imports—defeated discrimination and renewed the original act.[54]

The French chargé d'affaires lodged a protest with the Secretary of State under threat of retaliation. Because the act placed the friendly commerce of France on the same basis as a commerce loaded with pains and penalties, it actually discriminated against France. Jefferson could not quarrel with the spirit of this protest, though he disagreed with Versailles's view that the law violated the letter, as well as the spirit, of the treaty of commerce. He faced a dilemma. If the United States conceded the tonnage exemption claimed by France under the treaty, it would be obliged to make the same concession to other countries with which it had "most favored nation" treaties. Yet the consequences of refusal, jeopardizing the position of American commerce in France, were equally bad. He sought escape through an act of Congress that would place French vessels on the footing of natives in consideration of the favors granted by the royal decrees of 1787 and 1788. No other nation would receive this remarkable privilege without similar concessions. Once again he was backing into a navigation act.[55]

The Secretary of the Treasury opposed the recommendation. In his opinion the proposed concession was too high a price to pay for the favors France had granted, and it would excite unfriendly feelings in Britain. Moreover, the fund from the tonnage law was mortgaged to the payment of the public debt. "I feel a particular reluctance," he said, "to hazard any thing in the present state of our affairs which may lead to commercial warfare with any power."[56] The Treasury coffers were filled with the revenue of British trade. Until the United States could manufacture for itself, Britain was its surest supplier, almost its only creditor, and its best market. Hamilton was, therefore, despite earlier preachments to the contrary, reconciled to the subordination implicit in the British connection.

Jefferson had not expected to hear these opinions in the highest

[54] The debate in the House is reported in 1st Cong., 2d sess., *ibid.*, II, 1623-1635, 1712-1714.
[55] Report on Tonnage Law, [Jan. 18, 1791], in Ford, ed., *Writings of Jefferson*, V, 266-273.
[56] Hamilton to Jefferson, Jan. 13, 1791, in Harold Syrett and Jacob Cooke, eds., *The Papers of Alexander Hamilton* (New York, 1961—), VII, 426.

quarters of the new government. He had clashed with Hamilton before, but not on a major issue. This confrontation in the winter of 1790-91, a full month before the division of opinion on the Bank, involved for Jefferson a fundamental question of national policy. Should the United States push on toward the liberal commercial goals of the American Revolution, or, trapped in the web of debt, credit, and revenue, acquiesce in British maritime dominion? Seeing the issue in this way, Jefferson also began to see the larger implications of Hamilton's financial system. Indeed, for the first time, Hamilton's different measures assumed in Jefferson's mind the character of a system. It was permeated with fiscalism, of course; and from what he had seen of France and learned of Britain, fiscalism was the parent of monopoly and oppression. It was very partial in its distribution of benefits, enriching a few Eastern merchants and speculators, holding nothing material for Southern planters dependent on foreign markets, and, in general, checking the nation's agricultural expansion. In foreign affairs it tied the government into British politics. Despite new British attacks on American commerce, Jefferson wrote to James Monroe in April 1791, the Treasury takes the line of "passive obedience and non-resistance, lest any misunderstanding with them should *affect our credit, or the prices of our public paper.*"[57] Jefferson was not indifferent to these fiscal considerations; but he believed that Hamilton, in making credit rather than commerce the engine of national power, drew the country into many evils.

Although the President backed Jefferson's recommendation on the tonnage law, it was defeated in the Senate, and he had to scramble with the French as best he could. As the year wore on, it became increasingly apparent that Franco-American commerce, instead of approaching a new epoch, was sliding back into an old one. The Revolution brought the merchants of the coastal cities to power in the National Assembly. They had never subscribed to liberal commercial ideas, and they considered the American trade a losing proposition, only made worse by the tonnage law. It was hard for Jefferson to believe that a liberal revolution could turn reactionary in commercial policy. The indisputable evidence came first on the article of tobacco. The Farmers-General was destroyed, but the Assembly imposed a discriminatory duty, nearly prohibitive, on tobacco carried in American bottoms. Jefferson was outraged. French na-

[57] To James Monroe, Apr. 17, 1791, in Ford, ed., *Writings of Jefferson*, V, 319-320.

194

tionalism seriously embarrassed his commercial diplomacy; yet he did not abandon it, and continued to press for the negotiation of a new and far-reaching commercial treaty which the National Assembly had earlier promised in the compassion evoked by Franklin's death.[58]

The counterpart of the Secretary's advocacy of French commerce was his continued opposition to British commerce. Not long after the Report on the Tonnage Law, he sent to Congress his Report on the Cod and Whale Fisheries. The subject was familiar. He had become an expert on the whaling trade and whale oils, in particular, while in France. Now he marshaled the facts to show that the plight of the fisheries owed much to British bounties and restrictions. It could be overcome only by stiff counter regulations. The French, on the other hand, he praised as "co-operators against a common rival." "Nor is it the interest of the fisherman alone, which calls for the cultivation of friendly arrangements with that nation; besides five-eights of our whale oil, and two-thirds of our salted fish, they take from us one-fourth of our tobacco, three-fourths of our live stock . . . a considerable and growing portion of our rice, great supplies, occasionally, of other grain. . . ."[59] The contrast between British oppression and French liberality was unmistakable. The British consul in Philadelphia was not wrong in his estimate of Jefferson's Report: "designed," he said, "as the introduction of a series of proceedings calculated to promote measures very hostile to the commercial interests of Great Britain."[60] The cumulative impact of Jefferson's various reports on French and British affairs, together with a nudge by the President, led a committee of the House of Representatives to report a bill barring the importation of non-British goods in British vessels. Like previous essays at a navigation act, the bill was sidetracked. Congress, instead, referred the whole subject of commercial policy to the Secretary of State for study and recommendations.[61] It was this resolution of February 23, 1791, that finally produced Jefferson's Report on Commerce.

[58] See George F. Zook, "Proposals for a New Commercial Treaty between France and the United States, 1778-1793," *South Atlantic Quarterly*, VIII (1909), 267-283.

[59] Report on the Cod and Whale Fisheries, Feb. 1, 1791, in Lipscomb and Bergh, eds., *Writings of Jefferson*, III, 140.

[60] Phineas Bond to the Duke of Leeds, Mar. 14, 1791, in J. Franklin Jameson, ed., "Letters of Phineas Bond . . . ," *Annual Report of the American Historical Association for the Year 1897*, I (Washington, 1898), 475.

[61] 1st Cong., 3d sess., *Annals of Congress*, II, 2022.

The threat of retaliatory legislation also contributed to the decision of the British government, at long last, to send a minister plenipotentiary to the United States. George Hammond was apprised of the "extremely discordant" rift in the administration and instructed to make the most of it in order to combat the movement against British commerce.[62] With the assistance of the Secretary of the Treasury, he would do just that. Jefferson was under no illusions as to Hammond's intentions. He was in possession of a secret British report on commercial policy. This report, submitted in January 1791 by the Committee of the Privy Council for Trade and Plantations, gave a very flattering picture of Anglo-American commerce since the Revolution. Britain's share of the shipping had increased; the tonnage and tariff duties of the United States were less by about one half than those levied by the states individually in 1787; British exports to the former colonies had fallen off about one third, but the loss was more than offset by expanded markets in the remaining North American colonies; and since imports from the United States had declined drastically, the balance of trade was actually more favorable to Britain than before the war. The report might have been subtitled, "How to Grow Rich by Losing an Empire." It was a thorough vindication of Josiah Tucker, Lord Sheffield, and the architects of British commercial policy in 1783-84. "Government has indeed not been altogether deceived—," said the committee, "the new system [in the United States] is certainly more favorable to British navigation. And there can be no doubt from the proceedings of Congress, and from all that passed in their debate during the last two sessions, particularly in the *American Senate, that a party is already formed in favor of a connection with Great Britain,* which by moderation on her part, may perhaps be strengthened, as to bring about in a friendly way, the object in view."[63] The object: to detach the United States from France and to strengthen the connection with Britain. Commercial diplomacy was advised chiefly as a check on retaliatory measures, for nothing was to be conceded or concluded. Such were Hammond's instructions, as Jefferson accurately surmised, with respect to commerce. As for the hint in a British state paper of collusion

[62] Bernard Mayo, ed., *Instructions to the British Ministers to the United States, 1791-1812,* in *Annual Report of the American Historical Association for the Year 1936,* III (Washington, 1941), 9-13.

[63] Report on the Committee of the Privy Council for Trade and Plantations, Jan. 28, 1791, Jefferson Papers, Library of Congress, Washington, D.C. (underscoring in the manuscript).

with a party in the government of the United States, many things combined in the early months of 1791 to convince Jefferson that such a party existed and that Hamilton was its leader. The British report helped to complete the picture. In Hamilton's subsequent course of conduct, Jefferson could discover only unlimited hostility to his commercial diplomacy.[64]

Jefferson's desire to pursue this diplomacy in 1793 was at the bottom of the controversy on American neutrality. Hamilton proposed at the outset to revoke, or suspend, the French treaties, an act as unwarranted as it was unnecessary, which must have the effect, Jefferson thought, of throwing the United States into the arms of Britain. Given the balance of forces in the transatlantic world, he considered the survival of the French republic necessary to the security of the American; and, though the risks were high in 1793, he proposed to make the European war serve his purposes with respect to both belligerents. Britain should not be offered American neutrality as a gift but be required to bid for it. He had a particular end in view: British recognition of the broadest neutral privileges, embracing the modern principle of "free bottoms make free goods," contained in American treaties of commerce.[65] He agreed, reluctantly, to the President's Proclamation of April 22 believing it still left him room for maneuver with Britain. The Secretary at once instructed Thomas Pinckney, the American Minister, to advise Whitehall of his government's desire for a fair neutrality, *"on condition* that the rights of neutral nations are respected in us, as they have been settled in *modern* times."[66] As it turned out, Jefferson had no room for maneuver at all. Events moved too fast; French precipitancy placed the government on the defensive against that nation; and the Proclamation, which Jefferson regarded as an announcement of the *status quo* in foreign relations, was construed as a definitive Proclamation of Neutrality. The gloss Hamilton put on it, as *Pacificus,* effectively obscured the motives and purposes of Jefferson's diplomacy.

[64] Since this article was written, a thorough documentation of Hamilton's unofficial connections with agents of the British government has appeared in Julian P. Boyd's *Number 7, Alexander Hamilton's Secret Attempts to Control American Foreign Policy; With Supporting Documents* (Princeton, 1964).

[65] Opinion on Neutral Trade, Dec. 20, 1793, in Ford, ed., *Writings of Jefferson,* VI, 485-488. See also, Opinion on French Treaties, Apr. 28, 1793, *ibid.,* 219-231.

[66] To Thomas Pinckney, Apr. 20, 1793, in Lipscomb and Bergh, eds., *Writings of Jefferson,* IX, 67.

With France Jefferson hoped the exigencies of war would revive the spirit of commercial liberality and concord. He was not disappointed. The West Indies ports were thrown entirely open, fulfilling a decade long objective of American policy. The French Minister, Genêt, brought instructions to negotiate a new treaty of commerce on Jefferson's favorite plan of mutual naturalization. In this glittering emissary of the French republic, the Secretary of State saw a fresh embodiment of the dream of Franco-American partnership, though he also saw that it was crazily mixed up now with frenzies of war and revolution besetting the peace of the United States. The policy of neutrality, which he honorably supported, obtained an assured integrity during his tenure in the State Department. Yet on the baffling issues that arose from day to day in the divided cabinet, Jefferson's opinion as invariably squinted toward France as the opinions of his arch rival squinted toward Britain—neutrality was found, very imperfectly, somewhere in the field between these deviations. The conduct of both men was colored by policy commitments outside the straight and narrow path of neutrality. As an absolute concept, "neutrality" was a political fiction, exploited by both sides, but much more effectively by the British and their friends as the means of negating the French alliance. In this they were aided unwittingly by the French Minister. The little zealot played "the whole game . . . into their hands," as Jefferson said, discrediting the system pegged to friendship with France.[67] Genêt had to be abandoned, and with him went the prospect of improved commercial collaboration. The Jacobins now ruled in Paris. They repudiated Genêt, disowned the dazzling ocean-girdling ambitions of the Girondins, revived mercantilism, and proclaimed total war—at home and abroad, commercial and military—directing against Great Albion the same practices she had so successfully employed against her enemies.

These developments made a shambles of Jefferson's policy. To be sure, the damage was offset in some limited degree by the British Provision Order of June 8 authorizing the seizure of neutral vessels ladened with flour and grain for France. Jefferson vigorously protested this attack on American neutrality, and in other ways sought to deflect the rising public anger from France to Britain. But if these proceedings hurt one power, they did nothing to close the breach with the other. The deterioration of Franco-American relations was an unmitigated disaster from Jeffer-

[67] To James Madison, July 14, 1793, Jefferson Papers, Lib. Cong.

son's standpoint. He was not responsible for it, and indeed managed to prevent it from becoming total; but the damage to his system was probably irreparable.

Viewed in this decade-long perspective, Jefferson's Report on Commerce put the capstone on a system outmoded by events and shaken to its foundations. It was, in a sense, Jefferson's "farewell address," though he must have wondered if there was any future for the policy it advocated. In its origins, it was not *his* system but the system of the Continental Congress. It arose out of the compelling need for new markets, and it expressed a revolutionary new outlook on the "wealth of nations." It was carried forward in the general European plan of 1784, of which Jefferson was a principal architect and executor. As Minister to France, acting in response to stubborn facts, Jefferson redirected the policy toward Franco-American collaboration. This change of tactics had a limited success, at least on the American side; but in practice universal goals became increasingly bilateral, and the lengthening chain of obligation to France would prove embarrassing in the future. The policy entered still another phase when Jefferson became Secretary of State. He began to see it as "my system," a personal possession, but the possession, too, of the emerging Republican party, which championed it against the British modeled fiscal system of Hamilton and the Federalists. While at first the French Revolution seemed to place Jeffersonian policy on a stronger footing, the effect proved to be altogether different. The crucial defeat came in 1793, and the Jay Treaty finished it.

The record is one of failure. It is also, however, a record of persistent search for a national system of political economy capable of advancing the interests of the American republic upon the principles identified with its revolutionary birth. This was a reasonable, a progressive, even a necessary undertaking, conducted on Jefferson's part with admirable skill and intelligence. Quixotic he certainly was not; the odds were against him, and he knew it, but the stakes in the game were high and the very presence of the United States was changing the rules of the players. The venture failed finally not because it was wrong or visionary or insufficiently attuned to the national interest, but because forces and events, domestic and foreign, caused political preference to be given to another line of policy. It worked. But whether it worked better or worse than an ascendant Jeffersonian policy is a question admitting no satisfactory answer.

Jefferson himself, less inclined than most men to question the principles of his action, continued for years to insist upon the rightness of his policy. The government had chosen the wrong road in 1793-94, inviting further British aggression, the humiliation of the Jay Treaty, the inevitable resentment of France, and "all the obliquities of the public mind" that fashioned the war hysteria in 1798. Had his own policy prevailed, he said, war with either of the great powers would have been avoided, commerce extended, and justice rendered. "War," he wrote in a memorable restatement of his position, "is not the best engine for us to resort to, nature has given us one *in our commerce,* which, if properly managed, will be a better instrument for obliging the interested nations of Europe to treat us with justice. If the commercial regulations had been adopted which our legislature were at one time proposing, we should at this moment have been standing on such an eminence of safety and respect as ages can never recover."[68] To get back on the track, having wandered so far from it, was full of difficulties. Jefferson never surmounted them, nor did he develop a satisfactory alternative to the system of policy that had been so emphatically rejected. Fragments of it remained after 1800— the protective instrument of "peaceable coercion," for instance—but they formed part of no coherent system.

And suppose that system could have been fairly and fully tried in the incipiency of the new government? Would it have forced a change in British policy and the direction of history to 1812? Would the United States have cemented bonds of trade and friendship with France and other European nations? Would the federal government have met its domestic responsibilities within a political fabric less threatening to the rights of states and individuals than the Hamiltonian one? Would the enlightened principles of free and pacific intercourse have gained an earlier and stronger foundation in the policies of nations? On such questions there is no end to speculation. Fruitless as it may be, it should not foreclose scrutiny and understanding of historical strivings and promises, like those contained in Jeffersonian commercial policy, to which the course of events proved untrue.

[68] To Thomas Pinckney, May 29, 1797, to Doctor John Edwards, Jan. 22, 1797, and to Archibald Hamilton Rowan, Sept. 26, 1798, all in Ford, ed., *Writings of Jefferson,* VII, 129, 113, 280-281.

𝒩otes and 𝒟ocuments

Republicanism and American Foreign Policy: James Madison and the Political Economy of Commercial Discrimination, 1789 to 1794

Drew R. McCoy*

I N probing the political economics of leading Jeffersonian Republicans, historians have generally focused on Thomas Jefferson, to the comparative neglect of James Madison. Yet a close analysis of Madison's thought can draw cogent connections between what historians have recently discovered as "republican ideology," attitudes toward economic development, and the evolution of American commercial policy in the early national period.[1] Scholars have invariably noted the coherence of Alexander Hamilton's "system," in which fiscal policy and economic growth were intimately tied to the need for amicable Anglo-American commercial relations; they have failed to develop, however, the parallel relationship between Madison's commitment to commercial discrimination against Great Britain and his approach to internal economic development.[2] An examination of Madison's commercial policy

* Mr. McCoy is a doctoral candidate at the University of Virginia.

[1] For an excellent discussion of the growth of "republicanism" (or "republican ideology") as a concept in American historiography see Robert E. Shalhope, "Toward a Republican Synthesis: The Emergence of an Understanding of Republicanism in American Historiography," *William and Mary Quarterly*, 3d Ser., XXIX (1972), 49-80. Edmund S. Morgan has taken the first step toward linking this system of thought to economic policy in "The Puritan Ethic and the American Revolution," *ibid.*, XXIV (1967), 3-43, while Roger H. Brown's *The Republic in Peril: 1812* (New York, 1964) suggests the utility of examining American foreign policy from the general perspective of republicanism.

[2] For a concise description and explanation of the Hamiltonian "system" and its incompatibility with Madison's commercial policy see Paul A. Varg, *Foreign Policies of the Founding Fathers* (East Lansing, Mich., 1963), 77-78, and Joseph Charles, *The Origins of the American Party System: Three Essays* (Chapel Hill, N. C., 1956), 13, 30-31. For related and more extensive discussions of economic thought and policy in this period see esp. Charles A. Beard's classic *Economic Origins of Jeffersonian Democracy* (New York, 1915), and E. A. J. Johnson, *The Foundations of American*

from the perspective of his republicanism can suggest that he had a "system" of his own, directed toward the fulfillment of a specific pattern of politico-economic development in the new nation.

Central to this discussion is the question of Madison's attitude toward the development of manufactures. Historians have labeled Madison as anything from a rather naive, Virginia-oriented "agrarian" to a sophisticated "mercantilist" more committed to encouraging American manufactures than even his adversary Hamilton.[3] I would suggest that although Madison was neither naive nor narrowly provincial, his aversion to the development of *large-scale* manufacturing enterprises in the United States was central to his nationalist outlook. This aversion was grounded in the web of associated ideas and prejudices known as "republicanism" and stemmed from Madison's desire to secure American economic independence. His definition of economic independence, however, differed sharply from that of many of his contemporaries, especially from Hamilton's. A careful consideration of Madison's policy of commercial discrimination during the period 1789 to 1794 can uncover the origins of that definition, show how it was expressed in concrete policy suggestions, and further expose the interdependence of domestic and foreign policy objectives in this critical period of ideological conflict.

As one of the more prominent members of the First Congress, Madison moved immediately in the spring of 1789 to implement his program for economic independence.[4] The cornerstone of that program was commercial discrimination—a distinction in tonnage and tariff laws between nations in and out of commercial treaty with the United States. The

---

Economic Freedom: Government and Enterprise in the Age of Washington (Minneapolis, Minn., 1973).

[3] For a typical "agrarian" approach see Varg, *Foreign Policies*. William Appleman Williams develops the "mercantilist" argument in *The Contours of American History* (Cleveland, 1961), esp. 111-223. Williams undoubtedly built on the analysis of Madison's biographer, Irving Brant, who stresses that Madison was strongly in favor of encouraging domestic manufactures. Brant argues, for example, that Madison had no quarrel with the general purpose of Hamilton's Report on Manufactures—"for years he had been urging the national advantage of industrial development"—but objected only to the secretary's preference for bounties as a means of encouragement. *James Madison: Father of the Constitution, 1787-1800* (Indianapolis, 1950), 348, 392-393. Those scholars who take the "mercantilist" approach to Madisonian political economy stress that commercial discrimination was designed to promote the development of American manufactures. As I will argue below, this point of view misinterprets Madison's fundamental motives and the thrust of his program, while often failing to make necessary distinctions between different types of manufacturing.

[4] The proceedings and debates may be found in U. S. Congress, 1st Congress, 1st session, in Joseph Gales, comp., *The Debates and Proceedings in the Congress of the United States* . . . (Washington, D. C., 1834-1856), I, 107ff; hereafter cited as *Annals of Congress*.

target was Great Britain, which had refused since the peace of 1783 to enter into mutually acceptable commercial arrangements with its former colonies. As befitted a staunch republican and Virginia planter, Madison bemoaned the existing structural ties between the American and British economies. Credit, for example, was a curse used by experienced British merchants to divert American commerce from its "natural channels." Influenced strongly by the commercial liberalism of Adam Smith, Madison predicated his analysis on a rather vague but consistent reference to an ideal, "natural" international economic order. Despite political independence, Americans were still tied to the old system of British mercantilism; not only did British merchants and capital dominate American trade, thereby restricting foreign markets for American exports, but they directed it into "artificial" and politically dangerous channels of dependence. Madison's aim was to remove these onerous shackles from American commerce; his vehicle was retaliatory commercial legislation in the form of discrimination.[5]

Discrimination was designed to accomplish several purposes. First, it would encourage the development of American shipping, an objective dearer to Madison than to most southerners at that time. Proclaiming to Congress that he was "a friend to the navigation of America" who would always "be as ready to go as great lengths in favor of that interest as any man on the floor," Madison insisted that an independent navigation industry was necessary both for naval defense and for easy, dependable access to foreign markets.[6] Second, discrimination would force the British to grant America a just reciprocity in commerce; it would occasion a relaxation of the British navigation acts and thus loosen the deadly grip of British credit and redirect American commerce into more "natural" channels. Madison was particularly interested in promoting direct trade with France, a nation in commercial treaty with the United States, by reducing the lucrative (and unnatural) British reexport trade of American produce. Another primary target was American trade with the British West Indies, as Madison intended to force open this "most natural and valuable" channel of commerce that the British had closed to American vessels in 1783.[7] Confidence in the efficacy of com-

[5] *Ibid.*, 193, 209-210. In discussing British restrictions on American commerce, Madison often stressed the more fundamental danger of political "corruption" which transcended mere economic inconvenience; it was necessary, he argued in 1794, to consider "the influence that may be conveyed into the public councils by a nation directing the course of our trade by her capital, and holding so great a share in our pecuniary institutions, and the effect that may finally ensue on our taste, our manners, and our form of government itself." *Ibid.*, 3d Cong., 1st sess., IV, 215.

[6] *Ibid.*, 1st Cong., 1st sess., I, 247. See also 197, 290-292.

[7] *Ibid.*, 193; Madison to Jefferson, June 30, 1789, in Julian P. Boyd *et al.*, eds., *The Papers of Thomas Jefferson* (Princeton, N. J., 1950-   ), XV, 226.

mercial coercion had characterized American Revolutionary thought, but never was the policy more articulately promoted and defended than by Madison in this initial period of nation building. To understand why he was convinced that an "infant country" had sufficient power to coerce the mightiest nation on the globe, it is necessary to examine the assumptions on which the rationale for discrimination was based.

From a twentieth-century perspective, Madison had a peculiar analysis of the comparative nature and strength of the American and British economies. Great Britain was in a precarious position. "Her dependence, as a commercial and manufacturing nation," Madison argued, "is so absolutely upon us that it gives a moral certainty that her restrictions will not, for her own sake, be prejudicial to our trade."[8] The United States produced "necessaries" for export—food and raw materials—and imported "superfluities" in the form of British manufactures. Great Britain was "under a double dependence on the commerce of the United States"; her West Indies could not subsist without American supplies, and her manufacturers could not subsist without American customers. Madison usually emphasized the latter dependence, asserting the general rule that "in proportion as a nation manufactures luxuries must be its disadvantage in contests of every sort with its customers."[9] The United States, on the other hand, was blessed with an economy that provided a unique and relatively untapped source of natural power. Arguing that "the produce of this country is more necessary to the rest of the world than that of other countries is to America," Madison contended that "we possess natural advantages which no other nation does." Therefore, "if we have the disposition, we have abundantly the power to vindicate our cause."[10]

Several of Madison's fellow congressmen were at a loss to penetrate this logic and hardly shared his perception either of the latent strength of an undeveloped American economy or of Britain's dependence on it. They found it difficult to regard British clothing and hardware as "superfluities," and, unlike Madison, they feared the dire consequences of British economic power should commercial discrimination provoke a full-scale commercial war with that nation.[11] Madison's blanket view of American imports from Britain as "superfluities" stemmed in part from his conviction that the United States had the potential to manufacture

---

[8] *Annals of Congress*, 1st Cong., 1st sess., I, 256. See also 214, 248.
[9] *Ibid.*, 3d Cong., 1st sess., IV, 157, 215-216.
[10] *Ibid.*, 1st Cong., 1st sess., I, 214.
[11] Rep. John Lawrence of New York led the opposition to discrimination in Congress. *Ibid.*, 184, 212, 243. In private correspondence Congressman Fisher Ames of Massachusetts proved to be a determined foe of Madison's policy. See letters from Ames to George Richards Minot, May 27, 29, and July 2, 1789, in Seth Ames, ed., *Works of Fisher Ames*, I (Boston, 1854), 45-46, 48-50, 59.

any "necessaries" that it currently imported, and that the young Republic could, if necessary in the unlikely event of a commercial war, be converted very quickly into a society of self-sufficient yeomen who spun their own clothing at home. But this in itself seems insufficient to explain Madison's extreme view of British weakness and dependence on America, a view disputed by several of his contemporaries and, most importantly, actively opposed by the secretary of the Treasury.[12]

It is apparent that Madison's weltanschauung was strongly grounded in the structured intellectual paradigm now referred to as American "republican ideology." As several scholars have recently demonstrated, the vocabulary and concepts generated by minority opposition to government in eighteenth-century England permeated the American mind throughout the Revolutionary era.[13] "Corruption" signified more than bribery or dishonesty in government; it was an ideological catchword that connoted fundamental social and moral decay. American republicanism had its immediate origins in English "country" thought, which had flourished in the wake of England's post-1688 financial revolution and the crown's increased use of an enlarged patronage power. Radical Whig "Comnonwealthmen," led by John Trenchard and Thomas Gordon, had shared with the nostalgic Tory Lord Bolingbroke a moral and aesthetic aversion to certain features of the new politico-economic order consolidated under Robert Walpole.[14] To these critics, the growth of a new system of public finance, accompanied by the emergence and development of large moneyed companies (most notably the Bank of England) and the institutionalization of a stock and money market in London, brought into existence social types (rentiers, speculators in

---

[12] *Annals of Congress*, 1st Cong., 1st sess., I, 248. See also *ibid.*, 3d Cong., 1st sess., IV, 215, 382. For a detailed discussion of Hamilton's initial opposition to "Jeffersonian" commercial policy see the editorial note in Boyd *et al.*, eds., *Jefferson Papers*, XVIII, 516-558.

[13] Shalhope, "Toward a Republican Synthesis," *WMQ*, 3d Ser., XXIX (1972), 49-80. See esp. Bernard Bailyn, *The Ideological Origins of the American Revolution* (Cambridge, Mass., 1967); Gordon S. Wood, *The Creation of the American Republic, 1776-1787* (Chapel Hill, N. C., 1969); and two essays by J. G. A. Pocock, "Civic Humanism and Its Role in Anglo-American Thought," and "Machiavelli, Harrington and English Political Ideologies in the Eighteenth Century," both reprinted with slight revisions in Pocock, *Politics, Language, and Time: Essays on Political Thought and History* (New York, 1971), 80-103, 104-147.

[14] See Caroline Robbins, *The Eighteenth-Century Commonwealthman: Studies in the Transmission, Development and Circumstance of English Liberal Thought from the Restoration of Charles II until the War with the Thirteen Colonies* (Cambridge, Mass., 1959), and Isaac Kramnick, *Bolingbroke and His Circle: The Politics of Nostalgia in the Age of Walpole* (Cambridge, Mass., 1968). Pocock develops the concept of "country" thought in the essays cited above and in the review article, "Virtue and Commerce in the Eighteenth Century," *Journal of Interdisciplinary History*, III (1972-1973), 119-134.

public funds, placemen and the like) whose influence on government and society was pernicious; their predominance signaled the decline of English liberty and the corruption of the moral and social fabric. After 1760 most Americans came to share this view, and the Revolution became, in part, the necessary struggle to save America from that same corruption.[15] This "country" image of eighteenth-century England furnished the rationale for commercial discrimination, for it depicted an unhealthy, debauched society whose strength and prosperity were illusory—a society mired in fiscalism, with a national debt, privileged corporations, paper money, "stockjobbers," and all the attendant moral evils, in which large numbers of citizens, suffering under the burden of institutions incompatible with republican liberty, lacked "independence" and "virtue."[16]

Economically, then, Great Britain was "dependent" on the United States precisely because so many of its citizens were not free in either an economic or a political sense. In particular, British manufacturers of "superfluities" could never be independent, since they depended for subsistence on a capricious, often transient demand for their products. In both his essay "Fashion," published March 20, 1792, in Philip Freneau's *National Gazette,* and later in congressional debates on commercial discrimination, Madison pointed to the pathetic plight of twenty thousand English buckle manufacturers and employees who were devastated by a sudden preference for shoestrings and slippers. To him these victims of the "mutability of fashion" offered a disgusting example of "the lowest point of servility."[17] An economy characterized by such industries was particularly vulnerable to customers who exported "necessaries" that would always command a "sure market." Blessed with plentiful natural resources (primarily an abundance of open land) and a healthy political culture, the United States, by comparison, was a young and virile society of independent and industrious republicans.[18] Madison never doubted that American power was latent, sown in nature, and fully capable of shattering the British restrictions on American

[15] Pocock, *Politics, Language, and Time,* 93-97. My brief description of "country" ideology and its origin is, of course, selective and oversimplified. As Pocock notes, it was part of a tradition anchored in the Florentine Renaissance and looking back to classical antiquity.

[16] For an explicit and extended development of this general argument in relation to commercial discrimination by William Branch Giles, a fellow Virginian and one of Madison's congressional allies, see *Annals of Congress,* 3d Cong., 1st sess., IV, 281-285.

[17] Gaillard Hunt, ed., *The Writings of James Madison,* VI (New York, 1906), 99-101; *Annals of Congress,* 3d Cong., 1st sess., IV, 216.

[18] *Annals of Congress,* 3d Cong., 1st sess., IV, 212; "Fashion," in Hunt, ed., *Writings of Madison,* VI, 99-101.

commerce that threatened the virtue and autonomy of the new Republic.[19]

Commercial discrimination was thus to be Madison's vehicle for building an independent American economy. But his conception of economic independence did not necessarily imply extensive domestic manufactures, the development of a great home market, or a diminishing reliance on foreign markets for American agricultural exports. His intention was not to use commercial regulations as a means of raising semipermanent tariff walls to encourage "industrial growth," a balanced internal economy, and American self-sufficiency. There did exist a radical strain of republican thought in America with strong anticommercial, even anticapitalist overtones, which called for the United States to isolate itself completely from the corrupting influence of the rest of the world.[20] But other republicans, including Madison, did not share this suspicious antipathy to commerce, provided it could flow in its proper "natural" channels. They regarded commerce as a civilizing force that would expand the human mind, remove local prejudices, and extend an empire of humanity and benevolence throughout the world.[21] The retaliatory duties provided for by Madison's discrimination program were a means to this end, temporary regulations that would promote the development of an international economic order in which restrictions would be unnecessary.[22] Madison's prescription for American economic

[19] Madison could have found confirmation both of his comparative view of the American and British economies and of the potential viability of commercial coercion in Adam Smith's *Wealth of Nations* (1776). See esp. Book IV, chap. VII, pt. III, in which Smith portrays the British economy as unbalanced and dangerously precarious, particularly vulnerable to the very type of scheme Madison was advancing 15 years later. Adam Smith, *An Inquiry into the Nature and Causes of the Wealth of Nations*, ed. Edwin Cannan (reprint ed. New York, 1937 [orig. publ. London, 1776]), 590-593.

[20] For examples of this strain of thought see Amicus, "An Essay on the Fatal Tendency of the Prevailing Luxuries, . . ." *American Museum*, II (1787), 216-220; "An Oration Delivered at Petersburgh, Virginia, on the 4th of July, 1787, . . ." *ibid.*, 419-424; and extracts from "An Enquiry into the Causes of the Present Grievances of America," *ibid.*, V (1789), 254-257. The author of the Petersburg oration bluntly asserted that "foreign trade is in its very nature subversive of the spirit of pure liberty and independence, as it destroys that simplicity of manners, native manliness of soul, and equality of station, which is the spring and peculiar excellence of a free government." *Ibid.*, II, 421.

[21] Clear statements of the economic implications of this more moderate strain of republican thought may be found in Enos Hitchcock, *An Oration: Delivered July 4, 1788,* . . . (Providence, R. I. [1788]), and William Hillhouse, Jr., *A Dissertation, in Answer to a late Lecture on the Political State of America* . . . (New Haven, Conn. [1789]). These republicans usually argued that only commerce and the demand of foreign markets could stimulate the virtues of industry and frugality among Americans.

[22] Madison repeatedly professed his adherence to "a very free system of commerce," in which "industry and labor are left to take their own course," free from "unjust, oppressive, and impolitic" commercial shackles. *Annals of Congress*, 1st

independence did not require isolation from foreign markets as long as Americans continued to export the right kind of products—"necessaries." To be in a "dependent" relationship to a foreign customer or nation the United States would have to become a producer of whimsical "superfluities." Madison particularly regretted to see the day when Americans should resort to the production of articles like brass buckles for export; pointing to the British example, he warned that "in proportion as a nation consists of that description of citizens, and depends on external commerce, it is dependent on the consumption and caprice of other nations."[23]

In addition to dependence on foreign customers, Madison was determined to avoid another type of dependence—that of one class of citizens upon another within the United States. Here he referred in part to the problem of wage laborers who depended for subsistence upon the will of their employers. At the core of republican ideology was an intense concern with the autonomy or "independence" of the individual, and with the material or economic basis for that autonomy.[24] The individual who was "dependent" on others for subsistence was in a particularly deplorable situation, for he could be made to serve the will of his patrons, thus sacrificing the moral integrity necessary for the exercise of proper civic virtue. Once there were large numbers of "dependents" in a society, republican government was doomed. It seems clear that Madison, steeped in "republicanism," subscribed to James Harrington's maxim that the form of government followed the distribution of wealth, particularly landed wealth, and that republican government required a wide distribution of property among small independent landowners.[25] It was for this reason that Madison was so concerned with the potential economic and political ramifications of rapid population growth in America; in Europe, a human "surplus" had contributed to, if not induced, the general pattern of corruption, decay, and misery.[26]

Cong., 1st sess., I, 116. For the system to function properly between nations, however, all nations had to comply. Madison was determined to induce compliance from Great Britain.

[23] See "Fashion," in Hunt, ed., *Writings of Madison*, VI, 100-101.

[24] For a detailed discussion of the development of this concept of "independence" in 17th-century English political thought see C. B. Macpherson, *The Political Theory of Possessive Individualism: Hobbes to Locke* (Oxford, 1962). More recently, Edmund S. Morgan has discussed this matter in relation to Jefferson and the slavery problem in "Slavery and Freedom: The American Paradox," *Journal of American History*, LIX (1972-1973), 5-29.

[25] For an extended discussion of Harrington and the "balance of property" element in republican thought see Pocock, *Politics, Language, and Time*, 80-103, 104-147.

[26] See Madison's several statements on this matter in the Constitutional Convention in *Notes of Debates in the Federal Convention of 1787, Reported by James*

Madison had no aversion to household manufactures, which constituted "the natural ally of agriculture," but he did not look forward to the development of large-scale manufacturing enterprises that would employ large numbers of "dependent" wage laborers who neither owned their own land nor possessed much personal property. In his essay, "Republican Distribution of Citizens," which appeared in the *National Gazette* on March 3, 1792 (shortly after the delivery of Hamilton's Report on Manufactures to Congress), Madison wrote in reference to "the regular [i.e., non-household] branches of manufacturing and mechanical industry" that "whatever is least favorable to vigor of body, to the faculties of the mind, or to the virtues or the utilities of life, instead of being forced or fostered by public authority, ought to be seen with regret as long as occupations more friendly to human happiness, lie vacant."[27] He hoped that the United States would not be forced to turn to such manufacturing or to the production of "superfluities" by the pressures of an expanding population, a contracting supply of land, or inadequate foreign markets for American agricultural surpluses. Expansion across the continent and the expansion of foreign markets were the two surest ways to forestall this calamity; both strategies were central to Madison's political economics and foreign policy.[28]

While he drew upon much of the same republican heritage as Madison, Alexander Hamilton's intellectual world had a far different texture. Influenced heavily by David Hume's defense of luxury in modern commercial society, Hamilton's republicanism was less intense, less classical, and less rigid. By the 1790s his style of thought was closer to the English "court" mainstream than to the "country" opposition that had predominated in Revolutionary America.[29] His economic system—

Madison (Athens, Ohio, 1966), 194, 375. In an often-cited letter to Jefferson of June 19, 1786, Madison fretted about the apparent truism that "a certain degree of misery seems inseparable from a high degree of populousness." Boyd *et al.*, eds., *Jefferson Papers*, IX, 660.

[27] Hunt, ed., *Writings of Madison*, VI, 99. See also *Notes of Debates*, 194, 375. For an example of the dependence of wage laborers on their employers in Europe as, ironically, it was extolled (in the name of efficiency) by one promoter of large-scale manufacturing in America see John F. Amelung, *Remarks on Manufactures* . . . ([Frederick, Md.], 1787). There had been a definite trend in the direction of factory production in America between 1786 and 1792; if Madison was aware of this trend, it could only have exacerbated his fears. Curtis P. Nettels, *The Emergence of a National Economy, 1775-1815* (New York, 1962), 125.

[28] For Madison's favorable view of westward expansion see his essay "Population and Emigration," published Nov. 21, 1791, in the *National Gazette* and reprinted in Hunt, ed., *Writings of Madison*, VI, 43-66.

[29] See Gerald Stourzh's recent study, *Alexander Hamilton and the Idea of Republican Government* (Stanford, Calif., 1970), and Pocock, "Virtue and Commerce," *Jour. Interdisc. Hist.*, III (1972-1973), 130-131.

tied to a funded debt, a national bank, and fluid capital—was a bold but politically explosive initiative in a society of "country" republicans who were ideologically prone to view it is an insidious replica of the system that had corrupted Augustan England. The developing opposition to Hamilton should thus be viewed on two different levels; first, on the level of strictly tactical and strategic differences among intellectuals, competing interest groups, and geographic regions, and second, on the level of ideological resistance to an alleged conspiracy to corrupt American society and smash the republican experiment by imitating British forms, manners, and institutions. This ideological resistance was triggered for Madison and many others by the scramble for the stock of the Bank of the United States on the part of speculators (some of whom were congressmen) in the summer of 1791 and the ensuing panic of March 1792.[30] Madison was outraged by what he saw to be a corrupted legislature, manipulated by Hamilton from his vantage point in the Treasury and tied to a fiscal system that encouraged bad morals and habits in the society at large. Particularly frightening to Madison in this respect was Hamilton's Report on Manufactures, issued to Congress in December 1791.[31]

In his private correspondence Madison's objections focused on Hamilton's treatment of the "general welfare" clause of the Constitution. In urging pecuniary bounties as the best means of encouraging American manufactures, Hamilton had argued that Congress had virtually un-

---

[30] See Madison's general correspondence during this period—for example, Madison to Jefferson, Aug. 8, 1791, in Hunt, ed., *Writings of Madison*, VI, 58n-59n, and Madison to Henry Lee, Apr. 15, 1792, in *Letters and Other Writings of James Madison*, I (Philadelphia, 1865), 553-554. Madison also published during this general period an extended series of 13 essays (of which "Fashion" and "Republican Distribution of Citizens" were a part), focusing on threats to republicanism in America. See also, in particular, "Spirit of Governments," in Hunt, ed., *Writings of Madison*, VI, 93-95. Perhaps the best discussions of the intellectual origins of the Jeffersonian side of the ideological struggle of the 1790s are two unpublished doctoral dissertations: Douglass Adair, "The Intellectual Origins of Jeffersonian Democracy" (Yale University, 1944), and Lance G. Banning, "The Quarrel with Federalism: A Study in the Origins and Character of Republican Thought" (Washington University, 1972). See esp. Chap. 5 of Banning's dissertation and his recent article, "Republican Ideology and the Triumph of the Constitution, 1789 to 1793," *WMQ*, 3d Ser., XXXI (1974), 167-188. Richard Buel, *Securing the Revolution: Ideology in American Politics, 1789-1815* (Ithaca, N. Y., 1972), fails to exploit fully the ideological depth of the "republican" opposition to Hamilton's system.

[31] The final version of the Report on Manufactures may be found in Harold C. Syrett and Jacob E. Cooke, eds., *The Papers of Alexander Hamilton*, X (New York, 1966), 230-340.

limited power to interpret that clause, and Madison clearly feared the ominous potential of an unrestrained and "corrupted" legislature.[32] Staunch "republicans" suspected that the secretary of the Treasury would use this spurious constitutional interpretation to create corporate monopolies that would ruin small producers and create un-republican inequalities of wealth. Hamilton's Report left little doubt that he was most interested in large-scale factory production; this was corroborated by his aid in the establishment of a grandiose corporate enterprise, the "Society for Useful Manufactures," at Paterson, New Jersey, which prompted an outpouring of antimonopoly rhetoric.[33] There seems little doubt, moreover, that Hamilton's Report helped provoke Madison's essays "Fashion" and "Republican Distribution of Citizens," which raised republican objections to certain types of manufacturing enterprises.

Beyond this, the Report on Manufactures directly challenged Madison's fundamental system of political economy and the rationale for commercial discrimination. Hamilton insisted that foreign markets, limited by the restrictions of European mercantilism, would be increasingly insufficient for the absorption of burgeoning American agricultural surpluses. He admitted that if the doctrine of perfectly free commerce were universally practiced, arguments against the development of American manufactures would have great force; he contended, however, that "an opposite spirit" regulated "the general policy of Nations," with the unfortunate consequence that "the United States are to a certain extent in the situation of a country precluded from foreign Commerce."[34] Hamilton's unstated assumption was that the United States did not have the power necessary to destroy or significantly alter the prevailing European system of commercial intercourse. He thus denied Madison's assertion that the nature of the American economy provided power sufficient to overturn British commercial restrictions; instead, he explicitly developed the general theory that nations with extensive manufactures had overwhelming advantages in their intercourse with predominantly agricultural nations.[35] Since Hamilton's view

[32] See Report on Manufactures, *ibid.*, 302-304; Madison to Edmund Pendleton, Jan. 21, 1792, James Madison Papers, Library of Congress; and Madison to Henry Lee, Jan. 1, 1792, in Hunt, ed., *Writings of Madison*, VI, 81n.

[33] Hamilton made an indirect reference to the Society for Useful Manufactures in the Report when he announced that "measures are already in train for prosecuting on a large scale, the making and printing of cotton goods." Syrett and Cooke, eds., *Hamilton Papers*, X, 328. The most thorough study of the Society and the ideological attacks on it is in Joseph S. Davis, *Essays in the Earlier History of American Corporations*, II (Cambridge, Mass., 1916), 349-522.

[34] Report on Manufactures in Syrett and Cooke, eds., *Hamilton Papers*, X, 262-263. See also 256-260, 287-288.

[35] *Ibid.*, 287-290.

of England was not shaped by the assumptions of classical republicanism and Country ideology, Madison's idea of American "necessaries" and British "superfluities" was totally alien to his structure of thought. For Hamilton, the insufficiency of foreign markets for American surpluses pointed directly to the need for governmental assistance in the development of domestic manufactures and a more dependable home market for American produce. The result, he argued, would be a more balanced, sectionally interdependent economy that would gradually enhance American power to the point where the United States might effectively contend for commercial reciprocity.[36]

By denying the viability of commercial coercion and asserting that the development of government-subsidized manufacturing enterprises on a large scale was necessary to insure an adequate vent for American agricultural surpluses, Hamilton put Madison in an increasingly precarious position. He threatened to sustain the momentum already generated by the establishment of public credit (largely on his terms) and the Bank of the United States, and further consolidate the "system" that Madison thought antithetical to republicanism in America. Madison's counterattack came in January 1794, on the heels of Secretary of State Thomas Jefferson's Report on Commerce, when he attempted to exploit a growing diplomatic crisis with Great Britain by reviving his program of commercial discrimination.[37] The secretary of the Treasury had frustrated Madison's repeated attempts to enact the policy into law during each session of the First Congress, in part because his "system," tied to British credit and the revenue from Anglo-American trade, could not stand the risk of a serious rupture with England.[38] Madison's 1794 resolutions touched off a momentous congressional debate in which Representative William Loughton Smith of South Carolina led the opposition by delivering a brilliant, day-long speech that had been prepared by Hamilton. Echoing the implicit assumption of the Report on Manufactures, Smith ridiculed "the impracticability and Quixotism of an attempt by violence, on the part of this young country, to break through the fetters which the universal policy of nations imposes on their intercourse with each other."[39] During the course of the

[36] John C. Miller, *Alexander Hamilton: Portrait in Paradox* (New York, 1959), 292-295, 301. See also the conclusion of a speech written by Hamilton and delivered to Congress by William Loughton Smith in early 1794. *Annals of Congress*, 3d Cong., 1st sess., IV, 208.

[37] See Merrill D. Peterson, "Thomas Jefferson and Commercial Policy, 1783-1793," *WMQ*, 3d Ser., XXII (1965), 584-610.

[38] For a good account of Madison's repeated failures see Jerald A. Combs, *The Jay Treaty: Political Battleground of the Founding Fathers* (Berkeley and Los Angeles, 1970), 31-33, 50-51, 58.

[39] *Annals of Congress*, 3d Cong., 1st sess., IV, 196. For the whole debate see *ibid.*, 155ff. For a secondary account see, among many others, Varg, *Foreign Policies*, 99-101.

debate the crisis with Britain worsened, and Madison's resolutions were put aside in favor of more appropriate measures. While he concurred in the need for additional action, Madison stubbornly maintained that his resolutions were "in every view and in every event proper to make part of our standing laws till the principle of reciprocity be established by mutual arrangements."[40] Implementation of discrimination was to be indefinitely postponed, however, for the ultimate upshot of the 1794 crisis was the Jay Treaty, which prohibited for ten years the type of anti-British commercial program Madison had championed.

I would suggest that the full economic implications of Madison's aggressive commitment to commercial discrimination have been obscured by a failure to examine his motives within the broader context of his republicanism. Twentieth-century historians, anxious to prove that Madison was not a parochial or short-sighted agrarian, have stressed that his program would have promoted American manufactures and, therefore, that this objective must have been central to his purpose. To the limited extent that he expected his policy to encourage manufactures, however, Madison clearly spoke of those "carried on, not in public factories, but in the household or family way, which he regarded as the most important way."[41] Above all, Madison intended to demonstrate the ability of America's "natural" economic power to shatter Old World mercantilist restrictions. His primary politico-economic goal was not to stimulate manufactures but to undercut one of the key assumptions behind Hamilton's program for industrial development and insure the opening of adequate foreign markets for American agricultural surpluses. This in turn would encourage further westward expansion and, most importantly, secure the institutional and moral base for an American political economy conducive to republicanism. Viewed in this context, commercial discrimination was part of a determined attempt to preserve and expand across space the predominantly agricultural character of American society.[42] To this degree, Madison, as

[40] Madison to Jefferson, Mar. 19, 1794, Madison Papers.

[41] *Annals of Congress,* 3d Cong., 1st sess., IV, 221. As John C. Miller notes, Madison's commitment was thus to manufacturing that could be carried on as well in the southern states as in the North or East. *The Federalist Era, 1789-1801* (New York, 1960), 144n; *Annals of Congress,* 3d Cong., 1st sess., IV, 221-222. For a parallel discussion of Jefferson's political economics and its relation to commercial policy in this period see William D. Grampp, "A Re-examination of Jeffersonian Economics," *Southern Economic Journal,* XII (1945-1946), 263-282.

[42] See Adair, "Intellectual Origins." As J. R. Pole has recently noted, Madison always feared the political ramifications of industrial growth and widespread urbanization. *Political Representation in England and the Origins of the American Republic* (London, 1966), 360-361, 530-531. For an interesting and relevant discussion of later Whig and Democratic conceptions of economic development see Major L. Wilson, "The Concept of Time and the Political Dialogue in the United States, 1828-48," *American Quarterly,* XIX (1967), 619-644.

much as Hamilton, had a "system" in which foreign policy objectives were integral to his approach to economic development and to his vision of a future America. Hopefully, on a broader scale, this exploratory essay has suggested the need to extend our growing understanding of "republicanism" and American "republican ideology" into the areas of economic thought and foreign policy.

The Virginia Magazine

OF HISTORY AND BIOGRAPHY

Vol. 92   January 1984   No. 1

THE HAMILTONIAN MADISON

A Reconsideration

by Lance Banning*

When Alexander Hamilton submitted his Report on Public Credit to the First Federal Congress, he was dismayed to learn that his proposals for funding the Revolutionary debt would be opposed by the most influential member of that body. He had accepted his position at the Treasury, he wrote, in the conviction that "a similarity of thinking" and personal good will would guarantee James Madison's support. "Aware of the intrinsic difficulties of the situation and of the powers of Mr. Madison, I do not believe I should have accepted under a different supposition." [1]

Hamilton had cause to feel betrayed and reason for concern. From their earliest acquaintance—in the Confederation Congress during the emergency of 1783—he and Madison had joined repeatedly in efforts to secure a more effective central government. The bolder, younger man had been accustomed to defer to the Virginian's talents as a parliamentary leader. His admiration was sincere, and he was not without substantial grounds for his assumption that Madison would use his talents to guide the funding and assumption

* Mr. Banning is an associate professor of history at the University of Kentucky. Portions of this article were read in an earlier version to the Shelby Cullom Davis Seminar at Princeton University. The author is grateful to the members of the seminar for criticisms which prompted further thinking.

[1] Hamilton to Edward Carrington, 26 May 1792 (Harold C. Syrett et al., eds., *The Papers of Alexander Hamilton* [26 vols.; New York and London, 1960-79], XI, 426-45). The whole of my summary of Hamilton's analysis is taken from this letter. I have modernized spelling and punctuation and given abbreviations in full here and throughout the article.

plan through the House of Representatives. In 1783 James Madison had been the first public figure to propose a federal assumption of state debts. Madison's Address to the States of 26 April 1783 had defended a congressional request for new federal revenues in terms that condemned discrimination against secondary holders of the public debt. In a private conversation at the Constitutional Convention, Hamilton reported, Madison had once again endorsed assumption. In all their talks, "down to the commencement of the new government," he had never hinted at a change of mind.

Before the House of Representatives initiated its debate on the report, Hamilton approached his friend and contrasted his position of 1790 with his stance in 1783. Madison explained that massive transfers of the debt from its original to secondary holders during the years since 1783 had "essentially changed the state of the question" concerning discrimination, which he now intended to support. He also said that he had always envisioned a federal assumption of state debts, to which he was still not opposed in principle, as those debts had stood at the peace, but not as they stood in the aftermath of differential efforts by the states to retire them.

This explanation hardly satisfied the secretary of the treasury, nor has it satisfied the numerous historians who have shared Hamilton's puzzlement. An assumption of the mass of debts the states had already retired, together with the obligations not yet met, would have added enormously and unnecessarily to the federal burden, perhaps endangering the government's success. Transfers of the Revolutionary debt had been continuous since it was first incurred. Why was it only now that Madison expressed an inclination to distinguish between original and secondary holders?

Hamilton's befuddlement increased. In the congressional session following his opposition to the funding plan, Madison denounced creation of a national bank, although he had moved at Philadelphia to add a federal right to create such corporations to the enumerated powers of Congress. He also gradually revealed, in Hamilton's opinion, a "womanish attachment to France and a womanish resentment against Great Britain," which could produce an open war with the latter in six months' time. Finally, he joined with Thomas Jefferson to bring Philip Freneau to Philadelphia to establish a newspaper which consistently opposed administration measures. Indeed, as Hamilton perceived it, "in almost all the questions great and small" which arose after the first session of Congress, Madison sided with those "disposed to narrow the federal authority." His opposition to administration policies culminated in support for measures deliberately designed to drive the secre-

James Madison (1751-1836)

Virginia Historical Society

tary of the treasury from office. By March of 1792, Hamilton had openly declared his intention to treat his former ally as a foe.

As the other major author of *The Federalist*, Hamilton knew that Madison had long and recently maintained that "the real danger in our system was the subversion of the national authority by the preponderancy of the state governments." After 1789, however, "all his measures have proceeded on an opposite supposition." Hamilton could not conceive how he and Madison, "whose politics had formerly so much the same point of departure," could have reasoned to such contradictory conclusions in so short a time. He could only conclude that he had been mistaken in believing that the other "Publius" was a principled and candid man.

Insisting on a concord of opinion through the first session of Congress, Hamilton dismissed the possibility that fundamental principle could account for Madison's position of 1792. He considered other motives. He suspected that Jefferson's pernicious influence had played some part in the reversal, yet he knew that Madison's decision on the funding plan had antedated Jefferson's arrival on the scene. He decided, in the end, that Madison had been "seduced by the expectation of popularity and possibly by the calculation of advantage to the state of Virginia." After all, there had been a wave of sentiment among the people for a discrimination between original and secondary holders of the debt, a sentiment widely shared among Virginians. It was certainly a fact that Virginians overwhelmingly opposed a federal assumption of state debts. Most Virginians were wary of the new government itself. In the aftermath of the ratification contest, Virginia's legislature had refused to send Madison to the Senate. Under Patrick Henry's influence, the legislature had established congressional districts that forced him into a disagreeable campaign to win election to the House. Entirely reasonable was Hamilton's conclusion that his old ally, wishing to retain the veneration he had earned at Philadelphia and in the first session of Congress, prompted too by an insecure position in Virginia, had sacrificed his principles to the pressures of the moment.

Defeated on discrimination and assumption, blocked again in the argument over a national bank, and countered in the meantime in his efforts to secure a provision for commercial discrimination against Great Britain, Madison gradually became so thoroughly disgruntled, in Hamilton's analysis, that he would risk subversion of the government itself in order to destroy the secretary of the treasury. Principle had given way, at first, to political exigency. Then, under the frustrating influence of repeated checks, principles themselves reversed. The nationalist of the 1780s was transmuted into a proponent of states' rights. The former friend of governmental strength and wisdom became the idol of the American Jacobins. Madison grew so accustomed to "sounding the alarm with great affected solemnity at encroachments meditated on the rights of the states," to "holding up the bugbear of a faction in the government having designs unfriendly to liberty," that he eventually came to believe it. In time, he managed to convince himself that notions he had originally "sported to influence others" were actually true: There was "some dreadful combination against state government and republicanism."

Hamilton's analysis was searching and persuasive. Acknowledging the probity for which his foe was famous, the critique was so plausible that it has powerfully affected nearly everyone who has attempted to explain Madison's conduct during the 1780s and 1790s. Recent writings overwhelmingly agree that Madison reversed his course as swiftly and as completely as Hamilton maintained, probably for reasons similar to those that Hamilton suggested.[2] They do so in the face of Madison's own notorious insistence that no political figure of his time was actually less open to a charge of inconsistency.

Madison's own evaluation of his conduct should not, of course, be too readily accepted. Early in their training, historians are cautioned to beware of self-serving statements, and the crux of Hamilton's complaint was indisputably correct. As late as 1789, Madison feared that even under the new Constitution, the necessary powers of the central government would prove vulnerable to encroachments by the states. By 1792, his fears were on the other side. If Hamilton had said no more than that, his accusation would present no problem. If modern scholars said no more, this article would have no purpose. But Hamilton and Madison had never been at "the same point of departure," and Madison's intentions and assumptions were not what most historians have taken them to be.

Hamilton misunderstood his colleague. Sharing some of Hamilton's assumptions, most historians have shared to some degree in his misjudgment.

---

[2] "Madison had completely reversed his former position" on assumption and discrimination and offered a "dubious" explanation for doing so; his opposition to Hamilton's plan was "probably a tactical maneuver . . . dictated by political expediency," a move to strengthen his position in Virginia and Virginia's position in national politics (E. James Ferguson, *The Power of the Purse: A History of American Public Finance, 1776-1790* [Chapel Hill, 1961], 297-99). Ferguson's is among the most persuasive presentations of an interpretation whose shadings range from the emphasis on Madison's self-interest and hypocrisy in Forrest McDonald, *Alexander Hamilton: A Biography* (New York, 1979), pp. 175, 177-86, 199-201, to the sympathetic explanation of Madison's constitutional reversal in the biographies cited in n. 8 below.

Indeed, there are at least two ways in which the thrust of modern scholarship may even have compounded Hamilton's mistake. The dominant interpretation of Madison's thought and conduct during the two decades surrounding the ratification of the Constitution has come to be more "Hamiltonian" than Hamilton himself advanced. The resulting account of the great Virginian would have pained and puzzled Madison and might have seemed surprising even to his staunchest foe. It is sufficiently at odds with the perceptions of contemporaries as to demand a sympathetic reexamination of Madison's own views.

Reconsideration might begin by calling for a different set of questions. The usual inquiries are: How did Madison, the nationalist of the 1780s, become the Jeffersonian proponent of states' rights? How was the "father of the Constitution" transfigured into the author of the Virginia Resolutions of 1798? They ask for information that was vital to the secretary of the treasury and continues so for everyone who wants to understand the origins of the new government and its eventual disruption in a civil war. But these questions incorporate a bias with which Hamilton began, insisting that the most important issue of these years was a contest for power between the nation and the states, implying that resistance to the new administration's definition of the scope of federal authority must have involved a change of attitude about the new regime itself. The phrasing interjects a tangle of connected problems which impede an effort to recover Madison's intentions. The questions assume a polarity between Madison's objectives during the 1780s and during the 1790s, between his original understanding of the Constitution and his stand in 1798, that was simply not characteristic of his thought.

James Madison was never a "nationalist," not if that word is loaded with many of the connotations it has come to carry in recent histories of the 1780s.[3] Nor did his Virginia Resolutions advocate the sovereignty of the states. Even as he led the nation through the framing and ratification of the Constitution, Madison expressed a lively fear of distant, energetic government, a fear he had displayed throughout the 1780s.[4] Innovative though he was, he maintained that the purposes and powers of the central government were not so much altered by the new Constitution as were the means

---

[3] Lance Banning, "James Madison and the Nationalists, 1780-1783," *William and Mary Quarterly*, 3d ser., XL (1983), 227-55.

[4] Speech of 29 June 1787 (Max Farrand, ed., *The Records of the Federal Convention of 1787* [1911-37; reprint ed.; 4 vols.; New Haven, 1966], I, 464-65); Jacob E. Cooke, ed., *The Federalist* (Middletown, Conn., 1961), No. 41, pp. 270-75.

by which those ends could be attained.[5] As he conceived it, the fundamental flaw of the Confederation had not been a radically mistaken definition of the proper objects of the state and central governments, but ineffective mechanisms for enabling the federal government to act effectively within its proper sphere. The great accomplishment of constitutional reformers had not been a radical redistribution of responsibilities from state to federal hands, but structural reforms allowing Congress to meet the needs that it had always been intended to secure. The innovations of 1787, from this point of view, were essentially conservative in their intent. So were the arguments of 1798, with which Madison's early understanding of the Constitution was not in conflict.

From the ratification contest through the nullification controversy, which came upon the country during his retirement, Madison consistently defined the new regime as neither national nor purely confederate. Created by the bodies politic of the several united states, the Constitution, as he understood it, rendered the central government supreme within its sphere and strictly limited that sphere to needs that could not be satisfied by the separate states. The Constitution marked the proper boundaries between concurrent governments, all of which possessed a right to call attention to infractions of the charter and none of which possessed the ultimate authority to interpret the organic law.[6] In 1787 as in 1798 Madison desired a well-constructed, federal republic—not, as Hamilton did, because nothing better could be secured—but because no other form of government seemed consistent with the American Revolution. In the 1780s as in the 1790s, Madison's essential purpose was to nurture and to defend a revolutionary order of society and politics, not to widen or to contract the sphere of federal authority. His starting point for constitutional reform and his conception of the finished Constitution were never anything but incompatible with Hamilton's.

Historians, of course, have not lost sight of all of these essential differences. Several have contrasted Madison's federalism, which was friendly to the states, with Hamilton's continuing hostility to state attachments.[7] Madison's biographers do not believe that he was motivated principally by political

---

[5] Cooke, *Federalist* No. 45, p. 314; speech of 11 June 1788 (Jonathan Elliot, ed., *The Debates in the Several State Conventions on the Adoption of the Federal Constitution...*, III [Washington, D.C., 1854], 259).

[6] The point is particularly well made in Edward McNall Burns, *James Madison: Philosopher of the Constitution* (New Brunswick, 1938), pp. 178-79 and passim.

[7] For example, Gottfried Dietze, *The Federalist: A Classic on Federalism and Free Government* (Baltimore, 1960), pp. 260-64, 267-71 and passim; Alpheus Thomas Mason, "The Federalist—A Split Personality," *American Historical Review*, LVII (1952), 625-43; Douglass Adair, *Fame and the Founding Fathers: Essays by Douglass Adair*, ed. Trevor Colbourn (New York, 1974).

expediency.[8] Yet Madison's defenders have been no less ready than was Hamilton to detect a quick retreat from nationalism in the years after 1789. While clearing Madison of charges of one sort of inconsistency, they have introduced an accusation that the subject might have found still more offensive: a sudden reversal from broad to strict construction of the Constitution. Meanwhile, other modern studies have increasingly relied on the tenth *Federalist* as a key to Madison's position in the years to 1789. Together these two thrusts of recent scholarship have added final touches to a current portrait of a youthful Madison who stands much closer to Alexander Hamilton than any contemporary would have believed. Certain aspects of his thought and conduct have been clarified while other aspects equally important to a balanced view have been obscured.

Modern scholarship owes an enormous debt to Irving Brant's magnificent biography. Often accused of being too defensive of his hero, Brant, nevertheless, was primarily responsible for removing Madison from the shadow cast by Thomas Jefferson and for restoring him to his contemporary standing as a major leader in his own right, both before 1787 and after 1789. While sometimes adding greatly to our knowledge, every subsequent biographer has started with Brant's masterwork, and there have been few challenges to several of his most important themes.

Brant's biases, however, pervaded his six volumes and led him to interpret Madison in ways that may persistently have misled later scholars. Brant was a New Dealer. He approved of Hamiltonian means to Jeffersonian ends. The youthful Madison, as Brant perceived him, also blended an expansive attitude toward federal authority with a commitment to civil liberties and a deep hostility to the abuse of government by special interests. From the moment when he reaches Philadelphia to take his seat in the Continental Congress, Brant's Madison is an enthusiastic leader of a persistent effort to enlarge the powers of the central government. His nationalism grows progressively more intense, culminating in the Constitutional Convention, where compromises demanded by the inflexible smaller states then engendered second thoughts. These second thoughts, in Brant's interpretation, turned into a profound change of course under the pressure of Hamilton's successes after 1789. Madison's hostility to governmental favors for the few

---

[8] Hamilton and Madison "disagreed from the outset on social and economic matters. This disagreement grew until it produced a change in Madison's political and constitutional views" (Irving Brant, *James Madison* [6 vols.; Indianapolis, 1941-61], II, 217). Madison shifted "his view of the powers that could be safely consigned to the federal government in order to *preserve* consistency on the vastly more important matter of republican freedom" (Ralph Ketcham, *James Madison: A Biography* [New York and London, 1971], pp. 314-15).

overrode his wish for a more vigorous regime, and he became committed to a politics that forced him, for the rest of his career, to hide the fervent nationalism of his youth.

Brant's interpretation, seldom challenged in general outline and undeniably insightful, is problematic at a number of important points. Of all these, the one that has seemed least debatable would almost certainly have proved the most disturbing to Madison himself. Without exception, subsequent historians have followed Brant's suggestion that the Virginian moved from broad to strict construction of the Constitution after 1789. During his years in the Confederation Congress, Brant maintained, Madison believed in "easy discovery" of federal powers where none were explicitly granted, conducting a deliberate campaign to expand the boundaries of federal authority by way of a doctrine of implied congressional powers. At the Constitutional Convention, he and other members of the committee on unfinished business silently inserted the general welfare clause, which was a deliberate and substantive grant of power. Advancing arguments for broad construction and implicit powers in *The Federalist* and holding to them during the first session of the new Congress, Madison abruptly switched positions only when confronted with Hamilton's plan for a national bank.[9]

Nowhere did Brant's biases encourage a more serious misreading of his subject. Surviving evidence conclusively suggests that Madison was always a strict constructionist, that a profound regard for chartered limitations of authority was as central to his thinking during the 1780s as it was after 1789.[10] Hamilton did not maintain the contrary. Nor did any other of Madison's contemporaries. Yet recent studies of the new republic uniformly say that the Virginian was a sudden convert to a strict construction of the Constitution.[11] It has even been repeatedly suggested that Hamilton's defense of the constitutionality of the bank was derived from Madison's argument in *Federalist* No. 44.[12]

---

[9] Brant, *Madison*, II, 110-11, 118; III, chap. 10 and pp. 180-81, 332-33.

[10] Banning, "Madison and the Nationalists," *WMQ*, 3d ser., XL (1983), 235-37, 239.

[11] Even Harold Schultz, the biographer most resistent to describing Madison as a nationalist during the 1780s, believes that "Madison's views on specific policies came first and . . . the constitutional argument was derivative and secondary, . . . an instrumentality for blocking undesirable federal legislation" (*James Madison* [New York, 1970], pp. 97-99).

[12] Since Brant, numerous historians have pointed particularly to this number as evidence that Madison advanced a doctrine of broad construction and implied powers (Brant, *Madison*, III, 180-81; Cooke, *Federalist*, pp. 304-5). If the often-quoted sentences are put in context, though, Madison clearly was arguing that the necessary-and-proper clause is not a grant of extensive additional powers. Madison defended the phrasing of the clause as well calculated to make it unnecessary for Congress to usurp by implication and construction authority transcending its chartered limits. Madison's numbers of *The Federalist*, not to mention his other writings, are peppered with defenses of specific grants of power on grounds that these will obviate unavoid-

More must be said about the implications of this view below, for the Virginian's consistent strict constructionism is an indispensable, neglected starting point for better understanding. First, however, a second way in which Madison has been forced into a mold that even Hamilton did not discern must be described.

Of Brant's contemporaries, none added more to comprehension of the Revolutionary generation than Douglass Adair, not least in several essays on *The Federalist*.[13] Among their many contributions, Adair's exceptionally fine essays added impetus to an increasing interest in *Federalist* No. 10, which scholars since Charles Beard have seen as an especially important key to Madison, to the Federalist movement, and to a transition from a classical to a more modern mode of political thinking. In this, there has been no mistake. Madison's most distinctive contribution to the Federalist movement was probably his insistence that constitutional reform address the vices of republican government within the revolutionary states as well as the debilities of the Confederation. The tenth *Federalist* was his fullest presentation of the idea—novel even if anticipated by David Hume—that enlarging the sphere of republican government might counteract the characteristic evil of a democratic system: the majority's pursuit of special interests at the expense of others' rights. Extension of the sphere may have been the most effective argument against the most persuasive criticism of the Constitution, and Madison's analysis of the relationships among a people who could not be differentiated into two social orders was a significant advance toward modern thought. The essay fully merits repeated readings.

Two difficulties nonetheless arise from our particular attention to this famous essay. It strengthens the prevailing inclination to exaggerate the author's nationalism, and it can easily result in serious misunderstanding of Madison's intentions.[14] In *Federalist* No. 10 and elsewhere, Madison

---

able usurpations. He repeatedly decried a wish that the framers had written into the Constitution prohibitions that necessity would eventually have forced Congress to find a way around. These would have been "worse than in vain"; they would have planted "in the Constitution itself necessary usurpations of power, every precedent of which is a germ of unnecessary and multiplied repetitions" (see *Federalist* No. 41, p. 270; No. 42, p. 280; No. 43, p. 297).

13 These are conveniently reprinted in Adair, *Fame and the Founding Fathers*, ed. Colburn, pp. 27-106, 251-58.

14 The history of modern interest in the tenth *Federalist* is too nearly a tale of the replacement of one misreading by another. Adair corrected Beard's assertion that Madison anticipated an economic interpretation of political behavior; this opinion has few current advocates. More persistent has been a "pluralist" misreading, which, in its crudest form, asserts that Madison approved a clash of special interests and identified the product of such clashes with the public good (Paul F. Bourke, "The Pluralist Reading of James Madison's Tenth *Federalist*," *Perspectives in American History*, IX [1975], 271-95). Despite rebuttals, a subtler version of a pluralist interpretation persists among some able analysts who would regard the essay as the culmination of a long-term trend toward the acceptance of interest-group politics and an ideology of pluralistic

maintained that the large electoral districts required by the Constitution would favor the selection of men of extensive reputation, proven talent, and magnanimous vision over petty politicians willing to flatter the voters' prejudices and devote themselves to the majority's pursuit of partial interests. He argued that large electorates were more likely to choose representatives wise enough to discern the general good and virtuous enough not to sacrifice the good of all to lesser ends. Although he scrupulously avoided any reference to a "natural aristocracy," in private letters as in published writings, he preferred a more enlightened leadership and hoped the Constitution would encourage its emergence. Madison, after all, was writing in a republican tradition which contrasted an inevitable conflict of interests between different hereditary orders with the natural identity of interests between a non-hereditary leadership and its electors. To identify the concept of a filtration of talent as the centerpiece of Madison's attempt at reconciling majority control with liberty is to misread Madison as wishing for representatives who can ignore the demands of their constituents. Thus, from the argument for an extension of the sphere is inferred that Madison's most fundamental object was to transfer power from the hands of demagogic and illiberal state politicians to this special group of federal supermen.[15] For Alexander Hamilton, the critical necessity of the 1780s and 1790s was very much a massive transfer of authority from state to federal hands—and even to the hands of federal officials least responsive to the people's immediate will. Madison's most basic wishes were quite different.

Filtration of the people's will was a secondary and subsidiary point of the tenth *Federalist*—more than an afterthought, but much less than the vital core of Madison's thinking.[16] Madison did hope for an improvement in the quality of representation and decision-making, but he neither expected nor

individualism (see Kenneth A. Lockridge, "Social Change and the Meaning of the American Revolution," *Journal of Social History*, VI [1973], 403-39). Lockridge builds on Gordon S. Wood, *The Creation of the American Republic, 1776-1787* (Chapel Hill, 1969), esp. chap. 15, "The American Science of Politics." But Lockridge neglects Wood's frequent warnings that no American of 1789, certainly not Madison himself, had fully assimilated the theory toward which their developing ideas were pointing.

15 This reading of the essay emerges most fully in Garry Wills, *Explaining America: The Federalist* (New York, 1980). Yet even Wood, who is a sensitive and cautious student of Madison, may overemphasize the centrality of this concept in Madison's own thinking if not in that of some of his allies (Wood, *Creation of the Republic*, chap. 12 passim, esp. p. 505).

16 The concept is not mentioned, for example, in Madison's letter to Jefferson of 24 Oct. 1787, which offered a preliminary version of the argument of the famous essay and will be discussed more fully below. The possibility of an improvement in the quality of representation is mentioned only briefly, as an "auxiliary desideratum" of good government, in the "Vices of the Political System of the United States" (William T. Hutchinson et al., eds., *The Papers of James Madison* [Chicago and Charlottesville, 1962-], IX, 357). It is clearly identified as a secondary consideration in the tenth *Federalist* itself (Cooke, *Federalist*, p. 63).

wished for federal representatives who would not reflect the character and interests of their constituencies. The major argument of the tenth *Federalist* is that the large republic will incorporate so many different interests as to render unlikely the formation of majorities in pursuit of objects incompatible with the good of all. This reasoning would immediately collapse if the character and conduct of representatives were not assumed to mirror the variety among the people. Laws which threaten people's rights are passed by legislatures, and only if the legislators actually reflect the pluralistic structure of the great republic will the multiplicity of interests tend to check a union of a majority for factious ends.[17]

Madison emphatically did not suggest that any sort of large republic would provide superior protection for liberty. His argument for an extension of the sphere was premised on the limited authority and federal structure of the new regime. The constrained authority of federal officials seemed to him among the necessary guarantees of a continuing identity of interests between the people and their rulers, without which an extension of the sphere would not have been a democratic answer to a democratic problem. In *Federalist* No. 10, the praise of large electorates is closely followed by a major qualification: "There is a mean on both sides of which inconveniencies will be found." A small electorate is likely to elect men so thoroughly attached to local interests and perspectives as to be unfit "to comprehend and pursue great and national objects." Too large a suffrage, however, can result in representatives "too little acquainted with . . . local circumstances and lesser interests." Large electorates are therefore safe and preferable only when such local interests lie outside their province.

Madison's support for an enlarged republic as an essential safeguard for minorities was characteristically accompanied with a recognition of the danger of creating a government unresponsive to the majority. Madison recognized that too much authority in hands too distant from the people would pose the risk of tyranny.

The larger the society, *provided it lie within a practicable sphere*, the more duly capable it will be of self government. And happily for the republican cause,

---

[17] Hamilton grasped this point immediately when he first heard Madison's great speech in the convention on enlarging the sphere. "The Assembly when chosen will meet in one room if they are drawn from half the globe," he jotted, and "paper money is capable of giving a general impulse" (that is, of creating a majority faction) among the people and thus in the national legislature (Farrand, *Federal Convention*, I, 146). Among additional indications that Madison assumed that federal representatives would reflect the local interests and prejudices of their constituencies, one of the clearest is *Federalist* No. 46 (Cooke, *Federalist*, pp. 318-19).

the practicable sphere may be carried to a very great extent, by a judicious modification and mixture of the federal principle.[18]

For Madison, in short, the Constitution struck a delicate mean between an excess of democracy and the antidemocratic perils of consolidation, "the great and aggregate interests being referred to the national, the local and particular to the state legislatures," each of which would be responsible for and responsive to the needs they were particularly equipped to meet.[19]

Every part of the tenth *Federalist* must be considered in relationship to every other part and to the essay's total context. Fascination with the essay, proper in itself, too readily encourages a tendency to turn to it or even to a part of it in isolation from the other writings, including other numbers of *The Federalist*, which clarify its central concepts and qualify its place in Madison's thinking.[20] Madison considered an expanded territory to be an important barrier to formation of majority factions, but not because he hoped the result would be representatives removed from their constituents' control. Unresponsive rulers would not be republican at all. A large republic would break the force of majority interest without endangering majority rule because a large variety of concerns would be represented in a Congress whose authority would not extend beyond those national subjects on which its members would adequately reflect their constituents' desires.

Finally, Madison did not consider an extension of the sphere, important though the concept was, to be a complete solution to the difficulties suggested by the conduct of the revolutionary states. If the tenth *Federalist* had been the sum of his thinking, he need not have written twenty-eight additional numbers. With most of his contemporaries, Madison assumed that the legislature would be the dominant branch of the federal government, as the legislatures were in all the states. With an extension of the sphere, majority abuse of power would become less likely, representatives more enlightened. But majority faction would not be precluded, nor was the problem of majority abuse of power the only one with which republican statesmen had to be concerned. Madison also remained alert to the dangers of minority faction, most especially to the possibility that rulers, once independent of the people, could become the most dangerous minority of all. To *Federalist* No. 10 he therefore added several other essays on the necessity of checks and balances and on the distribution of authority between the federal

---

[18] Cooke, *Federalist* No. 10, p. 63; No. 51, p. 353. My italics.

[19] Ibid., No. 10, p. 63; No. 51.

[20] This is to reemphasize central themes of Neal Riemer, "The Republicanism of James Madison," *Political Science Quarterly*, LXIX (1954), 45-64, and "James Madison's Theory of the Self-Destructive Features of Republican Government," *Ethics*, LXV (1954), 34-43.

government and the states. When he wrote *The Federalist*, he anticipated that state encroachments would prove the characteristic danger to the new regime. At no point, though, did he lose sight of dangers on the other side. At no time was he able to embrace the prospect of excessive concentration of authority in federal hands or in the hands of unresponsive branches of the federal government. In private letters, he was careful to make clear that the authors of *The Federalist* were not responsible for one another's numbers, hinting his discomfort with some of Hamilton's views.[21] He admitted that some advocates of the new Constitution carried their alarm with the American majority too far.[22] The Constitution he endorsed provided for a compound, not a unitary government, a federal republic that would remain under popular control.

What difference does it make, however, if Hamilton and later critics started with assumptions, terms, or questions that might have seemed inherently misleading to Madison himself? What if we have misread or overemphasized a single essay, or come too close to thinking that Madison and Hamilton had shared "the same point of departure?" What would a more Madisonian Madison be like?

Entering the Continental Congress at age twenty-nine, Madison acquired an early reputation as a capable proponent of Virginia's distinctive desires: denial of the great land companies' claims to vast tracts beyond the mountains; treaties recognizing an American right to navigate the Mississippi River; and a Western boundary for the United States encompassing, at minimum, Virginia's western claims. As the War for Independence moved into the South, urgent problems shoved him toward support of larger powers for Congress—as, indeed, these problems pushed a large majority of delegates in the same direction. Madison was not an early or enthusiastic leader of this general shift toward centralizing change. Distrusting the New Englanders, locked constantly in bitter battles with the landless states, and theoretically inclined toward rather strict construction of the Articles of Confederation, he opposed congressional control of commerce and initially resisted both a national bank and the impost proposal of 1781. Not until the fall of 1782, when the financial crisis peaked, did he begin to work consistently with the reformers from the middle states. Even then, his differ-

---

[21] Madison to Jefferson, 11 Aug. 1788 (Hutchinson et al., *Papers of Madison*, XI, 227). Firmer, but more suspect, was Madison's late-life statement that he and Hamilton soon dispensed with their attempt to read each other's essays prior to publication partly because neither wished "to give a positive sanction to all the doctrines and sentiments of the other; there being a known difference in the general complexion of their political theories" (Elizabeth Fleet, ed., "Madison's 'Detached Memoranda,'" *WMQ*, 3d ser., III [1946], 565).

[22] Madison to Philip Mazzei, 10 Dec. 1788 (Hutchinson et al., *Papers of Madison*, XI, 389).

ences from men of more consistent consolidating vision led him to break ranks with Hamilton and Robert Morris as the Newburgh crisis reached its climax.[23]

During his years in Congress, Madison made important contributions to the movement to strengthen the central government. Urging mutual concessions and almost instinctively inclined to associate Virginia's interests with the long-term needs of the country as a whole, he played a major role in the creation of a national domain. He repeatedly wrote home to urge attention to Confederation needs and forbearance in the face of irritating jealousies of the Old Dominion. His compromise proposals were the core of the recommendations prompted by the emergency of 1783.

Still, Madison's eventual commitment to a thoroughgoing alteration of the federal system did not rise as a response to the sort of problems the central government encountered during his years in Congress. His plan did not take a form consistent with the solutions envisioned from that time by Hamilton and Morris. While it is accurate to say, with proper cautions, that Hamilton preferred a radical concentration of authority and attempted from the early eighties to nationalize the American system, Madison's objectives cannot be understood in similar terms. In 1783, Hamilton already wished for a general convention that would transform the federal system. Madison opposed this measure.[24] He believed that Congress could not continue to rely "on a punctual and unfailing compliance by thirteen separate and independent governments with periodical demands of money."[25] But he did not yet look, with Hamilton, toward the complete replacement of the Articles of Confederation, nor did he share in Hamilton's or Morris's desire "to achieve political centralization by fiscal reform."[26]

Madison had entered Congress a republican with a continental perspective, conditioned from his youth to look beyond Virginia for the fortunes of the Revolutionary cause. The years in Congress intensified his continentalism and confirmed his belief that the fate of the union and the fate of the Revolution were inseparably entwined. But Madison had also entered Congress a committed American Revolutionary. By 1780 he held intensely to the range of concepts identified with the Revolution's early thrust: hostility to privilege, commitment to written constitutions founded on consent, the

---

[23] Elaboration and support of my discussion of Madison's years in the old Congress may be found in "Madison and the Nationalists," *WMQ*, 3d ser., XL (1983), 227-55.

[24] Syrett et al., *Papers of Hamilton*, III, 420-26; Stephen Higginson to Henry Knox, 8 Feb. 1787 (Edmund C. Burnett, ed., *Letters of Members of the Continental Congress*, VII [Washington, D.C., 1934], 123 n. 4).

[25] Speech of 28 Jan. 1783 (Hutchinson et al., *Papers of Madison*, VI, 143-47).

[26] Ferguson, *Power of the Purse*, p. 292.

belief that republics rest on virtue, and a concern with the social and economic foundations of virtuous conduct. These convictions, together with his role as a delegate from Virginia, shaped and limited his contributions to reform.

While in Congress, Madison usually attributed the difficulties of the central government to sectional disputes, in which he was continuously involved, or to financial disabilities resulting from the war. He hoped that peace would meliorate these problems.[27] Through these years, he quarreled neither with the central principles of the Articles of Confederation nor with the Revolutionary constitution of the several states. Only after he returned from Congress to struggle year by year in the Virginia House of Delegates with paper money, tax abatements, and assessments for religion, only as Virginia and the other states repeatedly displayed their inability to grapple separately with Britain's navigation laws, did he begin to think in terms of far more radical reform. Only then did he begin to question the republican precept that the majority is the safest repository of civil liberty, that in republics right and might are one.[28] Not until he achieved an intellectual advance linking the difficulties he had learned about in Congress with his mounting discontent as a state legislator, did he make the leap to authorship of the Virginia Plan. Even then, his early Revolutionary arbor and long experience in Congress defending Virginia's unpopular claims remained essential aspects of the context in which he shaped his brilliant and distinctive solution to the problems he perceived.

What Madison was seeking at the Constitutional Convention was far from a consolidated system. Recently—and properly—historians have emphasized the provision in the Virginia Plan for a federal veto on state laws. Madison proposed a federal veto that would reach to all state legislation, as the royal prerogative once had done. He argued strenuously for this provision, under which the central government would have exercised a power more intrusive and more plainly unacceptable to most contemporaries than anything the great convention actually proposed. He was intensely disappointed when the convention rejected even a limited veto, and this has seemed to some interpreters to be clear evidence that he would really have preferred as centralized a system as Hamilton himself desired.[29]

---

[27] See the preface for his notes on debates in the Constitutional Convention (Farrand, *Federal Convention*, III, 542-43).

[28] "Vices of the Political System" (Hutchinson et al., *Papers of Madison*, IX, 350-51, 354); "Observations on Jefferson's Draft of a Constitution for Virginia" (ibid., XI, 287-88).

[29] Charles F. Hobson, "The Negative on State Laws: James Madison, the Constitution, and the Crisis of Republican Government," *WMQ*, 3d ser., XXXVI (1979), 215-35.

And yet the federal veto on state acts, as Madison conceived it, was to be a purely defensive power, wielded by a federal government whose positive authority would be of limited extent. It could not have consolidated the states into a unitary government such as the British one. Madison saw the veto as a necessary tool for checking state encroachments on the delegated powers of the central government. It seemed the only certain instrument for correcting the ills of republicanism within the several states, assuring the intervention of an impaired federal umpire whenever a local majority transgressed the bounds of justice or threatened the personal rights of a minority. The federal veto, though, was not to be an instrument with which the central government could set a positive direction. It was to be a negative on acts that breached a solemn compact or contradicted the most basic principles of a republican revolution, thereby threatening the popular commitment to a republican regime.

In the Constitutional Convention and as "Publius," Madison repeatedly insisted that America should not approve a Constitution inconsistent with revolutionary principles. The central theme of his particular contributions to *The Federalist* was the perfectly republican character of the proposed reform. Both there and in the private letter which contains his most complete defense of the federal negative on state laws, Madison said clearly that revolutionary principles were inconsistent with a wholly national regime.

In this famous letter, which anticipated the tenth *Federalist,* Madison explained to Jefferson the danger of majority oppression in republics. He suggested that the evil might be overcome by enlarging the sphere of republican government and taking in such a wide variety of different interests that a factious, oppressive majority would seldom appear. Then he immediately admitted, as he almost always did, that "this doctrine can only hold within a sphere of a mean extent." "In too extensive" a republic, he continued, a "defensive concert may be rendered too difficult against the oppression of those entrusted with the administration." A federal negative had seemed appropriate because the new government would be "sufficiently neutral" between different interests in the states "to control one part from invading the rights of another, and *at the same time* sufficiently controlled itself, from setting up an interest adverse to that of the entire society."[30] Madison called the new regime a "feudal system of republics," but fundamentally unlike a feudal system in that its head would not be "independent" of subordinate authorities, as well as limited by them, but "derived entirely

---

[30] Madison to Jefferson, 24 Oct. 1787 (Hutchinson et al., *Papers of Madison,* X, 214). My emphasis.

from the subordinate authorities." The federal government would therefore serve as an impartial umpire of contentions between its subjects in the several states, much as a feudal monarch was supposed to be. Yet "by its dependence on the community," the central government would "be at the same time sufficiently restrained" from sacrificing the happiness of all.

In the gathering at Philadelphia, Madison sought, as he said in the tenth *Federalist*, "a republican remedy for the diseases most incident to republican government." Relying on the federal principle to help define the "practicable sphere" of the new regime, he hoped to create a central government that would secure a revolutionary American order: by conducting a foreign policy which would foster the social and economic conditions on which a healthy republican polity must rest; and by avoiding the injustices and inconstancies which were endangering the people's faith in the revolutionary experiment. In the aftermath of the convention, he speedily began to hope that the new Constitution would prove adequate despite the failure to include the federal veto. As he defended the convention's work, he overcame his early doubts. He also came to understand more clearly than he had before that the objectives he associated with the plan for constitutional reform could not be reconciled with the policies that Alexander Hamilton would soon propose.[31]

In 1789 Madison assumed a central role in putting into action the government that he had done so much to create and to defend. He helped prepare George Washington's inaugural address to Congress, wrote the House of Representatives' reply, and then helped author Washington's response. Together with his opposition to the Senate's wish for a majestic title for the president, these actions went a good way toward establishing the tone he thought essential for the new regime. He also took a major part in the creation of executive departments. At the Constitutional Convention, Madison had been convinced that only a unitary executive would prove a responsible one; now he helped defeat attempts to associate the Senate in the removal of executive officials and to place the Treasury in the hands of a commission. He was principally responsible, as well, for quick addition to the Constitution of a Bill of Rights. Two basic goals appear to have guided him through the critical first session of the federal Congress. He wanted to complete a central government with the capacity to secure the republican revolution. He was equally determined to reconcile the host of honest men who wondered whether revolutionary principles could long survive the alteration of the federal system.

---

[31] Ibid., pp. 210, 214; Cooke, *Federalist* No. 10, p. 65.

No federal initiative was more important to both ends, in Madison's opinion, than retaliatory measures against the British for their debilitating restrictions on American commerce. Madison accepted the need for radical constitutional reform when he concluded that only federal action could compel Great Britain to relax its navigation laws. He conceived this as the critical first step toward a world of freer trade which he considered indispensable to American economic independence and to sustaining America's revolutionary course.[32] Toward this end, Madison attempted in 1789 to write into the first federal tariff a discrimination against nations that had not concluded commercial treaties with the United States. He was defeated. He tried again during the winter of 1790-91. Once again, he failed. He failed, in part, because the secretary of the treasury resisted a commercial confrontation that could poison Anglo-American relations and seriously disrupt the flow of revenues on which his plans for managing the debt depended.

Hamilton had no more cause to feel betrayed when Madison opposed his plans for an assumption of state debts and for a national bank than Madison had cause to feel betrayed by Hamilton's opposition to commercial discrimination. Arguably, Hamilton had much less. From the experiences of 1783, Hamilton had reason to anticipate that Madison would oppose any federal measure patently inequitable for Virginia, as the original proposal for assumption was. Madison had also shown repeatedly that a respect for constitutional limitations of authority was central to his republican convictions. Once the Constitution had endured the gauntlet of the ratifying conventions, Madison regarded it as an organic law. As he saw it, the Federal Convention had declined to authorize creation of a national bank, and the people had not ratified a Constitution containing such a clause.

Hamilton might even have expected the Virginian's opposition to his funding plan. A persistent revulsion against speculative gains at public expense and a reiterated commitment to a social order characterized by comparative equality, honest industry, frugality, and simple manners made discrimination a natural choice for Madison.[33] He had on more than one occasion pronounced his opposition to a "prolonged" or "perpetual" debt.[34] Nor did his proposal for discrimination really mark a complete reversal of

---

[32] Banning, "Madison and the Nationalists," *WMQ*, 3d ser., XL (1983), 252-53; Drew R. McCoy, *The Elusive Republic: Political Economy in Jeffersonian America* (Chapel Hill, 1980), esp. chap. 3; McCoy, "The Virginia Port Bill of 1784," *Virginia Magazine of History and Biography*, LXXXIII (1975), 288-303.

[33] This is the area of consistency emphasized by Brant and Ketcham.

[34] Among other places, in the very response to Hamilton's request for his opinions about funding to which the latter referred in his complaint to Carrington.

his position of 1783. In the Confederation Congress, Madison had opposed the kind of distinction between original and secondary holders that would have involved a partial repudiation of the debt and thus a violation of national morality: revaluation of the portion of the debt that had passed out of the hands of its original holders. In 1790 Madison still insisted that the government must meet its obligations in full. His alternative to Hamilton's proposal would actually have been, in certain ways, more consistent with a scrupulous regard for public faith than the secretary's own, since it did not involve a virtually compulsory reduction of the interest that the government had promised.[35]

Many revolutionaries resisted a funding plan that would entail a massive transfer of wealth into the hands of a relative few who would depend on the government for a significant proportion of their fortunes. Madison shared the feeling that this would be poor policy for a republic. He shared the view that asking original creditors, who had been forced by a defaulting government to sell its promises for fractions of their value, to sacrifice again to pay taxes on the debt into the indefinite future would be poor justice.[36] His alternative was part of a continuing attempt to secure popular commitment to the new regime by just, republican policies. His discrimination plan was intended to keep faith with those whose sacrifices had created the national debt and may also have reflected a desire to counter all proposals hinting at a breach of contract, Hamilton's as well as those of the repudiationists in Congress.[37]

Hamilton, by contrast, had suggested that an effort to retaliate against

---

[35] In characterizing Madison's proposal of 1790 as a sharp reversal of his previous position, Ferguson, like Hamilton, does not remark these differences. Madison's proposal of 1790, like Hamilton's own, would have paid the debt at its full face value and at a full 6 percent interest. Ferguson is also misleading when he suggests that Madison explained his support for discrimination as a consequence of "speculation attending Hamilton's report." Madison actually had been referring to transfers of the debt since 1783. But Ferguson's discussion is most suggestive in some other ways (*Power of the Purse*, pp. 293-302). See n. 37 below.

[36] Lance Banning, *The Jeffersonian Persuasion: Evolution of a Party Ideology* (Ithaca and London, 1978), pp. 141-47.

[37] When Ferguson calls Madison's proposal "a false issue" and an "unrealistic alternative," he does not mean that it would have been impossible to identify the original holders to whom the Virginian wished to return a portion of the money the government owed. Rather, he means to point out that Madison's plan might have made an assumption of state debts impossible and, more importantly, that it had only very narrow support. The really popular alternative to Hamilton, he suggests, would have been revaluation of the debt. This, together with a reduction of interest, is what had been suggested to Madison by William Maclay and what was being urged in the House by Samuel Livermore, Thomas Scott, James Jackson, and Thomas Tucker. I suspect that Madison had not given close consideration to the details of a proper funding plan until after he saw Hamilton's report. Then, disliking several features of Hamilton's plan and aware of the sizable sentiment in favor of what amounted to a partial repudiation, Madison developed an alternative that might conciliate the opposition while simultaneously fulfilling the government's pledges (and thus restoring public credit) at least as faithfully as Hamilton's own.

the British would be one of the first measures of a stronger federal regime.[38] He had eloquently explained how, under the new system, the several states would retain the capacity to intervene effectively against transgressions by the federal government of the constitutional limits of its power.[39] If there was a reversal of positions after 1789, Hamilton's was clearest. And as his policies unfolded one by one, they manifestly squinted at a new American order that the other "Publius" had long since identified as incompatible with revolutionary ends. When Madison contrasted his desires for the United States with the alternatives reflected in the current state of Europe, he expressed his horror at the prospect of "corruption" on the British model, at overgrown executives, and at a people whose liberties were crushed by standing armies and high, perpetual taxes necessary to support such forces and to manage a permanent national debt.[40]

Alexander Hamilton may well have been, as he insisted in the letter with which we began, "affectionately attached" to the cause of republican government. Few revolutionary leaders had better reason to condemn a social and political order based on accidents of birth. Yet Hamilton was also committed to the view that firm executive guidance and a sizable professional army were among the necessary means to national greatness. Hamilton's financial program was consciously designed to use a long-term, funded debt to separate the interests of a critical segment of the American elite from the prevailing inclinations of the body of the people.

Hamilton and Madison were both aware that the United States had not developed any counterpart to England's national elite. To both of them this fact was fully as important as it has been said to be in recent historical efforts comparing political developments in the two countries.[41] England's political nation was virtually identical, for certain purposes, with its landed gentlemen. The gentry were a cohesive social group which sat atop an

---

[38] Cooke, *Federalist* No. 11.

[39] Ibid., No. 28.

[40] In convention on 29 June 1787, after denouncing the "vicious representation" in Britain, Madison "prayed" the smaller states "to ponder well the consequences of suffering the Confederacy to go to pieces. . . . Let each state depend on itself for security . . . and the languishing condition of all the states . . . would soon be transformed into vigorous and high-toned governments." This would prove "fatal to the internal liberty of all. . . . A standing military force, with an overgrown executive, will not long be safe companions to liberty" (Farrand, *Federal Convention*, I, 464-65). In *Federalist* No. 41, he insisted that "nothing short of a Constitution fully adequate to the national defense and the preservation of the union can save America from as many standing armies" as there are separate states or confederacies and thus from the fate of Rome or contemporary Europe, where liberty was everywhere "crushed between standing armies and perpetual taxes" (Cooke, *Federalist*, pp. 272, 274).

[41] John M. Murrin, "The Great Inversion, or Court versus Country: A Comparison of the Revolution Settlements in England (1688-1721) and America (1776-1816)," in *Three British Revolutions: 1641, 1688, 1776*, ed. J. G. A. Pocock (Princeton, 1980), pp. 368-453.

integrated social order and normally supported an administration whose patronage and economic policies linked the executive with the landed representatives in Parliament and at the same time with financial, commercial, and officeholding segments of the elite.[42] The political nation of revolutionary America was a great deal larger and, like its economy, assumed a state and regional, not a national, configuration. For Madison this was America's great strength. The pluralistic structure of American society was mirrored in the irreducibly pluralistic character of its elite. Such diversity held out the promise that a polity erected on popular participation would prove consistent with protection of the fundamental liberties of all. For Hamilton the state and regional attachments of America's elite were obstacles to the pursuit of national ends, which must be overcome by governmental inducement of a class of influentials whose economic interests would tie them to the national regime. Hamilton intended to create a practical alternative to the pluralistic structure on which Madison had grounded his great dream.[43]

Madison objected to the Hamiltonian system, as Drew McCoy has best explained, because he considered its economic and social orientation inappropriate for a republican people. He disapproved of its tendency to aggrandize the executive branch of the federal government and to give that branch influence over those inside and out of Congress whose economic fortunes would be linked to the federal treasury's.[44] He protested the funding and assumption plan for unduly favoring certain states and certain citizens at the risk of alienating others from the union. He thought congressional approval of a national bank would bend the federal charter into shapes that its creators had not meant, altering the structure of the polity in ways that would eventually endanger its republican form.

Madison's opposition to the national bank on constitutional grounds has usually been seen as a convenient screen for other motives and a sharp reversal of a hitherto expansive attitude toward federal power. It was neither. As he continued to refine a continental vision of his own—in private letters, at the Constitutional Convention, as "Publius," and in a

[42] J. G. A. Pocock, "1776: The Revolution against Parliament," in ibid., pp. 265-88.

[43] Since the early 1780s, Hamilton had argued the necessity of creating among the nation's leadership a class of influentials tied to the federal government and capable of counterbalancing the influentials currently tied to the states. Genuine federal power, he insisted, required a union of the government's resources with those of a monied and officeholding class directly dependent on that government for promotion of their economic interests. See especially Hamilton's letters to an unknown recipient, to James Duane, and to Robert Morris, together with the conclusion of "The Continentalist" (Syrett et al., *Papers of Hamilton*, II, 234-51, 400-418, 604-35; III, 99-106).

[44] McCoy, *Elusive Republic*; Banning, *Jeffersonian Persuasion*.

series of letters to the *National Gazette*—Madison was more and more inclined to define a republican system in contrast to regimes in which political authority was independent of the people.[45] From 1790 forward, he saw with growing clarity that Hamiltonian measures opened the way to an exercise of influence on the federal government by special-interest factions.[46] Those policies created in the government and in its hangers-on an interest distinct from the public's as a whole.[47] With even greater perspicacity, he saw that Hamilton's construction of the Constitution allowed rulers to escape their proper dependence on society. The elective character of the government was the primary assurance of this dependence, but chartered limitations of authority and the federal structure defined in the organic law were additional supports. Madison's strict construction of the Constitution did not mark a change of course, for he had never been inclined toward any other view. His constitutional objections to Hamilton's designs were not politically convenient covers for more basic motives, not simply instrumental to his other wishes. They were integral components of a republican philosophy.

Late in life, Madison was asked why he had deserted Hamilton. He replied,

> "I deserted Colonel Hamilton, or, rather, Colonel Hamilton deserted me ... from his wishing to ... administer the government (these were Mr. Madison's very words), into what he thought it ought to be; while, on my part, I endeavored to make it conform to the Constitution as understood by the Convention that produced and recommended it, and particularly by the state conventions that adopted it."[48]

---

[45] On this point see also Robert J. Morgan, "Madison's Analysis of the Sources of Political Authority," *American Political Science Review*, LXXV (1981), 613-25.

[46] In the debate on the national bank, Madison reminded colleagues of "the great and extensive influence that incorporated societies had on public affairs in Europe. They are a powerful machine, which have always been found competent to effect objects on principles, in a great measure independent of the people" (Hutchinson et al., *Papers of Madison*, XIII, 384).

[47] Madison came as close to outrage as it was possible for him to do in response to the speculation attendant on the opening of the national bank—"a mere scramble for so much public plunder"—and on a further assumption of state debts during the summer of 1791. Such abuses, he told Jefferson, "make it a problem whether the system of the old paper under a bad government, or of the new under a good one, be chargeable with the greater substantial injustice. The true difference seems to be that by the former the few were victims to the many; by the latter the many to the few. . . . My imagination will not attempt to set bounds to the daring depravity of the times. The stock-jobbers will become the pretorian band of the government, at once its tools and its tyrant; bribed by its largesses, and overawing it by clamors and combinations" (Hutchinson et al., *Papers of Madison*, XIV, 43, 69).

[48] Interview with Nicholas P. Trist, 27 Sept. 1834 (Farrand, *Federal Convention*, III, 533-34). Perhaps the plainest evidence that Hamilton did hope to administer the government toward consolidation is his memorandum on the Constitution's prospects, 17-30 Sept. 1787 (Syrett et al., *Papers of Hamilton*, IV, 275-77).

The people, he insisted, had established a limited, federal republic. To force the federal charter into a different mold by broad construction would be to break the government's foundation in popular consent, a usurpation of the same sort as had moved the British colonies to revolution. Madison believed that usurpations were to be resisted on their first appearance, as they had been then. This one required greater seriousness of purpose because a concentration of authority in national hands would necessarily entail an end of union or a central government that must eventually approximate hereditary forms.[49]

Madison was a Virginia continentalist. This does not mean he rose in opposition to the funding and assumption plan in order to protect a faltering prestige at home; his reputation in his state and district were never that seriously at risk.[50] Nor is it very likely that he was seeking popularity, although he certainly believed that the success of the new government depended on its ability to win the veneration of the people with the equity and wisdom of its policies. He opposed assumption because he saw it as unfair to Virginia. He said as much, and said it with no feeling of embarrassment, for he believed that a representative had a duty to defend his constituents' legitimate interests. But this was not the most important way in which his stand reflected the interests and situation of his state. Unionist though he had always been—and Madison was one of the great early nationalists in his insistence on the bonds that made Americans a single people—his special kind of continentalism was a distinctive product of his experiences and perspective as a statesman of the Old Dominion.

Madison learned much from his opponents in the contest over ratification of the Constitution, but he required no help from Antifederalists to sense the dangers posed by what contemporaries called "consolidation." His comprehension of the nature of America's federal politics had been forged by several years of difficult defense of his state's particular interests in a Confederation Congress whose majority was usually unsympathetic to and jealous of Virginia. As a southern continentalist and former member of that Congress, as former leader of the Federalists in the state convention of 1788,

---

[49] Madison's most systematic explanation of the anti-democratic consequences of consolidation would come in his report to the House of Delegates on the responses to the Virginia Resolutions of 1798 (Gaillard Hunt, ed., *The Writings of James Madison*, VI [New York, 1906], 357-59).

[50] In the decidedly Antifederalist state legislature, following a powerful attack on Madison's principles by an embittered and magnetic Patrick Henry, the balloting for two senators produced 98 votes for Richard Henry Lee, 86 for William Grayson, and 77 for Madison. In a congressional district deliberately gerrymandered (or henrymandered) to place Madison's county in an Antifederalist district, he defeated James Monroe 1,308 to 972, winning more than 57 percent of the vote.

Madison understood the depth of sectional differences in the United States. He knew that a successful union must accommodate those differences. Interests and authority were simply too diffuse in the United States, both sectionally and vertically, for there to be a viable solution to its problems along the lines suggested by the course of English history to other Federalists of 1787-89.

Early in the 1780s, as thoughts turned from the difficulties of the war years to the prospects for America in time of peace, many continental-minded men began a long retreat toward what we might describe as a conventional solution to the problems Congress faced and a conventional vision of the path toward national greatness. They wished to imitate the undeniable success of eighteenth-century British statesmen with a system of administration and political economy that had helped to raise the little island to an envied height of happiness, stability, and international prestige. As they grew increasingly disgruntled with state politics and policies, many of them also came to a conclusion that private rights and public good could not be guaranteed in the United States by anything much short of a near imitation of the British constitution. Hamilton's great speech at the convention, proposing a life term for the executive and senators and a clear subordination of the states, urged exactly that.

Through the middle 1780s, Madison shared the growing discontent with the Articles of Confederation. No one felt a more profound revulsion with state politics. Still, Madison's experiences and background made it impossible for him to share the wish for a conventional solution. As an ardent revolutionary, he could not accept the argument that any government derived from an elective process could be called republican, no matter how remote its members were from a dependence on the people. As a Virginian, he was sharply conscious of the limits beyond which the union could not push its parts. He discovered his solution in the very differences between the states and their peoples that other continental-minded men considered problems. He concluded that these differences could feed into a properly constructed great republic in a manner that would break the force of majority faction without encountering the risk of recreating a regime in which a governing minority would eventually rule.

Madison's continentalism was a newer vision, in the end, than Hamilton's. It was better grounded in American realities. Hamilton sought to override the differences between the states by forging an alternative to their existing political elites. This was both premature and out-of-date. Too many of the country's economic regions simply lacked the monied and commercial interests required by Hamilton's vision, while regions with the right materials possessed a body politic too large, too little deferential, and too irreducibly diverse for Hamilton's elite to lead them. What Hamilton succeeded in creating, as Madison insisted, was a minority faction which ruled as long as special circumstances shielded them with Washington's prestige and reinforced them with large numbers who dreaded a collapse of traditional order. Hamilton's "Court" politics were bound to fail, as Madison expected, on the impassable barrier of the new republic's social and economic structure. Meanwhile, the Virginian necessarily opposed a set of policies that threatened to upset the grand design he hoped would preclude preference of factional objectives to the common good.

A MUDDY MIDDLE OF THE ROAD

The Politics of Edmund Randolph, 1790-1795

by JOHN GARRY CLIFFORD [*]

IN late spring of 1790 the president of the United States could view the prospects of the new federal experiment with considerable optimism. The fierce partisanship which had characterized each state's ratification of the Constitution had largely dissipated. Men of talent were flocking to national service under George Washington's leadership. And the chief executive placed greatest hopes in that small circle of advisers soon to be labeled the cabinet. To a friend in France, Washington wrote enthusiastically, "I feel myself supported by able co-adjutors, who harmonize extremely well together." [1]

Five years later Edmund Randolph, the last of Washington's original quartet of "able co-adjutors," with bitterness resigned his post as secretary of state. Just two days earlier, on August 18, 1795, the president had formally ratified Jay's Treaty with Great Britain—an act which, in the consensus of modern scholars, crystallized the development of national political parties in the young republic. [2] Clashes over fiscal and foreign policies had disrupted the harmony which Washington expected. Nowhere had this dissonance been so shrill as in the president's cabinet.

It was not insignificant that Randolph's departure from the government signaled open warfare between Federalists and Republicans over the Jay Treaty. Whether as attorney general seeking to bridge the widening gap between Alexander Hamilton and Thomas Jefferson, or as secretary of state attempting to moderate the views of Hamilton, Timothy Pickering, and Oliver Wolcott, Randolph had striven to rise above faction. With a certain

---

[*] Dr. Clifford is assistant professor of political science at the University of Connecticut, Storrs, Connecticut.

[1] Washington to LaFayette, June 3, 1790, J. C. Fitzpatrick, ed., *The Writings of George Washington*, (Washington, 1931-1941), XXXI, 47.

[2] See Joseph Charles, *The Origins of the American Party System* (Williamsburg, 1956), pp. 91-140; Noble E. Cunningham, Jr., *The Jeffersonian Republicans: The Formation of Party Organization* (Chapel Hill, 1957), pp. 77-85; William Nisbet Chambers, *Political Parties in a New Nation: The American Experiment, 1776-1809* (New York, 1963), pp. 78-93; Harry Ammon, "The Formation of the Republican Party in Virginia, 1789-1796," *Journal of Southern History*, XIX (1953), 310; Ammon, "The Genet Mission and the Development of American Political Parties," *Journal of American History*, LII (1966), 725-741; and Thomas J. Farnham, "The Virginia Amendments of 1795: An Episode in Opposition to Jay's Treaty," *Virginia Magazine of History and Biography*, LXXV (1967), 75-88.

proud obstinacy he had justified to the president this "long-settled determination never to attach myself to party," arguing that "my opinions . . . arise solely from my views of right" and "fall sometimes on one side and sometimes on the other."[3]

But compromise had proven barren. The young Virginian's middle-of-the-road course eventually was so muddied by partisanship that the charges of treason which precipitated his resignation blackened his reputation for more than a century.[4] Why did nonpartisanship fail? Was Randolph an inconsequential "trimmer," as some individuals charged, or was he the tragic victim of factional poison? Why did his policies become untenable? Did the rise of political parties make Randolph's pattern of compromise completely impossible?

The thirty-six-year-old Williamsburg lawyer, who became America's first attorney general in May 1790, was described by a contemporary at the Virginia bar as

a figure large and portly; his features uncommonly fine; his dark eyes and his whole countenance lighted up with an expression of the most conciliating sensibility; his attitude dignified and commanding; his gesture easy and graceful; his voice perfect harmony; and his whole manner that of an accomplished and engaging gentleman.[5]

For one so young, Randolph carried impressive credentials into federal service. A revolutionary patriot, he had broken with his Loyalist father on the independence issue. Such distinguished Virginians as Thomas Jefferson, Patrick Henry, and Benjamin Harrison had recommended him as aide to General Washington; and at twenty-three Randolph had been elected to the convention of 1776 which drew up the state's first constitution. That same year he became attorney general of Virginia, following in a distinguished family tradition which had seen both his father and uncle occupy the same post under the Crown. After the war Randolph won the governorship, served as delegate to the Annapolis convention, and in the more important conclave at Philadelphia in 1787 he presented the famous Virginia Plan of union.[6]

Randolph's stance in regard to the proposed federal constitution was

---

[3] Randolph to Washington, April 19, 1794, in Peter V. Daniel, ed., *A Vindication of Edmund Randolph, Written by Himself and Published in 1795* (Richmond, 1855), p. 43, hereinafter cited as Randolph, *Vindication.*

[4] See Irving Brant, "Edmund Randolph: Not Guilty!" *William and Mary Quarterly*, 3rd ser., VII (1950), 180-183.

[5] William Wirt, *Letters of a British Spy* (New York, 1832), p. 207.

[6] For Randolph's early years, see Moncure Daniel Conway, *Omitted Chapters of History Disclosed in the Life and Papers of Edmund Randolph* (New York, 1888) pp. 1-135.

somewhat equivocal, foreshadowing subsequent cabinet behavior. Because he feared that a strong executive might endanger republican principles, he had refused to sign the final instrument at Philadelphia. But at the Richmond ratifying convention Randolph reversed himself as the eloquent ally of James Madison against Patrick Henry and the strong antifederalist faction. However statesmanlike this dramatic espousal of federalism, it forfeited for Randolph his widespread popularity in Virginia.[7] Thereafter his expanding reputation and the special confidence placed in him by President Washington made the federal capital the logical place to continue his public career. Thus, when Washington offered the post of attorney general late in 1789, Randolph, after some hesitation, accepted and moved his growing family to New York.[8]

Experience in codifying the laws of Virginia and an extensive background in French and English law made Randolph an ideal choice to head the department of justice—an official whose constitutional duties were sufficiently amorphous to allow him to mold administrative precedent.[9] The attorney general busied himself with such divergent tasks as rendering opinions on the constitutionality of pending legislation, determining the legality of the disputed 1792 gubernatorial election in New York, and jousting with the Supreme Court over judicial jurisdiction.[10]

Sometimes these administrative functions assumed political implications. Randolph's concurrence with Jefferson's stand against the constitutionality of Hamilton's bank proposal merely reflected the split which the secretary of the treasury's fiscal measures had precipitated in Congress.[11] Randolph's argument as attorney for the plaintiff in the famous case of *Chisholm v. Georgia*—that states were amenable to private suits in federal courts—demonstrated that Randolph's republicanism was something more subtle and independent than a slavish devotion to state sovereignty.[12] Nor was he any less

---

[7] Randolph had favored a second Constitutional Convention and a bill of rights, but accepted the results of Philadelphia in lieu of continued frustration under the Articles of Confederation. See *ibid.*, pp. 102-112; David J. Mays, *Edmund Pendleton: A Biography, 1721-1803* (Cambridge, 1952), II, 231; Irving Brant, *James Madison* (Indianapolis, 1941-1959), III, 142-157; Kate Rowland Mason, *The Life of George Mason* (New York, 1892), II, 308.

[8] The abnormally low salaries offered federal appointees provided the main obstacle to Randolph's entering federal service; see Randolph to Madison, October 8, 1789, Conway, *Omitted Chapters*, pp. 129-30. For further discussion of this problem of federal salaries, see Stephen G. Kurtz, *The Presidency of John Adams* (New York, 1961), pp. 239-260.

[9] Leonard D. White, *The Federalists: A Study in Administrative History* (New York, 1948), pp. 164-172.

[10] Conway, *Omitted Chapters*, pp. 137-155.

[11] Cunningham, *The Jeffersonian Republicans*, pp. 50-51; Dumas Malone, *Jefferson and His Times* (Boston, 1948-1970), II, 341-342.

[12] Conway, *Omitted Chapters*, pp. 167-181.

steadfast in defense of prerogative when Jefferson, in search of weapons in the struggle against Hamilton, proposed in 1793 to circumvent the attorney general by erecting a special Board of Advice to give opinions on constitutional questions.[13] Randolph, by thwarting this and other attempts to diminish his influence, strengthened his well-deserved reputation as a strong administrator.[14]

The office of attorney general took on even greater political importance in light of the special use made by George Washington of his cabinet chiefs. In his experience as military commander and plantation manager Washington had systematically sought the best advice available before acting on the question at hand. As president, in the absence of any statutory executive council, he relied increasingly on the opinions of his department heads, generally abiding by the opinion of the majority.[15] And with Washington possessing "a deliberative, rather than an argumentative" mind, cabinet procedure became something of an essay contest with each secretary's written arguments competing for executive endorsement.[16] The result was a consistent split. Hamilton's incisive briefs were generally echoed by easygoing Henry Knox, the corpulent secretary of war. Jefferson stood in adamant opposition. In such a situation the attorney general's opinion was often decisive. However exaggerated, Jefferson's complaint that "everything . . . now hangs on the opinion of a single person [Randolph]" and "the Government is now solely directed by him" was not without its grain of truth.[17]

As a rule Randolph sided against the Federalists. Though hardly violent, his opposition to Treasury programs was steady. In addition to declaring against the National Bank, the attorney general took exception to funding the debt at par and objected to Hamilton's manipulation of funds designated for payment of the Revolutionary debt to France.[18] He did not oppose federal assumption of state debts, but neither did Jefferson.[19] Although Ran-

---

[13] Conway, *Omitted Chapters*, p. 186; White, *The Federalists*, pp. 168-169.

[14] Leonard D. White writes: "Since its incumbent early won a place in the Cabinet, the Attorney General played a role of substantial importance in the general policy of the Federalist era" (*The Federalists*, p. 172).

[15] Douglas Southall Freeman, *George Washington: A Biography* (New York, 1948-1957), VI, 335.

[16] Leonard D. White, "George Washington: Administrator," in Edward D. Saveth, ed., *Understanding the American Past* (Boston, 1954), pp. 153-154.

[17] Jefferson to Madison, May 12 and August 11, 1793, as quoted in Dice Robins Anderson, "Edmund Randolph," Samuel Flagg Bemis, ed., *The American Secretaries of State and Their Diplomacy* (New York, 1927), II, 99-100.

[18] Edmund Randolph, *Political Truth: Or . . . an Inquiry into the Truth of the Charges Preferred Against Mr. Randolph* (Philadelphia, 1796), pp. 12-13.

[19] Randolph to Hamilton, November 9, 1791, in Harold C. Syrett, ed., *The Papers of Alexander Hamilton* (New York, 1961-   ), IX, 486.

dolph remained personally friendly with Alexander Hamilton, his political disposition was such that while attorney general his opinion coincided with Jefferson's on sixteen of the nineteen party questions raised in the cabinet.[20]

Randolph had much in common with the secretary of state. Both were intimate friends of James Madison. Both were professed deists. The attorney general shared his colleague's interest in France—if not his enthusiasm. When Jefferson abandoned the profession of law in 1774, he turned over his Virginia practice to Randolph.[21] The two men were even related by blood, and there was no question that Randolph espoused the substance of his cousin's celebrated republicanism.

As early as the summer of 1791 Randolph was willing to defend the cause. Earlier that year Jefferson had penned a private endorsement of Thomas Paine's *The Rights of Man* which was appended, without permission, to the American edition of that work. Because it seemed to be a direct refutation of John Adams's conservative *Discourses on Davila*, the "preface" whipped up such a public storm that Jefferson was moved to direct an earnest apology to the vice-president.[22] Less timid, Randolph deemed it "a fair opportunity for a declaration of certain sentiments."[23] With the secretary of state's lukewarm support, he attempted to secure for Thomas Paine the recently vacated office of postmaster general. But President Washington's choice of the Hamiltonian candidate, Timothy Pickering, quickly put an end to the republican gesture.[24]

The following summer presented another chance to "declare certain sentiments." The smoldering antagonism between Hamilton and Jefferson had finally erupted in the public press. Accusing the secretary of state of subsidizing editor Philip Freneau's partisan assaults on administration policy, Hamilton wrote a series of anonymous letters in the *Gazette of the United States* which soon degenerated into outright slander. Appalled, Randolph hastened to assure James Madison (also under attack) that "no consideration upon earth shall prevent me from being useful to you, where you concede

[20] In the spring of 1793 Hamilton even extended to Randolph a timely personal loan to cover financial distress (Philip M. Marsh, "Randolph and Hamilton," *Pennsylvania Magazine of History and Biography*, LXXII [1948], 252; see also Randolph to Hamilton, April 3, 1793, Syrett, *Papers of Alexander Hamilton*, XIV, 278-279). The list of cabinet votes appears in Conway, *Omitted Chapters*, pp. 198-199. Although Conway ignores some subtle differences between Jefferson and Randolph, his numbers are substantially accurate.

[21] John M. Hamphill II, ed., "Edmund Randolph Assumes Thomas Jefferson's Practice," *Virginia Magazine of History and Biography*, LXVII (1959), 170-171.

[22] Malone, *Jefferson*, II, 354-370.

[23] Randolph to Madison, July 21, 1791, in Conway, *Omitted Chapters*, p. 188.

[24] Malone, *Jefferson*, II, 364.

that I can be so."[25] Shortly thereafter, Hamilton encountered in that same *Gazette* a challenger. Calling himself "Aristides," Randolph took up the cudgel by describing Jefferson's "calumniator" as "a cowardly assassin" whose assorted pseudonyms were mere masks for a "certain head of department."[26] "Aristides' " barbs goaded Hamilton to even greater virulence, but by then Madison and James Monroe were also rallying to Jefferson's defense. By the end of the year these republican stalwarts had blunted Hamilton's attacks. It was Edmund Randolph who had spoken first.

Within a year, however, Jefferson could write of this man whose republican loyalties seemed beyond dispute:

R[andolph] is the poorest cameleon [sic] I ever saw, having no color of his own, and reflecting that nearest him. When he is with me he is a whig, when with H[amilton] he is a tory, when with the P[resident] he is what he thinks will please him. . . . I have kept on strict terms of friendship hitherto, that I might have some good out of him, and because he has some really good private qualities; but he is in a station infinitely too important for his understanding, his firmness, or his circumstances.[27]

The intervening months had seen the United States undergo the first strains of neutrality toward the Wars of the French Revolution. The party struggle, which had begun over domestic matters, spilled over into foreign policy. With the Federalists identifying themselves with England, and the Republicans with France, statesmanship and party loyalties often conflicted. Both Randolph and Jefferson were affected.

As early as February 1793, before news reached America of Louis XVI's execution, international problems pushed the attorney general into political decision. Facing possible famine, France had instructed its minister in Philadelphia to request that the United States make an immediate advance on the French debt of 3,000,000 livres—a sum to be paid in provisions. Since the government was already behind in its payments and because a new installment fell due presently, Jefferson heartily recommended approval of the French request.[28] Randolph was more cautious. He feared that nations at war with France might take exception to "a *voluntary* payment of what is not yet due"; yet he saw also that refusal might stir up "the zealous partizans of French politics in America."[29] The attorney general's compromise sugges-

[25] Randolph to Madison, August 12, 1792, in Conway, *Omitted Chapters*, II, 189.
[26] Marsh, "Randolph and Hamilton," *Pennsylvania Magazine*, LXXII, 248-250.
[27] Jefferson to Madison, August 11, 1793, quoted in Conway, *Omitted Chapters*, pp. 190-191.
[28] Jefferson to Washington, February 12, 1793, in Paul Leicester Ford, ed., *The Works of Thomas Jefferson* (New York, 1904), VII, 226-234.
[29] Randolph to Washington, February 14, 1793, Reel 103, Washington MSS, Library of Congress.

tion that the United States pay immediately what was in arrears with "the residue of the requisition" to follow later did not, however, secure presidential support. More impressed by Randolph's warnings of public censure, Washington decided against delay and, rejecting Hamilton's negative opinion, agreed in full to the French request.[30]

A week later Randolph's views were instrumental in maintaining Gouverneur Morris as minister to France. Reports, some of them through official channels, had reached President Washington implying that Morris's outspoken aristocratic sympathies were making enemies among Parisian republicans. Jefferson seized on these complaints to propose that Washington effect an exchange of ministers: Thomas Pinckney would replace Morris in Paris, with Morris occupying Pinckney's London post.[31] Randolph, however, doubted "whether any determination ought *yet* to be made," at least not until France formally requested Morris's removal. An exchange of envoys was especially out of the question. According to Randolph, such a maneuver would not silence Morris's American critics, and his transfer to a country soon to be at war with France could serve only as a direct affront to the Girondin Ministry.[32] The president accepted this logic and left Morris in Paris, where he remained for another year.[33]

Decisions and disputes of even greater import were yet to come. On April 12, 1793, having learned officially of war between England and the French Republic, Washington instructed his secretary of state to prepare "immediate precautionary measures" for maintaining "a strict neutrality."[34] Here indeed was a delicate problem.

Jefferson advocated restraint, insisting that "it would be better to hold back the declaration of neutrality as a thing worth something to the powers at war."[35] He hoped that such bargaining tactics would entice concessions from the British—both in recognition of neutral rights and in observance of the 1783 peace treaty.[36] But the dangers of war seemed more urgent to the attorney general, who ranged alongside Knox and Hamilton in voting down

---

[30] See John A. Carroll and Mary W. Ashworth, *George Washington: First in Peace* (New York, 1957), pp. 27-29. This volume concludes Douglas Southall Freeman's biography of Washington.

[31] "Anas," February 20, 1973, Ford, *Works of Jefferson*, I, 253-256.

[32] Randolph to Washington, February 22, 1973, Reel 103, Washington MSS.

[33] Carroll and Ashworth, *George Washington*, pp. 30-32.

[34] Washington to Jefferson, April 12, 1793, Fitzpatrick, *Writings of Washington*, XXXII, 415-416.

[35] Jefferson to Madison, June 23, 1793, Ford, *Works of Jefferson*, VII, 408.

[36] Samuel Flagg Bemis, *Jay's Treaty: A Study in Commerce and Diplomacy* (Rev. ed., New Haven, 1962), pp. 191-192.

Jefferson's project.[37] The result was an immediate executive proclamation of "a conduct friendly and impartial toward the belligerent Powers."[38] And it was appropriate that the secretary of state relinquished to Randolph the task of drafting this crucial state paper.[39]

On two closely related questions Randolph returned to the Jeffersonian fold. Together, the two Virginians battered down Hamilton's arguments against full diplomatic recognition of the new French minister, Citizen Edmond Charles Genet; they also refuted Hamilton's contention that the French Alliance of 1778 had lapsed with the death of Louis XVI.[40] The decision to reaffirm all French treaties did not, however, reconcile privileges granted in these treaties with the president's announced determination to preserve a strict and "impartial" neutrality. Over the question of privateers and prizes, there appeared new rifts in the cabinet.

Who would enforce America's neutrality? Who would patrol seaports, guarding against illegal outfitting of privateers and reporting all infringements to federal authorities? Hamilton suggested that such duties be assigned to customs agents, who would inform the collector of revenue of all violations. That official could then refer appropriate cases to the secretary of the treasury, with indictment and prosecution to follow under the attorney general. Washington liked the plan, but on Randolph's advice, he directed that port collectors instead be responsible to federal attorneys in their districts, thus relieving the treasury department of almost exclusive supervision of American neutrality.[41]

When Jefferson learned of these decisions on May 7, he could scarcely conceal his irritation. To Randolph he declared:

I cannot possibly conceive how the superintendance of the laws of neutrality or the preservation of peace with foreign nations can be ascribed to the Department of the Treasury. . . . The collectors are to be made an established corps of spies . . . against their fellow citizens.[42]

In reply, the attorney general defended the choice of customs agents as the best one possible because they would be closest to the scene of probable vio-

---

[37] Carroll and Ashworth, *George Washington*, pp. 48-52. Randolph's biographer does not mention the neutrality proclamation as an instance where he and Jefferson divided (Conway, *Omitted Chapters*, p. 202).

[38] *American State Papers, Foreign Relations* (Washington, 1832), I, 140.

[39] Malone, *Jefferson*, III, 71.

[40] Charles M. Thomas, *American Neutrality in 1793: A Study in Cabinet Government* (New York, 1931), pp. 60-65; Carroll and Ashworth, *George Washington*, pp. 60-61.

[41] Washington to Hamilton, May 5, 1793, Fitzpatrick, *Writings of Washington*, XXXII, 447-451; Carroll and Ashworth, *George Washington*, p. 64.

[42] Jefferson to Randolph, May 8, 1793, Ford, *Works of Jefferson*, VII, 315-319.

lation. He further argued that the subordination of these officials to federal attorneys instead of the Treasury "goes very far into your main objection."[43] But Jefferson would not be mollified. To Madison he wrote sarcastically that Randolph had "found out a hair to split, which, as always, became the decision." The attorney general had become a fence-straddler who "always contrives to agree in principle with one, but in conclusion with the other."[44] Jefferson's extreme reaction is difficult to explain. Certainly he was more suspicious than Randolph of Hamilton's motives, and he could not understand his colleague's willingness to temporize. He may also have been jealous of Randolph's growing influence with the president, particularly in matters pertaining to foreign affairs. Whatever the reason, Jefferson's bitterness was not easily erased.[45]

For the remainder of the year Randolph's independence continued to irritate the secretary of state. In mid-May controversy arose over the English brigantine *Little Sarah*. A privateer outfitted under French commission at Charleston had captured this vessel on the high seas and taken it into Philadelphia as prize. The British minister, George Hammond, demanded full restitution, and was seconded by Hamilton and Knox.[46] Jefferson and Randolph disagreed. Because the privateer had embarked from its southern port before the United States had sufficient time to enforce the declaration of neutrality, they argued that the British had no legitimate claim and that forfeiture of the *Little Sarah* would be unjust and vindictive to France.[47] But the attorney general again moved toward the middle of the road. He proposed that "to vindicate the sincerity of our neutrality" the government ought at least to prosecute those Americans who had enlisted as crew to the Charleston privateer.[48] Impressed by this reasoning, Washington issued orders accordingly.[49]

---

[43] Randolph to Jefferson, May 9, 1793, quoted in Carroll and Ashworth, *George Washington*, p. 65 n.

[44] Jefferson to Madison, May 12, 1793, Ford, *Works of Jefferson*, VII, 323-225; see also, Jefferson to Monroe, May 5, 1793, *ibid.*, VII, 308-311.

[45] Randolph's biographer ignores Randolph's dispute with Jefferson over the port collectors (Conway, *Omitted Chapters*, p. 199). Jefferson's latest and most scholarly biographer is rather critical of the secretary of state's extreme reaction to Randolph's independence (Malone, *Jefferson*, III, 85).

[46] Hamilton to Washington, May 15, 1793, Syrett, *Papers of Alexander Hamilton*, XIV, 451-460.

[47] Jefferson to Washington, May 16, 1793, Ford, *Works of Jefferson*, VII, 332-35; Randolph to Washington, May 17, 1793, J. C. Hamilton, ed., *The Works of Alexander Hamilton* (New York, 1850-51), IV, 403-406.

[48] *Ibid.*

[49] Jefferson's "Anas," May 20, 1793, Ford, *Works of Jefferson*, I, 269-271; Carroll and Ashworth, *George Washington*, pp. 77-78.

The degree to which Randolph's stature had risen in Washington's estimate was evidenced by the attorney general's journey to Virginia the following month. At the president's behest he attempted to ascertain to what extent Citizen Genet's recent trip through that state had swayed political sentiment. Jefferson and his intimates were anxious that Randolph receive the
proper information. The secretary of state inquired of James Madison:
"Have you the time and the means of impressing Wilson Nicholas [Ran-
dolph's brother-in-law], (who will be much with ER) with the necessity of
giving a strong and perfect understanding of the public mind?" [50] Randolph's
reports confirmed rumors of serious dissent in Virginia toward government
policy, particularly the treasury department's forced collection of British
debts. But the attorney general remained hopeful that the president "by
candid and frequent publications" could retain popular support for his neutral foreign policy. [51] Back in Philadelphia, even Jefferson grudgingly admitted that "ER . . . on the whole . . . has quieted uneasiness here." [52]

The furor over Genet, which reached its peak later in the summer, found
Randolph again steering toward mid-channel. Siding with Hamilton and
Knox, the attorney general favored the use of peremptory, rather than deli-
cate language in requesting Genet's recall. But he swung back in support of
Jefferson by opposing Hamilton's appeal for a public remonstrance against
the French envoy. In both instances Washington upheld Randolph's views. [53]

Then in early November 1793, with the United States still awaiting a
formal successor to Genet, Randolph, not Jefferson, ironically became the
Frenchman's sole defender within the cabinet. Reliable reports of French-
organized freebooting expeditions against Spanish Louisiana had, by this
time, turned even the secretary of state against Genet. His patience exhausted, Washington was about to cancel all prerogatives and order the obnoxious envoy from the country. But the attorney general, with Jefferson
remaining silent, persuaded the president that it would be more diplomatic
to allow France to recall its representative in due time. [54] Genet remained.

Such studied objectivity from the young department head was especially

50 Jefferson to Madison, June 2, 1793, Ford, *Works of Jefferson*, VII, 357-358.
51 Randolph to Washington, June 24, 1793, Conway, *Omitted Chapters*, pp. 151-153
52 Jefferson to Madison, July 21, 1793, Ford, *Works of Jefferson*, VII, 455-56. Actually,
Jefferson believed that Randolph's reports, however reassuring, misled Washington as to the
growing republican opposition in Virginia to administration foreign policy (Ammon, "The Genet
Mission and the Rise of Political Parties," *Journal of American History*, LII [1966], 727).
53 Carroll and Ashworth, *George Washington*, pp. 111-113; "Anas," August 1, 1793, Ford,
Works of Jefferson, I, 305.
54 "Anas," November 8, 1793, Ford, *Works of Jefferson*, I, 324-328; Carroll and Ashworth,
George Washington, p. 140.

pleasing to the president. Thomas Jefferson's retirement loomed ahead. Randolph, whose views in recent months had coincided with Washington's own, seemed a logical replacement.[55] When, several months earlier, Washington had requested his opinion of Randolph's qualifications, Jefferson had been noticeably reticent, mentioning only that the attorney general's financial problems might hamper effective performance at the state department.[56] But the president knew his man and, in late December, offered the post to his long-time associate.[57] Randolph accepted gratefully, affirming that "nothing shall relax my attention or warp my probity . . . [in] this new and important business."[58]

Immediately on taking office, the new secretary of state entered a plea for administrative harmony. Addressing his colleagues at the war and treasury departments, Randolph suggested that each official be more candid with his fellows in criticizing and explaining departmental policy:

I will check any opinion, until I can obtain an explanation, which I will ask without reserve. By these means I shall avoid the uneasiness of suspicion; and I take the liberty of requesting, that the same line of conduct be pursued with respect to myself.[59]

But Randolph could not stifle partisan discord with a single conciliatory gesture.

For one thing, the new department head was an exceedingly unpopular figure in early 1794. If the president had come to appreciate the merits of compromise, Randolph's determination "to be of no party" had earned only enmity elsewhere.[60] Equivocal or not, his general opposition to Hamiltonian measures won no friends in Federalist ranks. And in one of his last official acts as attorney general, Randolph had incurred the wrath of Republican partisans by rejecting the legality of a libel suit by Citizen Genet against Chief Justice John Jay and Senator Rufus King.[61] From the sanctum of Monticello Jefferson wrote of his successor: "The choice of Randolph . . .

---

[55] Carroll and Ashworth, George Washington, pp. 147-147.

[56] "Anas," August 6, 1793, Ford, Works of Jefferson, I, 314.

[57] Washington to Randolph, December 24, 1793, Fitzpatrick, Writings of Washington, XXXIII, 216.

[58] Randolph to Washington, January 2, 1794, Reel 10, Washington MSS.

[59] Randolph to Hamilton and Knox, January 2, 1794, Syrett, Papers of Alexander Hamilton, XV, 604.

[60] Randolph, Political Truth, p. 20.

[61] Genet had attempted to sue Jay and King for their public censure of his appeals to the American populace over the head of President Washington. Because there was no evidence of libel, Randolph's dismissal of the case was inevitable (Robert Ernst, Rufus King: American Federalist [Chapel Hill, 1968], pp. 192-93; Carroll and Ashworth, George Washington, p. 147 n).

is the most unpopular one the President could have made. It is hard to conceive how much he is despised."[62]

Diplomatic developments became a further barrier to successful nonpartisanship. A growing crisis in Anglo-American relations stirred party loyalties to an even greater degree. American neutrality became more difficult to maintain. In the tangle of foreign and domestic politics which followed, the success or failure of Randolph's diplomacy was to determine, to a large extent, the fate of nonpartisan principles.

Seizure of American commerce on the high seas and threats of Indian attacks from Canada were the two sparks which touched off a war scare between England and the United States in the spring of 1794. When word reached Philadelphia in late February that British cruisers, under a secret order in council, had seized more than 250 American merchantmen trading with the French West Indies, indignation raged in Congress.[63] These acts on the high seas, when coupled with an inflammatory speech to the western tribes by Lord Dorchester, Governor General of Canada, seemed a direct military challenge to the young republic. Randolph's report to Congress on March 5 that French men-of-war, as well as British, were despoiling American ships in the Caribbean did little to cool the rising war fever.[64] Violations of the 1783 treaty still rankled. For many Republicans and some Federalists, the time had come to settle old scores.[65]

Cooler heads sought to prevent rupture with Britain. Fearful that the Republican majority in the House of Representatives would revive and extend old threats of commercial discrimination against England, a small group of Federalist senators hit on the scheme of sending a special envoy to the Court of St. James.[66] On March 12 Oliver Ellsworth of Connecticut suggested to the president that Alexander Hamilton would be the perfect agent to ward off conflict between the two countries.[67] Washington seemed skeptical, but before long Federalist designs gained support from an unexpected quarter.

Because of the real danger of war, Edmund Randolph looked favorably upon an extraordinary mission to London. But he opposed the choice of Hamilton. Some other "distinguished character, sent fresh from the feelings

---

[62] Jefferson to Monroe, March 22, 1794, Reel 1, James Monroe MSS, Library of Congress.

[63] Bemis, *Jay's Treaty*, pp. 216, 264.

[64] *American State Papers, Foreign Relations*, I, 423-424.

[65] For a convenient survey of war sentiment in March 1794, see Carroll and Ashworth, *George Washington*, p. 159.

[66] Charles, *Origins of the Party System*, pp. 101-104.

[67] Ernst, *Rufus King*, pp. 198-199.

of the U. S., would with more confidence assert, & with more certainty impress."[68] The Federalists knew of such a man. Cleverly foiling the opposition to himself, Hamilton proposed the nomination of John Jay—"the only man in whose qualifications for success there would be thorough confidence, and him whom alone it would be advisable to send."[69] Randolph pointed out the impropriety of sending "a Chief Justice . . . [on] *executive* honors . . . while he retained his judicial seat," but Washington was convinced.[70] By a vote of 18 to 8, the Senate, on April 18, confirmed this crucial diplomatic appointment.

Such were the origins of the Jay mission, the ultimate fruits of which the historian Samuel Flagg Bemis has aptly entitled "Hamilton's Treaty."[71] From the outset, party considerations made it difficult for the secretary of state to guide diplomacy. It was Hamilton's pen which drafted the bulk of John Jay's instructions. Randolph objected to the wide powers granted, particularly those permitting Jay to negotiate a commercial treaty. Only at the secretary's most strenuous insistence was a reference inserted to "the possibility of sounding Russia, Sweden, or Denmark as to an alliance on the principles of the Armed Neutrality."[72] But, as Bemis has shown, Hamilton eventually blocked even this meager channel of maneuver when he informed the British minister that Washington's cabinet had decided not to join such a neutral alliance.[73]

Randolph found himself in an anomalous position as Jay set sail for England on May 12, 1794. Whatever his diplomatic experience and abilities, the envoy extraordinary was of a different political persuasion from the secretary of state. Jay's instructions, which Randolph had played such a small part in formulating, afforded virtually a free hand in conducting negotiations.[74] Months could pass before Randolph's letters reached London; in fact, Jay signed a treaty before the secretary of state's criticisms of the tentative drafts arrived.[75] Randolph was compelled to mark time while this

[68] Randolph to Washington, April 6, 1794, Reel 10, Washington MSS.

[69] Hamilton to Washington, April 14, 1794, Henry Cabot Lodge, ed., *The Works of Alexander Hamilton* (New York, 1885-1886), V, 114-115.

[70] Randolph to Washington, April 19, 1794, Conway, *Omitted Chapters*, pp. 218-219.

[71] Bemis, *Jay's Treaty*, p. 373.

[72] As quoted in Anderson, "Edmund Randolph," *American Secretaries of State*, II, 137.

[73] Bemis, *Jay's Treaty*, pp. 337-340.

[74] Samuel Flagg Bemis writes: "Perhaps never in the history of the United States has a plenipotentiary been vested with more unfettered discretion than was Jay in the critical negotiations of 1794" (*ibid.*, p. 291).

[75] Anderson, "Edmund Randolph," *American Secretaries of State*, II, 130-131.

Federalist representative, alone, set out to rescue peace and commerce with Great Britain.

Duties in Philadelphia kept the secretary occupied. Cabinet discord had not ceased, as Hamilton continued to interfere with the daily conduct of diplomacy. Constant criticism of his dealings with the British minister not only irritated Randolph, but served also to illustrate how vulnerable his position had become during the period of the Jay mission. As the official spokesman for American policy, Randolph, while ignorant of events in England, had to sustain a proper diplomatic posture toward all foreign representatives, especially those of England and France. The secretary continued to protest against Britain's frontier violations and seizures of American ships. Such protests probably helped to relieve certain personal frustrations. Then, at the same time, Randolph had to reassure the new French minister, Joseph Fauchet, that Jay's instructions precluded any alteration of America's obligations to her sister republic. With political tension increasing throughout 1794, Randolph's narrow course quite naturally became the target of partisan suspicions.

With Fauchet, the secretary started out successfully. The arrival in February of this successor to Citizen Genet had dispelled much of the bitterness aroused by the latter envoy. Moreover, the simultaneous replacement of Gouverneur Morris in Paris with James Monroe was, in Randolph's words, "a fresh proof of our sincere desire to maintain peace with your nation."[76] By the summer of 1794 Randolph's relations with the French minister had grown so cordial that Fauchet reported enthusiastically to Paris that "this Mr. Randolph is without doubt an excellent man, very much a partisan of our Revolution. But I believe him to be of weak character; it is easy to penetrate his secret when one stirs him."[77] Randolph, it seems, had been momentarily indiscreet. Embittered by Federalist maneuvers which had resulted in the Jay mission, he made exaggerated claims concerning President Washington's hostility toward England and declared that no machinations by the "monocratic" faction could sway American friendship for France.[78] Because such statements did not fit Randolph's usual determination to be of "no party," his initial rapport with Fauchet could lead to eventual disillusionment.

---

[76] Randolph to Fauchet, April 21, 1794, as quoted in Conway, *Omitted Chapters*, p. 339.

[77] Fauchet, Dispatch No. 3, June 4, 1794, "Correspondence of the French Ministers to the United States, 1791-1797," Frederick Jackson Turner, ed., *American Historical Association Annual Report for 1903* (Washington, 1904), II, 376-377.

[78] *Ibid.* For Randolph's explanation, see Randolph, *Vindication*, pp. 62-64.

The Whiskey Rebellion later in the summer became a test of the secretary's political sympathies, and once more his middle-of-the-road inclinations pleased neither French nor British partisans. When the growing antagonism of Allegheny farmers to Hamilton's excise measures finally burst into armed insurrection in July 1794, Randolph remained the most restrained of Washington's cabinet advisers. Unlike Knox, Hamilton, and Attorney General William Bradford, he argued against immediate use of military force. Fearing that precipitate action would unite critics of the administration and perhaps drive westerners into the arms of Britain, the secretary urged caution and delay. In particular, he wanted recruitment of the militia to be postponed until peace commissioners had ample opportunity to investigate the situation in Western Pennsylvania.[79] According to Fauchet, Randolph became so disturbed at the danger of British partisans stirring up civil war that he solicited French support in financing Republican pacification measures.[80] Randolph later denied that he had asked money for himself and Fauchet eventually confirmed the secretary's denials; nevertheless, it was clear that Randolph's nonpartisan position was becoming increasingly difficult to maintain.[81]

In a cabinet meeting on August 6, Washington decided to call up militia forces at once, but also tacitly heeded Randolph's counsels of delay by awaiting the return of the commissioners from Pittsburgh before embarking on any campaign.[82] Shortly thereafter, in an apparent reversal of opinion, Randolph proposed that recruitment be increased from 12,500 to 15,000 troops. The secretary later justified this move on humanitarian grounds, saying that "the unhappy people would be intimidated by so large a force," but his retreat from earlier arguments was unmistakable.[83]

Later that autumn, as the western insurrection dragged to its conclusion, further statements by Randolph aroused even greater indignation among Republicans. The secretary of state became Washington's chief supporter in his condemnation of the Democratic Societies. Disavowing his previous belief that the British had instigated the Whiskey Rebellion, he declared to the president:

---

[79] Randolph to Washington, August 5, 1794, Randolph, *Vindication*, pp. 79-82.

[80] Fauchet, Dispatch No. 6, September 6, 1794, Turner, "Correspondence of the French Ministers," *American Historical Association Annual Report, for 1903*, II, 411₈418. Randolph thought that Fauchet could lend money to several republican leaders who were in debt to the British, thus allowing them to act more openly. Randolph was not asking for a bribe.

[81] Randolph, *Vindication*, pp. 7-10, 13-16.

[82] Carroll and Ashworth, *George Washington*, pp. 191-192.

[83] Conway, *Omitted Chapters*, p. 197.

I never did see an opportunity of destroying these self-constituted bodies [the Demo-cratic Societies] until the fruit of their operations was declared in the insurrection at Pittsburg[h]. Indeed I was, and still am, persuaded that the language which was understood to be held by the officers of government in opposition to them con-tributed to foster them. They may now I believe be crushed. The prospect ought not to be lost.[84]

Nor was the "prospect lost." In his annual message to Congress on November 18, Washington explicitly condemned "certain self-created societies" for their defiance of federal authority in Pennsylvania. Randolph may have hoped that the president's prestige would stifle American Jacobinism and "establish perfect tranquility to the government," but partisan response was immediate.[85] The Republican-dominated House of Representatives omitted any reference to the democratic clubs in their formal reply to Washington. James Madison called the act of censure "perhaps the greatest error of his [Washington's] political life."[86] For Jefferson it was "one of the extraordinary acts of boldness . . . from the faction of monocrats."[87] Randolph answered the president's critics with a series of powerful letters signed "Germanicus," which afterwards circulated in pamphlet form.[88] His biting distinctions between American liberty and Jacobin anarchy were not calculated to win approval from friends of France.[89]

By this time Randolph's relations with Fauchet had grown noticeably cool. News of Robespierre's downfall in July placed the young Jacobin envoy in a delicate position. He now had to justify his less than successful diplomacy to new masters in the Directory. Moreover, the likelihood that Jay's mission to England would be detrimental to French interests increased Fauchet's apprehensions. To the state department, he railed against America's continued "servile submission" to British maritime violations.[90] And to his superiors in Paris, Fauchet made Randolph his scapegoat. That the secretary of state had "played sincere and made me false confidences" became the theme of French diplomatic correspondence.[91]

---

[84] Randolph to Washington, October 11, 1794, in Conway, *Omitted Chapters*, p. 195.
[85] Randolph to Washington, November 6, 1794, *ibid.*, p. 231.
[86] Madison to Monroe, December 4, 1794, Gaillard Hunt, ed., *The Writings of James Madison* (New York, 1900-1910), VI, 221-222.
[87] Jefferson to Madison, December 28, 1794, quoted in Carroll and Ashworth, *George Washington*, p. 223 n.
[88] Conway, *Omitted Chapters*, p. 231.
[89] Even Federalists resented Randolph's efforts; see Carroll and Ashworth, *George Washington*, p. 224 n.
[90] Fauchet to Randolph, September 8, 1794, *American State Papers, Foreign Relations*, I, 601-603.
[91] Fauchet to Minister of Foreign Relations (Dispatch No. 16), February 4, 1795, Turner, "Correspondence," p. 562. "*Il joua . . . le sincère et me fit de fausses confidences.*"

Randolph's reputation was no higher in British circles. In the eyes of Minister Hammond, the secretary of state openly pursued a pro-French course and was given to talking in "terms of arrogance and menace" toward Great Britain.[92] Randolph found an even more formidable adversary in Foreign Minister Lord William Grenville, who thought the secretary of state manifested "a Spirit of Hostility towards Great Britain."[93] He was particularly incensed at a rather effusive letter of friendship which Randolph had written to the French Convention. The fact that Randolph published his notes of protest against British maritime seizures was also annoying. Shortly after putting his signature on Jay's Treaty, Grenville voiced his sentiments to Hammond in Philadelphia:

> you should converse confidentially on this Subject with those persons in America who are Friends to a System of amicable Intercourse between the two Countries, in the view that Some step may be taken in respect to the Affair so as either to convince Mr. Randolph of the necessity of his adopting a different Language and Conduct, or at least, to place him in a Situation where his personal Sentiments may not endanger the Peace of Two Countries.[94]

With such ominous words the Treaty of Amity, Commerce, and Navigation began its journey across the Atlantic.

An official copy of Jay's Treaty did not reach Randolph in Philadelphia until March 7, 1795. The Senate had dispersed just three days before. Anticipating the treaty's arrival, Washington had informed the legislators that "certain matters touching upon the public good" required their return on June 8.[95]

As the president and secretary of state examined the results of Jay's diplomacy, they could not have been pleased. Of twenty-eight articles in the treaty, only Article II, England's promise to withdraw from the western posts, seemed a major accomplishment. Nearly all the commercial clauses were unfavorable. Grenville's only real concession was to open British East Indian ports to American trade. The stipulations regarding the more important West Indian trade were especially outrageous. Under Article XII no American vessel of over seventy tons could enter British ports in the Caribbean; nor were any size ships allowed to carry certain staple cargoes

[92] Hammond to Grenville, April 28, 1795, Bernard Mayo, ed., "Instructions to the British Ministers to the United States, 1791-1812," *American Historical Association, Annual Report for 1936* (Washington, 1941), III, 83 n.

[93] Grenville to Hammond, November 20, 1794, *ibid.*, p. 73.

[94] *Ibid.*, p. 75.

[95] Washington to Vice-President of the United States, March 3, 1795, Fitzpatrick, *Writings of Washington*, XXXIV, 131.

(cotton, cocoa, coffee, molasses, and sugar) to French or neutral harbors. The lucrative transshipment trade was thus denied to American merchants. Jay fared no better in protecting American principles of neutrality. The treaty failed to mention the obnoxious British practice of search and impressment. Moreover, under Article XVIII, England reserved the right to declare and seize, as contraband of war, provisions and foodstuffs. Free ships no longer meant free goods.[96]

From the standpoint of party struggle, Great Britain's friends had gained a powerful weapon. Because the commercial clauses of the treaty were to remain in effect for twelve years, Anglo-American trade was safe from Republican interference. Madison and Jefferson could no longer frighten Federalists with threats of non-intercourse and discrimination against the British.[97] According to Jefferson, "a bolder party stroke was never struck."[98]

But Washington and Randolph were of neither party and, as such, could view Jay's Treaty with more objectivity. Though neither man was overjoyed at what he read, each saw that, if it did nothing else, the treaty would at least preserve peace between the United States and the world's foremost naval power.[99] War with England would throw everything out of kilter, intensify party feelings, and make the country too dependent on France. Both men wanted to maintain neutrality. As the secretary explained in a letter to James Monroe:

the *invariable* policy of the President is to be as independent as possible, of every nation upon earth; and this policy is not assumed now for the first time . . . but it is wise at all times, and if steadily pursued, will protect our country from the effects of commotion in Europe. . . . [W]ithout a steady adherence to *principles* no Government can defend itself against the animadversions of the world, nor procure a permanent benefit to its own citizens.[100]

Whether the Jay Treaty was in accord with these principles, Randolph and Washington did not undertake to judge. Together, holding the terms of the treaty in strictest secrecy, they decided to await a verdict from the Senate.[101]

---

[96] For an able analysis of the treaty, article by article, see Bemis, *Jay's Treaty*, pp. 346-373.

[97] Charles, *Origins of the American Party System*, pp. 101-103.

[98] Jefferson continued: "For it certainly is an attempt of a party, which finds they have lost their majority in one branch of the legislature, to make a law by the other branch of the executive, under color of a treaty, which shall bind up the hands of the adverse branch from ever restraining the commerce of their patron nation" (Jefferson to Madison, September 21, 1795, Ford, *Works of Jefferson*, VIII, 193).

[99] Carroll and Ashworth, *George Washington*, p. 239.

[100] Randolph to Monroe, April 7, 1795, as quoted in Louis M. Sears, *George Washington and the French Revolution* (Detroit, 1960), p. 234.

[101] Randolph, *Vindication*, p. 18.

For the next five months, Edmund Randolph became Washington's most intimate adviser. Knox and Hamilton had retired from the cabinet at the beginning of the year and were no longer on hand to contend with Randolph's ideas. Their respective successors, Timothy Pickering and Oliver Wolcott, Jr., did not yet possess the president's full confidence. Thus, to the disappointment of Federalist partisans, Washington kept his eyes focused on the middle of the road.

By the end of May, however, Randolph reluctantly had made his judgment "as to the propriety of ratifying" the treaty.[102] And such was the decision of the Senate. Ably led by Senator Rufus King of New York, Federalist supporters of the instrument on June 24 secured a bare two-thirds endorsement.[103] Responsibility then passed to the president.

Complications prevented immediate ratification. In order to gain the necessary majority, King and the other Federalist senators had found it expedient to omit Article XII (dealing with the West Indian trade restrictions) from the approved treaty. This produced a constitutional dilemma. Was the Senate resolution "intended to be the final act," inquired Washington of his cabinet, or did the legislators expect that the article, when renegotiated, would "be resubmitted to them before the treaty takes effect?"[104] The department heads unanimously asserted that the president could and should ratify the treaty in its present, amended form.[105]

Then, while Washington still hesitated, the terms of the treaty made their first appearance in the public press. Ignoring strictures on secrecy, a Republican senator leaked a copy of the treaty to the Philadelphia *Aurora*, whereupon that newspaper's editor, Benjamin Franklin Bache, printed and circulated copies throughout the entire northeast. Almost immediately the cry rose up in opposition. Anti-treaty manifestos and protest parades materialized in many towns and cities. In New York Hamilton was jeered and stoned as he spoke out in defense of the treaty, while in Philadelphia a mob hung John Jay in effigy and stoned the residence of minister Hammond. Federalist leaders quailed at the initial onslaught. From Boston the pessimistic "high priest" of Federalism, Fisher Ames, exclaimed: "Our Federal

---

[102] Randolph to John Jay, May 30, 1795, quoted in Anderson, "Edmund Randolph," *American Secretaries of State*, II, 140.

[103] Ralston Hayden, *The Senate and Treaties, 1789-1917* (New York, 1920), p. 76; Ernst, *Rufus King*, p. 206.

[104] Washington to Department Heads, June 29, 1795, Fitzpatrick, *Writings of Washington*, XXXIV, 224-225.

[105] See Randolph to Washington, undated, in Worthington C. Ford, ed., "Edmund Randolph on the British Treaty, 1795," *American Historical Review*, XII (1906-1907), 590.

ship is near foundering in a millpond."[106] In time, the public clamor would penetrate even President Washington's calm reserve.

More distressing was the arrival of news in Philadelphia early in July that British warships were once again seizing neutral vessels carrying foodstuffs bound for France. Had Great Britain reinstituted the hated order in council of June 8, 1793—the infamous "provision order" which had been one of the main causes of the Anglo-American crisis in the first place?[107] Sharing none of the Federalists' unshakeable confidence in the British Crown, Washington sought the counsel of his secretary of state.

Randolph had a plan. "The order for capturing provisions," he wrote in a long, eighteen-page memorandum dated July 12, "is too irreconcilable with a state of harmony of the treaty to put in motion during its existence."[108] He proposed that Hammond be informed of Washington's decision to ratify the treaty without resubmitting it to the Senate, but so long as the "provision order" remained in application he would refrain from so doing. Here was a solution to both the constitutional and diplomatic problems facing Washington. He instructed Randolph to proceed accordingly.

The secretary of state informed Hammond of Washington's decision on July 13. The response was far from gratifying, as the British envoy suggested that his government might temporarily rescind the order in council, then renew it a suitable period after the exchange of ratifications. When Hammond further inquired if the president were "irrevocably determined" to withhold ratification as long as Britain failed to withdraw the order, Randolph, at the moment, could give no definite reply. On hearing of Hammond's sentiments, however, Washington exploded, vowing that "he would never ratify if the provision order was not removed out of the way."[109] Randolph was then directed to draft an official statement to Lord Grenville, advising him of the reasons for American reluctance to exchange ratifications. With the secretary of state thus occupied, Washington on July 15 departed for his usual summer sojourn at Mount Vernon.[110]

---

[106] Ames to Oliver Wolcott, Jr., July 9, 1795, quoted in George Gibbs, ed., *Memoirs of the Administrations of Washington and John Adams* (New York, 1846), I, 210.

[107] Actually the new order in council (April 25, 1795) was not a restatement of the earlier "provision order" which had merely authorized the seizure of foodstuffs as contraband with adequate compensation. The latest British action was couched in terms of seizing *enemy* goods in *neutral* bottoms, a practice sanctioned by Article XVII of the Jay Treaty. British captains were to assume that the foodstuffs seized had already been purchased by French agents (as, indeed, was often the case). Thus, though the practice was the same, the principle was different (Josiah T. Newcomb, "New Light on Jay's Treaty," *American Journal of International Law*, XXVIII [1934], 685-693).

[108] Randolph to Washington, July 12, 1795, Reel 11, George Washington MSS.

[109] Randolph, *Vindication*, p. 21.

[110] Carroll and Ashworth, *George Washington*, pp. 261-265.

Three crucial, anxious weeks followed. Republicans continued to storm against the Jay Treaty. Even the president felt the blasts, as he wrote to Hamilton of "French machinations" and "poisonous foes of order." [111] But with Randolph laboring diligently in Philadelphia and Washington deliberating at his Virginia retreat, Federalist leaders were becoming desperate. Oliver Ellsworth wrote forebodingly: "if the President decides wrong, or does not decide *soon*, his good fortune will foresake him." [112] Another Federalist warned Rufus King that only Washington's voice could save the country, for "without it you may despair." [113] And Stephen Higginson of Massachusetts predicted that the whole nation would split in two if Washington failed to ratify, and "our race will be finished." [114] While the fate of the treaty hung in the balance, it seemed, in the words of one historian, that the frustrated "inner circle of the Federalist Party fairly held its breath." [115]

Such frustration sprang from a lack of information and consequent inability to influence policy. In essence, only one man had the ear of the distant chief who would pronounce the final verdict. This was Randolph, a suspicious, if not hated, figure in Federalist eyes. While at Mount Vernon the president did write frequently to Alexander Hamilton, but these letters pale in comparison with the policy-determining missives which Washington exchanged with his secretary of state. To his other cabinet advisers, the president wrote practically nothing. [116]

Not until July 22 did Washington instruct Randolph to inform the other department heads of his plans. "Conditional ratification," he wrote, "(if the later order which we have heard of respecting provision vessels is not in operation) may, on all fit occasions, be spoken of as my determination." [117]

Chafing at their impotence and aroused by the anti-treaty agitation, Pickering and Wolcott grew increasingly suspicious. "We have been amused by

---

[111] Washington to Hamilton, July 29, 1795, Fitzpatrick, *Writings of Washington*, XXXIV, 262-264.

[112] Ellsworth to Oliver Wolcott, Jr., August 15, 1795, Gibbs, *Memoirs of Washington and Adams*, I, 225.

[113] Christopher Gore to King, August 14, 1795, in Charles R. King, ed., *The Life and Correspondence of Rufus King* (New York, 1894), II, 24.

[114] Higginson to Timothy Pickering, August 16, 1795, in J. Franklin Jameson, ed., "Letters of Stephen Higginson, 1783-1804," *American Historical Association, Annual Report for 1896* (Washington, 1897), I, 793.

[115] Charles, *Origins of the American Party System*, p. 106.

[116] For Washington's correspondence while at Mount Vernon, see Fitzpatrick, *Writings of Washington*, XXXIV, 247-270.

[117] Washington to Randolph, July 22, 1795, *ibid.*, XXXIV, 244.

Randolph," Wolcott wrote, "who has said the President was determined to ratify. The *precise* state of business has never been communicated till within a few days. The affairs of his department are solely conducted by himself." [118] These two men, viewing the situation through partisan blinders, could not appreciate the subtleties of Washington's diplomacy. They did not recognize that hasty ratification with the "provision order" still in effect might lead to war with France. Whether or not Britain had violated the treaty did not seem to matter. To Pickering and Wolcott, decisive action by the president alone could stem the "Jacobin" uproar. With Washington absent, the uninformed cabinet officers focused their frustration on Randolph, the one who was seducing their leader from his proper duties. The British Foreign Office was happy to encourage these anti-Randolph sentiments.

Shortly after the president had departed for Virginia, Minister Hammond received a packet from London containing certain letters sent by Joseph Fauchet to his superiors in Paris, which had been intercepted. Dispatch Number Ten (October 31, 1794) had several ambiguous, but highly important passages. At first glance, Fauchet's report seemed to imply that Randolph had asked him for money so as to influence American policy in a pro-French direction. Because his instructions from Grenville stated that "the communication of some of [the information in Fauchet's dispatches] to well disposed persons in America may possibly be useful to the King's service," Hammond invited the "well disposed" Wolcott to his home on July 26. [119]

Hammond's oral translation of pertinent passages of Number Ten readily convinced Wolcott that Randolph was a traitor. Securing the original document along with a certified copy, Wolcott alerted Pickering to the unexpected windfall. Then, armed with a hasty translation, Pickering, on July 31, posted a special letter to Mount Vernon. "On the subject of the treaty," the secretary of war wrote, "I confess that I feel extreme solicitude; and for a *special reason* which can be communicated to you only in person, I entreat that you return with all possible speed." [120]

Washington arrived in Philadelphia on August 11 and was enjoying dinner with Randolph when the bombshell burst. Pickering interrupted the meal and, drawing the president aside, told him the shocking news. Washington remained outwardly unruffled and resumed the evening routine as if

118 Wolcott to Hamilton, July 30, 1795, Hamilton, *Works of Hamilton*, VI, 28.

119 Grenville to Hammond, May 9, 1795, Mayo, "Instructions to the British Ministers," *American Historical Association Annual Report for 1936*, III, 83. Fauchet's diplomatic packet had been captured by an English frigate on March 28 and sent directly to London.

120 Pickering to Washington, July 31, 1795, Reel 107, Washington MSS.

all were normal. Late that night he undoubtedly examined the incriminating documents.[121]

Pickering's erratic translation of Number Ten provided ample "evidence" to convince someone already suspicious of Randolph's guilt. By transliterating such phrases as "précieuses confessions" into "precious confessions" (the words actually meant "valuable disclosures"), the secretary of war had transformed what was an ambiguous document at worst into an incriminating one.[122] Nevertheless, if Washington had proceeded from the premise that his long-time associate was innocent until conclusively proven otherwise, he could have discovered enough in Fauchet's dispatch to prevent heedless judgment. For example, repeated references by Fauchet to two previous letters whose examination could have thrown light on obscure passages in Number Ten made little impact on Washington. Not until just before the final confrontation with Randolph did the president consider applying to the new French Minister, Pierre Adet, for permission to look at the two documents in question. Even at the last moment he drew back, yielding to the dissuasion of Pickering and Wolcott.[123]

Washington could also have considered more closely the position in which Fauchet found himself when he had penned his dispatch the previous autumn. Was it not possible that the young Jacobin diplomat, only recently aware of the events of Thermidor, exaggerated and embellished these lurid tales of Randolph in order to ingratiate himself with the Directory, while laying a smokescreen over his own failures in connection with the Jay mission? But such charitable thoughts did not enter Washington's mind that August night. To all intents, the president passed immediate and unfavorable judgment on his secretary of state.[124]

The next day, still outwardly calm, Washington summoned a cabinet meeting. He invited the department heads to give their views about ratifying the treaty. Pickering and Wolcott championed immediate endorsement by the president to stifle the Republican clamor. Even Attorney General Bradford, then mortally ill, gravitated to this position of urgency. Randolph reiterated his thoughts with regard to the "provision order." Then, "to my

[121] Fauchet's Dispatch Number Ten is printed in the French in Turner, "Correspondence," *American Historical Association, Annual Report for 1903*, II, 444-445. An extensive analysis, paragraph by paragraph, appears in Randolph, *Vindication*, pp. 46-73. The best explanation, however, is in Brant, "Edmund Randolph: Not Guilty!", *W. & M. Quart.*, 3rd ser., VII, 180-198.
[122] Brant, "Edmund Randolph: Not Guilty!" *W. & M. Quart.*, 3rd ser., VII, 193.
[123] Washington to Secretaries of Treasury and War, August 18, 1795, Fitzpatrick, *Writings of Washington*, XXXIV, 275-276.
[124] Brant, "Edmund Randolph: Not Guilty!", *W. & M. Quart.*, 3rd ser., VII, 191-192.

unutterable astonishment," as Randolph later reported, "I soon discovered that you [Washington] were receding from your *determination*." [125] After hearing the arguments, Washington announced abruptly that he would ratify. The British minister was to be notified and an official memorial delivered to him—without the stipulations Randolph had advocated. Washington then adjourned the meeting.

The following week was taut. Not wanting to do anything which might hamper ratification, the president continued his pantomime with Randolph. On August 14 Washington had him countersign the ratification form. Still loyal, the secretary then presented the official memorial to Hammond. According to the British envoy, "Mr. Randolph did not attempt to conceal his chagrin . . . but voluntarily confessed that his opinion had been overruled in the President's Cabinet." [126] Finally, with preparations completed, Washington formally ratified the Jay Treaty on Tuesday, August 18, 1795.

The next day he confronted Randolph. Pickering and Wolcott were in attendance, eyeing the victim like hawks. Washington handed him Dispatch Number Ten, pronouncing coldly, "Mr. Randolph! here is a letter which I desire you to read, and make such explanations as you choose." [127] The secretary's impromptu defense was valiant, but fore-doomed. Then, suddenly perceiving the deception which had been practiced for the previous week, Randolph saw no course but abrupt resignation. Indignantly he severed his ties with the president:

Your confidence in me, Sir, has been unlimited and, I can truly affirm, unabused. My sensations then cannot be concealed, when I find that confidence so immediately withdrawn without a word or distant hint being previously dropped to me! [128]

The rest was anticlimax. Randolph frantically set out to secure proof of his innocence. Fortunately he was able to overtake Fauchet at Newport before the latter's ship weighed anchor for France. With Fauchet's testimony, affidavits by Minister Adet as to Dispatches Number Three and Six, and state department documents, Randolph pieced together his famous *Vindication*, which appeared as a 103-page pamphlet in November 1795. Notwithstanding the persuasive defense of his conduct, Randolph's *Vindication* had one glaring defect—its tone. By self-righteously attacking President Washington, Randolph transformed his attempted public rehabilitation into a per-

[125] Randolph, *Vindication*, p. 41.
[126] Hammond to Grenville, August 14, 1795, as quoted in Conway, *Omitted Chapters*, p. 297.
[127] Randolph, *Vindication*, p. 1.
[128] Randolph to Washington, August 19, 1975, reproduced in Carroll and Ashworth, *George Washington*, pp. 287-288; also reel 107, Washington MSS.

sonal feud. Convinced that he was the victim of "a conspiracy . . . deeply laid and systematically pursued," he told James Madison that he was "happy at my emancipation from an attachment to a man who has practised upon me the profound hypocrisy of Tiberius."[129] But Randolph could not hope to win a popularity contest with the Father of His Country. Consequently, the *Vindication* convinced hardly anyone in the heated atmosphere of 1795. "As to Randolph," Hamilton wrote, "I shall be surprised at nothing."[130] For Jefferson, he was still a turncoat who "has generally given his practice to one party and his principles to the other, the oyster to one, the shell to the other."[131] Even Madison reacted unfavorably: "His [Randolph's] greatest enemies will not easily persuade themselves that he was under a corrupt influence of France, and his best friends can't save him from the self-condemnation of his political career, as explained by himself."[132] Randolph remained a man without a party.

Certainly it was a considerable loss that for the remaining eighteen years of his life Edmund Randolph could make no further contribution to public affairs, save, ironically, to become chief defense counsel at Aaron Burr's treason trial. Randolph was a far abler man than the Pickerings, Wolcotts, and other second-raters who rose in his place. But if the years after 1795 were tragic, what Randolph had done earlier was not.

Even in an era where political groups regarded one another with a hostility far removed from present-day attitudes of loyal opposition, Randolph was able to maneuver successfully between both extremes. For five crucial years this unpredictable and independent cabinet officer wielded an influence almost unmatched by any party leaders. The source of Randolph's power was, of course, George Washington. Studied nonpartisanship might provoke Federalist antagonism and destroy Republican friendships, but as long as he retained the ear of his revered chief, the middle of the road remained smooth.

Randolph's independence did not preclude unswerving loyalty to the president's final decisions. He could adapt, as his erratic behavior during the Whiskey Rebellion testified. And, with his position crumbling, he had faithfully countersigned the final ratification of Jay's Treaty. When Randolph resigned, it was not over questions of policy, but on a point of honor. Herein lay the difficulty of Randolph's nonpartisanship. His whole posi-

---

[129] Randolph to Madison, November 1, 1795, Reel 1, Madison MSS, Library of Congress.
[130] Hamilton to Washington, October 3, 1795, Hamilton, *Works of Hamilton*, VI, 40.
[131] Jefferson to Giles, December 31, 1795, Ford, *Works of Jefferson*, VIII, 201-204.
[132] Madison to Monroe, January 26, 1796, quoted in Brant, *James Madison*, III, 425-426.

tion depended upon Washington, and Washington, contrary to legend, was only human. Beset by partisan pressures, the president acted hastily and withdrew his trust. Randolph, by his outraged reaction, only compounded the error and irrevocably alienated the one man who could sustain nonpartisan principles.

Alexander Hamilton once wrote that Washington "was an *Aegis very essential to me.*"[133] If this leader of the Federalist party saw the necessity of shielding his programs behind Washington's prestige, a man of neither party needed even greater protection. Edmund Randolph and successful nonpartisanship lost this protection in August 1795.

---

[133] Hamilton to Tobias Lear, January 2, 1800, Lodge, *Works of Hamilton*, X, 537.

George Washington and the Reputation of Edmund Randolph

Mary K. Bonsteel Tachau

The case of Edmund Randolph provides a classic example of how difficult it is to prove one's own innocence. For almost two hundred years, a cloud of suspicion has surrounded his reputation. Randolph resigned as secretary of state in 1795 after his fellow cabinet members accused him of having held improper communications with the French minister to the United States and of having solicited a bribe from him — charges that President George Washington evidently found tenable. Randolph countered with an impassioned denial, *A Vindication of Mr. Randolph's Resignation*, which contained an exculpatory statement from the minister, but the president and his Federalist colleagues remained unmoved. Afterward; they additionally charged Randolph with having misspent public funds, but even a later recognition of the misleading implications of antiquated accounting methods has brought him no redemption. In the public mind Edmund Randolph's innocence is unproved.

Yet Randolph has had eloquent defenders. Among them are Irving Brant, Moncure Daniel Conway, and a grandson, Peter V. Daniel, Jr. Washington's most knowledgeable modern biographers believe that Randolph stated his case accurately and was not guilty.[1] But all of his defenders are defeated by the attitude of the one person who knew Randolph best: his mentor and the aegis of his career, George Washington. Washington held Randolph's fate in his hands. He might easily have restored Randolph to public esteem and chastened his detractors, but did not. Indeed, for the remainder of Washington's life, he had no contact at all with a man who had been his loyal supporter and intimate associate for twenty years. Like his contemporaries, most historians have followed Washington's lead. If Randolph was guilty, the president's reaction is entirely reasonable. But if Randolph was innocent, Washington's reaction invites further speculation.

Mary K. Bonsteel Tachau is professor of history at the University of Louisville. Research for the article was sponsored by a grant from the Graduate School, University of Louisville, and by a Fellowship in Legal History from the American Bar Association. Earlier versions of the article were presented at the annual meeting of the Society for Historians of the Early American Republic, Siena College, Loudonville, New York, July 24, 1981; and at The Filson Club, Louisville, Kentucky, April 5, 1982. Materials from the Connecticut Historical Society, the Historical Society of Pennsylvania, and the Massachusetts Historical Society are cited by permission.

[1] Irving Brant, "Edmund Randolph, Not Guilty!" *William and Mary Quarterly*, 7 (1950), 179–98; Moncure Daniel Conway, *Omitted Chapters of History Disclosed in the Life and Papers of Edmund Randolph, Governor of Virginia; First Attorney-General United States, Secretary of State* (New York, 1888); Peter V. Daniel, Jr., ed., *A Vindication of Edmund Randolph, Written by Himself and Published in 1795* (Richmond, 1885); John Alexander Carroll and Mary Wells Ashworth, *George Washington: First in Peace* (New York, 1957), 279–98, 315–36.

No additional proofs beyond those already available may ever be found in Randolph's defense. Yet an examination of records not previously associated with Randolph's case, coupled with an analysis of his behavior after he was accused, offers a new perspective on the context in which Washington responded to the charges against Randolph. The incident that precipitated Randolph's resignation occurred in 1795, but the causes for his departure lie in the administration's response to the Whiskey Insurrection of 1794. Together with an understanding of the president's posture toward the world and of Randolph's position in the cabinet, the data offer a new explanation for Washington's behavior. They suggest that Randolph was right, after all, when he wrote that he had been "the meditated victim of party spirit," framed by his enemies and abandoned by his hero, without cause.[2]

Randolph's formal association with Washington began in 1775, when he declined to join his Loyalist father's flight to England and instead served as an aide-de-camp to the general in Boston. A few months later Randolph went back to Virginia to handle family affairs and, as it turned out, to begin a career in politics. He was a delegate to Virginia's constitutional convention and the commonwealth's first attorney general. He married his childhood sweetheart, Elizabeth Nicholas, and in 1779 tried to manage both his state office and membership in the Continental Congress. When that proved to be impossible, he resigned from the Congress and settled in Richmond. Near the end of the war, he was again elected to the Congress. When he returned to Virginia, he was once more elected attorney general and, in 1786, governor of the commonwealth. Throughout the years he had kept in touch with Washington, and their friendship was renewed at the Constitutional Convention in 1787. Randolph, however, refused to sign the document when it was completed, although he defended it during the ratification struggle in Virginia.[3]

Randolph's waffling on the Constitution was the despair of such friends as James Madison. What appeared to others as undependability appeared to Randolph as independence on issues. That characteristic had its usefulness to Washington as Randolph hitched himself to Washington's star. When Randolph became the nation's first attorney general, he gave his loyalty totally to the president, subordinating his antifederalist sympathies to the greater purpose of serving Washington in whatever way he could. Randolph kept his eyes and ears open on the president's behalf and tried to minimize dissent in the cabinet. It was not a role that made him popular with his peers. Alexander Hamilton was probably jealous of him. Thomas Jefferson was contemptuous, describing Randolph as "the poorest chameleon I ever saw, having no color of his own and reflecting that nearest him. When he is with me, he is a whig. When with Hamilton he is a tory. When with the president, he is that [which] he thinks will please him."[4]

---

[2] Edmund Randolph to George Washington, Oct. 24, 1975, [Edmund Randolph], *A Vindication of Mr. Randolph's Resignation* (Philadelphia, 1795), 17; Mary K. Bonsteel Tachau, *Federal Courts in the Early Republic: Kentucky 1789–1816* (Princeton, 1978), 65–74, 95–126; Whiskey Rebellion Papers, Records of the Internal Revenue Service, RG 58 (National Archives).
[3] John J. Reardon, *Edmund Randolph: A Biography* (New York, 1975), 18–23.
[4] Thomas Jefferson to James Madison, Aug. 11, 1793, Carroll and Ashworth, *George Washington*, 115n100.

Edmund Randolph, by Constantino Brumidi. Mural in United States Capitol.
Courtesy Library of Congress.

Randolph was not eager to succeed Jefferson as secretary of state, but he knew how difficult it was for Washington to maintain sectional balance in the cabinet and to persuade men of substance to hold public office far from their homes—and the president's wishes came first. So Randolph let his law practice slip and remained in Philadelphia, worrying about his wife's health and his children's futures, and wearied by chronic impecuniousness. Washington reciprocated that devotion by relying on Randolph for special assignments, such as sounding out public opinion on controversial issues, handling the president's personal legal affairs (which Randolph did without fee), and looking after Martha Washington during the president's temporary absences from the city (as during the Whiskey Insurrection).[5]

By 1794 it was impossible for anyone but Washington to claim that he was above party, but Randolph tried to do that, too, and succeeded only in further alienating his earlier allies. Although written later, Jefferson's correspondence provides an acerbic description probably widely shared by other Republicans: "The fact is that he has generally given his principles to the one party and his practice to the other; the oyster to one, the shell to the other. Unfortunately the shell was generally the lot of his friends the French and Republicans, and the oyster of their antagonists."[6]

The policy of neutrality that the president insisted on after the outbreak of war in Europe in 1793 seemed designed for Randolph to implement. He followed his leader and plodded straight down the middle of the road, determined to deal as evenhandedly as possible with the ministers of Great Britain and France, even though his personal sympathies probably lay with the latter. Neither of them, of course, was satisfied. The British minister, George Hammond, knew that he was getting fewer oysters from the secretary of state than were provided by Secretary of the Treasury Hamilton, especially when John Jay's mission to London took shape. The French minister, Jean Antoine Joseph Fauchet, considered the very fact of the mission a violation of the permanent treaty that had bound America to France since 1778—a handful of shells for America's earliest ally. Hammond's mistrust and Fauchet's frustration were to have tragic consequences for Randolph because he became a victim of their parties' spirits, also.

Fauchet had arrived in the United States with a warrant for the arrest of his predecessor, Edmond Charles Genêt, a casualty of the Girondists' fall from power. Fauchet was afraid that the Americans' overture to Great Britain might be viewed by his own sponsor, Maximilien Robespierre, as evidence that he, too, was an ineffective advocate for the Republic of Virtue. But the French minister was a resourceful man. He compensated for his lack of success in molding United States foreign policy by exaggerating his own intimacy with the American secretary of state and the secretary's influence over the president—and gambled that no one in Paris would contradict his claims. Further, he tried to divert attention from his ignorance about foreign affairs by writing as little as possible about them and by expounding to the point of tedium what he learned about domestic issues.

[5] Reardon, *Edmund Randolph*, 232–38, 276–78.
[6] Jefferson to W[illiam] B[ranch] Giles, Dec. 31, 1795, Paul Leicester Ford, ed., *The Works of Thomas Jefferson* (10 vols., New York, 1904–1905), VIII, 202.

As it happened, Fauchet was remarkably well informed about some of them. Although Genêt had failed in his efforts to get George Rogers Clark to lead an army of Kentuckians against the Spanish in New Orleans, he had left a legacy of agents and informers in the West who freely reported the disaffection that western settlers felt toward the central government. Westerners wanted protection from hostile native Americans, access to the Northwest Territory, and a treaty with Spain that would grant free navigation of the Mississippi River. Most of all, they wanted the government to repeal the internal revenue taxes on stills and domestically distilled liquors, which were major components of Hamilton's 1791 fiscal program. Because of the difficulties and expense of transportation, thousands of western farmers had become, in Albert Gallatin's words, "distillers through necessity, not choice, that [they] may comprehend the greatest value on the smallest size and weight." From a trans-Appalachian perspective, the government did not provide what they needed for survival or security, but it taxed their only exportable product. Throughout all of Kentucky and western Pennsylvania, and in a number of western counties in Virginia, North Carolina, and South Carolina, the farmer-distillers steadfastly refused to pay the tax. Three years of sending petitions and memorials to Philadelphia had produced, in return, nothing but proclamations demanding submission; most of the amendments to the original statute were designed to extend the jurisdiction of the tax collectors and to make collection more rewarding and efficient. As a consequence, Hamilton came to be thought of as an enemy of the West—just as was Jay, who was believed to have offered to bargain away navigation of the Mississippi in the Jay-Gardoqui negotiations in 1786. By the summer of 1794, continued resentment of Hamilton and his taxes was changing what had been principally a peaceful protest into one increasingly marked by violence. That was a development that could not be ignored in Philadelphia.[7]

Fauchet's dispatches described those things at some length, but his information was not exclusive. What he reported was fairly common knowledge. Eastern newspapers printed copies of the remonstrances that Kentuckians and Pennsylvanians adopted to protest the excise tax and the government's failure to be responsive to their needs. Certainly the president and all the members of his cabinet knew what was going on in the West, as their internal correspondence shows. Personal letters sent to members of the House of Representatives and the Senate kept them informed. Inspectors of the revenue wrote to Hamilton about their inability to collect the excise and the violence experienced by collectors who tried to do so. Officials and clerks in the Treasury and in the internal revenue office knew that no taxes had been received from the area, as did every member of Congress who read the annual reports of the secretary of the treasury. And, of course, the noncomplying distillers and their families in the West and all of their friends knew it, too.[8]

[7] Albert Gallatin, *Writings*, ed. Henry Adams (3 vols., New York, 1960 [Philadelphia, 1879]), I, 3; Walter Lowrie and Walter S. Franklin, eds., *American State Papers, Finance: Documents, Legislative and Executive of the Congress of the United States* (5 vols., Washington, 1834), I, 250–51, 280–81, 390–91; Richard Peters, ed., *The Public Statutes at Large of the United States of America* (17 vols., Boston, 1855–1873), I, 999, 267, 275, 378.
[8] Joseph Fauchet to Minister of Foreign Affairs, June 4 (Dispatch No. 3), Sept. 5 (Dispatch No. 6), Oct. 31 (Dispatch No. 10), 1794, Original Papers on the Vindication of Edmund Randolph (Manuscript Division, Library

By the summer of 1794, it must have seemed to some members of the administration that the kind of Great Fear that had spread throughout rural France in 1789 was being ignited in the West. In early June Washington asked his cabinet how to respond to a particularly inflammatory remonstrance from Kentucky that had been precipitated by the news that Jay, of all people, had been sent to Great Britain to negotiate a treaty—when it was a treaty with Spain that westerners needed. (The cabinet advised him to ignore it.) That decision was still in everyone's mind when it was learned, near the end of July, that Marshal David Lenox—who had earlier served thirty-nine writs without incident—was prevented from carrying out his duties in Pennsylvania when he was accompanied by the revenue inspector, Gen. John Neville. A mob then laid siege to Neville's house and burned it. In the exchange of gunfire, one of the mob's leaders was killed, and the resulting fury over the killing set off two other chains of events, one in the West and another in Philadelphia. The former resulted in a series of mass meetings and angry statements; the latter led to a consideration of stronger measures by the government.[9]

For two years Hamilton had advocated using force to compel compliance and to quash public meetings that adopted "treasonous" statements.[10] He could always count on support from Secretary of War Henry Knox, but until the end of 1793, the cabinet was evenly divided because Jefferson and Randolph were unalterably opposed to using force against farmers who were exercising their First Amendment rights of free speech and petition.

But the cast was different in 1794. The president had become far more amenable to Hamilton's positions on many issues, and he was clearly reaching the end of his patience with westerners. Knox was still in Hamilton's corner, and Attorney General William Bradford was less concerned with the First Amendment than his predecessor had been. But Jefferson was out of the cabinet, having taken himself off to Monticello on what later seemed like a sabbatical from politics. Only Randolph remained an obstacle, and his faithfulness and devotion to the president's interests made his influence with Washington a problem to the Hamiltonians. And Randolph still counseled moderation and still opposed the use of force.

An analysis of the process of decision making in the cabinet on the question of using military power against defiant distillers must now take into account evidence revealed by Kentucky federal court records and an internal revenue file discovered in 1954, which show that the decision makers knew that opposition to Hamilton's

of Congress). Alexander Hamilton to Washington, July 13, 1794, George Washington Papers (Manuscript Division, Library of Congress); Henry Knox to Washington, July 14, 1794, *ibid*.; Randolph to Washington, July 15, 1794, *ibid*.; Attorney General [William Bradford] to Washington, July [15?], 1794, *ibid*.; Proceedings of the President, July 14, 1794, *ibid*.; [Philadelphia] *Gazette of the United States and Daily Evening Advertiser*, June 23, 1794; "Extract of a Letter from Kentucky Dated Lexington, Jan. 25, 1794," enclosed in Randolph to Washington, Feb. 27, 1794, Miscellaneous Letters, Department of State, 1789–1906, General Records of the Department of State, RG 59 (National Archives); Letters Sent by the Commissioner of the Revenue and the Revenue Office, 1792–1807, Whiskey Rebellion Papers; Lowrie and Franklin, eds., *American State Papers, Finance*, I, 355–56, 386–87.
  [9] Randolph to Bradford, Hamilton, and Knox, July 11, 1794, Harold C. Syrett, ed., *The Papers of Alexander Hamilton* (26 vols., New York, 1961–1979), XVI, 589; Carroll and Ashworth, *George Washington*, 184.
  [10] Hamilton to Tench Coxe, Sept. 1, 1792, Syrett, ed., *Papers of Alexander Hamilton*, XI, 305–10; Hamilton to Washington, Sept. 1, 1792, *ibid*., 311–13; Hamilton to John Jay, Sept. 3, 1792 *ib..J.*, 316–17.

policies and evasion of the excise extended far beyond Pennsylvania's four western counties. As the administration weighed the risks of civil war or anarchy and talked about a display of force giving strength to the government, it was seeing a far broader canvas than has formerly been realized.[11]

The ultimate decision had two parts: One was to characterize what was going on in western Pennsylvania as an insurrection and to take steps to end it. The other involved sending an emissary to Kentucky but pretending that there was no rebelliousness, violence, or tax evasion there or elsewhere and later covering up the evidence that those things had occurred.[12] Of course, it would have been enormously expensive to send federalized militia so far west, and supply problems would have been a nightmare. Moreover, to march troops into Kentucky while that state's own mounted volunteers were fighting Indians with Anthony Wayne's army in northwestern Ohio might have precipitated civil war or secession, or both. Yet to use military force in one state while sparing another carried its own dangers. Might not the chief executive be accused of failing to execute the laws evenhandedly throughout the nation? What did the concept of equal justice under law mean if some were punished severely and others were ignored?

Thus Randolph was a pivotal figure. His office was second in prestige to the presidency. Until a few months earlier, he had been attorney general, the administration's principal interpreter of the Constitution and federal law. He knew more about what was going on in Kentucky than anyone else in the cabinet. If he had not estranged himself from the Hamiltonians earlier, he certainly did so in August 1794 because he stood in their way. And Randolph, to the acute discomfort of everyone else, had the Constitution on his side.

Under Article IV, federal troops can be sent into a state only on the request of the legislature, or of the governor if the legislature is not in session (and Pennsylvania's was not). Gov. Thomas Mifflin of Pennsylvania doubted whether his state's militia would respond to a call-up, declined to test the waters, and strongly resisted sending in the federalized militia of any other states. Mifflin, moreover, had the support of other Pennsylvania officials: Chief Justice Thomas McKean, Secretary of State Alexander James Dallas, and Attorney General Jared Ingersoll.[13] But Hamilton would not be turned back—not by Randolph, not by Pennsylvania's top officials, and not by Article IV.

The idea of bypassing Article IV and, instead, employing the provisions of the Militia Act of 1792 bears the mark of Hamilton's political ingenuity. The Militia Act

[11] Richard H. Kohn, "The Washington Administration's Decision to Crush the Whiskey Rebellion," *Journal of American History*, 69 (Dec. 1972), 567–84; Edward Carrington to Washington, July 14, 1794, Proceedings of the President, Washington Papers; Knox to Washington, May 7, May 12, 1794, *ibid.*; Washington to Charles Mynn Thruston, Aug. 10, 1794, John C. Fitzpatrick, ed., *The Writings of George Washington from the Original Manuscript Sources, 1745–1799* (39 vols., Washington, 1939–1944), XXXIII, 464; Whiskey Rebellion Papers.

[12] Randolph to Washington, Aug. 7, 1794, Domestic Letters, Department of State, General Records of the Department of State; Randolph to James Innes, Aug. 22, Sept. 5, 1794, *ibid.*; Mary K. Bonsteel Tachau, "A New Look at the Whiskey Rebellion," in *The Whiskey Rebellion: Past and Present Perspectives*, ed. Steven R. Boyd (Westport, 1985), 97–118.

[13] "Conference Concerning the Insurrection in Western Pennsylvania," *Pennsylvania Archives: Second Series* (19 vols., Harrisburg, 1887–1896), IV, 144–46.

was an implementation of the clause in section 8 of Article I that gave Congress the power "to provide for calling forth the Militia to execute the Laws of the Union, suppress Insurrections and repel Invasions." The statute gave the president authority to summon the militia of a state on notification by an associate justice of the United States Supreme Court or by the federal judge of the district "whenever the laws of the United States shall be opposed, or the execution thereof obstructed, in any state, by combinations too powerful to be suppressed by the ordinary course of judicial proceedings, or by the powers vested in the marshals." If the militia of that state refused or was insufficient, the president was empowered to call up the militia of other states, which, if Congress was not in session, would serve for thirty days after the next session began. Although the Militia Act required notification in the specific language of the statute, it did not set a standard of proof that needed to be met before a judge issued the statement.[14]

For Hamilton it was pure luck that there happened to be an associate justice of the Supreme Court who was a Federalist, who was in Philadelphia, and who, because he was facing bankruptcy, was vulnerable to pressure from the powerful. This was James Wilson, whose distinguished public career included signing the Declaration of Independence and being a member of the Constitutional Convention. In the summer of 1794, however, he was desperately trying to stave off his creditors. The administration gave him a deposition and some letters describing events in the western part of the state and awaited his decision. Hamilton, in fact, hovered over the justice, barely maintaining a proper arm's length. He need not have worried. Without personal knowledge of what was going on in the West or evidence that would have been acceptable in a trial, Wilson produced the desired notification. He asserted that "in the Counties of Washington and Allegany . . . Laws of the United States are opposed, and the Execution thereof obstructed by Combinations too powerful to be suppressed by the ordinary Course of judicial Proceedings, or by the powers vested in the Marshal of that District."[15]

As far as Hamilton was concerned, that took care of the constitutional issue. Randolph was still not convinced. He pointed out that Wilson mentioned only two of the four counties and failed to specify which laws were opposed. Moreover, the secretary of state argued that "a judge ought not a priori to decide, that the marshall is incompetent to suppress the combination by the posse comitatus." Randolph went on to list eleven reasons why the militia ought not to be called out and urged the president, instead, to issue a proclamation and to appoint a commission to negotiate with the westerners. If the commissioners failed, the offenders could still be prosecuted, as the excise statutes provided. Randolph insisted that the government ought not to resort to military action unless all other legal procedures had been taken and the judiciary had been "withstood."[16]

---

[14] Peters, ed., *Public Statutes*, I, 264. Probably the reason why the Federalists always used the word *insurrection* was to reinforce their reliance on the Militia Act of 1792. The term "Whiskey Rebellion" is of later origin.

[15] Journal, July 8, 1794–Aug. 25, 1794, vol. 5, Papers of James Wilson (Historical Society of Pennsylvania, Philadelphia); Hamilton to Coxe, Aug. 1, 1794, Syrett, ed., *Papers of Alexander Hamilton*, XVII, 1; Whiskey Rebellion, vol. 1, Pennsylvania Miscellany (Manuscript Division, Library of Congress).

[16] Randolph to Washington, Aug. 5, 1794, Washington Papers.

For a time Randolph prevailed over Hamilton and Knox. Washington issued a proclamation and appointed a commission composed of Attorney General Bradford, Pennsylvania Supreme Court Justice Jasper Yeates, and United States Sen. James Ross, a Federalist lawyer from Washington, Pennsylvania. Randolph wrote their instructions as the president directed but had a State Department clerk attach to the file copy a statement expressing his own reservations about some of the provisions. Washington evidently felt some confidence in the plans and told Secretary Knox that he could go off to Maine, as Knox had earlier requested (but had been refused), in order to look after some land claims.[17]

That confidence was not initially shared by the commissioners. Yeates and Bradford set out nervously, having arranged to meet Ross in western Pennsylvania. Eventually, however, the absence of opponents along their journey allayed their fears. In retrospect their mission does not seem to have been unsuccessful, especially considering the time constraints imposed by the possibility of a military campaign that would have to begin before winter set in. The commissioners had only about three weeks to get to the scene and to obtain oaths of submission from distillers in more than forty townships. Yet when in Brownsville their proposals won by "only" thirty-four votes to twenty-three, the administration believed that the commission had failed. On September 9 Hamilton's orders went out, calling up a militia army of twelve thousand men—more than Washington had ever commanded during the War for Independence. Hamilton had won.[18]

With Knox far away (and later denied permission to join the army when he did return to Pennsylvania), Hamilton rode at Washington's side as the president proceeded to Carlisle and on to Bedford. It was a triumphal procession. The autumn weather was splendid most of the time, and in all the towns and villages the citizenry honored the man who was the nation's truly authentic hero. They placed the finest houses along the route at Washington's disposal and filled his evenings with banquets.[19] At the time, the total absence of any opposition only added to the glory of the occasion. When Washington left the army at Bedford in order to be present when Congress convened in Philadelphia—which was necessary to get an extension of time for the unopposed troops—he must have felt that his own prestige as well as the government's had surely been augmented by the magnificent and untroubled display of military power. But he also knew that there was no insurrection to justify the expense of the militia army.

Where Hamilton won, Randolph lost. His reluctance to use force, his delaying tactic involving the commission, and his stated belief that the strength of the government lay not in military might but in the affection of its people—all were deficits in the Hamiltonians' closely computed accounts. Randolph was the odd man

[17] Memorandum by G. T., Jr. [George Taylor, Jr.], Aug. 5, 1794, Whiskey Rebellion, vol. 1, Pennsylvania Miscellany; Washington to Knox, Aug. 8, 1794, Henry Knox Papers (Massachusetts Historical Society, Boston).

[18] Bradford to Elias Boudinot, Aug. 1, Sept. 5, 1794, vol. 2, Wallace Papers (Historical Society of Pennsylvania); Jasper Yeates to Mrs. Jasper Yeates, Aug. 21, Sept. 25, 1794, box 1, Jasper Yeates Papers, ibid.; Hamilton to Thomas Mifflin, Sept. 9, 1794, Syrett, ed., Papers of Alexander Hamilton, XVII, 210; Hamilton to Samuel Hodgdon, Sept. 10, 1794, ibid., 215; Hamilton to Thomas Sim Lee, Sept. 10, 1794, ibid., 218.

[19] Carroll and Ashworth, George Washington, 199–213.

out, and the Federalists were determined to isolate him and to destroy his influence with the president.

In January 1795 Oliver Wolcott succeeded Hamilton as secretary of the treasury, and Timothy Pickering succeeded Knox as secretary of war. They shared their predecessors' views about Randolph but apparently decided to await events and to take advantage of whatever opportunity might arise. By that time Randolph had acquired other powerful enemies: the Grenville ministry in London and its emissary George Hammond in Philadelphia. Those Englishmen were true professionals when it came to sabotaging an obstructionist. They had taken full advantage of Hamilton's information about Jay's instructions, and they enjoyed exacerbating the differences within Washington's cabinet. Hammond, of course, had vastly increased his own value to the ministry both by his relationship with the Hamiltonians and by conscientiously carrying out George Grenville's carefully worded suggestions. Usually his orders were phrased permissively: "You will, if possible, be pleased to . . . ," "pray consider yourself free to . . . ," or "it appears that it might be helpful to. . . ." But in November 1794 Grenville had sent Hammond new instructions, couched in imperative language:

> It will therefore be absolutely necessary that . . . you should converse confidentially . . . with those Persons in America who are friends to a System of amicable Intercourse between the two Countries, in the view that some step may be taken . . . so as either to convince Mr. Randolph of the necessity of his adopting a different language and Conduct, or at least, to place him in a Situation where his personal Sentiments may not endanger the Peace of Two Countries between whom I trust a permanent union is now established. You will readily see that this is to be done with prudence and delicacy on your part.[20]

That was an order: If Randolph will not change his ways, *get him out of the way.* Hammond must have been delighted to be turned loose against a secretary of state whose cautious and plodding adherence to the middle of the road had been no help at all to Great Britain in its war with France. The fact that neutrality was the official policy of the United States government was irrelevant to the British. They wanted a secretary of state who was more responsive to their interests.

Within a matter of months, the means to accomplish that purpose came to hand through an accident of war. A packet of dispatches that Fauchet had written to his government was found on a French ship captured by the British on the high seas. In May 1795 the ministry sent them on to Hammond to use as he saw fit. After he received them at the end of July, the minister wrote back: "The originals of the French letters are peculiarly interesting, and will, I am persuaded, if properly treated, tend to effect an essential change in the public sentiment of this country with regard to the character and principles of certain individuals, and to the real motives of their political conduct."[21]

---

[20] [George Grenville] to George Hammond, Nov. 20, 1794, vol. 19, Foreign Correspondence, America, British State Papers [transcribed by Henry Adams] (Manuscript Division, Library of Congress).
[21] Hammond to Grenville, July 27, 1795, *ibid.*

The proper treatment was to give them to the friends of Great Britain so that they could be used against its enemy—in other words, to give them to the Hamiltonians for use against Randolph. Hammond immediately got in contact with the secretary of the treasury and gave him Fauchet's Dispatch No. 10, written the previous autumn. Wolcott, in turn, shared it with Pickering, his closest ally in the cabinet, and soon after, with Bradford.[22]

For unscrupulous men the dispatch was pure serendipity. The French language slowed them down, but Pickering (who just a year earlier had written to his son that he was handicapped by his lack of fluency) got out his grammar and dictionary and went to work.[23] Like all amateur translators, he seized on apparent cognates, two of which were especially germane to his purposes. Fauchet had reported that Randolph shared "précieuses confessions" with him. Moreover, in referring to Dispatch No. 6, which he had written earlier, Fauchet hinted rather ambigiously that Randolph had made overtures to him relating to money with "un air fort empressé." Pickering, of course, translated the first phrase as "precious confessions" instead of "valuable disclosures" or "invaluable acknowledgments," either of which would be more accurate. Even worse, he translated the second phrase as "an air of great eagerness" instead of "a countenance expressive of much anxiety"—which gives a totally different impression. Fauchet's attempts to enhance his own importance by exaggerating his relationship to Randolph (and Randolph's to Washington) would have serious consequences for the secretary of state. The seriousness of those consequences was exponentially increased by Pickering's mistranslation.[24]

The dispatch provided the opportunity so long sought by the Federalists—to get rid of Randolph—and just in time. When Hammond gave it to Wolcott, the news about Jay's Treaty was spreading throughout the nation. In community after community crowds of people rejected its provisions and excoriated its negotiator. They were angry with the Senate, which had secretly ratified it, even though the Senate had done so only conditionally. The Federalists in the cabinet were afraid that the secretary of state, no friend of Great Britain, might well advise the president not to sign it, especially because they had learned about a British Order-in-Council again authorizing the seizure of American grain bound for France. This, then, was the moment to get Randolph out of the way once and for all. Hammond's gift of the intercepted dispatch provided the opportunity that Randolph's enemies had wanted for at least one year, and probably three.

Wolcott and Pickering moved quickly. They tricked Randolph into urging the president to return to Philadelphia from Mount Vernon and presented Pickering's translation to him. Washington, who must have been stunned to read that his faithful servant had made "precious confessions" to the French minister, took seven-

---

[22] Carroll and Ashworth, *George Washington*, 279–80; Brant, "Edmund Randolph," 185. Cf. W. Allen Wilbur, "Oliver Wolcott, Jr., and Edmund Randolph's Resignation, 1795: An Explanatory Note on an Historic Misconception," Connecticut Historical Society, *Register*, 38 (1973), 12–16.

[23] Timothy Pickering to John Pickering, June 17, 1794, p. 73, vol. 4, Timothy Pickering Papers (Massachusetts Historical Society).

[24] Carroll and Ashworth, *George Washington*, 281–283; Brant, "Edmund Randolph," 193–96.

teen pages of notes in order to study the dispatch further.[25] Unfortunately for Randolph, Washington did not read French either and therefore was entirely dependent on Pickering's artless (and sometimes erroneous) translation.

What Randolph's grandson and other defenders did not know is the likelihood that Washington was even more stunned to learn what Fauchet had reported to his government: that the Whiskey Insurrection was not what it was purported to be. Dispatch No. 10 was dated October 31, 1794, ten days after Washington had left the army in order to be in Philadelphia for the opening of Congress. Fauchet described the administration's decision to send troops into western Pennsylvania as evidence of Hamilton's vindictiveness against simple farmers who opposed his whiskey tax. At the very least it was disconcerting to the president to learn that Fauchet had told his government all about the partisan divisions in the new republic, the extent of opposition to Hamilton's (and thus the administration's) policies, and the widespread discontent of westerners. It was profoundly embarrassing to read Fauchet's statement that "a commotion of some hundreds of men, who have not since been found in arms . . . were not symptoms which could justify the raising of so great a force as 15,000 men." In his own notes Washington underlined—as Fauchet had done in the original, referring to something written earlier in Dispatch No. 3—the minister's allegation that Randolph had told him that "*under the pretext of giving energy to the government it* [the sending of troops to western Pennsylvania] *was intended to introduce absolute power, and to mislead the President in paths which would conduct him to unpopularity.*" It all made the commander in chief, who had commanded in person, look like a dupe or a fool. Washington must have wondered what else Randolph had said and Fauchet had reported in dispatches that had not been intercepted.[26]

Irving Brant based his defense of Randolph on Pickering's misleading translations, which implied that Randolph had told Fauchet things he ought not to have told him and had even asked for money. That is an important contribution because it helps explain why Washington shifted his trust from Randolph to Wolcott and Pickering. But neither Brant, nor Moncure Daniel Conway, nor Peter V. Daniel, Jr., could have known that the vigor of Washington's response was due to the *subject* of Fauchet's dispatch, because they accepted—as do most historians today—the Federalists' assertion that there had been a genuine Whiskey Insurrection that ended with the appearance of the militia army and that the administration's timely use of military might gave strength to the government. Randolph's defenders did not know, as Washington knew, that the glorious advance of the troops was, in many ways, a charade.

Even if Washington had believed in September 1794 that military action was necessary—whether to show the strength of the government, to defeat the Pennsyl-

[25] "Copius Extracts of Intercepted Letter dated Oct. 31, 1794," Washington Papers.

[26] Fauchet to Minister of Foreign Affairs, Oct. 31 (Dispatch No. 10), June 4 (Dispatch No. 3), Sept. 5 (Dispatch No. 6), 1794, Original Papers on the Vindication of Edmund Randolph. A convenient published source for Dispatch No. 10 and sections of Dispatch No. 3 and of Dispatch No. 6, providing the French text where relevant, is Reardon, *Edmund Randolph*, 367–80.

vanians, or to threaten the noncomplying Kentuckians, western Virginians, western North Carolinians, and western South Carolinians, or to do all of those—he knew by August 1795 that military action had not succeeded even in gaining compliance with the excise laws, and it was doubtful whether the government had been strengthened. As long as troops remained in the area, Pennsylvania distillers registered their stills and paid their taxes. When the troops left, collections dried up. A year after the so-called insurrection had been put down, no returns had yet been received from Kentucky, the Northwest Territory, western South Carolina, western Virginia, or what would soon become Tennessee.[27] Kentucky still had no federal attorney, and sporadic violence against collectors continued there and elsewhere. Washington realized, therefore, that Fauchet's contemptuous comments about sending a huge army against "some turbulent men at their plough" were embarrassingly close to the mark.

The whiskey "rebels" were not far from the president's mind, anyway. As recently as July 10, he had issued a general pardon for those Pennsylvanians who had been exempted from the general amnesty; in June he had pardoned the two men who had been convicted of treason. The charges themselves must have troubled him; they resulted from orders that Hamilton had given on his own authority as acting secretary of war, shortly after Washington had left the army to return to Philadelphia. By November 17 the secretary of the treasury had commanded the arrest and imprisonment of 150 men for having committed treason.[28]

It is doubtful whether any of the farmer-distillers had done anything that met the constitutional definition in Article III, which specifies that "treason against the United States, shall consist only in levying war against them, or in adhering to their enemies, giving them aid and comfort." The president knew that there had not been any actual levying of war. He also knew that citizens, however disgruntled, are not enemies. He must have remembered that the constitutional definition was designed to repudiate the numerous grounds on which treason charges could be brought in England; it was generally considered to be an important improvement over English practice.[29] He may also have recalled that Hamilton himself had written in No. 84 of *The Federalist* that one of the reasons that a bill of rights was not needed was because the Constitution already provided a series of protections from the misuse of governmental power—among which, ironically, was this narrow definition of treason.

The basis for the charges in Pennsylvania was not the constitutional definition but a doctrine of "constructive levying of war," which, like the English doctrine of "constructive treason," had the effect of broadening the grounds on which alleged offenders could be brought to trial. Attorney General Bradford and William Rawle, the federal attorney for the District of Pennsylvania, argued that a combination of

[27] After 1795 the commissioner of revenue reported amounts *payable*, not amounts *paid*. Lowrie and Franklin, eds., *American State Papers, Finance*, I, 355–56, 390–91, 562, 593, 618.

[28] Hamilton to Washington, Nov. 17, 1794, Syrett, ed., *Papers of Alexander Hamilton*, XVII, 380–81.

[29] See, for example, James Wilson's 1790–1791 law lectures in Robert Green McCloskey, ed., *The Works of James Wilson* (2 vols., Cambridge, Mass., 1967), II, 663–68. See also Harry Innes, "Address to the Grand Jury," [Jan. 12, 1792], pp. 2–123, vol. 13, Harry Innes Papers (Manuscript Division, Library of Congress).

individuals united for the common purpose of forcibly preventing the execution of a public law and the actual or threatened use of force to prevent execution of the law constituted a treasonous levying of war. Although their argument was upheld by Justice William Paterson, grand jurors were less cooperative. They returned only fifty-one indictments, of which thirty-one were for treason. When the cases came to trial, petit jurors were even less convinced, and they convicted only two.[30]

The trials took place in May 1795, the pardons in June and July. It was less than three weeks later that Hammond gave Fauchet's intercepted dispatch to Wolcott and set in motion the events that led to Randolph's resignation. Wolcott's dismay about Randolph's apparent disloyalty was compounded by that reminder, in Fauchet's words, of Randolph's reluctance to support Hamilton on many issues. Wolcott revered Hamilton and saw the dispatch as a way of getting rid of Randolph, at last. With Pickering's and Bradford's support, the secretary of the treasury turned to Washington.

As for the president, however shaken he may have been by the suspicion that his trusted confidant had been disloyal, he was equally disturbed that the French government had been given that kind of information about what had happened—and what had not happened—in Pennsylvania. He knew, better than the secretaries of war and the treasury that, despite all the angry talk, no one had opposed the militia army. He knew that he had refused to halt the march, even when implored to do so by prominent representatives of the western counties who believed that they could gain total compliance if they were given just a little more time.[31]

And by August 1795 Washington knew also that he was no longer immune to criticism. As the terms of Jay's Treaty spread throughout the nation, the president himself came under attacks more virulent than he had ever before experienced. Doubtless they, too, were being reported by Fauchet's and Hammond's successors. Washington did not need to know about the letters from the Venetian ambassadors (whose three centuries of reports on English politics are still influential primary sources) in order to appreciate the damage that the French ambassador's dispatch might do to his own public image in the capitals of Europe.[32]

Whatever he may have felt, the president kept his head and, for eight days, his thoughts to himself. But on the question of how to deal with Fauchet's dispatch, it was Wolcott and Pickering whom he consulted, not Randolph, his faithful Dobbins. To him, Washington did not breathe a word about the dispatch, although the two met and dined together frequently. Yet within twenty-four hours of reading it, Washington repudiated the strategy regarding Jay's Treaty that he and Randolph had agreed on a month earlier—to delay signing it until the Order-in-Council was rescinded. Instead, he announced that he would sign immediately, as Wolcott and

[30] United States v. Mitchell, A[lexander] J[ames] Dallas, Reports of Cases Ruled and Adjudged in the Several Courts of the United States, and of Pennsylvania, Held at the Seat of the Federal Government, II (Philadelphia, 1798), 348–56; Minutes of the United States Circuit Court for the Eastern District of Pennsylvania, May 6, May 7, May 25, May 27, 1795, Records of the District Courts of the United States, RG 21 (National Archives).
[31] Carroll and Ashworth, George Washington, 205–208.
[32] Calendar of State Papers, Venetian (9 vols., London, 1864–1898).

George Washington (The Landsdown Portrait), by Gilbert Stuart, 1796.
Bequest of William Bingham.
Courtesy Pennsylvania Academy of the Fine Arts.

Pickering urged him to do. Randolph was chagrined; Hammond and the Federalists gloated.

It was only after Randolph had completed all of the official business relating to the treaty that Washington, having arranged to have Wolcott and Pickering present, gave Randolph a copy of Fauchet's dispatch and asked him to explain it. Randolph read it through but found nothing remarkable. Although others might disagree with Fauchet's assertions about motivation and about who was influential with whom, the basic information that he had reported was public knowledge and could be found in the newspapers. There were no secret "précieuses confessions." On request, Randolph commented on the dispatch, paragraph by paragraph, puzzled that so much was being made over the minister's account of the Whiskey Insurrection, however biased it was. It was some time before he realized that Washington believed the charges so painstakingly framed by Wolcott and Pickering: that he had been traitorous in his communications with Fauchet and had solicited money from him.[33]

Then it was Randolph's turn to be stunned. He was stunned by the solicitation charge—based, in fact, on Dispatch No. 6, which neither he nor the president had seen but which may have been known to the others—and even more stunned to realize that Washington might imagine him disloyal or dishonest. Randolph left in a trance, gave instructions that his office be locked so that no one could charge that he had tampered with evidence, and wrote out his letter of resignation.[34]

It is unlikely that a guilty man would have done what Randolph did next. He hurried up the East Coast to catch Fauchet (who had been recalled) before he sailed for France, in order to get an exonerating statement from him. The most compelling section of Randolph's *A Vindication* is his verified account of that wild journey. It may also be the best evidence of his innocence. Only Fauchet, after all, could prove Randolph's guilt or establish his innocence, because only the two of them knew whether Randolph had spoken indiscreetly or had solicited a bribe. If Randolph were guilty, surely he would have let Fauchet return to France and then shed crocodile tears about his absence and consequent inability to give testimony. Fauchet had been recalled because Robespierre had fallen from power and had been executed; it was entirely possible that Fauchet, too, might face the guillotine on his homecoming. If Randolph were guilty, Fauchet's departure would end forever the chance that Fauchet might testify against him.

There is a further reason why Randolph would not have pursued Fauchet had he been treasonous. Randolph neither liked nor trusted the minister; they did not have the kind of relationship that would have led him to expect Fauchet to write a false statement out of friendship. Exactly three weeks before the confrontation with the cabinet over the dispatch, Randolph had written a private letter to James Monroe, who was then in Paris. Ironically, it was highly critical of Fauchet because

---

[33] Washington to Oliver Wolcott and Timothy Pickering, [Aug. 12–Aug. 18, 1795], Fitzpatrick, ed., *Writings of George Washington*, XXXIV, 275–76; Wolcott to John Marshall, June 29, 1806, Oliver Wolcott Papers (Connecticut Historical Society, Hartford); Timothy Pickering, "Miscellaneous Notes," p. 184, vol. 3, Timothy Pickering Papers; Carroll and Ashworth, *George Washington*, 290–96.

[34] Randolph to Washington, Aug. 19, 1795, Washington Papers.

he had been insufficiently attentive to Washington. Randolph stated in the letter that the minister had "wrapped himself round with Intrigue; from the first moment of his career in the U. States."[35] Randolph would have been unlikely to plot with someone he considered unreliable, and a man whom he disliked would have been unlikely to perjure himself out of sympathy.

But if Randolph was innocent, he had much to gain and little to lose by trying to reach Fauchet in order to get a statement that would quash forever any suspicions of improper behavior. He therefore took off on a journey as full of suspense as any movie serial of the 1930s. Randolph finally found the minister at Newport, Rhode Island, ready to board the French ship *Méduse*. Its captain was impatient to sail, but he could not leave because the British ship *Africa* lay outside the harbor, hoping to capture so rich a prize. Fauchet promised to prepare a certificate by the following morning. Randolph, exhausted, found lodgings for himself and a stable for his horse and went to bed. Early the next morning he called for the statement, but Fauchet had not finished writing it. Then the weather became a factor in Randolph's fate. During the night a storm had come up, and the *Africa* had to abandon its sentinel post for shelter in Narragansett Bay. That was the opportunity the captain of the *Méduse* had been awaiting for weeks. He sent for Fauchet and weighed anchor. When Randolph returned to Fauchet's lodgings at the hour they had agreed on, he found the minister gone—and no certificate. Frantically, Randolph got the local marshal to help him hire someone to overtake the *Méduse* despite the high seas. After what must have seemed an interminable time, Randolph's man returned and said that he had failed. Randolph must have felt completely defeated.[36]

Then, at last, his luck changed. The pilot who had guided the *Méduse* out of the harbor appeared with a letter from Fauchet. It said that the certificate and other papers had been sent to the new French minister in Philadelphia, Pierre Adet. Randolph stayed in Newport long enough to collect affidavits from almost every witness to his adventure and departed.[37]

His return was not uneventful, but he finally reached Philadelphia and prepared to write an account that he expected would vindicate him. Pickering, who had been appointed acting secretary of state in his absence, tried to withhold documentation in State Department files, and Randolph had to appeal to Washington. The president remained coldly aloof but did order access to the necessary papers. (We know now that Washington drafted a rather testy personal reply to Randolph but decided not to send it.) As the weeks passed, Randolph's sense of injury and frustration transposed into anger.[38]

[35] Randolph to James Monroe, July 29, 1795, transcript, *ibid.* The authenticity of this letter is doubtful because the original copy has not been located. Dorothy Twohig to Tachau, Jan. 22, 1982 (in Tachau's possession). See also Reardon, *Edmund Randolph*, 461–62n27. George Washington's biographers think that the letter hurt Randolph's case. Carroll and Ashworth, *George Washington*, 289.

[36] [Randolph], *Vindication of Mr. Randolph's Resignation*, 4–11; Reardon, *Edmund Randolph*, 313–14; Original Papers on the Vindication of Edmund Randolph.

[37] [Randolph], *Vindication of Mr. Randolph's Resignation*, 12; Reardon, *Edmund Randolph*, 315; Original Papers on the Vindication of Edmund Randolph.

[38] Randolph to Washington, Oct. 8, Oct. 24, 1795, [Randolph], *Vindication of Mr. Randolph's Resignation*, 15–16; Washington to Randolph, Oct. 25, 1795, Carroll and Ashworth, *George Washington*, 317.

The intemperance of Randolph's *A Vindication* suggests that he wrote it without consulting anyone. The pamphlet provides translations—unfortunately, as poor as Pickering's—of the three dispatches and of the statement that Fauchet had written and sent to Adet. Fauchet certified that Randolph had not been indiscreet and had never communicated anything of an improper nature. His certificate is accompanied by one from the new French minister, saying that a review of Fauchet's papers showed that he had always described Randolph as an honest and upright man. As for the charge of soliciting a bribe, Fauchet wrote that Randolph had urged him to fulfill French purchasing contracts made earlier with grain merchants so that they would not be at the mercy of their British creditors but had never asked for money for himself on that or any other occasion. The pamphlet also includes an accurate account of the journey to Newport and back, with supporting affidavits. All of that is accompanied by Randolph's explanations and his assertion that he had been "the mediated victim of party spirit."[39]

But *A Vindication* contains more, much more, too much more. Randolph sets his defense within the context of a diatribe against Washington, and the pamphlet almost explodes with Randolph's anger and hurt. He describes the intimacy of his working relationship with Washington as evidence that he had been badly treated for his years of devoted service. He quotes from letters the president had sent him and from letters he had written as secretary of state to show that he had been undercut by his colleagues in the cabinet. Most important of all, he bitterly attacks the president for having prejudged and misjudged him. Over and over again he lashes out at Washington, leaving him no room to maneuver, no room to save face.[40]

By the time that *A Vindication* was published in December 1795, Randolph was back home in Richmond, trying to reestablish his law practice, licking his wounds, and awaiting some gesture of reconciliation from Washington. (The president consulted with Hamilton, who agreed that Washington should not reply.)[41] No gesture, no letter, no private message ever came. The silence that the president had maintained publicly—and had required of the cabinet—continued for the rest of his life. Washington was a proud and austere man, and it would have been difficult for him to have said that he was sorry or had been mistaken under any circumstances. It was impossible for him to reestablish contact with Randolph under these circumstances. Whether he eventually became convinced of Randolph's innocence, no one will ever know with certainty.[42] But it was intolerable to him that Randolph had attacked him so bitterly and had described their working relationship so indiscreetly. He could not forgive Randolph for publishing Fauchet's dispatches, especially Dispatch No. 10. Publication gave nationwide circulation to the minister's observations that Washington had been used by Hamilton when he led the militia army westward

[39] [Randolph], *Vindication of Mr. Randolph's Resignation*, 12–27, 41–48, 61–96; Reardon, *Edmund Randolph*, 322–31; Original Papers on the Vindication of Edmund Randolph.
[40] [Randolph], *Vindication of Mr. Randolph's Resignation*, 23–24, 26–27, 49, 57, 96–97; Reardon, *Edmund Randolph*, 322–31; Original Papers on the Vindication of Edmund Randolph.
[41] Washington to Hamilton, Dec. 22, 1795, Fitzpatrick, ed., *Writings of George Washington*, XXXIV, 404.
[42] Washington's biographers not only believe in Randolph's innocence themselves but also think that Washington believed in it, too. Carroll and Ashworth, *George Washington*, 333.

against phantom opponents. Publication also exposed part of the role that the British minister had played, for it was after Washington read the dispatch that he changed his mind and decided to sign the controversial treaty with Great Britain. Any reply that the president made to Randolph in 1795 or later might have lent credence or given further publicity to matters that were, from Washington's standpoint, best left alone.

A *Vindication* did not vindicate Randolph, because the president did not respond. Only he could have restored Randolph to his former position of honor and trust. No one offered to act as intermediary between the two men, because Randolph had always put his loyalty to Washington ahead of everything and everyone else, principles and friends alike. Madison, who was one of the earliest of his colleagues, wrote to Monroe that "his greatest enemies will not easily persuade themselves that he was under a corrupt influence of France, and his best friends can't save him from the self condemnation of his political career." Jefferson's analysis was similar; the distribution of shells and oysters had had its effect on both men.[43] Madison and Jefferson were probably the only people secure enough to have attempted a reconciliation between the president and his former secretary of state, and they were not moved to do so.

As for the Federalists, the odd man out was at last truly out of the way, and none of them was about to try to change that long-awaited result. Further, as far as they were concerned, the now published Fauchet dispatches were not innocuous. Although they and the minister's certificate may have exonerated Randolph from the charges of bribery and improper communication—at least to the dispassionate— they presented evidence that the minister of a foreign power knew the embarrassingly thin grounds on which twelve thousand troops had been called up to put down a rebellion that never took place. No Federalist wanted to be reminded of that, especially when so many thousands of people knew that no action at all had been taken against Kentucky and the western counties of Virginia, North Carolina, and South Carolina. A year earlier Hamilton's determination to compel compliance had been gravely threatened when Randolph refused to cooperate; now the treaty with Great Britain lay in the balance. The Federalists wanted Randolph isolated. To make sure that he would remain isolated, Wolcott later charged that Randolph had left a deficit of $49,154.89 in diplomatic and consular funds. The secretary of the treasury knew that State Department accounts often remained open because receipts were lost at sea or in accidents of war; yet he apparently delighted in planting the suspicion that Randolph had personally absconded with the money.[44]

---

[43] Madison to Monroe, Jan. 26, 1796, James Madison Papers (Manuscript Division, Library of Congress); Jefferson to W[illiam] B[ranch] Giles, Dec. 31, 1795, Ford, ed., *Works of Thomas Jefferson*, VIII, 202. See also John Garry Clifford, "A Muddy Middle of the Road: The Politics of Edmund Randolph, 1790-1795," *Virginia Magazine of History and Biography*, 80 (1972), 286–311.

[44] The government had no procedures for clearing the books of open accounts. Leonard D. White, *The Jeffersonians: A Study in Administrative History, 1801–1829* (New York, 1951), 166. The "debt" was paid by Randolph's brother-in-law, to whom Randolph assigned most of his real and personal property. Reardon, *Edmund Randolph*, 356–57. John Alexander Carroll and Mary Wells Ashworth explain the history of the allegations about Randolph's default (which continued through 1887) in an appendix to their biography of Washington. That continuation undoubtably contributed to clouding Randolph's reputation. Carroll and Ashworth, *George Washington*, 635–36.

If there had been any who were neutral on the question of Randolph's guilt or innocence, there were none after that disclosure. The silence from the public suggests also that Randolph's expressed bitterness toward the president was seen as being in exceedingly bad taste. Theirs was a generation that carried on its public quarrels under pseudonyms (usually the names of Roman republicans), but Randolph had ignored that convention. Despite the criticism of Washington for signing Jay's Treaty, he was nevertheless "first in war, first in peace, and first in the hearts of his countrymen." The more Randolph had battered away, the more he had bloodied himself. Washington stood above the fray.

Yet Randolph was right, all along. He was right in opposing the sending of troops into western Pennsylvania. He was right in trying to buy time to avoid a military confrontation. He was right in objecting to the constitutionally flimsy grounds on which the militia army was raised. He was right in persuading Washington to send a personal emissary to Kentucky and to reopen negotiations with Spain. He was right in recommending that the president not sign the treaty with Great Britain unless the Senate's rejection of Article XII was honored and the British Order-in-Council that authorized the seizure of American ships was withdrawn. He was right in denying that he had solicited a bribe or shared state secrets with Fauchet. But Randolph was wrong in the strategy he pursued in *A Vindication*.

In Randolph's world a gentleman's reputation was his most important asset. He was understandably angry when his own integrity was questioned by the man who knew him best. Blinded by that anger, he pursued a strategy that offended and threatened the only person who could vindicate him. Without Washington's support he was condemned to political exile.

Randolph's failure to achieve vindication had consequences that extended far beyond his own good name. It contributed to discrediting the opposition to the Washington administration's actions in the Whiskey Insurrection, a process that was reinforced a decade later when Hamilton's untimely death lent his policies an apotheosis that not all of them deserved. As a result, the Federalist version of the history of that event remained largely unchallenged for almost two centuries.

Edmund Randolph was the "meditated victim" of the Grenville ministry, which manipulated people to its own advantage whenever it could. He was certainly the "meditated victim" of his colleagues in the cabinet, who were ready to believe the worst about him. George Washington ought to have known better. He acquiesced in the sacrifice of Randolph's reputation in order to preserve his own.

The Compromise of 1790

Jacob E. Cooke*

THE Compromise of 1790 is generally regarded as one of the most important bargains in American history, ranking just below the better known Missouri Compromise and the Compromise of 1850. It was arranged by Hamilton, Madison, and Jefferson over the dinner table at Jefferson's house on or around June 20,[1] surely one of the most famous dinner parties in our history. The compromise was on two controversial issues, the location of the national capital, which Virginians fervently wished to be situated on the Potomac River, and the assumption of state debts, a measure which Hamilton regarded as an indispensable feature of the fiscal program he had proposed in his Report on the Public Credit, submitted to Congress some five months previously. A compromise linking the two issues appeared possible because the Potomac site, urged by the Southerners, had been opposed successfully by Northern votes while assumption, supported by many Northerners, had been defeated some two months earlier, largely by its Southern opponents. The arrangement agreed upon was that certain provisions of the assumption which Virginians regarded as inequitable would be modified; that Madison, while not voting for it, would not oppose the amended measure; that Hamilton would round up enough votes for passage of the residence bill; and that Jefferson or Madison would then secure enactment of assumption by persuading two Virginia congressmen—

* Mr. Cooke is a member of the Department of History, Lafayette College, and associate editor of The Papers of Alexander Hamilton. An earlier version of this paper was read before the Columbia University Seminar on Early American History and Culture, New York, Feb. 10, 1970.

[1] Dumas Malone, Jefferson and the Rights of Man (Boston, 1951), 299-306, states that the dinner took place sometime between June 17 and June 22. Irving Brant, James Madison: Father of the Constitution, 1787-1800 (New York, 1950), 316, concurs but more specifically sets the date between June 20 and June 22. Julian Boyd, on the other hand, argues that the dinner was held on June 15 (see Julian P. Boyd, ed., The Papers of Thomas Jefferson, XVII [Princeton, 1965], 163-172 [hereafter cited as Jefferson Papers]), a contention that is convincingly refuted by Kenneth R. Bowling, Politics in the First Congress, 1789-1791 (unpubl. Ph.D. diss., University of Wisconsin, 1968), 324-325. Bowling asserts that the meeting "may well have been on the 20th itself." Ibid., 184.

Alexander White and Richard Bland Lee—to support it. The three principals to the bargain kept their promises and within a month or so the two measures were enacted. So the traditional account goes.

Although virtually all American historians accept this account of the well-known bargain,[2] the story should be modified in a number of important particulars. Its validity, as with so many historical interpretations, measurably depends not only on the evidence but on the mind-set with which the historian examines it. If one's research is underpinned by acceptance of the traditional account, his reading of contemporary letters and congressional debates will seem to provide ample documentation. On the other hand, if one starts by questioning the account, he soon finds that available evidence renders it suspect.

Only the most perverse iconoclast would challenge the fact of the dinner meeting or the agreement there made. But one has only to read the debates of Congress and examine congressional roll calls to doubt that that agreement was responsible for the passage of the residence bill or assumption. If the parties to it believed otherwise, this was because they, humanly enough, overestimated their influence on Congress which a year previously may have been, in William N. Chambers's phrase, "a leaderless herd,"[3] but which in 1790 had, if anything, too many leaders, at least on these two issues. It should be added, however, that two of the principals to the deal, Hamilton and Madison, made no such claim and, indeed, made no explicit reference to it, much less to its implementation. Jefferson was the only participant who left a record of the bargain, and to challenge his account of it is not to question his veracity but rather to challenge his exaggerated claim that it was responsible for the passage of the residence and assumption measures.[4]

[2] The best account is Bowling, Politics in the First Congress, a model monograph which accepts the traditional story while revising it in important particulars. In his excellent study of public finance during the Confederation era, E. James Ferguson demonstrates that the settlement of state accounts was an essential part of the famous compromise. E. James Ferguson, The Power of the Purse (Chapel Hill, 1961), 322-325. The traditional account of the bargain can best be followed in any of the multivolumed biographies of its participants, the most interesting of which is Malone, Jefferson and Rights of Man, 299-306. Although he accepts the details of the compromise on the authority of Jefferson's record of it, Malone implicitly expresses considerable doubt about some of its features.

[3] William N. Chambers, Political Parties in a New Nation: The American Experience, 1776-1809 (New York, 1963), 38.

[4] Jefferson recorded three versions of the bargain: (1) an undated document which was presumably written in 1792; (2) a letter to George Washington of Sept.

Since funding and the residence were far and away the most important issues of the second congressional session, January 4-August 12,
1790, they were sometimes linked in congressional debate and there was
occasional talk, in newspapers[5] and elsewhere, of combining them in a
compromise.[6] But the bargain worked out by Jefferson, Madison, and
Hamilton was not consummated. For one thing, the number of congressmen involved in it was too small to provide even the swing votes
on either measure. More important, different coalitions assured the success
of the two bills. Each was treated separately and its passage was owing
to sub rosa congressional negotiations and compromises relating only
to that measure. Thus, the bargain over the residence was arranged by
Pennsylvania and Virginia congressmen before the famous dinner meeting; the crucial bargain over assumption did not involve the residence
but a reallocation of the amount of state debts to be assumed and a
compromise on the interest rate to be paid on the funded debt. The
dinner table bargain, finally, involved votes in the House of Representatives, whereas the crucial battle for both assumption and the residence
took place in the Senate. If Madison or Jefferson had had any measurable
influence on the Senate vote on the assumption, no evidence of it has
been found;[7] Hamilton's efforts (if, indeed, he made any) to assure

---

9, 1792; and (3) an account written in 1818 as part of the introduction to the collection of his notes which he designated *Anas. Jefferson Papers*, 171. Boyd asserts
that "on essential points all are in agreement." Jefferson's most detailed record of the
compromise, and the one on which I have relied, is the undated document to which
Boyd ascribes the date 1792.

[5] That newspaper articles would link the two is understandable. They were, after
all, the most controversial issues of the congressional session. Opponents of assumption, moreover, eagerly sought to discredit that measure by charging that its proponents were engaged in secret machinations to assure its passage. For such articles
see *New York Daily Advertiser*, June 3, 1970; *New York Journal*, July 27, 1790;
Pennsylvania Mercury, quoted in *N. Y. Jour.*, June 29, 1790.

[6] This was particularly true of the Pennsylvania delegation. As early as Feb. 28,
1790, for instance, Thomas FitzSimons observed that because his state favored funding
while not being adverse to assumption Pennsylvania "holds the balance." Pennsylvania congressmen, he said, are "trying to make some Advantage of our Situation. . . ." FitzSimons to Tench Coxe, Coxe Papers, Historical Society of Pennsylvania, Philadelphia.

[7] Jefferson stated that Madison agreed that the assumption measure "should be
again brought before the house by way of amendment from the Senate." *Jefferson
Papers*, 206. That Madison could have arranged this, however, appears highly unlikely.

passage of the residence bill, in the Senate as in the House, were un-successful.

For three months after the introduction of Hamilton's Report on the Public Credit on January 9, 1790, its fate in the House was uncertain. That his proposals for funding the debt of the central government would pass, whether or not in modified form, appeared certain, the more so after the defeat on February 22 of Madison's motion for a discrimination between original and current holders of the public debt.[8] Assumption was quite another matter. The position taken by most congressmen depended not only on their opinion of Hamilton's effort to enhance the power of the national government, but on the extent to which their own state stood to benefit by the measure. Massachusetts and South Carolina, whose large Revolutionary debts remained virtually unpaid, strenuously supported Hamilton's proposal, as did Connecticut. Maryland, Virginia, North Carolina, and Georgia, much of whose debts already had been paid, just as vigorously opposed assumption. A majority of congressmen from other states—New Hampshire, New York, New Jersey, Delaware, and Pennsylvania—were uncommitted. The swing state, so its congressmen believed, was Pennsylvania.[9]

Just as important as the constitutional questions raised by assumption and the desire of some states to unload their heavy debts was the problem of the final settlement of the debts of the Union.[10] This settlement had been underway since the appointment of a Board of Commissioners in 1787 and presumably would be completed by 1791 or 1792. Wishing immediate relief from their burden of debt, Massachusetts and South Carolina demanded that state debts be assumed before a final settlement; states that had paid most of their debts (Maryland, Virginia, North Carolina, and Georgia) demanded that settlement precede assumption. Not only did they believe that the final settlement might find them large creditors of the Federal government but they were persuaded that an immediate assumption might jeopardize such a settlement or obviate it altogether. They also wished a change in the rules respecting the type of evidence required by the Board of Commissioners to substantiate expenditures,

---

[8] [Annals of Congress.] *Debates and Proceedings in the Congress of the United States, 1789-1824* (Washington, 1834-1856), I, 1298.

[9] FitzSimons to Coxe, Feb. 28, 1790, Coxe Papers.

[10] This is the conclusion of Ferguson whose *Power of the Purse* is the definitive study of the financial intricacies of funding and assumption. See *ibid.*, esp. 307-310.

evidence which they were unable to provide. "The substance of the matter," as E. James Ferguson remarks, "was that one side wanted assumption of state debts before anything else, the other a settlement of accounts before anything else."[11]

On March 8, 1790, the former appeared to have won. By a vote of 31-26, a Committee of the Whole House endorsed assumption.[12] Such a slender margin, as Hamilton's supporters well knew, was dangerously close. The representatives from North Carolina who were known to oppose assumption were expected momentarily and other representatives who voted affirmatively were by no means firm allies. Such fears were well founded, for on April 12 the question was again taken up in a Committee of the Whole and this time negatived by a vote of 32-29.[13] Owing to the arrival of three North Carolinians, the addition of the vote of one representative who had not voted earlier, and a switch in the votes of two previous supporters, a five-vote margin for assumption had turned into a three-vote margin against it. This, however, is only partly attributable to opposition to assumption per se. As Thomas FitzSimons, himself a large public creditor, remarked, it was "another proof that avarice often disappoints itself." "I consider the opposition to the assumption," he explained, "as a measure of the holders of Contl Securitys who supposed their security would be lessened by the Measure. The Correspondence of some of that class with the Members of our house has I am sure influenced their votes."[14] In any event, the failure of repeated efforts in the House to restore this controversial clause of the funding bill indicated that assumption, if not dead, would have to be revived by the Senate.

During these months the residence issue was deceptively absent from congressional debate. It was discussed, however, at caucuses of the various delegations and at unofficial gatherings of congressmen to some of whom —certainly those of Pennsylvania, New York, and Virginia—it remained the vital issue. On April 13, the day after the crucial vote on assumption, Thomas FitzSimons described to Tench Coxe the anger of the Pennsylvania delegation on discovering "a combination between S. Ca. and Mass.

[11] *Ibid.*, 310-311.
[12] Charles A. Beard, ed., *The Journal of William Maclay* (New York, 1927), 204. Hereafter cited as *Maclay Journal*.
[13] *Annals of Congress*, II, 1525. Individual votes were not recorded.
[14] To Coxe, Apr. 13, 1790, Coxe Papers.

with New York to disappoint any expectation of the Removal of Congress. If my apprehension shall be realized," he added, "we shall not be long together for the Irritation is so great that it would be vain to hope for any union of sentiment on any other question."[15]

The Pennsylvanians, employing a modified form of their strategy in the first session,[16] decided to remove the irritant and to further congressional progress by removing the capital to Philadelphia, ostensibly as the temporary site but they hoped the permanent one.[17] "The little scheme we laid," as Senator William Maclay described the plan,[18] was hatched late in April or early in May at one of the frequent meetings of the Pennsylvania delegation and called for the introduction of similar motions in the House and Senate. "We have again revived the Question on a Removal and not without hopes of success," the Speaker of the

[15] Ibid.

[16] From the day the First Congress assembled in New York in Apr. 1789, the Pennsylvania delegates were determined to move the capital to their state. Soon after the issue was formally introduced late in Aug. 1789, they struck a bargain with Southern congressmen by which they agreed to vote for the Potomac as the permanent site in exchange for Southern support of Philadelphia as the temporary capital. Actually, the Pennsylvanians were banking on the possibility that once moved to Philadelphia the government would be unwilling to leave. A coalition of New England and New York congressmen, however, successfully blocked this bargain by moving that the permanent location be on the Susquehanna River, and the temporary capital in New York, a motion the Pennsylvanians were bound to support. Despite the angry opposition of the Southerners, a bill designating the Susquehanna site passed the House of Representatives one week before adjournment. The Senate, owing largely to the backstairs negotiations of Robert Morris of Pennsylvania, substituted Germantown for the banks of the Susquehanna. In the ensuing parliamentary wrangle, opponents of a Pennsylvania site managed to table the bill until the next session.

[17] The Pennsylvanians were not alone in believing that once Congress went to Philadelphia it would never leave. This conviction was repeatedly voiced in Congress, for example, by John Lawrence of New York, Elbridge Gerry of Massachusetts, Joshua Seney of Maryland, and Aedanus Burke, William Smith, and Thomas Tucker of South Carolina. Annals of Congress, II, 1624, 1662, 1663, 1665, 1667, 1672, 1675. Sen. William Maclay, speaking of a letter from Congressman George Clymer to the mayor and corporation of Philadelphia, wrote "there was a clause in Clymer's letter of advice to erect a new building for Congress, for the giving the State House to Congress would furnish a reason for removing the seat of Government elsewhere." Although Maclay was "much pleased" with this arrangement, he observed a few days later that the Philadelphians would be disappointed in their expectation that Congress would never leave their city. Maclay Journal, 325, 331.

[18] Maclay Journal, 238. On Apr. 30, Maclay wrote to Coxe that the latter's friends were "fervent" for "an adjournment to Philada. It will certainly be right to try this measure as even a miscarriage can place us in no worse situation than we now are." Coxe Papers.

House told Coxe on May 2.[19] "We anxiously wait for the arrival of Mr. Bassett as the Question is first to be put in the Senate."[20] Having failed to persuade Senators Richard Bassett of Delaware, John Langdon of New Hampshire, or Richard Henry Lee of Virginia to introduce the motion,[21] Robert Morris offered it himself on May 24,[22] hoping that the coalition contrived by Maclay and himself would carry it. The coalition consisted of the senators from New Hampshire, Pennsylvania, Delaware, Maryland, Virginia, New Jersey, North Carolina, and James Gunn of Georgia.[23] Morris and Maclay were disappointed[24]—Paterson of New Jersey (to Maclay's unwarranted surprise), Gunn, and the North Carolinians voted for a postponement of Morris's motion, which was carried 11-13.[25]

Now the initiative passed to the House where on May 27 FitzSimons offered the same motion.[26] It was promptly attacked by members from New England, New York, and South Carolina who, in an attempt to block the attempt to move to Philadelphia, proposed amendment after amendment. Nevertheless, on May 31 the original motion was carried by a decisive vote of 38-22,[27] which found half of the Massachusetts delegation deserting their allies.[28] Coxe, believing that his long labors on behalf of his native state would soon be rewarded, was jubilant. "The

[19] Coxe Papers.
[20] Ibid.
[21] Maclay Journal, 239.
[22] Annals of Congress, I, 978.
[23] Maclay Journal, 261, 265, 266, 267. Maclay implies that he and Morris believed the North Carolina senators would support them. After the introduction of Morris's motion, he commented, the proponents of New York City "flew about. The people they mostly attacked were Governor Johnston, Hawkins, and Gunn. . . ." Ibid., 265. Presumably the attacks were effective, since all three men voted two days later for postponement.
[24] In this instance Morris appears to have been particularly unsuccessful in influencing his colleagues. He was convinced that he had persuaded Tristam Dalton of Massachusetts to vote with the Pennsylvanians and was certain, as was Maclay, that William Paterson of New Jersey could be counted on. Ibid., 261-262, 263.
[25] No vote is given in Annals of Congress, I, 979. It is recorded in Maclay Journal, 268.
[26] Annals of Congress, II, 1620.
[27] Ibid., 1626.
[28] This perhaps was owing to a meeting which Pennsylvania congressmen Fitz-Simons and Clymer held with the New England congressmen on the preceding evening. According to Maclay, "Last night Fitzsimons and Clymer called on us. They agreed to call on Goodhue, Gilman, Huntington, and some other of the New England men, and tell them calmly that the Pennsylvanians would not stay in New

Senate is now the place," he wrote. "A very judicious North Carolinian assures me both their Senators will be with us, and the opinions seem much in our favor. Several things will operate for us. So large a majority of the Representatives, the fear of a proposition for the *permanent* seat in Pennsylvania, and some other considerations will affect the votes of the Southern people."[29] Perhaps Coxe's Pennsylvania congressional friends, more conscious of the Senate maneuverings which had defeated their hopes in the previous session, were less optimistic. They should have been.

On May 31, the very day that Philadelphia triumphed in the House, it presumably was no coincidence that in the Senate Pierce Butler of South Carolina, a consistent opponent of that city's claims, was granted permission to bring in a residence bill. Two days later it was assigned to committee, along with the House resolve of May 31, whose report was taken up on June 8. It was, as Senator Maclay remarked, a "day of confusion in the Senate."[30] First came a defeat for Pennsylvania when a motion to take up the House resolve of May 31 failed by a vote of 11-13, precisely the same vote by which Morris's similar motion previously had been postponed and proof that Morris's and Maclay's scheme had been blocked. Second came a defeat for the Senate committee which the previous day had reported a bill fixing the Potomac as the permanent seat and leaving open the question of the temporary residence.[31] This brought to the floor Butler's original bill in which the sites of the permanent and temporary capital had been left blank. Motions to locate the former on the Potomac and in Baltimore were decisively rejected.[32]

It was the 1789 situation all over again, except that this time the

---

York; that if they of New England would persist in voting for New York, the Pennsylvanians would agree to any other place whatever; and from here they would go. I readily agreed to join Mr. Morris in a similar service with respect to the Senate." *Maclay Journal*, 270.

[29] To Tench Francis, May 31, 1790, Coxe Papers.

[30] *Maclay Journal*, 277.

[31] It was defeated by the casting vote of the vice-president. *Annals of Congress*, I, 985.

[32] The Potomac motion was defeated 9-15, Baltimore by a vote of 7-17. The repeated defeat of the Potomac on June 8 had been preconcerted by its advocates. Maclay explained: the Pennsylvanians "agreed to send for all the Senators who were friends of moving to Philadelphia. Eleven attended—Virginia, Maryland, Delaware, Pennsylvania, Dr. Elmer from New Jersey, and New Hampshire. Much desultory discourse was held. Virginia and Maryland manifested a predilection for the Po-

Pennsylvanians, instead of playing the gratifying game of heads I win, tails you lose, by gaining either the temporary or permanent capital, appeared likely to win neither.[33] The Philadelphia boosters expressed indignation that "the determination of a very great majority of the House had been overruled in an unprecedented and extraordinary manner by the Senate" and insisted that the House "ought in justice to themselves, and to their constituents, who were greatly interested in the issue of the question, to insist on their former vote." Josiah Parker of Virginia rallied to the aid of the Pennsylvanians by moving that the House do precisely that. Other congressmen, however, concluded that such a question "of a mere local nature . . . ought not to be brought forward at the present moment, to interrupt the great and important business before the House."[34] The latter were in a majority, for on June 11 the House approved a motion amending Parker's motion by "striking out Philadelphia and inserting Baltimore" by a vote of 31-28. The amended bill was adopted on the same day by a deceptively decisive vote.[35] Since the Senate repeatedly had rejected Baltimore, a compromise was in order.

Or so it seemed to Hamilton. Frantically searching for some means of assuring the passage of assumption and believing the residence to be a comparatively unimportant issue, he presumably decided to offer to surrender what it was not within his power to sacrifice, the residence. Aware that five of the eight Pennsylvania representatives were opposed to assumption, and of their persistent attempts to bargain for the capital, Hamilton's first move was to approach them through a fellow Pennsylvanian, Coxe, who recently had been appointed assistant secretary of the Treasury. Coxe was designated to meet with George Clymer and Fitz-Simons in order to "negotiate a bargain: the permanent residence in Pennsylvania for her votes for the assumption."[36] The task was doubtless congenial, for Coxe, despite his attachment to Philadelphia, had warmly

---

tomac; but the final resolutions, in which Virginia led the way, were as follows: 'That as the business of a permanent residence was brought forward evidently with a design of dividing us, we would uniformly vote against every plan named for the permanent residence.'" *Maclay Journal*, 277.

[33] See n. 16 above.

[34] *Annals of Congress*, II, 1635.

[35] *Ibid.*, 1637. It was deceptive because the House rules forbade the reintroduction of Philadelphia and because many congressmen were bewildered by the parliamentary wrangle.

[36] *Maclay Journal*, 284.

supported a bill proposed during the first session of Congress which placed the capital on the Susquehanna, a site which he well knew a majority of the Pennsylvania congressmen also favored. The Pennsylvania congressmen presumably were receptive, but a major obstacle remained—Senator Morris, who had been largely responsible for the defeat of the Susquehanna site in the 1789 congressional session. Using assumption as the bait, he might now be caught. The secretary of the Treasury himself, at Morris's insistence, undertook this delicate task. Maclay told the story as related to him by Morris: "I wrote a note to Colonel Hamilton that I would be walking early in the morning on the Battery, and if Colonel Hamilton had anything to propose to him he might meet him there, as if by accident. I went in the morning there, and found him *on the sod before me*. Mr. Hamilton . . . wanted one vote in the Senate and five in the House of Representatives; . . . he was willing and would agree to place the permanent residence of Congress at Germantown or Falls of the Delaware, if he [Morris] would procure him these votes." Morris agreed to consult members of the Pennsylvania delegation, and then, doubtless to Hamilton's surprise if not dismay, "proposed that the temporary residence of Congress in Philadelphia should be the price."[37] In fact, Hamilton had asked for what Morris could not deliver; Morris, in turn, had proposed what Hamilton was unable to grant. Morris may or may not have been able to deliver one Senate vote,[38] but he had no chance of winning over the opponents of assumption among the Pennsylvania representatives (at least five in number) who, distrusting the senator because of the role he had played during the capital fight of the first session, looked to FitzSimons as the "key negotiator" for their state[39] and who, in any event, were more likely to enter into a bargain to defeat assumption than one to assure its success.[40] Indeed, only a few days

---

[37] *Ibid.*, 284-285.

[38] He obviously had no chance at all of persuading his colleague, Maclay. The usual account, based on Maclay's *Journal*, is that Morris won over Sen. George Read of Delaware. *Ibid.*, 285.

[39] Bowling, Politics in the First Congress, 171.

[40] Whether or not Morris recognized this fact, Hamilton misunderstood the sentiments of the Pennsylvania delegation. This was revealed when he deputized Coxe to sound out Sen. Maclay on the possibility of a bargain by which Pennsylvania would vote for assumption in return for the location of the permanent capital on the Susquehanna River which Maclay's lands adjoined. *Maclay Journal*, 284. If Hamilton had been following the Senate debates, as he presumably had, he should have known that Maclay's opposition to assumption was inflexible.

earlier they had done just that.[41] For his part, Hamilton was being uncharacteristically fanciful if he believed, even momentarily, that he could cajole the New York delegation into surrendering their own claim to their arch-rival. Hamilton thus may have been disappointed but Morris scarcely could have been surprised when the secretary of the Treasury reported the following day that he could "not think about negotiating about the temporary residence; that his friends will not hear of it." To Maclay, Morris confided that "I think he has some other assurances."[42]

Hamilton did not, but he immediately began searching for them. A week or so later, the secretary of the Treasury met Jefferson, whether by chance or design, in front of the president's house. Hamilton's look, Jefferson recalled, "was sombre, haggard, and dejected beyond description. . . . He asked to speak with me. We stood in the street near the door. He opened the subject of the assumption of the state debts, the necessity of it in the general fiscal arrangement and it's indispensible necessity towards a preservation of the union." If the measure could not be passed, Hamilton said he "was determined to resign," but he reminded Jefferson that "the administration and its success was a common concern" and that they should "make common cause in supporting one another." The secretary of state who from the beginning had viewed assumption as "a choice of evils"[43] concluded that "the first step towards some conciliation of views would be to bring Mr. Madison and Colo. Hamilton to friendly discussion of the subject" and invited the two men to dine with him the following day. According to Jefferson's record, the result of the friendly meeting was

Mr. Madison's acquiescence in a proposition that the question should be again brought before the house . . . , that tho' he would not vote for

[41] Early in June Fisher Ames observed that in return for House approval of Philadelphia as the temporary capital, Pennsylvania congressmen had made a bargain with Virginia to defeat assumption. Seth Ames, ed., *Works of Fisher Ames,* I (Boston, 1854), 79-80. Ames's biographer writes that "rumors had been rife two months earlier that the Pennsylvanians, who held a balance of power, might be willing to sacrifice assumption in order to gain the temporary capital." Winfred E. A. Bernhard, *Fisher Ames: Federalist and Statesman, 1758-1808* (Chapel Hill, 1965), 151. They were the more willing to do so because, as FitzSimons wrote to Coxe, they had been deeply angered by the persistent efforts of the New England-New York-South Carolina coalition "to disappoint any expectation of the removel of Congress." FitzSimons to Coxe, Apr. 13, 1790, Coxe Papers.

[42] *Maclay Journal,* 285.

[43] *Jefferson Papers,* 166.

it, nor entirely withdraw his opposition, yet he should . . . leave it to it's fate. It was observed, I forget by which of them, that as the pill would be a bitter one to the Southern States, something should be done to soothe them; that the removal of the seat of Government to the Patowmac was a just measure. . . . It was agreed to speak to Mr. White and Mr. Lee . . . [and induce them] to yield to the assumption. This was done. . . . The measure came down by way of amendment from the Senate and was finally carried by the change of White's and Lee's votes. But the removal to Patowmac could not be carried unless Pennsylvania could be engaged in it. This Hamilton took on himself, and chiefly, *as I understood,* through the agency of Robert Morris, obtained the vote of that state, on agreeing to an intermediate residence at Philadelphia. This is the real history of the assumption.[44]

Although there is no reason to doubt the accuracy of Jefferson's description of the bargain made, there is good reason, as I said, to doubt that it was responsible for the passage of either the assumption or the residence acts. That Jefferson believed otherwise is understandable enough—the two Virginians were persuaded to change their votes, Madison remained silent during the House debate, and, so far as Jefferson knew, Hamilton secured the votes necessary to carry the residence measure. He did not round up even one,[45] but as things turned out, there was no point in his doing so. The Pennsylvanians already had committed themselves to the Potomac-Philadelphia measure. They had agreed to such a compromise in the previous session, only to have it aborted by the shrewd maneuver of New Englanders to locate the permanent capital

[44] See *ibid.,* 205-207, [italics added], where Jefferson's narrative is ascribed to the year 1792. A phrase in Jefferson's account which he deleted stated that "Mr. Madison undertook" to persuade Lee and White. *Ibid.,* 208.

[45] Although concluding that Hamilton did not "persuade any Northern voters to switch to the Potomac," Bowling argues that the secretary did succeed in breaking "the northern coalition by preventing New York and its allies," specifically Massachusetts, "from interfering with the evolving Virginia-Pennsylvania agreement." Bowling, Politics in the First Congress, 185, 188, 189. This interpretation is untenable for three reasons: (1) As Bowling himself says "the votes of the Massachusetts representatives were not crucial to the bargain"; (2) the representatives from Massachusetts continued to vote with their allies for New York rather than Philadelphia, for Baltimore rather than the Potomac; and (3) the familiar coalition, owing to the defection of two South Carolinians and the support of only two Marylanders, was unable to block the Philadelphia-Potomac measure in the House by substituting another site. Nor could it have done so in the Senate, the critical battleground, where Marylanders voted against their own city and in favor of Philadelphia and the Potomac. *Annals of Congress,* I, 995. See also n. 56 below.

on the Susquehanna.[46] Convinced that the advantages of Philadelphia were so great that the capital, once located there, would never again move, they had decided early in the second session again to work out a bargain with the Southerners.[47] The advantages of such an arrangement were not lost on the Virginians who, aware that the two delegations had eighteen congressmen (or a third of the House), realized that it was the best, perhaps the only, way of winning the coveted prize.[48]

The bargain was arranged before Jefferson's dinner party on June 20.[49] The Virginians, disturbed by the House vote for Baltimore, took the initiative by proposing, through an ally, Congressman George Matthews of Georgia, an extended stopover in Philadelphia for the Pennsylvanians' support of the Potomac.[50] Their acceptance of the offer, as well as their duplicity, was described by Congressman Peter Muhlenberg. "The Southern Members have hitherto acted with great Candour on this occasion," he informed Benjamin Rush, "and I am more inclined to accede to their proposal, because no Conditions are annext that may be thought dishonorable, and because in the course of 15 or 20 years, Circumstances

[46] Even before the second session began, Morris concluded that if Germantown were rejected as the permanent site, then his state should support the South's demand for the Potomac in exchange for that section's vote for Philadelphia as the temporary capital. Bowling, Politics in the First Congress, 171.

[47] Maclay Journal, 167-170, 184-188, 218, 237-238, 258. Maclay argued that if Congress would agree to make Philadelphia the temporary capital enough votes could be secured to make it the permanent capital. As the session progressed, the Pennsylvanians remained firm in the belief that a bargain with Virginia was necessary if they were to secure the temporary capital.

[48] Bowling, Politics in the First Congress, 171-172.

[49] Jefferson may or may not have known of the earlier bargain of the Virginians. On June 15, according to Maclay, Morris told his senatorial colleague that "he had had a communication from Mr. Jefferson of a disposition of having the temporary residence fifteen years in Philadelphia and the permanent residence at Georgetown." On the other hand, it is possible that Maclay's account is inaccurate. The senator himself doubted it. "I certainly had misunderstood Mr. Morris at the Hall," he wrote, "for Jefferson vouched for nothing." Maclay Journal, 294.

[50] Bowling, Politics in the First Congress, 182. According to Rufus King, sometime between June 14 and June 28 a bargain was made "between Pennsylvania, Delaware, Maryland and Virginia to remove at the end of the session to Philadelphia, there to remain for ten years and afterwards to remove to, and permanently remain at the Potomack." Charles R. King, ed., The Life and Correspondence of Rufus King, I (New York, 1895), 384. If King is correct, such a bargain may well have been made after the famous dinner party agreement. But there is no evidence that the bargain among these states and the compromise reached at Jefferson's dinner table were connected.

may alter cases."[51] The essential bargain on the residence, then, was between Virginia and Pennsylvania congressmen, was set in train even
before the famous dinner meeting, and had nothing to do with the
assumption of state debts. Writing some two years later, William Smith
of South Carolina, an ardent proponent of New York as the capital,
wrote that "the Residence Bill . . . was the offspring of a political cohabi-
tation (for it cannot be called a marriage) between Pennsylvania and
Virginia . . . it was begotten in darkness and its Nurses were afraid of its
being exposed to the light—having forced its way through the Senate
(to which it was first introduced) by a large majority, it was ushered into
the house of Representatives, where it underwent the solemn farce of a
discussion."[52]

The crucial vote on the residence, as Smith observed, was in the Senate and not, as the traditional account has it, in the House. On June 28
the residence bill, introduced by Butler of South Carolina and dormant
since the confused debate on June 8, again came before the Senate. After
defeat of a motion to make Baltimore the permanent seat,[53] the Potomac
won the coveted prize by the surprisingly decisive vote of 16-9. It was
the familiar story of New England against the South, but this time with
some critical character changes: Maryland now supported the Potomac
as did South Carolina, previously the firm ally of the New England-
New York coalition. But if a bargain had been made to give Philadelphia the temporary capital, some of the partners to it reneged. After an
unresolved squabble about the date of removal to the Potomac, New
York was selected as the temporary capital. The combination which
Maclay and Morris had tried to put together a month earlier would not
coalesce, or so it appeared. Although one North Carolina senator—
Hawkins—voted with the Pennsylvanians, Samuel Johnston of that state
supported New York as did Paterson of New Jersey, while Gunn of

[51] Muhlenberg to Rush, Gratz Collection, Historical Society of Pennsylvania.
The final agreement, of course, called for a stopover in Philadelphia of ten years.
Maclay, who apparently had been left out of the negotiations because of his known
insistence that the permanent residence must be in Pennsylvania, was not informed
of the bargain until June 24 when Sen. John Walker of Virginia informed him of
it. The Pennsylvania senator acquiesced only because he concluded that "a house
divided against itself could not stand." *Maclay Journal*, 297, 298.
[52] *Jefferson Papers*, 180.
[53] The vote was 10-15. *Annals of Congress*, I, 995.

Georgia did not vote.[54] The decision was not final, however, for on the following day, June 29, the reopening of the question of the date of removal also reopened the question of the temporary capital. In an inexplicable reversal, New York now lost, the Massachusetts senators, Butler of South Carolina, and William Few of Georgia having changed their votes.[55] The most likely explanation of the switch is the wish of the two Southern senators to get the capital to the Potomac whatever the decision on its temporary location and the realization on the part of the Massachusetts delegates that to persist in championing New York might well mean that the capital fight would dominate the rest of the session, destroying whatever chances assumption might have.[56] That this was a tactical retreat rather than a surrender, however, was indicated when Massachusetts voted on the same day against a subsequent motion in favor of Philadelphia.[57] Nevertheless, the Pennsylvanians were within sight of the promised land. The vote (13-12) on the Philadelphia motion was the same as that by which that city had been defeated and New York selected on the previous day except that Gunn of Georgia now came through and voted for Philadelphia, thus creating a tie, 13-13. To the

[54] The vote was 13-12. *Ibid.*, 997.

[55] *Ibid.*, 998. The vote was 9-16. Gunn of Georgia did not vote on June 28, but voted against New York on June 29; Benjamin Hawkins of North Carolina, who voted against New York on June 28, did not vote on June 29.

[56] On June 30, 1790, King of New York, in a memorandum to Caleb Strong, implied that Hamilton had sought to persuade the Massachusetts delegation to abandon their New York allies and to support the Potomac. Commenting on his own efforts to round up votes for a five-year temporary residence in New York and the selection of Balitimore as the permanent seat, King observed that "Massachusetts declined." The refusal, King recorded, "was explained by the Sec'y of the Treasury, who called on Mr. K . . . and informed him, *He had made up his mind thus:* The funding System, including the assumption is the primary national object; all subordinate points which oppose it must be sacrificed; the project of Philadelphia and Potomack is bad, but it will insure the funding System and the assumption: agreeing to remain in New Yk will defeat it: agreeing to N. Yk and Baltimore will defeat it, so that in the present state of things nothing but Philad. or Phila and Potomack will insure it. Massachusetts therefore will not agree to N. Yk and Baltimore because her object is the assumption." King, ed., *Rufus King*, I, 384-385. Although Hamilton may merely have been predicting that Massachusetts would subordinate the residence to achieve her overriding goal of assumption, King may correctly have inferred that the secretary had made an "arrangement" with Massachusetts. For a plausible argument in its support see Bowling, Politics in the First Congress, 189, 190-191. If so, it was not successful, for Massachusetts subsequently voted consistently against both the Potomac and Philadelphia. See n. 45 above.

[57] *Annals of Congress*, I, 999.

chagrin, but perhaps not to the surprise, of the Pennsylvanians the vice-president broke it by a negative vote.[58] A switch of only one vote was necessary to reverse the decision and, so far as the Pennsylvanians were concerned, it came from an unexpected quarter, South Carolina. Butler, who steadfastly had supported New York and just as vehemently denounced Philadelphia, came to the rescue of the latter.[59] Why did he change? Perhaps Morris or FitzSimons persuaded him. More likely he, like so many other congressmen whose states were not in the race, decided it was time to solve this issue which, more than any other, had agitated the First Congress. In any event, on June 30 the Southerners, with the help of one of their own, Butler, got what they wanted—the capital on the Potomac—and the Pennsylvanians captured the consolation award for which they so long had bargained and cajoled and which some of them believed might yet be turned into the grand prize. Madison was right when, a week or so earlier, he remarked that if the Potomac were selected it would be the effect of "a coincidence of causes as fortuitous as it will be propitious,"[60] a statement which historians, in the face of the clear meaning of the words, have misinterpreted to support the traditional bargain story. The result was fortuitous and, from Madison's point of view, propitious. Despite a long tradition in American historical writing, fortuity is perhaps as often responsible for the course of events as hidden causes or conspiracies.

The debate in the House was anticlimactic. Despite the efforts of the Massachusetts-New York-South Carolina group to defeat the measure, whether by logic, ridicule, or parliamentary strategy, other congressmen who formerly had opposed it now came to its support. This was not because of backstairs manipulation by Hamilton or anyone else but rather because there appeared no alternative save the indefinite postponement of any decision at all. Michael Stone of Maryland spoke for this group when he said that "had the bill come down from the Senate with Baltimore inserted instead of Potomac, he should have had no difficulty in determining how to act." As it was, he "should vote for the Potomac; and on this idea he was willing to make some sacrifice. He considered the subject as one of the most painful and disagreeable that could be

[58] Ibid.

[59] Ibid., 1000. The vote was 14-12.

[60] To Edmund Pendleton, June 22, 1790. Gaillard Hunt, ed., The Writings of James Madison, VI (New York, 1906), 17n.

agitated, and he wished to have the business finally and unalterably fixed."[61] Nor was it passed, despite the hints made by Lee of Virginia,[62] as part of a residence-assumption compromise. To the contrary, some ardent assumptionists doubtless agreed with Aedanus Burke of South Carolina who charged that the Potomac-Philadelphia bill was "calculated . . . to arrest the funding system, and to throw every thing into confusion."[63] To some supporters of the residence bill, on the other hand, failure to accept the Senate measure would defer any decision on funding, with or without assumption. That the Pennsylvanians secured the temporary capital, finally, was not attributable to the persuasiveness of Morris, much less of Hamilton. If any individual can be assigned major responsibility, he was, as I have said, FitzSimons whose persistence and lobbying finally won what he so eagerly wanted at a price he all along had been willing to pay.[64] His tenacity even overrode, if it did not still, the fear that Philadelphia once chosen as the temporary capital would become the permanent one. Perhaps also some congressmen were won over by Madison's

[61] *Annals of Congress,* II, 1664. It was also pointed out that there was no point in substituting Baltimore for the Potomac since the former had been "repeatedly rejected" by the Senate. *Ibid.,* 1660.

[62] Almost certainly Lee and White were consulted by Madison or Jefferson and were parties to the dinner table bargain. In a speech of July 6, supporting the Senate residence bill, Lee threw out not-so-thinly-veiled threats that the South, fearful of being "swallowed up" by the "strongest parts of the Union," would accept no permanent residence save the Potomac and "drew an alarming picture of the consequences to be apprehended from disunion, ambition, and rivalship." He also threw out equally obvious hints of Southern acquiescence in assumption should the North concede the capital. "He then gave a pleasing sketch of the happy effects to be derived from a national, generous, and equal attention to the Southern *and* Northern interests." *Ibid.,* 1661, [italics added].

[63] *Ibid.,* 1662. A similar complaint had been made weeks earlier by Benjamin Goodhue of Massachusetts: "The future residence of Congress has a long time past been secretly the cause why we have not accomplished the great business, the public has justly expected from us," he wrote to Michael Hodge on June 12, 1790. "It has now burst forth and in the conflict between N York and Pennsylvania in which no other states are much interested, the great concerns of the Nation are suspended and put in extream jeopardy. . . . I have only to lament our situation in which all important public measures must give place to paltry and local considerations." *Essex Institute Historical Collections,* LXXXIV (1948), 159-160.

[64] Maclay, for one, recognized this fact. Believing that his colleague, Morris, was negotiating, through Elias Boudinot of New Jersey, with the New England congressmen to locate the capital at Trenton, Maclay promptly called FitzSimons out from the House chamber and "told him of Boudinot's being in treaty with Mr. Morris, and begged him to counteract everything of this kind. He promised that he would." *Maclay Journal,* 262.

sage advice that such suspicions, however well founded, should give way to the overriding practical consideration that Congress could do nothing more than pass a law. "It is not in our power to guard against a repeal," he said. "Our acts are not like those of the Medes and Persians, unalterable. A repeal is a thing against which no provision can be made . . . I flatter myself that some respect will be paid to the public interest, and to the plighted faith of the Government."[65]

Similarly, acceptance of assumption cannot be interpreted as the outcome of the Hamilton-Jefferson-Madison bargain, although their individual influence, particularly Hamilton's, was greater in this instance than in the residence dispute. The story of assumption in Congress can be briefly told. After its defeat on April 12, proponents in the House employed every strategy they could devise to revive it. As FitzSimons, himself a supporter of assumption, remarked: "While I lament the probable consequences, I cannot but condemn the Conduct of some of the Supporters of the Measure. They have pressed it without discretion and really so as to disgust some who gave into it more with a view to National Accomodation than from Conviction of the Justice or Necessity of it."[66] Whether because they aroused "disgust" or because enough congressmen agreed with FitzSimons's judgment that it was "improper" to couple assumption and funding and expedient to let the latter "rest upon its merits," advocates of assumption failed to persuade their colleagues. On June 2 the House adopted a funding bill with no provision for the debts of the states.[67] What had been lost in the House, however, might be regained in the Senate, a possibility that may have been in part responsible for the intemperateness of assumption's ardent advocates who "contrived to waste . . . time in Useless disquisitions merely to force the other part of the house into their measures."[68]

Whether or not the Senate was impressed, it obliged. Some two weeks later, on June 14, the committee to which the House bill had been

[65] Ibid., 1666.
[66] FitzSimons to Coxe, Apr. 13, 1790, Coxe Papers.
[67] Annals of Congress, II, 1269.
[68] FitzSimons to Coxe, Apr. 27, 1790, Coxe Papers. The Senate would be the decisive battleground because as many congressmen realized the House was so divided that it would not be able itself to initiate passage of the bill. Gerry, of Massachusetts, for one, recognized this when he insisted on June 14 that the Senate had the right to originate assumption and remarked that he was opposed to taking up the pending bill on distilled spirits until the opinion of the Senate on assumption was known. Ibid., 1638, 1639.

referred recommended that the funding bill proposed by the House be amended to incorporate the assumption of state debts.[69] On July 2 this report was referred to another special committee which, ten days later, reported favorably.[70] The critical debate on the proposed bill providing for the public debt, including assumption, began on July 13, and centered on the rate of interest the debt should carry. In his Report on the Public Credit, Hamilton, convinced that the debt assumed must be balanced against the resources of the federal government, had recommended a reduction of the 6 per cent interest rate pledged by the Confederation Congress. Instead, he proposed "differential methods of funding" designed to pare down the immediate interest to around 4 per cent.[71] This reduction was obstinately opposed by an influential coterie of the secretary's otherwise ardent supporters, most notably Robert Morris, Philip Schuyler, and Rufus King, who demanded that national honor be salvaged (and, though they did not even imply it, themselves enriched) by honoring the promise to pay 6 per cent. Their obstinacy was matched by Oliver Ellsworth, Charles Carroll, George Read, and others, who insisted that the maximum interest on the Continental debt should be 4 per cent.[72] To Hamilton's dismay each group threatened to vote against assumption if its demands were not met. To fund at 6 per cent or 4 per cent, that was the question, not whether to take the capital to the Potomac or Philadelphia. Aware that by opposing his own allies he might obviate both funding and assumption, Hamilton worked out a compromise—6 per cent would be paid on the principal of the public debt; arrears of interest on that debt would bear only 3 per cent.[73] This was the last and an essential compromise, but the "sugar coating" which made the measure palatable to former opponents—notably the Virginians—already had been applied. It was not, as Jefferson supposed, the location of the capital on the Potomac but two concessions unrelated to that decision. The first was an increase in the amount of credits allowable to some states. Of the $21,500,000 which the Senate measure proposed to

[69] *Ibid.*, I, 988.

[70] *Ibid.*, 1003, 1005. Charles Carroll of Maryland was chairman.

[71] Ferguson, *Power of the Purse*, 294.

[72] Theodore Sedgwick to Pamela Sedgwick, July 13, 1790, Sedgwick Papers, Massachusetts Historical Society, Boston.

[73] William L. Smith to Edward Rutledge, July 14, 17, 1790, as cited in George C. Rogers, Jr., *Evolution of a Federalist: William Loughton Smith of Charleston* (Columbia, S. C., 1962), 197.

assume, "New Hampshire, Connecticut, Massachusetts, and South Carolina got no extra allowances, but New York and Pennsylvania each received $200,000. Delaware's allowance was raised by $100,000. Southern opposition was mollified by conceding $500,000 more to Virginia, $800,000 to North Carolina, and $200,000 to Georgia."[74] The second was a solution to the nettlesome problem of the settlement of state accounts which pacified Virginia, North Carolina, Georgia, and Maryland.[75] Not only was a satisfactory arrangement worked out for apportioning the common charges of the war, but the time limit for submitting claims was extended to July 1, 1791.[76] These, then, were the critical Senate compromises, and they were successful. On July 16, the Senate, by a vote of 15-11, agreed "that the resolutions for the assumption be added to the funding bill and the whole measure made one system."[77] Hamilton's appearance which Jefferson described less than a month earlier as "sombre, haggard, and dejected" had changed. Two South Carolina congressmen on their way to Federal Hall ran into the secretary who, they reported, wore "a smile on his countenance."[78]

He should have, for House debate, on the funding bill as on the residence, was something of an anticlimax. True, the vote was close, as it repeatedly had been, but the speed with which the Senate bill was approved and the laconic debate suggest that many congressmen were weary of the subject, if still unwilling to accept a decision adverse to their own principles. In the recorded debates only James Jackson of Georgia, indefatigable opponent of assumption, and William Smith of South Carolina, its tireless proponent, spoke at any length. The only other recorded speaker was Elbridge Gerry of Massachusetts who concluded

[74] Ferguson, *Power of the Purse*, 321.

[75] The position of these states was succinctly stated by Madison who recommended to Congress on Feb. 24 that assumption should include "effectual provision . . . for liquidating and crediting to the States, the whole of their expenditures during the war, as the same hath been or may be stated for that purpose; and, in such liquidation, the best evidence shall be received that the nature of the case will permit." Arguing that many of Virginia's claims unfairly had been barred, Madison also proposed that an extension of time be granted. *Annals of Congress*, II, 1339-1341.

[76] Ferguson, *Power of the Purse*, 322.

[77] *Annals of Congress*, I, 1012.

[78] Rogers, *Evolution of a Federalist*, 197. The final vote on the bill, as amended, was 14-12, a change owing to the switch of Few of Georgia who presumably realized that the measure could be carried without his support and so voted his principles and his state's interest.

his brief remarks with the warning that it would be disastrous to postpone the bill to another Congress. "What will be the result?" he asked. "The Government will be in danger of a convulsion—the revenue will probably be impaired or lost, and citizens attached to you will no longer be able to support your administration."[79] On July 24, three days after receipt of the Senate bill, the House negatived a proposal by Jackson of Georgia to reject it by the close vote of 32-29. Historians have compared this vote to that of April 12 which defeated assumption by a similar vote of 32-29 and have concluded that the critical difference was a switch of two votes, those of Lee and White. Superficially, this seems plausible. On examination, however, the comparison is clearly invalid. The composition of the House was not the same on the two dates, nor can it be assumed that all congressmen, save Lee and White, voted the same way.[80] Although an accurate comparison of the two roll calls is not possible because the votes of individual members on April 12 were not recorded, an approximate estimate of the number of votes needed was doubtless made by Hamilton who told Morris in mid-June that five votes in the House were necessary. Thus, at least three votes in addition to those of the Virginians were needed; if, as seems likely, two Marylanders also changed their position, there remains one mystery vote. Although this numbers game can be played almost any way, it cannot be fairly played in such a way as to bear out Jefferson's account.[81] The fact is that posi-

[79] *Annals of Congress,* II, 1710.

[80] For example, Thomas Hartley of Pennsylvania voted for assumption on Apr. 12 (see *Maclay Journal,* 230) but against it on July 24. *Annals of Congress,* II, 1712. Henry Wynkoop of Pennsylvania, on the other hand, was absent on Apr. 12 and voted in the affirmative in July. Although these votes cancelled each other, there were other changes which obviate the position that only a 2, or even a 4, vote switch was necessary. Two votes for assumption were needed to offset the negative votes of the two North Carolinians—John Sevier and John Steele—who arrived after Apr. 12. One affirmative vote was needed to replace that of Theodorick Bland of Virginia who had supported assumption and who died on June 1. Had all other congressmen remained of the same opinion, the vote in July thus would have been 33 against assumption, 28 for it. This meant that 6 votes *for* assumption had to be found.

[81] It could be pointed out, for example, that since a change of more than 2 votes was necessary to carry the measure, any one of them was as crucial as the other. It could also be observed that even if the two Virginians had voted *for* Jackson's motion it would not necessarily have defeated the Senate bill. Although at first glance it would appear that had they done so, the motion would have won by a vote of 31-30, this is not an accurate depiction of the situation. Daniel Huger of South Carolina who did not vote on Jackson's motion (but who voted *for* assumption two days later) would undoubtedly have voted against the motion, creating a tie which would

tions so fluctuated from month to month, even from week to week, that the most clairvoyant counter of congressional heads could not have foretold the outcome. The Pennsylvania delegation, for example, was particularly unpredictable. According to Senator Maclay—to cite only one instance—Clymer's final decision would depend on "whether his wish of popularity" subdues "his pride and obstinacy" and Thomas Hartley was "too giddy and unsettled for anyone to determine how he will vote."[82]

On July 26, the advocates of assumption happily came to the end of the rough legislative road they had traveled with such single-minded determination. The House vote was 34-28, the gain over the vote on Jackson's motion being attributable to a switch by Sumter of South Carolina and an affirmative vote by Huger of the same state who had not voted two days previously. The coalition was markedly different from that which had put through the residence bill some two weeks earlier, so different, in fact, that correlation is meaningless.[83] Each measure had passed on its merits, and doubtless would have succeeded had Jefferson, Madison, and Hamilton not struck a bargain a month or so earlier. In brief, Hamilton was not responsible for passage of the residence bill and the votes of Lee and White did not carry assumption. Nor was the cooperation of Jefferson and Madison, as Irving Brant remarks, "won by the dangled bait of a southward seat of government."[84] What Brant writes of Madison was equally true of Jefferson: "His letters written before the meeting with Hamilton make it plain that he would have accepted assumption without the capital, had that been necessary.

---

have meant the loss of the motion. In any event, acceptance of Jackson's motion would have put the amended bill before the House, where it presumably would have been carried with the votes of the two South Carolinians who voted for it on July 26.

[82] *Maclay Journal*, 223. Other examples of indecisiveness and unpredictability cited by Maclay were Hugh Williamson and John Ashe of North Carolina and Frederic Muhlenberg of Pennsylvania. *Ibid.*, 217, 239.

[83] Twenty-two congressmen who voted *against* the residence bill voted *for* the funding and assumption bill. Twenty-one congressmen who voted *for* the residence bill voted *against* the funding and assumption measure. In other words, 43 out of 61 changed their votes. Eleven congressmen voted "yea" both times; 7 voted "nay" both times.

[84] Brant, *James Madison*, 317. Nor were Lee and White lured by the Potomac bait. The explanation of their change was provided in a letter which one of them wrote to a correspondent in Alexandria: "It appears impractical to go on with the government without it in some shape or another. I was therefore among those who

His primary concern was to prevent national credit from being ruined and the Union destroyed by a group of blackmailing financiers in and out of Congress."[85]

That Jefferson believed otherwise is doubtless explained by his preoccupation with other affairs and his failure to follow closely the course of the measures through Congress. As Julian Boyd writes: "Jefferson had been ill, was immersed in his report on weights and measures, and had formed a strict resolution to confine himself to his own department and not to intermeddle in legislative questions."[86] Had he paid close attention to the details of the congressional session, he would have seen that the passage of the two bills was not owing to the compromise arranged at his dinner party but to separate and unrelated congressional coalitions. Jefferson had contributed to the success of assumption, it is true, but so, too, had others. His exaggerated account of the bargain may also be attributed, in Brant's phrase, to "Jefferson's deep hunger for posthumous fame."[87] This was personally unfortunate, for had he known the true story of assumption he might have been spared the enduring and deep regret for what he once termed the greatest "of all the errors of my political life."[88] But perhaps it was as well. If he mistakenly believed that he had carried a torch for assumption, he was at least unaware that Hamilton had been unable to light even a taper for the Potomac.

---

agreed to it under certain modifications, which have either removed, or greatly lessened, my original objections." Cited in *Jefferson Papers*, 182 (from an extract of a letter from a member of Congress to a gentleman in Alexandria, July 28, 1790, *N. Y. Daily Advertiser*, Aug. 13, 1790). Boyd quite plausibly conjectures that the letter must have been from either White or Lee.

[85] Brant, *James Madison*, 318. Madison and Jefferson were not alone. As early as June 17 Congressman Benjamin Goodhue reported that "there is reason to believe the Virginians and others who have been so much opposed to the assumption begin to be alarmed with the critical situation of our affairs without it, and have privately come forward to us with propositions which I am in hopes may lead to an accommodation on that subject." Goodhue to Hodge, June 17, 1790, *Essex Inst. Hist. Coll.*, LXXXIV, 160.

[86] *Jefferson Papers*, 166.

[87] Brant, *James Madison*, 315.

[88] *Jefferson Papers*, 171-172.

Slavery, Economics, and Congressional Politics, 1790

By HOWARD A. OHLINE

No FEATURE OF AMERICA'S REVOLUTION HAS DISTURBED THE contemporary generation of historians more than the failure of the Founding Fathers to abolish slavery. Recent historians have explained this failure chiefly in cultural and ideological terms. Winthrop D. Jordan, for example, has argued that the opportune moment to eliminate slavery after the Revolution was lost because whites could not overcome their negative racial attitudes toward blacks.[1] David Brion Davis has pointed to economic and ideological factors within the Revolution itself that checked emancipation.[2] Edmund S. Morgan has analyzed American belief in republicanism to explain the paradox of accepting slavery within a society dedicated to freedom.[3] These attitudes cut across sectional lines. Thus, even though sectionalism or regionalism shaped much of the political behavior and many of the policies of Revolutionary America,[4] the general culture and ideological consensus on blacks and slavery limited the possibilities of antislavery politics.

Valuable as such studies are to an understanding of American values, ideas, and politics, they often overlook the more concrete role of interest-group politics in setting the nation's course on slavery. Interest-group politics refers to the tendency of individual congressmen to pursue the priorities of his constituents while shap-

[1] Jordan, *White over Black: American Attitudes Toward the Negro, 1550–1812* (Chapel Hill, 1968), 342, 374.

[2] Davis, *The Problem of Slavery in the Age of Revolution, 1770–1823* (Ithaca and London, 1975), 249–62.

[3] Morgan, "Slavery and Freedom: The American Paradox," *Journal of American History*, LIX (June 1972), 5–29; and *American Slavery, American Freedom: The Ordeal of Colonial Virginia* (New York, 1975), 363–87.

[4] Joseph L. Davis, *Sectionalism in American Politics, 1774–1787* (Madison, 1977); H. James Henderson, *Party Politics in the Continental Congress* (New York and other cities, 1974); Rudolph M. Bell, *Party and Faction in American Politics: The House of Representatives, 1789–1801* (Westport, Conn., and London, Eng., 1973); and Mary P. Ryan, "Party Formation in the United States Congress, 1789 to 1796: A Quantitative Analysis," *William and Mary Quarterly*, 3d Ser., XXVIII (October 1971), 523–42.

MR. OHLINE is assistant professor of history at Temple University.

THE JOURNAL OF SOUTHERN HISTORY
Vol. XLVI, No. 3, August 1980

ing the policy of the whole nation. A case in point was the debate and action of Congress on slavery in the spring of 1790. The Revolution had generated both the desire for antislavery reform and the need for national solutions to economic problems. In 1790 both came before Congress at almost the same time, one in the form of petitions to Congress to define its powers over slavery, the other in Alexander Hamilton's Report on Public Credit. It is the thesis of this essay that the policy of the new republic toward slavery was set not in the federal Constitutional Convention but during the second session of the First Congress in the spring of 1790[5] and that it was set because congressmen from New England and Middle Atlantic states, however much influenced by cultural and ideological factors, in the end were moved equally as much by the desire to win southern support for Hamilton's Report on Public Credit. Afraid of alienating possible southern support for assumption of state debts, no northerner consistently supported the first abolitionist attempt to transform Revolutionary antislavery ideals into the explicit policy of the national government. The consequence was a lost opportunity, a chance to establish the ideal that the new government did not approve of slavery and had some responsibility to end it, if not immediately, at least in the future.

The origins of the congressional debate of 1790 on slavery were complex. Antislavery Quakers from the Middle Atlantic states had been waging an anti-slave trade campaign for a decade. Their Philadelphia Yearly Meeting had petitioned the Confederation Congress in 1783 to end the trade. When told that under the Articles of Confederation the central government had no power to regulate commerce, the Quakers turned to state governments, winning a number of laws during the late 1780s against the foreign slave trade. Laws against the foreign slave trade, in contrast to laws against the importation of slaves, prohibited merchants from transporting slaves from Africa to foreign markets.[6] This campaign was part of an international movement against the slave trade. John Pemberton, a member of a prominent Philadelphia Quaker family, personified the international dimension of the movement. During the late 1780s he went to England and organized a petition campaign to Parliament. Returning to the United States, he played a major part in

[5] William M. Wiecek in *The Sources of Antislavery Constitutionalism in America, 1760–1848* (Ithaca and London, 1977) has suggested that a "federal consensus" existed in the Constitution which prohibited federal power over slavery "in the early years of national independence" (p. 15). Professor Wiecek, however, has not explained when and how the "federal consensus" developed historically.

[6] William E. Burghardt Du Bois, *The Suppression of the African Slave-Trade to the United States of America, 1638–1870* (New York and other cities, 1896), 231–34.

lobbying against the slave trade and slavery in the first federal Congress.[7]

In 1790, after the new Constitution went into effect, the Quakers again petitioned Congress to end the slave trade. Although the Constitution referred to slavery obliquely when it explained procedures having to do with representation, commercial powers, and interstate extradition of criminals and fugitives, it was not explicit about the powers or limitations of the new government over the institution of slavery. The text could be interpreted to mean that Congress might regulate slavery, or that only the states could control domestic slavery, or even that the national government was obliged to protect slavery. All these interpretations were in fact expounded during the ratification debates.

In the South opponents of the new Constitution warned that slavery would find no protection under it. George Mason, in the Virginia convention, attacked it because there was "no clause in the Constitution that will prevent Northern and Eastern States from meddling with our whole property of that kind."[8] Patrick Henry warned that the national government would become a tool of abolitionists, who had been stopped in Virginia during the 1780s. The Constitution contained, he warned, "ten thousand *implied powers* which they may assume, they may, if we be engaged in war, liberate every one of your slaves . . . ." Henry feared that in the future a congressional conspiracy "will search that paper, and see if they have power of manumission."[9]

Southern supporters of the Constitution, however, argued that not only did the states retain jurisdiction over slavery but that the federal government even had power to protect slavery under the new frame of government. James Madison claimed that the fugitive-slave clause established "a better security than any that now exists." But Madison knew that the issue had not been resolved at the Constitutional Convention in Philadelphia and that it would be settled in the arena of national politics. He promised that the South could depend upon New York, New Jersey, and Connecticut. Together they would "oppose any attempts to annihilate this species of property."[10] In addition, in an anonymous article written expressly

[7] Davis, *The Problem of Slavery*, 213–54; Betty L. Fladeland, *Men and Brothers: Anglo-American Antislavery Cooperation* (Urbana and other cities, 1972); and Roger Anstey, *The Atlantic Slave Trade and British Abolition, 1760–1810* (Atlantic Highlands, N. J., 1975).

[8] Jonathan Elliot, ed., *The Debates in the Several State Conventions on the Adoption of the Federal Constitution* . . . (5 vols., Philadelphia, 1876), III, 270.

[9] *Ibid.*, 589–90; first quotation on p. 589, second on p. 590.

[10] *Ibid.*, 453, 459; Robert McColley, *Slavery and Jeffersonian Virginia* (Urbana and other cities, 1973), 167–71.

for consumption by delegates to the Virginia ratifying convention, Tench Coxe, a supporter of the Constitution from Philadelphia, writing on the slave trade and emancipation, asserted the state governments could not "be controuled or restrained, by the federal legislature."[11]

In northern ratifying conventions the sides were reversed, Antifederalists claiming that the Constitution did not do enough against slavery and supporters of the document denying that this was so. James Wilson of Pennsylvania, along with other northern Federalists, argued that the clause which gave Congress the power to prohibit the importation of slaves in twenty years would set into motion a chain of events that would destroy the institution of domestic slavery. Wilson, bidding for Quaker support of the Constitution, argued that the clause gave Congress the "power to exterminate slavery from within our borders."[12] Tench Coxe, arguing differently than when he wrote for Virginians, promised that the Constitution laid "a solid foundation . . . for exploding the principles of negro slavery, in which many good men of all parties in Pennsylvania and throughout the union, have already concurred." Mathew Carey supported the same idea.[13] In Massachusetts Thomas Dawes relied on Wilson's argument, suggesting that slavery "has received a mortal wound, and will die of a consumption."[14]

Northern federalists offered a second line of argument in response to those who claimed the Constitution accepted the moral evil of slavery and thus implicated its supporters in this sin. William Heath in the Massachusetts convention denied that joining the new government would involve New Englanders in supporting sin. Slavery was local. "If we ratify the Constitution," he asked, "shall we do any thing by our act to hold the blacks in slavery? or shall we become the partakers of other men's sins?" Answering "neither," he added, "Each state is sovereign and independent to a certain degree, and the states have a right, and they will regulate their own internal affairs . . . ." Slavery was not sanctioned by the Constitution as a national institution. New Englanders would not be "partakers of other men's sins; for in nothing do we voluntarily en-

[11] "Address to the honourable the Members of the Convention of Virginia . . . ," *American Museum*, III (May 1788), 426–33, 544–48; quotation on p. 429. The essay was also published in the Philadelphia *Pennsylvania Gazette*, May 21, 28, 1788, and the Richmond *Virginia Gazette and Weekly Advertiser*, June 5, 1788; Jacob E. Cooke, *Tench Coxe and the Early Republic* (Chapel Hill, 1978), 120–21.

[12] Elliot, ed., *Debates*, II, 484; Charles Page Smith, *James Wilson: Founding Father, 1742–1798* (Chapel Hill, 1956), 274.

[13] Coxe, "Letters on the Federal Government . . . ," *American Museum*, II (October 1787), 387 (quotation); Carey, "Selected Poetry . . . ," *ibid.*, 411.

[14] Elliot, ed., *Debates*, II, 41.

courage the slavery of our fellowmen."[15] Those who offered this argument, however, did seem to be conceding that power over the institution of slavery lay entirely with the states. Thus, Heath's arguments were at odds with Wilson's. On the other hand, there was agreement among the northern Federalists that the Constitution did not sanction slavery.

The debates over the issue of slavery in the ratifying conventions reveal that there was no clear and definitive understanding about the powers of the new government over slavery, although which interpretation was advanced seemed to have depended upon whether the speaker favored or opposed the Constitution in general. The abolitionist petitions of 1790, therefore, quite reasonably sought a clear definition of the new government's powers.

A second reason for the slavery debate of 1790 lay in a jurisdictional uncertainty created by the Constitution. Congress had been given the power to prohibit the importation of slaves only after 1808. Congress was also given power to regulate foreign commerce, but the Constitution did not say whether this power also included regulation of the foreign slave trade. If it did, was Congress's power an exclusive power, and were the state laws against slave trading from Africa to the West Indies still valid? During 1788 and 1789 some northern merchants who operated in the trade argued that power to regulate foreign commerce was now the exclusive power of the federal government and that the recently passed state laws prohibiting the foreign slave trade were void. Enough New York assemblymen supported this view to stall abolitionist efforts to win a law against the foreign slave trade in New York. As a result, merchants who wished to avoid the watchful eyes of antislavery societies in other ports transferred their operations to associates in New York City.[16] The jurisdictional uncertainty thus threatened to limit and possibly destroy the effectiveness of other states' laws. Worse still, this was occurring just at the time that Spain opened her colonial empire to free trade in slaves. Between 1788 and 1790 the American share of the foreign trade was increasing.[17] Abolitionists feared that Americans, already carrying more Africans into slavery than before the Revolution, would soon become the major suppliers

[15] *Ibid.*, 115.
[16] John Murray to James Pemberton, February 4, 1790, Papers of the Pennsylvania Society for Promoting the Abolition of Slavery (cited hereinafter as *PASP*); Edmund Prior to James Pemberton, July 4, 1789; Moses Brown to James Pemberton, September 2, 1789, Pemberton Papers; John Parrish to James Madison, May 28, 1790, Cox-Parrish-Wharton Papers. All three collections are in the Historical Society of Pennsylvania, Philadelphia, Pa.
[17] Herbert S. Klein, "North American Competition and the Characteristics of the African Slave Trade to Cuba, 1790 to 1794," *William and Mary Quarterly*, 3d Ser., XXVIII (January 1971), 88, 91, 102; Anstey, *The Atlantic Slave Trade*, 38.

of slaves to Cuba as well. A clarification of the jurisdictional question was vital if the abolitionist campaign against the slave trade was not to collapse.

Finally, Quaker petitions against slavery and the slave trade in 1790 functioned to preserve their antislavery testimony and to indicate their acceptance of the new government at the same time. Many Quakers were unhappy with specific parts of the Constitution. They felt betrayed because the importation of slaves was not stopped immediately. James Pemberton complained that the men of the Convention "have not only fallen greatly short of the wishes of the multitude, but erred against conviction, and their acknowledged duty . . . ."[18] Moses Brown, who led the campaign against the slave trade in Rhode Island, feared that the twenty-year delay against the importation of slaves would have a bad effect on state laws. "States may fall back," he suggested, "from their present sights into great darkness on this subject and the recovery from this Gross Evil, for which the Land Mourns, be long obstructed."[19] While disturbed, however, many Philadelphia Quakers supported the Constitution. They resolved their dilemma by supporting a petition campaign that went beyond the issue of the importation of slaves. Brown advised Quakers to testify against all the slavery provisions of the Constitution, and Pemberton agreed that "the advocates for the enslaved negroes" should send Congress a "suitable remonstrance" against the parts that violated Quaker testimony for "emancipation and the abolition of the iniquitous traffic."[20]

Because of the various problems created by the ambiguity of the Constitution and the anti-slave trade campaigns three antislavery petitions appeared in Congress during February 1790. On February 11 Quakers from Pennsylvania, New Jersey, Delaware, and the western parts of Maryland and Virginia petitioned Congress to hold a "sincere and impartial inquiry" into "the licentious wickedness of the African trade for slaves."[21] On the same day representative John Laurance from New York submitted another petition from Quakers in his state, concerning the jurisdictional confusion over the foreign slave trade caused by the silence of the Constitution.[22] A third petition was submitted by the Pennsylvania Abolition Society on February 12. This petition asked Congress to specify its powers over the whole institution of slavery. The society had prepared an

[18] James Pemberton to James Phillips, May 4, 1788, Pemberton Papers.
[19] Moses Brown to James Pemberton, October 17, 1787, ibid.
[20] James Pemberton to Moses Brown, November 16, 1787, ibid.
[21] Annals of Congress, 1 Cong., 2 Sess., 1224–25 (February 11, 1790).
[22] John Pemberton to James Pemberton, February 11, 1790, PASP.

antislavery petition in 1787 for presentation to the Constitutional Convention in Philadelphia, but divisions over timing led to postponement. Now in 1790 numerous members of the Pennsylvania Abolition Society, in their desire to make the new republic conform to their notion of good government, wanted Congress to adopt James Wilson's antislavery interpretation of the Constitution. Their petition, signed by Benjamin Franklin, "observed, with real satisfaction, that many important and salutary powers were vested in you [Congress] for 'promoting the welfare and securing the blessings of liberty to the people of the United States' . . . ." If Congress had the power to promote the welfare of the people and secure their liberty, did not this imply a grant of power against African slavery? The petition expressed the hope that the blessings of liberty would be administered "without distinction of color, to all descriptions of people." Congress should not only resolve the confusion over the slave trade but discuss "all justifiable endeavors to loosen the bands of slavery . . . ."[23]

Abolitionists could not have known at the time that the issue they raised would become entangled with economic measures in Congress. On February 8 the House of Representatives had begun debate on Hamilton's Report on Public Credit.[24] Hamilton's primary goal was to secure the nation's credit by establishing a funded national debt. Stable credit would encourage investment and economic growth. Hamilton's proposals divided Congress, and a political opposition developed. On February 11 James Madison emerged as an opponent of Hamilton's plan, delivering a speech critical of the plan's failure to discriminate between original creditors and the then holders of national debt certificates. On the same day the two Quaker petitions on slavery were presented to Congress. After a brief debate, in which a few southerners argued violently and abusively, the Quaker petitions were tabled, and Congress returned to the issue of public credit. The next day, however, debate on that issue was again suspended in order to consider the petition of the Pennsylvania Abolition Society. Perhaps owing to Benjamin Franklin's signature or possibly because the supporters of Hamilton needed time to prepare arguments against Madison, the society's petition was received more favorably than those of the Quakers. The entire legislative day was given over to consideration of whether to create a special committee to prepare a report specifying the powers of Congress over slavery.[25]

[23] *Annals of Cong.*, 1 Cong., 2 Sess., 1239–40 (February 12, 1790).

[24] Linda Grant DePauw *et al.*, eds., *Documentary History of the First Federal Congress* . . . (3 vols., Baltimore and London, 1972–1977), III, 289.

[25] *Annals of Cong.*, 1 Cong., 2 Sess., 1234–36 (February 11, 1790).

There was no clear North-South division on the question of creating a special committee. While the Deep South opposed it, the upper South generally supported it, as did the North. Representatives from the Deep South who opposed submitting the antislavery petitions to a special committee included William Loughton Smith, Thomas Tudor Tucker, and Aedanus Burke from South Carolina and James Jackson and Abraham Baldwin from Georgia. These representatives attacked the Quakers for meddling in the affairs of the states. Jackson accused them of distributing "dirty pamphlets representing Negroes." He charged them with hypocrisy, claiming that their sincerity against slavery would be believed only when they organized a bank to compensate slaveholders for any loss of property. Jackson stung the Quakers with the double charge that the emerging banking activity in Philadelphia was a self-interested business instead of a socially beneficial institution and that Quakers were asking southern planters to sacrifice their property without any material sacrifice from the Quakers.[26] William Loughton Smith warned that the creation of a committee would mean sedition and civil war. This would be especially so if such a committee and Congress were to support emancipation after supporters of the Constitution in South Carolina had said during ratification that Congress would have no power to emancipate slaves. During his campaign for Congress in 1788 Smith had promised his constituents that he would not only protect slavery but would also convert northerners to the necessity of slavery.[27]

Michael Jenifer Stone of Maryland also opposed the creation of a committee. No action should be taken by Congress, he argued, because the Quakers did not own slaves and were not "exclusively interested." Stone assumed that antislavery petitions were improper in a republic. Republican representatives functioned to protect the interests of their constituents. Government should not act upon petitions unless the petitioners had a material interest in the issue. Persons could petition to protect their own property, as the holders of Continental debt certificates had, but not to deny another's property. Humanity unconnected with material interest was not within the limits of republic legislative actions.[28]

Virginians like James Madison and John Page, on the other

[26] John Pemberton to James Pemberton, February 11, 1790, *PASP.*

[27] George C. Rogers, Jr., *Evolution of a Federalist; William Loughton Smith of Charleston, 1758–1812* (Columbia, 1962), 162–66; Merrill Jensen and Robert A. Becker, eds., *The Documentary History of the First Federal Elections, 1788–1790* (1 vol. to date, Madison, 1976), I, 180–81.

[28] *Annals of Cong.,* 1 Cong., 2 Sess., 1225–27, 1233 (February 11, 1790); quotation on p. 1226; action to table on p. 1233.

hand, reflecting the anti-slave trade sentiment of their state, declared that Congress could support the trade's abolition through regulation and by preventing importation to the western territories. Thomas Scott of western Pennsylvania hoped that a congressional statement against the principles of Negro slavery would influence judges to protect the freedom of blacks in judicial proceedings. Western Pennsylvania already was having difficulty with Virginians trying to capture blacks and return them to slavery.[29] Elbridge Gerry argued that Congress had the right to buy slaves and free them. Many other northerners simply agreed with the antislavery position of the abolitionists. Thus, on February 12, by a vote of forty-three to eleven, the House voted to create a special committee to determine what powers Congress should have over the institution of slavery. It is clear from this vote and from the debates that preceded it that many representatives in 1790 by no means accepted the view that Congress was prohibited from touching the institution of slavery in any way at all.[30]

The composition of the special committee augured well for a sympathetic consideration of the petitions. The committee included Abiel Foster of New Hampshire, chairman, Benjamin Huntington of Connecticut, Elbridge Gerry of Massachusetts, John Laurance of New York, Thomas Sinnickson of New Jersey, Thomas Hartley of Pennsylvania, and Josiah Parker of Virginia. Parker, the only southerner of the group, had already, in 1789, proposed legislation against the slave trade.[31]

Hoping that the Senate would also appoint a committee, the abolitionists submitted the petitions to the Senate on February 15. They acted apparently on the advice of Senator John Langdon of New Hampshire that a large majority in the Senate supported the cause of abolition. This may indeed have been so, but no senator assumed leadership in support of the petitions. Ralph Izard and Pierce Butler, senators from South Carolina, however, were prepared. They "railed at the society; [and] called them fanatics . . . ." Butler attacked Benjamin Franklin and "charged the whole proceeding to anti-Federal motives."[32] Butler's argument that the abolition petitions were motivated by antifederalism was politically and historically wrong, but like Smith in the House, he believed it his

[29] *Ibid.*, 1245–46 (February 12, 1790); William R. Leslie, "A Study in the Origins of Interstate Rendition: The Big Beaver Creek Murders," *American Historical Review*, LVII (October 1951), 63–76; Thomas D. Morris, *Free Men All: The Personal Liberty Laws of the North, 1780–1861* (Baltimore and London, 1974), 19–22.
[30] *Annals of Cong.*, 1 Cong., 2 Sess., 1240–47 (February 12, 1790).
[31] Du Bois, *The Suppression of the African Slave-Trade*, 78, 74.
[32] John Pemberton to James Pemberton, February 15, 1790, *PASP.*

responsibility to convince northerners that antislavery politics was
not a proper function of Congress.

Meanwhile important senators like the New Englander Rufus
King, then representing New York, refused to support antislavery
action.[33] Those on whom the antislavery forces had counted for
support rationalized that the Senate did not need to act because the
House, which was more friendly to the cause, had already acted.
Further, Vice-President John Adams who presided over the Senate
was unsympathetic. At the least, it was a matter of priority: Congress should finish the business of funding the debt without intru-
sions of this sort. The day before the abolitionists submitted their
petitions to the Senate he had written that he was pleased "to see a
returning disposition . . . to pay debts, and to do justice by holding
property sacred . . . ." Like Hamilton, Adams assumed that the
funding of the debt would establish national political and economic
stability.[34] Thus, he delayed the presentation of the antislavery memorials, and when he did submit them "He did it rather with a
sneer . . . ." Adams objected to pressure on the Senate from these
"self-constituted" societies.[35] He was suspicious of the abolitionists' intentions and confused about the motives of "the eastern
members" for supporting "the silly petition of Franklin and his
Quakers," while the question of the debt was still pending.[36] The
Senate decided not to create a committee to review the problem.

Meanwhile the House had turned again to its work on Hamilton's
Report on Public Credit. The debate on discrimination resumed on
February 15, and on the twenty-second the House voted to reject
Madison's proposal and fund the domestic debt without dis-
criminating between the original and the then holders of the debt.[37]
That issue settled, debate then began on the issue of assumption of
state debts.[38] After two weeks of debate the House, sitting as the
Committee of the Whole, voted in favor of assumption by the
margin of thirty-one to twenty-six.[39] All understood, however, that
this narrow vote did not settle the issue, in part because North Carolina representatives who would have voted in the negative had not

[33] Joseph L. Arbena, "Politics or Principle? Rufus King and the Opposition to Slavery,
1785-1825," Essex Institute, *Historical Collections*, CI (January 1965), 56-77.
[34] Page Smith, *John Adams* (2 vols., Garden City, N. Y., 1962), II, 787.
[35] Edgar S. Maclay, ed., *Journal of William Maclay: United States Senator from Pennsylvania, 1789-1791* (New York, 1890), 196.
[36] Adams to Thomas Crafts, May 25, 1790, Adams Papers (Massachusetts Historical Society, Boston, Mass.).
[37] *Annals of Cong.*, 1 Cong., 2 Sess., 1344 (February 22, 1790).
[38] *Ibid.*, 1356-74, 1374-80 (February 23, 24, 1790).
[39] Winfred E. A. Bernhard, *Fisher Ames: Federalist and Statesman, 1758-1808* (Chapel
Hill, 1965), 141.

been present. Indeed, a month later the House again in Committee of the Whole once more voted on assumption, this time defeating it by thirty-one to twenty-nine.[40] Thus, the assumption issue remained a central and unresolved question throughout March and into April.

Sometime during the latter part of February John Pemberton and Warner Mifflin, a Quaker abolitionist from Maryland, prepared a list of issues for Foster's special House committee to examine. First, they wanted the committee to consider what Congress could do to prevent merchants from using New York City "for the purpose of fitting out ships for the African Trade?" Second, they suggested that Congress declare the limits of its power over domestic slavery, believing that Congress had power "to frame such regulations respecting the conditions of the oppressed Africans now held in Bondage in these States." Pemberton and Mifflin did not ask the committee to declare that Congress had an immediate power of abolition, but that it had the right to regulate the conditions of "oppressed Africans" so that they would be advanced "nearer to an equality with their fellow man and render them in time more fit for a state of freedom." Third, they wanted Congress to study the legal status of some "poor Blacks in North Carolina," and "the circumstance of a Number of Negroes in Virginia." In both states, Pemberton and Mifflin argued, blacks had suffered enslavement in violation of state laws. The two states, they believed, had used ex post facto laws, now illegal under the Constitution, abridging the freedom of blacks. Fourth, they wanted Congress to recommend that the states pass laws against the slave trade, regardless of the constitutional limitation on congressional power over the importation of slaves. Such a recommendation would "open the Eyes of the people to see and acknowledge the inequity and injustice of the Slave Trade." Finally, in what seems like an afterthought, they wanted to know "whether an impost of ten Dollars a head on slaves sent from one state to another can be levied." This might have been the first expression of the idea that congressional power extended to the interstate slave trade, although it is more likely that Pemberton and Mifflin believed such power was derived from Congress's constitutional right to levy a ten-dollar tax on imported slaves.[41]

The most important issue for the future of antislavery politics was raised in Pemberton and Mifflin's second point. They assumed that

[40] *Annals of Cong.*, 1 Cong., 2 Sess., 1525 (April 12, 1790). By this time three representatives from North Carolina had taken their seats. They were Hugh Williamson, John Baptista Ashe, and Timothy Bloodworth. There was, however, no roll call on the vote.

[41] "Friends Remarks to the Committee of Congress at New York," February 1790, Pemberton Papers.

Congress had power to regulate the institution of domestic slavery. They believed such power to lie in the constitutional injunction to "promote the general Welfare, and secure the Blessings of Liberty to ourselves and our Posterity . . . ."[42]

Foster's committee finished its work on a preliminary report on March 1 and sent it to the House on March 5. The general spirit of the report was antislavery although the abolitionists did not get all they sought. The report contained seven sections. Each explained a power or a lack of power vested in Congress "relating to the abolition of slavery." Section One restated the constitutional prohibition against congressional action on the importation of slaves "until the year one thousand eight hundred and eight." Section Two stated that Congress was "equally restrained from interfering in the emancipation of slaves . . . within the period mentioned . . . ." Although the report did not say more on that subject, by reasonable inference this seemed to say that at the time Congress gained the power to prohibit importation of slaves it would also acquire some power over domestic slavery. This had been James Wilson's interpretation during ratification. The committee, however, explicitly rejected the abolitionists' idea that the power to regulate domestic slavery existed in the preamble to the Constitution. John Pemberton reported that they were defeated on this issue by the tie-breaking vote of Abiel Foster. The committee included three members who were willing to use the preamble to extend congressional power over slavery. Pemberton did not identify the three. He did believe, however, that Foster voted against the abolitionists' proposal because he feared the violent response of the southerners.[43]

Section Three of the report stated that Congress did not have power to interfere with "the internal regulations of particular States." Only the states could regulate the religion, clothing, accommodations, subsistence, marriage, rights, separation of families, medicine, transportation, and sale of blacks. Section Three, however, also expressed the hope that states would "promote the objects mentioned in the memorials, and every other measure that may tend to the happiness of slaves." The committee thus appeared to be saying that it was appropriate that the national government encourage humane treatment even though Congress did not have power to regulate immediately. Moreover, it would be fair to assume that if Congress could interfere with "the emancipation of

[42] John Pemberton to James Pemberton, March 14, 1790, *PASP*. The quotation is from the preamble to the Constitution.
[43] John Pemberton to James Pemberton, March 2, 1790, *PASP*. The committee report is found in DePauw *et al.*, eds., *Documentary History*, III, 340–41; subsequent quotations are from this source.

slaves" after twenty years, its powers might also extend to internal regulation of the institution.

The remaining sections of the report focused on the problems of the slave trade. Section Four declared that Congress had power to tax each imported slave, but the report said nothing about taxing the interstate slave trade, leaving that query raised by Pemberton and Mifflin unanswered. Section Five of the report stated that Congress had the power "to interdict" the foreign slave trade and "to regulate" the treatment of slaves sold to foreigners and imported into the United States. While Congress did not have power to stop the importation of slaves until 1808 the committee assumed that it had power to regulate the trade immediately. On this and the power to prohibit the foreign trade, the committee granted Congress powers not specified in the Constitution. Section Six held that Congress could prohibit foreigners from participating in the foreign slave trade from ports in the United States. The concluding paragraph, Section Seven of the report, promised the abolitionists "that in all cases, to which the authority of Congress extends, they will exercise it for the humane objects of the memorialists, so far as they can be promoted on the principles of justice, humanity and good policy."

The Foster report was, as noted, presented to the House of Representatives on Friday, March 5, whereupon it was tabled until the following Monday. At this point its fate became entangled with two other pieces of legislation. One was the issue of assumption, discussed above. The second was the North Carolina cession bill. This bill, passed by the Senate in February, dealt with the cession by North Carolina to the federal government of its territory west of the Alleghenies. It included a provision to prohibit Congress from interfering with slavery in the new territory. Thus, even as the Foster committee was putting the final touches on a report favorable to antislavery, the Senate had sent to the House a bill denying congressional power over slavery in the territory ceded by North Carolina. The cession bill was received by the House on March 5, given its second reading on March 8, and scheduled for debate on March 11, with a vote presumably to follow soon afterward. The Foster report was scheduled to come off the table on Monday, March 8.[44] If consideration of the report was delayed, the cession bill might well be enacted first and be taken as Congress's statement on its powers over slavery. This would undercut and possibly destroy the chance of getting the Foster report adopted.

Pemberton was alarmed. He could not comprehend how a nation

[44] DePauw *et al.*, eds., *Documentary History*, III, 317, 319.

could "declare all men are by nature free and then declare they shall not be made free."[45] On the same day that the North Carolina cession bill was read to the House, he and Warner Mifflin persuaded Representative Thomas Hartley to move prompt consideration of the Foster report. Hartley did so on Monday, March 8.[46]

Hartley's motion touched off a preliminary skirmish in which opposing interpretations about the power of the national government over slavery were aired. Roger Sherman, calling the Foster report "prudent, humane, and judicious," favored consideration and assumed that the power over the slave trade implied the beginning of gradual abolition. For the same reason William Loughton Smith objected to taking up the report, "saying what Congress could not do until 1808 implied that then they might set every slave in the Continent free."[47] The House agreed to begin debate in one week because, significantly, the report or parts of it "represented the sentiments of the Legislators."[48]

Even after the Hartley motion, Quakers feared that Congress, preoccupied with Hamilton's Report on Public Credit, would postpone consideration of the Foster report again. Pemberton worried that Smith's "violence" against the report would intimidate northerners, preventing its adoption.[49] During the following days they lobbied intensively. Elias Boudinot of New Jersey and John Vining of Delaware reluctantly agreed to prevent further delay.[50] Mifflin went to President George Washington for support on March 16. According to Washington, Mifflin stressed "the immorality—injustice—impolicy of keeping these people in a state of Slavery . . . ." As Washington interpreted the visit, Mifflin wanted him to support a policy of gradual abolition, but the President replied that for official reasons he "was not inclined to express any sentiments of the merits of the question . . . ."[51] Washington was also probably aware of displeasure in Virginia over the antislavery petitions.[52] Like John Adams in the Senate, he regarded the issue as the business of the House, not an executive problem.

On the afternoon of March 16 the House of Representatives be-

[44] John Pemberton to James Pemberton, February 23, 1790, *PASP.*
[46] *Annals of Cong.,* 1 Cong., 2 Sess., 1465 (March 8, 1790).
[47] John Pemberton to James Pemberton, March 8, 1790, *PASP.*
[48] *Annals of Cong.,* 1 Cong., 2 Sess., 1465–66 (March 8, 1790).
[49] John Pemberton to James Pemberton, March 9, 1790, *PASP.*
[50] John Pemberton to James Pemberton, March 14, 1790, *ibid.*
[51] John C. Fitzpatrick, ed., *The Diaries of George Washington, 1748–1799* (4 vols., Boston and New York, 1925), IV, 104.
[52] David Stuart to Washington, March 15, 1790, John C. Fitzpatrick, ed., *The Writings of George Washington from the Original Manuscript Sources, 1745–1799* (37 vols. and index, Washington, 1931–1944), XXXI, 28n.

gan debate on the Foster committee's report. Supporters were relieved that despite the schedule set earlier by the House, the cession bill had not yet been called up. Thus, debate on their own measure would now precede vote on that bill. On the other hand, assumption had by no means been settled, and was very much on the minds of most House members.

Opponents from the Deep South followed a strategy of delay and filibuster, repeatedly trying to table the Foster report. On the first day of debate James Jackson of Georgia consumed several hours arguing that blacks were in misery in Africa; that the slave trade to Georgia was an act of humanity; that abolition was religious fanaticism; and that Quakers like Mifflin were not really concerned with the happiness of society but with expiating their own sins. The next day William Loughton Smith filibustered for three and a quarter hours.[53]

From the gallery John Pemberton watched the debate with a sense of unease. Smith, he wrote to his brother, "was heard with more patience than he deserved, for he wearied himself and his hearers . . . except his friend Jackson."[54] Northern congressmen not only avoided engaging Jackson and Smith, lamented Pemberton; "many of the New England men slipped away and some . . . [even] voted against it being revived . . . who here to fore professed highly respecting freedom."[55]

Pemberton was right. No prominent New England or Middle Atlantic congressman assumed leadership in defending the report on the floor of the House. George Clymer of Pennsylvania left Congress before the debate began. Thomas Fitzsimons, who had submitted the first antislavery petition to Congress and had helped to keep the issue alive, excused himself for two weeks. Jeremiah Wadsworth of Connecticut left Congress after expressing sympathy for the Quaker position.[56] Egbert Benson, a New Yorker, actually made one of the motions to send the report back to committee.[57]

Pemberton thought he knew the reason why northerners were not taking on Smith, Jackson, and the proslavery position: northerners favored antislavery, but they favored assumption of state debts more, and with the vote on that issue promising to be close, they wished to do nothing that might alienate support of proslavery southerners. "The funding system is so much their darling," Pemberton wrote in disgust, "that they want to obtain the favor of those

[53] John Pemberton to James Pemberton, March 17, 1790, *PASP; Annals of Cong.*, 1 Cong., 2 Sess., 1499, 1503–14 (March 16, 17, 1790).
[54] John Pemberton to James Pemberton, March 17, 1790, *PASP.*
[55] John Pemberton to James Pemberton, March 16, 1790, *ibid.*
[56] John Pemberton to James Pemberton, March 18, 1790, *ibid.*
[57] Philadelphia *Pennsylvania Packet,* March 30, 1790, reporting debate of March 18.

from Carolina and Georgia."⁵⁸ Indeed, some New Englanders did admit privately that the assumption of state debts took precedence over antislavery.⁵⁹ Wadsworth said as much as he left Congress, and Theodore Sedgwick of Massachusetts clearly agreed. Sedgwick privately condemned the Foster report as an irritant which endangered assumption, and he believed the decision to press it and the debate which followed "a very foolish thing and very indiscreetly managed."⁶⁰ Benson, who had moved recommittal, was known to be a friend of Hamilton's financial program. At least one southerner, Abraham Baldwin of Georgia, played directly on northern concerns about assumption in speaking for returning the report to committee without further debate. The debate had caused such agitation, Baldwin observed, that "the most important business of the union has been arrested in the midst of its progress . . . the plan for the support of public credit—the necessary arrangements for the formation of the state of North Carolina into districts . . . are all laid aside as of no account."⁶¹ The storm which the report had already created, he suggested, was sufficient reason to set it aside.

Attempts to table the Foster report failed, but not because of strong northern resistance. Rather, they failed because the South itself was divided. Representatives from South Carolina and Georgia hoped to strangle debate. But Virginians, although opposing those sections which would lead to the abolition of "Negro property," supported "the immediate parts of the report respecting the Discouragement of the Trade."⁶² They played a crucial role in keeping the debate alive. Virginians may well have had another reason: they opposed assumption,⁶³ and a long debate on the Foster report would allow time for North Carolina's representatives, who also opposed assumption, to get to New York City and vote against it.

On March 18 the House proceeded to take up the first section, which reaffirmed the constitutional settlement prohibiting congressional interference with the importation of slaves for twenty years. Debate revolved around the fact that the report contained different wording than the Constitution. The Foster committee stated that

⁵⁸ John Pemberton to James Pemberton, March 16, 1790, *PASP*.
⁵⁹ Nathaniel Gorham to Henry Knox, April 17, 1790, Henry Knox Papers (Massachusetts Historical Society); Gorham to Theodore Sedgwick, April 18, 1790, Theodore Sedgwick Papers (Massachusetts Historical Society); Stephen Higginson to Oliver Wolcott, Jr., May 6, 1790, Oliver Wolcott (1760-1833) Papers (Connecticut Historical Society, Hartford, Conn.).
⁶⁰ Sedgwick to Ephraim Williams, March 17, 1790, Sedgwick Papers.
⁶¹ Philadelphia *Pennsylvania Packet*, March 30, 1790, reporting debate of March 18, 1790.
⁶² John Pemberton to James Pemberton, March 17, 1790, *PASP*.
⁶³ Norman K. Risjord, *Chesapeake Politics, 1781-1800* (New York, 1978), 336-69.

the central government could not restrain importation of such persons "as any of the states now existing shall think proper to admit, *until* the year one thousand eight hundred and eight." The Constitution contained the phrase *"prior to* the year one thousand eight hundred and eight." Whether the change of wording was intentional or not, it favored the South Carolinian view of Congress's power over the slave trade. The use of the word "until" implied uncertainty whether the power contemplated would ever be exercised. The phrase "prior to," however, meant *before* and implied that after 1808 Congress would act against importation. Antislavery representatives therefore proposed a motion to change the wording to "prior to." Ironically, Smith of South Carolina argued against the change, preferring the uncertainty of the word "until" in the report. The motion passed, Smith complaining that the House was under the "influence" of Quakers. Privately, John Pemberton interpreted the change in wording as an anti–slave trade victory.[64]

This vote turned out not to be a true test of strength. When the House discussed Section Two, which, in prohibiting Congress "from interfering in the emancipation of slaves . . . within the period mentioned . . . ," implied a power over emancipation in the future, James Madison moved to amend. Madison proposed that Sections Two and Three, which listed the things Congress could not do, be replaced with the statement "That Congress have no authority to interfere in the emancipation of slaves, or in the treatment of them within any of the States; it remaining with the several States alone to provide any regulations therein, which humanity and true policy may require." Madison's amendment would make impossible a construction that after 1808 congressional power could extend to domestic slavery.[65]

Although this was a critically important change that destroyed the antislavery implications of the report, northerners did not resist it. Opposition to Madison came not from the North but from William Loughton Smith, who did not believe that Congress had any right to suggest that state laws on slavery should conform with "humanity and true policy." Smith tried to amend Madison's amendment by removing the concluding phrase "humanity and true policy," but the representatives rejected his motion. Northerners were in favor of state laws which contained humanity but in the political context of 1790 they would go no further.

Madison was thus able to mold the first three sections of the

[64] John Pemberton to James Pemberton, March 18, 1790, *PASP.*
[65] The wording of the amendment comes from the amended report, DePauw *et al.*, eds., *Documentary History,* III, 340–41; quotation on p. 340. John Pemberton identified Madison as its sponsor in his letter of March 18, 1790, to his brother James.

report to his liking. With the help of John Page, he assumed leadership in the debate. In the situation, Madison was able to appear as a moderate. He attacked the "bawling" of the South Carolinians and supported the abolitionists against the slave trade. At the same time he circumscribed the power of Congress over domestic slavery. His moderate posture assured the House that it would be able to move through the rest of the report without any serious conflict.[66]

Many northerners were relieved. Henry Wynkoop, representative from Pennsylvania, described the general satisfaction after the progress of the debate on March 18. It was, he claimed, the fair weather after a storm. He was thankful that the slavery debate was coming to an end, but he expressed no resentment towards Madison's amendments of Sections Two and Three. In fact, Wynkoop was worried more that the debate would disgrace the national government than he was about conflict over the antislavery implications of the Foster report. He hoped that it would be possible "to cast a Veil over the Debate of the two past days . . . ."[67]

Debate over the rest of the report followed the pattern which had emerged by March 18. Representatives from South Carolina and Georgia continued to ridicule the Quakers and obstruct. Virginians, particularly Madison and John Page, continued as moderates, defending the essence of the remaining sections while suggesting changes. Northerners, with a few exceptions, remained in the background.

Section Four of the Foster report, which declared Congress's power to levy a ten-dollar tax on each imported slave, was removed after Egbert Benson, acting as chairman of the Committee of the Whole, broke a twenty-four to twenty-four tie. The South Carolinians wanted it removed because it did not follow the exact wording of the Constitution. John Page of Virginia believed Section Four "unnecessary, because Congress will have the power given by the constitution, whether declared by the House or not." He sensed that Congress was not inclined to tax the slave trade anyway. Thus, a declaration of its power to tax imported slaves without passing such a tax would "look like temporising with the Quakers."[68]

On the same day, March 19, the representatives debated Section

[66] John Pemberton to James Pemberton, March 18, 1790, *PASP*. Description of debate on the first three sections of the report depends on this letter. Neither the *Annals of Congress* nor the newspapers contain a record of the debate on Madison's action to amend Sections Two and Three.

[67] Henry Wynkoop to Dr. Reading Beatty, March 18, 1790, Joseph M. Beatty, Jr., ed., "The Letters of Judge Wynkoop, Representative from Pennsylvania to the First Congress of the United States," *Pennsylvania Magazine of History and Biography*, XXXVIII (April 1914), 191–92; quotation on p. 192.

[68] Philadelphia *Pennsylvania Packet*, March 30, 1790, reporting the debate of March 19.

Five which stated that Congress had power "to interdict" or "to regulate" the foreign slave trade and also to provide "humane treatment of slaves, in all cases, while on their passage to the United States, or to foreign ports . . . ." Madison proposed a substitute amendment which changed the wording but not the substance of Section Five. Smith condemned the whole idea of regulating the foreign slave trade as "an indirect violation of the constitution." Regulation of the trade was not mentioned in the Constitution.[69] Smith warned that any regulations of the trade could become a pretext for stopping it. If Congress passed any law that said "that Negroes shall be brought into the country in any other way than as Brutes . . . [Congress] must interdict the trade."[70] Madison's cooperation with the abolitionists and his conflict with Smith pleased John Pemberton, who concluded that Madison was the abolitionists' major ally in Congress.[71] Madison's amendment passed.[72]

The House finished voting on the report on March 22 and 23. Elias Boudinot of New Jersey emerged as the major defender of Section Six which prohibited foreigners from fitting out vessels in American ports in order to supply other foreigners with slaves. Boudinot was a supporter of Hamilton's financial program, but he was also close to the Quaker community in New Jersey. Defense of Section Six was politically safe, for it did not affect Americans directly. His major argument in debate focused on the integrity of the Quakers instead of the institution of slavery. Thus, he was able to satisfy the Quakers, who believed his actions contributed to their testimony, while not antagonizing southerners. Moreover, he did not take a major position on the report until after Madison had altered Section Two. Like most northerners, he was relieved when the House was "done with the Negro Business, which has been . . . carried by the Southern Gent to a most unmeasurable length."[73] Fisher Ames agreed that the southerners had "teased and bullied the House out of their good temper, and driven them to vote in earnest on a subject which at first they did not care much about." Ames was more interested in solving the problem of assumption. He believed that the debates on slavery were "a matter of moonshine."[74]

[69] *Ibid.*

[70] John Pemberton to James Pemberton, March 20, 1790, *PASP.*

[71] *Ibid.;* John Pemberton to James Pemberton, March 9, 1790, *ibid.*

[72] John Pemberton to James Pemberton, March 20, 1790, *PASP.*

[73] Boudinot to William Bradford, Jr., March 25, 1790, John William Wallace Papers (Historical Society of Pennsylvania); *Annals of Cong.,* 1 Cong., 2 Sess., 1517–22 (March 22, 1790).

[74] Ames to George Richards Minot, March 23, 1790, in Seth Ames, ed., *Works of Fisher*

Abolitionists were disappointed that the Congress had not accepted their interpretation of the Constitution. Hoping to salvage something, Warner Mifflin remained in New York City in the hope of finding a congressman who would at least prepare a bill that would regulate the slave trade.[75] In an open letter to the Congress he suggested that the dignity of republican American would be achieved by obstructing the trade through regulation "without infringing the constitutional right of any branch of confederation . . . ." Federal regulation, he prophesied, would be "a light to surrounding powers and empires" of America's virtue.[76] But Mifflin could find no takers. Abolitionists hoped Madison would continue as the congressional leader against the slave trade, but he refused. Madison admitted that the foreign trade was growing, but he believed that after the turmoil over the Foster report "a renewal of the subject in Congress would be equally unseasonable."[77] Four years would pass before Congress enacted a law regulating the foreign slave trade. In the meantime abolitionists could only rationalize that the debates of 1790 "served to disseminate our principles, by exciting a commotion on the subject . . . ."[78]

It is clear that one of the chief reasons the Foster report was not adopted by the House of Representatives in its original antislavery form is that representatives from New England and the Middle Atlantic states, who had been thought to be antislavery, did not take an active part in fighting for it. Their support, when it came, was half-hearted, but there were two major reasons for their lack of enthusiasm. One was the racial attitudes of many of the representatives and their constituents. Oliver Wolcott, Sr., a leading Federalist in Connecticut, preferred "the white people of this country to the black—after they have taken care of the former they may amuse themselves with the other people—"[79] And a friend of George

---

Ames . . . (2 vols., Boston, 1854), I, 76. It is impossible to determine the character of the conflict in the House through vote analysis because the votes on each section were not reported. The only recorded vote was on a motion to include the original committee report and the amended report in the House journal. It was approved. One, however, cannot assume that a vote to include the reports in the journal meant support for the original or the amended report. Moreover, representatives like Fisher Ames, who took no role in debate, voted against publication of the reports. He did not believe Congress should declare its powers in any but legislative actions. He thought that the reports would commit Congress to "dogmas which may be hereafter denied . . . ." *Ibid.,* 76. See also Bernhard, *Fisher Ames,* 141, 143–44.

[75] John Pemberton to James Pemberton, March 23, 1790, *PASP.*

[76] "Warner Mifflin's Address to Congress . . . ," *American Museum,* VIII (October 1790), 158, 156.

[77] Madison to John Parrish, June 6, 1790, Cox-Parrish-Wharton Papers.

[78] "Address of the Pennsylvania Abolition Society to the Paris Society," quoted in W. J. Buck, Manuscript History of the Pennsylvania Abolition Society, I, 77, *PASP;* Pennsylvania Society to London Society, October 25, 1790, *ibid.*

[79] Oliver Wolcott, Sr., to Oliver Wolcott, Jr., April 23, 1790, Wolcott Papers.

Thacher's, an antislavery representative from the Maine district of Massachusetts, wrote him that the Quakers should go to "hell" where "the Negroes . . . [could] wait on them."[80] To the extent that these racial attitudes infected northern congressmen and their supporters—and thus affected their support or lack of it for the Foster report—the record supports Winthrop Jordan's view that racial attitudes restricted antislavery in the early republic.

A second reason, however, was the immediate pressure of special-interest politics. The evidence is compelling that many northerners were embarrassed by the introduction of the entire issue at this time and acquiesced in the emasculation of the major antislavery provisions of the report because they feared the effects of this issue on assumption. It has already been noted how some northerners were absent from Congress in order to avoid the conflict. Those who stayed did not fight Madison's amendments. A northern defense of the Foster report would have prolonged the debate, intensifying southern fears about national power, and probably eliminated any chance of compromise over the assumption of states' debts. John Pemberton had concluded in his dealings with the legislature that congressmen were not guided by principles but by a pragmatic "wisdom which is earthly and sensual." The politics of the first Congress were "too much like scratch me and I will scratch thee."[81]

Some New Englanders found themselves in a political dilemma. George Thacher, strongly in favor of antislavery principles, encouraged Quakers to "persevere in the glorious cause of general freedom until we see the whole human race equally partaking of its Blessings."[82] At private parties in New York he tried to convince congressmen to support antislavery.[83] In private he expressed frustration and amazement that southerners would attempt "to prove the lawfulness and good policy of slavery." He feared that "a stranger would . . . imagine that slavery is the only sacred thing in the United States—whilst Religion, Law and Liberty are only of consequence as they are made subservient to the establishment of the most odious slavery and despotism."[84] But Thacher took no public lead in defense of Foster's report and did not fight Madison's amendments to Section Two.

In this, Thacher and others merely reflected the views of their

[80] Jeremiah Hill to George Thacher, undated, Chamberlain Collection, George Thacher Papers (Boston Public Library, Boston, Mass.).
[81] John Pemberton to James Pemberton, February 23, 1790, *PASP*.
[82] Thacher to Warner Mifflin, June 12, 1790, George Thacher Papers (Massachusetts Historical Society).
[83] Mifflin to Thacher, May 5, 1790, Chamberlain Collection, George Thacher Papers.
[84] Thacher to Hezekiah Rogers, March 21, 1790, George Thacher Papers, MHS.

constituents, many of whom believed that antislavery harmed assumption. John Adams tried to convince friends that the problem of slavery and the loss of assumption were not connected, but the events occurred so closely in time that the public understandably perceived a causal relationship.[85] Nathaniel Gorham, who had helped prepare the Constitution, was annoyed that the antislavery petitions were "so zealously pushed in the infancy of the government and at a time when . . . they ought to have avoided everything that would tend to irritate." He reported to Theodore Sedgwick and Henry Knox, secretary of war, that New Englanders "who feel very sore upon the loss of the assumption, attribute it in a great measure to this Negro Business."[86] In the same letter in which Oliver Wolcott, Sr., expressed racist views he also argued that antislavery was an issue that interfered with the interests of New England. The slave trade was "scandalous," but it was more important to "take care of ourselves first—"[87] Stephen Higginson complained that the "antifederalists" were using the situation to prove that effective republican government could not be established beyond the geographical limits of Connecticut.[88] Tench Coxe, who had become assistant secretary of the Treasury, agreed that antislavery harmed the success of economic reforms. Until economic problems were solved the issue of slavery should be avoided. Coxe knew that different views on slavery had arisen during ratification and feared that sectionalism would now delay agreement on economic issues, preventing creation of a national economy.[89]

Interestingly, historians have always understood the southern position on slavery and the slave trade as an expression of special-interest politics. This was clearly the case with James Jackson and William Loughton Smith, who fought to protect Georgia's and South Carolina's peculiar interests. It was also the case with the Virginians, whose interests were strongly connected with the continuation of slavery but not of the slave trade. Thus, John Page found himself in political trouble at home because his constituents believed that at one point in the debate he had "advocated the abolition of slavery by Congress."[90] In a short circular letter clarifying his actions Page insisted he had done nothing which would deprive any Virginian of his slaves. Slavery was the basis of his own subsis-

---

[85] Adams to Thomas Crafts, May 25, 1790, Adams Papers.

[86] Gorham to Sedgwick, April 18, 1790, Sedgwick Papers; Gorham to Knox, April 17, 1790, Knox Papers.

[87] Oliver Wolcott, Sr., to Oliver Wolcott, Jr., April 23, 1790, Wolcott Papers.

[88] Higginson to Oliver Wolcott, Jr., May 6, 1790, ibid.

[89] Coxe to James Madison, March 31, 1790, James Madison Papers (Manuscript Division, Library of Congress, Washington, D. C.); Cooke, Tench Coxe, 109, 145-49.

[90] St. George Tucker to Page, March 29, 1790, PASP.

tence, he noted, and he opposed any action which would create "confusion and ruin." Misrepresenting the antislavery petitions, he claimed that they raised only the question of the slave trade. And he expressed his belief that no government, not even Virginia's, had the power to emancipate slaves. To certify his defense of slavery he also published endorsements by Aedanus Burke and Thomas Tudor Tucker who vouched for his proslavery behavior in Congress. Burke affirmed that "in public and private I have heard his sentiments . . . and think him to be as strenuous in securing to the holders [of] that kind of property as anyone in Congress."[91]

Madison, too, was pursuing special-interest politics in the spring of 1790. During the debate Madison wrote Edmund Randolph that the political situation was perfect for obtaining "an assertion of the powers of Congs. [along with] a recognition of the restraints imposed . . ." on Congress.[92] Northerners could not afford to lose southern support for Hamilton's report by fighting for the antislavery sections of Foster's report. Madison's amendments to the slavery report were a reflection of his constituents' view. They were "as favourable as the proprietors of that species of property could have expected considering the great dereliction to Slavery in a large part of this Union."[93] While the debate itself had raised fears and lessened confidence in Congress, the final amended report satisfied public opinion in Virginia.[94] Further, by manipulating the situation so as to delay the final vote on assumption until North Carolina representatives arrived in New York, Madison advanced another of Virginia's interests, the defeat of assumption.

The reason that historians have failed to understand that northerners, too, were engaged in special-interest politics in 1790 on this issue is that they have looked at the issue entirely in terms of slavery versus antislavery. When, however, the added factor of the North's desire for assumption is understood one can see the role of interest politics in shaping the new republic's policy toward slavery. Many northerners were antislavery and very possibly at another time might have taken the lead in pressing for Foster's report in its original form. In the spring of 1790, however, the issue had become complicated for northerners by the appearance of another issue

[91] "To the FREEHOLDERS of the DISTRICT OF ESSEX," Richmond Virginia Independent Chronicle, August 11, 1790.

[92] Madison to Randolph, March 21, 1790, Gaillard Hunt, ed., The Writings of James Madison: Comprising His Public Papers and His Private Correspondence . . . (9 vols., New York, 1900–1910), VI, 9.

[93] George Washington to David Stuart, June 15, 1790, Fitzpatrick, ed., The Writings of George Washington, XXXI, 52.

[94] Adam Stephen to Madison, April 25, 1790; Edward Carrington to Madison, April 7, 1790, Madison Papers.

which had for them a greater and more immediate importance—assumption. They chose to extend federal power over the debts of the states instead of over domestic slavery.

One reason for the abolitionists' failure to convince northerners that antislavery should be an immediate priority of the new republic lay in their own eighteenth-century view of politics. That view stressed individual conscience over interest and practicality and harmony over faction. Warner Mifflin, for instance, believed that republican representatives should act according to their "conscience and judgment." They should not "induce one member of a legislature to promote any matter contrary to his judgment but that after a proper investigation of facts he should vote as was consistent with his judgment, let it please or displease . . . ."[95] Abolitionist petitions tended to be supplications to do justice instead of requests loaded with arguments that would appeal to a congressman's practical interests. During the debate Mifflin repeatedly assured the representatives that he wanted to preserve "the Harmony of Government." To maintain this approach, however, required the demonstration that antislavery was a fundamental national interest. Mifflin even tried to convince William L. Smith of South Carolina "that we were embarked in the same bottom with them; that the objective of the movement was to promote the peace of families, the peace of neighborhoods, and surely the peace of the Government . . . ."[96] This view of politics made it difficult for abolitionists to organize their activity in a politically effective way. Mifflin spent too much time trying to convert Smith instead of mustering a majority against him. He sought political harmony without fully recognizing that he was functioning as a lobbyist with a special interest.

Abolitionists were also unable to define their goals in modern political terms. Mifflin believed that his "concern" for antislavery arose "from apprehension of the duty to Him that made me." It was impossible to convince legislators who were cultural products of the American Enlightenment to act merely for religious reasons, yet Mifflin's antislavery thought was fundamentally religious. The liberation of slaves would be, he thought, "of greater advantage to the Master than to the slave . . . ." Slavery was an offense to God, but "true Liberty came to a society only when God was pleased."[97] Thus, these abolitionists were ill-suited for the task of defining the

[95] Mifflin to William Tilghman, February 24, 1789, William Tilghman Papers, Etting Collection (Historical Society of Pennsylvania).
[96] Mifflin to Benjamin Rush, June 19, 1790, Cox-Parrish-Wharton Papers.
[97] Mifflin to William Tilghman, February 24, 1789, Tilghman Papers.

new nation's goals. They were psychologically vulnerable because they had not developed a political mentality which prepared them for secular interest politics of a modern nation.

Nevertheless, the abolitionists would have had a majority, if northerners had united in support of the antislavery assumptions of Foster's report. Numerous factors shaped their decision not to do so: their fundamental belief in the protection of private property, their desire to maintain sectional harmony, and surely their racist attitudes towards the Afro-American. But the issue in 1790 was ultimately determined by political priorities. John Sullivan from Massachusetts complained to Elbridge Gerry, who had sat on Foster's committee, "That Congress should think of a permanent place of residence, or of quakers or negros, before they had settled their system of finance, and settled it upon principle, is a galling thing to the men who love the honor of the nation and delight in those sentiments which lead to purity of politicks and the love of freedom."[98] Obviously, Sullivan's and other northern conceptions of national honor and "freedom" in 1790 differed fundamentally from Mifflin's understanding of "true liberty."

The 1790 discussion of the slavery issue was an important event in the history of antislavery politics. It established what William M. Wiecek has called the "federal consensus." The debate made explicit for the first time the policy that "only the states could abolish or in any way regulate slavery within their jurisdictions," and "the federal government had no power over slavery in the states."[99] This policy had not been settled in the Constitutional Convention. It was declared in the second session of the First Congress. At least the abolitionists could take hope in the fact that Congress did not declare it must protect slavery.

As republicanism helps one to understand why Americans accepted slavery in a society dedicated to freedom, special-interest politics helps one to understand why congressmen who claimed to be antislavery accepted slavery as they constructed a modern political system bound together by economic self-interest. The belief of northern congressmen that the national government should foster economic stability and growth created a functional relationship between slavery and economic measures. In 1790, as later, the price of economic development was to ignore the antislavery thrust of the American Revolution. The political priorities of northerners in 1790

---

[98] John Sullivan to Gerry, [July] 18, 1790, as quoted in Betty L. Fladeland, "Compensated Emancipation: A Rejected Alternative," *Journal of Southern History,* XLII (May 1976), 171–72.

[99] Wiecek, *The Sources of Antislavery Constitutionalism,* 16.

encouraged them to avoid the question of slavery in order to obtain intersectional support for Hamilton's Report on Public Credit. The tendency of the national government to ignore slavery continued until a later generation of northerners constructed their own anti-slavery view of the Constitution. That development, like the conflict in 1790, would also be shaped by the way northerners perceived and integrated their economic self-interests with attitudes toward slavery.[100]

[100] Eric Foner, *Free Soil, Free Labor, Free Men: The Ideology of the Republican Party Before the Civil War* (New York, 1970).

Protecting the Frontiers:
Defense Policy and the Tariff Question in the
First Washington Administration

Gerard Clarfield*

O N December 5, 1791, Alexander Hamilton presented his Report on Manufactures to the House of Representatives. Three months later a bill for the implementation of certain aspects of this important proposal began a troubled journey through Congress. The result was the Tariff of 1792, another in the string of legislative successes that marked Hamilton's career as secretary of the Treasury. It is surprising that the political contest over the enactment of this tariff has never been detailed, for the Federalist period has long been an attractive area of historical investigation. Moreover, the victory did not come easily. The struggle of Hamilton and his congressional supporters with the emerging opposition led by James Madison was so bitter that by the time Congress adjourned in May 1792 Hamilton was in an extremely agitated mental and emotional state. In a long and revealing letter to Virginia's Edward Carrington he explained that for some time, in spite of differences that had developed between them, he had been unwilling to believe that Madison was really his political enemy. "It was not till the last session," he wrote, that certain events had forced him to the reluctant conclusion that Madison, together with Thomas Jefferson, headed a faction that was *decidedly hostile to me and my administration.*"[1]

According to Hamilton, two events proved decisive in convincing him of the enmity of the Virginians. Of secondary importance were some

* Mr. Clarfield is a member of the Department of History, University of Missouri–Columbia. He wishes to thank the Research Council of the University of Missouri for research support.

[1] Alexander Hamilton to Edward Carrington, May 26, 1792, in Harold C. Syrett and Jacob E. Cooke, eds., *The Papers of Alexander Hamilton* (New York, 1961-   ), XI, 429, hereafter cited as *Hamilton Papers*. This extraordinary letter has received a great deal of attention. See, for example, Irving Brant, *James Madison: Father of the Constitution, 1787-1800* (Indianapolis, 1950), 351-353, and Dumas Malone, *Jefferson and His Time*, II: *Jefferson and the Rights of Man* (Boston, 1951), 453-456.

"insidious insinuations" that Madison had made late in the session relating to Hamilton's probity in handling certain Treasury Department funds.[2] Of far greater consequence was an issue that was curiously related to the tariff question. Hamilton charged that although the responsibility was clearly his under the law, Madison had offered constitutional objections to a House resolution requesting a Treasury Department report on ways and means of funding a forthcoming military expedition against the western Indian tribes. Specifically, Madison had argued that the doctrine of separation of powers forbade the executive branch to interfere in the legislative process in this way. The issue was so significant, Hamilton continued, that had the House supported Madison, he would have been compelled to resign.[3]

Hamilton's letter to Carrington was not designed to be a balanced recounting of the troublesome events of the congressional session just concluded. It was in the nature of a lawyer's brief, and its object (it was in all likelihood intended for selective circulation) was to encourage Hamilton's sympathizers in the Old Dominion to organize politically in his behalf. A partisan document, it revealed only one fragment of an extended political contest that took place in the House of Representatives during the first session of the Second Congress.[4]

As Hamilton alleged, Madison had made a nearly successful attempt to limit the extensive powers of the Treasury Department. Afterward, however, Hamilton turned the tables. He used an unrelated but important political issue—the question of an increase in army appropriations that arose after Gen. Arthur St. Clair's humiliating defeat in November 1791 at the hands of the western Indians—to force the passage of the tariff. These closely related issues produced one of the most important legislative confrontations of that session of Congress.

To gain perspective on the politics of the tariff question it is useful to begin at an unexpected point, with an analysis of public attitudes toward the Indian war that had been going on intermittently since the end of the Revolution. Originally the warring tribes had been members of the Iroquois Confederacy. After the War for Independence, however, the old confederacy fragmented. Contemptuous of American military power and embittered by the unscrupulous attempts at land grabbing that characterized federal Indian policy during the Confederation period,

---

[2] Hamilton to Carrington, May 26, 1792, *Hamilton Papers*, XI, 434.
[3] *Ibid.*, 432-433; Malone, *Jefferson and the Rights of Man*, 437-438.
[4] Malone, *Jefferson and the Rights of Man*, 453-456.

the Shawnee, Chippewa, Miami, Wabash, Wyandot, and several other western tribes broke with the Six Nations, sought to form their own confederacy, and insisted on the right to an Ohio River boundary. In asserting that claim, they carried on a constant border war with the Virginians and Kentuckians who lived along the Ohio, as well as with the whites who dwelled north and west of the river in what is now southern Ohio.[5]

The war itself had never enjoyed widespread popularity, but until the St. Clair debacle criticism had been muted. In its aftermath, however, the opposition grew strident. According to one view, if whites could be restrained from violating established boundaries and killing innocent Indians, the problem would disappear. It would be far more just, said one congressman, to "check the roving disposition" of frontier settlers than to continue the war. He urged Congress to force western Americans to remain on lands clearly within the boundaries of the United States and develop communities that would contribute to the strength and well-being of the nation, instead of provoking the Indians and involving the country in wars that could not be won.[6] This sentiment was widely expressed. Oliver Wolcott of Connecticut, for example, confessed his willingness to see America's "white savages" governed as were her blacks if that was what was required to bring peace to the area.[7]

While some blamed the frontiersmen for the continuing warfare, others held the Washington administration primarily responsible. The War Department was even accused of practicing genocide. The war's real purpose, one newspaper essayist alleged, was to "extirpate" the Indians in order to take their lands.[8] St. Clair's defeat, a writer in the *Connecticut Courant* observed, was not the cause of the sudden expression of national

---

[5] Reginald Horsman, *Expansion and American Indian Policy, 1783-1812* (East Lansing, Mich., 1967), 84-96; Francis Paul Prucha, *The Sword of the Republic: The United States Army on the Frontier, 1783-1846* (New York, 1969), 17-20; Anthony F. C. Wallace, *The Death and Rebirth of the Seneca* (New York, 1970), 154-159. Before their victory over St. Clair the Indians would in all likelihood have accepted a less advantageous boundary. The altered battlefield situation of early 1792, however, made them overconfident. See Reginald Horsman, *Matthew Elliott, British Indian Agent* (Detroit, 1964), 66-67.

[6] [*Annals of Congress*] *Debates and Proceedings in the Congress of the United States, 1789-1824* (Washington, D. C., 1834-1856), 2d Cong., 1st sess., Jan. 26, 1792, 338, hereafter cited as *Annals of Congress*. During this particular debate the stenographer did not identify the speaker by name.

[7] Oliver Wolcott, Sr., to Oliver Wolcott, Jr., Mar. 3, 1792, in George Gibbs, ed., *Memoirs of the Administrations of Washington and John Adams*, I (New York, 1846), 75.

[8] *National Gazette* (Philadelphia), Jan. 9, 1792.

discontent. It had simply focused public attention on what had been from the start an immoral and unjustifiable war.[9]

A North Carolina senator, Benjamin Hawkins, deeply aroused by the injustice of the war, saw other dangerous tendencies emerging from its continuance. In a letter to President George Washington he charged that continued fighting on the frontier was part of a War Department conspiracy to create a large standing army and to make profits for the contractors who did business with Secretary of War Henry Knox. This, Hawkins alleged, explained why the administration had made only the most "feeble" efforts to negotiate a settlement. The men who made policy, as well as "all who are dependent on the department," were "for war."[10] "Braddock," a critic of the war whose pen name had obvious connotations and whose essays, published originally in the *Boston Independent Chronicle*, gained wide notoriety, made the same point. In a remark pointedly directed at the obese Knox, he warned Americans not to allow a "few ambitious, 'overgrown' individuals to force a continuation of the war."[11]

Not all of those who demanded an end to the fighting did so from moral conviction. Many land speculators with holdings on the Pennsylvania and New York frontiers also urged a cessation to hostilities. These men were strange bedfellows for those who attacked the war as immoral and unjust, but they were powerful allies nonetheless. As early as March 1791 Rufus King reported to Hamilton that speculators all over the northeast were unhappy about the protracted warfare. To that point the Six Nations had stayed out of the fighting, but who could say how long they would remain neutral? If they joined in the war, hundreds of warriors would be loosed on New York and Pennsylvania. This, he warned, would "break up our whole frontier" and drive land values down. King thought that the war should only be continued if there were no other way of gaining a permanent settlement, and under no circumstances should it be allowed to go on beyond the summer of 1791.[12] In early 1792, however, the war was by no means over. In fact, the American situation had grown worse, and some northeastern speculators were more concerned than ever.

---

[9] *Connecticut Courant* (Hartford), Jan. 16, 1792. This article was reprinted in the *Natl. Gaz.*, Jan. 26, 1792.

[10] Benjamin Hawkins to George Washington, Feb. 10, 1792, Washington Papers, Presidential Microfilm Edition, Ser. IV, reel 101, Library of Congress, hereafter cited as Washington Papers. Although Hawkins left Washington himself out of the supposed conspiracy, the chief executive was furious at these allegations. See Washington's memorandum for a reply to Hawkins, Feb. [?], 1792, *ibid.*

[11] *Philadelphia Aurora*, Jan. 4, 1792.

[12] Rufus King to Hamilton, Mar. 24, 1791, *Hamilton Papers*, VIII, 213.

Charles Stevenson, a British army officer who visited New York City in early 1792, was deeply impressed by the strength of the antiwar sentiment there. The situation, he reported to Lt. Gov. John Graves Simcoe of Upper Canada, offered Britain a remarkable political opportunity. Public sentiment was running so strongly against the war, he wrote, that in all likelihood the government would be forced to settle with the western tribes on terms that would leave them in control of the entire area northwest of the Ohio, including the disputed northwestern posts. Should the administration insist on continuing the war, he thought it quite possible that the United States might simply disintegrate.[13] Although in this and other ways Stevenson's judgments were off the mark, even Knox admitted that a great majority of the American people was strongly opposed to the continuation of the war, at least until further efforts at negotiation had been attempted.[14]

Although on balance national public opinion seems to have been heavily weighted against the war, there was nevertheless a significant minority viewpoint. In Pennsylvania, for example, Hugh Henry Brackenridge, an influential spokesman for that state's western settlers, was only one of several who published essays supporting continued military action.[15] Even Philip Freneau, whose National Gazette served as the vehicle for numerous antiwar statements, endorsed administration militancy, calling upon the government to take decisive steps to "check the progress of savage desperation."[16]

In the South, supporters of the war were more numerous, especially in Virginia, Kentucky, South Carolina, and Georgia. Jefferson, Madison, and Washington had their differences, but the three Virginians agreed that the Indians would have to be defeated if peace were to be permanently established on the frontier.[17] Virginia's governor, Henry Lee, agreed. After St. Clair's defeat he wrote Washington urging that another and

[13] Charles Stevenson to J. G. Simcoe, Jan. 3, 7, 1792, in E. A. Cruikshank, ed., The Correspondence of Lieut. Governor John Graves Simcoe, I (Toronto, 1923), 95-96, 100-101.

[14] Henry Knox to Anthony Wayne, Sept. 7, 1792, in Richard C. Knopf, Anthony Wayne, A Name in Arms: The Wayne-Knox-Pickering-McHenry Correspondence (Pittsburgh, 1960), 83-86.

[15] Natl. Gaz., Feb. 2, 13, 1792.

[16] Ibid., Jan. 23, 1792.

[17] Thomas Jefferson to James Monroe, Apr. 17, 1791, in Paul Leicester Ford, ed., The Writings of Thomas Jefferson (New York, 1892-1899), V, 319, hereafter cited as Writings of Jefferson; James Madison to Edmund Pendleton, Jan. 21, 1792, Madison Papers, Presidential Microfilm Ed., Ser. I, reel 4, Lib. Cong., hereafter cited as Madison Papers; Washington's memorandum for a projected letter to Hawkins, Feb. [?] 1792, Washington Papers, Ser. IV, reel 101.

more powerful army be promptly sent against the Indians.[18] Such important South Carolina leaders as Gov. William Moultrie and Gen. Charles C. Pinckney added their voices to a chorus of southerners who urged continued war.[19]

The reason for this southern endorsement of the war is obvious: it was being fought along the Kentucky and Virginia borders. The fifteen hundred men, women, and children whom Knox reported to have been slain by Indians before 1790 were almost all from these regions.[20] Farther south, the frontier was menaced by the Cherokees, Creeks, Choctaws, and Chickasaws, powerful enemies who might spread the war if the more northerly tribes were not first checked.[21]

Southern support notwithstanding, the public outcry against the war rocked the administration. Washington even took the unusual step of going directly to the people for support, instructing Knox to issue a rebuttal to the critics of administration policy.[22] The president remained convinced that the only way to arrive at a settlement with the western tribes was to crush them militarily. This, however, would require a substantial increase in the size of the army. Although many, including Secretary of State Jefferson, advised it, Washington refused to consider relying on western militiamen to do the fighting. His Revolutionary War experiences had left him with little regard for part-time soldiers. Moreover, the Treasury Department believed that in the long run paying western militia to do the fighting would be more expensive and bring less decisive results than enlarging the army for two or three years.[23]

---

[18] Henry Lee to Washington, Dec [?] 1791, Washington Papers, Ser. IV, reel 101.

[19] William Moultrie to Washington, Dec. 29, 1792, Charles C. Pinckney to Washington, Jan. 8, 1792, *ibid.*

[20] *Annals of Congress*, 2d Cong., 1st sess., 345-346. See also "The Causes of the Existing Hostilities Between the United States and Certain Tribes of Indians," Jan. 26, 1792, *ibid.*, 1046-1052.

[21] Lee to Washington, Dec. 1791, Pinckney to Washington, Jan. 8, 1792, Washington Papers. Both men predicted that the war would expand to include the southern Indians in 1792. See also a report from Charleston in the *Natl. Gaz.*, Mar. 5, 1792. The Cherokees were described as celebrating wildly over news of St. Clair's defeat. Freneau explained that a "universal prejudice against us is taking place among the Indian Nations."

[22] Washington to Knox, Jan. 16, 1792, Washington Papers, Ser. II, reel 35.

[23] O. Wolcott, Jr., to O. Wolcott, Sr., Feb. 14, 1792, in Gibbs, ed., *Memoirs,* I, 73. See also the substance of a conversation between Hamilton and Col. George Beckwith on May 15, 1792. Hamilton told Beckwith that he believed that the western settlers actually wanted the war to continue for some time. They had "interested motives," he said, "as an Indian war leads to the spending money in their country as well as to the gratification of their individual resentments." *Hamilton Papers,* VIII, 343.

On January 18, 1792, Washington sent Knox to the House of Representatives with a confidential report relating to the progress of the Indian war and proposing a large increase in the army. According to John Steele, a North Carolina congressman, a "warm debate" followed. An informal vote taken at the end of the first day's discussion indicated that a substantial majority in the House would support the administration. Steele, who was especially anxious to arrange the repeal of the excise on whiskey, was furious. If the army were enlarged, current revenues would be insufficient to meet increased costs. Under such circumstances, there would be little likelihood of repealing the excise tax. Most irritating to Steele was the fact that so many southern congressmen, who agreed that the whiskey excise ought to go, nevertheless supported the army.[24]

Acting promptly on Knox's recommendations, the House appointed a committee to draft legislation for augmenting the army. A few days later, on January 25, Madison, acting for the committee, submitted a bill "for making further provision for the protection of the frontier."[25] This proposal authorized the president to bring the tiny regular army, one battalion of artillery and two regiments of infantry, up to full strength. It also projected the recruitment of three new regiments of infantry to be made up entirely of three-year volunteers. Although the total would still be small, fewer than six thousand men, these additions would more than double the size of the army.[26]

Opposition to the proposal developed quickly. Antiwar congressmen moved an amendment deleting the bill's critical second section that authorized the three new regiments. They defended their position with a powerful array of moral, ideological, and practical arguments reflecting the wide range of antiwar sentiment in the country. They also made a good deal of the extraordinary costs entailed by such a large army. The public would be outraged, one congressman charged, by such an expense, especially since the size of the proposed army was out of all proportion to its ostensible purpose. In his public defense of administration policy Knox had incorrectly described the hostile Indians on the frontier as a rabble, a gathering of outcasts from their tribes. It was "strange policy," this lawmaker argued, to raise between five and six

---

[24] John Steele to Joseph Winston, Jan. 22, 1792, in H. M. Wagstaff, ed., *The Papers of John Steele*, I (Raleigh, N. C., 1924), 82-83.

[25] *Natl. Gaz.*, Jan. 30, 1792. The *Gaz.* named Madison as the man who reported the bill to the House.

[26] *Annals of Congress*, 2d Cong., 1st sess., 1343-1346. The three additional regiments were to be kept in service until the end of the Indian war or for three years, whichever came first.

thousand men to oppose such a handful of "Indian banditti." Surely, he hinted darkly, that could not be the real reason the administration was seeking so large an increase. The government, he continued, was "preparing to squander away money by millions," yet "no one, except those who are in the secrets of the Cabinet, knows for what reason the war has been thus carried on for three years."[27]

Although Madison did not speak in opposition to the amendment, two Virginia congressmen, both closely aligned with him, did. Alexander White and Andrew Moore denied that the administration had any ulterior motives in seeking to increase the army. A much larger force was patently needed to win the war. Using information provided by the War Department, White and Moore rebutted the charge that the war was the result of white aggression. The Indians, they insisted, were clearly at fault. Moreover, there was no truth to the criticism that the government had failed to make serious efforts to negotiate an end to the war. The Indians simply did not want peace; they would continue their attacks on the frontier until they were defeated militarily. Under the circumstances, there was no choice but to carry the war to its inevitable conclusion. As to the expense, Moore and White admitted that the excise tax on whiskey might have to be increased. They insisted, however, that one could not stop to measure costs when the lives of American citizens were at stake.[28]

It was, all things considered, a remarkable debate. The excise tax was one of the most unpopular features of Hamilton's developing "system." Madisonian congressmen and the opposition press attacked it regularly. Yet on this occasion roles were reversed. Madisonians in the House urged the expansion of the army and suggested that the excise be raised to pay for it, while antiwar congressmen, many of whom supported the administration's economic program, opposed the plan. In the upshot, the amendment to delete section two of Madison's bill was easily defeated, 34 votes to 18, by a coalition made up primarily of southern and Middle Atlantic representatives. Seventeen of the majority votes, including Madison's, came from southern states, while only seven southern congressmen voted for the amendment.[29] With the exception of North Carolina, whose

[27] Ibid., 342-343. The debates on this issue are recorded in such a manner as to make it impossible to learn more than the names of the congressmen who spoke and the side that they took on the amendment. There is no way of telling precisely which of the several congressmen who spoke on this side of the issue made these particular remarks.

[28] Ibid., 345-346.

[29] Ibid., 354-355. Significantly, 9 of the 13 New England congressmen who

five-man delegation unanimously supported the amendment, almost the entire southern contingent in the House enthusiastically endorsed the augmentation of the army.[30]

In the Senate the bill ran into further stiff resistance. As in the House, the opposition focused on the crucial second section. In this instance, however, instead of attempting to delete it, the bill's critics introduced an amendment that would have required the administration to use the militia instead of raising more men for the regular army. This was a proposal that many southerners could and did support. As a result, the sectional divisions that had been evident in the House failed to materialize in the Senate.[31]

The opposing sides were evenly matched in the debate on the Senate amendment. According to Jefferson, who favored using the militia rather than expanding the army, supporters of the amendment managed at one point to win passage. On reconsideration, however, one senator changed his vote and the amendment was lost.[32] Henry Knox, who watched the progress of the bill with great concern, made no mention of the passage of the amendment in his report to Washington. He did, however, emphasize the critical importance of Aaron Burr's vote to the administration's success. According to Knox, the New York senator had been miffed because the administration had not given its support to an earlier unidentified piece of legislation that he had introduced. He was therefore not inclined to support an increase in the army. It was only with great difficulty that the amendment's opponents managed to persuade him to change sides. At that, he only consented to join the opposition after it was agreed that the number of men in each of the three new regiments—"already too few," according to Knox—should be cut from 960 to 912.[33]

---

voted on this measure supported the amendment.

[30] The views of the North Carolina delegation are nowhere fully stated. The delegation's attitude, however, was probably influenced strongly by the fact that the state had no frontier problem. It may well be that this, combined with the certainty that the excise tax could not be repealed if the army were enlarged, motivated the North Carolinians. John Steele, the only one of the state's delegates whose views are recorded, opposed the enlargement of the army on just these grounds. He was not opposed to the war per se. He hoped, however, to force the administration to use less expensive militiamen to do the fighting. For Steele's views see *ibid.*, Dec. 20, 28, 1792, 750, 762-768. Benjamin Hawkins, a senator from North Carolina, fully expressed his feelings in the very provocative letter to Washington cited in n. 9.

[31] *Annals of Congress*, 2d Cong., 1st sess., 89, 90-93.

[32] Jefferson to Archibald Stuart, Mar. 14, 1792, *Writings of Jefferson*, V, 454.

[33] Knox to Washington, Feb. 18, 1792, Washington Papers, Ser. IV, reel 101. The agreement to reduce the size of each new regiment evidently broke down later. The

Having doubled the army, Congress next came to consider means of paying for it. At that point the issue of frontier defense became the vehicle for a continuation of the legislative dueling already characteristic of relations between Madisonians and Hamiltonians in the House.

A previous report from the Treasury Department made it clear that an enlarged army would require increased federal revenues.[34] On March 7, 1792, a resolution was therefore introduced in the House asking the president to direct Hamilton to provide legislative recommendations. House rules prohibited the executive branch from submitting bills or unsolicited reports to Congress. But if the House asked a cabinet officer's opinion, an opportunity was created for executive leadership in the legislative process. This was especially true with regard to the Treasury Department. The House in 1792 had no Committee on Ways and Means to originate money bills. Instead, Hamilton's office was charged with the responsibility for making financial estimates and advising the House on methods of raising new revenues and otherwise meeting its financial obligations.[35] Hamilton had used this authority during the First Congress to originate far-ranging and controversial legislative proposals. Select committees of the House, responding to Hamilton's leadership, had drafted bills that reflected his ideas, and a cooperative Congress had enacted these into law.[36]

The resolution of March 7, which was in effect an invitation to Hamilton once again to provide legislative leadership, touched off an intense debate in which Madison led the opposition. Hamilton noted that during most of the Second Congress, Madison had not taken a leading role in House debates. On this occasion, however, he was clearly visible. The secretary of the Treasury thought he understood why. "My overthrow was anticipated as certain and Mr. Madison, *laying aside his*

---

law called for regiments of 960 men exclusive of officers. See *Annals of Congress,* 2d Cong., 1st sess., 1343-1346.

[34] "Report of the Treasury Department on Reduction of the Public Debt," Jan. 23, 1792, *ibid.,* 1059-1070.

[35] Ralph Volney Harlow, *The History of Legislative Methods in the Period Before 1825* (New Haven, Conn., 1917), 132; Joseph Cooper, "Jeffersonian Attitudes Toward Executive Leadership and Committee Development," *Western Political Quarterly,* XVII (1965), 47-49.

[36] Hamilton's influence in Congress cannot be precisely gauged. Ralph Harlow, however, suggests that he was very influential. Basing his analysis on isolated entries in Sen. William Maclay, *The Journal of William Maclay: United States Senator from Pennsylvania, 1789-1791* (New York, 1927), Harlow concluded that Hamilton could control the legislative process from beginning to end. "Congress may go home," Maclay once wrote. "Mr. Hamilton is all-powerful, and fails in nothing he attempts." Harlow, *History of Legislative Methods,* 141-145.

wonted caution, boldly led his troops as he imagined to a certain victory."[37]

Although he was being a bit melodramatic, Hamilton was quite right. Madison hoped to convince a majority in the House to reject executive leadership in the framing of legislation. If this could be accomplished, Hamilton's influence in the House would be sharply reduced. The idea was enticing because a strong argument could be made that current practices were in violation of the principle of the separation of powers. The Maryland congressman, John Mercer, thought even more was at stake. He believed that in accepting Hamilton's leadership the House was actually surrendering "the power of the purse" to the executive.[38]

There were indications that some congressmen who in the past had supported Hamilton's financial policies might now be brought to endorse the opposition's view on the constitutional question. On January 2, 1792, a full two months before the debate exploded on the House floor, Jefferson had explored this possibility over dinner with two congressmen, Thomas Fitzsimons of Pennsylvania and Elbridge Gerry of Massachusetts. Both men agreed that Treasury Department leadership in the origination of economic legislation violated the principle of the separation of powers and ought to be stopped. The secretary of state came away from this meeting optimistic about the chances for cutting Hamilton's direct line to the House.[39]

Jefferson's memorandum on this conversation suggests a certain casual air, as though it came about almost by accident. This may have been so. Yet Jefferson could hardly have selected two more ideal subjects for such a discussion. Neither Fitzsimons nor Gerry was firmly in the Hamiltonian camp, although both tended to support Hamilton on important economic questions. Moreover, both men had played leading roles in earlier congressional attempts to frame economic legislation independently, without recourse to executive leadership. Gerry had been the chairman of the first temporary committee organized to "report estimates of expenditures" to the House. Fitzsimons chaired the committee that succeeded Gerry's, until that too was disbanded, its duties taken over by the Treasury Department in September 1789. Finally, in January 1790 Gerry had led the opposition that defeated Hamilton's attempts to take the floor of the House in person to explain and defend his Report on the Public Credit.[40]

[37] Hamilton to Carrington, May 26, 1792, *Hamilton Papers*, XI, 433.

[38] *Annals of Congress*, 2d Cong., 1st sess., 349-351.

[39] Jefferson's memorandum, Mar. 10, 1792, Jefferson Papers, microfilm, reel 25, Lib. Cong., hereafter cited as Jefferson Papers; Malone, *Jefferson and the Rights of Man*, 438.

[40] Patrick J. Furlong, "The Origin of the House Committee of Ways and

Madison's speech in opposition to the March 7 resolution is unfortunately not recorded in the *Annals of Congress*. But Theodore Sedgwick, the Massachusetts Federalist, summarized it in a speech defending executive leadership. Madison was in an awkward position. In 1789, during the debate on the bill establishing the Treasury Department, he had been on the other side of this argument. He had then supported a proposal to vest Hamilton with the power "to report financial plans to Congress on his own initiative."[41] Because of his earlier endorsement of such wide-ranging executive power, Madison was anxious to convince his congressional colleagues that he was not being inconsistent. His argument, as summarized by Sedgwick, was at best weak. He insisted that during the 1789 debates he had never intended that the secretary of the Treasury should do more than report facts and provide information for Congress to act upon. Hamilton, he alleged, had gone far beyond this by actually suggesting in his reports the form that legislation should take. According to Sedgwick, Madison contended that in order to preserve the integrity of the House while utilizing the expertise of the secretary of the Treasury, it was necessary first for the House to call on the secretary for a statement of the facts of a given economic situation, nothing more. Then it was up to the House to decide its own course, without executive guidance. Finally, the proposed legislation should be sent back to the Treasury Department, but only for advice on how best to implement it. Strictly speaking, Madison was not attacking Hamilton; he was simply defending the Constitution. In effect, however, he was proposing a vast reduction in the power of the Treasury Department to influence the legislative process.[42]

As Congressman Steele later pointed out, the Madisonian argument was marred by inconsistency. The same men who were then attacking the Treasury Department's right to make legislative recommendations on the ground that to do so would violate the principle of the separation of powers had, only a short while before, moved quickly to accommodate

---

Means," *William and Mary Quarterly*, 3d Ser., XXV (1968), 587-589; Cooper, "Jeffersonian Attitudes," *Western Political Qtly.*, XVII (1965), 47.

[41] *Annals of Congress*, 2d Cong., 1st sess., 439-440. On Feb. 28, 1792, only a few days before the debate on the Mar. 7 resolution began, Jefferson expressed his fears of Treasury Department power in a very frank conversation with Washington. He warned the president that Hamilton "possessed already such an influence as to swallow up the whole Executive powers, and even the future Presidents (not supported by the weight of character which himself possessed) would not be able to make head against this department." *Writings of Jefferson*, I, 174.

[42] *Annals of Congress*, 2d Cong., 1st sess., 439-440; Harlow, *History of Legislative Methods*, 129-134; Cooper, "Jeffersonian Attitudes," *Western Political Qtly.*, XVII (1965), 47.

Secretary of War Knox when he recommended the enlargement of the army.[43] Steele was quite right. At the time, although Madison and his friends insisted on the principle of legislative autonomy, they had no consistent approach to the question of executive participation in the framing of legislation. Their assault on the resolution of March 7 was primarily a political tactic. In future congresses they would be more consistent. After 1801, however, when executive power changed hands, they reversed themselves again. Jeffersonian executives would be intimately involved in the shaping of legislation.[44]

At the close of debate on March 7, Madison was sanguine about his chances for success. A majority in the House seemed to be falling into line behind him.[45] The constitutional issue had evidently attracted support. Hamilton, on the other hand, was nearly frantic. Had Madison won this vote, he later explained, "a certain consequence was my resignation." If stripped of his broad powers, he declared, he would have had no interest in making the "pecuniary sacrifices" or continuing the "life of extreme drudgery" required of him in government service.[46]

It was not until the debate actually began that Hamilton learned what Madison was planning. He was therefore reduced to last minute lobbying to avert defeat on this critical issue. These "measures of counteraction," as he referred to his activities on the evening of March 7, were successful. On the following day, when the vote was taken, Madison lost by the narrow margin of 31 to 27.[47]

It is seldom possible to piece together the behind-the-scenes arrangements that influence legislative decisions. In this instance, however, there is enough material to warrant some interesting speculations. Jefferson's analysis of the narrow defeat suggests that Hamilton managed to win the votes of some South Carolina congressmen who might otherwise have

[43] *Annals of Congress*, 2d Cong., 1st sess., 445-446.
[44] Noble E. Cunningham, Jr., *The Jeffersonian Republicans in Power: Party Operations, 1801-1809* (Chapel Hill, N. C., 1963), 94-100; Cooper, "Jeffersonian Attitudes," *Western Political Qtly.*, XVII (1965), 55-57.
[45] Jefferson's memorandum, Mar. 10, 1792, Jefferson Papers.
[46] Hamilton to Carrington, May 26, 1792, *Hamilton Papers*, XI, 433.
[47] *Annals of Congress*, 2d Cong., 1st sess., 452; Hamilton to Carrington, May 26, 1792, *Hamilton Papers*, XI, 433. Hamilton here states that he took steps to counteract Madison's attack. He does not, however, go into detail. Although it is never easy to trace the activities of a lobbyist, Hamilton evidently did his share. He admits it in his letter to Carrington. Jefferson discusses it in his memorandum of Mar. 10. Maclay noted the same sort of activity on another occasion in early 1790. According to the Pennsylvania senator, Hamilton was "uneasy" about the prospects of his funding plan. "He was here early to wait on the Speaker, and I believe spent most of his time in running from place to place among the members." *Journal*, 185.

supported Madison. South Carolina was particularly eager to see the further assumption of state debts by the federal government. Jefferson believed that the votes of at least two of that state's congressmen had been influenced by Hamilton's linking of the future of assumption to his continued ability to make legislative recommendations. He noted that Thomas Tudor Tucker, who was generally more sympathetic to Madison than to Hamilton, nevertheless voted for the resolution. Another South Carolinian, Thomas Sumter, did not vote at all. Although Sumter was almost always on Madison's side, on this occasion he left the House chamber at the time of the vote, "debauched for the moment," Jefferson thought, "because of the connection of the question with a further assumption." Several other unnamed· congressmen, Jefferson believed, also absented themselves because they found it politically inexpedient to oppose the resolution.[48]

Jefferson also took note of the strange behavior of Gerry, who supported Hamilton on this occasion. During the first day of the debate the Massachusetts congressman seemed to be securely in Madison's camp. His turnabout was especially confusing because he had a well-earned reputation as a strong defender of legislative autonomy and had only recently assured Jefferson that he believed that Treasury Department interference in the legislative process directly violated the principle of the separation of powers. What could have influenced Gerry? At the time Jefferson did not speculate. Later, however, John Page, a Virginia congressman, implied that an agreement had been reached by which votes on this issue were traded for a bill that subsequently passed, granting a federal subsidy to Massachusetts's ailing fishing industry.[49]

In spite of their narrow setback, neither Madison nor Jefferson was discouraged. They believed that the constitutional argument had made many converts. For example, all of Pennsylvania's delegates, Israel Jacobs excepted, had voted against the resolution; Hamilton had formerly been able to count on far better backing from that quarter. Furthermore, much of Hamilton's support had been the result of his ability to connect the vote to other important political issues. At some future time, when Hamilton had less leverage, a similar resolution might pass. On balance, both men felt that Hamilton had been "deeply wounded" by what had happened on March 7 and 8. The Treasury secretary's influence in Congress, Jefferson wrote, seemed to be "tottering." Another time it might collapse entirely.[50]

[48] Jefferson's memorandum, Mar. 10, 1792, Jefferson Papers.
[49] Ibid.; Annals of Congress, 2d Cong., 1st sess., 569.
[50] Jefferson's memorandum, Mar. 10, 1792, Jefferson Papers; Annals of Congress,

A few days after Madison's unsuccessful attack on the resolution of March 7, Hamilton took the political offensive. The government's sudden need for money stemmed from the passage of legislation that had been coauthored by Madison and strongly endorsed by many of his southern friends. None of this was lost on Hamilton, who knew a superb political opportunity when he saw one. Madison had attempted to block passage of the March 7 resolution in order to stop the secretary of the Treasury from making important legislative recommendations. Hamilton now pro-. posed to use the opportunity created by the resolution's passage to do just that.

During the debate on the bill "for the protection of the frontiers," Madisonian congressmen had proposed an increase in the excise tax as one method of funding the augmented army. Benjamin Goodhue of Massachusetts, a devoted Hamiltonian, had at the same time suggested borrowing the money.[51] On March 16 Hamilton made his own recommendations. His report began with some good financial news. Despite the extraordinary expenses caused by the Indian war, the last quarter of 1791 had produced greater revenues than had been expected, creating a federal surplus of $150,000. Unfortunately, however, the enlarged army would require an extra $525,000. There were, Hamilton went on, three ways to raise the funds. The government could sell its stock in the Bank of the United States, borrow the money, or resort to new taxes.

Hamilton, of course, opposed selling the bank stock. The government, he thought, ought never to do this. Apart from the merits he found in remaining permanently in the banking business, he argued that it would be financially irresponsible to sell at that particular moment, for the market price had only recently fallen very low. The situation was not desperate, and there was no reason for the government to accept such a loss.[52]

Hamilton also objected to borrowing the money, although he admitted that this course would be better than selling the bank stock. His argument against borrowing was sweetly ironic, considering the amount of ink

---

2d Cong., 1st sess., 569.

[51] *Annals of Congress,* 2d Cong., 1st sess., 566-567. The reference to Goodhue was made in a speech by John Page.

[52] "Report of the Secretary of the Treasury," Mar. 16, 1792, *ibid.,* 1099-1105. After a long period of speculation and rising prices, the stock market peaked in January 1792. In March, just at the time Hamilton presented his report, it broke. The panic in financial centers continued into the autumn. See Malone, *Jefferson and the Rights of Man,* 434. For reasons unknown to me, Madisonians never pressed the idea of selling the government's holdings in the bank.

his critics were then spilling in denouncing his financial program and the national debt as joint instruments of tyranny. Taking a page from the opposition's book, he warned against the dangers posed by the national debt. There was no better argument against borrowing the money or in favor of increased taxation, he wrote, than the imperative need to extinguish the national debt as quickly as possible.[53]

This was a strange argument coming from Hamilton, and it is hardly to be taken seriously except in respect to the political situation. In effect, Hamilton was warning Madison and his friends that they could not have it both ways. They would have extreme difficulty in maintaining a convincing posture as opponents of Hamilton's growing "system" while simultaneously urging an increase in the national debt to support the unpopular Indian war.

But was a loan feasible? Hamilton forthrightly admitted that it was. The national credit was sound, and in spite of the break in the market, the nation was enjoying genuine prosperity.[54] Moreover, prospects were good. The cause of the inflated War Department budgets, the Indian war, could not continue long. Many observers predicted that one successful military campaign would end it. This suggests that the government was looking forward to large reductions in military spending and to increased surpluses. In short, although Hamilton rejected the idea, there was no good financial reason not to borrow.

Yet Hamilton insisted that an upward revision of the tariff would be the best means of financing the army. Since a loan was feasible and increased taxes, in the form either of an excise or of tariffs, would have been unpopular, the question that immediately arises is why Hamilton dismissed the idea of a loan in favor of tariff revision. In his report he suggested two important reasons. First, he hoped to discourage a growing tendency among Americans to purchase too many foreign manufactures on credit, thus overextending themselves.[55] Second, he hoped to encourage the growth of industry. A "spirit of Manufacturing," he wrote, "prevails at this time in a greater degree than it has done at any antecedent period; and as far as an increase of duties shall tend to second and aid this spirit they will tend to promote essentially, the industry, the wealth, the strength, the independence, and the substantial prosperity of the country."[56]

[53] "Report of the Secretary of the Treasury," Mar. 16, 1792, *Annals of Congress,* 2d Cong., 1st sess., 1100.
[54] *Ibid.,* 1099-1100.
[55] *Ibid.,* 1101.
[56] *Ibid.*

Specifically, Hamilton sought full tariff protection for iron and steel makers, very high tariffs on wines and spirits, a 50 percent increase in the general revenue tariff to a rate of 7.5 percent ad valorum (to be reduced to 5 percent after the costs of the Indian war had been fully paid), a 15 percent ad valorum duty on chinaware, most kinds of glass, and fire arms and other weapons, and a 10 percent duty on almost all other ordinary manufactures entering the country.[57]

Hamilton has been called the father of protection in the United States, and his advocacy of full tariff protection for America's iron and steel makers clearly gives him a claim to the title. But his proposal for a 15 percent duty on chinaware, glass, and most weapons, and a 10 percent rate on other important manufactured goods was not aimed at protecting the home market. Not only were there few manufacturers to protect, but a protective attitude would have been contrary to Hamilton's basic foreign policy, which emphasized peace with England and the cultivation of the so-called "British connection." Hamilton's 15 percent and 10 percent ad valorum tariff proposals constituted an attempt to encourage the development of American manufacturing by providing a substantial competitive edge for aspiring industrialists while simultaneously maintaining close economic ties with the English. The key word in Hamilton's conception was *encouragement,* not *protection.*

As on earlier occasions, a select committee of Congress produced a bill that mirrored precisely the suggestions outlined in Hamilton's report of March 16. Its description as a bill "to raise a further sum of money for the protection of the frontiers" was an unsubtle reminder to Madison and his supporters of the reason for the increased revenues. Had circumstances been different, it is extremely doubtful that this tariff proposal would have stood much chance in Congress. By linking military appropriations to the impost, however, Hamilton managed to neutralize a good deal of the opposition. Northern antiwar congressmen who supported the plan for encouraging manufacturing found it difficult to oppose this measure. More important, many of Madison's southern supporters, who would otherwise have refused to endorse the upward revision of tariffs on manufactures, were forced to acquiesce because they supported the Indian war.

From the time the bill was first introduced Madison thought it would pass. He had good reason to think so, for Hamilton had expertly manipulated the political situation to his own advantage. Had Madison and his friends tried the only feasible alternative and recommended a loan, they would have seemed grossly inconsistent—and in an unpopular cause at

[57] *Ibid.,* 1101-1103.

that. At the same time, as Madison explained to Edmund Pendleton, the exigencies of the military situation necessitated some sort of increased taxation. Too many congressmen who supported the continuation of the war and were unwilling to endorse other, more unpopular forms of taxation would go along with Hamilton.[58]

Because of their inability to offer a reasonable alternative, Madisonians in and out of Congress failed to mount an effective opposition to the tariff. A few hostile articles did appear in the Republican press. Early in April, for example, "Sidney," an anonymous author who regularly published attacks on Hamilton's policies in the *National Gazette,* devoted one column to the issue, but confined himself to the broader question of Treasury Department involvement in the legislative process.[59] Eleven days later another author, signing himself "A Farmer," made a much stronger attack on the tariff itself. Such increases as Hamilton proposed, he charged, would ultimately lead to higher costs for America's agriculturalists. He predicted retaliatory tariffs against American agricultural exports in the European marketplace, and higher prices for manufactures at home.[60] Aside, however, from a scattering of such protests, and one petition against increased tariffs submitted by a group of Philadelphia merchants, little opposition developed.

Despite the seeming hopelessness of the situation, Madison and a hard core of his supporters in Congress fought the new impost proposal. It took almost a full month to get the bill out of the Committee of the Whole for consideration by the House. Echoing arguments used by "A Farmer," opponents charged that it was biased against the nonindustrial sector of the economy. Manufacturers would benefit from the legislation, but agriculturalists would lose by it. Hamilton's friends in the House responded to this early version of what would later become a cry of southern outrage by offering some concessions of questionable worth. Hemp, cordage, and, most important, cotton, were added to the list of items to be protected against foreign competition. At this some northern congressmen protested. Fisher Ames opposed forcing Massachusetts cotton manufacturers to purchase essential raw materials at other than the free market price.[61] John Laurance of New York attacked the decision to protect hemp and cordage as a tax on commerce.[62] But by and large, the

[58] Madison to Pendleton, Mar. 25, 1792, Madison to Henry Lee, Apr. 15, 1792, Madison Papers.
[59] *Natl. Gaz.,* Apr. 12, 1792.
[60] *Ibid.,* Apr. 23, 1792.
[61] *Annals of Congress,* 2d Cong., 1st sess., 560-562.
[62] *Ibid.*

Hamiltonians in the House agreed that these concessions were important to the accomplishment of their general goal. For example, Maryland's William Vans Murray, who usually voted with Hamilton, supported these amendments as conducive to sectional conciliation.[63]

By April 15 Madison had to admit that he and his supporters had exhausted their arguments. Earlier, Virginia's Governor Lee had urged him to do his utmost to stop the bill. Sadly Madison informed Lee that it was no use. The worst was "that many of the new duties are made permanent."[64] Perhaps it was simply the act of putting these words to paper that gave Madison the idea. Whatever the stimulus, he suddenly realized that he was not through yet. There was one last move to be made. A few days later, counting on the support of those who endorsed the tariff proposal only because they felt an immediate need to finance a western military campaign in 1792, the Madisonians introduced an amendment to the bill limiting its life to just one year, time enough to collect the revenues needed for the war.[65]

The sharp legislative skirmish produced by the introduction of this amendment is very revealing. According to John Francis Mercer of Maryland and John Page of Virginia, the opponents of the amendment made it clear that funding the army was only one of a number of objectives they had in mind. Permanent tariff revision, they argued, was crucial for "the encouragement of manufactures." Beyond that, it would produce "stability in commercial arrangements," add to the sinking fund, provide for a "variety of new purposes," and compensate for some unspecified "former deficiencies."[66]

The results of the vote on the amendment are equally revealing. They

[63] Ibid., 569-570.
[64] Madison to Lee, Apr. 15, 1792, Madison Papers.
[65] Annals of Congress, 2d Cong., 1st sess., 562. Fisher Ames, a supporter of permanent tariff revision, believed that Madison's amendment would pass. Ames to Thomas Dwight, Apr. 19, 1792, in Seth Ames, ed., Works of Fisher Ames, I (Boston, 1854), 116.
[66] Annals of Congress, 2d Cong., 1st sess., 349-354. The speech by Mercer has been placed out of context in the Annals. It appears under the date Jan. 27, 1792, as part of the debate over Madison's bill for protecting the frontiers. However, both the Natl. Gaz. and the Annals report that Mercer first took his place in the House on Feb. 6, 10 days after he was supposed to have delivered this address. Moreover, the speech is an attack on a Treasury Department bill that fits the description of the measure introduced in mid-March. The reason for the confusion appears to lie in the fact that both Madison's bill and the tariff proposal were described as measures designed for the protection of the frontiers.

Unfortunately, the views of those who opposed the amendment are not recorded in the Annals. It is necessary, therefore, to rely on Madisonian sources for a recapitulation of their arguments.

clearly indicate that many congressmen who ultimately either refused to oppose or even supported tariff revision did so because they sought immediate funding for the Indian war. The amendment very nearly passed. After the roll call, the vote stood at 32 to 31 in its favor. Then Jonathan Trumbull of Connecticut, Speaker of the House, saved the situation for the Hamiltonians. In an extremely unusual parliamentary maneuver, he left the chair to vote against the amendment and thus create a tie. The amendment was defeated for lack of a majority.[67]

John Page next tried to have the bill sent back to committee. Emphasizing again the danger of allowing the executive branch to interfere in the legislative process, he argued that the House was abdicating its responsibilities by thoughtlessly endorsing recommendations made by Hamilton. In addition, he declared it improper to pass a law that, while ostensibly designed for the defense of the frontiers, was in reality calculated to encourage manufacturing and increase the sinking fund. Page's impassioned plea was ignored and his motion to recommit defeated.[68]

William Vans Murray led the move for final passage. He denied any impropriety in the preparation of the bill. Congress needed over $500,000 to finance the war in the West. It had sought expert guidance from the Treasury on how to raise the money. There was nothing wrong in that. Nor had the House surrendered any of its powers in doing so. Early in the debate some had charged that the bill was designed to help northern economic interests at the expense of the rest of the country. Murray denied this. Making precisely the sort of nationalist appeal Hamilton himself might have used, he noted that the bill as amended protected not only iron makers but cotton and hemp producers as well. It was good for all sections and for the nation as a whole. "In this bill the raw materials of the more Southern states are protected and made to serve the purposes of industry and manufacture in the more Northern states."[69]

In fact, Murray's nationalist appeal was far less persuasive than were the increasing military imperatives in the spring of 1792. Winter had been a quiet time on the Ohio frontier. But with the coming of good weather it was generally predicted that the Indians would return to the attack. In February the *National Gazette* reported a meeting of a small group of settlers on the Ohio at which resolutions were passed "to support the present frontier to the last extremity." An "Indian invasion" was fully ex-

---

[67] *Annals of Congress*, 2d Cong., 1st sess., 562.
[68] *Ibid.*, 566-568.
[69] *Ibid.*, 569-572.

pected.[70] Even such larger settlements as Gallipolis and Marietta expected the worst. With no troops to protect them, one settler predicted, the people of Marietta would have to choose between abandoning their homes and the prospect of a massacre.[71] Early in April the *Pittsburgh Gazette* reported the renewal of Indian depredations along the Ohio. A few days later the *National Gazette* carried an even more disturbing story. Reports from Kentucky indicated that the hostile Indians had "infested" the territory south of the river. Fourteen persons had been murdered by Indians in that region since the beginning of March.[72]

If the Indian war were to be brought to a successful conclusion, funds for the army would have to be found. The longer the Indians on the Ohio remained uncontrolled, the greater was the danger that the southern tribes and the Six Nations might join them. Under this kind of pressure, and because tariffs were the least obnoxious of all revenue-raising measures, a great many congressmen who had no use for Hamilton's latest scheme nevertheless felt impelled either to vote for the measure or to abstain. The bill passed easily in the House by a vote of 37 to 20. The Senate proved no obstacle and the bill was signed into law on May 2, 1792.[73]

Alexander Hamilton deserves credit, perhaps even admiration, for the skillful way in which he managed the passage of the Tariff of 1792. By linking the issues of frontier defense and the impost he overcame the opposition of some in the North who might otherwise have opposed increasing military spending. More significantly, he gave southern congressmen who supported the Indian war no choice but to allow an unpalatable tariff to become law.

It is difficult to assess the broader political significance of this contest. Scholars tend to agree that 1792 saw a hardening of political differences between Madison and Hamilton. The tariff fight certainly contributed to that development. In his letter to Carrington, Hamilton went so far as to suggest that Madison's opposition to the resolution of March 7 was of decisive political importance. By Hamilton's own testimony, this episode convinced him that there existed an unbridgeable gap between himself and Madison and Jefferson. To suggest, however, that any single issue

[70] *Natl. Gaz.,* Feb. 27, 1792.
[71] *Ibid.,* Mar. 12, 1792.
[72] *Ibid.,* Apr. 16, 19, 1792.
[73] *Annals of Congress,* 2d Cong., 1st sess., 1364-1370.

was preeminently significant in explaining the political polarization that became manifest in 1792 would be a serious perversion of our historical understanding. Hamilton was responding to an accumulation of grievances dating back to the First Congress. The same was true of Madison, who, tired of losing repeated legislative encounters with Hamilton, was making his own preparations for the coming elections. Of the related questions of defense appropriations and the tariff, it is best to suggest nothing more than that they constitute an important and hitherto largely overlooked link in a long chain of events. The end product was of course the development of political parties in America.

GENERAL CHARLES SCOTT, THE KENTUCKY MOUNTED VOLUNTEERS, AND THE NORTHWEST INDIAN WARS, 1784-1794

Paul David Nelson

The United States during its first decade of independence was vexed by a simmering conflict between settlers in the West and Indians in the territories north of the Ohio River. Citizens of Kentucky were particularly harassed by Indian raids, and they responded by striking back with mounted volunteers, led by various militia officers. One of these commanders, General Charles Scott, was an especially prominent and effective leader of the mounted volunteers in the years 1790-1794, and he, along with his fellow citizen soldiers, played an important role in the Indian wars of that time. It seems useful, therefore, to examine the role of Scott and the Kentucky mounted volunteers in the Indian wars, while at the same time using this opportunity to reconsider, and perhaps settle, a point that partisans bickered about while the wars went on: whether the United States should suppress the Indians by relying exclusively upon *either* Kentucky mounted volunteers *or* the regular army (under its various leaders). It seems, after examining the evidence, that President George Washington was correct to insist upon combined militia-regular operations; this essay will argue that point as the story of Scott and the Kentucky militiamen unfolds.

General Scott's role as a rough-and-tumble Indian fighter had come naturally to him. While a young man, he had served as a private under Edward Braddock in the ill-fated British campaign of 1755 against

---

Mr. Nelson is a member of the Department of History at Berea College in Berea, Kentucky. He wishes to thank the Appalachian Center, University of Kentucky, for awarding him the James Still Fellowship which enabled him to complete this article.

JOURNAL OF THE EARLY REPUBLIC, 6 (Fall 1986). © 1986 Society for Historians of the Early American Republic.

Fort Duquesne, and during the American Revolution he fought as a colonel and brigadier general in the battles of Trenton, Monmouth, and Stony Point. After the war, he lived quietly for a few years as a Virginia gentleman farmer, and in 1785 he moved westward to Virginia's "District of Kentucky." Settling in Woodford County, he fitted himself into the routine of his new life, visiting with his close friends James Wilkinson and Harry Innes, discussing politics, expounding at length (according to Wilkinson) "upon ways to defend the [Kentucky] settlers" from Indian attacks, and ruminating over the possibility of planting a military colony at the mouth of the Yazoo River on the Mississippi.[1] By the end of the 1780s, Scott's entire attention was engrossed in military matters, and he devoted his time in the next few years to fighting Indians. Shortly after his arrival in Kentucky, he had lost a son in an Indian raid. Thereafter, according to Theodore Roosevelt, he was consumed by a passionate hatred of the Indians and "delighted in war" against them. To be sure, the general was not averse to fighting, for during the first half of the 1790s he spent more time on active service than any other senior Kentucky officer. And while he may not have been the military equal of George Rogers Clark, he still was a good soldier, making up for any deficiencies with his ardor for warfare.[2]

When he enlisted in the Indian wars in early 1790, Scott inherited two military traditions from the militia that during the past decade had taken on the force of doctrine. First, he was bequeathed the organization called the "mounted volunteer corps," which had supplanted the unglamorous, slow-moving, foot-soldier regiment as the standard militia unit for the "District of Kentucky." By hit-or-miss experimentation, the Kentuckians had learned that a militia upon horseback, supplied by packhorses carrying reserves of ammunition and provisions, had such obvious advantages of speed in moving troops

---

[1] Samuel M. Wilson, "Charles Scott," *Dictionary of American Biography*, XVI, 487; Francis B. Heitman, *Historical Register of Officers of the Continental Army During the War of the Revolution* (Washington 1914), 485; J. W. Whickcar [Whicker], "General Charles Scott and His March to Ouiatenon," *Indiana Magazine of History*, 21 (Mar. 1925), 98; James Ripley Jacobs, *Tarnished Warrior: Major-General James Wilkinson* (New York 1938), 71, 73; Thomas Robson Hay and M. R. Werner, *The Admirable Trumpeter: A Biography of General James Wilkinson* (Garden City, N.Y. 1941), 62, 104; Thomas Marshall Green, *Spanish Conspiracy: A Review of Early Spanish Movements in the South-West* (Cincinnati 1891), 134.

[2] Richard G. Stone, Jr., *A Brittle Sword: The Kentucky Militia, 1776-1912* (Lexington, Ky. 1977), 17-18; Theodore Roosevelt, *The Winning of the West* (4 vols., New York 1889-1896), III, 301-302.

General Charles Scott, ca. 1739-1813
Courtesy of Indiana Historical Society

to rendezvous and battle that this tactical arrangement must be adopted.[3] In addition, the Kentuckians had discovered that their service as mounted volunteers entitled them to a monthly salary of twenty dollars from the federal government (which nationalized them for duty against the Indians), rather than the mere three dollars per month they earned as poor, slogging foot soldiers. Finally, their service as mounted infantrymen was perceived by them to be more glamorous and better suited to their proud temperaments than serving as "mere" infantrymen.

Second, and obviously interrelated with the first point, Scott inherited from the Kentuckians the military dogma that the only way to fight Indians was to carry out swift, punishing, and relatively brief campaigns deep into Indian territory, always in retaliation for an

---

' Stone, *A Brittle Sword*, 15.

"atrocity" perpetrated by Indians against "innocent" Kentucky citizens. The Kentuckians had begun to use this method of warfare in the 1780s. They had observed the ineffectiveness of the regular United States army, consisting of six hundred men commanded by Lieutenant Colonel Josiah Harmar, in stopping Indian raids southward across the Ohio River, despite Harmar's establishment of a series of forts (Washington, Finney, Harmar) to interdict such raids. In 1786 Virginia Governor Patrick Henry, under heated pressure from his Kentucky constituents, instructed the Kentucky militiamen "to concert some system for their own defense," and it was at that time that they determined to deliver militia retribution upon the Indians. That summer, Benjamin Logan led eight hundred Kentuckians in a raid against Shawnee villages on the Miami River, and George Rogers Clark conducted an abortive and inept operation into the Wabash country. A year later, Colonel John Logan launched an expedition against the Chickamaugas, entering Cherokee territory in Tennessee to do so and defying a United States treaty with that nation. Shortly thereafter, Robert Todd led a raid on another tribe of northwest Indians, this time without sanction either from the governor of Virginia or from the United States government.[4]

Soon the westerners and many persons in the East were quarreling vigorously with each other about the effectiveness of the Kentuckians' tactics, trading mutual recriminations and shedding little light upon the problem. Military strategists in the East, such as Henry Knox, the Confederation government's secretary of war, inclined to see such raids as aggravating the problem, turning otherwise friendly Indians into hostiles. Arthur St. Clair, federal governor of the Northwest Territory, put it best when he declared that the Kentuckians were "in the habit of retaliation . . . without attending precisely to the nations from which the injuries are received." The Kentuckians, for their part, were convinced that their critics were totally out of touch with their needs; not only was the United States army too weak and scattered to defend the Ohio River line but also its tactics and leadership were totally inadequate to the challenge of Indian warfare.[5]

---

[4] Richard H. Kohn, *Eagle and Sword: The Federalists and the Creation of the Military Establishment in America, 1783-1802* (New York 1975), 62-65, 93; Stone, *A Brittle Sword,* 23; Green, *Spanish Conspiracy,* 67-68, 81-82.

[5] Arthur St. Clair to George Washington, Sept. 14, 1789, in William Henry Smith, ed., *The St. Clair Papers* (2 vols., Cincinnati 1882), II, 124; Henry Knox to Washington, June 15, 1789, George Washington Papers (Library of Congress); Kohn, *Eagle and Sword,* 93.

When President Washington took office in 1789, he was faced with near-crisis conditions in the West, for the dying Confederation government had allowed its policies for that region to drift for the past two years. Washington decided as a stopgap measure to negotiate with the northwestern tribes, in hopes of attaining a peaceful solution to tensions in that region. Like Knox, his secretary of war, he was afraid that all-out war with the Indians would lead the Kentuckians into a campaign of extirpation. Moreover, as Knox informed him, such a war would require a regular army of at least 2,500 men and would cost $200,000 annually—an expense both men considered beyond the ability of the United States at that time to afford.[6] But, by early 1790, Washington was aware that his policy of negotiating with the Indians was an abject failure, and he began to move more directly toward war preparations. At that time, he adopted the military policy that he would adhere to throughout the Indian wars: the enrolling of both militia and regulars to serve in a combined force, under command of an overall federal officer. Although he and Knox would have preferred to depend solely on the United States army, military and political constraints (not least anti-army sentiment in Congress and the Kentuckians' desire to kill Indians) necessitated that he adopt St. Clair's proposal to call upon frontier militiamen for national service in cooperation with regulars. Clearly, Washington put this program into place as much to conciliate the Kentuckians and his political foes in Congress as to deal with the Indians from strength.[7]

The president's decisions were none too soon, as far as Scott and his neighbors were concerned. For besides their resentment of easterners for lack of protection from Indian raids, they feared the federal government would not support their right to free navigation on the Mississippi River through Spanish New Orleans. Moreover, they were negotiating with Virginia for statehood. Washington knew that Wilkinson and other Kentuckians had long been involved in a conspiracy to place Kentucky under Spanish hegemony, so he realized he must act with haste to placate Virginia's western citizens. The president hoped that his new policy of regular-militia cooperation would effect this purpose, at the same time heading off an all-out Indian war. Nevertheless, he feared that he may not yet have handled this matter "effectually"

---

[6] Knox to Washington, June 15, 1789, Washington Papers; Kohn, *Eagle and Sword*, 95-96.

[7] Knox to Josiah Harmar, June 10, 1789, Josiah Harmar Papers (William L. Clements Library [WLCL], University of Michigan, Ann Arbor); Arthur St. Clair

and that he might soon be forced into such a war, despite his best efforts to avoid one.[8]

It was at this time that Charles Scott emerged as a major actor in the unfolding drama on the western frontier. In April 1790 he volunteered as a private citizen to bring forward a contingent of Kentucky volunteers and join Josiah Harmar in a joint regular-militia raid against the northwest Indians. The latter gentleman was at Limestone (present-day Maysville) on the Ohio River, preparing, under new orders from Knox, to launch an expedition against some Indian towns on the upper waters of the Scioto River, and he had sent a call to Kentucky for mounted volunteers to join the effort. On the 18th of the month, Harmar with 160 regulars and Scott with 230 Kentucky mounted volunteers, mostly from Bourbon and Fayette counties, marched north-northeastward from Limestone to the upper Scioto, then almost due southward to the mouth of that stream, emerging on the Ohio near the present town of Portsmouth.[9] This foray, while accomplishing nothing against the Indians, was an even more dismal failure—as Scott and Harmar well knew—in that Scott and the Kentuckians had developed an aversion to Harmar's leadership which made them vow never to have anything more to do with him. Consequently, Harmar's future effectiveness as a leader of combined regular-militia forces was compromised irrevocably.

The Scioto raid of April 1790 was intended by Harmar and Governor St. Clair, Washington's servants in the West, to be merely a warm-up for a full scale assault against the northwestern Indians later that year. In early June, St. Clair arrived at Fort Washington to draw up plans with Harmar and Robert Elliot, an army contractor, for the larger operation. It was decided by these three gentlemen that Harmar in the fall would lead a force of 1,500 men, more than half of whom would be Kentucky militia volunteers, in an attack on the Miami Indians on the Maumee and upper Wabash rivers.[10] In September, when the militiamen for this expedition began to collect at Fort Washington, Commander Harmar was dismayed by their poor qual-

---

to Washington, Sept. 14, 1789, Henry Knox's "Summary Statement," May 27, 1790, Knox to St. Clair, June 7, 1790, in Smith, ed., *St. Clair Papers*, II, 124, 146-148; Knox to Harmar, June 7, 1790, *American State Papers: Indian Affairs* (2 vols., Washington 1832), I, 97-98; Kohn, *Eagle and Sword*, 96-98.

   [8] Donald Jackson and Dorothy Twohig, eds., *The Diaries of George Washington* (6 vols., Charlottesville 1976-1979), VI, 15.

   [9] Federal Writers Project, Works Projects Administration, *Military History of Kentucky* (Frankfort 1939), 53-54.

   [10] Kohn, *Eagle and Sword*, 102-103.

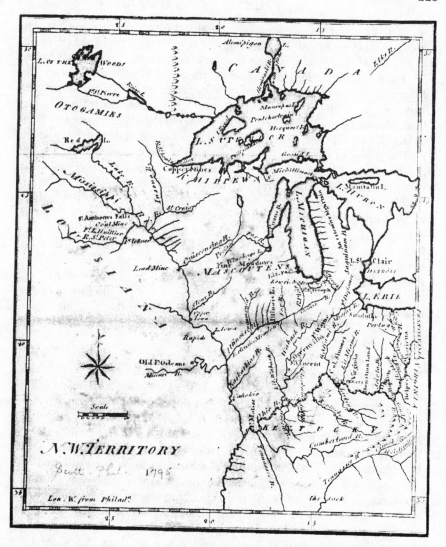

Map of the Northwest Territory, 1795
Courtesy of Indiana Historical Society

ity. He was even more chagrined when he learned that the principal military leaders of Kentucky, such as Scott, Benjamin Logan, and Robert Todd, refused to serve under him. Hence, at the very outset of his campaign, Harmar, whose limited ability as a military leader had already reduced American chances of success, was crippled even more by the inferior nature of his soldiers and officers.

The Harmar expedition soon collapsed into American defeat, and it escaped being a total disaster only because its leader had sense enough to realize at a crucial moment that he must retreat and cut his losses. In early October, Harmar moved his army northward toward the Miami towns, which he entered unopposed on the 17th and destroyed. But then a militia detachment under Colonel John Hardin was ambushed and compelled to retreat helter-skelter back to Harmar's main camp. At that point, Harmar began a return march southward, but on the night of October 21 he detached a force of 400 regulars and militia under Major John P. Wyllys to return to the villages and surprise the Indians, who were returning to their homes. Instead of ambushing the Indians, however, Wyllys allowed part of his own force to be routed with the loss of himself and almost fifty men. The remainder of his detachment then escaped back to Harmar's main encampment. Two weeks later the thoroughly demoralized Harmar and his army reached the safety of Fort Washington, whereupon Harmar and St. Clair publicly claimed a great victory over the Indians. Yet, both these men knew the opposite was the case. "Our loss is heavy, heavy indeed," a distraught Harmar had written to St. Clair during his return march. This was an obvious enough fact to both the Americans and their Indian foes.[11]

Although Harmar's lack of success against the northwest Indians was to some degree the fault of Scott and the other Kentuckians (since they had refused to march with him), they were by no means willing to accept any blame. Instead, they used this occasion to argue forcefully to Washington that Harmar's failure proved irrefutably their long-held opinion that regular army troops and leaders were ineffective in fighting Indians and that only Kentucky mounted volunteers would be able to do the job. Petitioning Washington some time in late 1790, the Kentuckians in the Virginia General Assembly deplored "the Late Unfortunate Defeat" of Harmar's expedition—although they were quick to praise the president for his "very Early Attention to the Safety and protection" of Kentucky. The basic problem, as the petitioners saw it, was that "the present System will never produce the wished for Effects," because "Regular Officers and Soldiers" were incapable of fighting Indians, and "an Intermixture of them with Militia promises nothing better." Only the Kentuckians themselves, acting alone, could carry out "an Enterprize against the Indians from our Country" with

---

[11] Harmar to St. Clair, Oct. 24, 1790, Northwest Territory Collection (Indiana Historical Society Library, Indianapolis); Stone, *A Brittle Sword*, 24-25; Mann Butler, *A History of the Commonwealth of Kentucky* (Cincinnati 1836), 191-194.

the necessary "Utmost Secrecy and Dispatch," for only the "veteran Officers" of that district, "long accustomed to [Indian] methods of Warfare . . . and well Accustomed to the use of Riffles and Both arouzed and put in motion by the most pressing of all obligations— the preservation of themselves their wives and Children," would have either the talent or the desire to succeed. Moreover, declared the Kentuckians, "the Confidence of the Militia in their own officers can never be Sufficiently Transferred to or Reposed in those in the Regular Service." Therefore, the petitioners prayed that the president "would be pleased to Appoint Such of [our militia officers] as you may think fit to Take the Command of us," and they specifically suggested that it "would Be highly pleasing to us" if Scott were appointed a major general and Logan and Isaac Shelby brigadier generals.[12]

These political pressures from the Kentuckians upon eastern politicians had immediate and important consequences for both Scott and his Kentucky neighbors. First, although President Washington did not follow their advice to commission Scott, Logan, and Shelby as officers in federal service, Governor Beverley Randolph of Virginia (perhaps upon Washington's suggestion) appointed Scott on December 30, 1790, a brigadier general of Virginia militia with command of the entire "District of Kentucky." Second, Washington accepted the recommendation of Congressman John Brown, a Kentuckian, to accredit Brown, Isaac Shelby, Benjamin Logan, Charles Scott, and Harry Innes as a Kentucky Board of War, with responsibility for organizing the Kentucky militia for federal service.[13] Immediately, Scott began his new duties by writing (at the request of Governor Randolph) a number of Kentucky officials about the possibility of setting up a series of defensive frontier stations along the Ohio River. He met with the Kentucky Board of War in April to make final arrangements for these establishments, and then proceeded with the board's permission to draft 326 privates for a period of sixty days to man them.[14]

Meanwhile, Scott was monitoring the number of Indian raids

[12] "Representatives of the Counties Composing the District of Kentucky now in the General Assembly of Virginia" to Washington, [1790], Charles Scott Papers (Margaret I. King Library, University of Kentucky, Lexington).

[13] *Kentucky Gazette*, Feb. 5, 1791; Charles Gano Talbert, *Benjamin Logan: Kentucky Frontiersman* (Lexington, Ky. 1962), 250; Stone, *A Brittle Sword*, 25; Richard H. Collins, *History of Kentucky* (2 vols., Covington 1874), I, 173; Butler, *Kentucky*, 196.

[14] Charles Scott to "Comdt of Rangers," Feb. 23, 1791, Minutes of Board of War, Apr. 8, 1791, Scott Papers; *Kentucky Gazette*, Dec. 17, 1791; WPA, *Military History*, 56; Joseph Allen Thacker, Jr., "The Kentucky Militia from 1792 to 1812" (M.A. thesis, University of Kentucky 1954), 4.

against white settlers along the Ohio and sending news of them to
Randolph. On April 8, he noted that since his accession to command
there had been at least a half dozen serious incidents, mostly involving Indian ambushes of flatboats on the Ohio and resulting in the
deaths of many individuals as well as whole families. Although he admitted to the governor that the Indians in these altercations always
seemed to suffer higher casualties than the whites, he and his neighbors
received little comfort from such statistics. And although Scott's survey
of Kentucky's eligible military manpower in the spring of 1791 (by
order of Randolph) showed that there were almost 11,000 men of
military age in the district—a force that was vastly superior to any
that the Indians could muster—Scott was not impressed. As he well
knew, and as he made quick to inform the governor, the exigencies
of finance and the Kentuckians' own economic survival made it impossible for him to muster more than a fifth of that total number at
any one time.[15]

Despite his problems in the spring and summer of 1791, Scott
was not overly perturbed about Kentucky's defenses, for he realized
that he was only marking time until the Washington administration
could take more effectual steps against the northwest Indians later in
the year. In January, the president had made the decision to launch
an all-out military invasion of the Indians' homelands, in hopes of
bringing them to heel. His plan—despite the Kentuckians' earlier protests against combined regular-militia operation—called for the organization of an army of 3,000 men at Fort Washington under St. Clair
(who was appointed to command in March), one third to be Kentucky
volunteers enlisted for four months' service, the rest regulars, to march
against the Indian towns on the Maumee River. General Scott, who
stood high in the esteem of military planners in Philadelphia, was chosen
to lead the Kentuckians as a subordinate officer of St. Clair, and he
was apprised of this fact by a friend in mid-February. Therefore, Scott
was genuinely confident during the first half of 1791 (despite his misgivings about combined regular-militia operations) that he and the Kentucky volunteers would march northward in the fall with St. Clair's
regulars and utterly destroy Indian power in the Northwest Territory.[16]

---

[15] Henry Lee to Scott, Mar. 22, 1791, Scott to Beverley Randolph, Apr. 2,
1791, Scott Papers; Scott's Return of Militia Strength, Spring, 1791, in "Virginia
Justices of the Peace and Military Officers in the District of Kentucky Prior to 1792,"
Register of the Kentucky Historical Society, 25 (Jan. 1927), 55-62.
[16] Knox, Report to Washington, Jan. 22, 1791, *American State Papers: Indian Affairs*, I, 112; Jno. Belli to Scott, Feb. 17, 1791, Scott Papers.

As a prelude to St. Clair's major expedition, General Scott was ordered by Washington to initiate "surprise and sudden attacks" on the Wabash Indian towns during the spring of 1791. The aim of these raids, as Knox explained to Scott, was to keep the Indians off balance while St. Clair prepared for his big push and also to give the Kentucky militiamen, who had suffered impatiently during the winter under Indian assaults along the Ohio River, something to keep them employed until they could join St. Clair's main expedition. Accordingly, Scott secured permission from the Kentucky Board of War in April to call for a rendezvous of all "interested" Kentucky mounted volunteers at Frankfort on May 15, "there to enter under [his] command" and ride against the northwest Indians.[17] The response to the general's call was heartening, and in early May he was deeply involved in preparing for the upcoming raid.

On the 8th of the month, however, Scott received unwelcome news that he might have to delay his plans indefinitely. That day, St. Clair visited him at his home in Woodford County and informed him that John Proctor, a peace envoy sent by Washington to parley with the Miamis, had not yet returned from the Northwest Territory. Until Proctor reappeared, Scott must not launch his raid—even if such a delay meant that the Kentuckians remain quiescent until they joined St. Clair's main operation later in the year. This news, the general was quick to let St. Clair know, would not sit well with the Kentuckians, for they were already distrustful of easterners and itching to get at the Indians after a season of inaction. Although St. Clair was distressed at Scott's blunt words, he realized that Scott did not exaggerate the Kentuckians' restlessness, and he dare not alienate them more, lest they refuse him assistance later in the year. Therefore, he compromised his orders from Philadelphia and asked Scott only to "dawdle" on his muster for two weeks, after which, if nothing had been heard from Proctor, the Kentuckian could proceed with his operations. Finally, Proctor was not heard from, having returned to Philadelphia without informing the westerners of the failure of his mission, and Scott, still unaware of (and not overly concerned about) Proctor's fate, proceeded with his raid.[18]

---

[17] Knox to Scott, Mar. 9, 1791, *American State Papers: Indian Affairs*, I, 129-131; Minutes of Board of War, Apr. 8, May 2, 1791, Scott Papers; Jacobs, *Tarnished Warrior*, 112.

[18] St. Clair to Scott, May 18, 1791, to Knox, May 26, 1791, in Smith, ed., *St. Clair Papers*, II, 207-209, 212-216; Arthur St. Clair, *A Narrative of the Manner in Which the Campaign Against the Indians in the Year One Thousand Seven Hundred and Ninety-*

Scott's expedition into the wilderness set out from Fort Washington on May 24, 1791. His destination was a group of Indian towns on the Wabash River (near present-day Lafayette, Indiana) about 155 miles away, which were known as Ouiatenon. The general's army was impressive, according to a contemporary newspaper account, composed as it was "of the first class of citizens, a member of Congress, members of the Senate and Assembly, marshals, Colonels, Mayors, Captains, Lawyers, and others serving as privates in the field." Yet, as Scott later reported to St. Clair, this proud group of men was a bedraggled lot after eight days of hard riding through "deep Clayey Bogs, from one to five miles in width, rendered almost Impervious by brush and Briers," across innumerable rivers and streams, with rain falling "in torrents every Day; with frequent blasts of Wind and Thunder storms." Before long, the Kentuckians and their horses were worn down, their provisions were spoiled, and they were obliged to scavenge blackberries along the route of march (thus giving the name "Blackberry Campaign" to this expedition). But Scott pressed on.[19]

At last, on the morning of June 1, the Kentuckians emerged into open prairie near their destination, and the commander, realizing the great danger of being detected by the Indians during their approach, proceeded with haste toward Ouiatenon. Sure enough, noted Scott later, just as the troopers entered the "Ocean of Prairie I perceived a man on horseback a few miles to my right," who rode like the wind to warn the villagers. So, "Finding myself discovered, I determined to advance with all the rapidity my circumstances would permit," and by one o'clock in the afternoon the general's guides informed him that he was only four miles from the main towns. At that point, Scott detached a party of men under Colonel John Hardin to attack two villages on his left, then proceeded "with my main body in order of Battle, towards the Towns, the smoke from which was discernable." As he approached the Indian villages, located on bottomland "bordering on the Wabash," he ordered Captain William Price and forty men to assault a lone house standing between his troops and the villages,

One, Was Conducted . . . (Philadelphia 1812, rep. New York 1971), 2-3; Frazer Ellis Wilson, The Peace of Mad Anthony (Greenville, Ohio 1909), 53-54.
    [19] St. Clair to Knox, May 26, 1791, in Smith, ed., St. Clair Papers, II, 212-216; Scott to St. Clair, June 20, 1791, Scott Papers; Kentucky Gazette, June 23, 1791; Elmore Barce, The Land of the Miamis (Fowler, Ind. 1922), 183; H[umphrey] Marshall, History of Kentucky (2nd ed., 2 vols., Frankfort 1824), I, 373-374; Paul W. Beasley, "The Life and Times of Isaac Shelby, 1750-1826" (Ph.D. diss., University of Kentucky 1968), 102-103; [Whicker], "General Charles Scott," 95; Roosevelt, Winning of the West, IV, 29.

which they did "with great gallantry, killing two warriors." Thereupon, Scott "gained the margin of the eminence, which overlooks the Villages," and "discovered the enemy in great confusion, endeavouring to make their escape in canoes over the Wabash." Instantly, he "ordered Lt. Colo. Cmdt Wilkinson to rush forward with the first Battallion" in order to cut off the Indians' route of retreat, and although his orders were "executed with promptitude," the Kentuckians "gained the bank of the River, just as the rear of the enemy had embarked" under the protective fire of other Indians in a Kickapoo village on the far side of the Wabash.

General Scott was now determined to assault this Indian village, but to his "great mortification" he discovered that "the Wabash was many feet beyond fording at this place," and so he must seek other places to cross. Immediately, he detached Wilkinson and a body of mounted troops toward a possible fording site two miles upriver, which his guides informed him was "practicable," and he sent another force under Major Thomas Barbee in the opposite direction for the same purpose. Although Wilkinson found no ford and only managed to rout a few more defenseless Indians from another small village before returning to the main army, the force under Major Barbee had more success. Barbee's men got across the Wabash and into battle formation, noted Scott, "before they were discovered by the enemy," whereupon the Indians once again fled in great disarray before their superior enemies. After this raid, Barbee and his men rejoined General Scott, as did Colonel Hardin, who announced proudly upon his arrival at camp with fifty-two Indian prisoners that he had killed six enemy warriors. At this point, Scott halted military operations for the day because, as he reported, all Indian villages for miles about by now had been abandoned by the terrified Indians, and he expected to achieve little more in Ouiatenon than a leisurely destruction on the following day of the natives' crops, houses, and livestock.[20]

Scott decided, however, during the evening of June 1 that Wilkinson upon the morn should continue the raids against Indian towns by attacking Kethtipecanunck (or Tippecanoe), an important village about eighteen miles upriver. Although Scott intended that 500 of his troops ride with Wilkinson, only about 300 volunteered for the service, and so it was this number that departed camp on the morning of the 2nd, for what turned out to be the final operation of the campaign. As Wilkinson later reported to Scott, he came upon

---

[20] Scott to St. Clair, June 20, 1791, Scott Papers; [Whicker], "General Charles Scott," 97-98; Barce, *Miamis*, 185.

Kethtipecanunck at 4:30 p.m. on the 2nd and immediately ordered an assault against its inhabitants. He discovered, however, that they had fled in canoes across the unfordable river. After exchanging an ineffectual fire with them for a time, he burned the village, mustered his troops, and marched back to Scott's headquarters.[21]

While Wilkinson was thus engaged, Scott's troops systematically ravaged the Indian towns that were Ouiatenon, ceasing their labors only when the entire region lay in smoldering ruin. That duty done, the general commenced his march toward the Ohio River, without having lost a single man killed and only five wounded; by comparison, his enemies had suffered thirty-eight deaths and the capture of fifty-seven prisoners. Scott bemoaned his inability to "Carry Terror and desolation to the head of the Wabash," but the weather, lack of provisions, and exhaustion of his horses made such a march impossible. In any case, he was convinced that he had already accomplished enough to "increase the Panick" of the Indians and distract their councils in favor of "the views of government." Meantime, "to gratify the impulsion of Humanity," he released sixteen of "the weakest and most infirm" of his prisoners, sending them back to their people with a "talk" encouraging peace negotiations with the United States. On the 14th of June, he brought his men safely back to Fort Finney (present-day Clarksville, Indiana), where he delivered his remaining forty-one prisoners into the hands of the United States army. Then he and his famished troops gratefully accepted Colonel John Campbell's invitation to "refresh themselves at his house" from a "plentiful supply of food and liquor," served upon tables that "were kept continually spread."[22]

Although Scott and his Kentucky neighbors were delighted with the results of the raid against Ouiatenon, the Washington administration was even more so, for the president garnered much praise from westerners for his support of them in "avenging" past Indian insults. On three separate occasions during the next few months, Knox lauded the Kentucky Board of War for its bellicosity and encouraged it to dispatch the mounted volunteers on other such missions. St. Clair also did his part to encourage Kentucky militia raids by suggesting on June

---

[21] James Wilkinson to Scott, June 3, 1791, "Letters of James Wilkinson," *Register of the Kentucky Historical Society*, 24 (Sept. 1926), 259-267; Marshall, *Kentucky*, I, 374; Barce, *Miamis*, 186-187.

[22] Scott to St. Clair, June 20, 1791, Scott Papers; *Kentucky Gazette*, June 25, 1791; WPA, *Military History*, 58. In his report, Scott said that he returned to "Fort Steuben," but it is obvious from the context that he misnamed the fort.

24 that the Board of War send a party of 500 officers and men upon another Wabash expedition. At the same time, he ordered that the Kentuckians disband their frontier guard posts, organized the previous April, so that federal expenses could be reduced and manpower freed for what war planners in Philadelphia now considered the more important duty of raiding Indian towns. Scott, skeptical of these proposals, noted that 500 men were insufficient for any new operation, and he suggested that the guardsmen remain in place until the results of St. Clair's intended expedition were known. The board, however, had its orders, and despite Scott's views voted to remove all the guards by July 15, except for a group of Bourbon Countians who were protecting an ironworks there. The board also ordered Scott to call together the Kentucky volunteers, as St. Clair had directed, for another raid into the Wabash country.[23]

During July, Scott proceeded as best he could to carry out the dual orders of the board. His first item of business was to persuade his colleagues on the board to leave guardsmen at two other vital locations, Great Bone Lick, a salt source, and the mouth of the Kentucky River, a strategic post. Succeeding in this business (luckily for the Kentuckians, since a month later Indian parties tried—unsuccessfully, thanks to Scott's foresight—to seize Great Bone Lick and deny settlers access to salt), Scott also ordered the militia to rendezvous on July 19 at Limestone for a quick raid against the Sandusky Indians. When 300 men had been mustered for service, Scott appointed Colonel John Edwards of Bourbon County to lead them, and they proceeded to march northward. Before they had effected much, Edwards ordered his men home, much to the disgust of his fellows, who accused their commander of cowardice. Another mission that Scott helped organize in early August, this one led by James Wilkinson against the Indian village of Kenapacomaqua (or L'Anguille, on the Eel River, six miles from present-day Logansport, Indiana), was more successful.[24]

While Scott and the Kentuckians were kept "amused" during the spring and summer of 1791 with desultory raids against the northwest

[23] Knox to Board of War, June 30, 1791, Scott to Board of War, June 29, 1791, Harry Innes Papers (Library of Congress); Knox to Board of War, Aug. 3, Sept. 29, 1791, in Temple Bodley, ed., *Reprints of Littel's Political Transactions* . . . , Filson Club *Publications*, 31 (1926), 120-121; St. Clair to Board of War, June 24, 1791, in Smith, ed., *St. Clair Papers*, II, 222-223; Kohn, *Eagle and Sword*, 113; Talbert, *Logan*, 254-255.

[24] Scott to St. Clair, July 18, 1791, to _____, Aug. 20, 1791, Scott Papers; St. Clair to Scott, July 19, 1791, Wilkinson to St. Clair, Aug. 24, 1791, in Smith, ed., *St. Clair Papers*, II, 226-227, 233-234; WPA, *Military History*, 59-60.

Indians, St. Clair at Fort Washington proceeded with plans for his major operation. By late summer, prospects for his expedition seemed to have lowered from just months before, for St. Clair himself, at the age of 57, now frankly admitted that he was unfit for active soldiering. Also, like Harmar before him, he had inspired little confidence in his ability as a soldier during the time of his command, either among regulars or militiamen. Hence, Scott, like Wilkinson, was by the fall of 1791 "damn skittish" that his reputation might be ruined by cooperating with St. Clair. And Scott was in less than a willing mood to comply either with instructions from the governor of Virginia on August 4 to cooperate with St. Clair or from St. Clair himself to lead the Kentucky volunteers in a combined regular-militia army. Finally, Scott did acquiesce to St. Clair's orders to call for a muster of volunteers for federal service, but he, like every other general officer in Kentucky, pleaded illness (or made other excuses) to avoid leading those who came forward. Under these circumstances, it was not surprising that the militia rank and file also balked at volunteering their services. Finally, as a last resort, Scott and the board were compelled to draft 1,000 reluctant citizens to serve under St. Clair. These less than ardent soldiers Scott put under command of Colonel William Oldham, who was the highest ranking Kentuckian the board could find to lead them.[25]

Under the circumstances, it is not surprising that St. Clair's expedition came to grief on the morning of November 4, 1791, when his army was surprised in camp by a powerful Indian army. Before that *rencontre* was over, St. Clair had lost 600 men killed, and 300 more wounded, out of a total force of only 1,400 soldiers. The Kentucky militia did not cover itself with glory in this fight, for during the Indian attack the citizen soldiers disintegrated into a panic-stricken mob, and Colonel Oldham was killed. Their poor performance, however, did not deter either the survivors of the debacle or their stay-at-home brothers from blaming the entire disaster upon St. Clair and the administration's policy of combined regular-militia operations against the natives. Already convinced that regulars were worthless for Indian warfare, the westerners' experience under St. Clair (despite the fact that the regulars stood and fought for two hours after the militia fled) only confirmed their worst fears. Regulars, growled John Cleves Symmes, a land speculator in Ohio, "will never answer our purposes for fighting of Indians," and they ought to be confined in fixed garrisons, while

---

[25] Stone, *A Brittle Sword*, 25; Jacobs, *Tarnished Warrior*, 114; Marshall, *Kentucky*, I, 376.

the frontiersmen, who understood the Indian and his methods of war, should be allowed to conduct operations in the field. "One hundred Marlboroughs," Symmes fumed, "could not fight fifty Indians in the woods with success." These views were widely held in both the East and West after St. Clair's disaster in late 1791.[26]

When word of St. Clair's defeat reached Scott, he immediately grasped the magnitude of the emergency now facing Kentucky. Quickly recovering from his "illness," he ordered his county lieutenants to muster volunteer horsemen on November 15 at Craig's Mill, twenty miles north of Lexington, "completely equipped" and ready to ride northward. The safety of Kentucky and the lives of "brave men," he said, were in danger, "and the circumstances require the greatest dispatch." Despite Scott's tone of urgency, however, the Kentuckians did not seem unduly perturbed, and it was not until November 24 that the general, with only 200 mounted volunteers, finally did join St. Clair at Fort Washington. Even at this late date, St. Clair intended to recommence operations against the Indians if he could but scrape up enough soldiers to replace his staggering losses of twenty days before. He grasped, therefore, at Scott's assurances that Benjamin Logan was also on the march with many more troops and would arrive within three days. But St. Clair, who even under circumstances more auspicious had not been sanguine about his chances of success, was now more pessimistic. "I am not," he told Knox on the day of Scott's arrival, "without my fears that the project will blow up." Sure enough, it did, for Logan and his men did not come forward and the luckless St. Clair had no opportunity to redeem either his own or his country's misfortunes.[27]

By late 1791, President Washington finally realized that he had a full-fledged Indian war on his hands, and he began a major push in Philadelphia to increase the size and potency of the regular army. At the same time, he insisted that his policy of negotiation with the Indians be not only continued but also reinvigorated by every responsible official of government. In a word, he declared, there were from

---

[26] Kohn, *Eagle and Sword*, 114, 118 (quotation); Stone, *A Brittle Sword*, 25. St. Clair's belated *apologia* for his actions during the expedition are in his *Narrative of the . . . Campaign Against the Indians*, 26-58, published in 1812.

[27] Scott to County Lieutenants, Nov. 12, 1791, *Universal Magazine of Knowledge and Pleasure*, 90 (1792), 76-77; St. Clair to Knox, Nov. 24, 1791, in Smith, ed., *St. Clair Papers*, II, 269-271; Talbert, *Logan*, 256. A romantic story that Scott in late 1791 marched to the site of St. Clair's defeat and slaughtered two hundred Indians in refuted by Butler, *Kentucky*, 205-206.

now on to be no half measures in either the diplomatic or the military sphere. Hence, while Washington's negotiations with the Indians were vocal, public, and pursued in deadly earnest, he advocated to Congress the build-up of a large, regular army under a tough, professional, and prudent commander. On January 11, 1792, the president sent to Congress proposals, which were enacted on March 6, 1792, authorizing an army of just over 5,000 men, to be arranged in legionary form (that is, into four sub-legions, each of which possessed its own units of musket-armed infantry, riflemen, cavalry, and artillery), designed specifically for warfare against the Indians of the Northwest Territory. One provision of this new law especially interested Scott and the Kentuckians, for it empowered the president, as a continuation of the old policy, to call up mounted volunteer militia to operate in conjunction with the Legion of the United States. That Washington intended to avail himself of the opportunity to reaffirm the old policy was never in doubt, and so it was clear to everyone that he would continue to field mixed regular-militia forces.[28]

Scott, however, had another, more personal reason to be intrigued by the new military arrangements, for a Philadelphia friend, George Walker, informed him that he was being considered by President Washington to command the entire Legion force rather than just the Kentucky volunteers. Delighted with this news, Scott openly lusted for the position, and Wilkinson (who also happened to be in the running for the job) described Scott as "a poor old wretch . . . galled and chafed with jealousy and impatience of office." Alas for Scott, when Washington came to the final choice, he decided that the Kentuckian, although "brave" and well intentioned, was "of inadequate abilities" and a drunkard. He selected instead a less unpalatable candidate, Anthony Wayne of Pennsylvania, even though Wayne too was overly fond of the bottle and likely to be "drawn into scrapes." The Kentuckians—including Scott and Wilkinson—were not impressed with Washington's choice; according to Congressman John Brown, most preferred Wilkinson. Brown, however, was willing to give Wayne the benefit of the doubt, for he recognized that the new commander's record of service in the revolutionary war had been outstanding. As for Scott, his hurt feelings were assuaged on June 4 by the General Assembly of the newly created Commonwealth of Kentucky, when that body

---

[28] Knox, "Statement relative to the Frontier Northwest of the Ohio," Dec. 26, 1791, *American State Papers: Indian Affairs,* I, 197-199; "Organization of the Army," Dec. 27, 1792, *ibid.*: *Military Affairs* (7 vols., Washington 1832-1861), I, 40-41; Extract of Act of Congress, Mar. 6, 1792, Scott Papers.

appointed him, along with Benjamin Logan, a major general in the Kentucky state militia.[29]

The Washington administration's flurry of military activity in the first few months of 1792 promised future security for Kentuckians, but it did almost nothing to bring them immediate relief. With the spring came renewed Indian raids upon the state, such as a strike by a party of warriors against Mason County in April that resulted in the loss of thirty-six stolen horses. Although Knox had forbidden Kentuckians once more to carry out raids into the Northwest Territory (because of the administration's continuing attempts to achieve a negotiated settlement with the Indians), the citizens of Mason County immediately organized a force of twenty-six men that pursued the Indian party forty miles up the Little Miami River in an attempt to retrieve the horses. When a night assault against the warriors' camp did not do the trick, the Mason Countians went home, secured reinforcements, and returned to the chase. They recovered many of their steeds, even if in a manner heartily disapproved of by Washington and his advisors. Most Kentuckians, however, applauded their resourcefulness, including newly elected Governor Isaac Shelby, who on April 9, in defiance of federal policy, empowered Scott to call up small parties of militia for as much as thirty days' service to protect "the inhabitants of the frontier."[30]

In the next few months, Scott's policy was to exercise Shelby's orders only under the most pressing of circumstances; but his fellow citizens had no such qualms. Thus, on May 10, Colonel Samuel McDowell and 180 Kentucky volunteers crossed the Ohio River, in defiance of Scott's orders, to strike a Wyandot village on the lower Sandusky River (near present-day Fremont, Ohio). When Knox learned of this raid, he wrote a letter to Wayne imploring him to halt such filibusters, for they imperiled the mission and life of Rufus Putnam, Washington's latest peace envoy to the Indians. Wayne complied with

---

[29] George Walker to Scott, Apr. 20, 1792, Scott Papers; Wilkinson to Harry Innes, Feb. 29, 1792, John Brown to Innes, Apr. 13, 1792, Innes Papers; Washington's "Opinion of the General Officers," Mar. 9, 1792, in John C. Fitzpatrick, ed., *The Writings of George Washington* (39 vols., Washington 1931-1944), XXXI, 509-515; *Kentucky Gazette*, July 7, 1792; Royal Ornan Shreve, *The Finished Scoundrel: General James Wilkinson . . .* (Indianapolis 1933), 93; Beasley, "The Life and Times of Isaac Shelby," 128; Jacobs, *Tarnished Warrior*, 126; Talbert, *Logan*, 260-261; Kohn, *Eagle and Sword*, 120. The most recent biography of Anthony Wayne is Paul David Nelson, *Anthony Wayne: Soldier of the Early Republic* (Bloomington, Ind. 1985).

[30] Thacker, "Kentucky Militia," 54-55; WPA, *Military History*, 62; Beasley, "The Life and Times of Isaac Shelby," 119-120.

Knox's instructions by writing the county lieutenants of Kentucky to cease and desist, and his strictures must have had some effect, for Scott's subordinates stopped their raiding into the Northwest Territory until October. In that month, however, John Adair and 100 of his neighbors launched a punitive expedition toward Fort St. Clair, where they claimed to have met a warrior band led by Little Turtle and routed his force at the expense of six Indians killed.[31]

While the Kentuckians filibustered, General Wayne labored at his headquarters in Pittsburgh to organize and train the Legion of the United States. When he arrived at his new post in June 1792, he found fewer than 100 soldiers under his command, and even by the end of the year he had collected a mere 2,000 recruits, only forty percent of his congressionally allotted strength. Nevertheless, he worked with diligence to whip the army into shape, moving the Legion in late November away from the fleshpots of Pittsburgh to a new site about twenty-two miles downstream on the Ohio River, which he named Legionville. As he organized his army, he also reflected upon an overall strategy for the future, and he mused long and hard on how best to employ the Kentucky mounted volunteers, which by the president's specific orders were to be an integral part of his forces. In August, he wrote Knox a long letter detailing the plan of operations that he intended to put into effect, and by and large it was this scheme that he finally utilized. His thoughts upon employment for the Kentucky volunteers, however, would alter drastically as time went on.[32]

In his original outline for the campaign, Wayne suggested to Knox that "two strong desultory parties of Operations composed of Mounted Volunteers (& I am pleased to find an avidity for this kind of service)" ought to be launched in the spring of 1793, "the one against Sandusky . . . the other against the Indians who have removed from the Miami Villages to St. Joseph's river, where by recent accounts there are several new towns of Hostile Indians." These expeditions, he said, would only be set in motion when "every thing was in readiness for a forward move of the Legion from fort Jefferson" (a post to the north of Fort Washington and the departure point for his expedition). The Kentuckians' raids, Wayne felt sure, would "be crowned with briliant success," but even if they had no other effect than to "distract

---

[31] Knox to Anthony Wayne, June 15, 1792, Wayne to County Lieutenants, June 23, 1792, Anthony Wayne Papers (Historical Society of Pennsylvania [HSP], Philadelphia); Beasley, "The Life and Times of Isaac Shelby," 130.
[32] Wayne to Knox, June 15, 1792, Anthony Wayne Papers, WLCL; Knox to Wayne, Sept. 7, 1792, Wayne Papers, HSP.

the savage Councils—& create a Jealousy for the safety of their Women & Children,'' they would have served a good purpose. Once these forays were finished, all the mounted volunteers would be discharged, ''except a chosen corps . . . who shou'd fall in with & join the Legion as Auxiliaries to the Regular Dragoons—In order to Assist in Escorting further supplies from Fort Jefferson to the Miami Villages or to strike at other Hostile towns lower down the river as Occasion might present.''[33]

Wayne's plan, which had much to recommend it in terms of allowing the most expeditious use of available resources, was predicated upon three primary considerations. First, as he well knew, the Kentuckians had no desire to serve in a combined regular-militia army. Second, Wayne himself had an aversion to militia soldiers, which he had developed during the revolutionary war, and which led him to believe that the mounted volunteers would be of more harm than good if they were incorporated into his main army. Third, the general in 1792 was sure that his Legion army eventually would reach its authorized strength, thereby eliminating the necessity for him to depend upon any militia force at all.

By the time Wayne moved his army to Fort Washington in the spring of 1793, however, he had been compelled to revise entirely his plans on how to use the Kentucky volunteers. On April 20, the secretary of war notified him that despite the administration's best efforts to recruit the army to its full strength, only 3,000 men would be forthcoming eventually (and even this estimate proved overly optimistic). Therefore, Wayne must incorporate into his main army ''such number of mounted Volunteers of Kentucky . . . as shall make your real force superior to the highest force of the Enemy.'' These proud westerners, Knox told Wayne on May 17, must be allowed to join the army as mounted volunteers, for they delighted ''to serve on Horseback and it is alledged in that case the bravest and best Men of the State may be brought into the field''; but they would flatly refuse to serve ''as mere Militia'' and if compelled to do so would send forward second-rate substitutes.[34]

Neither Wayne nor the twice-burned Kentuckians were pleased with Knox's news that they must cooperate with each other in a combined regular-militia army. Yet they had no choice in the matter and had to accept the secretary's verdict with as much equanimity as they

---

[33] Wayne to Knox, Aug. 14, Sept. 14, 1792, Wayne Papers, HSP; Stone, *A Brittle Sword*, 26.

[34] Knox to Wayne, Apr. 20, May 17, 1793, Wayne Papers, HSP.

could muster. Three times during May and June, Wayne wrote Governor Shelby, asking him to embody a force of about 1,500 men by the middle of July for service with the Legion. Shelby complied with Wayne's requisition by ordering Generals Scott and Logan to muster the state's militia, while Wayne supplemented the governor's correspondence by appealing to these gentlemen himself. Although Logan flatly refused to work with any federal officer, believing the idea of combined operations not to be "consistent with good policy," Scott agreed to go along—but only if Wayne would ignore his orders from Knox and allow the mounted volunteers to act as an independent force.[35]

Wayne was appalled at the responses of Logan and Scott, and he refused to concede the latter's request, for he now (if only of hard necessity) found the idea of an independent mounted militia force abhorrent. "Nothing," he growled to Knox on June 20, "shall induce me to commit the honor & dignity of Government nor to expose the Legion (unnecessarily) to the whole Combined force of the enemy—whilst *two thousand* mounted Volunteers . . . of the State of Kentucky (in pay of the United States) were stealing a March very wide from the Army— in order to burn a few Wigwams & capture a few women & Children & in which . . . they cou'd not meet with any Opposition, until they returned *triumphantly & safe* to their respective homes—leaving the. Legion to contend with the difficulty & danger." He hoped the Kentuckians would see the error of their ways, and he wrote the governor, Scott, and Logan assurances that he would be more successful than Harmar and St. Clair before him. Luckily, he persuaded Scott to his point of view much to Governor Shelby's relief. On July 1, Wayne commissioned Scott (who had joined him in camp for a few days) as an officer in the United States army. Five weeks later, Scott wrote his new commander from Lexington that the mounted volunteer force was enlisted to full strength and awaiting his summons to join the Legion—despite opponents of the raid, who were "etarnally throwing cold water on the Volunteer business."[36]

---

[35] Knox to Wayne, Apr. 20, May 17, 1793, Wayne to Shelby, May 18, June 14, 1793, to Scott, June 14, 1793, to Benjamin Logan, June 14, 1793, Shelby to Wayne, June 24, 1793, Wayne Papers, HSP; Wayne to Shelby, July 1, 1793, Shane Collection (Presbyterian Historical Society, Philadelphia); Shelby to Wayne, May 27, 1793, Scott Papers; Logan to Wayne, June 24, 1793, Wayne Papers, WLCL.

[36] Wayne to Knox, June 20, July 7, 1793, to Scott, Aug. 5, 1793, Scott to Wayne, Aug. 1, 10, 1793, Wayne Papers, HSP; Wayne to Shelby, July 1, 1793, to Scott, Aug. 13, 1793, Shane Collection; Scott's commission, July 1, 1793, Edward E. Ayer Collection (Newberry Library, Chicago).

The call that Scott anticipated was not long in coming, for in mid-September Wayne decided to move his Legion army northward from his camp on the Ohio River to a new post at or near Fort Jefferson, about fifty miles north of Cincinnati. At this new encampment he intended to spend the winter, preparing his army for a final drive against the Indians during the summer of 1794. In a letter to Scott on September 12, Wayne informed the Kentucky general that the mounted volunteers would be needed in this operation to serve as guards against a surprise Indian attack; Scott was to come forward immediately with his men and join Wayne at Fort Washington for the march northward. To Wayne's surprise and dismay, he learned from Scott on the 22nd that only 200 horsemen were still embodied and that the Legion commander could expect few more than that to join him later. Wayne growled to Scott in late September that the armed forces of the United States—Scott's militiamen included—were not involved in "a common or little predatory war made by a few tribes of Indians" but a "confederated war forming a chain of circumvallation around the frontiers of America." Kentuckians, he declared, had more to lose ("the lives of many, very many thousands of helpless women & Children") than did most citizens of the United States, and therefore they ought to join the Legion army in "One United & Gallant effort" to extirpate the menace once and for all.[37]

Although Scott agreed with Wayne and was embarrassed by the lackadaisical attitude of his neighbors, he nevertheless was compelled to tell the Legion commander on September 30 that only a draft order by Wayne would serve to fill the Kentucky militia ranks. This was a "Dernier resort," noted Wayne to Knox on October 5, with "little hopes of success," and although a measure that he felt compelled to take, he decided only two days later to commence his movement toward Fort Jefferson without the Kentuckians in support. Hence, by the time Governor Shelby and General Scott effected a draft call and gathered 1,000 mounted militiamen for service, Wayne had already reached his intended winter quarters, thus negating the very reason that the Kentucky militia had been embodied in the first place. Yet, it was now necessary—primarily because of political considerations—for Wayne to allow Scott and the citizen soldiers to join him. On October 21, as an anonymous Kentucky militiaman noted in his diary, General

[37] Wayne to Scott, Sept. 12, 18, Oct. 5, 1793, to Knox, Oct. 5, 1793, Scott to Wayne, Sept. 16, 1793, Wayne Papers, HSP; Scott to Wayne, Sept. 22, 1793, Wayne Papers, WLCL; Wayne to Scott, Sept. 26, 1793, Hardin Family Collection (Chicago Historical Society).

Scott's troops rode into the Legion camp, which was located "6 miles advance[d] of Ft. Jefferson . . . on a Level open Oak Land." Although Wayne was not of a mind to welcome the Kentuckians with open arms, he did admit privately to Senator John Edwards that they were impressive soldiers and "well officered."[38]

Wayne now decided that since Scott's men, whether needed or not, were going to draw their federal pay, they might as well be put to some useful purpose. He called together the Kentucky generals, Scott, Wilkinson, Robert Todd, Thomas Barbee, and Thomas Posey, on October 31, to propose a winter raid by the mounted militia against the Auglaize Indian villages on the Maumee River, about a hundred miles to the north. Although Wayne pointed out to the generals that the idea for the expedition came from Governor Shelby rather than himself, they rejected it out of hand. As Scott explained to Wayne, "the enterprise . . . is two [sic] Hazardous for the Volunteers alone," for only 900 troopers were well enough for service, all the horses were exhausted and hungry, and probably the entire Indian warrior force of 2,000 was collected at Auglaize. Finding Scott's arguments sensible, Wayne ordered him instead to carry out an expedition against a small Delaware Indian town about fifty miles south-southwest of the Legion camp, destroy this "source of frequent predatory parties," and then move on to Fort Washington for mustering out of the service.[39]

As it turned out, Wayne did not even get to launch this minor foray, for when Scott ordered the Kentuckians on November 4 to commence their march toward the Delaware town, they refused and demanded to be sent home immediately. Scott and the other militia officers, acutely discomfited by their troops' churlishness, reminded them of the " consequence of thier [sic] disorderly behavour but with out success." Finally, more than half of them simply decamped without orders and set out for home, leaving a chagrined Scott and a disgusted Wayne to decide what to do with the remaining 488 soldiers. Since the corps now had too few men to serve any good military purpose, the commander dismissed them as well, at the same time admonishing Scott to be prepared in the spring of 1794 to have his troops take

---

[38] Scott to Wayne, Sept. 30, 1793, Wayne to Knox, Oct. 5, 1793, to John Edwards, Oct. 22, 1793, Wayne Papers, HSP; *Kentucky Gazette*, Oct. 5, 1793; Richard C. Knopf, ed., "Two Journals of the Kentucky Volunteers, 1793 and 1794," *Filson Club History Quarterly*, 27 (July 1953), 253; Thacker, "Kentucky Militia," 57-58.

[39] Council of War, Oct. 31, 1793, Thomas Barbee to Wayne, Nov. 1, 1793, Wilkinson and Thomas Posey to Wayne, Nov. 1, 1793, Robert Todd to Wayne, Nov. 2, 1793, Wayne to Scott, Nov. 2, 1793, Wayne Papers, HSP; Scott to Wayne, Oct. 31, Nov. 1, 1793, Scott Papers.

the field once more. That evening, Scott left camp with the remnants of his corps, some of whom were still in a "noisy and troublesom mood." Their march southward was uneventful but for an inconsequential—and ineffective—raid against a five-man Indian camp along the way, and on November 14 they reached Cincinnati and were mustered out of the service. Wayne, meantime, vented his spleen against militia forces, snapping to Knox that the "dereliction of Five Hundred" of the Kentuckians "in the course of One night . . . will best shew whether that prejudice" he had earlier shown against citizen soldiers "was well founded or not." He then pleaded with Knox, "Let the Legion be completed, & I wish no *further or other force*" to destroy the "haughty savages."[40]

By the end of 1793, from all appearances, Wayne and the Kentuckians had suffered an irreparable breach in relations and Washington's hopes of eventually defeating the Indians were destroyed. Yet, things were by no means as bad as surface appearances would indicate. Wayne, for all his bluster against the Kentucky militia, had found them good soldiers and also had developed a respect for Scott; he continued to plan for the Kentuckians' use again in the coming year. (In fact, he had no choice, for Knox informed him in May 1794 that he must rely on them again in order to have sufficient manpower for the campaign.) The Kentuckians, for their part, had discovered during their two weeks' service with Wayne that he —unlike Harmar and St. Clair—was not making empty boasts when he declared that he knew how to fight Indians and could be trusted as a commander. There was one more bout of tension between Wayne and the militiamen in the early months of 1794, when Knox threatened to withhold pay from those soldiers who had "deserted" the previous year, and Wayne was accused by the Kentuckians of encouraging Knox's foot dragging in the matter. Finally, Wayne, with Scott's assistance, got the salary question cleared up to the westerners' satisfaction, and everyone spent the remainder of the winter impatiently marking time until a new campaign season opened. Scott in fact was now so enthusiastic about future service under Wayne's command that, in March 1794, he gave Knox a guarantee (according to Knox) that his "cordial co-operation" with the Legion commander could be "relied upon."[41]

---

[40] Wayne to St. Clair, Nov. 7, 1793, Arthur G. Mitten Collection (Indiana Historical Society Library); Scott to Wayne, Nov. 9, 22, 1793, Wayne to Knox, Nov. 15, 1793, Wayne Papers, HSP; *Kentucky Gazette*, Nov. 16, 1793; Knopf, ed., "Two Journals," 255-258; Thacker, "Kentucky Militia," 59; Stone, *A Brittle Sword*, 27.

[41] Scott to Wayne, Jan. 25, 1794, Scott Papers; Wayne to Scott, Feb. 10, 1794,

Scott's assistance, it transpired, was needed much sooner than either Wayne or Knox had anticipated, for early in 1794 James Wilkinson, who was second in command of the Legion army, began a concerted campaign of anonymous vilification against Wayne, both within the army and in Philadelphia, in hopes of destroying Wayne's reputation and gaining command of the army for himself. Although Washington and Knox knew that Wilkinson was orchestrating the attacks against their commander, they kept Wayne ignorant of the fact for almost a year, until after the Indians had been defeated at Fallen Timbers, because they did not wish to increase Wayne's mental burdens in the midst of vital military operations. In any case, Wayne's popularity with the people was not being hurt by the "disorganizers," as Knox informed Wayne on March 13, for the administration was doing all it could to defend him from "imbecillity" and "misrepresentations." General Scott, who was on leave in Philadelphia during early 1794 and heard reports "in Sirculation very injurious to the Commander in Chief of the Legion," greatly assisted Washington's program by writing the secretary of war an unsolicited letter on April 30, denying the allegations. "During my stay" in Wayne's camp, declared Scott, "I found him with great Sobriety & extream attention to the Duty of the army"; at all times "he paid the most Unwearied attention to every the most minute thing possible *in person*." Gratefully, Knox seized upon Scott's letter of praise for Wayne and with the Kentuckian's authorization published it widely. As for Wilkinson, whose consuming ambition was temporarily thwarted, he now added Scott to the considerable list of persons whom he hated for one reason or another.[42]

In May, as part of his final preparations to push the Legion army northward in a final drive against the Indians, Wayne called upon Governor Shelby to muster the Kentucky mounted volunteers for service. His letter caught the governor in a sour mood, for during the previous winter the Indians had kept up their raids upon Kentuckians, and Shelby believed Wayne had not done enough to curtail them. Shelby's response, therefore, was a curt suggestion to the general that, rather than calling militia to arms for service in the Northwest Territory, he ought to be paying more attention to defending Kentucky's borders against Indian harassment. Wayne, taken aback by Shelby's

---

to Knox, May 7, 1794, Knox to Wayne, May 7, 1794, Wayne Papers, HSP; Stone, *A Brittle Sword*, 27.

[42] Knox to Wayne, Mar. 13, 1794, Wayne Papers, HSP; Wayne to John Armstrong, Apr. 20, 1794, Northwest Territory Collection; Scott to Knox, Apr. 30, 1794, Scott Papers; Nelson, *Wayne*, 257.

sharpness, tried to convince the governor of the enormity of the Indian menace by sending a courier, Captain Thomas Lewis, on May
26 with a personal message. Soon it was clear to him that Shelby was
dawdling in calling the volunteers and that they would not possibly
be available until mid-July, but he had no one else to appeal to in
Kentucky, for Scott was still in Philadelphia and would not return
home until June at the earliest. In a fury against militiamen, Wayne
wrote Knox on May 26, "Wou'd to God that early & proper means
had been adopted by Congress for the Completion of the Legion; I
wou'd not at this late hour have to call for Militia . . . from Kentucky
who may not have a relish to meet this Hydra now preparing to attack us." But rage as he might, Wayne could only wait throughout
June for the newly arrived Scott to muster the mounted volunteers,
and he was vastly relieved when Scott and 1,500 Kentuckians finally
arrived at Fort Greeneville (which Wayne had founded the previous
winter) on July 27.[43]

With everything at last prepared for his march, General Wayne
gave the order for the Legion army and its Kentucky auxiliaries to
march northward, and his troopers swung out of the gates at Fort
Greeneville with optimism. Scott was particularly proud on this occasion, for Wayne the month before had paid him the compliment of
announcing that Scott was to succeed to the command of the Legion
should anything happen to Wayne. The commander, who was unaware
of Wilkinson's scheming against him, had no other motive in this matter
than to assure the most competent succession for his army in case
of emergency, but Wilkinson took the decision as a personal slight
and merely one more example of Wayne's favoring his "pets." He
protested to Wayne in a stiffly worded letter of June 8, only to have
Wayne shrug the whole matter off as being a mere formality necessitated
by military etiquette. Wilkinson, refusing to be placated, now launched
a sub-rosa campaign of vilification and slander against Scott, referring to his erstwhile friend as an "incompetent," a "fool, a scoundrel, and a poltroon."[44]

As he drove northward through the wilderness, Wayne adhered
to a fixed order of march for his army, which now consisted of 2,169

---

[43] Shelby to Wayne, May 7, 1794, Wayne Papers, WLCL; Wayne to Shelby,
May 21, 1794, to Knox, May 26, 1794, Wayne Papers (Kentucky Historical Society
Library, Frankfort).

[44] Wayne to Wilkinson, June 8, 1794, Wilkinson to Wayne, June 8, 1794, Wayne
Papers, HSP; Wilkinson to Innes, Jan. 2, 1795, Innes Papers; Jacobs, *Tarnished Warrior*, 140.

General Anthony Wayne, 1745-1796
Courtesy of Indiana Historical Society

regulars in addition to Scott's 1,500 Kentucky militiamen. He had his troops advance in double column with dragoons protecting their flanks, a picked body of Kentucky mounted volunteers under Major William Price scouting far in their front to reduce the risk of ambush, and the remainder of the Kentuckians stationed in the rear to guard the army's communications. Enjoining the soldiers to exercise constant vigilance, General Wayne each night had his men build a fortified camp for their protection, in order to escape the fate of St. Clair, who had been caught in the open with his guard down. Moving rapidly, Wayne seized the recently evacuated Indian town of Grand Glaize, located at the confluence of the Auglaize and Maumee rivers on August 8. There he halted his advance for a week and constructed a permanent stronghold, which he named Fort Defiance. (It was Scott who suggested this name when he exclaimed to Wayne, upon seeing the almost-completed works, "I defy the English, Indians & all the devils in hell to take it.") While the fort was abuilding, Wayne ordered a number of mounted volunteer patrols to ride eastward, down the Maumee, and scout out enemy strength in that direction. On the 10th, two soldiers in a five-man patrol were wounded at Roche de Boeuf while capturing two Indian prisoners, and two days later a larger contingent of 200 volunteers probed ten miles downriver to an Indian village named Tawa, looking for signs of enemy activity. The intelligence that Wayne garnered from both these patrols made it clear that an Indian army of about 2,000 warriors was rapidly gathering at Roche de Boeuf, under protection of about 400 British regulars, commanded by Major William Campbell, who had recently occupied and refurbished an old citadel named Fort Miami.[45]

Wayne now realized there was not a moment to lose in recommencing his army's march, so on August 14 he put his troops in motion eastward along the north bank of the Maumee River. Pausing in his advance only long enough to throw up a rude stockade (Fort Deposit) for protection of stores not needed in battle, Wayne pushed toward Fort Miami with his Legion, tempting the Indian army to stand and fight. Although his plans called for his trained regulars to bear the brunt of any full scale battle by engaging the enemy in a bayonet assault, he nevertheless had three important tasks reserved for Scott and the Kentucky mounted volunteers. First, he continued to dispose Major Price's "select Battalion" of Kentuckians in his Legion's vanguard, where they would be first to engage the enemy. Second, he posted General Robert Todd's brigade—about half the total number of volunteers—on the extreme left flank of his army to assault the Indians from that direction and get into their rear. Third, he ordered the remaining Kentuckians, General Thomas Barbee's brigade, into reserve, fully expecting that they would be called into battle at just the right moment to rout the Indians from the field.[46]

On the morning of August 20, as Wayne rode forward with his troops, Major Price probed with his vanguard toward the waiting Indians. Suddenly, at about 8:45 a.m., Price ran into the Indian army, which was hidden in the woods and grasslands between the Legion and Fort Miami, and the battle of Fallen Timbers was on. When Price's men reeled back from the fire of the warriors, Wayne and Scott rode forward to reconnoiter the Indians' positions. Immediately they realized that their enemy had chosen the site with care, for the warriors occupied an area that once had been swept by a tornado and was covered

[45] R. C. McGrane, ed., "William Clark's Journal of General Wayne's Campaign," *Mississippi Valley Historical Review*, 1 (Dec. 1914), 423; Knopf, ed., "Two Journals," 263.

[46] Wayne to Knox, Aug. 28, 1794, Wayne Papers, HSP; General Orders for Volunteers from General Scott, Aug. 4, 1794, Shane Collection; Thacker, "Kentucky Militia," 60.

with a thicket of uprooted trees and underbrush. This nearly impenetrable tangle, as Wayne later noted to Knox, made it difficult "for calvary to act" and afforded the Indians good cover. Despite these disadvantages, Wayne promptly ordered his regulars to charge with bayonets, which they did "with spirit & promptitude" until they came close enough to deliver a deadly aimed fire at the enemy. Then they rushed forward, screaming at the top of their lungs, so unnerving the warriors that they threw away their guns and fled in panic. Over the next hour and a half, the routed Indians were pushed back more than two miles, swirling around and beyond the tightly closed gates of Fort Miami, which Major Campbell refused to open for them. So total was the triumph of Wayne's regulars in this action that Scott's Kentucky horsemen on the American left barely managed to engage the enemy at all. Only in the last half hour of the contest, according to an anonymous Kentucky diarist, did Scott and Todd finally maneuver their troops close enough to "dismount and move forwards in a lo swampy ground with a great dale of fallen Timber and thick brush." Even then, according to Wilkinson's disparaging account of the Kentuckians' actions, "not more than three hundred" troopers got into the fight for any time at all. So, after an inconsequential amount of firing at the fleeing Indians, the militiamen were ordered by Scott to retrace their steps over their recent battleground, collect their seven dead and thirteen wounded comrades who had fallen during the charge, remount their horses, and rejoin Commander Wayne's main army near Fort Miami.[47]

In the days immediately following the American triumph at Fallen Timbers, Scott and his volunteers were not allowed to rest from their recent military labors. For almost a week, Wayne lingered at Roche de Boeuf, vainly attempting to dislodge Major Campbell's British garrison from Fort Miami without precipitating a shooting war with Great Britain. Meantime, he had the Kentuckians patrolling downriver toward Lake Erie to interdict any supplies that might be coming toward the fort by barge. (There were none, so the duty was relatively easy.) Then Wayne marched his army back to Fort Defiance, whence he wrote Knox a long letter describing the battle of Fallen Timbers and praising Scott's Kentucky militiamen. "I never discover'd more true spirit & anxiety for Action," he declared, "than appeared to pervade

---

    [47] Wayne to Knox, Aug. 28, 1794, Wayne Papers, HSP; Dresden W. H. Howard, ed., "The Battle of Fallen Timbers, as told by Chief Kin-Jo-I-No," *Northwest Ohio Quarterly*, 20 (Jan. 1948), 46; Knopf, ed., "Two Journals," 266; Thacker, "Kentucky Militia," 61; Stone, *A Brittle Sword*, 29-30.

the whole of the Mounted Volunteers; I am well persuaded that had the Enemy maintained their favorite ground but for one half hour longer they wou'd have most severely felt the prowess of that Corps." (Wilkinson, also describing the battle, denigrated his fellow Kentuckians' role on the 20th and expressed the opinion that their leader, Scott, was a "worthless Old scoundrel," who deserved the "contempt of the whole army.")[48]

In retrospect, it is clear that the triumph of Wayne and Scott at Fallen Timbers had broken the will of the northwest Indians further to resist American might. It was only a matter of time until the natives sued for peace, however reluctantly, and signed a peace treaty—which they did a year later at Fort Greeneville. The generals, however, not being privy to this comfortable foreknowledge, continued to wage war against the Indians after their arrival at Fort Defiance, by ravaging villages and crops within a distance of fifty miles on all sides. Wayne then decided in early September to march his army westward to the Miami villages, the site of Harmar's defeat in 1790, seize the natives' most vital lands, and construct a permanent military post upon them. He set out on the 15th to effect this final military maneuver of the campaign of 1794, accompanied by Scott and the mounted volunteers. By this time, the Kentuckians were once more becoming restless under Wayne's orders. It seems that in late August they had been assigned the onerous duty of packing much needed supplies from Forts Greeneville and Recovery northward on their valuable riding horses, and they were sending Wayne "petitions with out number" protesting this service's brutalization of their privately owned animals. Finally, on October 2, some of Barbee's men, whose time it was to make a run to Fort Recovery, mutinied, insisting that they had been promised by their officers "to be discharged." Although Scott delivered them a peroration on their duty, they were unimpressed. That night, some of them got drunk, and there was "a great nois and Quarreling in Camp," quelled only when Wayne paid them a visit at one o'clock the following morning and promised that they "should be discharged" upon the return of Barbee's men to camp, if they would only make one more supply trek. Scott's troopers agreed to this arrangement, but their hearts were not in it.[49]

---

[48] Wayne to Knox, Aug. 28, 1794, Wayne Papers, HSP; Wilkinson to John Brown, Aug. 28, 1794, James Wilkinson Papers (Detroit Public Library); Knopf, ed., "Two Journals," 267; Stone, *A Brittle Sword*, 28, 30.
[49] Wayne to Scott, Sept. 8, 1794, to Knox, Sept. 20, 1794, Wayne Papers, HSP;

During the next ten days the Kentuckians remaining with Scott in camp, while Barbee's men trudged to and from Fort Recovery, completed their tour of duty in what was now clearly the winding down of their decade-long war against the northwest Indians. The volunteers' final services were mind-numbingly prosaic, for they were merely laborers in fatigue parties, constructing a new stronghold that later would be named Fort Wayne. Although relations between Wayne and Scott remained cordial during this time, the army commander continued to find fault with the rank and file militiamen, noting in a typical fit of temper on October 4 that the volunteers were cutting wood for their fires which he had intended to use in erecting his fort. These outbursts notwithstanding, Wayne had developed a genuine respect for the Kentucky troops, and he expressed this regard both to Knox and to Governor Shelby. "The conduct of both Officers & men of the Corps in general," he declared in mid-October, "has been better than any Militia I have heretofore seen in the field for so great a length of time." The United States House of Representatives, agreeing with Wayne's assessment, on December 4, 1794, included specific mention of Scott and the mounted volunteers in a resolution of thanks to Wayne and the army for the victory at Fallen Timbers.[50]

Wayne, however, did not wish to leave the Washington administration with the impression that he had altered his views on militia troops, for he hastened to inform Knox that he still thought it a "mistaken policy & bad economy" to substitute "Mounted Volunteers in place of regular troops." Congress, he asserted, must support a strong regular military establishment for garrisoning his newly constructed posts in the Northwest Territory, or else "we have fought bled & conquered in vain." As for Scott and the Kentuckians, while they had certainly found Wayne by far the best federal commander with whom they had done business over the past decade, they nevertheless continued to believe that they could have handled the Indians more easily and inexpensively than the regulars had. General Wilkinson spoke for many of his fellow Kentuckians when he asserted that Wayne's achievement at Fallen Timbers with an expensive regular army could have been accomplished by the Kentucky volunteers alone in only thirty days'

Knopf, ed., "Two Journals," 268-269, 271, 273-274; Thacker, "Kentucky Militia," 63.

[50] Wayne to Shelby, Oct. 13, 1794, to Knox, Oct. 17, 1794, Jan. 24, 1795, Knox to Wayne, Dec. 5, 1794, Wayne Papers, HSP; Knopf, ed., "Two Journals," 274; Joseph Gales, comp., *Debates and Proceedings in the Congress of the United States* . . . (42 vols., Washington 1834-1856), IV, 956-966; Stone, *A Brittle Sword*, 30.

campaigning.[51] It seems clear from the evidence that both Wayne and the Kentuckians were arguing positions at variance with the facts, and that President Washington's adherence to the policy of combined regular-militia operations throughout the Indian wars was the only sensible, or even possible, way of achieving a victory.

On October 13, Scott at last received from Wayne orders that he and his soldiers had so long awaited: to march immediately for Kentucky. Although Scott only four days before had been "very much indisposed" with a fever, he now recovered quickly, ordered the mounted volunteers to ride for home, and after a final farewell to his old comrade in arms, Major General Anthony Wayne, swung into the saddle and joined the exodus. Seven days later, after a placid and uneventful march southward, he arrived at Fort Washington with his triumphant soldiers, mustered them out of the service and departed the military field for the last time. In future years, Charles Scott would serve the Commonwealth of Kentucky in various positions, and would culminate his career by occupying the governor's chair. In none of his civilian offices, however, did he do greater service for his fellow citizens than he had as general of militia in the Indian wars of the 1790s.[52]

---

[51] Wayne to Knox, Oct. 17, 1794, Wayne Papers, HSP; Wilkinson to John Brown, Aug. 28, 1794, Wilkinson Papers.

[52] Wayne to Scott, Oct. 13, 1794, Wayne Papers, HSP; *Dictionary of American Biography*, XVI, 487; Knopf, ed., "Two Journals," 275-276.

"Among the Most *Techy Articles of Civil Police*": Federal Taxation and the Adoption of the Whiskey Excise

William D. Barber*

COMMENTING in 1791 on the difficulties of paying the national debt, the Philadelphia merchant and political economist Pelatiah Webster warned, *"Taxes* are ever ranked among the most *techy articles of civil police,* and require very *delicate* management. . . ."* The federal revenue system was *"very young, tender,* and not ripened enough into *firm, general habit"*; yet it was being asked to carry a heavier burden than the country had ever felt before. "Any plan that *tends to embroil the finances,* and furnish *objections* and *murmurs* against the revenue," he added, "ought to be *reprobated* as the most *dangerous* and *fatal* measure that can be devised." Webster's solution—"to *reduce the debt* by *docking off some part* of it"—found no favor at the United States Treasury and little in Congress, but even the staunchest Federalist politicians admitted that the alternate approach of raising enough revenue to finance Alexander Hamilton's funding plan did demand the most delicate management.[1]

For the Federalists, tax policy involved far more than simply replenishing the treasury since taxes could determine political relationships, help shape an economy, or even affect the morals of a people. A comprehensive federal revenue system would establish the superiority, or at least the equality, of the national government in relation to the states and impress individual citizens with the energy of the new regime. Americans, however, had resisted taxation both by the British Crown before the Revolution and by their own legislatures afterwards. Federalist plans for restoring vigor, order, and discipline in government and society under the new constitution required extensive use of federal tax powers,

---

* Mr. Barber is a member of the Department of History, State University College, Oneonta, New York.
[1] Pelatiah Webster, *Political Essays on the Nature and Operation of Money, Public Finances, and Other Subjects* . . . (Philadelphia, 1791), 362-363, 372.

but too strong and sudden an application of this powerful remedy might convulse the patient. Only skilled political practitioners "acquainted with the general genius, habits and modes of thinking of the people at large and with the resources of the country" could fashion the most productive and least burdensome system of finance. "There is no part of the administration of government," declared Hamilton, "that requires extensive information and a thorough knowledge of the principles of political economy so much as the business of taxation."[2]

Taxes, according to the political economist of the eighteenth century, fell into two main classes, direct and indirect. Direct taxes included those on polls and real estate and general assessments on property of all kinds. Indirect taxes were excises and customs duties. Unfortunately for the practicing politician, every method of extracting revenue fell short of perfection. The common direct taxes on lands and polls were productive and easy to administer, but, particularly in the case of the poll tax, they did not distribute the tax burden in relation to wealth. Customs duties and excises, although relatively difficult and expensive to collect, largely solved the distribution problem since a citizen's expenditures would usually be proportional to his income. In theory, the consumer ultimately paid these levies and found them convenient, even unnoticeable, because they were blended into the price of goods which he might buy or not as it suited him.[3]

While most political economists endorsed indirect taxes, they cautioned that such measures did have significant disadvantages. Taxation of a domestically produced luxury would make that industry vulnerable to foreign competition, and a tax on a necessity oppressed the poor and would eventually injure the economy by causing an increase in wages. Most importantly, even well-planned indirect taxes were costly and troublesome to enforce since evasion was easy and maintaining adequate surveillance over a country's commerce demanded a large force of in-

[2] Jacob E. Cook ed., *The Federalist* (Middletown, Conn., 1961), 221-222.

[3] Adam Smith, *An Inquiry into the Nature and Causes of the Wealth of Nations*, ed. Edwin Cannan (New York, 1937), 777-779, 821; Malachy Postlethwayt, *A Dissertation on the Plan, Use, and Importance, of the Universal Dictionary of Trade and Commerce; Translated from the French of . . . Monsieur Savary, Inspector-General of the Manufactures . . . at the Custom-House of Paris: With Large Additions and Improvements . . .* , 2d ed. (London, 1757), II, 785; William Kennedy, *English Taxation, 1640-1799; An Essay on Policy and Opinion* (*Series of the London School of Economics and Political Science*, XXXIII [London, 1913]), 26-50, 82-94, 123-150.

trusive revenue officers. Excises suffered particularly from this drawback both because their very nature made them harder to administer than customs duties and because Englishmen had developed a hearty dislike for them.[4]

England's excise system relied on harsh and arbitrary enforcement for its effectiveness. The chief excise officials, for example, could try offenders without resorting to juries or the common law, and lesser officers had extensive powers of search and seizure which seemed to violate the principles of English liberty. Moreover, from its inception the excise fell heavily on the necessities of life despite theoretical admonitions to the contrary, and it proved to be a "growing" tax under which the rates increased as did the number of commodities covered.[5] The inhabitants of England's colonies on the American mainland had their own excises in the form of retail sales taxes on wine and liquor but retained the traditional English attitude toward them.[6]

When the Americans declared their independence, they compounded the tax problems known to political economy and English tradition by adopting a federal form of government. This made taxation a vital determinant of the relationship between the central authorities and the states. Those who shaped the Articles of Confederation feared giving the national government any right to tax. After a decade of experience with insolvency and democracy, the members of the Philadelphia Convention hardly questioned granting Congress almost unrestricted power "to lay and collect taxes, duties, imposts, and excises."[7]

The taxation issue became the most important specific charge in the

[4] Ibid., 113-122; Smith, Wealth of Nations, ed. Cannan, 821-824, 837-839, 847-850; for a summary of English denunciations against excise, see Townsend Ward, "The Insurrection of the Year 1794, in the Western Counties of Pennsylvania," Contributions to American History (Historical Society of Pennsylvania, Memoirs, VI [Philadelphia, 1858]), 120-125.

[5] Smith, Wealth of Nations, ed. Cannan, 850; Kennedy, English Taxation, 51-81, 104; Stephen Dowell, A History of Taxation and Taxes in England from the Earliest Times to the Year 1885, 2d ed. rev. (London, 1888), II, 8-14, 61-62, 72-79, 96-105, 137-143.

[6] Paul S. Boyer, "Borrowed Rhetoric: The Massachusetts Excise Controversy of 1754," William and Mary Quarterly, 3d Ser., XXI (1964), 328-351; Worthington C. Ford et al., eds., Journals of the Continental Congress, 1774-1789 (Washington, D. C., 1904-37), I, 109.

[7] Max Farrand, ed., The Records of the Federal Convention of 1787 (New Haven, 1911), I, 243-244, 589-593; II, 181-183, 353-354, 357-359, 382, 408-410, 414-417, 434, 446, 449-453, 473, 610, 614; III, 203.

Antifederalist indictment of the Constitution for granting more power of all kinds to the central government than was safe. According to the Antifederalists, the states would be destroyed by federal encroachment on their revenues. The national government had sole possession of the impost and concurrent power with the states over other taxes. It was axiomatic that all governments found a use for as much money as they could raise, and so Congress would enter into an intense struggle with the states for the sources of revenue over which they had joint jurisdiction. Victory would inevitably go to the federal tax collectors since they would be supported by the regular army, the federal courts, and even the state militia which could be summoned by the central authorities to enforce their edicts.[8]

To the individual citizen unlimited federal taxing power would mean higher taxes levied in inconvenient ways and collected by tyrannical officials. As Congress increased expenditures to maintain federal officers, including a vast array of tax collectors, in the manner to which they would soon become accustomed, it would lay all kinds of taxes and impoverish the people.[9] Eventually "a standing army of ravenous collectors" would threaten liberty as well as property. A delegate to the Massachussetts ratifying convention warned, "In an age or two, this will be the case; and when the Congress shall become tyrannical, these vultures, their servants, will be the tyrants of the village, by whose presence all freedom of speech and action will be taken away."[10]

Most Antifederalists wanted to limit rather than totally eliminate the federal government's taxing powers. They would yield the impost willingly and the excise reluctantly but balked at the direct tax. The states needed to retain one reserved source of revenue, and this was the key one from the Antifederalist viewpoint. It was the basic tax power, the one by which the states raised most of their revenue and the one whose exercise was "the highest act of sovereignty."[11]

[8] Jonathan Elliot, ed., *The Debates of the Several State Conventions on the Adoption of the Federal Constitution* . . . (Washington, D. C., 1836), II, 330-337; III, 147-149, 166-169, 322-323, 411-412; IV, 93, 289. Jackson T. Main discusses the Antifederalists' fears of consolidation with some special attention to the tax power in *The Antifederalists; Critics of the Constitution, 1781-1788* (Chapel Hill, 1961), 120-126.

[9] Elliot, ed., *Debates*, II, 72; III, 157, 263-266, 320-322; IV, 80-81, 87-88. Farrand, ed., *Records*, III, 215-216.

[10] Elliot, ed., *Debates*, II, 73-74.

[11] *Ibid.*, III, 29-31, 214, 280; IV, 75-77. Main, *Antifederalists*, 143-145, 184-185.

The federal power to lay excises left the Antifederalists in a quandary, for this sort of tax was indirect like the impost but internal like land and poll taxes. Although it lacked the peculiar relationship to sovereignty of the direct tax and from a practical standpoint would be a logical supplement to customs duties, it would threaten the states and oppress the individual. The power to levy excises was "very *odious* in its nature, since it authorizes officers to go into your *houses,* your *kitchens,* your *cellars,* and to examine into your *private concerns,* the Congress may impose *duties* on every *article* of *use* or *consumption.* . . ."[12] Military force could be used to secure compliance; moreover, a man might be dragged hundreds of miles to a federal court for perhaps justifiable resistance to federal officers. Excise officers would increase federal patronage while the collections would cut into the revenues of the states.[13] Nevertheless, most of the Antifederalists would have agreed with Samuel Spencer of North Carolina when he grudgingly admitted, "I would give them power of laying imposts; and I would give them power to lay and collect excises. I confess that this is a kind of tax so odious to a free people, that I should with great reluctance agree to its exercise. . . ."[14]

Antifederalists and Federalists argued not only about the eventual consequences of adopting the Constitution but also about what the immediate tax policy of Congress would be. Naturally the Antifederalists assumed the worst, the imposition of a full range of heavy taxes, including even direct ones.[15] Most Federalists replied that the impost would provide the bulk of federal revenue, very moderate excises would be necessary to supplement these duties, and direct taxes would probably be reserved for wartime emergencies. Some Federalists claimed, or at least implied, that in normal times the new nation would require only the impost.[16]

In *The Federalist,* Hamilton's analysis of the taxation problem stressed the practical difficulties of raising revenue in the United States and

[12] Farrand, ed., *Records,* III, 204.
[13] Elliot, ed., *Debates,* III, 167-168, 323, 412.
[14] *Ibid.,* IV, 75. The amendments to the Constitution supported by the Antifederalists fully reflected their views on federal tax powers. In eight states they formally proposed eliminating or restricting federal direct taxes; in four states they did the same for excises. *Ibid.,* I, 322-323, 325, 329, 336; II, 545, 551-554; III, 659; IV, 245-251. Main, *Antifederalists,* 144-146.
[15] Elliot, ed., *Debates,* II, 76-77, 101-102; III, 109; IV, 77-78, 188-190.
[16] *Ibid.,* II, 60, 106, 341-343, 501-502; III, 109; IV, 77-78, 188-190.

presaged his later recommendations as secretary of the treasury. He naturally accepted the proposition that the federal government required unlimited taxing power and added prophetically "that *in the usual progress of things, the necessities of a nation in every stage of its existence will be found at least equal to its resources.*" This was embarrassingly true in the United States, a country peculiarly deficient in productive revenue sources.[17] The recent past had proved that large sums could not be raised by direct taxes. "The popular system of administration, inherent in the nature of popular government, coinciding with the real scarcity of money, incident to a languid and mutilated state of trade," declared Hamilton, "has hitherto defeated every experiment for extensive collections, and has at length taught the different Legislatures the folly of attempting them." The impost should be the main source of revenue, supplemented by very limited excises cautiously applied. According to Hamilton, anyone devising a tax system for Americans would be narrowly circumscribed by prejudice and economic reality. "The genius of the people" would "ill brook the inquisitive and peremptory spirit of excise laws." On the other hand, real estate taxes would produce only small sums from reluctant farmers, and personal property was "too precarious and invisible a fund to be laid hold of in any other way, than by the imperceptible agency of taxes on consumption."[18]

Despite his advocacy of the impost, Hamilton carefully cautioned against total reliance on customs duties and avoidance of the more unpopular excise which would be needed to provide additional revenue and to create a balanced federal tax system. Too much emphasis on customs revenue could force industry out of its natural channels, oppress the merchant who would have to absorb part of the duty (and thus make importing states pay more than their fair share of federal taxes), encourage smuggling, and give an unfair advantage to manufacturing states which consumed relatively fewer imported goods than other states. Recourse to excises would be necessary, and although there were few proper objects for such taxes, an excise system could be devised that would be productive and not injurious to infant industries. Even in 1788 the country had one industry that might very properly be excised—the manufacture of ardent spirits.[19]

After winning the contest over ratification, the Federalists turned to

[17] Cooke, ed., *Federalist,* 190, 229.
[18] *Ibid.,* 74-76.
[19] *Ibid.,* 190, 216-218; Elliot, ed., *Debates,* II, 369.

the business of fixing the new government firmly on the country, and they thought no part of that task more important than collecting taxes effectively. Benjamin Lincoln, the future collector of the port of Boston, commented to John Adams, the newly elected vice-president, that if the federal government could get its revenue system into operation under officers who would do their duty uninfluenced by popular pressure, "we may consider the work as nearly done. . . ." Habitual obedience to national authority and the deference due a full treasury would soon assure permanent success.[20] Still, Congress would have to combine discretion with energy. "The Collection of a Revenue in all Governments seems to be the most nice and Critical part of it," a prominent Federalist merchant from Rhode Island advised Adams, "and if we consider the opposition that has been made to the Federal Constitution, and the many Prophetick sayings of the Antis, I hope and Trust that every step will be taken to Conciliate the People, and yet as to have good Government, by which Life Liberty and Property will be secured and Defended."[21]

The House of Representatives had barely finished organizing itself in April 1789 when James Madison proposed a temporary impost to secure "the object of revenue" without being "oppressive to our constituents."[22] No one disputed the need for immediate revenue, but the question of what would oppress a constitutent and the consequent dangers to the government caused controversy. Western congressmen complained about a heavy salt duty which would irritate the turbulent frontiersmen and perhaps lead to secession, but the loudest outcry arose over a proposed molasses duty of five cents a gallon which outraged New England. Business interests complained that the stills of Massachusetts were to be sacrificed to the breweries of Pennsylvania, and politicians warned that public opinion in the northeast, the nation's chief commercial section, would countenance smuggling as in the years before 1776 if tariff rates were set too high.[23] Yet the outlook was by no means totally dark. The

[20] Lincoln to Adams, July 14, 1789, The Adams Papers, Massachusetts Historical Society, Boston. Permission to quote from this and subsequent references to the Adams Papers has been granted by the Adams Manuscript Trust at the Mass. Hist. Soc.

[21] Jabez Bowen to Adams, Apr. 28, 1789, ibid.

[22] Apr. 8, 1789, in U. S. Congress, The Debates and Proceedings in the Congress of the United States . . . (Washington, D. C., 1834-56), 1st Cong., 1st sess., I, 102; hereafter cited as Annals of Congress.

[23] Apr. 16, 17, 27, 28, May 8, 9, 11, 12, 1789, ibid., 158-167, 209-231, 291-318,

merchants of the seaports had largely supported the Constitution and seemed ready to cooperate with a reasonable revenue system. "And the People in the Country," commented a Boston lawyer, "have not yet learnt the language of Complaint against Taxes where the Merchant is the Paymaster."[24]

On the whole, the first tariff was as well received and administered as any friend of the Constitution could have wished. The trading and shipping interest favored the new government, and their patriotism and honesty were extolled and encouraged by Federalist editors and clergymen. Recalcitrants who feared neither press nor pulpit were kept honest by the vigorous and efficient customs service organized by Alexander Hamilton.[25]

Congress had set the duties low to encourage compliance, and consequently, even before enacting the tariff of 1789, congressmen had begun warming toward an excise for additional revenue. Madison had favored a high molasses duty partly as a substitute for an excise on domestic distilleries, but New England congressmen had argued that this was a crude expedient for taxing the distillers and preferred an excise which would fall on southern whiskey as well as New England rum. By the middle of May, Madison feared it would be impossible to establish a reasonable ratio between taxes affecting imported and domestic rum without an excise. "The dilemma between that expedient and a palpable inequality in the burden, and injury to the Treasury," he complained privately, "is a perplexing one."[26] At the same time, Fisher Ames of Massachusetts, who had been the leading New England spokesman on the molasses issue and mistakenly assumed that Madison was still firmly aligned with other southerners in opposition to an excise,

---

324-328, 330-335; for a summary of the House debates on revenue measures during the first session of the First Congress, see Richard Hildreth, *The History of the United States of America* (New York, 1863), IV, 65-101. New England's reaction is reflected in William Tudor to John Adams, Apr. 22, 1789, Adams Papers; Abigail Adams to John Adams, May 1, 1789, *ibid.*; William Smith to John Adams, May 19, 1789, *ibid.*

[24] William Tudor to John Adams, May 18, 1789, *ibid.*

[25] Jeremy Belknap to John Adams, Sept. 19, 1789, *ibid.*; Leonard D. White, *The Federalists; A Study in Administrative History* (New York, 1948), 460-465, 515.

[26] Madison to James Monroe, May 13, 1789, in U. S. Congress, *Letters and other Writings of James Madison, Fourth President of the United States* (Philadelphia, 1865), I, 469-470; Apr. 27, 28, May 9, 11, 12, 1789, *Annals of Congress*, 1st Cong., 1st sess., I, 211-212, 214-216, 220, 302, 310-311, 327-328, 330-332.

found his zeal kindling over "the most evident necessity" for drawing some revenue from that source.[27]

More than a desire for equitable taxation and the need for revenue prompted taking the politically risky step from customs to excise since the question involved vital considerations of commercial control and political power. Ames realized that if the excise were left to the states, they might defeat the protective features of any tariff by taxing American manufactures.[28] Like many Federalists, John Adams was concerned about establishing "the Superiority, the Sovereignty of the national govt" since the states still had so much power as to make "thirteen Omnipotences against one Omnipotence." All sorts of collisions were possible, and one of the most likely subjects of conflict was taxation. "Can there be a greater danger than for the national gov't to take the Impost and leave the Excises in the State gov'ts . . . ?" the Vice-President asked worriedly. But if Congress took both, the states would probably be unable to continue financing their debts, and their creditors would oppose the national government. Was "there any other security against this danger than for Congress to take upon itself to pay all the State Debts. . ."? By the middle of June, Adams reported that "many gentlemen" favored a national excise and "some" advocated assumption.[29]

Still, going further than the impost meant venturing into hazardous fields of taxation. William Grayson, an Antifederalist senator from Virginia, disliked the tariff bill of 1789 since he thought that it favored the North over the South and that problems of enforcement would make it the most expensive way to raise money possible. Yet he could take some grim delight in the discomfiture of the Federalists as they hesitated to attempt more than the impost:

The cry here is, raise every thing this way; and to be sure this is good policy with the States east of Maryland; some of the other states join in the cry, not because it is their interest, but because they are afraid of trying any other mode of taxation. An excise is talked of, also a stamp duty, and I believe seriously aimed at by a good many—but whether there will be found a majority in both houses for this sort of business is more than

[27] Ames to George Richards Minot, May 14, 1789, in Seth Ames, ed., *Works of Fisher Ames with a Selection from his Speeches and Correspondence* (Boston, 1854), I, 37.
[28] *Ibid.*
[29] Adams to [Nathaniel P.] Sargeant, May 22, 1789, and Adams to [Cotton] Tufts, June 12, 1789, Adams Papers.

I can pretend to determine—If the Antis have their uneasy sensations, in my opinion the federalists are not altogether on a bed of roses—The creditors of the domestic debt (the great supporters of the new government) are now looking steadfastly on their friends for a permanent provision for their interest—But how is this to be accomplished—The Impost, after deductions for smuggling—Cutters—tide waiters, Searchers, naval officers, collectors and controllers etc. etc., will not yield, after supporting the expences of government, more than will pay the French and Dutch interest, if so much—what is then to be done? Ah! there is the question—[30]

According to the estimate of the House's own committee, the gap between expected expenditures and revenue was almost as broad as Grayson indicated. Income from the tariff and tonnage fees was estimated at $1,467,000 a year while the annual operating expenses of the government would amount to $596,000, interest on the foreign debt to $477,000, and interest on the domestic debt to $1,643,000 without making any allowance for arrearages. Hamilton later put the cost of paying 6 per cent on the whole domestic debt and arrearages at $2,545,000 and estimated that assuming the state debts on the same terms would add a million and a half dollars to the bill.[31]

Under these circumstances, the new government's original success in levying taxes could prove ephemeral. The tariff act of 1789 obviously provided inadequate revenue for existing federal requirements; excises would probably be necessary in any case; and assumption might well mean direct taxes.[32] Even if the cost of carrying the domestic debt were scaled down in some manner, there would presumably still be a sizable deficit. The Federalists had exhausted the easy answers to the revenue question since the tariff rates had reached the level where congressmen began to fear political repercussions, smuggling, and diminishing returns through reduced imports. Even taxing liquor, the favorite recourse of the politician, threatened to grow complicated. Simply raising the impost

[30] Grayson to Patrick Henry, June 12, 1789, in William W. Henry, *Patrick Henry; Life, Correspondence and Speeches* (New York, 1891), III, 393-394.

[31] The committee made its expenditures report on July 9 and its revenue report on Sept. 24, 1789. Walter Lowrie and Matthew St. Clair Clarke, eds., *American State Papers: Documents, Legislative and Executive, of the Congress of the United States. Finance* (Washington, D. C., 1832-61), class III, I, 11-12, 14. Harold C. Syrett, ed., *The Papers of Alexander Hamilton* (New York, 1961—), VI, 86-87.

[32] *Connecticut Courant* (Hartford), Dec. 21, 1789.

without resorting to other forms of taxation seemed economically and politically unsound, but either direct taxes or excises were bound to be unpopular. Many congressmen had started to think seriously of an excise which would not only produce revenue but also alleviate some of the difficulties connected with higher customs duties. On the other hand, such a proposal would tend to confirm the Antifederalist prophecy of a centralized tyranny suppressing individual liberty and the states. Also the effect on state revenues might necessitate assumption which would produce more political difficulties and the need for more federal taxes.

After passing tariff and tonnage acts, Congress left the fiscal problem to the ingenuity of the incoming secretary of the treasury; and during October, as part of his preparations for his report on funding, Hamilton began systematically seeking advice on commercial regulations, the management of the national debt, and means of obtaining further revenue. "Considering plans for the increase of our revenues," the secretary commented to Madison, "the difficulty lies, not so much in the want of objects as in the prejudices which may be feared with regard to almost every object. The Question is very much What further taxes will be *least* unpopular?"[33]

Madison, William Bingham, and Stephen Higginson supplied the most useful recommendations concerning the revenue problem. All three suggested increasing the impost and adopting excises, but beyond that their opinions varied widely. Madison advocated a spirits excise based on the size of the still to obviate complaints about prying excise officers, an accompanying increase in the duties on imported liquor, a stamp tax limited to the proceedings of the federal courts to avoid popular prejudices, and a land tax. The latter suggestion, despite its continued support by many southern politicians, was probably bad advice.[34] Bingham

[33] Hamilton to Madison, [Oct. 12, 1789], in Syrett, ed., *Papers of Hamilton,* V, 439; VI, 56, n. 34.

[34] Madison favored a land tax because of "its simplicity, its certainty, its equity, and the cheapness of collecting it." Still showing the nationalism of this period in his career, he also commented that the federal government should establish itself in this field of taxation and divert the states from real estate to direct taxes on other objects. Madison to Hamilton, Nov. 19, 1789, *ibid.,* V, 525-527. Later other southern congressmen claimed that their section would prefer a land tax to an excise, but little evidence supports the contention. Shortly after Madison mailed his advice on the revenue system, two members of the Virginia legislature, which was considering possible amendments to the federal constitution at the time, warned him about the unpopularity of direct taxes. Henry Lee

proposed a broad spectrum of taxes including a general stamp tax on legal and financial documents, a levy on liquor licenses, an inheritance tax on federal bonds, and increased imposts and excises on articles of general consumption. The Philadelphia merchant pointed to Great Britain as proof of the comforting axiom that skillfully imposed taxes would "in Some measure beget the Means of paying them." He added encouragingly, "The present Period is very favorable for carrying into Effect a System of Taxation, as the Affections of the People are So riveted to the new Government, that their Mind will be easily conciliated to all its operation."[35]

Higginson, a prominent Boston businessman and the one of the three who came closest to suggesting the course that Hamilton eventually followed, recommended reducing the interest on the national debt and then advised, "But the great Object is, first, to get a revenue equal to this or any other plan. I have no Idea, that any thing can be drawn from the States by requisition, or direct taxes. Imposts and Excises are the only Sources that can be relied upon; and those you must have exclusively to make the most of them." Furthermore, the two modes of taxation complemented each other, for together they not only gave the federal government control over commerce without state interference but also could "be so framed as to aid and check each other," an important point considering the low state of public morality.[36]

In his report on public credit of January 9, 1790, Hamilton proposed stretching the national revenues to the limits of prudence and perhaps beyond. Even after reducing interest rates to 4 per cent on the nation's domestic obligations, the existing federal debt plus the government's operating expenses would require $2,839,000 during the ensuing year, and this sum the secretary proposed to raise by increasing the customs duties on coffee, tea, wine, and liquor, and by laying an excise on domestically produced spirits. He estimated that the existing system would yield $1,710,000 and that the suggested alterations would add $1,133,000 of which $557,000 would come from excises. Although his recommendation

---

cautioned, "Never adventure direct taxation for years. The event now would be attended with serious consequences." Lee to Madison, Nov. 25, 1789, and Hardin Burnley to Madison, Nov. 28, 1789, The Papers of James Madison, Library of Congress, Washington, D. C.

[35] Bingham to Hamilton, [Nov. 25, 1789], in Syrett, ed., Papers of Hamilton, V, 548-549.

[36] Higginson to Hamilton, Nov. [11], 1789, ibid., 508, 511.

for assuming the state debts would call for an additional million dollars in revenue, Hamilton offered no plan for obtaining the sum since it would not be needed immediately.[37]

The report on public credit embodied a closely coordinated fiscal system designed to achieve Federalist goals with a minimum of risk and a maximum of efficiency. The key elements of the scheme were the excise, assumption, and the reduction of interest on the debt. By selecting a few luxuries, especially liquor, to bear the burden of increased taxes, Hamilton had placed himself in a strong position from the standpoints of both morality and political economy. He had also made an excise immediately necessary to finance the domestic debt. This new mode of taxation would provide essential revenue and administrative support for the impost. Moreover, the two taxes would establish federal dominance over all types of indirect taxation. Assumption, more palatable for being unconnected with any specific tax measures, would avoid "competition for resources" with the states and "mutual jealousy and opposition" between two rival groups of public creditors.[38] Reducing the interest on the national and state debts made assumption conceivable without later having to ask Congress for a land tax, a proposal likely to be rejected and also one likely to be dangerous and unproductive if adopted. Hamilton's recommendations would give the federal government an integrated system of taxation which would extend national influence beyond the seaports, avoid a direct confrontation with the states, and hopefully prove acceptable to the public.

The excise marked a new departure for the federal revenue system, but it was both administratively and politically the next logical step for the Federalists beyond the existing customs arrangements. In Hamilton's opinion, the proposed changes in the tariff would make the potential profits of smuggling so great that more extensive provisions for enforce-

[37] *Ibid.*, VI, 86, 97-99, 109, 137; E. James Ferguson, *The Power of the Purse* (Chapel Hill, 1961), 292-297. The revenue figures are approximate since Hamilton did not phrase his report in this way. I have credited the existing system with the revenue that would have been raised by its duties on imported liquor, tea, and coffee.

[38] Syrett, ed., *Papers of Hamilton*, VI, 78-81, 99-101. Hamilton's heavy reliance on taxing wines and liquors made control of indirect taxation and effective enforcement of great practical concern to him. According to his plans at the beginning of 1790, the federal government was to derive almost 44 per cent of its gross revenues from customs duties, excises, and retail sales taxes on these commodities. *Ibid.*, 137, 287-289.

ment would be necessary. Experience in other nations had proved that the only answer to the problem was the surveillance in depth provided by a network of excisemen covering the interior of the country and supplementing the efforts of the customs officers at the ports.[39] The excise also had other administrative advantages of a more political nature, however, and the measure was aimed at least as much at restraining the states as at curbing smugglers.

Despite their protestations during the struggle over ratification, many Federalists had believed that concurrent jurisdiction over taxes, at least over indirect taxes, by the state and federal governments would prove unworkable. As Hamilton later put it, while "the subordination of the State power of taxation to that of the General Government, or the confining it to particular objects, would probably have been an insuperable obstacle to the adoption of the Constitution," the existing arrangement involved "inherent and great difficulties." He had proposed to sever "the Gordian-knot of our political situation" by leaving "the States under as little necessity as possible of exercising the power of taxation."[40] The Constitution had given Congress sole possession only of the impost, and even this provision could be undermined if the states excised imported articles. Hamilton intended to extend the federal monopoly to all indirect taxes by levying a national excise and assuming the state debts.

Assumption would not only unite the interest of all public creditors, but it would also allow the central government to control indirect taxation and avoid any interference with its revenue system or attempts to direct the nation's economy. If forced to pay their own debts, the states would rely heavily on excises, and the result would be "collision and confusion." Productive objects for indirect taxes were scarce in the United States. Should either the state legislatures or Congress engross these objects, the other's revenue system must falter, and its creditors grow resentful. Should both parties tax the same commodities, no proper balance could be struck. Either certain branches of commerce and industry would be overburdened, or the state and national governments would try to make allowances for each other's levies and fail fully to exploit the country's resources. In any case, there must be inefficiency—

[39] *Ibid.*, 100-101.
[40] "Defence of the Funding System," II, [c. 1790], quoted in Richard B. Morris, ed., *Alexander Hamilton and the Founding of the Nation* (New York, 1957), 251-252.

and consequently recourse to less agreeable taxes.[41] By placing a substantial federal excise on liquor, Congress would lay its claim to this type of tax and appropriate the most suitable object for itself while assumption would make indirect taxation by the states unnecessary.

Hamilton's concern over state excises was by no means an abstract one. Connecticut and Massachusetts both had such taxes which were under attack by merchants who preferred a national excise and branded the laws Antifederal for interfering with the impost. In Massachusetts the Antifederalists were reported to be supporting the local excise law to gain the allegiance of the state creditors. Both states repealed their legislation in 1790—Massachusetts doing so only after Congress agreed to assume the state debts.[42]

A federal excise did have its potential drawbacks as well as advantages, but Hamilton had planned to mitigate these difficulties, fit the legislation to American conditions, and disarm his critics. As for objections to taxing a native industry, he argued that his entire revenue program actually protected American producers since duties on imported spirits would be raised and even a differentiation made in excise rates on liquor distilled from domestic materials and that manufactured from foreign ones like molasses. Thus, depending on the proof of the product, the American distiller of Monongahela rye or peach brandy would pay nine to twenty-five cents per gallon in taxes while the New England rum manufacturer paid eleven to thirty cents and the importer of Dutch gin or Jamaica rum twenty to forty cents.[43]

[41] Report Relative to a Provision for the Support of Public Credit, [Jan. 9, 1790], in Syrett, ed., Papers of Hamilton, VI, 78-81.

[42] Oliver Wolcott, Sr., to Oliver Wolcott, Dec. 23, 1789, in George Gibbs, ed., Memoirs of the Administrations of Washington and John Adams, Edited from the Papers of Oliver Wolcott, Secretary of the Treasury (New York, 1846), I, 33; John Trumbull to John Adams, June 5, 1790, Adams Papers; H[enry] Jackson to Henry Knox, Jan. 24, 1790, The Henry Knox Papers, Mass. Hist. Soc.; C[hristopher] Gore to Rufus King, Jan. 24, 1790, in Charles R. King, ed., The Life and Correspondence of Rufus King, Comprising his Letters, Private and Official, his Public Documents and his Speeches (New York, 1894-1900), I, 385-386; Connecticut Courant (Hartford), Dec. 21, 1789, Jan. 7, 1790; Columbian Centinel (Boston), Jan. 20, 23, 1790; Boston Gazette, June 21, 1790; Pennsylvania Packet (Philadelphia), Oct. 1, 1790.

[43] Syrett, ed., Papers of Hamilton, VI, 138-139, 143-145. The actual advantage to American distillers was slight. Those processing foreign materials gained very little over the rates in the tariff of 1789; those using domestic materials generally had other problems, such as raising cash for taxes, more important than foreign competition. Annals of Congress, 1st Cong., 2d sess., II, 2129.

The secretary of the treasury met the most important traditional complaints against excise by limiting his proposal to spirits and taking "the most scrupulous care" to make its enforcement compatible with American liberties. Any levy on liquor, commonly considered the most suitable object of taxation, could always be defended as turning vice and luxury to the public good. To avoid both political objections to prying excisemen and the practical administrative problems of maintaining close surveillance over the thousands of country stills in the southern and middle states, Hamilton suggested that distillers operating outside cities, towns, and villages should have the option of paying a flat annual rate of sixty cents a gallon on the capacity of their stills rather than so much a gallon on their actual production. In addition, revenue officers were to be legally amenable for all transgressions, and unlike their British counterparts, they had no right of indiscriminate search or summary jurisdiction. The United States government would go so far as to pay damages in suits against excisemen when the jury exonerated the defendant by finding probable cause for his seizure of the goods but held that the plaintiff had suffered a loss. The sugar coating on the draft of the bill even extended to Hamilton's proposed title which claimed that the measure was "as well to discourage the excessive use of those Spirits, and promote Agriculture, as to provide for the support of the Public Credit."[44]

The House of Representatives gave little attention to the revenue problem until it had settled on a plan for funding the domestic debt, but when the members turned to assumption, the tax question inevitably arose. Those who favored assuming the state debts contended that a uniform federal system of imposts and excises would raise revenue more efficiently and avoid internecine clashes between the state and national governments. However, some proponents of Hamilton's program, especially the Massachusetts delegates, feared granting any excise to the federal government until assumption had been assured. As one Massachusetts congressman put it, "Where the resources go the debts must follow."[45] Those suspicious of assumption revived the former Antifederalist arguments about revenue and power and extolled the ability

[44] Syrett, ed., *Papers of Hamilton*, VI, 99-101, 104, 138, 154-156, 158-160.
[45] Feb. 23, 25, 26, 1790, *Annals of Congress*, 1st Cong., 2d sess., II, 1309-1311, 1319-1320, 1357-1359, 1372. For the best complete account of the congressional struggle over assumption, see Ferguson, *Power of the Purse*, 306-325.

of state legislatures to fit taxation to local prejudices and economic situa-tions "by known and accustomed methods, handed down to them by their ancestors." The American people had given Congress full powers of taxation but had not expected all of them to be exercised except in a national emergency.[46]

Hamilton's report had left the revenue measures necessary to finance the state debts undefined. His supporters spoke airily of small increases in imposts and excises, but his opponents contended that the end result might be a general excise and even direct taxes. On the other hand, with-out assumption even the liquor excise might be avoided. Alexander White of Virginia's Shenandoah Valley, who claimed to fear direct taxes, proposed asking Hamilton to present a plan for raising the funds, and after considerable debate the House agreed by one vote. Within only two days the secretary responded with a report outlining further increases in the import duties, a carriage tax, a tobacco excise, federal legal licenses and stamp taxes, levies on auction sales, and taxes on the retail sale of wines and liquors. Perhaps a few other undefined measures might be required, but assumption could certainly be financed "without the necessity of taxing, either houses or lands, or the stock or the produce of the farms."[47]

In his whole revenue plan Hamilton attempted to accommodate Fed-eralist aims to practical problems and popular prejudices, and in doing so he disturbed some fellow Federalists who felt that by losing his nerve the secretary was failing to rivet the new system firmly on the country. John Trumbull, the Hartford Wit, expressed a common anxiety when he demanded of John Adams: "When, in the name of Common Sense, are direct Taxes to be wanted, when can they with propriety be demanded, if not now? Does he mean to give them up forever, and lose the most important resource of the Empire? Is he ignorant that direct Taxation to a moderate amount is the strongest link in the chain of Government, and the only measure, which will make every man feel that there is a power above him in this world?" Trumbull advocated ramming assumption and a direct tax through Congress together since both would meet an equal amount of opposition from the same quarters.[48]

[46] Feb. 24, 25, Mar. 1, 1790, *Annals of Congress*, 1st Cong., 2d sess., II, 1312-1316, 1328-1331, 1339, 1344-1345, 1350, 1365-1366, 1379-1380.

[47] Feb. 24, 25, Mar. 2, 1790, *ibid.*, 1330, 1344-1346, 1396-1405; Report on Funds for the Payment of the Interest on the States' Debts, Mar. 4, 1790, in Syrett, ed., *Papers of Hamilton*, VI, 289.

[48] Trumbull to Adams, June 5, 1790, Adams Papers; see also Chauncey Good-

Hamilton's guarantee against direct taxation failed to quiet the critics of his funding plan. Still urging delay, they contended that a miscalculation might result in a direct tax while leaving the state debts undisturbed would probably enable the national government to rely solely on the impost and permit the country to escape any federal excise whatsoever. After almost two months of debate, the House rejected assumption at the end of April, and later attempts by New England congressmen to reverse the decision and maintain the integrity of Hamilton's entire program failed. On June 2 a funding bill with no provision for assumption was passed, and then the representatives turned to the tax question. By the middle of the month they seemed ready to approve Hamilton's original bill, including the excise, without assuming the state debts.[49]

The struggle over the tax bill, however, had reached such a complexity that the ultimate outcome remained in doubt. Southern congressmen led the opposition against both the excise and assumption with those from backcountry constituencies emerging as the strongest champions of the family still. John Steele, a Federalist from western North Carolina and normally a loyal ally of the treasury, warned that the government dared not risk "a convulsion" at present and added, "This bill extends so far as to embrace little private fruit, or grain stills employed in the country. This, I confess, appears to me to be a *wild goose chase* after revenue. . . . Have gentlemen considered the extent of this country, the number of counties? The inundation of excisement and reptile collectors that must be let loose upon the people?"[50] On the other hand, the delegations from Massachusetts and Connecticut strongly favored both assumption and the excise, but they were prepared to scuttle that tax or even the whole revenue bill if the states were not relieved of their debts. On June 18 representatives from both groups made separate attempts to eliminate the excise. Josiah Parker of Virginia, an inveterate opponent of the measure, offered a resolution to have Hamilton report another revenue plan without excise while Elbridge Gerry of Massachusetts proposed striking the key excise provisions from the existing bill. Both

rich to Oliver Wolcott, Mar. 28, 1790, and Oliver Wolcott, Sr., to Oliver Wolcott, Apr. 23, 1790, in Gibbs, ed., *Memoirs of the Administrations*, I, 44-45.

[49] Mar. 9, 30, Apr. 1, 26, 27, May 24, 25, 26, June 2, 8, 9, 11, 14, 18, 1790, *Annals of Congress*, 1st Cong., 2d sess., II, 1417-1418, 1488, 1507-1509, 1544-1548, 1587-1616, 1619, 1629, 1633-1634, 1636-1639, 1642-1643; Broadus Mitchell, *Alexander Hamilton* (New York, 1957-62), II, 72-76; John C. Miller, *Alexander Hamilton, Portrait in Paradox* (New York, 1959), 247-248.

[50] *Pennsylvania Packet* (Philadelphia), June 25, 1790.

motions failed—Gerry's in part because some southerners felt that this
change without others in the customs duties would give New England
distillers an unreasonable amount of tariff protection. Three days later,
however, the two factions united against engrossing the whole bill.
Moderates like Madison, an opponent of assumption and excise, and
Thomas Fitzsimons of Pennsylvania, an advocate of both, supported
the act in hopes of salvaging some sort of revenue program, but they
went down to defeat by a vote of thirty-five to twenty-three.[51]

Every member of the Massachusetts and Connecticut delegations but
one voted to reject the bill. As Fisher Ames explained, he and his allies
were engaged in political blackmail to counteract both the failure of
assumption and a possible deal between the South and Pennsylvania to
place the capital first at Philadelphia and then on the Potomac. Disrupting the whole revenue system should cause their opponents to reconsider
and produce a more equitable arrangement.[52]

Ames's forecast of an accommodation with "those who love peace,
and those who fear the consequences," was actually already well on the
way to fulfillment since shortly before the defeat of the revenue bill
Hamilton and Madison had reached their accord at Thomas Jefferson's
famous dinner. Nevertheless, the New Englanders' maneuver had not
been wasted since the obvious difficulties facing the tax program in the
House had been an important factor in bringing about a compromise.
"The assumption still hangs over us," Madison had observed shortly
before his meeting with Hamilton. "The negative of the measure has
benumbed the whole revenue business. I suspect that it will yet be un-
avoidable to admit the evil in some qualified state."[53]

Moreover, even after Jefferson's dinner party every added bit of pressure for a settlement helped, since the understanding between Hamilton
and the Virginians did not automatically guarantee that the state debts
would be assumed. Jefferson, who presumably was the one to approach

---

[51] *Ibid.*, June 23, 25, 1790; June 18, 21, 1790, *Annals of Congress*, 1st Cong.,
2d sess., II, 1642-1644.

[52] Ames to George Richards Minot, June 23, 1790, in Ames, ed., *Works of
Ames*, I, 81-83.

[53] In the same context Madison also mentioned the fading hope of locating the
capital on the Potomac and the uncertain fate of the funding bill in the Senate.
Madison to James Monroe, June 17, 1790, quoted in Dumas Malone, *Jefferson and
the Rights of Man* (Boston, 1951), 298. The agreement that saved assumption
probably was made between June 17 and June 20.

the Virginia congressmen whose votes would be required for the compromise, expected that proposals to protect the low debt states and the plan to place the permanent capital on the Potomac would win the necessary support for assumption. He did, however, foresee strong continued resistance by congressmen who preferred state taxation, especially by those who during the struggle over ratification had argued that Congress would probably never levy taxes when the states could do so effectively and who now feared the reaction of their constituents.[54]

Once the compromise succeeded, the whiskey tax became inevitable. James Jackson of Georgia in a last ditch attack on assuming the debts claimed that the excise had begun "to set the Continent in a flame" and asked if his colleagues in the House meant to "foster it in secret, while they apparently reject it." Although the connection between the tax and assumption was certainly no mystery, the representatives did find themselves in the happy position of being able to fund without taxing since no interest would fall due immediately on the assumed state debts, and they proceeded to take advantage of the situation. The House approved assumption at the end of July, increased the impost to fund the original national debt at the beginning of August, and then discreetly adjourned without making any further provision for revenue other than requesting another report on the subject from Hamilton. As for Jackson's kindled continent, public reaction to the excise alone had not been especially vehement, but interest in the measure began intensifying since the tax was the only major part of Hamilton's funding program that still required congressional action.[55]

When the First Congress reconvened during December 1790, the secretary of the treasury informed its members that they faced a $38,000 deficit in the financing arrangements for the former national debt as well as the unfunded annual interest of $788,000 on the assumed state debts which would begin to accrue after 1791. To raise the needed

[54] *Ibid.*, 301; Jefferson to James Monroe, June 20, 1790, in Julian P. Boyd, ed., *The Papers of Thomas Jefferson*, XVI (Princeton, 1961), 536-538.

[55] July 23, Aug. 6, 9, 1790, *Annals of Congress*, 1st Cong., 2d sess., II, 1694-1695, 1721, 1723, 2296-2299; James Madison to James Madison, Sr., July 31, 1790, and a circular letter by James Madison, Aug. 13, 1790, Madison Papers. Most of the popular reaction to the excise issue came after the debts had been assumed. I have been able to find references to only two public meetings on the subject before Aug. 1790—one in Philadelphia and the other in Newbern, North Carolina. *Pennsylvania Packet* (Philadelphia), June 23, Aug. 17, 1790; *Boston Gazette*, July 12, 1790.

funds he recommended consummating his plan of January 1790 by
further increasing import duties on liquor to the levels that he had
proposed and adopting the excise. An assumed debt smaller than expected and customs receipts larger than estimated had made unnecessary the miscellaneous taxes in the report of March 4. Besides, those
proposals had no special importance to Hamilton beyond their monetary
return. This time his revenue program was almost assured of passage
since assumption had swung the entire Massachusetts and Connecticut
delegations behind the excise while for southerners like Madison who
disliked the tax but supported it, the fiscal needs of the country now
left "scarce an option." Direct taxes would probably be more unpopular,
and hard liquor was the least objectionable article that the government
could excise.[56]

The measure's irreconcilable opponents in the House renewed all
their former arguments, seeking at least to delay action until the newly
elected Congress convened and some actual experience had been gained
concerning the fiscal effects of assumption.[57] After failing to strike out
the bill's key sections, they turned to supporting amendments that would
reduce the supposed political dangers hidden in its administrative provisions. Abraham Baldwin of Georgia indicated the assumptions behind

[56] First Report on the Further Provision Necessary for Establishing Public
Credit, [Dec. 13, 1790], in Syrett, ed., *Papers of Hamilton*, VII, 225-228; Jan. 17,
27, 1791, *Annals of Congress*, 1st Cong., 2d sess., II, 1870, 1884; James Madison
to Edmund Pendleton, Jan. 2, 1791, in U. S. Congress, *Letters of Madison*, I, 525.

[57] Eighteen members eventually voted for eliminating the excise from the revenue bill (total vote 16 yeas to 36 nays), against engrossing the bill on its third
reading (35-20), or against final passage (35-21) without voting inconsistently on
any of these questions. They included one of five representatives from New York
voting, three of seven from Pennsylvania, one of five from Maryland, three of
eight from Virginia, five of five from North Carolina, two of three from South
Carolina, and three of three from Georgia. Eight of these men, if one includes all
the Georgians, had been elected from frontier districts. (Only two representatives
from such districts voted consistently for the bill, and one of them was Alexander
White of Virginia, who had strongly resisted an excise before the bargain locating
the capital on the Potomac had won his support for assumption.) Four more of
the bill's opponents were Antifederalists. (The only other Antifederalists voting,
both from Massachusetts, favored the excise.) One representative from New York
(Jeremiah Van Rensselaer from a frontier district), two from Maryland, and one
from Virginia opposed eliminating the excise but then voted against passing the
whole bill. Thomas Scott of Pennsylvania, who was elected at large but had been
put on the Federalist ticket to give it western balance, voted to eliminate the excise
but also favored engrossing the bill. Jan. 5, 6, 11, 17, 25, 27, 1791, *Annals of Congress*, 1st Cong., 2d sess., II, 1842-1852, 1857-1861, 1870, 1883-1884.

this line of attack when he commented that "the genius and whole structure of the government" showed it had been designed for national purposes "such as the general regulation of trade, coinage, post-offices and post-roads, peace and war. . . . It should be precluded, as far as possible, from attempting to go down to intimate and particular legislation. . . . Whenever it gets upon that ground, it will appear, by its want of power, to be out of its element, and that it is not furnished with the necessary tool to carry on the work." Enacting the excise or a direct tax would mean more federal revenue officers, probably an extension of the federal judiciary to the justice of the peace level, and generally the minute regulation of Americans by their national government. The exercise of these taxing powers might prove essential in an emergency, but once used even under those conditions, "there would . . . be great reason to doubt, whether the government would ever again return to its former ground."[58]

Hamilton's recommendations regarding the administration of the law intensified the fears of its opponents since he favored leaving most matters such as the boundaries of the internal revenue districts, the number of excisemen, and their salaries to the discretion of the president—an arrangement that would provide the necessary flexibility to manage an undertaking with which the government had no previous experience. Congressmen distrustful of the secretary of the treasury and his allies naturally suspected his motives, but some supporters of the bill also disliked giving so much authority to the executive department without including some safeguards. In the House amendments were offered to restrict the number of revenue officers that could be appointed in any area, to fix their salaries by law, to place a two-year limit on the authorization for paying them, and to restrain their personal political activity solely to casting a vote in elections.[59] In the Senate the administrative provisions of the bill also produced an uneasiness among

[58] *Augusta Chronicle*, Apr. 9, 16, 1791.
[59] None of these amendments became part of the act. The major safeguard against burgeoning executive influence that Congress enacted was one which Hamilton had suggested—limiting the total compensation of the revenue officers to a fixed percentage of the amount raised by the act. Syrett, ed., *Papers of Hamilton*, VI, 139-140; Jan. 18, 20, 21, 24, Feb. 19, 22, 25, 1791, *Annals of Congress*, 1st Cong., 2d sess., II, 1872-1882, 1966, 1968, 1971, 2321-2322, 2339-2340; Fisher Ames to Timothy Dwight, Jan. 24, 1791, in Ames, ed., *Works of Ames*, I, 92-93; White, *Federalists*, 395-397.

some members that was intensified when Hamilton secured the addition
of a clause which specifically empowered the president to establish
revenue districts by transferring territory "from the great to the lesser
States." This peculiar wording was designed to soothe the smaller states
by guaranteeing them against dismemberment for federal purposes, but
a few administration Senators argued that the Senate should go even
further and not *pay any more attention to the State boundaries than to
the boundaries of the Cham of Tartary.*[60]

Such sentiments from his colleagues only confirmed the misgivings
of the ever suspicious William Maclay of Pennsylvania whose political
paranoia often magnified the fainter forebodings of less virtuous and
egotistical republicans and threw a refracted but revealing light on
national affairs. On this occasion the Senator discerned a plot to annihilate the states and American liberty. In Maclay's opinion, Hamilton
and his adherents in Congress had already promoted the Indian war in
the Northwest Territory to create a standing army and were preparing
to use the difficulties with the Algerian pirates to justify a navy. "With
these two engines, and the collateral aid derived from a host of revenue
officers," Maclay warned, "farewell freedom in America." If not tyranny,
perhaps revolution lay ahead. After the final vote on the excise act,
Senator William S. Johnson of Connecticut remarked to Maclay, "All is
over, and the business is complete. We have a revenue that will support
the Government and every necessary measure of Government." The
Pennsylvanian morosely replied "that the Government might, and perhaps would, fall by her overexertion to obtain support."[61]

Maclay recorded that his colleague "seemed a little struck" by the
comment, and the traditional unpopularity of excises combined with
the hostile reaction of several state legislatures to Hamilton's fiscal
policies did give Maclay's observation some credibility. To the con-
sternation of the Federalists, state assemblies had begun passing resolutions on federal affairs and in some cases claiming the right to
instruct their senators. During December 1790 the Virginia legislature
and the Maryland House of Delegates, which reversed itself five days

[60] William Maclay, *The Journal of William Maclay, United States Senator from
Pennsylvania, 1789-1791* (New York, 1927), 374-378, 386-387. Maclay's quotation
from the bill paraphrases the language of the act as passed. *Annals of Congress*, 1st
Cong., 2d sess., II, 2322.
[61] Maclay, *Journal of Maclay*, 378-379.

later, denounced assumption while the North Carolina legislature adopted several resolutions including one opposing federal excises and direct taxes and another urging a policy of "republican economy," especially in regard to "the enormous salaries given to the public officers."[62] A more widely publicized attack on the excise came a month later when the Pennsylvania House of Representatives called the tax "subversive of peace, liberty and the rights of the citizens." The common residence of the state legislature and Congress in Philadelphia plus a popular petition campaign against the excise made the Pennsylvania situation particularly obnoxious to good Federalists.[63]

Staunch supporters of the Washington administration deprecated the "ferment" in North Carolina, the "mobbish Disposition" of Philadelphia, and Maryland's inclination "to lead down the Virginia Dance." They questioned the propriety of the state legislatures debating matters that were the responsibility of Congress—a practice which Fisher Ames branded as anarchy. The resolutions seemed just the first shots opening a general battle for supremacy between the states and the national government. Besides, these expressions of legislative opinion combined with the "indiscreet violence" of the speeches delivered by congressional opponents of the excise would make the law even more obnoxious to the public than it was already.[64]

With considerable justice some observers questioned both the extent of popular discontent and the sincerity of the excise's political critics. Auditor of the Treasury Oliver Wolcott found it difficult to form any sound opinion of conditions in the southern states since the speeches of the region's politicians made their constituents appear on "the eve of a rebellion" but the national revenues were collected there with no more difficulty than elsewhere. In Pennsylvania Maclay expected the excise issue would "vanish in air." Politicians from the old Constitutional

[62] Miller, *Hamilton*, 255-256; *Maryland Gazette* (Annapolis), Dec. 23, 1790; Walter Clark, ed., *The State Records of North Carolina* (Goldsboro, N. C., 1886-1907), XXI, 855-856, 859-860, 902-903, 961-963, 991-992, 1028-1030, 1040-1041, 1044, 1048-1049; Benjamin Hawkins to Alexander Hamilton, Feb. 16, 1791, in Syrett, ed., *Papers of Hamilton*, VIII, 45.

[63] *Dunlap's American Daily Advertiser* (Philadelphia), Jan. 13, 15, 20, 21, 22, 24, 29, 1791; *Gazette of the United States* (Philadelphia), Jan. 22, Feb. 2, 1791.

[64] Henry Marchant to John Adams, Feb. 19, 1791, Adams Papers; Fisher Ames to Thomas Dwight, Jan. 6, Jan. 24, 1791, in Ames, ed., *Works of Ames*, I, 91-94; Benjamin Lincoln to Alexander Hamilton, Dec. 4, 1790, in Syrett, ed., *Papers of Hamilton*, VII, 196-198.

party, like Albert Gallatin and William Findley, who championed the anti-excise resolutions in the state legislature had nothing in mind except using a popular issue to secure themselves "niches in the six-dollar temple of Congress," the United States Senate. Certainly those individuals had never shown any interest in repealing the state's own excise law on the grounds that it threatened liberty.[65]

Whatever the original motives of its exploiters, the excise issue did become a continuing embarrassment to the Washington administration. The spirits excise was assumption made manifest in taxation; to many people it proved that "what may be Called the monied Interest—the speculators in the publick Securities . . . seem to have obtained too great an Influence in the General Government, and to support their Luxury, Idleness, and extravagance the bulk of the people of the U States must be loaded and oppressed with Taxes. . . ."[66] The tax signified political as well as economic oppression, for English politicians had been denouncing such levies as threats to the citizens' rights for a century and a half while in America the Antifederalists had recently added the states to the potential victims of excisemen and standing armies. The existence of an estimated 5,000 stills in Pennsylvania and still more to the south assured that the excise would bring the Hamiltonian system forcibly to the attention of many backcountry farmers, thus stirring up opposition to the administration and at the same time committing the government to the enforcement of an unpopular law in inconvenient places. Congressmen and other politicians who found the whiskey tax a useful issue continued their attacks on the act. When the Whiskey Rebellion occurred, the federal government's reaction seemed only to confirm the premonitions of those who had discerned the Federalist plot against liberty less than four years before.[67]

[65] Oliver Wolcott to Oliver Wolcott, Sr., Feb. 12, 1791, in Gibbs, ed., *Memoirs of the Administrations*, I, 62-63; Maclay, *Journal of Maclay*, 379, 384-385; *Dunlap's American Daily Advertiser* (Philadelphia), Jan. 22, 24, 1791.

[66] Thomas Pleasants, Jr., to James Madison, Mar. 4, 1791, Madison Papers.

[67] For example, compare Maclay's comments on the passage of the excise act with those of James Madison on the Federalists' reaction to the Whiskey Rebellion and Washington's denunciation of the democratic societies in his annual address to Congress of 1794. Madison to Thomas Jefferson, Nov. 30, 1794, Madison to James Monroe, Dec. 4, 1794, in U. S. Congress, *Letters of Madison*, II, 21-25. Charles A. Beard gives a good succinct account of the later course of the excise controversy in *Economic Origins of Jeffersonian Democracy* (New York, 1915), 248-267.

Even in 1791 the sensitivity of the Federalists to any attack on the excise had indicated their realization of the risk involved in enacting the measure and its fundamental importance to their program. Congress had been very cautious in writing the tariff of 1789, but, given the financial condition of the new government and their own predilections, Federalist politicians could only view that law as a temporary expedient. They needed to draw more money and more authority from the federal tax system than modest customs duties could provide. Yet further taxation required very delicate management in a country with sensitive taxpayers, a federal system of government, and few productive revenue resources. Higher tariffs alone would invite evasion and do nothing to extend federal influence. Direct taxation represented the most straightforward bid for authority and, therefore, could prove the most provocative to taxpayers and state legislatures. Excises would encounter the usual prejudice against them and also encroach on important state revenues. Depending solely on the tariff might appear the safest course, but most Federalists felt that the unused tax powers would atrophy while the United States Treasury lacked funds, the states competed successfully for supremacy with the central authorities, and the citizens remained unawed by their national government. Indeed, when the secretary of the treasury chose to add only excise to comparatively noncontroversial impost, some of his allies thought "that a system a little bolder would have been more safe; and that it would have been better to have begun at once with a small direct tax, a pretty liberal Stamp tax, and an Excise as well as an impost on Merchandise and Tonnage."[68]

Hamilton's more moderate and adroit proposals, which appeared bold enough in the light of future events, still fulfilled the financial needs of the government and the political requirements of the Federalists. Basing a revenue system largely on the indirect taxation of luxuries followed the accepted teachings of political economy, although excising whiskey might prove little less noticeable or burdensome than a direct tax in regions where many small farmers owned stills. The excise complemented the customs system administratively and made placing heavy duties on a few selected objects feasible. The corps of internal revenue agents could also provide the nucleus of a force to collect other internal taxes such as further excises, a stamp tax, or even

[68] John Adams to [John] Trumbull, Mar. 31, 1791, Adams Papers.

a direct tax on land if necessary, and, without being given more duties, these excisemen would still make federal authority felt throughout the whole country. Moreover, the spirits excise combined with assumption should establish a federal hegemony over all indirect taxation so that Congress could raise revenue or shape the national economy unhindered by obtrusive state legislation. With the passage of the excise act Hamilton's funding plan had achieved not only fiscal but also administrative and political symmetry—a fearful symmetry in the eyes of those who recalled English history and the prophecies of the Antifederalists.

The Washington Administration's Decision to Crush the Whiskey Rebellion

RICHARD H. KOHN

O NE of the fundamental questions raised in the debates over the Constitution in 1787 and 1788 was on what foundation the ultimate authority of government rested. When they discussed the problem men who differed over the Constitution as much as James Madison and Richard Henry Lee agreed that government was based either on law or on force and that law was the only firm basis on which to build a healthy republican society. And they also agreed that once the law failed, either through individual disobedience or riot and rebellion, force would be necessary to restore order and compel citizens to fulfill their social obligations.[1]

The first test of this doctrine came in 1794 with the Whiskey Rebellion, a clear-cut case of the failure of law and the necessity for coercion, at least to the Federalist leaders who were responsible for executing the laws. Yet a question which had been wholly neglected in the discussion six years earlier was how force should be applied and how physical coercion could restore respect for the law. Historians have also missed this problem. Prevailing interpretations of the rebellion, whether sympathetic to the rebels or to the Washington administration, have presented a picture of a federal executive dominated by the advice and philosophy of Alexander Hamilton moving quickly and eagerly to crush the insurrection with force. The only major historiographic controversy has been over whether Hamilton provoked the rebellion in order to enhance the government's stature with a show of military power.[2]

Richard H. Kohn is assistant professor of history in Rutgers University. The author acknowledges the financial assistance of the American Philosophical Society and the National Endowment for the Humanities.

[1] James Madison in Jonathan Elliot, ed., *The Debates in the Several State Conventions on the Adoption of the Federal Constitution, as Recommended by the General Convention at Philadelphia, in 1787. Together with the Journal of the Federal Convention, Luther Martin's Letter, Yates's Minutes, Congressional Opinions, Virginia and Kentucky Resolutions of '98–'99, and other Illustrations of the Constitution* (5 vols., Philadelphia, 1861), III, 384, 413-15; Richard Henry Lee to Edmund Pendleton, May 22, 1788, Box 5, John Lamb Papers (New-York Historical Society). See also Oliver Ellsworth in Elliot, ed., *Debates*, II, 197; Charles Pinckney, "Observations on the Plan of Government Submitted to the Federal Convention In Philadelphia, on the 28th of May, 1787," Max Farrand, ed., *The Records of the Federal Convention of 1787* (4 vols., New Haven, 1937), III, 118-19.

[2] Jacob E. Cooke, "The Whiskey Insurrection: A Re-Evaluation," *Pennsylvania History*, XXX (July 1963), 316-46. For arguments that Alexander Hamilton was running the government, see Merlin Vincent Wills, "Hamilton and the Whiskey Insurrection" (master's thesis, University of Pittsburgh, 1930), 41-46; Joseph

Historians have been correct in arguing that the administration was united in its determination to enforce the law, but they have missed the most critical issue involved: not whether to suppress the rebellion, but how to suppress it. The most vexing problems for George Washington and his advisers were whether it was possible to use force, and if it was feasible to do so, whether a military expedition would restore order and respect for the law or provoke civil war and deeper disrespect for the whiskey excise and the federal government's authority generally. These issues—essentially ones of tactics—divided the cabinet and forced the President to delay sending the militia to Pittsburgh for nearly two months. Washington came to the final decision with neither the speed nor the confidence historians have supposed. The process by which the government decided to crush the rebellion was actually a series of disjointed and incongruous decisions which revealed that the President was far less a tool of Hamilton, and far more perceptive politically, than historians have thought. A study of these decisions not only illustrates the inner workings of the Washington administration, the relationship between Hamilton and Washington, and the political skills of each, but also raises intriguing questions about the use of force.

When Washington and the cabinet first learned of the attack on excise collector John Neville's estate in July 1794, their reaction was just as historians have supposed. Without a hint of internal disagreement, they set in motion the machinery for the use of force. If anything the speed and unity of their response was even greater than most accounts have suggested. Within ten days, however, this policy was reversed; and in the light of the initial reaction, this reversal is all the more fascinating.

To understand the administration's first reactions, the rebellion must be viewed in the wider context in which Federalists placed it. The rebellion was not simply a response to violence and intimidation of excise officials in western Pennsylvania, even though this had been mounting steadily since the tax took effect in 1791. The reaction was equally as much a product of the growing Federalist paranoia about the motives of their Republican opponents and the bitterness that had come to characterize national politics. When Federalists in public and in private tried to explain the rebellion, the near universal charge

Charles, *The Origins of the American Party System* (Chapel Hill, 1956), 38, 41-44, 46-48, 52-53. For biographers who avoid the issue or imply the opposite, see Broadus Mitchell, *Alexander Hamilton: The National Adventure, 1788-1804* (New York, 1962), 310-28; Broadus Mitchell, *Alexander Hamilton: The Revolutionary Years* (New York, 1970), 308-17; Nathan Schachner, *Alexander Hamilton* (New York, 1946), 334-37; John C. Miller, *Alexander Hamilton: Portrait in Paradox* (New York, 1959), 404-07; Stuart Gerry Brown, *Alexander Hamilton* (New York, 1967), 95-97. See also William Findley, *History of the Insurrection in the Four Western Counties of Pennsylvania* ... (Philadelphia, 1796), 312-13; William Findley to Alexander Addison, Nov. 30, 1792, Alexander Addison Papers (Darlington Memorial Library, University of Pittsburgh); Leland D. Baldwin, *Whiskey Rebels: The Story of a Frontier Uprising* (Pittsburgh, 1939), 269-70.

was that it stemmed from faction: "a set of *leading partizans*" who "had always maintained a systematic opposition" to the government.[3] As early as 1792, Hamilton accused Madison and Thomas Jefferson of deliberate "subversion of measures, which ... would subvert the Government."[4] Thereafter, every political controversy, large and small, led Federalists to a more conspiratorial and seditious interpretation of the opposition; and this spiral of suspicion became reciprocal.[5] By late 1793, Jefferson was repeating third hand stories of Federalist conversations about the necessity of a "President for life, and an hereditary Senate."[6] One Federalist congressman even received a murder threat from "15 Republicans and boys of Liberty to exterpate Torys" who had admittedly "form[ed] a conspiracy" to "mangle [his] body."[7] By the outbreak of the rebellion, politics was such a morass of hate and suspicion that Attorney General William Bradford could easily see it as part of "a formed and regular plan for weakening and perhaps overthrowing the General Government."[8]

A second element which helps to explain the administration's determination to use the militia was the episode in 1792 when resistance to the excise in western Pennsylvania led Hamilton to recommend government intervention with force. There had been resistance to the law from the very beginning. In August 1792, it took a more serious turn when local leaders resolved to "persist" in "legal" measures "that may obstruct the operation of the Law."[9] Subsequent

[3] Philadelphia *Gazette of the United States*, Aug. 2, Sept. 6, Dec. 22, 1794. See also New York *Minerva*, Sept. 30, 1794; Oliver Wolcott, Jr., to Oliver Wolcott, Aug. 16, 1794, George Gibbs, ed., *Memoirs of the Administrations of Washington and John Adams from the Papers of Oliver Wolcott* (2 vols., New York, 1846), I, 157; George Washington to Burges Ball, Sept. 25, 1794, John C. Fitzpatrick, ed., *The Writings of George Washington* (39 vols., Washington, 1931-1944), XXXIII, 506.

[4] Hamilton to Washington, Sept. 9, 1792, Harold C. Syrett and Jacob E. Cooke, eds., *The Papers of Alexander Hamilton* (15 vols., New York, 1961-), XII, 349. See also Hamilton to Edward Carrington, May 26, 1792, *ibid.*, XI, 426-45.

[5] See Hamilton to—, May 18, 1793; Stephen Higginson to Hamilton, July 26, 1793, Rufus King to Hamilton, Aug. 3, 1793, *ibid.*, XIV, 473-76, XV, 127-28, 173; King, memorandum on the opposition, 1793, Box 3, Rufus King Papers (New-York Historical Society); Lee to [Washington?], Sept. 17, 1793, *Lee Family Papers* (Microfilm edition, reel 7, exp. 856) (Charlottesville, 1966); Hugh Williamson to Hamilton, May 27, 1794; Francis Corbin to Hamilton, July 12, 1794; Hamilton, draft of essay, 1794, Alexander Hamilton Papers (Manuscript Division, Library of Congress); James McHenry to John Bleakley, Feb. 9, 1794, James McHenry Papers (Maryland Historical Society); Zephaniah Swift to David Daggett, April 17, 1794, Franklin B. Dexter, ed., "Selections from the Letters Received by David Daggett, 1786-1802," *Proceedings of the American Antiquarian Society*, IV (1887), 372. See also Marshall Smelser, "The Federalist Period as an Age of Passion," *American Quarterly*, X (Winter 1958), 391-419; John R. Howe, Jr., "Republican Thought and the Political Violence of the 1790s," *ibid.*, XIX (Summer 1967), 147-65. But see Richard Hofstadter, *The Idea of a Party System: The Rise of Legitimate Opposition in the United States, 1780-1840* (Berkeley, 1969), ix-x, 7-9, 16-18, 34-35, 84-111. The fear of conspiracy and sedition were more widespread and surfaced earlier than Marshall Smelser implies, however, and by 1794 was directly affecting government policy.

[6] Franklin B. Sawvel, ed., *The Complete ANAS of THOMAS JEFFERSON* (New York, 1903), 183.

[7] Anonymous to William L. Smith, 1794, William Loughton Smith Papers (Manuscript Division, Library of Congress).

[8] William Bradford to Elias Boudinot, Aug. 1, 1794, John William Wallace Papers (Historical Society of Pennsylvania).

[9] Minutes of the meeting, Aug. 21-22, 1792, Syrett and Cooke, eds., *Papers of Hamilton*, XII, 308n-09n.

resolutions called for more rallies, the creation of county committees of correspondence, and the intimidation of anyone who favored or obeyed the law.
Neville, who as excise inspector was responsible for collecting the tax, immediately informed his superior in Philadelphia that the law was now unenforceable
and that he could not enter Washington County, the seat of the most determined resistance, without risking his life. The day after Neville sent off the
report, a mob fired on one of his inspection stations and threatened to murder
the owner for allowing the house to be used for registering stills.[10]

Hamilton had been waiting for such an incident. Earlier, when he heard of
riots against the excise in North Carolina, he told the Virginia supervisor of
revenue that "the thing must be brought to an issue"; and he asked if Virginia's
militia was reliable.[11] The situation in Pennsylvania, he told John Jay, marked "a
crisis in the affairs of the Country."[12] Hamilton's first active move was to send
Pennsylvania supervisor George Clymer to Pittsburgh—a "preparatory step."[13]
Then he asked Attorney General Edmund Randolph for a legal opinion of the
question and the government's options. To the President, however, Hamilton
was more blunt: "Moderation enough has been shewn—," he argued, " 'tis time
to assume a different tone." First the government should "exert the full force of
the Law against the Offenders." Then if court action proved impossible, "as is
rather to be expected," the President could mobilize troops.[14]

Hamilton's eagerness to use force, however, was not matched by Randolph,
Jay, or Rufus King, to whom Hamilton wrote for advice. Jay and King cautioned him to wait until Congress convened so that "all the Branches of
Gov[ernmen]t. [can] move together" backed by public opinion. Tough talk
without a follow-up might "render the operations of administration odious."[15]
Randolph also emphasized the dangers of overreaction. The mere resolutions of
a meeting could not justify legal prosecution, he told Hamilton, and "improper
interference" by the President might "inlist against him even those who exec-
rate the spirit of the Pittsburgh proceedings." For a variety of reasons Randolph
agreed to a presidential proclamation, but he edited Hamilton's draft to remove
what he considered provocative language—words like "criminality" and any
mention whatsoever of the military.[16]

[10] John Neville to George Clymer, Aug. 23, 1792, ibid., 306n, 310n. The first incidents of violence had led
Neville to conclude that "it will be impossible to carry the law into effect without an armed force." Neville to
Clymer, Nov. 17, 1791, Oliver Wolcott, Jr., Papers (Connecticut Historical Society).

[11] Hamilton to Carrington, July 25, 1792, Syrett and Cooke, eds., Papers of Hamilton, XII, 84.

[12] Hamilton to John Jay, Sept. 3, 1792, ibid., 316-17.

[13] Hamilton to Tench Coxe, Sept. 1, 1792, ibid., 310.

[14] Hamilton to Washington, Sept. 1, 1792, ibid., 311-13.

[15] Jay to Hamilton, Sept. 8, 1792; King to Hamilton, Sept. 27, 1792, ibid., 334-35, 493-94.

[16] Edmund Randolph to Hamilton, Sept. 8, 1792, ibid., 336-40.

Washington accepted the idea of a proclamation. He would enforce the law, he confided to Hamilton, to the point of using force if necessary. But if the regular army was used, "there would be the cry at once, 'The cat is let out; We now see for what purpose an Army was raised.'" Force could only be the "dernier resort."[17]

The debate over how to respond in 1792 matched almost exactly the one that would develop in 1794. Hamilton already leaned toward military suppression. Randolph was inclined to be more lenient, more concerned with public opinion and the government's image. Washington took middle ground. He accepted Hamilton's premises about the necessity for strict enforcement lest the laws and government itself be undermined, but he was cognizant that force would not only need public support but also have political overtones beyond the simple enforcement of the law. But most important, the whole episode in 1792 strengthened the tendency to react more harshly in 1794. The government was lenient in 1792, almost circumspect. Yet the violence continued. In early 1794 it began to mount in tempo and frequency, and finally culminated in an armed attack on Neville. Given the continual incidents in western Pennsylvania, the view that political opposition was actually a conspiracy to subvert governmental institutions, and the obvious failure of lenience in 1792, neither the President nor any member of his cabinet had any reason to doubt their informants in Pittsburgh who described the assault on Neville as the beginning of a "civil War."[18] Hamilton was speaking for all when he told representatives of the Pennsylvania government that "the crisis was arrived when it must be determined whether the Government can maintain itself. . . ."[19]

What forced the administration to pause in 1794—in fact what changed the whole nature of the crisis and led to the split in the cabinet—was a flood of obstacles to the mobilization of the militia, obstacles that forced the President to waver and to consider the possible dangers in a policy of immediate military suppression. First news of the attack on Neville reached Philadelphia on July 25.[20] After sending the letters to state authorities, Washington met with the cabinet and decided to lay the facts before Supreme Court Justice James Wil-

[17] Washington to Hamilton, Sept. 17, 1792, *ibid.*, 390-92. See also Washington to Hamilton, Sept. 7, 1792, *ibid.*, 331-33.

[18] John Gibson to Thomas Mifflin, July 18, 1794; Isaac Craig to Henry Knox, July 18, 1794; Thomas Butler to Knox, July 18, 1794, *Pennsylvania Archives: Second Series* (19 vols., Harrisburg, 1887-1896), IV, 58-60; Neville to Coxe, July 18, 1794, *Bulletin: Carnegie Library of Pittsburgh*, XVI (1911), 193-94.

[19] "Conference at the President's," Aug. 2, 1794, *Pennsylvania Archives*, IV, 124.

[20] Philadelphia *General Advertiser*, July 25, 1794; Philadelphia *Independent Gazetteer*, July 26, 1794.

son.[21] Under the 1792 Militia Act, a federal judge had to certify that the judicial process had collapsed before the executive could call up troops.[22] Wilson was a longtime political ally and a good Federalist. But the administration was so eager to act quickly that when Wilson did not reply immediately, Washington and his advisers grew anxious. Suddenly they realized that only correspondence supported the existence of actual rebellion, and it was by no means certain what kind of evidence Wilson would require.[23]

The other alternative was to ask the state of Pennsylvania to call up its militia. Here the problems were immense. Similar situations in the past had caused confusion, discord, and crippling delays. In 1783, when army recruits had surrounded Congress waving their muskets and demanding back pay, the state had refused to act. During Shays' Rebellion coordination between national and state governments had been extremely difficult despite agreement on both sides that force was mandatory.[24] But the most potent obstacles were political: Pennsylvania's administration was solidly Republican. Governor Thomas Mifflin had been Washington's enemy ever since his service on the Board of War and his involvement in the Conway Cabal, and his chief adviser, Secretary of State Alexander Dallas, was the leading member of the Philadelphia Democratic Society. Their only response to the rebellion had been to instruct judges and county officials to round up the rioters for trial.[25] Moreover, formal relations between the federal government and the state were already sour. In May, Washington had forced Pennsylvania to suspend a project to lay out the town of Presque Isle so as not to provoke neighboring Indians into joining the hostile tribes fighting in the Northwest. Mifflin had exploded at this interference in state affairs, and after an angry exchange of letters, Washington and Secretary of

[21] There is no record of this cabinet meeting. But see Randolph to Washington, Aug. 5, 1794, George Washington Papers (Manuscript Division, Library of Congress), which mentions a meeting at which it was decided to submit the facts to James Wilson. Bradford to Boudinot, Aug. 1, 1794, Wallace Papers, also indicates that the meeting took place.

[22] *The Public Statutes at Large of the United States of America, from the Organization of the Government in 1789* ... (83 vols., Boston and Washington, 1854-), I, 264-65.

[23] Bradford to Boudinot, Aug. 1, 1794, Wallace Papers. To buttress their case, Hamilton secured testimony from Francis Mentges, an army colonel who had been in Pittsburgh between July 22 and 25, 1794. See Mentges' deposition in Hamilton's handwriting, Aug. 1, 1794, Wolcott Papers.

[24] For these episodes, see Richard H. Kohn, "The Federalists and the Army: Politics and the Birth of the Military Establishment, 1783-1795" (doctoral dissertation, University of Wisconsin, 1968), 118-20, 177-82; Broadus Mitchell, *Alexander Hamilton: Youth to Maturity, 1755-1788* (New York, 1957), 315-23; Joseph Parker Warren, "The Confederation and the Shays Rebellion," *American Historical Review*, XI (Oct. 1905), 42-67.

[25] Alexander Dallas to Jared Ingersoll, July 25, 1794; Dallas to the judges, etc. (circular), July 25, 1794; Dallas to John Gibson, July 25, 1794; Dallas to Knox, July 26, 1794, *Pennsylvania Archives*, IV, 66-67. According to the administration's information, county officials had been involved in the rioting. See Neville to Coxe, July 18, 1794, *Bulletin: Carnegie Library of Pittsburgh*, XVI, 194.

War Henry Knox began to doubt the governor's willingness to honor national obligations.[26]

In spite of these difficulties, by August 1 the administration felt it had no choice. Even if Wilson freed them to mobilize militia, Washington and the cabinet would need the help of the Pennsylvanians to use state forces. Therefore, on August 2, at its own request the administration met with Mifflin, Dallas, state Chief Justice Thomas McKean, and state Attorney General Jared Ingersoll.[27] Most accounts have used this conference only to gauge the mood of the administration. Actually, it marked a major turning point in policy; in order to gain cooperation from the state, the administration was forced to delay a military expedition.

Washington began the conference by declaring that events around Pittsburgh struck "at the root of all law & order." "[T]he most spirited & firm measures were necessary . . . for if such proceedings were tolerated there was an end to our Constitution & laws." In evidence he cited correspondence, depositions, and newspaper extracts showing that the insurgents had robbed the mail and were planning another meeting to organize military resistance. He then asked for help from the Pennsylvanians. Randolph followed with a direct request to call out troops under a 1783 state militia law. The state officials were silent. Finally Ingersoll replied that this law had been repealed and McKean, evidently presenting the official Pennsylvania position, claimed that "the judiciary power" was still "equal to the task" and that "the employment of a military force, at this period, would be as bad as anything that the Rioters had done—equally unconstitutional and illegal."

Then Hamilton spoke. "[C]o-operating sources of opposition to the Constitution and laws," he said, had produced a "crisis" over "whether the Government can maintain itself." "[A]n immediate resort to Military force" was necessary simply to compel "obedience to the laws." But the Pennsylvanians refused to budge and the two sides began quarreling over Judge Alexander Addison's opinion that the courts could restore order and that force would only unite the rioters and swell their numbers.[28]

What then passed has been lost. Undoubtedly it was bitter because Mifflin adamantly refused to call out his forces immediately. And he argued heatedly

[26] Knox to Mifflin, May 24, 1794, Henry Knox Papers (Massachusetts Historical Society); Washington to Knox, June 25, 1794, Fitzpatrick, ed., *Writings of Washington*, XXXIII, 410-11. See also Harry Marlin Tinkcom, *The Republicans and Federalists in Pennsylvania, 1790-1801: A Study in National Stimulus and Local Response* (Harrisburg, 1950), 113-31; Kenneth R. Rossman, *Thomas Mifflin and the Politics of the American Revolution* (Chapel Hill, 1952), 232-46.

[27] "Conference at the President's," Aug. 2, 1794, *Pennsylvania Archives*, IV, 122. The state officials "were invited." Dallas to William Irvine, Aug. 7, 1794, William Irvine Papers (Historical Society of Pennsylvania).

[28] "Conference at the President's," Aug. 2, 1794, *Pennsylvania Archives*, IV, 122-24.

that out of hatred for the excise, unwillingness to march on fellow citizens, or desire to avoid a long expedition, large numbers of the militia might ignore his orders.[29] The administration believed it.[30] Certainly without the governor's aid, the Pennsylvania militia would be useless. To gain his help, the administration struck a bargain. In return for Mifflin's cooperation in mobilization, the President agreed that he would initiate any call for troops, justify the measure publicly, and then give Mifflin time to convene the legislature and open negotiations with the rebels. The terms were deliberately vague, probably to avoid irrevocable commitments, but the administration had agreed informally to suspend military suppression for several weeks.[31]

Clearly Mifflin's intransigence and the fear that the militia might not turn out forced Washington for the first time to question whether he had the public backing to justify force. An immediate call to arms might reveal the government's military weakness and stimulate a divisive public debate over government reaction, especially if Mifflin, a leading Republican, publicly declared that force was unnecessary. The recommendations from the cabinet to the President reflected this dilemma, and for the first time in the crisis the cabinet split. Hamilton and Knox stuck to a military solution: raise immediately 12,000 men, a "super abundant" force, to disabuse the insurgents of success and to demonstrate "at home and abroad" the "power of the Government to execute the laws."[32] But Bradford, Randolph, and Mifflin, the latter in a long and probably unsolicited letter justifying his earlier opposition, advised delay.[33] And it was Randolph's eloquent recitation of the dangers that finally persuaded the President to reverse the government's earlier intention to use force immediately.

"Unnecessarily harsh action" without any "spirit of reconciliation," wrote the secretary, would only broaden the opposition to the government, perhaps even unite the whole West in civil war. The militias were unstable, the expense would be huge, and party politics already had produced bitter national division.

[29] See Mifflin to Washington, Aug. 5, 12, 1794, and Randolph to Mifflin, Aug. 7, 1794, *American State Papers. Documents, Legislative and Executive, of the Congress of the United States, from the First Session of the First to the Second Session of the Tenth Congress . . . : Miscellaneous* (2 vols., Washington, 1834), I, 97-103; Dallas to Irvine, Aug. 7, 1794, Irvine Papers; Bradford to Randolph, Aug. 8, 1794, Pennsylvania Miscellany (Manuscript Division, Library of Congress).

[30] Both Bradford and Randolph expressed great fears on this point. See Bradford to Boudinot, Aug. 7, 1794, J. J. Boudinot, ed., *The Life, Public Services, Addresses, and Letters of Elias Boudinot, LL.D.: President of the Continental Congress* (2 vols., Boston, 1896), II, 86-87; Randolph to Thomas Pinckney, Aug. 11, 1794, United States Miscellany (Manuscript Division, Library of Congress).

[31] "Memoranda of an Executive Conference" [Aug. 2, 1794], *Pennsylvania Archives*, IV, 70.

[32] Knox to Washington, Aug. 4, 1794, Washington Papers. See also Hamilton to Washington, Aug. 2, 1794, Henry Cabot Lodge, ed., *Works of Alexander Hamilton* (9 vols., New York, 1885-1886), V, 485-89. Both estimated that the insurgents could muster as many as 7,000 armed men.

[33] Bradford to Washington, Aug. 1794, Randolph to Washington, Aug. 5, 1794, Washington Papers; Mifflin to Washington, Aug. 5, 1794, *American State Papers . . . : Miscellaneous*, I, 97-99.

The best alternative was to negotiate with the rebels, as the President was then considering. But if the administration offered "reconciliation ... with one hand" while brandishing "terror ... in the other," it would be "considered delusive by the insurgents and the rest of the world," a trick "only to gloss over hostility; to endeavour to divide; to sound out the strength of the insurgents; and to discover the most culpable persons" for punishment. Issue a proclamation against the rebels and back a peace commission, Randolph urged. If it failed, prosecute the rebels. If the courts failed, then call out the militia.[34]

On August 4, Wilson finally certified the situation beyond the "ordinary course of judicial proceedings"; and, by the end of the cabinet meeting on August 6, the President had decided on a course of action, one that was far closer to Randolph's rather than Hamilton's recommendations.[35] The key was a federal commission to negotiate with the rebels, partly to divide the rebels and gain intelligence, but mostly to blunt any possible public criticism and to gain the time to prepare the public should force prove ultimately necessary.[36] At the same time Washington decided to issue a preliminary call to the militia—to test their loyalty, to convince the rebels of his determination, and to gain the time needed to organize an expedition. The whole package was a compromise designed to keep all options open and to anticipate the widest possible range of reactions from the public, the militia, and the rebels. Above all, it was predicated on public opinion. "[T]he Pres[iden]t means to convince [the rebels] and the world ... of the *moderation* and *the firmness* of the Gov[ernment]," Bradford explained to his father-in-law. If after the negotiations the rebels refused to submit to the law, "the weight of the public opinion will give energy to the *dernier* resort."[37] On August 7, the government issued a proclamation ordering the rebels to disperse and stating the government's intention to ready the

[34] Randolph to Washington, Aug. 5, 1794, Washington Papers.

[35] Wilson to Washington , Aug. 4, 1794, *American State Papers ... : Miscellaneous*, I, 85.

[36] The idea of negotiating was discussed in the August 2 conference. "Memoranda of an Executive Conference," [Aug. 2, 1794], *Pennsylvania Archives*, IV, 70. It was also mentioned by Randolph in his letter to Washington but there is no ironclad proof that a federal peace commission was agreed upon until August 7 when Bradford actually left on the mission. Preliminary steps were taken by August 5, however, when draft instructions were ready. Randolph to Washington, Aug. 5, 1794, Washington Papers, Hamilton and Knox to Washington, Aug. 5, 1794, Lodge, ed., *Works of Hamilton*, V, 518. The decision was evidently made final at the cabinet meeting on August 6, since Bradford left Philadelphia on August 7. Minutes of the commissioners, Aug. 7, 1794, Pennsylvania Miscellany. The official instructions, signed by each cabinet officer, are dated August 7. Randolph to the commissioners, Aug. 7, 1794, *ibid.*

[37] Bradford to Boudinot, Aug. 7, 1794, Boudinot, ed., *Elias Boudinot*, II, 87. For Washington's thinking, see Washington to Charles Mynn Thruston, Aug. 10, 1794, Fitzpatrick, ed., *Writings of Washington*, XXXIII, 465; Washington to "Fellow-citizens of the Senate and of the House of Representatives," Nov. 20, 1794, *American State Papers ... : Miscellaneous*, I, 83-85; Randolph to the commissioners, Sept. 29, 1794, Domestic Letters of the Department of State (M-60, reel 7), General Records of the Department of State, RG 59 (National Archives).

militia; simultaneously Knox wrote the governors of four states to alert their troops, and Bradford hurriedly left for Pittsburgh to meet with the insurgents.[38]

The government was now committed to seeking a peaceful end of the rebellion. It was a shaky commitment, more a tactic than a policy, and indicative more of the President's uncertainty and fear than of a belief that force could be avoided. But in the two weeks after August 7, it was at least sincere. Between August 7 and August 24, the administration did not make any serious military preparations for an expedition. The peace commission was given very flexible instructions and the authority to grant a blanket amnesty for all unlawful acts as well as absolution from previously uncollected excise taxes.[39] Just how nervous and uncertain this policy actually was, however, was not revealed until August 24, when the first definitive reports from the peace commission reversed the policy again and turned the effort to negotiate into what Randolph called earlier a sham "to gloss over hostility."

Bradford left the moment his instructions were approved, before either Pennsylvania Supreme Court Justice Jasper Yeates or Senator James Ross, a trusted confidant of the President and a resident of the most rebellious county, could be informed of their membership on the federal commission. At Lancaster, Bradford was joined by Yeates (Ross was near Pittsburgh) and the two rode up to forty miles a day in order to arrive in time for a meeting of the insurgents scheduled for August 14 at Parkinson's ferry on the Monongahela.[40] As the two sped westward they became increasingly convinced that it would be impossible to restore order. Among the first people Bradford met on the journey were Neville and the federal marshal for the state, both of whom had narrowly escaped from Pittsburgh. They all but advised Bradford to turn back. By the time Bradford and Yeates reached Bedford, they learned that there were new

---

[38] Proclamation, Aug. 7, 1794, Fitzpatrick, ed., *Writings of Washington*, XXXIII, 457-61; Knox to [Governor of N. J.?], Aug. 7, 1794, Anthony Walton White Papers (Rutgers University Library); Knox to Mifflin, Aug. 7, 1794, *Pennsylvania Archives*, IV, 101-02; Minutes of the commissioners, Aug. 7, 1794, Pennsylvania Miscellany. There is no record of the August 6 cabinet meeting, but Hamilton and Knox asked for one for that date. Hamilton and Knox to Washington, Aug. 5, 1794, Lodge, ed., *Works of Hamilton*, V, 518. Since the government acted on August 7 and Bradford left for Pittsburgh that day, the meeting undoubtedly took place and most likely on August 6. Moreover, at the meeting, Washington asked Hamilton to prepare a document citing the opposition and acts of violence against the excise. See Hamilton to Washington, Aug. 5, 6, 1794, *ibid.*, 489-518, 519. It was not published until two weeks later. See Hamilton to Washington, Aug. 16, 1794, *ibid.*, VI, 17; Bartholomew Dandridge to Hamilton, Aug. 19, 1794, Washington Papers; Philadelphia *American Daily Advertiser*, Aug. 21, 1794.

[39] Randolph to commission, Aug. 7, 1794, Domestic Letters of the Department of State (M-60, reel 7), General Records of the Department of State. Another copy of this letter, also dated August 7, is in the Simon Gratz Collection (Historical Society of Pennsylvania). Therefore the published version is either misdated or was purposely backdated by the administration when it sent the document to Congress. Randolph to commission, Aug. 5, 1794, *American State Papers . . . : Miscellaneous*, I, 86-87.

[40] Minutes of the commissioners, Aug. 7-13, 1794; Bradford to Randolph, Aug. 6, 1794, Pennsylvania Miscellany; Edward Shippen to Jasper Yeates, Aug. 6, 1794, Gratz Collection.

riots, that a proclamation by Governor Mifflin was ridiculed by the rebels, and that the impending meeting would be stacked against more moderate westerners.[41]

Exhausted by a week's travel, already prejudiced about the situation and skeptical of their chances for success, Bradford and Yeates reached Parkinson's ferry on August 15. There they met Ross who had attended the meeting and who prejudiced them further. Actually moderates had been able to manipulate the proceedings into rejecting any further violence and negotiating with the federal commissioners. Yet to Ross, circulating among the spectators and delegates, listening to rumors and plans, this outcome only masked what he felt to be the basic intransigence of the populace, or at least a sizable and uncontrollable minority.[42]

Still tired and evidently a bit anxious about their personal safety, Bradford, Yeates, and Ross went on to Pittsburgh where they spent all day on August 17 conferring with leading residents of the town.[43] They were told that moderates were forced to play along with the fireaters or jeopardize their own safety and that of the town itself and that through intimidation and continual violence the extremists held the upper hand.[44] This testimony only reinforced what Bradford and Yeates had heard for a week on the road, and what Ross had deduced from observations on the scene. That night the commissioners decided to inform the government of their feelings even though they were not scheduled to meet the negotiating committee from the Parkinson's ferry meeting for another three days.

The faction at the meeting advocating civil war, they reported, was very small. But a second group, "numerous and violent," would resist the excise "at all hazards." These radicals were forcing the moderates—a majority—"to turn Hypocrites, and even to appear as the Leaders of these *Enragées*" out of fear of reprisal and doubts about legal protection. While they dominated the negotiating committee, the moderates were so "overawed" that they would not "express ... real opinions" much less press the insurgents to accept the government's terms. "We see not any Prospect of inforcing ... the Laws," concluded the commissioners, "but by the Physical strength of the Nation."[45] In a private letter Bradford used harsher language: the insurgents were really delaying until cold

[41] Bradford to Randolph, Aug. 8, 10, 12, 13, 1794, Pennsylvania Miscellany.

[42] Yeates and Bradford to Ross, Aug. 14, 1794; Minutes of the commissioners, Aug. 15, 1794; commissioners to Randolph, Aug. 17, 1794, *ibid.*; Yeates to wife, Aug. 17, 1794, Jasper Yeates Papers (Historical Society of Pennsylvania); Baldwin, *Whiskey Rebels*, 172-82; Raymond Walters, Jr., *Albert Gallatin: Jeffersonian Financier and Diplomat* (New York, 1957), 72-75.

[43] Yeates put on a brave front for his wife, but the tension in the letter reveals his mood. Yeates to wife, Aug. 17, 1794, Yeates Papers.

[44] Hugh H. Brackenridge, *Incidents of the Insurrection in the Western Parts of Pennsylvania In the Year 1794* (3 vols., Philadelphia, 1795), I, 100-01; Baldwin, *Whiskey Rebels*, 187-88.

[45] Commissioners to Randolph, Aug. 17, 1794, Pennsylvania Miscellany.

weather made military operations impossible. This would provide "time to strengthen themselves—to circulate the manifesto they are preparing—to tamper with ... Kentucky—to procure Ammunition and ... seduce the well-affected." As for negotiations, "any man who would openly recommend obedience ... would be in danger of assassination."[46] Thus barely two days after arriving, before meeting any of the rebels, and without consulting the state commission, the federal envoys recommended immediate mobilization.

When these reports reached Philadelphia on August 23, Washington called an emergency cabinet meeting, and within twenty-four hours, the administration's policy of peace died.[47] It was not just the information from the commissioners. Bradford's dismal letters on the road undoubtedly contributed to the doubts about suspending military preparations. The articles in the opposition press calling for lenience and the evidence that widespread hatred of the excise was giving the rebels sympathy also made the administration apprehensive.[48] But most of all, rumors abounded in Philadelphia that the insurgents had decided on secession and that they were buying up arms and seeking British aid.[49] Shortly before the letters arrived, British minister George Hammond was visited by two men, each claiming to represent the rebels and both proposing some kind of alliance with the crown.[50] The letters from Pittsburgh merely precipitated the new crisis.

Solemnly, for eight hours on August 24, Washington reviewed the situation with Hamilton and Randolph (Knox was in New England on private business). First the President asked whether the militia should be assembled at once. The

---

[46] Bradford to Washington, Aug. 17, 1794, *ibid.*, 74-76. On August 17, Isaac Craig wrote to Knox saying that the commissioners were convinced that reconciliation was impossible. He asked for something immediate "to excite Confidence in those that remain well effected to Government." Craig to Knox, Aug. 17, 1794, Isaac Craig Papers (Carnegie Library, Pittsburgh). Similar fears were voiced by Irvine, one of the state's negotiators. See Irvine to Dallas, Aug. 17, 1794, *Pennsylvania Archives*, IV, 142-43.

[47] For the arrival date, see the endorsement on commissioners to Randolph, Aug. 17, 1794, Pennsylvania Miscellany. For the reaction, see Randolph to Washington, Aug. 23, 1794, Miscellaneous Letters of the Department of State (M-179, reel 12), General Records of the Department of State; Randolph to commissioners, Aug. 25, 1794, Domestic Letters of the Department of State (M-60, reel 7), General Records of the Department of State. For the meeting, see Washington to Randolph, Aug. 23, 1794, Fitzpatrick, ed., *Writings of Washington*, XXXIII, 472. The letter is misdated August 21 in Fitzpatrick and the manuscript; Saturday, as it was marked, was August 23.

[48] Philadelphia *General Advertiser*, Aug. 12, 16, 20, 23, 1794; Henry Lee to Washington, Aug. 17, 1794, William Wirt Henry, *Patrick Henry: Life, Correspondence and Speeches* (3 vols., New York, 1891), II, 539-40. See also Carrington to Edward Heth, Aug. 13, 1794, Whiskey Rebellion, General Records of Internal Revenue Service, RG 58 (National Archives).

[49] Philadelphia *Gazette of the United States*, Aug. 24, 1794; Philadelphia *General Advertiser*, Aug. 21, 1794; Philadelphia *American Daily Advertiser*, Aug. 23, 1794; John Wilkins, Jr., to Randolph, Aug. 14, 1794, Miscellaneous Letters of the Department of State (M-179, reel 12), General Records of the Department of State. Evidently the rumors of overtures to the British had some substance. See Thomas McKean to Ingersoll, Aug. 29, 1794, Emmet Collection (New York Public Library).

[50] George Hammond to Lord Grenville, Aug. 29, 1794, British State Papers, Ford Transcripts (New York Public Library).

two secretaries, apparently now in agreement, recommended mobilizing Virginia's since Governor Henry Lee was an old friend of the President and had recently pledged his help unequivocally.[31] Washington then asked if additional forces were necessary and the two cabinet officers agreed that the total should be raised to 15,000. The three then decided where ánd when the units would assemble and where their supplies would be stockpiled. As soon as the meeting broke up, Hamilton, acting for the absent secretary of war, began ordering the arms and supplies. Although the decision was not irrevocable, the administration was committed to force prior to any word that negotiations had started. But public opinion was still a crucial consideration. Governor Lee was to keep his orders secret until September 1, to allow negotiations to proceed and to honor the informal agreement with Mifflin made in early August. And the peace commission was specifically ordered to continue the talks. The administration wanted to be certain that it could not be charged with insincerity or bad faith.[32]

Meanwhile in Pittsburgh the rebel negotiators unexpectedly agreed to recommend the government's terms to the committee of sixty, an executive group of township representatives, and to call the committee into session on August 28.[33] Suddenly the commissioners were hopeful. They wrote Randolph that to insure that the populace would submit to the law, they were requiring each citizen to declare his loyalty at his local polling place. Moderates, they added, were beginning to surface and the situation had improved to the point where they felt they could agree to withhold an expedition until the oath-signing took place on September 14. Bradford, Yeates, and Ross fully expected the committee of sixty to accept the terms, authorize local meetings, and—together with other moderates—silence the extremists, and convince the majority to abide by the law.[34]

These hopes proved short-lived. When the rebel negotiators recommended submission to the committee of sixty, the reaction was hostile. Fireaters immediately accused the negotiators of accepting government bribes. So great was the intimidation that the moderates on the committee demanded a secret ballot taken in such a way that their votes would not be disclosed by their handwriting. When the votes were tallied, approval of the government's terms—amnesty

[31] Henry Lee to Washington, Aug. 17, 1794, Wirt, *Patrick Henry*, II, 539-40.

[32] Cabinet notes [Hamilton's handwriting], Aug. 24, 1794, Pennsylvania Miscellany; Randolph to commissioners, Aug. 25, 1794, Domestic Letters of the Department of State (M-60, reel 7), General Records of the Department of State. For Washington's mood of determination and his reasoning, see his letter to Henry Lee, Aug. 26, 1794, Fitzpatrick, ed., *Writings of Washington*, XXXIII, 474-76. See also Hamilton to Henry Lee, Aug. 25, 1794, Ferdinand Dreer Collection (Historical Society of Pennsylvania); Hamilton to Samuel Hodgdon, Aug. 25, 27, 1794; Hamilton to Abraham Hunt, Aug. 27, 1794; Hamilton to George Gale, Aug. 27, 1794; Hamilton to Henry Lee, Aug. 27, 1794, Wolcott Papers; John Stagg to Knox, Aug. 30, 1794, Knox Papers.

[33] Minutes of the commissioners, Aug. 21-23, 1794, Pennsylvania Miscellany.

[34] Commissioners to Randolph, Aug. 21, 23, 29, 1794; Bradford to Hamilton, Aug. 23, 1794, *ibid.*; Yeates to wife, Aug. 22, 29, 1794, Yeates Papers; Bradford to wife, Aug. 22, 1794, Bradford to Boudinot, Aug. 29, 1794, Wallace Papers.

and future excise prosecutions in state courts in return for the oaths—won by only 34 to 23." Bradford and the other government representatives were stunned. If twenty-three leaders refused to obey the law, enforcement would be impossible. In their reports to Philadelphia, the three pointed this out and described the hostile mood. Military resistance had been openly advocated; nearly 1000 packhorses were seen on the way to Maryland to procure military supplies. If the vote had been public, submission would have lost and the commissioners viewed the actual vote as an accurate reflection of mass opinion. Their recommendation was "Military coercion."

With all hope of reconciliation gone, the commissioners decided to return to one of the original purposes of their mission—as they put it, leaving "the Government free from any reasonable grounds of censure." They informed the rebels that the militia would undoubtedly march and that those who resisted further would be punished. On September 11, the people must assemble at their local polling places to sign explicit oaths of loyalty. Under this pressure the rebels caved in. On September 2, the two groups of negotiators and the representatives of the state government agreed to the terms. The next day Bradford and Yeates left for Philadelphia; Ross remained to monitor the oath-taking and report the results.

From Bedford, Bradford and Yeates explained their actions to the administration. The Redstone meeting had posed a dilemma: to the "violent party" and most westerners, the fiery speeches and closeness of the vote had really represented a rejection of the government's offer. But to people "at a distance," it appeared to be a decision for submission. The rebels were willing to have the citizenry vote by ballot, for or against submitting, so that a large percentage of yes votes would make a military expedition seem unwarranted. To counter this stratagem, the commissioners "determined to address [themselves] to fears" and demand individual affirmations to abide by the excise. But force was still mandatory because the moderates had been promised "prompt and effectual" protection and because the rebels still believed that the militia would not turn out. Bradford and Yeates expected the voting to be meaningless. "Measures will still be taken," they predicted, "to procure . . . an expression" of submission from the people, but it "will not be such a one as Government can rely on."

³³ Baldwin, *Whiskey Rebels*, 193-97.
³⁴ Commissioners to Randolph, Aug. 30, Sept. 2, 1794; Bradford to [Randolph?], Aug. 30, 1794; Bradford and Yeates to Randolph, Sept. 5, 1794, Pennsylvania Miscellany.
³⁷ Bradford and Yeates to Randolph, Sept. 5, 1794, *ibid.*
³⁶ Minutes of the commissioners, Sept. 1-2, 1794, *ibid.*
³⁹ Bradford and Yeates to Randolph, Sept. 5, 1794, *ibid.* See also the report of the commissioners, Sept. 24, 1794, *American State Papers . . . : Miscellaneous*, I, 87-88.

The administration received the report on September 8.[60] Again the commission precipitated action—this time a final decision to send in the militia. No one in the administration had believed the commissioners' earlier optimism. Increasingly the administration had come to feel that the rebels' conviction that they were invulnerable to coercion, either because of public sympathy or the instability of the militia, was calling into question the whole fabric of governmental authority. Riots elsewhere in Pennsylvania and in Maryland indicated that the rebellion was spreading and that there was general disrespect for the government. On September 9, the President ordered all militia units to march to their rendezvous.[61]

The one decision left, if military suppression were to proceed, was to order the troops over the mountains from their rendezvous in Carlisle and Cumberland, Maryland. Once more the President delayed, and for the same reason: the government's public image. Morally the government had to wait for the results of the oath-taking, and not until the week after September 9 was the administration absolutely certain that public opinion unequivocally supported a military expedition. The tide turned with the publication of the description of the close vote at the Redstone meeting. Actually the administration had been publicizing the violence and preparing the public for action since mid August.[62] But on September 10, the Philadelphia militia responded enthusiastically to Mifflin's exhortations to march. The next day the Republican party newspaper came out with a strong endorsement of military suppression, and by September 15 Federalists were crowing about the numbers of people volunteering for the expedition.[63] "A federal and military spirit has at length awakened in this city," wrote Bradford gleefully, "and it carries every thing before it."[64] Even Randolph admitted that "the spirit, which the States manifested, is astonishing." "All

[60] The commissioners' letter of August 30 reached Philadelphia on September 7 and the letters of September 2 and September 5 on September 8. Randolph to Bradford and Yeates, Sept. 8, 1794, Domestic Letters of the Department of State (M-60, reel 7), General Records of the Department of State.

[61] Randolph to commissioners, Sept. 4, 1794, *ibid.*; Bradford and Yeates to Randolph, Sept. 5, 1794, Pennsylvania Miscellany; Hamilton to Thomas Sim Lee, Sept. 6, 1794, Maryland State Papers (Maryland Hall of Records, Annapolis); Philadelphia *General Advertiser*, Sept. 4, 1794; Hamilton to Mifflin, Sept. 9, 1794, *Pennsylvania Archives*, IV, 226-27; Stagg to Knox, Sept. 11, 1794, Knox Papers.

[62] Hamilton was the chief publicist. See "Tully" [Hamilton], Philadelphia *American Daily Advertiser*, Aug. 23, 26, 28, Sept. 2, 1794; Hamilton to Washington, Aug. 5, 21, 1794, *ibid.* There is little evidence about the state of public opinion until *after* September 10 when it became loudly pro-government.

[63] Philadelphia *General Advertiser*, Sept. 11, 15, 1794; Hamilton to Samuel Smith, Sept. 19, 1794, Samuel Smith Papers (Manuscript Division, Library of Congress); Hamilton to King, Sept. 17, 1794, Charles R. King, ed., *The Life and Correspondence of Rufus King: Comprising His Letters, Private and Official, His Public Documents and His Speeches, 1755-1794* (6 vols., New York, 1894-1900), I, 573-75; John Fenno to Joseph Ward, Sept. 14, 1794, Joseph Ward Papers (Chicago Historical Society); Presley Neville to Craig, Sept. 12, 1794, Craig Papers; Oliver Wolcott, Jr., to Oliver Wolcott, Sept. 23, 1794, Gibbs, ed., *Memoirs of the Administrations of Washington and John Adams*, I, 159.

[64] Bradford to Yeates, Sept. 19, 1794, Gratz Collection.

these circumstances," he added in an acknowledgment that the administration's patience had paid off, "furnish a conviction that the energy of the Government is and will be greatly increased."[65]

By September 18, the administration had received early returns of the oath-signing in western Pennsylvania. It was "just in the situation we expected," Bradford informed Yeates; "great divisions and some tumults."[66] In a later report Ross described "great diversity of opinion" in one county, and he enclosed letters describing intimidation and disorder at the polls and a plan to "waylay" him and steal the oaths.[67] The administration's hands were now free. While most westerners were "disposed to pursue the path of Duty," Hamilton told Mifflin, "there is a large and violent Party, which can only be controuled by the application of Force."[68] On September 25, with units from New Jersey, Maryland, and Virginia converging on Carlisle and Cumberland, Washington issued a long proclamation justifying "this resort to military coercion."[69] Five days later, he and Hamilton were on the road to join the army.

The rebellion has long been interpreted as a milestone in the creation of federal authority, and in most respects that is its chief significance. Certainly to the Federalists, who had long been striving for a strong national government, it was a major test: the new government successfully crushed organized and violent resistance to the laws. As Hamilton put it, the rebellion "will do us a great deal of good and add to the solidity of every thing in this country."[70]

Hamilton's whole approach to the rebellion was positive because to him force was a positive tool. As early as 1792 he pushed for a military solution to enforce the excise. In 1794 he opposed sending a peace commission until troops were actually poised at the mountains in a show of governmental power.[71] In his eagerness to crush the rebellion Hamilton agreed to organize the whole expedition while Knox was out of town, and it is even possible that Hamilton encouraged Knox to leave so that he, Hamilton, could be certain the operation was managed efficiently.[72] For Hamilton force made the government a grander

[65] Randolph to James Monroe, Sept. 25, 1794, James Monroe Papers (Manuscript Division, Library of Congress).

[66] Bradford to Yeates, Sept. 19, 1794, Gratz Collection.

[67] James Ross to Randolph, Sept. 11, 1794, John Woods to Ross, Sept. 12, 1794, Wilkins to Ross, Sept. 11, 12, 1794, Ross to Bradford, Sept. 13, 1794, Wallace Papers.

[68] Hamilton to Mifflin, Sept. 20, 1794, *Pennsylvania Archives*, IV, 281. See also Hamilton to King, Sept. 22, 1794, King, ed., *Life and Correspondence of Rufus King*, I, 574.

[69] Proclamation, Sept. 25, 1794, Fitzpatrick, ed., *Writings of Washington*, XXXIII, 507-09.

[70] Hamilton to Angelica Church, Oct. 23, 1794, quoted in Cooke, "Whiskey Insurrection," 326.

[71] See Hamilton's notation on Randolph to commissioners, Aug. 7, 1794, Pennsylvania Miscellany.

[72] This is speculation. Knox left on August 8, but he had been planning to leave for some time because his speculations in Maine were on the point of ruining him. Knox was not, however, the kind of man to sacrifice his public duty. While not a particularly outstanding administrator, he had been for ten years a patient, regular, and trustworthy secretary of war. One cannot see him deserting the government on the eve of a

machine, more impressive and more permanent. It spoke a language of its own, imparting confidence to friends and threatening punishment to enemies, endowing its wielders with prestige and respect."

Hamilton's views predominated among Federalists in 1794. A few Federalists, however, refused to see the rebellion in such simple terms. They realized that the government response constituted a crisis as great as the maintenance of the law. Carried to their logical conclusion, said Randolph, Hamilton's ideas "would heap curses upon the government. The strength of a government is the affection of the people.'"⁴ Washington agreed with Randolph. Once the confrontation with Mifflin forced him to reassess the situation, the President followed a policy based primarily on public opinion, on making the government appear moderate, just, and humane—saddened and distressed by the need to coerce its citizens."⁵ What he sensed in the midst of the crisis was that regardless of the excise or even the maintenance of the law, force itself was a controversial act. Randolph argued and the President accepted a theory that the manner and conditions surrounding the use of force can divide as well as unite the community and undermine a government or institution under attack as well as protect them. Washington and other Federalists undoubtedly sympathized with Hamilton's position and even his statement a few weeks later, when under attack for accompanying the militia to Pittsburgh, Hamilton declared that he had "long

military crisis of inestimable proportions—especially after his experience in Shays' Rebellion eight years earlier—unless assured that his absence would not harm the administration. Hodgdon to Craig, July 19, 1794, Craig Papers. For a more favorable estimate of Knox's stewardship, see Harry M. Ward, *The Department of War, 1781-1795* (Pittsburgh, 1962). Neither Hamilton nor Washington had much respect for Knox's administrative abilities. In 1792, after two disastrous Indian defeats, several important war department functions had been shifted to the treasury, where Hamilton could control them. Kohn, "Federalists and the Army," 276-77. At some point in the almost continuous meetings of late July and early August, Knox probably expressed his concern over his land speculations and his desire to travel to Maine in person. Because the crisis demanded quick and flexible leadership, Hamilton could well have encouraged the journey. It would give added reason for Hamilton to accompany the troops, which he certainly wanted to do in September, and probably thought of in early August because of Mifflin's reluctance to cooperate and the acknowledged instability of the militia. See Hamilton to Washington, Sept. 19, 1794, Lodge, ed., *Works of Hamilton*, VI, 441-42; Hamilton to Washington, Dec. 24, 1795, Washington Papers. Washington's very quick reply to Knox's request to leave suggests some kind of prior understanding about the trip. And Washington probably shared Hamilton's doubts about Knox's ability to organize a complex and delicate military operation on short notice. Knox to Washington, Aug. 8, 1794, Washington Papers; Washington to Knox, Aug. 8, 1794, Fitzpatrick, ed., *Writings of Washington*, XXXIII, 461-62.

⁷³ "Government can never said to be established," Hamilton may have argued in early August when the administration was wavering between delay and immediate action, "until some signal display has manifested its power of military coercion." The quotation is from Randolph to Washington, Aug. 5, 1794, Washington Papers. Randolph's statement sounds like a direct quote rather than a paraphrase. He did not name Hamilton specifically as the author. But the implication is overpowering that he meant Hamilton, and the statement not only has a Hamiltonian ring but fits his position at the August 2 conference. "Conference at the President's," Aug. 2, 1794, *Pennsylvania Archives*, IV, 122-24.

⁷⁴ Randolph to Washington, Aug. 5, 1794, Washington Papers.

⁷⁵ Washington to Randolph, Oct. 16, 1794, Washington to Jay, Nov. 1[-5], 1794, Sixth Annual Address to Congress, Nov. 19, 1794, Fitzpatrick, ed., *Writings of Washington*, XXXIII, 4, 17, 34.

since ... learned to hold popular opinion of no value."[76] But the President knew he could not govern on such principles.

What makes the President's maneuvering in 1794 so interesting today was its success. First of all it defused the crisis and prevented bloodshed. Even before the troops reached Pittsburgh, the leaders of the insurrection were running for cover and the militia met no resistance when it arrived.[77] "The Heads of the Hydra," boasted Ross, "were cut off by the Commissioners."[78] Second, because the cabinet sessions remained hidden and because the expedition was organized under the guise of rhetoric about peace and the necessity for prudent preparations, the government escaped from the rebellion with its image untarnished.[79] Again the reason was delay and negotiation. As Randolph put it in a letter of thanks, the commissioners had "amply prepared the public mind" for force.[80] Force does speak a language of its own, but applied clumsily, too quickly, or without clear-cut justification, it smacks of tyranny and repression. Used as Washington used it, however, it can, as Justice James Iredell told a grand jury in Richmond the next year, bring "Success beyond the most sanguine expectations" and be "a lesson to Governments and People."[81]

[76] Hamilton to Washington, Nov. 11, 1794, Lodge, ed., *Works of Hamilton*, VI, 64-65.

[77] Bradford to Mifflin, Oct. 4, 1794, Society Collection (Historical Society of Pennsylvania); Craig to James O'Hara, Oct. 17, 1794, Craig Papers; Randolph to Washington, Oct. 20, 1794, Domestic Letters of the Department of State (M-60, reel 7), General Records of the Department of State; Washington to Randolph, Oct. 9, 1794; Washington to Jay, Nov. 1[-5], 1794, Fitzpatrick, ed., *Writings of Washington*, XXXIII, 526, XXXIV, 18.

[78] Ross to Richard Peters, Oct. 12, 1794, Richard Peters Papers (Historical Society of Pennsylvania).

[79] The administration did not escape political fire from its opponents. But with the exception of Thomas Jefferson, and then in private, the opposition never questioned the existence of a rebellion. Instead they attacked the excise and Hamilton, arguing that the government had provoked the affair and then that excess force had been used to intimidate all dissenters and militarize the country. See Jefferson to William Branch Giles, Dec. 17, 1794; Jefferson to Madison, Dec. 28, 1794; Paul Leicester Ford, ed., *The Writings of Thomas Jefferson* (10 vols., New York, 1892-1899), VIII, 515, 516; Madison to Jefferson, Nov. 16, 1794, Madison to Monroe, Dec. 4, 1794, James Madison Papers (Manuscript Division, Library of Congress); Philadelphia *General Advertiser*, Sept. 5, 9, 11, Nov. 6, 1794; Donald H. Stewart, *The Opposition Press of the Federalist Period* (Albany, 1969), 31, 87-89. There is no evidence that these charges convinced any significant proportion of the public at the time, probably because of the administration's smooth tactics between July and October.

[80] Randolph to commissioners, Sept. 29, 1794, Domestic Letters of the Department of State (M-60, reel 7), General Records of the Department of State.

[81] James Iredell's charge to the grand jury, Nov. 23, 1795, Charles E. Johnson Collection (North Carolina Department of Archives and History).

THE WHISKEY REBELLION IN KENTUCKY: A FORGOTTEN EPISODE OF CIVIL DISOBEDIENCE

Mary K. Bonsteel Tachau

In the nineteenth century, civil disobedience was identified with Henry David Thoreau; in the twentieth, with Mohandas K. Gandhi, Martin Luther King, and opponents of American military involvement in Vietnam.* Yet the history of civil disobedience in America begins at least as far back as the eighteenth century and the first decade of the nation. In this particular episode, civil disobedience was not the act of a single man, stubbornly and eloquently defending his position behind the bars of a Massachusetts prison. Nor was it the act of charismatic leaders who disciplined their followers to resist violence by nonviolent methods. Neither was it the act of a committed minority. Leaders and followers there were, but they were not in the minority in their region: they included almost the entire population of Kentucky. Stubborn and committed they were, too, but except for a few petitions and remonstrances they did not waste much of their time verbalizing their position. In fact there are so few documents by the perpetrators — and no official acknowledgment of their law-breaking by the government — that this entire movement has been overlooked by historians.

But anything involving thousands of people in a literate

Ms. Tachau is a member of the Department of History at the University of Louisville in Louisville, Kentucky.

*Some of the material in this article has been excerpted from chapters 2, 3, and 5 in Mary K. Bonsteel Tachau's *Federal Courts in the Early Republic: Kentucky, 1789-1816*, copyright © 1978 by Princeton University Press, and is reprinted by permission of Princeton University Press.

JOURNAL OF THE EARLY REPUBLIC, 2 (Fall 1982). © 1982 Society for Historians of the Early American Republic.

society leaves bits and pieces of evidence that someday can be fitted together in the jigsaw puzzle of history. The evidence of this early example of massive civil disobedience lies in the records of the lower federal courts in Kentucky, the Harry Innes Papers in the Manuscript Division of the Library of Congress, and Revenue Office correspondence in a long-lost file in the National Archives. These are all rather obscure sources. But a hint of what was going on is in *American State Papers*, one of the most widely used collections for historians of the early American republic. Together, these fragments reveal a remarkable story of tax evasion. It is the account of how almost the entire population of Kentucky managed to resist the laws of the United States for fully eight years — and how, ironically, Hamilton's hated excise gained acceptance only after Jefferson became president.

Civil disobedience is a serious matter. It is perhaps understandable that great moral issues like war, political independence, and equality should evoke it. But to find massive, almost universal civil disobedience in response to an internal revenue measure is unusual. However burdensome it may have been, it was not taxation to support an unpopular war, and it was not taxation without representation. It was simply a tax to cover the cost of the states' Revolutionary War debts, and Kentuckians, like the citizens of other states, were promised equity in the final settlement.

The tax was laid on domestic distilled spirits during Washington's first term. In Massachusetts it was a rum tax, in some parts of the southeastern seaboard a brandy tax, and in the interior a whiskey tax. People from all regions protested, but those on the frontier took stronger measures. In Pennsylvania, the tax provoked what the administration perceived as an overt rebellion; in Kentucky, it provoked a covert one that the Federalists later agreed to cover up.[1]

---

[1] The standard works on the Whiskey Rebellion include Leland D. Baldwin, *Whiskey Rebels: The Story of a Frontier Uprising* (Pittsburgh 1939); Hugh H. Brackenridge, *Incidents of the Insurrection in the Western Parts of Pennsylvania, in the Year 1794* (Philadelphia 1795); Henry M. Brackenridge, *History of the Western Insurrection in Western Pennsylvania, Commonly Called the Whiskey Insurrection, 1794* (Pittsburgh 1859); Jacob E. Cooke, "The Whiskey Insurrection: A Re-evaluation," *Pennsylvania History*, 30 (July 1963), 316-346; William Findley, *History of the Insurrection, in the Four Western Counties of Pennsylvania . . .* (Philadelphia 1796); and Harold C. Syrett et al., *The Papers of Alexander Hamilton* (26 vols., New York 1961-1979), XVII, *passim*. Steven R. Boyd is preparing an anthology of new studies about the Whiskey Rebellion.

Then as now, whiskey was important to the economy of Kentucky. In the early years, whiskey was as significant as tobacco had been in seventeenth century Virginia, and as cotton would become in the South after Eli Whitney's cotton gin was widely adopted. Whiskey was used in place of money because specie and banknotes were scarce beyond the Appalachian Mountains. Practically everything could be paid for with the products of the backyard still, and in Kentucky practically everybody had a backyard still.

The part of Kentucky that was then settled — chiefly the bluegrass and the Green River country — was fertile even beyond the expectations of the settlers. Hemp and corn grew luxuriantly, and horses, cattle, and hogs thrived. But there was no way to get produce or animals to the markets of the eastern states or to Europe. Spain held the west bank of the Mississippi River and, below what is now Vicksburg, the east bank as well. It will be remembered that Spain forbade free navigation of the Mississippi and prohibited Americans from exporting goods at New Orleans unless they paid exorbitant fees.

Transporting grain or hemp or animals eastward up the rivers or over the mountains was an economic impossibility: values were consumed by transportation costs. The only product made in Kentucky that could be sold elsewhere for a profit was whiskey, which had the greatest worth for the least weight and volume. When Congress passed internal revenue statutes, the people of Kentucky protested publicly and determined privately not to pay. From their standpoint, the federal government was taxing their only exportable product and giving little or nothing in return.

What Kentucky needed then was protection from the Indians and cooperation from Spain. But the Washington administration was of little help with either. A general inattention to the Indian problem was followed by the disastrous defeats of Generals Harmar and St. Clair. The government seemed equally uninterested in securing free navigation of the Mississippi. Kentuckians recalled bitterly that Congress under the Articles of Confederation had considered sacrificing the Mississippi for commercial advantages that would benefit only the eastern states. In the mid-1790s, the Washington administration opened negotiations with Great Britain but appeared to ignore westerners' need for a treaty with Spain. The people of Kentucky decided that they would not support a government that did not support them, and the near unanimity of that decision became apparent as time went on.

President Washington signed the first of the internal revenue acts in March 1791, and it became effective the following July 1. (A series of later statutes amended the original, but none made the excise more acceptable in Kentucky.)[2] Kentucky was still a part of Virginia — another source of irritation — and fell within the jurisdiction of Edward Carrington, the Virginia supervisor of revenue. He appointed a family "connection" as the chief revenue officer for Kentucky.[3] This man was Colonel Thomas Marshall, father of the future chief justice of the United States and of fifteen other children, most of whom had accompanied him when he had moved west. The Marshall family, with its numerous sons and sons-in-law, comprised the core of the early Federalist party in what became the Bluegrass State. Colonel Marshall was initially delighted with his appointment and accepted it "with gratitude and pleasure."[4] But the pleasure, if not the gratitude, soon wore thin. The day before his acceptance he wrote Carrington complaining about "the spirit of opposition to the laws so visibly prevalent among the People."[5] Nevertheless, the colonel undertook his duties conscientiously, although in doing so, as a major historian of Kentucky has stated, he "incurred great obloquy."[6]

It was difficult to organize a tax collection system for the Kentucky district and find people willing to serve as collectors because resignations almost kept pace with appointments. Marshall combined assignments, switched people around, offered to add his one percent to their six percent commissions, and even refused to release a reluctant collector from his post because he could not find anyone else to fill it. Tench Coxe, the commissioner of revenue in Philadelphia, suggested that Marshall encourage complying distillers to inform on the non-compliers, but no one wanted to do

---

[2] Richard Peters, ed., *Statutes at Large of the United States of America, 1789-1873* (17 vols., Boston 1850-1873), I, 199, 267, 275, 504, 539, 547.

[3] Carrington's wife, Elizabeth Ambler Carrington, was the sister of Mary Ambler Marshall, the wife of John Marshall, and the daughter-in-law of Colonel Thomas Marshall.

[4] Thomas Marshall to Alexander Hamilton, Mar. 9, 1792, Whiskey Rebellion Papers, Records of the Internal Revenue Service, Record Group 58 (National Archives).

[5] Marshall to Edward Carrington, Mar. 8, 1792, *ibid.*

[6] Temple Bodley, *History of Kentucky* (4 vols., Chicago 1928), I, 501.

that even for half of the resulting penalties and forfeitures, the legally established reward.[7]

The statute's complexity aggravated Marshall's problems. Distillers were supposed to maintain records and make them available for inspection, but they simply ignored the paperwork. Stills under 400 gallons in cities, towns, and villages were taxable according to quantity and proof produced — a provision that favored those producing high proof whiskey and reinforced perceptions that the law was unfair. Country stills, however, were taxable according to capacity. But, as Marshall explained, it was impossible to measure them because they were all in constant operation. Further, penalties were not to be charged against distillers who had only one still with a capacity of less than fifty gallons. Farmers who fell into that category did not bother even to register their stills, and avoidance of the law proceeded apace with evasion.

Kentucky, like other states, had its own judicial institutions responsible for enforcing the law, but the state courts took no official notice of unpopular federal laws. That responsibility remained with the federal district court headed by Judge Harry Innes, a well educated Virginia lawyer who had come to Kentucky a decade earlier. He instructed Marshal Samuel McDowell to convene a grand jury at every term of his court.[8] McDowell served the processes, but the difficulties of travel made it hard to convene panels during the first few years. When they did meet, grand jurors seemed uninterested in charging anyone with anything. In fact, the only action taken by grand juries during the first four years was to approve the first census.[9] Their inactivity implied that Kentucky was a notably law-abiding place.

Of course the judge, the marshal, the grand jurors, and everybody else in Kentucky knew that the internal revenue laws were being ignored. The *Kentucky Gazette* regularly published notices

---

[7] Marshall to Carrington, Mar. 8, 1792, Whiskey Rebellion Papers; Tench Coxe to Marshall, Oct. 31, 1792, Letters Sent by the Commissioner of the Revenue and the Revenue Office, 1792-1807, M-414, reel 1, Records of the Internal Revenue Service, Record Group 58 (National Archives).

[8] United States Court for the District of Kentucky, Order Book A, June 21, 1791. (Kentucky's federal court records, in the custody of the Clerk of the United States Court for the Eastern District of Kentucky and stored in Frankfort, have been microfilmed, with copies in the Special Collection Department, Margaret I. King Library, University of Kentucky, Lexington.) McDowell was a Federalist and cousin of the Marshalls.

[9] *Ibid.*, Jan. 12, 1792.

about the statutes, often accompanied by complaints and threats from Colonel Marshall.[10] It is possible that the grand jurors felt justified in overlooking their obligation by attending strictly to the instructions that Judge Innes gave them. He regularly delivered eloquent addresses describing the matters that came within their cognizance. Among those were such traditional offenses as treason, misprision of treason, forgery, interference with the processes of the courts, bribery, perjury, and so on.[11] These were sometimes lengthy lists, but they had one obvious omission because violation of federal statutes was also within the grand jurors' purview. As long as the judge overlooked such widespread evasion, the jurors evidently felt no obligation to take the initiative and bring charges against their neighbors.

There was another time-honored procedure to compel compliance with federal laws: a federal prosecutor could prefer charges to the grand juries and, if they found probable cause, they could indict the suspects. The first federal attorney, however, did not bring a single action in the court, although he was present every term. After he resigned in 1792, no one could be found to succeed him. President Washington offered the job to an established lawyer (George Nicholas), and then to one just beginning his practice (John Breckinridge). Both declined. Marshall thought that neither of them would have been recommended had they not been known to be opponents of the law, and he may have been right. Even one of his sons-in-law (William McClung) turned down the job. As a Kentucky correspondent wrote Senator John Brown, "the Excise is so very odious that No lawyer who has a reputation to loose [sic] will accept Office."[12]

---

[10] *Kentucky Gazette* (Lexington), June 18, 1791; Mar. 24, Apr. 21, 28, Nov. 24, 1792; Jan. 12, July 27, Aug. 31, Nov. 23, 1793; Feb. 22, 1794.

[11] Draft address, undated but prepared for the grand jury that convened Jan. 12, 1792. Harry Innes Papers, XVIII, 2-123 (Manuscript Division, Library of Congress).

[12] George Nicholas to Marshall, Aug. 25, 1793, Whiskey Rebellion Papers; John Breckinridge to the Secretary of State, Jan. 13, 1794, Miscellaneous Letters, Department of State, 1789-1906, M-179, reel 11, General Records of the Department of State, Record Group 59 (National Archives); Edmund Randolph to George Washington, Oct. 22, 1794, Domestic Letters, Department of State, 1784-1906, M-40, reel 7, General Records of the Department of State, Record Group 59 (National Archives); "Extract of a Letter from Kentucky Dated Lexington, Jan. 25, 1794," enclosed in Randolph to Washington Feb. 27, 1794, Misc. Letters, Dept. of State, M-179, reel 11.

From the collection of the J.B. Speed Art Museum, Louisville, Kentucky.

Judge Harry Innes

Marshall was discouraged, but neither he nor the revenue office gave up. Coxe authorized him to employ private counsel and to offer "liberal fees" to anyone who would prosecute for the government. Marshall tried that, but was turned down. "[A]ll our former attorneys are now violent opposers of the law," he reported.[13] The treasury authorized Marshall to forgive arrearages for a limited period, if the distillers would promise to pay in the future. In 1793, it suggested forgiving arrearages for the first year of the tax — from July 1, 1791 to June 30, 1792. The distillers said that one year was not enough and asked for two years, but were refused. By 1795, Secretary of the Treasury Alexander Hamilton

---

[13] Marshall to Nicholas, Oct. 8, 1794, Carrington to Marshall, Dec. 31, 1793, Marshall to Coxe, May 24, 1794, Whiskey Rebellion Papers.

was willing to go further, but by then even three years' forgiveness was not sufficient.[14]

Eventually, Hamilton made a third proposal: that the distillers pay the excise in whiskey to be supplied to the western army. According to custom and statute, the army then furnished spirits to officers and men, as well as more conventional provisions like flour, meat, and coffee. Because everyone received from two to six rations daily, depending on rank, the army's requirements offered a substantial market for Kentucky whiskey. Further, as Hamilton pointed out, paying taxes in whiskey avoided problems associated with the scarcity of specie in the West. This was an ingenious idea, but the distillers saw it as a trick and would have none of it. That tactic was no more successful than the others had been.[15]

As time went on, the generally passive nature of the resistance gave way to sporadic acts of violence. Distillers stole collectors' records, attacked them in their sleep, threatened those who tried to inspect their stills, docked their horses' tails, and in at least one instance tarred a collector and rolled him in leaves.[16] Marshall kept Carrington and Coxe informed of these events, and they passed his letters on to Hamilton.[17] Of course, everybody in the revenue office was aware that no taxes were being paid, and that even these acts of violence were being ignored by the federal

[14] Thomas Jefferson to Nicholas, July 15, 1793, Domestic Letters, Dept. of State, M-40, reel 5; Nicholas to Marshall, Aug. 25, 1793, Hamilton to Coxe, Jan. 27, 1795, Whiskey Rebellion Papers.

[15] Coxe to Marshall, Jan. 22, 1796, Letters of Tench Coxe, Commissioner of the Revenue, Relating to the Procurement of Military, Naval, and Indian Supplies, 1794-1796, M-74, Records of the Bureau of Indian Affairs, Record Group 75 (National Archives). Evidently some distillers sold whiskey to the army, and their taxes were deducted from payment. All whose names appear in correspondence were themselves revenue collectors: the general population refused to take advantage of this or other "compromises." Coxe to Marshall, Nov. 24, 1796, Letters Sent, Revenue Office; Oliver Wolcott to Washington, Nov. 12, 1795, Oliver Wolcott Papers XLII, 5 (Connecticut Historical Society, Hartford); Wolcott to William Clarke, Oct. 23, 1797, ibid., XXXIII, 45; "Balances Due on the Supervisors' Accounts," Dec. 31, 1799, ibid, XI, 81.

[16] Coxe to Carrington, Mar. 27, 1793, Letters Sent, Revenue Office, M-414, reel 1; Nicholas to Marshall, Aug. 25, 1793, Whiskey Rebellion Papers; Marshall to Carrington, Mar. 20, 1794, ibid.; William Clarke to Coxe, May 11, 1797, Tench Coxe Section, Coxe Papers (Historical Society of Pennsylvania, Philadelphia).

[17] Until Hamilton resigned as Secretary of the Treasury in January 1795, all of the letters cited above as Whiskey Rebellion Papers were transmitted to him, as shown in Syrett, ed., Papers of Hamilton, passim.

court.[18] Every member of the cabinet knew that, too, but they did not acknowledge it publicly.[19]

What alarmed the administration about Kentucky even more than noncompliance or violence against revenue officers were reports that prominent Kentucky leaders were preparing to take matters in their own hands and secede from the Union, or seize for themselves what the government had not secured from Spain — free navigation of the Mississippi River. As early as August 1793, the Spanish commissioners in Philadelphia had complained to Secretary of State Thomas Jefferson that an expedition fomented by French agents was being organized in Kentucky. Governor Isaac Shelby initially denied that he knew anything about it. Still, rumors persisted that the western hero of the Revolutionary War, George Rogers Clark, was contracting for boats and supplies and raising troops who would travel down the Ohio and Mississippi rivers, attack Spanish garrisons stationed along the way, and invade Spanish Louisiana to force Spain to grant free navigation and the right to export from New Orleans. In March 1794, a Philadelphia newspaper carried an advertisement for volunteers to serve under Clark, who was identified as a Major General in the Armies of France and Commander in Chief of the French Revolutionary Legions on the Mississippi River. Apparently informed about the recruiting notice before its publication, the cabinet responded vigorously. President Washington issued a proclamation to the people of Kentucky forbidding anyone from enlisting or serving under the aegis of a foreign power.[20] Secretary of State

---

[18] The revenue office reported regularly to the House of Representatives. The absence of receipts from Kentucky, somewhat disguised as "accrued and payable," is shown in Walter Lowrie and Walter S. Franklin, eds., *American State Papers: Documents, Legislative and Executive, of the Congress of the United States . . .: Finance* (5 vols., Washington 1832), I, 250-251, 280-281, 390-391, 562, 593, 618.

[19] Jefferson knew because he had declined to extend the period for forgiveness of arrearages beyond June 30, 1792, as described above; his successor Edmund Randolph knew because he was informed by his brother-in-law George Nicholas and by Senator John Brown, and he passed his information on to Washington as indicated in note 15, *supra*; Knox knew, and transmitted similar information in Knox to Washington, May 7, 1794, George Washington Papers, reel 12 (Manuscript Division, Library of Congress); a notation on "Proceedings of the President," July 14, 1794, indicates that Marshall and Carrington had also written to the president, *ibid.*, reel 13; William Bradford knew because of cabinet consultations in 1794; Hamilton knew from the correspondence of Marshall, Carrington, and Coxe, and, of course, from treasury records.

[20] "Extract of a Letter from Kentucky . . .," in Randolph to Washington,

Randolph ordered Governor Shelby to stop the expedition by calling up the militia, if necessary. Secretary of War Knox ordered General Anthony Wayne, who was in the Northwest Territory, to station troops at Fort Massac (opposite the confluence of the Cumberland and Ohio Rivers) to prohibit any expedition from passing. Knox also suggested that Wayne include mounted Kentucky volunteers — who were expensive — in his planned summer campaign against the Indians, to preclude their participation in Clark's enterprise. Noncompliance with the whiskey tax seemed relatively unimportant, compared with the evident intention of those wayward frontiersmen to make war against a nation with whom the United States was at peace and to exacerbate relations with Great Britain, which were then at their nadir.[21]

Kentuckians got the message and obeyed the president, although perhaps with some reluctance. Clark's expedition fizzled out, but his compatriots remained unreconciled to the administration's policies. When they learned that John Jay, of all people, was en route to Westminster with confidential instructions to negotiate with the English — and that no one was yet en route to Madrid to negotiate with the Spanish — their short fuses once again ignited. (Jay was considered the enemy of the West because it was he who reportedly had been willing to sacrifice free navigation of the Mississippi during the Jay-Gardoqui negotiations of 1785-1786.) At a mass meeting in Lexington in May, hundreds gathered to hear and cheer what General Wayne described as "most inflammatory & invective language."[22] The crowd proceeded to adopt thirteen

---

Feb. 27, 1794, Misc. Letters, Dept. of State, reel 11; "Cabinet Meeting. Opinion on Expeditions Being Planned in Kentucky for the Invasion of the Spanish Dominions [Mar. 10, 1794]," Syrett, ed., *Papers of Hamilton*, XVI, 136-140; Jefferson to Isaac Shelby, Aug. 29, 1793, Domestic Letters, Dept. of State, reel 5, Knox to Washington, Mar. 24, 1794, Washington Papers, reel 105; Knox to Washington, May 7, 1794, *ibid.*, reel 12; *The Pennsylvania Gazette* (Philadelphia), Mar. 12, 1794. The cabinet's advice and the president's decisions are in "Cabinet Meeting. Opinion on a Proclamation Against Forces to be Enlisted in Kentucky for the Invasion of Spanish Territory [Mar. 18-19, 1794]," Syrett, ed., *Papers of Hamilton*, XVI, 162-163.

[21] Randolph to Shelby, Mar. 29, 1794, Domestic Letters, Dept. of State, reel 6; Knox to Anthony Wayne, Mar. 31, 1794, *American State Papers: Foreign Relations*, I, 458; Knox to Washington, May 12, 1794, Washington Papers, reel 105.

[22] Wayne to Knox, June 11, 1794, quoted in Syrett, ed., *Papers of Hamilton*, XVI, 589.

resolutions, one of which stated "that civil liberty is prostituted, when the servants of the people, are suffered to tell their masters, that communications which they may judge important ought not to be entrusted to them." The resolutions were sent to Philadelphia, together with a remonstrance to the president and Congress which declared that the absence of protection on the frontiers was "a grievance of the greatest magnitude."[23] A month later, a Philadelphia newspaper published the news from Kentucky, and again the president convened a cabinet meeting to determine a course of action.[24]

The question of what to do about Kentucky was not the only problem confronting the administration in the summer of 1794. Although it took the official position that opposition to the whiskey tax had subsided everywhere except in western Pennsylvania, in fact the entire cabinet and many members of Congress knew that it still existed in western South Carolina as well as in Kentucky. Further, it appeared that an Indian war was about to break out in Georgia, where American settlers were moving into Indian territory, despite a series of treaties and the possible intervention of Spain. Most important of all, events in Pennsylvania were reaching a climax. Within a week of the meeting to discuss Kentucky affairs, a mob fired on the home of John Neville, revenue inspector in Pennsylvania. Soon after, they burned it down, and the administration hesitantly reached the decision to crush the whiskey rebels in Pennsylvania with armed force.[25]

In the context of all the other contemporaneous acts of defiance, that decision may well have been reached out of frustration. Hamilton was unwilling to give up on the whiskey tax, and the administration was unwilling to admit how widespread was its opposition. In this same month, Hamilton recommended, and the administration approved, a new bill that would extend the excise to the southwestern and northwestern territories (soon to become the states of Tennessee and Ohio, respectively) and would increase

---

[23] *Kentucky Gazette*, May 31, 1794.
[24] Randolph to Bradford, Hamilton, and Knox, July 11, 1794, Domestic Letters, Dept. of State, reel 7.
[25] *American State Papers: Finance*, I, 279,380; Syrett, ed., *Papers of Hamilton*, XVI, 588-590, XVII, 1-6, 53-56; Richard H. Kohn, "The Washington Administration's Decision to Crush the Whiskey Rebellion, *Journal of American History*, 59 (Dec. 1972), 567-584.

the collectors' fees by one third.[26] It proved impossible to turn back the Georgians permanently, and the actions that led to the Yazoo scandal proceeded throughout the summer. It was also impossible to punish the Kentuckians. Wayne's campaign was underway with the mounted Kentucky volunteers leading the way; any action against the commonwealth at such a time would certainly have precipitated secession or reawakened Clark's sleeping dogs. Moreover, it would take weeks (and boats) to transport troops that far west, and supply arrangements already strained by Wayne's army would present insoluble logistical problems.

After nearly two centuries, it is still not clear whether it was Hamilton's will, Knox's absence, the pressure of events, the perceived need to demonstrate the government's strength through military power, a sincere belief that rebellion threatened, a shifting balance among human relationships — or all of these factors — that determined the administration's decision. In the end, it labeled the problems in Pennsylvania an insurrection and called up 15,000 militia on the strength of a declaration by a judge facing bankruptcy that the laws were "opposed . . . by combinations too powerful to be suppressed by the ordinary course of judicial proceedings"[27] It is clear from surviving documents that the odd man out in the cabinet was Edmund Randolph. It was he who counseled moderation, who noted that the judge had failed to specify which laws were opposed, and who pointed out that the available processes of the courts to compel compliance and punish violence had not yet been exercised.[28] It was also he who proposed a strategy to deal with Kentucky. On matters relating to Pennsylvania, he was for the most part overruled or ignored. But on the question of Kentucky, it was Randolph who prevailed. A year later, his independent position and his enemies' trumped up charges would force him from the cabinet and permanently estrange him from the president. Nevertheless, in 1794 Randolph preserved the peace in Kentucky by persuading the others to overlook the violence, the tax evasion, the mass meetings and remon-

---

[26] Peters, ed., *Statutes*, I, 378.

[27] The statement of Associate Justice James Wilson is in *American State Papers: Miscellaneous*, I, 85.

[28] Randolph to Washington, Aug. 5, 1794, Washington Papers, reel 106, states Randolph's reservations most forcefully, but the entire series of his communications throughout July and August reflect his reluctance.

strances. He convinced President Washington, at least, that instead of mounting an attack upon Kentucky, it was imperative to launch an attack on the cause of western discontent by initiating a new mission to Madrid.[29]

Randolph's strategy called for two appointments. Both required men with political experience and appropriate political credentials. Both also needed sufficient rank to impress their counterparts, sufficient persuasiveness to achieve results when the government could not guarantee much in the way of a *quid pro quo*, and sufficient determination to accomplish their missions. It took time to find such paragons.[30] During the weeks that the administration planned the invasion of western Pennsylvania, appointed commanders, raised troops, arranged supplies — and that Wayne defeated the Indians at Fallen Timbers — Randolph sought men to carry out his plan. About the time that the militia army proceeded westward, Thomas Pinckney prepared to go to Spain to try to get free navigation of the Mississippi, and James Innes (the older brother of the federal judge) set out for Kentucky. Innes' assignment was to persuade a skeptical population that the government was undertaking a new diplomatic initiative and was committed to its success — and to arrange, if he could, a truce with the distillers.[31]

Innes arrived in time to spend Christmas with his brother. He met with the governor and other leaders, and got the *Kentucky Gazette* to print his message so that it would have wide distribution. He also met with leading distillers and got some kind of

---

[29] Randolph to Washington, Aug. 7, 1794, Domestic Letters, Dept. of State, reel 7.

[30] Thomas Jefferson and Patrick Henry both declined the mission to Madrid, and it took extensive consultation to agree upon Thomas Pinckney, then in London but in a secondary role since Jay's appointment as minister plenipotentiary. James Innes was unenthusiastic about the Kentucky assignment because of a possible conflict with his position as attorney general of Virginia, his poor health, and questions about whether the administration would cover his expenses. Randolph to Jefferson, Aug. 28, 1794, *ibid.*; Randolph to Patrick Henry, Aug. 28, 1794, *ibid.*, Jefferson to Randolph, Sept. 7, 1794, Misc. Letters, Dept. of State, reel 12; Randolph to Washington, Oct. 2, 1794, Oct. 9, 1794, Oct. 15, 1794, *ibid.*; Randolph to James Innes, Aug. 22, 1794, Sept. 5, 1794, Domestic Letters, Dept. of State, reel 7; Randolph to Shelby, Aug. 15, 1794, Aug. 25, 1794, Nov. 16, 1794, *ibid.*

[31] "Instructions for Col. James Innes," Nov. 11, 1794, Domestic Letters, Dept. of State, reel 7.

promise that they would henceforth obey the excise law if arrearages accumulating before 1794 were forgiven. Eventually he returned to Virginia and filed his report. Later that year, the administration's efforts brought results. In August, Wayne concluded the
Treaty of Greenville, in which the Indians ceded most of what
became Ohio, making Kentucky far more secure from attack. In
October, Pinckney completed negotiations for the Treaty of San
Lorenzo, by which Spain granted a renewable three year right to
navigate the Mississippi and to deposit at New Orleans. Unfortunately, the Spanish authorities in America were slow to carry out
the terms of the treaty, and the Kentuckians were impatient. Unfortunately, also, the terms of Jay's treaty with Great Britain
became known that summer, and throughout the nation the
administration came under bitter attack. The resignation of
Edmund Randolph compounded the disaffection of Kentuckians.
For reasons known only to themselves but easily imagined by
others, the Kentucky distillers remained recalcitrant — unintimi-
dated by the government's actions in Pennsylvania, unmoved by
their agreement with Innes. Indeed, his "treaty" with them was
still not carried out in 1799, according to Oliver Wolcott, who was
then secretary of the treasury.[32]

It was not until nearly the end of 1796 that Washington
finally found someone to act as federal attorney in Kentucky. By
that time the office had been vacant for four years, and the
revenue acts had been in effect for five and a half years. Even then,
the president could not find anyone who had been in Kentucky for
any length of time; he appointed a recent arrival from Maryland
named William Clarke, who had been recommended by members
of the Marshall clan. (Colonel Marshall warned the revenue office
to furnish Clarke with copies of the revenue statutes, because none
was available in the commonwealth.)[33]

As the colonel had hoped, the mere appointment of a federal
attorney brought results. For the first time, a grand jury brought
presentments (criminal charges based upon their own knowledge)
against two men who were believed to have forcibly obstructed a

[32] *Kentucky Gazette*, Mar. 14, 1795; Wolcott to John Adams, Nov. 18, 1799,
Wolcott Papers, XL, 68.

[33] Washington to Timothy Pickering, Oct. 10, 1796, John C. Fitzpatrick, ed.,
The Writings of George Washington from the Original Manuscript Sources, 1745-1799
(39 vols., Washington 1931-1944), XXXV, 241; Marshall to Coxe, Aug. 14, 1796,
Whiskey Rebellion Papers.

revenue officer. At the following term of court, the next grand jury brought another presentment (based on a charge by a revenue collector) against a distiller for using an unregistered still, and an indictment (in response to a charge brought by Clarke) against another man for assault and battery against a collector. Clarke, too, was busy. With instructions from Coxe to go after influential people, he filed informations (formal criminal accusations initiated by an officer of the government) against Thomas Jones, a justice of the peace in Bourbon County, and against Senator John Brown, Judge Innes' closet friend. With all of this unprecedented activity in the federal court, Colonel Marshall thought that it was safe to leave enforcement to Clarke, and he resigned his position. It seemed to him that, at long last, the forces of law and order were winning over neglect of duty.[34]

But the colonel was mistaken. During the remaining terms of court in 1797, the federal marshal failed to convene grand juries, and Clarke failed to file any informations. Clarke had run head-on against the power structure, and it was not about to submit tamely to an outsider. The agents that he had instructed to seize Jones's stills were charged with trespass; the witnesses whom he had summoned to testify to the grand juries were denied compensation for their travel. Clarke complained to the treasury department, which initially sympathized with him, but it acknowledged that the judge was master in his own court.[35]

Clarke was additionally handicapped by James Innes' "treaty," which had provided that arrearages before 1794 would be forgiven. Some distillers who claimed that they had paid duties before that date argued that they should get refunds. Clarke agreed that their position was just, but of course he had no power to compensate them.[36] In any event, they must have been revenue collectors or people who sold their whiskey to the army through the good offices of Colonel Marshall. The records published in *American State Papers: Finance* do not indicate that any money was

---

[34] District Court, Order Book A, Dec. 21, 1796, Mar. 22, 1797; Wolcott to Coxe, June 27, 1796, Wolcott Papers, XXXI, 49; Wolcott to Coxe, June 27, 1796, Whiskey Rebellion Papers; Coxe to Marshall, June 30, 1796, Letters Sent, Revenue Office, reel 2; Marshall to Adams, Apr. 28, 1797, Misc. Letters, Dept. of State, reel 15.

[35] Clarke to Wolcott, May 11, 1797, Coxe Papers; Wolcott to Thomas T. Davis, Feb. 25, 1800, Wolcott Papers, XXXVII, 146.

[36] Clarke to Wolcott, May 11, 1797, Coxe Papers.

forwarded from Kentucky. Presumably, the only people who complied were those whose tax money was deducted from the payments they received for their whiskey, in accordance with Hamilton's earlier suggestion.[37]

Colonel Marshall was understandably frustrated, but in his frustration he employed a litigation strategy that would eventually prove significant. As a private citizen he could not bring a criminal charge (e.g., an information), but he could bring a civil suit, and he did. In November 1797, Marshall sued a distiller for the amount of money owed in taxes "for the benefit of the United States," and he got Supervisor Carrington to sue, also. Marshall and Carrington employed the common law form of action called "debt," a device hitherto overlooked, although it had been authorized by section 23 of the first Internal Revenue Act.[38] This strategy had the advantage of invoking the power of the court to compel obedience without raising the spectre of criminal charges against distillers whose "crime" was failure to register their stills and pay the required taxes. No evidence yet unearthed explains why no one used this form of litigation earlier — or why Marshall and Carrington initiated it when they did. In any event, it was an effective response to the problem of evasion. In the long run, it was the legal strategy that brought compliance.

But that day still lay in the future. The immediate conse-quence of Marshall's and Carrington's litigation was that it got Clarke moving again. Although he, too, could have used civil procedures and sued for debt, he did not choose to do so. Instead, he resumed criminal charges in March 1798 by filing an information against a distiller, and by getting the grand jury to issue a presentment on an information filed by a collector.[39] In

---

[37] See note 18, *supra*. An entry in the Wolcott Papers suggests that Marshall's successor James Morrison remitted $4,000 in October 1799, but this unique notation does not indicate whether he had collected money from the tax on distilled spirits or from other taxes imposed from 1794 to 1799 on carriages, selling wines and foreign distilled liquors, refined sugar, property sold at auction, snuff, tobacco, stamps, teas, foreign bills of exchange, and bills of lading. Wolcott Papers, XI, 81; Peters, ed., *Statutes*, I, 373, 376, 378, 384, 397, 426, 478, 495, 509, 527, 545, 547, 622.

[38] *Marshall v. Horine, Carrington v. Horine, Carrington v. Helm, Carrington v. Ravenscraft, Carrington v. Saunders*, District Court, Order Book A, Nov. 20-21, 1797.

[39] *Ibid.*, Mar. 12, 1798.

July, Clarke filed two more informations, but there was no grand jury that term. It was very slow going.

Suddenly, in November — more than seven years after the first Internal Revenue Act — Judge Innes announced a new rule in court that suggests the reason why the marshal had trouble getting grand jurors to serve, and why Clarke had trouble getting those who did serve to do much about enforcing the excise laws. Judge Innes' rule was that

> No person shall on whom any process shall be served returnable to this Court, or has a Suit depending herein, or who may be summoned as a witness in any suit or question depending in the Court, *or who is a distiller of Spirits within this district* [italics added], shall be summoned as a Grand Juror; and the Marshall [sic] before he summons a Grand Juror is directed to make the necessary inquiry agreeably to his Regulation.[40]

The new rule brought results: the grand jury issued presentments against five distillers for operating stills that had not been registered. Over the following four terms of court they cited twenty-five more distillers. Clarke filed five informations in November 1798, and two more in March 1799.[41] Compliance seemed assured.

Yet as these cases came to trial, it became clear that the distillers did not have much to worry about. In an early grand jury address, Judge Innes had stated that "[t]rials by jury . . . are the great bulwark which intervenes between the magistrate and the citizen," and these petit jurors obviously saw themselves as that great bulwark.[42] Whether the charges were initiated by Clarke or by revenue collectors or by grand juries made no difference: trial jurors regularly acquitted their neighbors of criminal charges. In Kentucky, violation of the revenue acts was simply not perceived as a crime. Not one of the fifty criminal charges brought during the four years of Clarke's tenure resulted in conviction. Default judgments were set aside, while other charges were abated by death, or quashed, dismissed, or discontinued. Seven cases went to trial, but the jurors found for the defendants every time, and the judge then ordered their accusers to pay the costs of the suits.[43]

---

[40] *Ibid.*, Order Book B., Nov. 26, 1798.

[41] *Ibid.*, Nov. 11, 19, 1798; Mar. 11-12, July 8, Nov. 18, 1799; Mar. 11, 1800.

[42] Draft address, Innes Papers, XVIII, 2-123.

[43] District Court, Order Book B, *passim.*

It seems never to have occurred to Clarke to use the civil procedures that Marshall and Carrington had used. But James Morrison, the colonel's successor as supervisor of the revenue, did pursue that strategy. In November 1798, Morrison filed six suits in debt, "For the use of the United States," against two major distillers who — significantly — were also revenue collectors. When their cases came to trial in July 1799, the government won its first major victory: petit jurors found for the government and assessed the defendants more than $1,400 — a huge sum of money.[44] Morrison must have thought that the key to gaining compliance had at last been found, and over the next year and a half, he filed 158 additional suits in debt.

But the government was foiled again, this time by the court. Clarke was sloppy in preparing the cases, and he was no match for the local lawyers or the judge. In the debt cases, Clarke sometimes sued in the name of the United States, instead of in the name of a government officer "for the use of the United States," as the statute required. Those cases were immediately thrown out. Sometimes he neglected to present evidence that a demand for payment had been made, and those cases also were thrown out. Sometimes he called revenue agents as witnesses, but their testimony was inadmissible in that era because they had a pecuniary interest in the result — so those cases joined the others in the trash bin.[45] If there were no other explanation for Clarke's failures, a reason may be found by checking the names of defendants against the lists of petit jurors. In one term of court alone, five members of the jury panels were themselves defendants in cases brought by Clarke. Yet there is no indication that he ever challenged them.[46]

In time, Clarke became as frustrated as Colonel Marshall had been earlier. He complained about the judge to the secretary of the treasury. Secretary Wolcott in turn complained that the distillers had never lived up to the 1795 agreement negotiated by the judge's brother. Judge Innes wrote to his representative in Congress to find out what was being written about him. Edmund Pendleton, in Virginia, wrote to Innes that he should not be intimidated. (The advice was not necessary.) Tench Coxe's successor wrote Colonel Marshall's successor, complaining about Clarke's poor judgment

---

[44] *U.S.* v. *Stith Daniel, U.S.* v. *Thomas Daniel, ibid.*, July 12, 1799.

[45] Harry Innes to John Brown, Mar. 5, 1800, Innes Papers, XXVIII, 9-217.

[46] The five were Dudley Mitcham, Robert Peeples, William Ellis, John Galbraith, and Ambrose Bush, District Court, Order Book B, Mar. 12, 1799.

and lack of legal skills. So many letters were written by so many people that it is astonishing that for two hundred years no one ever suspected what had gone on in Kentucky.[47]

After four years of confrontation, with few positive results and little appreciation for his efforts, Clarke eventually became such an embarrassment to the sponsoring Marshalls that they arranged to have him kicked upstairs to a judgeship in the new Indiana Territory.[48] Once again the office of federal attorney was vacant. Once again no suits were filed. Once again the distillers went about their business unhampered by the excise laws.

And the amount of their business was substantial. The revenue office reported that in the year ending June 30, 1798, $38,233.59-3/4 in excise taxes on whiskey had accrued and were payable in the Ohio District (Kentucky and what would become the state of Ohio.)[49] Because the tax ranged from 7 to 18 cents per gallon, according to proof, the revenue office's estimate indicates that there was a lot of untaxed whiskey being distilled in the district. At the very least (at the highest proof), it meant that 200,000 gallons were being produced annually. At the lowest proof, the estimate suggests that 500,000 gallons were produced. Whatever the proof, each year somewhere between a quarter and a half million gallons trickled, tax free, through those primitive stills and worms.

Finally, in the waning months of the Federalist era, President John Adams found a competent person to go after the Kentucky distillers. He appointed Joseph Hamilton Daveiss, another Federalist, and one soon to become a Marshall-by-marriage.[50] It took

---

[47] Wolcott to Clarke, Oct. 23, 1797, Wolcott Papers, XXXIII, 45; Wolcott to David, Feb. 25, 1800, Innes Papers, XXI, Pt. i, 1-89; Innes's inquiry is acknowledged in Davis to Innes, Feb. 28, 1800, ibid., XXVII, Pt. i, 8-2; Pendleton to Innes, Nov. 3, 1799, ibid., XXI, Pt. i, 1-87; William Miller to James Morrison, Oct. 23, 1799, Letters Sent, Revenue Office, reel 2.

[48] Wolcott to Clarke, Aug. 5, 1800, Wolcott Papers, XXXVIII, 38; John Marshall to Adams, Aug. 26, 1800, Clarence E. Carter, ed., The Territorial Papers of the United States, VII: The Territory of Indiana, 1800-1810 (Washington 1939), 18.

[49] American State Papers: Finance, I, 618. The 1794 statute specified this reorganization. Peters, ed., Statutes, I, 378.

[50] Humphrey Marshall, nephew and son-in-law of Colonel Marshall, evidently arranged Daveiss' appointment. Humphrey Marshall to Joseph Hamilton Daveiss, Nov. 24, 1800, Joseph Hamilton Daveiss and Samuel Daveiss Papers (The Filson Club, Louisville, Ky.).

Daveiss a year to begin work, but when he did in November 1801, the results were notable. On his first day in court he got an indictment from the grand jury that eventually resulted in the only guilty verdict against a distiller who had been charged by a grand jury during this entire period. Daveiss had chosen the defendant for criminal proceedings carefully: he was a friend of Thomas Marshall, Jr. who had shot and wounded officers who had come to serve a search warrant.[51] Earlier petit juries had acquitted defendants accused of assault and battery, but apparently using firearms to obstruct collectors was going too far, even in Kentucky.

Even more significant was Daveiss' decision to use *civil* proceedings to enforce the law. By this time it was obvious that juries would not convict distillers in criminal proceedings. Daveiss wisely abandoned them, and instead filed civil charges of debt, as Marshall, Carrington, and Morrison had done earlier. He did this on a grand scale: on his first day in court, he filed 121 debt cases, and added 40 more during the term. In succeeding terms he filed even more, making a total of 317 civil suits.[52] (The new federal marshal served so many processes — and thereby earned so many fees — that he became the highest paid federal marshal in the nation!)[53] And Daveiss was careful to observe the legal proprieties. None of *his* cases was thrown out of court for lack of evidence, improper witnesses, or lack of legal form.

It was this massive docketing of technically correct debt cases that finally brought results — of a kind. Ironically, compliance was secured during Jefferson's administration, and not under either of the Federalist presidents who supported this Federalist statute. it was only after Jefferson's promise of repeal that the Kentucky distillers capitulated. For the first time, the pages of the court records note that distillers by the dozens were coming into court, acknowledging their debts, and paying their taxes. The penalties and forfeitures that they owed were remitted by Secretary of the Treasury Albert Gallatin, who as a Pennsylvanian had tried to ameliorate the government's policies in his home state, and who

---

[51] Thomas Marshall, Jr., provided the $300 bail bond. *U.S.* v. *Mannen*, United States Court for the Sixth Circuit, District Court, Order Book C, Nov. 17, 1801; May 17, 1802; United States Court for the District of Kentucky, *ibid.*, Nov. 17-Dec. 6, 1802.

[52] The proceedings may be traced in District Court, Order Book C, *passim*.

[53] *American State Papers: Miscellaneous*, I, 303.

sympathized with the distillers far more than his predecessors had.[54]

But the story does not quite end in 1802, when the taxes were paid and the statute repealed, because it soon became evident that the revenue collectors were as delinquent as the distillers had been. As the years wore one, Daveiss had to bring the revenue officers into court to force them to remit their collections or forfeit their bonds. Virtually every one of the dozens of revenue officers in the district, with the notable exceptions of Colonel Thomas Marshall and James Morrison, were eventually charged with delinquency. And, as one might expect, juries were quick to convict *them*.[55]

The history of the first whiskey tax in Kentucky is thus a history of massive, if largely passive, resistance. There was little violence. Still, the covert rebellion is important in reflecting a public united in opposing what they always regarded as Hamilton's excise. The spontaneity and tenacity of the movement is truly remarkable, especially considering the primitive nature of communication in that era. The near unanimity with which Kentuckians avoided and evaded the statutes would have astounded even Thoreau, Gandhi, and King. In the history of civil disobedience, that first generation of Kentuckians made, for better or worse, a significant contribution.

---

[54] Authority to remit forfeitures and penalties began with the first internal revenue statute (Peters, ed., *Statutes*, I, 199, sec. 3) and was incorporated in its successors. The court records record these remittances.

[55] The records of the Solicitor of the Treasury (Record Group 206), the General Records of the Department of the Treasury (Record Group 56), and the Records of the Post Office Department (Record Group 28), as well as the Records of the Internal Revenue Service (Record Group 58) — all in the National Archives — provide extensive evidence of delinquency among minor public officials.